W9-DBK-890

Windows Vista Annoyances

Other Microsoft Windows resources from O'Reilly

Related titles

Windows Vista:
 The Definitive Guide
Windows Vista
 Administration:
 The Definitive Guide
Windows Vista in a
 Nutshell

Windows Vista: The
 Missing Manual
Windows Vista for Starters:
 The Missing Manual
Windows Vista Pocket
 Reference

Windows Books Resource Center

windows.oreilly.com is a complete catalog of O'Reilly's Windows and Office books, including sample chapters and code examples.

oreillynet.com is the essential portal for developers interested in open and emerging technologies, including new platforms, programming languages, and operating systems.

Conferences

O'Reilly brings diverse innovators together to nurture the ideas that spark revolutionary industries. We specialize in documenting the latest tools and systems, translating the innovator's knowledge into useful skills for those in the trenches. Visit *conferences.oreilly.com* for our upcoming events.

Safari Bookshelf (*safari.oreilly.com*) is the premier online reference library for programmers and IT professionals. Conduct searches across more than 1,000 books. Subscribers can zero in on answers to time-critical questions in a matter of seconds. Read the books on your Bookshelf from cover to cover or simply flip to the page you need. Try it today for free.

Windows Vista Annoyances

David A. Karp

O'REILLY®

Beijing · Cambridge · Farnham · Köln · Paris · Sebastopol · Taipei · Tokyo

Windows Vista Annoyances
by David A. Karp

Copyright © 2008 O'Reilly Media, Inc. All rights reserved.
Printed in the United States of America.

Published by O'Reilly Media, Inc., 1005 Gravenstein Highway North, Sebastopol, CA 95472.

O'Reilly books may be purchased for educational, business, or sales promotional use. Online editions are also available for most titles (*safari.oreilly.com*). For more information, contact our corporate/institutional sales department: (800) 998-9938 or *corporate@oreilly.com*.

Editors: John Osborn and
Laurel R.T. Ruma
Production Editor: Rachel Monaghan
Proofreader: Rachel Monaghan

Indexer: Lucie Haskins
Cover Designer: Karen Montgomery
Interior Designer: David Futato
Illustrator: Robert Romano

Printing History:

December 2007:   First Edition.

 This book uses RepKover™, a durable and flexible lay-flat binding.

ISBN-10: 0-596-52762-4
ISBN-13: 978-0-596-52762-4
[M]

Table of Contents

Preface

Why Am I Annoyed?

Imagine a windowless room in a nondescript office building. Inoffensive tan carpet lines the floors, fluorescent lights hum softly overhead, and 20 seated Microsoft employees flank a rectangular folding table in the center of the room. On the table rests a Windows PC, and at its helm, a slack-jawed cipher punches blindly at the controls in a vain attempt to carry out a task requested by the team leader.

"OK, here's the next exercise: find a picture of a badger on the Internet and print it out on that printer there," says the leader.

The observers—members of Microsoft's Usability Research Group—diligently note each click, keypress, and hesitation, hoping they'll learn the answer to the industry's big secret: why do so many people find computers difficult to use?

Over the years, Microsoft has uncovered many startling facts about PC users with this system, and the software has been changed accordingly. For instance, people new to computers apparently have a hard time with the concept of overlapping windows. (Did I say "startling"? I meant "idiotic.") So, Microsoft spent six years designing a "Glass" interface for Windows Vista with translucent borders that sort of show stuff underneath. Of course, most people new to PCs figure out the concept of stacking windows after about 10 minutes of fiddling, so is this actually a solution to a genuine usability problem, or just glitzy eye candy included to give those still using XP a compelling reason to upgrade?

Here's another one: lots of people seem to get lost searching through long menus for the tools they need, so once again, Microsoft snapped into action. The team's first attempt was "personalized menus"—a feature found in earlier versions of Windows (including XP) and Microsoft Office—which caused about half the items in a menu to vanish so *nobody* could find them. In Windows Vista, Microsoft took a different tack and removed the menus altogether. The good news is that you'll no longer get lost looking through menus. Of course, you won't be able to find anything, either.

Or take the fact that, for years, people have been complaining about the time it takes to load Windows. Rather than making the operating system leaner and cleaner so that it starts faster, Microsoft's designers have continued to add features and complexity to the software, which results in longer load times. The solution? Replace the Shut Down button in the Start menu with a *Sleep* button, so once Windows starts, it'll stay loaded in memory even when you shut it off. Thereafter, it'll take only a few seconds to get your desktop back.

Truth be told, features like Sleep have been around for years, but they've always sat on the sidelines, waiting for inquisitive people to discover them. But thanks to Vista, Sleep is now the main dish, which means Windows should start much faster now—whether you're the inquisitive type or not—and this should make a lot of people happy. The downside, of course, is that it takes a constant supply of electricity to keep Windows loaded in memory, causing your PC to suck power 24 hours a day, 7 days a week...even when you're not using it. This means shorter-lasting laptop batteries, higher electricity bills, and more pollution from the power plants that now have to power millions of sleeping Vista PCs.

What most people don't know is that Sleep is actually a hybrid of the old *Standby* and *Hibernate* power-saving modes, which means you can now completely power off your PC and still get it to load quickly. Once again, only the inquisitive—you, presumably—will be in the know, leaving the masses to leave their PCs on all night.

Probably the most substantive change in Vista's interface is the prominence of the Search tool. Rather than being a separate window, it's now permanently lodged in the Start menu and at the top of every Explorer window. What's more, Windows now invisibly indexes most of your data, making search results more or less instantaneous (a feat possible in earlier versions of Windows only with free add-on desktop search software).

Unfortunately, that speed comes at a cost—namely, that your searches may be out-of-date or incomplete, and you won't even know it. In some cases, you can search a folder full of JPEG images for *.jpg and get absolutely nothing, or worse, a partial listing with no warning that it may be incomplete. And when you do get the search results you want, there's no telling whether or not your favorite Details columns will be present since Vista seems incapable of saving your preferences from one session to the next.

In short, the new Search feature shows promise, but its competence is limited by a company that values marketable features over usable ones.

Hundreds of design decisions are made this way. Take *content protection*, Vista's copy-protection initiative for so-called "premium content" like high-definition movies from Blu-Ray and HD DVD discs. According to Microsoft's standards, software and hardware manufacturers are supposed to disable "premium content" across all *interfaces* that don't provide copy protection. One such interface is the S/PDIF digital audio port—usually in the form of a TOSlink optical plug—that comes on most high-end audio cards. Since S/PDIF doesn't support copy protection—meaning that you could theoretically plug it into another PC and rip the soundtrack off an HD movie—Vista requires that your TOSlink plug be disabled whenever you play back that HD movie on your PC. As a result, you'll only be able to use your analog audio outputs when watching HD content, and that expensive sound card you just bought is now trash. Why would Microsoft hobble an important feature? For you, the consumer? Of course not. Vista's content-protection feature is intended to appease piracy-wary movie studios, so Microsoft won't be left behind as the home theater industry finds new ways to rake in cash. And ironically, Microsoft boasts "content protection" as a feature of Vista.

Would Microsoft be making decisions like these if it had to compete fairly for your business? After Europe's second-highest court upheld a ruling that Microsoft had abused its market power and stifled innovation, Neelie Kroes, the European Union competition commissioner, stated that "the court has confirmed the commission's view that consumers are suffering at the hands of Microsoft."

So that leaves us lowly Vista users with a choice: do we continue to suffer with Windows' shortcomings, or take matters into our own hands?

Of Bugs and Features

The point of this book is to help you solve problems. Sometimes those problems are the result of bad design, such as the aforementioned shortcomings of Vista's search tool, and sometimes the problems are caused by bugs.

Take the *Blue Screen of Death*, a Windows mainstay for more than a decade. Yes, it's still alive and well in Vista, but now it has a cousin: the *Green Ribbon of Death*. As explained in Chapter 6, the Green Ribbon of Death—capable of bringing Windows Explorer to its knees—comes from a combination of poor design and bugs in its code. And thus the reason for distinguishing where an annoyance becomes clear: you need to know what you're dealing with in order to fix it.

The User Account Control (UAC) feature in Windows Vista is a perfect example of a feature gone awry. Most of the time, UAC does precisely what it was designed to do—prevent programs from doing harm to your PC, occasionally asking your permission when it deems it appropriate to do so—but the result is a system that frequently bothers you with UAC prompts, while intermittently breaking your applications without telling you why. Because this behavior isn't caused by a bug per se, fixing the problem is instead just a matter of customizing the system so that it suits your needs.

This inevitably leads to an important conclusion: one person's annoyance is another's feature. Although Microsoft may be motivated more by profit than excellence, often leading to products designed for the lowest common denominator, you're not bound to that fate. In other words, you should *not* be required to adjust the way you think in order to complete a task on your computer; rather, you should learn how to adjust the computer to work in a way that makes sense to you.

But I prattle on. Feel free to dive in to any part of the book and start eliminating annoyances.

How To Use This Book

Windows Vista Annoyances is not documentation; you can get that anywhere. Rather, it's a unique and thorough collection of solutions, hacks, and time-saving tips to help you get the most from your PC.

Most topics begin by describing the problem, annoyance, or task at hand, and include something you don't often find in technical references: why you'd want to complete the particular solution (and sometimes, why you wouldn't). Of course, if you're in a hurry, you can always skip ahead to the actual solution, easily identifiable by subheadings and numbered steps.

Although you certainly don't need to read the chapters in order, the solutions and chapters are arranged so that you can progress easily from one topic to the next, expanding your knowledge and experience as you go. You should be able to jump to any topic as you need it, but if you find that you don't have the proficiency required by a particular solution, such as familiarity with the Registry, you can always jump to the appropriate section (Chapter 3, in the case of the Registry).

There are nine chapters and two appendixes, as follows:

Chapter 1, *Get Started with Windows Vista*. Get the low-down on what's special about Vista, as well as what's annoying. Learn how to install (or reinstall) the operating system in a variety of scenarios.

Chapter 2, *Shell Tweaks*. Customize Windows Explorer, the desktop, the Start menu, and the Search tool to be less annoying and more useful. Then, learn a host of file management tricks to help you work with your stuff more effectively.

Chapter 3, *The Registry*. Dive inside Windows' giant database of settings and system configuration data, and learn about the various tools you can use to explore, hack, and manage this valuable resource.

Chapter 4, *Working with Media*. Improve your experience with videos, pictures, and music in Vista, and solve problems with CDs and DVDs.

Chapter 5, *Performance*. Speed up your PC and get it to work better. Get the new Glass interface working, and take care of your hard disk.

Chapter 6, *Troubleshooting*. Learn what to do when Windows won't start, when applications crash, and when Windows can't set up your new hardware. Deal with the Blue Screen of Death, fix the Green Ribbon of Death, and prevent data loss by backing up your PC.

Chapter 7, *Networking and Internet*. Get your local network up and running, get your wireless working (safely), and connect to the Internet. Once you've connected, close all of Vista's backdoors, and then improve your experience with the Web and email.

Chapter 8, *Users and Security*. Protect your privacy and your data with permissions, encryptions, and user account management. Tame the User Account Control (UAC) prompt, customize your login, and share your files and printers with others on your network.

Chapter 9, *Scripting and Automation*. Automate Vista with scripts, Command Prompt Batch files, Task Scheduler, and the new Windows PowerShell. Explore the good ol' DOS commands still used in the Command Prompt, not to mention the times when Windows won't boot.

Appendix A, *BIOS Settings*. This is a brief glossary of the often-neglected motherboard settings that can significantly affect the stability and performance of your PC.

Appendix B, *TCP/IP Ports*. Look up common network port numbers, used to identify data travelling on a network (or over the Internet), and essential for configuring and securing your network.

Conventions Used in This Book

The following typographical conventions are used in this book:

Constant width

Indicates text you're supposed to type, output from a command-line program, code examples, Registry keys, and paths to Registry keys.

Constant width italic

Indicates user-defined elements within constant-width text (such as filenames or command-line parameters). For example, Chapter 8 discusses a file encryption utility, *cipher.exe*, which has a variety of command-line options. A particular solution might instruct you to type:

    cipher /r:filename

The italicized portion of this code, filename, signifies the element you'll need to replace with whatever is applicable to your system or needs. The rest—the non-italicized portion—should be typed exactly as shown.

Bold

Identifies captions, menus, buttons, checkboxes, tabs, keyboard keys, drop-down lists and list options, and other interface elements. Bolding interface elements makes it easy to distinguish them from the rest of the text. For example, you may wish to turn off the **Force Windows to crash** option.

Window/dialog titles are typically not bolded, but some objects (such as Control Panel contents) can appear as icons or menu items, and therefore typically appear bolded.

Italic

Introduces new terms, indicates web site URLs, and sets apart file and folder names.

Italic is also used to highlight chapter titles and, in some instances, to visually separate the topic of a list entry.

{Curly braces}

Denote user-defined elements in paths or filenames, e.g., *C:\Users\ {username}\AppData\Roaming\Microsoft\Windows\Start Menu*.

"Quotation marks"

Are used sparingly in this book, and are typically used to set apart topic headings and emphasize new concepts. Note that if you see quotation marks around something you're supposed to type, you should type the quotation marks as well (unless otherwise specified).

Path Notation

Occasionally, the following shorthand path notation is used to show you how to reach a given user-interface element or option. The path notation is always presented relative to a well-known location. For example, the following path:

Control Panel → Date and Time → Internet Time tab

means "Open Control Panel, then open **Date and Time**, and then choose the **Internet Time** tab."

Keyboard shortcuts

When keyboard shortcuts are shown, a hyphen (such as **Ctrl-Alt-Del**) or a plus sign (Winkey+**R**) means that you should press the keys simultaneously.

This is an example of a tip, often used to highlight a particularly useful hint or time-saving shortcut. Tips often point to related information elsewhere in the book.

This is an example of a warning, which alerts you to a potential pitfall of the solution or application being discussed. Warnings can also refer to a procedure that might be dangerous if not carried out in a specific way.

Request for Comments

Please address comments and questions concerning this book to the publisher:

O'Reilly Media, Inc.
1005 Gravenstein Highway North
Sebastopol, CA 95472
800-998-9938 (in the United States or Canada)
707-829-0515 (international/local)
707-829-0104 (fax)

You can also send messages electronically. To be put on the mailing list or request a catalog, send email to:

elists@oreilly.com

To comment or ask technical questions about this book, send email to:

bookquestions@oreilly.com

The O'Reilly web site has a section devoted especially to this book, on which can be found errata, sample chapters, reader reviews, and related information:

http://www.oreilly.com/catalog/9780596527624/

For software mentioned in this book, as well as additional tips, online discussion forums, and Windows news, visit:

http://www.annoyances.org/

For more information about books, conferences, software, Resource Centers, and the O'Reilly Network, see the O'Reilly web site at:

http://www.oreilly.com/

Safari® Books Online

 When you see a Safari® Books Online icon on the cover of your favorite technology book, it means the book is available online through the O'Reilly Network Safari Bookshelf.

Safari offers a solution that's better than e-books. It's a virtual library that lets you easily search thousands of top technical books, cut and paste code samples, download chapters, and find quick answers when you need the most accurate, current information. Try it for free at http://safari.oreilly.com.

Acknowledgments

I'd like to start by thanking the folks at O'Reilly Media, Inc. It's a supreme pleasure to work with people who are dedicated to quality and are passionate about their work. Special thanks to Tim O'Reilly for his enthusiasm, support, and commitment to quality. Thanks to John Osborn, Laurel Ruma, Kyley Caldwell, and Rachel Monaghan for helping me get this edition together and out in time.

Thanks also to Debbie Timmins, Rob Cohen, and Tim Vander Kooi for their comments, and thanks to everyone on the team who worked on this book.

I'd like to thank my family, friends, and well-wishers—in that they didn't wish me any specific harm—all of whom put up with my deadlines and late-night writing binges.

Bye bye, Maeby.

Finally, all my love to Torey Bookstein.

CHAPTER 1

Get Started with Windows Vista

Windows Vista is like a papaya: sleek on the outside, but a big mess on the inside.

Love it or hate it, Vista is what Microsoft is serving up right now. Whether it goes down smoothly or gives you heartburn is up to you.

On the plus side, Vista gives you a new, faster Search tool; the shiny, translucent "Glass" interface; and a revamped Windows Explorer. It's also the first version of Windows where you can get Tablet PC and Media Center in the same package, which means you can use it to build a DVR (Digital Video Recorder) without a keyboard. And Vista handles videos and pictures much better than earlier versions of Windows, with improved thumbnail and metadata support built right into Windows Explorer.

As for the minuses, Vista seems intolerably slow compared with its predecessors, and its reliability leaves something to be desired. The *Green Ribbon of Death* is an everyday occurrence, bringing down Windows Explorer if you so much as bat your eyes at it. And the horrendously annoying User Access Control (UAC) prompt forces you to endure repeated prompts for even the most mundane tasks in Control Panel.

Fortunately, you can deal with most of the minuses. For instance, to tame UAC, see Chapter 8. Or, to fix the Green Ribbon of Death (or the *Blue Screen of Death* for that matter), see Chapter 6. And to make Vista run faster, check out Chapter 5. But if you want to take stock of what you have and install the operating system on your PC, then Chapter 1 is for you.

Editions of Vista

Internally, Windows Vista refers to itself as Windows 6.0. When held up against Windows 2000 (Windows 5.0) or XP (5.1), that means nothing more than the fact that Microsoft considers Vista to be a major milestone, and the basis for its operating systems for the next few years at least. (It's been seven years since Windows 2000.)

Windows Vista is available in several different editions, each of which is supposedly intended for a different market. They're all the same version—effectively, the same software—differing only in the toys included in the box.

The top of the line is the *Ultimate* edition, available at more than twice the cost of the baseline *Home Basic* edition. The *Home Premium* and *Business* editions include most of the extras found in Ultimate, but at a cost only slightly higher than Home Basic. On the fringe, you'll find the *Starter* and *Enterprise* editions, as well as *Windows Home Server*. See the "What Does 64-Bit Vista Get Me?" sidebar, next, for details on the 64-bit versions of Vista.

What Does 64-Bit Vista Get Me?

More bits gets you access to more memory. The processor inside your PC communicates with your system memory (RAM) with numeric *addressing*. Thus the maximum amount of memory a 32-bit processor can address is 2^{32} bytes, or 4 gigabytes. Newer 64-bit processors—not to mention the 64-bit operating systems that run on them—can address 2^{64} bytes of memory, or 17,179,869,184 gigabytes (16 exabytes) of RAM.

(17 million gigabytes may sound like a lot of space now, but it won't be long before you'll be taking baby pictures with an 8-gigapixel digital camera.)

Windows NT, released in 1993, was Microsoft's first fully 32-bit operating system. But it took eight years before the platform, which had since evolved into Windows 2000 and then XP, became mainstream. (For those keeping track, Windows 9x doesn't count because it was a hybrid OS that ran 32-bit applications on a 16-bit DOS foundation, which was one of the reasons it was so unstable.) 64-bit Windows became a reality in XP, but Vista is Microsoft's first serious attempt to make 64-bit computing mainstream. But the question is, how mainstream is it?

While 64-bit Vista can run most 32-bit applications without a problem, it's not compatible with 32-bit hardware drivers or 32-bit utilities like Windows Explorer extensions (e.g., context menu add-ons). This means that you need a native 64-bit driver for every device on your PC. And since 64-bit Vista won't load *unsigned drivers* (see Chapter 6), finding support for all your hardware may be a bit of a challenge, at least presently. Since most Vista installations are still 32-bit, most manufacturers aren't bothering to compile, test, and support 64-bit drivers and software.

—continued—

Now, 64-bit software running on 64-bit Windows has been known to run as much as 10% faster, which illustrates the other reason—aside from memory addressing—that people find 64-bit Vista alluring. Just be prepared for lackluster industry support, at least for the next few years until Microsoft releases a 64-bit-only OS. → $Win\ 7.0\ ?\ ?$

It should also be noted that, at the time of this writing, most 64-bit antivirus programs running on 64-bit Vista performed very poorly compared with their 32-bit counterparts. Of course, there aren't a lot of 64-bit viruses out there right now, but that doesn't mean a 32-bit virus can't do some harm.

All editions of Vista (except Starter) are available in both the 32-bit or 64-bit varieties; the retail Ultimate edition even includes both 32-bit and 64-bit DVDs right in the box. If you have 32-bit Vista (other than Ultimate), you can get the 64-bit version of your edition (*http://www.microsoft.com/windowsvista/ 1033/ordermedia/*), and assuming your license key checks out, you only pay shipping. But beware: once you "convert" your key to work with the 64-bit version, you won't be able to use it to reinstall the 32-bit version, should you decide to go back.

Regardless, all of the solutions in this book apply to both the 32-bit and 64-bit versions of Windows Vista unless otherwise noted.

The differences among the editions are outlined in Table 1-1. See the next section for ways you can make up the difference if you're not using the Ultimate edition.

Table 1-1. What you get (and what you don't) with the various editions of Windows Vista

	Home Basic	Home Premium	Business	Enterprise	Ultimate
Aero Glass interface		✓	✓	✓	✓
Back Up Files wizard	✓	✓	✓	✓	✓
Backup scheduler		✓	✓	✓	✓
Complete PC Backup and Restore			✓	✓	✓
Dual processor support			✓	✓	✓
Encryption – BitLocker drive encryption				✓	✓
Encryption – file and folder encryption (EFS)			✓	✓	✓
Fax and Scan			✓	✓	✓
Group Policy Editor (*gpedit.msc*)			✓	✓	✓

Table 1-1. What you get (and what you don't) with the various editions of Windows Vista (continued)

	Home Basic	Home Premium	Business	Enterprise	Ultimate
IIS (Internet Information Services) 7.0 Web server	✓	✓	✓	✓	
Join a corporate network domain			✓	✓	✓
Local Security Policy Editor (*secpol.msc*)			✓	✓	✓
Local Users and Groups Manager (*lusrmgr.msc*)			✓	✓	✓
Multi-Lingual User Interface				✓	✓
Offline files and folders (sync with network folders)			✓	✓	✓
Premium games (InkBall, Mahjong Titans, Chess Titans)		✓			✓
Remote Desktop			✓	✓	✓
Shadow Copies			✓	✓	✓
Subsystem for UNIX-based Applications (SUA)				✓	✓
System Memory supported (64-bit only)	8 GB	16 GB	128 GB	128 GB	128 GB
Tablet PC extras (Handwriting recognition, pen flicks, Windows Touch technology)		✓	✓	✓	✓
Windows DVD Maker		✓			✓
Windows Media Center		✓			✓
Windows Meeting Space	Join only	✓	✓	✓	✓
Windows Movie Maker high definition support	SD only	HD+SD	SD only	SD only	HD+SD
Windows SideShow support		✓	✓	✓	✓
Windows Ultimate Extras					✓

More Than This

Got Vista envy? Are you using the Home Basic, Home Premium, or Business editions, and wish you could have the benefits of Ultimate? Here are the big-ticket differences among the editions, and, when applicable, how to get the extra features at little or no extra cost:

Aero Glass
The translucent "Glass" interface is available on every edition except Home Basic, although Vista's basic Aero interface (without transparency effects) is available on all editions. See "Get Glass," in Chapter 5, for alternatives for Home Basic.

Backup and Restore Center
See "Preventive Maintenance and Data Recovery," in Chapter 6, for details on Windows' various versions of its backup software, as well as free alternatives.

BitLocker Drive Encryption
BitLocker, included only with the Ultimate and Enterprise editions, is a method by which you can encrypt an entire drive, as opposed to the more basic folder and file-level encryption features included in the Business, Enterprise, and Ultimate editions. Freeware alternatives include FreeOTFE (*http://www.freeotfe.org/*) and TrueCrypt (*http://www.truecrypt.org/*). See Chapter 8 for the skinny on encryption.

Group Policy Object Editor
Several solutions in this book use the Group Policy Object Editor (*gpedit.msc*) to change a few esoteric settings, but this tool isn't included in the Home Basic or Home Premium editions. If the *gpedit.msc* file isn't on your system, you can access most of these settings with Vista's net command-line tool (provided you open the Command Prompt in administrator mode), as explained in Chapter 8.

Local Security Policy
The Local Security Policy tool (*secpol.msc*) provides access to advanced settings, the useful ones relating mostly to Vista's UAC feature; see "Control User Account Control," in Chapter 8, for details.

Local Users and Groups
The Local Users and Groups tool (*lusrmgr.msc*) duplicates some user account management features found elsewhere in Windows, and offers a few extras. See "Log In As the Administrator," in Chapter 8, for a workaround if you don't have this tool.

Media Center
See Chapter 4 for free alternatives to the Media Center application included with the Home Premium and Ultimate editions.

Remote Desktop
TightVNC, a freeware remote control application, works with any version of Windows, or for that matter, Mac OS X, Linux, and even Apple's iPhone. See "Control Your PC Remotely," in Chapter 7, for details.

Shadow Copies
Vista's *Previous Versions* tool, which can be used to automatically back up files you're working on, makes use of the *Shadow Copies* feature in the Business, Enterprise, and Ultimate editions. See Chapter 6 for alternatives.

Tablet PC

You can use a tablet with any edition of Vista, as long as its manufacturer provides a native Vista driver. But the Tablet PC subsystem, which adds handwriting recognition and a few other gimmicks like *gestures*, isn't available in Home Basic. If you want handwriting in Home Basic, you may be able to use the "Microsoft Windows XP Tablet PC Edition 2005 Recognizer Pack"; just go to *http://search.microsoft.com/* and search for `TRPSetup.exe`.

Windows Movie Maker

You can download Windows Movie Maker for all editions of Vista; just go to *http://search.microsoft.com/* and search for `MM26_ENU.msi`.

Install Windows Vista

Installing an operating system is not among the 10 "must have" experiences in your life. Rather, it can be a slow, agonizing process, and can be unceremoniously aborted for a variety of reasons.

Depending on your hardware, just booting up the setup disc can be a headache. You then must sit and wait…and wait…for Windows to copy some 2,000 files to your hard disk and then go through the excruciating process of "configuring" your computer. When it finally boots—assuming it even makes it this far—you then have the unenviable task of having to download and install more than a hundred megabytes' worth of updates and fixes. And when all is said and done, you still will need to go through and turn off all of the annoying "features" littered throughout the interface and then fix the myriad of problems that are sure to pop up.

But the worst part is the feeling you can't shake: that you chose to install Windows Vista on your machine, and now you've got to live with it. (Of course, this may not apply to you if you got Vista preinstalled on a new PC, at least not yet….)

Both the steps to begin the installation procedure and the procedure itself can vary, depending on what's already installed on your system (if anything) and how you choose to approach the task. If you're installing over an older version of Windows, use Table 1-2 to cross-reference the old version with the edition of Vista you're installing and determine whether or not upgrading is an option.

Table 1-2. Vista upgrade compatibility chart; a checkmark (✓) means you can upgrade from within the older version, no checkmark means you need to perform a clean install

	Vista Home Basic	Vista Home Premium	Vista Business	Vista Ultimate
Windows XP Professional			✓	✓
Windows XP Home	✓	✓	✓	✓
Windows XP Media Center		✓		✓
Windows XP Tablet PC			✓	✓
Windows XP 64-bit				
Windows 2000				

Install Vista on a New (Clean) System

Use this method to set up Vista on a brand-new, empty hard disk, or if you don't want to upgrade an earlier version of Windows (discussed in the next section). See the upcoming sidebar, "Reduce Vista's Footprint," before you proceed if you want to customize the installation.

The Windows Vista installation disc is bootable, which means that you can pop it in your drive, turn on the computer, and the installation process will start automatically.

If your PC doesn't boot off your Vista disc, you'll need to do one of the following:

BIOS setup
Enter your BIOS setup utility (discussed in Appendix A), navigate to the **Boot** section, and change the **boot device priority** or **boot sequence** so that your DVD drive appears *before* your hard disk. Save your changes and exit BIOS setup when you're finished.

Boot menu
Alternatively, some PCs provide a "boot menu" that lets you choose the boot drive on the fly. Look for a message above or below the boot screen right after you power on your PC; usually, all you do is press the **F12** key (before the beep; don't dawdle), select your CD/DVD drive from a list, and hit **Enter**.

When your PC detects a bootable disc, you'll usually see this message for three to four seconds:

```
Press any key to boot from CD or DVD...
```

Reduce Vista's Footprint

When you install Vista, the setup program basically unpacks a standard installation from a disc image on the DVD. This is why there are so few questions asked during setup, no optional components to include, and no way to exclude the tons of sample media files Vista includes. Sure, once Vista is installed, you can subsequently go through it and thin out this bloated behemoth, but wouldn't it be easier to lighten the load before you install?

Fortunately, there's vLite, a free utility available at *http://www.vlite.net/*, which lets you customize your Vista installation before you install a single file to your PC. It requires a functional PC (and a DVD burner) to run, but, of course, you can always install Vista as-is first, and then wipe your hard disk clean before you install the vLite version.

Using your original setup disc as a template, vLite walks you through the process creating a new, custom disc, allowing you to:

- Integrate available Windows updates, language packs, and hardware drivers, so you don't have to install them later (a great time-saver if you're setting up more than one PC).
- Remove unwanted components.
- Tweak default settings, like disabling UAC, enabling Hibernation, and unhiding filename extensions in Windows Explorer.
- Split a DVD disc into CDs so you can install Vista on a PC without a DVD reader, or consolidate a set of CDs into a DVD-based install to save time.
- Embed your product key on the disc so you don't have to type it each time, or add other features to create an "unattended" installation.

When you're done, vLite burns your custom installer to a DVD you can use just like an ordinary Vista disc.

Press a key on the keyboard, and in a few moments, setup should load normally and display its Welcome screen. On the first screen, click **Next** to display the Install Windows screen shown Figure 1-1. From here, click **Install now** to proceed.

On the next page, setup asks for your product key, which you can read off the DVD sleeve or the sticker on your PC case. Mercifully, Microsoft now allows you to skip this step—leave the field blank, click **Next**, and then answer **No**—so you don't have to waste time fishing around for the sticker and typing the excruciating 25-digit key. This is a particularly nice time-saver in the event that setup fails and you have to start over, or if you're only setting up a temporary Vista installation for software testing or data recovery.

Figure 1-1. From this page, click "Install now" to begin setup, or "Repair your computer" to use the repair tools explained in Chapter 6

 If you complete setup without typing your key, make sure you choose the edition of Vista you actually own. If you choose the wrong edition, you won't be able to change it later without reinstalling from scratch. When Vista boots, it'll operate in a fully functional "evaluation mode" you can use normally for 30 days. If you don't enter a valid product key for the edition you chose during setup in time—through the System page in Control Panel—Vista goes into a lockdown mode. (See the next section, "Install clean with only an upgrade disc," for a way to extend this evaluation period.) So, if this installation ends up being a keeper, don't put this step off, lest you risk making the data on your hard disk more-or-less inaccessible.

A few pages later, you'll be asked "Which type of installation do you want?," at which point you can select **Upgrade** or **Custom (advanced)**. The Upgrade option is only available if you install Vista from within a previous version of Windows, as described later in this chapter. So, click **Custom (advanced)** to advance to the "Where do you want to install Windows?" page, and then click the **Drive options** link to reveal the partition editor shown in Figure 1-2. See Chapter 5 for more information on partitions and the tools included with Vista to manage them.

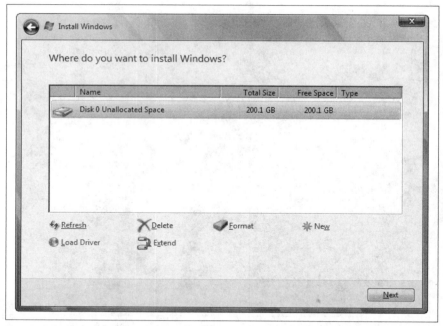

Figure 1-2. Click the "Drive options" link to show these drive preparation and partition editing tools

If the hard disk is clean, and you want to use the entire hard disk for your Vista installation, just click **Next** to proceed. Otherwise, use **Delete** to wipe out any existing partitions—as well as the data on them (*warning:* there's no undo here)—and **New** to create new partitions on the drive.

Follow the screens to complete setup. If setup crashes along the way, or Vista won't boot after you're done, see "Potential Problems During Setup," later in this chapter.

Install clean with only an upgrade disc

So you thought you'd save a little money by purchasing the "upgrade" version of Vista, but now you find yourself in a bit of a jam. Your hard disk crashed, and without a full backup (see Chapter 6), you need to rebuild your system. Or perhaps you've decided against upgrading XP directly to avoid passing on six years of accumulated junk to your new operating system. Either way, you've undoubtedly discovered that your upgrade disc won't install if it can't find an eligible Windows installation to upgrade.

In this scenario, Microsoft suggests that you install XP and then install Vista over it. Not bloody likely.

Instead, just follow these steps to get a fresh Vista installation from an upgrade disc:

1. Use your Vista disc to boot your PC, as described in "Install Vista on a New (Clean) System."

2. When setup loads, click **Install now** and proceed normally.

3. When prompted for the product key, leave the field blank, and just click **Next**.

4. Without the key, setup will ask you which edition of Vista you'd like to install; make sure you choose the edition you've actually purchased.

5. When setup is complete, you'll be operating in the 30-day evaluation period, but you won't be able to activate Vista until you enter your product key.

   To enter the product key, open a Command Prompt window in administrator mode, as explained in "Control User Account Control" in Chapter 8, and then type this at the prompt:

   ```
   cscript \windows\system32\slmgr.vbs -ipk xxxxx-xxxxx-xxxxx-xxxxx-xxxxx
   ```

   where *xxxxx-xxxxx-xxxxx-xxxxx-xxxxx* is your Vista product key, taken from the DVD sleeve or the sticker on your PC case. Press **Enter** to proceed.

 If this doesn't work, you may need to temporarily deactivate the UAC feature as described in Chapter 8, and then try again. Then, reactivate UAC when you're done (should you so desire).

6. Next, activate Vista with this command:

   ```
   cscript \windows\system32\slmgr.vbs -ato
   ```

   and press **Enter**. To verify that activation was successful, type this:

   ```
   cscript \windows\system32\slmgr.vbs -dlv
   ```

7. Type exit or close the Command Prompt window when you're done.

 Using a process known as *rearming*, you can extend Vista's evaluation period up to two or three times, for a total of 120 days. Just execute the *slmgr.vbs* script with the -rearm parameter. It will take 15–30 seconds to make the change, at which point you'll need to restart Windows.

Upgrade from a Previous Version

Microsoft suggests that anyone installing Vista on a PC that already has a recent version of Windows on it should use the *Upgrade* feature; that is, boot into the old Windows installation and start Vista setup from within. There are a few reasons you may want to do this:

Preserve your programs. If you upgrade to Vista from within, you won't have to reinstall all your applications and their settings. Of course, most of your programs will need to be updated or eventually reinstalled to work with Vista, but at least you won't have to do it all at once.

Preserve your settings. Some of your custom file type associations (Chapter 3) and Windows Explorer settings (Chapter 2) will be preserved during the upgrade, as will most of the settings (custom toolbars, etc.) in your installed programs.

Preserve your drive letters. If you have more than one hard disk (or more than one partition), the upgrade process preserves your drive letters. Sure, you can reassign drive letters at any time, with the exception of the Windows drive. When you do a "clean" install, setup insists on naming the Vista drive C:, regardless of the partition you choose during setup (see Figure 1-2, earlier).

Save time, sort of. It takes a lot less time, at least initially, to upgrade a previous version than to install Vista "clean" and subsequently install and set up all your programs. Of course, down the road, you'll spend a lot more time troubleshooting your upgraded system than you would a fresh install. And there's also the fact that a freshly installed Vista will easily outperform an upgraded one (more below).

It's easier. Upgrading is easier, but again, only initially.

As you can see, it's not all lollipops and rainbows. Here's why you may want to install fresh rather than upgrade a previous version:

Time for a little spring cleaning. How long have you been using that previous version of Windows? If you got XP when it came out, you've amassed as much as six years of junk—drivers, software, spyware, video codecs, and countless leftovers from software you don't even use anymore—that will continue to bog down Vista once you upgrade. If you take this opportunity to start anew, you'll have a leaner, faster PC when all is said and done, even if it does take more time to set up at the outset.

Be free of old hardware drivers. Even if Vista updates every hardware driver on your PC during an upgrade installation, pieces of the old drivers and support software—not to mention Registry settings from those old versions—will remain on your system and undoubtedly cause headaches down the road. Don't be surprised if you can't get your sound card—or any sound card, for that matter—to work on an upgraded Vista installation.

It's harder. OK, this may not seem like a selling point for a fresh install, but why back away from a challenge? It's not *that* much harder than upgrading.

Set up a dual-boot system. You'll need to install fresh if you want to keep your old Windows installation intact; see "Set Up a Dual-Boot System," later in this chapter, for details.

 Before upgrading or installing fresh on a hard disk containing data, you'd be wise to back up the entire system. But make sure the backup software you use—not to mention the backup *device*—will also operate in Windows Vista so you can read the media after the install is complete; otherwise, your backup will be worthless. See Chapter 6 for details on restoring data from a backup made in an earlier version of Windows.

So, if you want to proceed to upgrade your old software, just pop in the Vista disc and start the setup program. See "Install Vista on a New (Clean) System," earlier in this chapter, for details on some of the screens you'll encounter, and some tips about the product key. Otherwise, the upgrade pretty much takes care of itself. If setup crashes along the way, or Vista won't boot after you're done, see "Potential Problems During Setup," later in this chapter.

Special case: Reinstall Vista

You may find yourself in a position where you'll need to reinstall Windows Vista, usually in an effort to solve a nasty problem or to repair a damaged installation. The procedure you choose depends on the current state of your computer.

If Vista won't start, see "What to Do When Windows Won't Start" in Chapter 6. In most cases, you'll need to use your Vista setup disc, but you won't need to reinstall.

If you're able to start Vista and it's working well enough to reliably access your DVD drive, but poorly enough that you're considering reinstalling, then you'll need to decide whether to reinstall ("upgrade" as Vista setup puts it) or install a second copy on your PC.

An in-place reinstallation is the easiest way to go, and despite the warnings in the previous section, probably won't make things any worse. Just pop the DVD in your drive and follow the prompts. When asked what type of installation you want, select **Upgrade** and then follow the prompts.

But if your Vista installation is sufficiently munged, you may choose to install Vista fresh without harming your existing installation, as described next.

Fresh install on a dirty drive

As opposed to a "clean" drive, a *dirty* drive in this context is one that already has data on it. There are times you need to install Vista on a hard disk that already has a Windows installation, yet you don't want to perform an in-place upgrade or set up a dual-boot system.

For instance, if Vista won't start, and none of the solutions in Chapter 6 help you fix the problem, then you can do what's called a *parallel installation*, which allows you to start your PC and access your data. You may also want to do this if you have a Windows XP installation you don't want to upgrade.

 If you have more than one hard disk or partition, you can install Vista on a drive other than the one currently containing Windows. See "Set Up a Dual-Boot System," later in this chapter, for details.

To install Vista fresh on a drive with data on it, follow these steps:

1. Insert a Vista disc in your drive and boot off the DVD, as described in "Install Vista on a New (Clean) System," earlier in this chapter.
2. When you see the "Install Now" page, click the **Repair your computer** link at the bottom to get to the System Recovery Options window shown in Figure 6-3 (in Chapter 6).
3. From the list, select **Command Prompt**.
4. When the Command Prompt appears, change to your Windows drive, usually *C:*, by typing the drive letter and a colon (c:) and pressing **Enter**.
5. Rename the *Windows* folder to *windows.old*, like this:

   ```
   ren windows windows.old
   ```
6. Rename the *Program Files* folder to *programs.old*, like this:

   ```
   ren "program files" programs.old
   ```
7. Type exit or close the Command Prompt when you're done.
8. Restart your PC and boot onto the Vista setup DVD again.
9. Install Vista onto your Windows drive, as described earlier in this chapter.

When setup is complete, Vista will boot normally, at which point you'll be able to glean old files off of the *Windows.old* and *Programs.old* folders as needed. Eventually, you can delete these relics.

Potential Problems During Setup

The most common cause of a failed installation of Windows Vista is an out-of-date BIOS. If setup crashes, or if Vista won't boot after you finish installing, check with the manufacturer of your system or motherboard for any BIOS updates, and update your BIOS if needed. Better yet, make sure you have the latest BIOS before you begin installation, particularly if your PC is more than a year old.

Another common stumbling block to a successful Windows Vista setup is your video card (display adapter). If setup stops with an unintelligible error message, reboots unexpectedly during setup, or just hangs at a blank screen, your video card may be at fault. Unfortunately, setup will rarely, if ever, warn you about such an incompatibility before you begin. If replacing the video card permits Windows Vista to install, then the culprit is obvious.

Next, if you see an error that says something like "failed to open the windows image file," this is an indictment of your DVD drive. Setup installs Vista from a single, huge hard-disk image file, and some older drives can't handle files larger than 3 gigabytes in size. The solution is to replace the drive, or, if you're particularly attached to the drive *and* you're not in a hurry, purchase a copy of Vista setup on a stack of CDs (which Microsoft calls "alternate media") and try again.

Lastly, if it's an older disc, the culprit might be nothing more than a little dust; wipe the disk against your shirt and try again.

Set Up a Dual-Boot System

With a dual-boot (or multiboot) setup, you can install multiple operating systems side-by-side on the same computer, and simply choose which one to use each time you boot. So, why would you want to do this?

Both ends burning
If you rely on some software or hardware that won't operate in Windows Vista, you can install Vista and the other OS on the same system simultaneously. And there's no reason you can't install Vista alongside Linux, or even (if you have an Intel-based Mac) alongside Mac OS X. Or, if you're using the 64-bit version of Vista, you might need to keep that old XP installation around so you can run all that 16-bit software you use every day (16-bit software won't run on Vista-64).

Just testing

If you're in the process of upgrading from an earlier version of Windows to Windows Vista, you may wish to test Vista with your existing software and hardware without having to commit to the new OS until you're certain it will meet your needs. Of course, you can also do this with Microsoft Virtual PC 2007, freely available from *http://www.microsoft.com/virtualpc/*. Depending on your timing, you may even be able to download certain versions of Windows preinstalled on a Virtual Hard Disk that you can run in place on your PC; see *http://www.microsoft.com/vhd* for details.

Software testbed

Install two copies of Windows Vista on your system—one for normal use, and one as a testbed for new software and hardware. That way, you can try out a potentially buggy product without jeopardizing the main OS on which you rely. Again, you can also use Virtual PC for this purpose, but it's just so darn slow....

Backdoor

Got disk space to burn? Install Vista twice, and keep the second installation around to easily access your data in case your primary installation fails.

For that matter, you can set up a dual-boot system *after* a Vista installation fails, and get to your valuable data without first having to repair Windows.

Windows Vista comes with built-in support for a dual-boot system. The dual-boot feature, called the *Windows Boot Manager*, is installed automatically when you install Vista, whether you set up a dual-boot system or not. If, at the end of the installation, Windows Vista is the only operating system on your computer, it boots automatically without giving you a choice. Otherwise, you'll see a menu of installed operating systems, from which you can choose the OS you wish to use.

To set up a dual-boot system, you'll need at least two partitions: one for each operating system. Install the first OS on any drive you like. Then, during Vista setup, when you see the "Where do you want to install Windows?" page (Figure 1-2), just select the empty drive, and setup will do the rest.

 See Chapter 5 for more information on partitions, including a way to divide your current single-partition drive into two partitions *without* having to reformat.

In most cases, the boot manager of the most-recently installed operating system is the one that will be used for all your operating systems, so the sequence in which you install your operating systems is very important. Most of the time, you'll need to install older operating systems *before* newer ones. For instance, on a PC with Windows 98, just install Vista on a different drive, and voilà: you'll have a functional dual-boot system.

 Some other operating systems, such as FreeBSD and Windows 2000, have boot managers of their own, and can therefore be installed either before or after Vista is installed with little additional fuss. However, those operating systems *without* their own boot managers, such as Windows 9x/Me, will break the Windows Vista boot manager if installed subsequently.

Modify the Boot Manager configuration

The Windows Boot Manager is responsible for loading Vista, and, optionally, booting any other operating systems you may have installed.

The Boot Manager in both Windows XP and 2000 stored its configuration in a tiny, easily editable file called *boot.ini* in the root folder of your C: drive, but in Windows Vista, this file is no longer used. If you install Vista on an XP system, and then open the *boot.ini* file left behind, you'll see this message:

```
;Warning: Boot.ini is used on Windows XP and earlier operating systems.
;Warning: Use BCDEDIT.exe to modify Windows Vista boot options.
```

The BCDEdit (*bcdedit.exe*) tool that comes with Vista is a command-line tool, and isn't exactly user-friendly. Open a Command Prompt window (in administrator mode, as described in Chapter 8), type bcdedit and press **Enter**, and you'll see output that looks something like this:

```
Windows Boot Manager
--------------------
identifier              {bootmgr}
device                  partition=C:
description             Windows Boot Manager
locale                  en-US
inherit                 {globalsettings}
default                 {default}
displayorder            {ntldr}
                        {default}
toolsdisplayorder       {memdiag}
timeout                 3
```

```
Windows Legacy OS Loader
------------------------
identifier              {ntldr}
device                  partition=C:
path                    \ntldr
description             Earlier version of Windows

Windows Boot Loader
-------------------
identifier              {default}
device                  partition=D:
path                    \Windows\system32\winload.exe
description             Microsoft Windows Vista
locale                  en-US
inherit                 {bootloadersettings}
osdevice                partition=D:
systemroot              \Windows
resumeobject            {70c7d34d-b6b4-12db-cc71-d30cdb1ce261}
nx                      OptIn
detecthal               Yes
```

[handwritten annotation in left margin: "Windows Legacy OS Loader" with arrow pointing to the section]

What a mess. In short, the first section describes the menu you see when you first boot; the second section here—Windows Legacy OS Loader—describes the older version of Windows (XP); and finally, the third section—Windows Boot Loader—describes your new Vista installation.

If you type bcdedit /? at the prompt, you'll see a bunch of command-line parameters you can use to add or remove entries, choose a new default (the OS that's loaded if you don't choose one before the timer runs out), or run a variety of debugging tools.

But if all you want to do is choose a default and maybe change the timeout, there's a better tool. Open your Start menu, type msconfig in the **Search** box and press **Enter** to open the System Configuration window, and choose the **Boot** tab as shown in Figure 1-3.

Here, the easy options are truly self-evident, and the advanced options are at least accessible. On the right, you can adjust the **Timeout** from its default of 30 seconds; type 5 here, and you'll instantly shave off 25 seconds from your unattended boot time. (Don't use a value so small that you won't have time to change it, lest you set an inoperable installation as the default and have no way to get around it.)

To choose the default OS, select it in the list and click **Set as default**. (See "Make Your Own Windows Startup Logo," in Chapter 2, for an example of when you'd use the **No GUI boot** option.) When you're done, click **OK**, and then restart Windows to see your new settings.

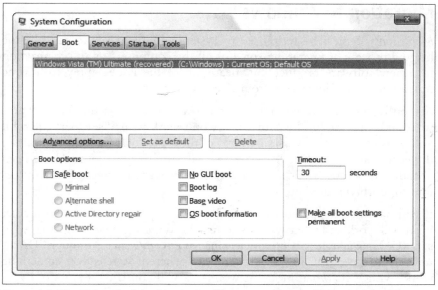

Figure 1-3. The Boot tab of the System Configuration tool provides most of the features of BCDEdit in a much more pleasant interface

Of operating systems and filesystems

When setting up a dual-boot system for day-to-day use, you'll need to consider the matter of sharing files between your operating systems.

In order to share files between operating systems, both partitions must use filesystems supported by at least one OS. For instance, if you have a dual-boot setup with both Windows Vista and Windows 98, you'll be able to see both drives while you're in Vista, but you'll only be able to see the 98 drive while 98 is running. (Although Vista can read drives formatted with the FAT32 filesystem, it can't be installed on one.) See Chapter 5 for details.

Now, if both your partitions use the NTFS filesystem—which is what you'd likely get if you set up a dual-boot system with Vista and XP—you also may have ownership problems to contend with. As explained in Chapter 8, every file and folder on your PC has an "owner," a user tied to a specific account on your PC. If, for instance, you create a file in Windows XP and then attempt to modify it in Vista, you may be denied permission until you "take ownership," as explained in "Protect Your Files with Encryption" in Chapter 8.

And in regards to protecting your data, encryption is also effective at preventing an intruder from reading your files by installing a second operating system on your PC.

Migration to Windows Vista

Migration is typically a term used by system administrators to describe the lengthy process of upgrading some or all the computers in an organization to a new software product, but nearly all of the issues apply to anyone upgrading to Windows Vista from an earlier version.

As you've probably discovered on your own, there are a number of hardware and software products that just won't work with Vista (particularly if you're using the 64-bit version). Some of these products are simply awaiting driver updates from their respective manufacturers, while others have been abandoned because their manufacturers don't want to invest the resources into supporting retired products.

If you haven't yet upgraded to Windows Vista, the easiest way to predict what will work and what won't is to use the Windows Vista Upgrade Advisor (UA), available at *http://www.microsoft.com/vista*. Although UA is unlikely to give you any false positives—wherein it tells you something works with Vista when in fact it won't—it will construct a laundry list of potential problems with which you can follow up on your own. (Unfortunately, UA won't run on 64-bit XP.)

For instance, UA might bring to your attention that your printer, antivirus software, backup software, CD burning software, and perhaps your Bluetooth adapter are all unsupported on Vista. So, this means you'll definitely need new versions of your antivirus and backup software (see Chapter 6) and your CD burning software (Chapter 4). You'll also need to check with the manufacturers of your printer and Bluetooth adapter to see whether they've released native Vista drivers; if not, and you don't want to wait, you'll need to replace those devices.

Sentimental Fool

Disorientation is not an uncommon sensation among those users coming to Vista from earlier versions of Windows. Here's where you can find some of the more elusive entities you may have grown accustomed to in Windows XP:

Add or Remove Programs
  This is still in Control Panel, but now it's called **Programs and Features**.

Address Bar
  The path box in Windows Explorer doubles as an address bar, so if you want to type a path or copy the current path to the clipboard, click just to the right of the text, and Explorer will show you a familiar, backslash-equipped folder path.

Display Properties

Right-click an empty area of the desktop and select **Personalize** (or open the **Personalize** page in Control Panel), and then click the **Display Settings** link at the bottom of the page.

File Types window

Sorry, you don't get one of these in Vista. The best Microsoft could do is the **Default Programs** page in Control Panel. If you want to edit your context menus, you'll need File Type Doctor, explained in Chapter 3.

Menus in Windows and Internet Explorer

Microsoft took the menus out of both Windows Explorer and Internet Explorer, and replaced them with drop-down buttons that do pretty much the same thing. But you can always press the **Alt** key on the keyboard to temporarily show the old, familiar menu bar in either application. See Chapter 2 if you want to make it permanent in Windows Explorer.

Network Connections

As explained in Chapter 7, the Network Connections window has been subjugated in Vista, and is now only accessible as a link on the left side of the Network and Sharing Center page.

Shut Down button

The red button at the bottom of the Start menu doesn't shut down Windows any more, but rather puts it to sleep. Click the tiny arrow to the right of the red button to shut down, restart, or log off. To reconfigure the red button to shut down instead, see Chapter 5.

System

The familiar System Properties window that has been around since Windows 2000, and the only way to change your PC's name on your network, is now buried under the **Advanced system settings** link on the System page in Control Panel. Alternatively, you can type SystemPropertiesAdvanced.exe in the Start menu's **Search** box and press **Enter** to open this window.

CHAPTER 2
Shell Tweaks

What makes an ideal user interface? Of course, the phrase "easy to use" springs to mind, but that could mean anything. Some of us find large, friendly controls that need no explanation to be "easy," while those more experienced may consider smaller, less obtrusive controls to be easier to use on a daily basis. And some might argue that the best interface is no interface at all.

At first glance, it seems like Microsoft messed around with the _shell_—the desktop interface, including the Start menu and Windows Explorer—more than anything else when assembling Windows Vista. Sure, Microsoft made tons of changes under the hood (covered in subsequent chapters), but to those familiar with, say, Windows XP, the most immediately apparent changes to the operating system have been made to Windows Explorer and its cohorts.

As a result, the sensation most seasoned Windows users will likely experience when they open Vista's Explorer for the first time is…disorientation.

Figure 2-1 shows Windows Explorer as it appears right out of the box.

The formal Windows Explorer shortcut is buried deep in the Start menu, under **All Programs → Accessories**, but you can open an Explorer window by double-clicking any folder icon on the desktop or selecting one of the locations on the righthand column of the Start menu (e.g., **Documents, Pictures, Music, Games**). Mercifully, Microsoft finally dropped the cutesy "My" prefix used in earlier versions of Windows, so the _My Pictures_ folder is now merely _Pictures_.

While the basic layout is more or less the same as versions of Explorer dating back to 1995, the menu and the title bar are both gone, replaced with many subtle—almost hidden—controls that surprisingly offer more functionality than any previous version. But that's only the beginning. The righthand pane of the window more closely resembles a restaurant menu than a list of files, which does end up making it look more friendly, if a little weird.

Figure 2-1. Windows Explorer may have been gussied up for Windows Vista, but everything you need is still within reach

And to the left, where you'd expect to find the folder tree, resides the **Favorite Links** pane (akin to the "Places" bar found in some file dialog windows in Vista).

The folder tree sits at the bottom left of the Explorer window, filled with a list of unfamiliar folders, such as *Contacts*, *Downloads*, and *Saved Games*. The little plus [+] and minus [–] boxes, once used to identify expandable branches in the folder tree, are now microscopic arrows: a right-pointing arrow signifies a collapsed branch, and a downward arrow signifies an expanded branch.

> Across the bottom of the Explorer window is the preview pane; it's resizable, so you can enlarge it to show more information, or shrink it out of the way. If you lose the preview pane and want to get it back, open the **Organize** drop-down and select **Layout → Preview Pane**.

Fortunately, the basic premise of the Explorer window remains the same: click a location (i.e., folder) on the left side to see the folder's contents on the right. To make Explorer look more like earlier versions, expand the

Folders pane by dragging the upper edge of the **Folders** title strip to the top of the window, covering **Favorite Links**. Use the **Views** drop-down to choose **Details**, or any other view more useful than **Tiles**. And if you want your menu bar back, just press the **Alt** key, or open the **Organize** drop-down and select **Layout → Menu Bar**. See Figure 2-2 for a visual rundown of everything you can do in Windows Explorer.

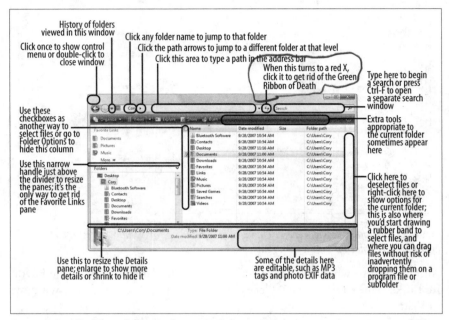

Figure 2-2. All of the subtle—and not so subtle—controls you can use to navigate folders and manage your files in Windows Explorer

Now, with improved security (covered in Chapter 8), included backup software at long last (Chapter 6), and a handy-dandy new Search tool (later in this chapter), Vista takes your stuff more seriously than any previous version of Windows. But the tools Vista gives you (Explorer, et al.) to manage your pictures, music, spreadsheets, email mailboxes, saved games, etc., fall short in a lot of ways. Fortunately, with some of the tricks and adjustments in this chapter, you should be able to transform the shell into a more useful tool that—at the very least—you actually won't mind using every day.

Customize Windows Explorer

Many aspects of the way Windows works can be controlled by changing settings scattered throughout the interface. When it comes to the look and feel of Windows Explorer, and the way it displays and handles your files, the

Folder Options window is a good place to start. In Explorer, open the Organize drop-down and select **Folder and Search Options** (or open **Folder Options** in Control Panel).

As explained in "Quick Access to Control Panel," Microsoft didn't finish revamping Control Panel before shipping Windows Vista. As a result, we have windows like Folder Options filled with holdover features that aren't really applicable anymore, such as these found under the **General** tab:

Tasks
This misnamed option has nothing to do with the Tasks links shown in some Control Panel pages. Rather, choose **Use Windows classic folders** to turn on the menu bar that's hidden by default, and hide the **Preview** and **Details** panes. Of course, you can temporarily show the menu bar at any time by pressing the **Alt** key, and customize all of Explorer's panes by selecting **Layout** from the **Organize** drop-down.

Browse folders
It doesn't make any difference which option you select here, unless you hide the folder tree in Windows Explorer by opening the **Organize** drop-down and selecting **Layout → Navigation Pane**.

Use the **Ctrl** key when double-clicking folder icons to override your choice here. Or, right-click any folder icon and select **Open** (not the bolded **Explore**) to open the folder in a new window.

Click items as follows
Set this to **Single-click to open an item** if you like the idea of navigating most of Windows as though it were a web site—in other words, without ever having to double-click to open an item.

If you choose the single-click interface, you'll no longer be able to click an item twice slowly to rename it; instead, you must either right-click and select **Rename** or carefully move the mouse pointer so that it is hovering over the icon and press the **F2** key.

The point of double-clicking is to prevent you from accidentally opening a program or folder when you're just trying to select, delete, move, copy, or rename the file. If you don't like double-clicking, but aren't comfortable with the single-click interface Explorer provides, most pointing devices (mice, styli, trackballs) with more than two buttons allow you to program the additional buttons to handle double-click duty.

The **View** tab (Figure 2-3) contains settings that affect how much information Explorer shows you, arranged in alphabetical order.

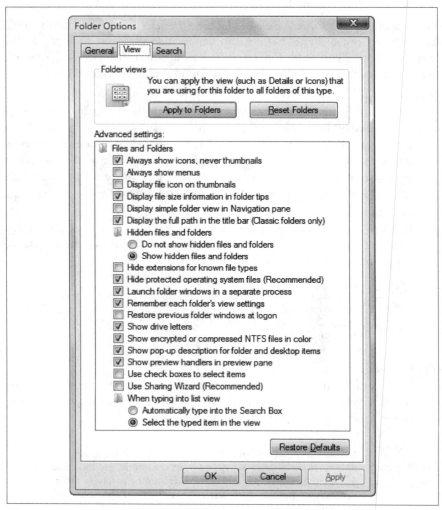

Figure 2-3. The most useful Explorer settings are in the View tab

Unfortunately, the defaults are set in favor of a "simpler" (read *dumbed-down*) interface, which has the unfortunate and ironic side effect of making many everyday tasks like organizing files, sharing folders over a network, or even opening certain folders, more difficult. But probably the most annoying thing is that Vista provides no help whatsoever for these settings, so they're explained in detail here.

Some of these options may not be available in all editions of Windows. Also, the use of some of these options can be very confusing, in that enabling them ends up turning something *off* in the interface, or vice-versa. But that's the nature of the beast....

Always show icons, never thumbnails. This is a setting Windows has been lacking for years. By default, Explorer automatically shows large thumbnails when a folder (or search results window) contains mostly image files. Turn on this option to disable thumbnails except when you specifically select **Thumbnails** from the **Views** drop-down. See "Green Ribbon of Death," in Chapter 6, for another reason to use this setting.

Always show menus. This self-explanatory option basically accomplishes the same thing as selecting **Use Classic Folders** on the **General** tab. Of course, you can display the menu bar at any time by pressing the **Alt** key.

Display file icon on thumbnails. Turn this off for cleaner-looking thumbnails, or turn it on if you want to more easily distinguish a JPG image from a Photoshop document. Better yet, turn off the **Hide extensions for known file types** option, described later in this section.

Display file size information in folder tips. Like many settings here, this option doesn't do exactly what it says. Turn it on, and the tool tip that appears when you hover your mouse over a folder icon will include information about the contents of the folder, including names of some of its subfolders and the size of the files contained therein. Turn off the option, and all you'll get is the date and time of the folder. To turn off folder tips altogether, use the **Show pop-up description for folder and desktop items** option, described later in this section.

Display simple folder view in Navigation pane. The *simple folder view* refers to the way the folder tree looks, and is turned on by default. Turn it off to show dotted lines connecting folders, like the folder trees in some earlier versions of Windows.

Display the full path in the title bar (Classic folders only). This setting does not affect the Windows Explorer title bar, nor does it have anything to do with "Classic" folders. Instead, it determines whether the full path or only the bare folder name appears in the taskbar button and in the task switcher (**Alt-Tab** window) for each open folder window.

Despite this setting, Explorer's title bar never contains any text at all, and the full path of the current folder is always shown in the Address box at the top of the window. See "Navigating files and folders," later in this chapter, for more information on the path box.

Hidden files and folders. Vista does not show hidden files by default in Explorer. If you set this option to **Show hidden files and folders**, any files with the *hidden* or *system* file attribute will be shown in Explorer, but their icons will still appear semi-transparent.

> To hide or unhide a file or folder, right-click it, select **Properties**, and change the **Hidden** option. For quicker access to a file's attributes, try the **Change file attributes** tool, part of Creative Element Power Tools (*http://www.creativelement.com/powertools/*).

Hide extensions for known file types. Some believe this feature to be one of Windows' biggest annoyances. Filename extensions—the last few letters after the dot in a file's name—are hidden by default in Windows, and have been in every Windows release since Windows 95. Filename extensions (e.g., *.txt, .jpg, .doc*) determine how Windows interacts with your documents, and hiding this information only makes it harder to distinguish different files. See "File Type Associations," in Chapter 3, for a further explanation of why you'll probably want to turn off this option and leave it off.

Hide protected operating system files. When this option is turned on (the default), files with the *system* file attribute are hidden in Explorer, regardless of the **Hidden files and folders** option, discussed earlier. So-called *system* files include most of the boot loader files discussed in Chapter 1, the *$RECYCLE.BIN* and *System Volume Information* folders found on every hard drive, the *hiberfil.sys* hibernation file (see Chapter 5), and a handful of other files. Leave this option turned on to protect these important files from accidental damage, or turn it off if you want to see and mess around with them.

Launch folder windows in a separate process. By default, the desktop, Start menu, and all open Explorer and single-folder windows are handled by the same instance of Explorer. That is, only one copy of the *Explorer.exe* application is ever in memory. If you turn on this option, each Explorer window will use a new instance of the program. Although this takes slightly more memory and may slightly increase the time it takes to open new Explorer windows, it means that if one Explorer window crashes—see "Green Ribbon of Death" in Chapter 6—it won't bring them all down.

To see this option in action, open a few Explorer windows. Then, right-click an empty area of the taskbar, select Task Manager, choose the **Processes** tab, and click the **Image Name** column header to sort the list alphabetically. If you've elected to launch folder windows in a separate process, you'll see multiple instances of *Explorer.exe* listed, one for each open window and one for the desktop. (Note that a problem that prevented Windows from reinstating a crashed desktop in previous versions of Windows has been more or less fixed in Vista.)

Remember each folder's view settings. This option, when enabled, forces Explorer to remember the "view" settings for the 20–30 most recently opened folders, such as the sort order and icon size. This "memory" overrides the default view settings, but only for the folders you've recently customized.

Unfortunately, this feature does cause problems from time to time. If you ever encounter a folder missing all its **Details** columns, for instance (only the **Name** column appears), then turn off this option temporarily to force Windows to forget the settings for the folder. Leave this option off if you want your folders to always be shown with your chosen default view settings.

To change the defaults used by *all* folders, click the **Apply to Folders** button at the top of the Folder Options window, as described in the section "Force Explorer to Remember Its Own Settings," next.

Restore previous folder windows at logon. Turn this option on if you want Windows to remember which folders are open when you shut down or log out, and then reopen them the next time you log in. Another way to do this is to not shut down at all, but rather use Vista's Sleep feature, explained in "Start Windows Instantly (Almost)" in Chapter 5.

Show drive letters. Turn this off to hide drive letters (e.g., C:, D:, N:) from Explorer's folder tree.

Show encrypted or compressed NTFS files in color. Among the additional services provided by the NTFS filesystem (see Chapter 1) are support for on-the-fly encryption and compression. Turn on this option to visually distinguish encrypted and compressed files and folders by displaying their names in blue. See "Protect Your Files with Encryption," in Chapter 8, for a way to customize the colors used for these files.

Show pop-up description for folder and desktop items. Commonly referred to as "tool tips," pop-up descriptions show additional details about the file or folder underneath the mouse pointer. Turn off this option to hide these tool tips. See also the **Display file size information in folder tips option**, earlier in this section, for a related setting.

Show preview handlers in preview pane. When the Preview pane is visible (open the **Organize** drop-down and select **Layout → Preview Pane**), Windows shows a thumbnail preview on the left unless this option is turned off.

Use check boxes to select items. If you enable this option, you'll be able to select multiple files without having to drag a *rubber band* or use the keyboard. See "Slicker Ways to Select Files," later in this chapter, for tips involving this feature.

Use Sharing Wizard. Disable this option to use the Advanced Sharing window instead of the feeble Sharing Wizard each time you right-click a folder or drive and select **Share**. Despite the fact that Microsoft apparently recommends that you use this feature, only the Advanced Sharing window lets you specify sharing permissions to properly protect your data. See Chapter 8 for details.

When typing into list view. See "Who Doesn't Love Keyboard Shortcuts?," later in this chapter, for tips involving this setting.

What it comes down to, of course, is that you should use what works best for you. Don't blindly accept the defaults just because they came out of the box that way.

The **Search** tab in this window is dissected in excruciating detail in "Search Tricks," later in this chapter.

Force Explorer to Remember Its Own Settings

One of the most common annoyances with Windows Explorer is, well, annoying, because it should've been so simple for Microsoft to get it right.

How many times have you selected the **Details** view in Explorer, only to find that it has reverted to the **Large Icons** view the next time you open the folder?

For the most part, Windows Explorer's apparent inability to remember its own settings is the result of a battle among three opposing forces: your saved settings, Vista's propensity to show thumbnail previews for media files, and some poor coding on Microsoft's part.

First, open the **Folder Options** window, turn on the **View** tab, turn on the **Remember each folder's view settings** option, and click **OK**. Thereafter, Windows Explorer will temporarily save the settings for roughly 30 of the most recently viewed folders. Most of the time, these saved settings override your saved defaults. But how do you change the defaults?

 Your choices are stored in the Registry (discussed in Chapter 3) rather than in the folders themselves, which not only explains the limit on the number of folders Explorer can remember, but exposes a rather annoying flaw in the system. Say you choose the view settings for a folder called *Lenny*. When you close and reopen *Lenny* right away, your settings will remain. However, if you rename the *Lenny* folder to, say, *Karl*, it will instantly revert to Explorer's defaults and forget the settings you made only seconds earlier.

If you're tired of constantly having to go back to Explorer's **View** drop-down to change the icon size, or having to click the column headers to sort file listings, you can set your own defaults. But Explorer's use of your defaults won't make much sense until you figure out Vista's clandestine template system.

A *template* is a collection of folder display settings that includes the view (e.g., Large Icons, Details, etc.), the sorting method, and the columns displayed. Each time you open a folder, Vista automatically picks one of the five preset templates, and uses those settings to configure the view. And herein lies the source of the problem: Vista is no good at picking the default template. You might open a folder full of HTML web page documents, and Explorer will choose the template for music files. Or, a folder with nothing but photos will show up in the **Details** view, rather than thumbnails (Large Icons).

Unfortunately, there's nothing you can do to change how Vista chooses its templates, nor can you remove or create your own templates. But you *can* customize the view settings for each template so that when Windows Explorer does get it right, you'll get the view you need. To choose a template for a folder and then customize it, see "Photos, Pictures, Images" in Chapter 4.

But you may soon realize that Windows gets it wrong too often, and customizing the templates just isn't enough. In this case, the solution is to duplicate your favorite view settings across every template, so no matter which template Windows picks, you'll get the view you need:

1. Open Windows Explorer and navigate to any folder with files in it. (This won't work with drives, so make sure the folder isn't a root folder.)

2. Right-click the folder in the tree, select **Properties**, and choose the **Customize** tab. Or right-click an empty area of the folder background and select **Customize This Folder**. (See the "Missing the Customize Tab?" sidebar, next, if these options aren't present.)

Missing the Customize Tab?

If you don't see the **Customize** tab in the Properties window for a folder, all you need is a quick Registry hack to fix the problem.

Open the Registry Editor (see Chapter 3) and expand the branches to HKEY_ CLASSES_ROOT\Directory\shellex\PropertySheetHandlers. Look for a subkey named {ef43ecfe-2ab9-4632-bf21-58909dd177f0}; if it isn't there, create a new key with that name by going to **Edit → New → Key**.

Navigate to HKEY_CURRENT_USER\Software\Microsoft\Windows\ CurrentVersion\Policies\Explorer. Double-click the NoCustomizeThisFolder value in the right pane, type 0 (zero) in the **Value data** field, and click **OK**. Do the same for the NoCustomizeWebView and ClassicShell values. (If any of these values are absent, skip 'em.)

And finally, navigate to HKEY_LOCAL_MACHINE\Software\Microsoft\Windows\ CurrentVersion\policies\Explorer, and if the Explorer key is present, set the same three values to 0 (zero). Close the Registry Editor when you're done, restart Windows, and try again.

3. From the **Use this folder type as a template** listbox, select the first entry, **All Items**, and then click **OK**.

4. Set your view settings, column headers, and sorting to your taste.

5. Open the **Organize** drop-down, select **Folder and Search Options**, and then choose the **View** tab.

6. Click the **Apply to Folders** button, answer **Yes**, and then click **OK**.

7. Repeat steps 3–6 for each of the other four templates: **Documents**, **Pictures and Videos**, **Music Details**, and **Music Icons**.

That's it; now you have five identical templates, and you no longer need to care whether or not Vista knows what kind of files are in each folder.

Start Explorer with Any Folder

For the most part, you get the same window when you double-click a folder icon on your desktop as when you use the **Windows Explorer** shortcut in your Start menu. But the latter, without a target, simply dumps you in your home folder.

To customize the folder that Windows Explorer opens by default, you need to create a custom Windows Shortcut. To start, right-click an empty space on your desktop and select **New → Shortcut**.

If you've removed **Windows Shortcut** from Explorer's Ne menu, another way to make one is to open your Start mer and type explorer.exe in the **Search** box (the *.exe* extensio is necessary). Using the right mouse button, drag th explorer.exe entry from the search results onto an empty area of your desktop, and then select **Create Shortcuts Here** from the menu that appears. Right-click on the newly created explorer.exe - Shortcut, select **Properties**, and choose the **Shortcut** tab.

Next, type the following text into the **Target** field:

    explorer.exe d:\myfolder

where *d:\myfolder* is the full path of the folder you want Explorer to open. You might see the text %SystemRoot% in front of explorer.exe, which can be left alone or removed as desired.

Click **OK** when you're done, and then double-click the new shortcut to try it out. There are actually a bunch of different parameters you can use, should you feel the need to fine-tune the appearance of the folder tree. The full syntax is as follows:

    explorer.exe [/n][,/e][,/root,object][[,/select],subobject]

The square brackets ([...]) show the optional nature of each of the parameters. Note that the syntax here isn't like most other programs that take command-line parameters; for instance, the parameters must be in order and separated by commas. However, unlike earlier version of Windows, you don't have to include the commas for omitted parameters.

/n   This opens a new window even if the folder is already open elsewhere.

/e   This shows the folder tree pane in the event you've turned it off.

/root,object

The /root,object parameter lets you choose what appears as the root of all folders in the new window, which is useful if you want an abbreviated tree for security reasons. The default, of course, is the desktop. You can specify an ordinary folder to be the root of the tree (i.e., /root,c:\stuff), or a system object by specifying its Class ID (see Chapter 3).

/select

If you include the /select switch along with a folder path (subobject, discussed next), Explorer opens the folder's parent and selects it in the right pane. Only if you omit /select does Explorer actually open the folder you specify. See the subobject entry, next, for an example of when this is useful.

subobject
> This is the path to open, shown in the first example. Unless you use the
> /select option, Explorer highlights *subobject* in the tree and shows its
> contents in the right pane.

For example, if you want Explorer to open to the *Computer* folder so that no
drive branches are initially expanded—which is handy if you have several
drives and you want to see them all on equal footing—type this:

```
explorer.exe /n,/e,/select,c:\
```

Or, to display an Explorer window rooted at *C:*, use this:

```
explorer.exe /n,/e,/root,c:\
```

In addition to launching Explorer with these parameters, you can open an
Explorer window in the context of any object on the screen and Windows
will send you to the right place.

For example, you can right-click on any visible folder icon (on your desktop, in an open folder, and even in the tree pane of another Explorer window) and select **Explore** to open a new Explorer window with the folder in
question highlighted. You can also explore from various system objects by
right-clicking and selecting **Explore**. This works on the **Start** button, any
folder in your Start menu, and folders in your file dialogs.

Get to the Desktop

If you have to reach over a pile of papers just to reach your keyboard, then
you're the type who likes surfaces. The Windows desktop is no exception,
and yours is probably full of files you need. Problem is, they're always
underneath everything else.

Here are some ways to get to the stuff on your desktop without much hassle:

Minimize everything
> Hold the Windows logo key (which we'll call *Winkey*, just to be cute)
> and press **D** to quickly show the desktop. Press Winkey-**D** again to
> restore your windows (although not necessarily in the same sequence). Do
> this many times to give yourself a headache. (If your keyboard has no Win-
> key, see "Who Doesn't Love Keyboard Shortcuts?," later in this chapter.)

Show Desktop
> Don't want to use the keyboard? Just locate the Quick Launch toolbar,
> the little row of tiny buttons on the far left of your taskbar, and click the
> **Show Desktop** button (the blue rectangle in Figure 2-4). Give the but-
> ton another click to restore the windows.
>
> If the Quick Launch toolbar isn't there, right-click an empty area on
> your taskbar and go to **Toolbars → Quick Launch**. If you don't see the

Show Desktop button, it may be buried inside the tiny white arrows; otherwise, see the "Make a Show Desktop Button" sidebar for tips.

You can also right-click an empty area of the Taskbar, and select **Show the Desktop** to do the same thing as the button. Then, to restore your windows, right-click the taskbar again and select **Show Open Windows**.

Figure 2-4. Use this handy button to show the Windows desktop without having to manually minimize all your windows

Make a Show Desktop Button

By default, the Quick Launch toolbar comes with a **Show Desktop** button, which allows you to quickly hide all open windows and access stuff on your desktop, and then quickly bring them all back when you're done. But what if your Quick Launch toolbar doesn't have one?

Unlike most other toolbar buttons, the **Show Desktop** button isn't a Windows Shortcut. Rather, it's a Shell Command File (*.scf*), which is really just a plain-text file containing a special command Windows understands. To create a new *.scf* file, open your favorite plain-text editor (or Notepad), and type the following five lines:

```
[Shell]
Command=2
IconFile=explorer.exe,3
[Taskbar]
Command=ToggleDesktop
```

Save the file as *Show Desktop.scf* (or any other name, provided that you include the *.scf* filename extension) anywhere you like, including your desktop. To have the icon appear on your Quick Launch toolbar, place the file in this folder:

C:\Users\{user}\AppData\Roaming\Microsoft\Internet Explorer\Quick Launch

If you like the **Show Desktop** button, but you don't like the clutter of the Quick Launch toolbar, you can simply eliminate the buttons you don't use by right-clicking each one and selecting **Delete**.

Next, right-click an empty area of the Taskbar, turn off the **Lock the Taskbar** option, and then shrink down the newly sanitized Quick Launch toolbar so it's no larger than the remaining button, like the example in Figure 2-4. When things are the way you like them, turn **Lock the Taskbar** back on.

Open Windows Explorer

Another approach is to simply open a Windows Explorer window and navigate to the *Desktop* folder at the top of the tree. That way, you can leave your open programs intact, making it easier to drag files onto them from the desktop.

 You can also drag files onto a minimized application, provided you have a steady hand and some patience. Just drag down to the taskbar and hover the file over the minimized application button you want to restore. Although you can't drop files on the buttons themselves, if you wait a second or two, Windows will restore the application window, at which point you can drag the file over to the window and drop it.

Icons on the taskbar

Right-click an empty area of the taskbar, select **Toolbars**, and then select **Desktop**. By default, the toolbar will probably be smushed up against the notification area (tray) and the clock, so right-click the taskbar again and turn off the **Lock the Taskbar** option so you can move the **Desktop** toolbar around. Next, right-click the **Desktop** title and select the **Show Text** option to fit more icons on the bar. It's not the most convenient interface, especially if you have a lot on your desktop, but it's there if you need it.

Save Your Desktop Layout

Let me guess: you sneezed and Windows rearranged your desktop icons.

This happens for a variety of reasons, most commonly any time Windows changes the screen resolution (often for games), when you update your display settings, or when you install a new video card driver. But it'll also happen whenever you use the Magnifier tool that comes with Vista, or when you change the desktop icon size (discussed next). Regardless of the trigger, it's a petty annoyance we all could do without.

There are a variety of tools designed to combat this problem, but most have died out for one reason or another. The quick and dirty—not to mention free—solution is to use an add-on released by Microsoft several years ago; with a little tweak, it works just fine in Vista (32-bit edition only). Here's how you install and use it:

1. Go to *http://www.annoyances.org/exec/software/layout* and download the *layout.zip* file, saving it to your desktop.

2. Open *layout.zip*, and inside you'll find two files. The *.dll* file you can find elsewhere on the Web, but the other (the *.reg* file) has been specifically modified for this book to work with Vista.

3. Copy the *layout.dll* file to your *C:\Windows\System32* folder.

4. Double-click the other file, *install.reg*, and answer **Yes** when asked whether you want to continue. (See Chapter 3 for more information on .reg files.)

5. Next, right-click an empty area of your desktop and select **Save Desktop Icon Layout**.

6. The next time Windows messes up your icons, just right-click an empty area of your desktop and select **Restore Desktop Icon Layout**.

Now, if Windows isn't spontaneously rearranging your desktop icons, but refuses to let you put them where you want them, there's a fix for that, too. This problem is caused by either one of two mechanisms designed to help keep your desktop icons tidy, and you'll have to turn at least one of them off to more freely place your desktop icons. Right-click an empty area of the desktop, select **View**, and turn off the **Auto Arrange** option. The other, **Align to Grid**, is discussed next.

Control the space between desktop icons

As any green grocer will tell you, the most efficient way to stack oranges is the face-centered cubic arrangement, wherein each piece of fruit is placed in the cavity formed by three adjacent oranges in the lower plane. (For more information, Google "Kepler Conjecture.") Sadly, Windows Vista doesn't have this option, but if you're content with Windows' rectilinear arrangement, you can fine-tune row and column spacing on the desktop.

Also in the aforementioned **View** menu is the **Align to Grid** option. Leave it on, and your icons will always appear lined up in rows and columns; turn it off to have complete flexibility when dragging your icons around the desktop.

To change the spacing, right-click an empty area of the desktop, select **Personalize**, and then click **Window Color and Appearance**. Click the **Open classic appearance properties for more color options** link, and then click **Advanced**. (Or, if you're not using Vista's Aero interface, just click **Advanced** here.) From the **Item** drop-down menu, choose **Icon Spacing (Horizontal)** and adjust the spacing by changing the **Size** value to indicate the number of pixels between the edges of adjacent icons.

A good value is approximately 1.3 to 1.5 times the width of an icon. To find the size of your desktop icons, right-click an empty area of the desktop and select **View**. If **Medium Icons** (the default) is checked, your icons are 44×44. For **Classic Icons**, they're the standard 32×32; for **Large Icons**, they're 86×86.

So, if you're using classic icons, specify 40 in the Advanced Appearance window to pack them pretty closely, or 50 to spread them apart. Next, change the **Icon Spacing (Vertical)** value; use the same number for both the horizontal and vertical measurements, and the result will look pretty good.

Quick Access to Control Panel

A lot of the clicking and scrounging in this book takes place in Control Panel, a window that provides links to many settings that affect the way Vista looks, sounds, and behaves. It's a hodge-podge of modern web-like pages and older, pre-Vista tabbed dialog windows. Some of the dialog windows date back more than a decade to Windows 95, and are still present merely because Microsoft presumably doesn't want to invest the resources to update or replace all their settings. (For examples, see the beginning of this chapter.)

As a result, it can be hard to find specific settings in Control Panel, and time-consuming to repeatedly return to dialogs to change certain settings. Fortunately, there are a few tricks that will help you find and change settings faster.

First, open Control Panel, and click the **Classic View** link on the left to show a complete list of all the top-level Control Panel pages and windows. Next, click the little path arrow to the right of the **Control Panel** text in the address bar, as shown in Figure 2-5. As you can see, this list is considerably shorter than the one in the main window.

Why? Because clicking the path arrows shows only the web-style Control Panel pages, not the older tabbed dialog windows. It seems as though Microsoft made an effort to convert Control Panel to the new, easier-to-use format, but didn't get around to finishing the job; it's estimated that only about 60% of the conversion was completed in time for the release of Windows Vista. Ultimately, this is more or less inconsequential, but once you understand the makeup of the program, it'll be a lot easier to navigate.

Search in Control Panel

Control Panel has a brand-new Search feature, and it actually works. Just click the **Control Panel Home** link on the left (in Classic View, search only looks through icon captions), and then type a word into the **Search** box on the upper right to find matching settings (see Figure 2-6). Then, just click a link in the search results to jump to the window with that setting.

Figure 2-5. Use the path arrows in the address bar to quickly jump to a Control Panel page

Control Panel's Search feature is slick, but not as comprehensive as Windows Explorer's Search tool. In other words, your search is conducted against a pre-programmed index of common settings referring only to Vista's own settings. This means that advanced settings like "Icon Spacing" (see "Save Your Desktop Layout," earlier in this chapter) and any settings in third-party Control Panel windows, such as QuickTime window (present if you've installed Apple iTunes) won't show up in search results.

Shortcuts to Control Panel pages

Many windows are buried several levels deep in Vista's Control Panel, so it can be a bit of a pain to make your way around the program. If you find yourself returning to the same spot often, there are several ways to make shortcuts and save yourself some time in the future.

The easiest way to make a shortcut is with drag-drop. If you're using the **Control Panel Home** (category) view, drag any link onto the desktop to make a shortcut, but don't be surprised if the shortcut doesn't take you as far as you wanted to go. For instance, drag the **Change desktop background** link, and you'll get a shortcut to the **Appearance and Personalization** page only.

You can get a little more control in the **Classic View** of Control Panel; just drag an icon to the desktop to make a shortcut.

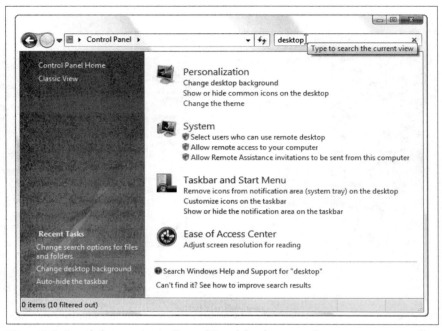

Figure 2-6. Search for a setting in Control Panel, but be aware that you may not see all the settings available

But if you want to get to a specific page or tab more directly, you can use any of the available command-line alternatives to open Control Panel pages and windows from shortcuts, the Start menu, or even from the **Start → Run** dialog. For example, you can open the **Advanced** tab in the Advanced System Properties window with this old-school syntax (around since the days of Windows 3.x in the 1980s, if you can believe it):

```
control.exe sysdm.cpl ,3
```

Or, you can use this new standalone executable to accomplish the same thing:

```
SystemPropertiesAdvanced.exe
```

For a complete list of these shortcuts, see Table 2-1.

Table 2-1. Command line access to Control Panel pages and tools

Control Panel	Command line
Add Hardware Wizard	`hdwwiz.cpl`
Administrative Tools	`control admintools`
Advanced System Properties → Advanced tab	`SystemPropertiesAdvanced.exe`

Table 2-1. Command line access to Control Panel pages and tools (continued)

Control Panel	Command line

Advanced System Properties → Computer Name tab	`sysdm.cpl`
	or
	`SystemPropertiesComputerName.exe`

Advanced System Properties → Advanced tab → Performance Options → Data Execution Prevention tab	`SystemPropertiesDataExecutionPrevention.exe`
Advanced System Properties → Hardware tab	`SystemPropertiesHardware.exe`
Advanced System Properties → Advanced tab → Performance Options	`SystemPropertiesPerformance.exe`
Advanced System Properties → System Protection tab	`SystemPropertiesProtection.exe`
Advanced System Properties → Remote tab	`SystemPropertiesRemote.exe`
AutoPlay	`control /name Microsoft.AutoPlay`
Backup and Restore Center	`control /name Microsoft.BackupAndRestoreCenter`
Backup and Restore Center → Backup Status and Configuration	`sdclt.exe`
BitLocker Drive Encryption	`control /name Microsoft.BitLockerDriveEncryption`
Bluetooth Devices	`bthprops.cpl`

Date and Time	`timedate.cpl`
	or
	`control date/time`

Display Settings	`desk.cpl`
Default Programs	`control /name Microsoft.DefaultPrograms`
Device Manager	`devmgmt.msc`
Disk Manager	`diskmgmt.msc`

Ease of Access Center	`access.cpl`
	or
	`Utilman.exe`

Folder Options	`control folders`
Fonts	`control fonts`
Game Controllers	`joy.cpl`
Indexing Options	`control /name Microsoft.IndexingOptions`
Internet Options	`inetcpl.cpl`
Keyboard Properties	`control keyboard`

Mouse Properties	`main.cpl`
	or
	`control mouse`

Table 2-1. Command line access to Control Panel pages and tools (continued)

Control Panel	Command line
Network and Sharing Center	`control /name Microsoft.NetworkandSharingCenter`

Network Connections	`ncpa.cpl`
	or
	`control netconnections`

Offline Files	`control /name Microsoft.OfflineFiles`
Parental Controls	`control /name Microsoft.ParentalControls`
Pen and Input Devices	`TabletPC.cpl`

People Near Me	`collab.cpl`
	or
	`p2phost.exe`

Performance Information and Tools	`control /name Microsoft.PerformanceInformationandTools`
Personalization	`control desktop`
Personalization → Window Color and Appearance → Classic Appearance Settings	`control color`

Phone and Modem Options	`telephon.cpl`
	or
	`control telephony`

Power Options	`powercfg.cpl`
Printers	`control printers`
Problem Reports and Solutions	`wercon.exe`
Programs and Features	`appwiz.cpl`
Programs and Features → Turn Windows features on or off	`OptionalFeatures.exe`

Regional and Language Options	`intl.cpl`
	or
	`control international`

Scanners and Cameras	`sticpl.cpl`
Secure Online Key Backup	`control /name Microsoft.SecureKeyBackup`
Security Center	`wscui.cpl`
Sound	`mmsys.cpl`
Speech Recognition Options	`control /name Microsoft.SpeechRecognitionOptions`
Sync Center	`mobsync.exe`
System	`control /name Microsoft.System`
Tablet PC Settings	`control /name Microsoft.TabletPCSettings`
Task Scheduler	`control schedtasks`

Table 2-1. Command line access to Control Panel pages and tools (continued)

Control Panel	Command line

Text to Speech	`sapi.cpl`
	or
	`control speech`

User Accounts	`nusrmgr.cpl`
	or
	`Netplwiz.exe`
	or
	`control userpasswords`

User Accounts (advanced)	`control userpasswords2`
Volume Mixer	`SndVol.exe`
Welcome Center	`control.exe /name Microsoft.WelcomeCenter`
Windows Defender	`MsAsCui.exe`

Windows Firewall	`Firewall.cpl`
	or
	`FirewallControlPanel.exe`

Windows Firewall Settings	`FirewallSettings.exe`
Windows Sidebar Properties	`control.exe /name Microsoft.WindowsSidebarProperties`
Windows SideShow	`control.exe /name Microsoft.WindowsSideshow`
Windows Update	`control.exe /name Microsoft.WindowsUpdate`

Cascading Control Panel menu

Another way to get to a specific Control Panel page quickly is to add a menu with all its contents to the Start menu:

1. In Control Panel, open **Taskbar and Start Menu** and then choose the **Start Menu** tab.

2. Click the currently enabled **Customize** button.

3. If you're using the modern, two-column Start menu (**Start menu** in the last window), find the **Control Panel** branch, and then select the **Display as a menu** option.

   If you're using the Classic Start menu, turn on the **Expand control panel** option in the **Advanced Start menu options** list.

4. Either way, click **OK** when you're done.

Now, instead of a single menu item in the Start menu, all the Control Panel icons are listed individually. To open the standalone Control Panel folder window from this interface, simply right-click **Control Panel** and select **Open**.

Unwanted icons and the Green Ribbon of Death

Does it take an inordinately long time to show Control Panel in Classic View? If you upgraded your PC from a previous version of Windows, there's a bug in Vista that can cause the Green Ribbon of Death (explained in Chapter 6). This bug, incidentally, is related to a specific "legacy" feature that lets you hide certain Control Panel icons; see the "Hide Unwanted Control Panel Icons" sidebar, next, for details.

Hide Unwanted Control Panel Icons

You can hide certain types of icons in Control Panel's Classic View with a quick Registry hack. Just open the Registry Editor (explained in Chapter 3), and expand the branches to HKEY_CURRENT_USER\Control Panel\don't load.

Then, create a new string value for each icon you want to hide. For the name, type the filename of the *.cpl* file responsible for the icon (see "Shortcuts to Control Panel pages," earlier in this chapter). Then, double-click the new value, type No for its data, and click **OK**.

Refresh the Control Panel window by pressing the **F5** key to see the change.

Now, there's a bug in Windows Vista that can crash Control Panel—or at least cause it to take a long time to load all its icons—if there's an errant entry in the don't load Registry key. If you're seeing the Green Ribbon of Death (see Chapter 6) whenever you open Control Panel, delete all the values in the don't load key and then try again.

Who Doesn't Love Keyboard Shortcuts?

Despite the fact that Microsoft has excised those little underlined letters—the ones that show you which letter you have to press while holding the **Alt** key to jump to that control—the keyboard is alive and well in Vista. In fact, there are tons of useful keyboard shortcuts that can be real time-savers in Windows, some even used in conjunction with the mouse. Following are some of the best ones.

Navigating files and folders

Properties
> Hold the **Alt** key while double-clicking on a file or folder to view the Properties sheet for that object. Or, press **Alt-Enter** to open the Properties window for the selected item without using the mouse at all.

History

Press **Backspace** in an open folder window to go back one step in the window's history to the last folder you looked at, which is not necessarily the parent folder.

You can also press the left or right arrow keys while holding **Alt** to go back and forth through the folder history; these work just like the two round arrow buttons in the upper left of any Explorer window.

Refresh/Reload

Press **F5** in almost any window (including web browsers and even Device Manager) to refresh the current view.

Folder tree

With the focus on Explorer's folder tree, press **Enter** to view the contents of the highlighted folder in the right pane. Also, use the left and right arrow keys (or + and -) to collapse and expand folders, respectively, or press the asterisk key (*) to expand all the folders and their subfolders in the current branch.

Jump to an item

With the focus on the right pane, press a letter key to quickly jump to the first file or folder starting with that letter. Continue typing to jump further. For example, pressing the **T** key in your *Windows* folder will jump to the *Tasks* folder. Press **T** again to jump to the next object that starts with T. Or, press **T** and then quickly press **A** to skip all the Ts and jump to *taskman.exe*. If there's enough of a delay between the **T** and the **A** keys, Explorer will forget about the T, and you'll jump to the first entry that starts with A.

 If you'd rather, you can have Windows Explorer begin a formal search as soon as you start typing. Open the **Organize** drop-down, select **Folder and Search Options**, and then choose the **View** tab. Scroll to the bottom of the **Advanced settings** list, and under the **When typing into list view** branch, click **Automatically type into the Search Box**.

New Explorer window

Press **Ctrl-N** to open another Explorer window at the same folder. Or, if you prefer, you can use **Ctrl-N** to create a new folder on the spot—something you can't otherwise do easily with the keyboard—by installing Creative Element Power Tools (*http://www.creativelement.com/powertools/*) and turning on the **Quickly create new folders** tool.

You can also press Winkey+E to open a new Windows Explorer window, even when you're not currently in Explorer.

Search

In Windows Explorer or on the desktop, press **Ctrl-F** or **F3** to open a separate search window so you can search without losing the current view. Or, press Winkey+F to open a search window no matter where you are. See "Search Tricks," later in this chapter, for other ways to improve search.

Show hidden context menu items

Hold the **Shift** key while right-clicking a file to show three new items in the file's context menu: **Pin to Start Menu** (normally shown only for programs), **Add to Quick Launch**, and **Copy as Path** (used to copy the full path of the item to the clipboard).

Address bar

Press **F4** to jump to the address bar so you can type or flip through recently visited folders. While you're there, press **Esc** twice to revert to the new-style path box so you can navigate parent folders without typing.

Cycle through all the controls

Press the **Tab** or **F6** keys to jump among the file pane, the file pane column headers, the address bar, the **Search** box, the Favorites pane (if it's visible), the folder tree divider, and then finally the folder tree itself.

Selecting and managing files

Select all

Press **Ctrl-A** to quickly select all of the contents of a folder, both files and folders.

Select range

Select one icon, then hold the **Shift** key while clicking on another icon in the same folder to select it and all the items in between.

Select multiple items

Hold the **Ctrl** key to select or deselect multiple files or folders, one by one. Note that you can't select more than one folder in the folder tree pane of Explorer, but you can in the right pane.

 You can select multiple files without using the keyboard by dragging a *rubber band* around them. Start by holding down the left mouse button in a blank portion of a folder window, then drag the mouse to the opposite corner to select everything that appears in the rectangle you just drew.

You can also use the **Ctrl** key to modify your selection. For example, if you've used the **Shift** key or a rubber band to select the first five objects in a folder, you can hold **Ctrl** while dragging a second rubber band to highlight additional files *without* losing your original selection.

Delete files

Select a file or folder and press **Del** to delete it. Or, press **Shift-Del** to delete it permanently without sending it to the Recycle Bin.

Rename

Press **F2** to rename the currently selected item.

Starting and switching programs

Start menu

Press the Windows logo key (Winkey) to open the Start menu, and then navigate with your arrow keys. You can also open the Start menu by pressing **Ctrl-Esc**. See the upcoming "Hack the Windows Logo Key" sidebar if you don't have a Windows logo key.

Switch to a different window

Press Winkey+**Tab** to show the fancy Flip 3D Rolodex-style task switcher, or **Alt-Tab** to show the classic means of switching from one open window to another. See "Get Glass," in Chapter 5, for a good alternative. Hold **Shift** (**Shift-Alt-Tab** or **Shift**-Winkey+**Tab**) to go backward.

If you're using an application with more than one document, press **Ctrl-Tab** to switch among the open documents. Or, press **Ctrl-Tab** to cycle through tabs in a tabbed window.

Drop the current window to the bottom of the pile

Press **Alt-Esc** to move the active window to the bottom of the stack and activate the one underneath it. Hold **Shift** to go backward.

Run

Press Winkey+**R** to open the Start menu **Run** box.

Minimize all windows

Press Winkey+**D** to show or hide the desktop, Winkey+**M** to minimize all open windows, or **Shift**-Winkey+**M** to restore minimized windows. See "Get to the Desktop," earlier in this chapter, for related tips.

Windows Explorer

Press Winkey+**E** to open a new Windows Explorer window.

Task Manager

Press **Ctrl-Shift-Esc** to open Task Manager (see Chapter 6).

Task bar

Press Winkey+**T** to send the keyboard focus to the taskbar, or press Winkey+**B** to send the focus to the notification area (tray).

Hack the Windows Logo Key

What if your keyboard has no Winkey? Strictly speaking, you don't really need it, but there are a bunch of nifty keyboard shortcuts you can only do with the Winkey, such as Winkey+**D** to show the desktop, Winkey+**R** to run a program, and Winkey+**Tab** to use the Flip 3D task switcher.

To give your keyboard a Winkey, or any other key it doesn't have, you need a keyboard remapping tool. Most tools use an obscure feature already built in to Windows, such as Sharpkeys (free, *http://www.randyrants.com/sharpkeys/*), KeyTweak (free, *http://webpages.charter.net/krumsick/*), and Microsoft's own Microsoft Keyboard Layout Creator (*http://www.annoyances.org/exec/software/mklc*).

First, pick a key on your keyboard you don't use—the righthand **Alt** key is usually a good candidate for the Windows Logo Key—and remap it to the key you want Windows to think you pressed. In SharpKeys, for instance, click **Add**, select **Special: Right Alt** from the **Map this key** list, select **Special: Left Windows** from the **To this key** list, and click **OK**. Back in the main window, click **Write to Registry**, and then log out and back in again for the change to take effect.

Of course, the Winkey isn't for everyone. On most keyboards, it's right next to the Space bar, which means it's easy to hit by accident. And since it's one of the few keys that takes the focus *away* from the active window, it can be decidedly inconvenient if you press it while you're typing.

To disable Winkey, all you do is use one of the aforementioned keyboard remapping tools to remap Winkey to something innocuous, like **Ctrl** or **Pause/Break**. Or, if you have the MyExpose task switcher installed (see "Get Glass" in Chapter 5), you can remap the Winkey to activate MyExpose instead.

While you're at it, you can likewise disable some other nuisance keys like **Insert** (**Ins**), so you'll never again inadvertently delete text as you type.

If you want to keep your Windows logo key, but you don't like the Winkey hotkey combinations (e.g., Winkey+**R**), you can turn those off with a quick Registry hack. Open the Registry Editor (see Chapter 3) and expand the branches to `HKEY_CURRENT_USER\Software\Microsoft\Windows\CurrentVersion\Policies\Explorer`. Create a new DWord value by selecting **Edit** → **New** → **DWord Value (32-bit)**, and then name the new value `NoWinKeys`. Double-click the new value, type 1 for its data, and click **OK**. You'll need to log out and then back in again for the change to take effect.

Quick Launch toolbar

Press the Windows logo key and a number key to open the Quick Launch icon at that position. For instance, press Winkey+**1** to open the first icon, Winkey+**2** to open the second, and so on.

Close the window

Press **Alt-F4** to close the current application, or **Ctrl-F4** to close the current document (if it's the type of program that can hold multiple documents). Press **Alt-F4** while the keyboard focus is on the desktop or taskbar to shut down windows.

View System Information

Press Winkey+**Pause/Break** to open the System page in Control Panel.

Get Windows Help

Press Winkey+**F1** to open Windows Help and Support.

Everything else

Clipboard

Press **Ctrl-C** to copy the selected item to the clipboard, **Ctrl-X** to cut (copy and then delete), and **Ctrl-V** to paste the item anywhere else.

Undo

Press **Ctrl-Z** to undo the last text edit, file operation, deletion, etc.

Menus

Press **Alt** or **F10** to jump to the menu bar (or show the menu if it's hidden).

Drop-down listboxes

Use the up and down arrow keys to flip through items in a drop-down box, or press **Alt**-down arrow to open the listbox.

Accessibility tools

Press Winkey+**U** to open the Ease of Access Center page in Control Panel. Press **Shift** five times to toggle *StickyKeys* on and off. Hold **Shift** for eight seconds to toggle *FilterKeys* on and off. Hold **Num Lock** for five seconds to toggle *ToggleKeys* on and off. Press **Alt-LeftShift-Num Lock** to toggle *MouseKeys* on and off. Press **Alt+LeftShift+Print Screen** to toggle *high contrast mode* on and off.

Log off

Press Winkey+**L** to log off Windows.

Massage the Start Menu

The Start menu has gotten a face-lift for Vista, and not a moment too soon. It's easier to configure and its arrangement makes quite a bit more sense than its predecessor, and if you find it too cluttered, you can get rid of just about anything you don't use.

Unfortunately, each element—or rather, elements in each region—are configured in slightly different ways, as shown in Figure 2-7.

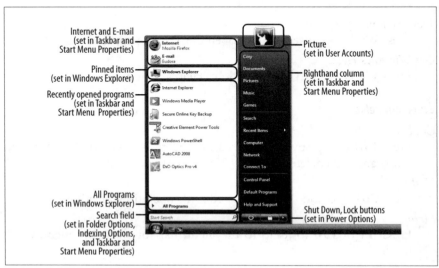

Figure 2-7. Each region of the Start menu gets configured in a different place

The contents of Vista's standard Start menu are divided into seven sections:

Pinned items

At the top of the lefthand column, above the horizontal line, is a list of programs you can customize. Right-click any application executable (*.exe* file) and select **Pin to Start Menu** to add it to the list (the command isn't available if you're using the "classic" Start menu discussed later). You can also drag shortcuts to add them to the list, right-click unwanted items and select **Remove from this list** to delete them, or drag the entries to rearrange them.

At the top of the list, you'll see two special entries—Internet and E-Mail—that aren't actually "pinned," but rather put in place by special settings in the Taskbar and Start Menu window in Control Panel. To get rid of them, right-click each one and select **Remove from this list**. You can replace them with ordinary pinned items, or use the settings designed for this purpose by right-clicking an empty area of the Start menu, selecting **Properties**, and then clicking **Customize**.

Shell Tweaks

The pinned items list is peculiar because, unlike the **All Programs** folders and the **Quick Launch** toolbar, the pinned items aren't shortcuts on your hard disk. Rather, the pinned items are stored in the Registry (see Chapter 3) in a format that makes them impractical to edit by hand. This means that application installers can't litter your pinned items list with unwanted icons, but it also introduces some annoying limitations for day-to-day use.

For example, if you rename a pinned item, Windows renames the *target* file! This means that if you pin *Photoshop.exe* or *diskmgmt.msc*—the executables for Adobe Photoshop and the Disk Management console file discussed in Chapter 5, respectively—and then remove the filename extensions to pretty up the pinned entries, you'll render the programs inaccessible. To work around this, create shortcuts to these items somewhere out of the way—perhaps a subfolder of *All Programs*, discussed shortly—and then pin the shortcuts instead.

Recently used applications

Below the pinned items on the left side is a dynamic list of recently used programs. The problem with this list is that it is always changing, making it a poor choice to store shortcuts to programs you need to use frequently.

To remove the list entirely, right-click an empty area of the Start menu, select **Properties**, and turn off the **Store and display a list of recently opened programs** option. Or, to change the size of the list, click the **Customize** button here, and in the **Start menu size** box toward the bottom, adjust the **Number of recent programs to display** value. (If the section is grayed out, it's because the aforementioned **Store and display** option is turned off.)

All Programs

At the very bottom of the left column is a single entry, **All Programs**, which contains the icons for the applications you've installed on your PC, and is the most customizable area of the Start menu.

The items in the **All Programs** menu are shortcuts on your hard disk, compiled from two sources. First, there are your personal shortcuts here:

C:\Users\{username}\AppData\Roaming\Microsoft\Windows\Start Menu\Programs

and then there's the common (or "All users") folder here:

C:\ProgramData\Microsoft\Windows\Start Menu\Programs

Although you can drag and drop shortcuts in this list, it's usually a whole lot easier to work with the folders directly in Windows Explorer, especially if you have a lot of things to change.

 Resist the temptation to consolidate your personal Start menu shortcuts and the All Users shortcuts. Among other things, this can mess with applications that place shortcuts in these locations automatically, and can cause problems like the same program being run more than once each time you start windows. Instead, just delete unwanted items from both places, and add your own items only to your personal Programs folder.

To remove the **All Programs** item from the Start menu, open the Group Policy Object Editor (*gpedit.msc*, which is not present on the Vista Home editions), and expand the branches to User Configuration\ Administrative Templates\Start Menu and Taskbar. Double-click **Remove All Programs list from the Start menu**, select **Enabled**, and click **OK**. You'll have to log out and then log back in for this change to take effect.

You can customize some of the aspects of this menu by right-clicking an empty area of the Start menu, selecting **Properties**, and then clicking **Customize**. If you turn on the **Enable context menus and dragging and dropping** option, you'll be able to drag shortcuts and even right-click them to customize them; turn off this option if you want them to stay put. Next, turn on the **Sort All Programs menu by name** option to keep the list sorted; or, if you turn it off, you can sort a single folder on the fly by right-clicking any entry and selecting **Sort by Name**.

Search box

This is more than just a **Search** box; it's also a quick and dirty replacement for the Run window. You can type any program here—either the application name or the executable filename—and press **Enter** to run the program. Or, type the first few letters of the program to launch, and then click the desired entry in the search results above.

If you've started a search you want to cancel, click the blue × button to the right of the search text field to get your Start menu back.

By default, search results here are limited to your personal documents, items in your **All Programs** menu, and special locations like Control Panel. To broaden your searches to include the entire index, right-click an empty area of the Start menu, select **Properties**, and then click **Customize**. Scroll down the list to the **Search files** branch, and select **Search entire index**. See "Search Tricks," later in this chapter, for details on the index.

Also in the Customize Start Menu window, you'll find three other search-related options. The first, **Search**, allows you to show or hide the **Search** entry in the righthand column of the Start menu (discussed shortly). The second, **Search communications**, includes email mailboxes and contacts from the Windows Mail program, and the third, **Search favorites and history**, adds Internet Explorer bookmarks and recently visited web sites to your searches. Turn off the latter two options to speed up searches made from your Start menu.

The Picture Box

To change the picture, open the User Accounts page in Control Panel (or just click the picture), and then click **Change your picture**. There's no way to remove the picture box—it's also used to provide visual feedback as you hover the mouse over items in the righthand column, as discussed next—but you can click **Browse for more pictures** and then choose a *.bmp*, *.jpg*, or *.gif* file of a solid color box if you want to de-emphasize it.

You can, however, remove your name from beneath the picture by right-clicking an empty area of the Start menu, selecting **Properties**, and then clicking **Customize**. Under the **Personal folder** branch, select **Don't display this item**, and then click **OK**.

Righthand column

You have control over everything in the right column, but not directly.

To get rid of any unwanted entries, right-click an empty area of the Start menu, select **Properties**, and then click **Customize**. In the list you'll find each of these items—there are 15 in all—interspersed with settings that affect other aspects of the Start menu. In most cases, just clear the checkbox for the item, or if it's shown as a folder here, just select **Don't display this item** to get rid of it.

The only right-column entry you won't see in the Customize Start Menu window is **Recent Items**. To get rid of this entry, close the Customize Start Menu window, and turn off the **Store and display a list of recently opened files** option, something you may want to do anyway for privacy and security purposes.

Among these items is also the Run command, which you may choose to hide even if you frequently use this feature. For one, the **Search** box, discussed earlier in this section, is a more convenient "run" tool; just type the filename or command you wish to run, and press **Enter**. Or, if you want the drop-down list of recently run items, you can hold the Windows logo key and **R** (Winkey+**R**) to open the Run window, even if Run isn't present in your Start menu.

Shut Down button

Last but not least is the red **Shut Down** button, which appears at the bottom of the right column along with a **Lock this computer** button and the tiny arrow that lets you switch users, restart, log off, put your PC to sleep (see Chapter 5), and shut down.

By default, Windows puts your PC to sleep when you click the red button. If you'd rather use this button to shut down your PC, see "Start Windows Instantly (Almost)" in Chapter 5.

To remove the **Shut Down** button et al., open the Group Policy editor (*gpedit.msc*, which is not present on the Vista Home editions), and expand the branches to User Configuration\Administrative Templates\ Start Menu and Taskbar. Double-click **Remove and prevent access to the Shut Down, Restart, Sleep, and Hibernate commands**, select **Enabled**, and click **OK**. You'll have to log out and then log back in for this change to take effect. Of course, once that's done, the only way to shut down or restart (necessary to undo the change) is to use the shutdown command-line tool described in "Control Your PC Remotely," in Chapter 7, or press the physical power switch on your PC.

When all is said and done, you'll have a leaner, cleaner Start menu that contains only the items you actually want and use. If you like, you can basically wipe the Start menu completely clean so that it looks like the one in Figure 2-8, adorned only with the **Search** box and your custom picture.

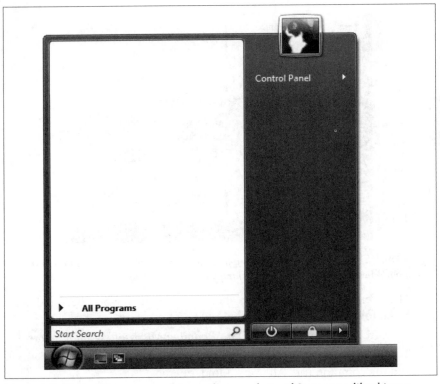

Figure 2-8. Minimalists may appreciate a clean, uncluttered Start menu like this one

Customize the Classic Start menu

The Classic Start menu style is not quite as flexible as the standard Vista Start menu in terms of the items that can be removed, but it's more flexible in the custom items you can add to the top level. The Classic Start menu is also simpler and smaller, and will feel more familiar to those coming from Windows 2000 or Windows 98. Figure 2-9 shows a somewhat slimmed-down Classic Start menu.

The Classic Start menu is divided into only three sections:

Custom programs
> The space above the horizontal bar is a fully customizable free-for-all, and somewhat of a saving grace for the Classic Start menu. In Figure 2-9, there's a single shortcut to Explorer, but you can place any type of shortcut here, and even include folders for further organization.

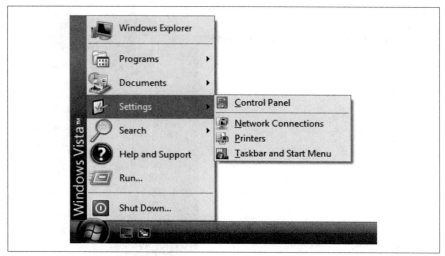

Figure 2-9. The Classic Start menu is simpler and cleaner than Vista's standard Start menu, but relies more heavily on overly jumpy cascading menus

These entries are merely the shortcuts stored in your personal *Start Menu* folder:

C:\Users\{username}\AppData\Roaming\Microsoft\Windows\Start Menu

and the common (or "All users") folder here:

C:\ProgramData\Microsoft\Windows\Start Menu

To get to these folders quickly, right-click the **Start** button and select **Explore**. Inside each of these locations is a *Programs* folder, containing the items shown in the **Programs** menu, discussed next.

Programs

At the top of the lower section is a single entry, **Programs**, which is the "classic" counterpart to the **All Programs** menu covered in the previous section.

When there are too many items in the **Programs** menu to fit on the screen, one of two things can happen. Either the menu "scrolls," which means you have to use the tiny arrows at the top and bottom of the menu to navigate, or the items are clumsily spread across multiple columns. To change this, right-click the **Start** button, select **Properties**, click **Customize**, and turn on or off the **Scroll programs** option. While you're here, you can also turn off the **Use Personalized Menus** option, which instructs Windows to stop hiding program icons you haven't used recently.

Windows items

The remaining entries in the lower part of the Start menu are all seemingly "hardcoded," in that you can't easily customize or hide most of them.

To hide the **Favorites** or **Log Off** entries, right-click the **Start** button, select **Properties**, click **Customize**, and turn off the **Display favorites** or **Display log off** options, respectively. To remove any other entries here, like **Search** or **Run**, open the Group Policy Object Editor (*gpedit.msc*, which is not present on the Vista Home editions), and expand the branches to User Configuration\Administrative Templates\Start Menu and Taskbar. For instance, to remove the **Documents** menu, double-click the **Remove Documents icon from Start Menu** entry, select **Enabled**, and click **OK**.

 If you hide the **Documents** menu, you may also want to double-click the **Do not keep history of recently opened documents** entry and select **Enabled**; this not only stops Windows from tracking what you do on your PC, but it clears the history lists shown in some applications' **File →Open** and **File → Save** windows.

Close the Group Policy Object Editor when you're done, and log out and then back in again for the changes to take effect.

Clean Up the Tray

The *notification area* as Microsoft calls it—or more commonly, the *tray*—is the box full of tiny icons on the far right side of your taskbar, next to the clock.

It made its first appearance in Windows 95, but it didn't take long for most trays to get cluttered with junk from every program installed on your PC. And since Microsoft wasn't too careful about establishing standards for the icons put there, applications weren't too careful about giving their customers control over those icons. As a result, many applications won't let you remove their icons, and of those that do, the process is different for each one.

Microsoft snapped into action to solve the problem, and five years later came up with the **Hide inactive icons** feature. To clean up your tray, right-click an empty area of the taskbar, select **Properties**, and choose the **Notification Area** tab. Turn on the **Hide inactive icons** option, and then click **Customize** to open the Customize Notification Icons window shown in Figure 2-10.

Figure 2-10. If you don't want to hide the tray completely, use this window to bury unwanted clutter under a collapsible panel

The active icons in your tray appear under **Current Items**, while those that have come and gone show up further down, under **Past Items**. To hide an icon, highlight it in the list, and then select **Hide** in the **Behavior** column. Click **OK** when you're done; the change takes effect right away.

If you've hidden at least one icon, a little white arrow appears to the left of the tray (meaning that you won't save any space if you hide only one icon). Just click the arrow to temporarily show hidden tray icons; move the mouse away, and the arrow hides them again.

Tired of dealing with tray icons on a one-by-one basis? If you're using the Vista Business or Ultimate edition, you can turn off the tray completely. Open the Group Policy Object Editor (*gpedit.msc*, which is not present on the Vista Home editions), and expand the branches to User Configuration\ Administrative Templates\Start Menu and Taskbar. Double-click **Hide the notification area**, select **Enabled**, and click **OK**. You'll have to log out and then log back in for this change to take effect.

Make Your Own Windows Startup Logo

The pompous Microsoft Windows Vista logo that appears for the 30 seconds or so it takes to boot your computer can be replaced with any image you choose; it just takes a little hacking.

First, find an image you'd like to use. It can be a photo you took with a digital camera or a picture you got off the Web. When you've got one, use your favorite image-editing application—or, barring that, Vista's Paint program (*mspaint.exe*)—to convert the file to the *.bmp* format. You'll actually need two *.bmp* files, one resized to 800×600 and the other resized to 1024×768, but both must have a 24-bit color depth. (If your photo doesn't conform to the 4:3 aspect ratio, you'll need to crop it or add padding so that it does.)

Next, download and install the free Vista Boot Logo Generator from *http://www.computa.co.uk/staff/dan/*. (Note that at the time of this writing, this program only works with the 32-bit edition of Vista.) Start the program, click **Browse for image** on the left side, and locate the 800×600 *.bmp* file you just made. Then, click **Browse for image** on the right side, and locate the 1024×768 version. When that's done, select **File → Save Boot Screen File As**, name the file winload.exe.mui (the default) and save it to your desktop, and then close the Vista Boot Logo Generator.

Open Windows Explorer and navigate to the *C:\Windows\System32\en-US* folder (if you're not using the United States–English edition of Windows Vista, choose the appropriate folder in place of *en-US*). Take ownership of the *winload.exe.mui* file in this folder, as described in "Set Permissions for a File or Folder" in Chapter 8, and then rename it to *winload.exe.mui.backup*.

Now that the original file is out of the way, drag your custom *winload.exe.mui* file into the *C:\Windows\System32\en-US* folder.

There's one more step: open the Start menu, type msconfig in the **Search** box, and press **Enter** to open the System Configuration window. Choose the **Boot** tab, and from the **Boot options** section, turn on the **No GUI boot** option. Click **OK** and then close the System Configuration window when you're done.

To try out your new boot screen, restart Windows!

See "Start Windows Instantly (Almost)," in Chapter 5, for other settings that determine how long the startup logo appears on screen, and "Customize the Welcome Screen Background," in Chapter 8, for a related hack.

Working with Files and Folders

What is Windows Explorer if not a file manager at heart? Sure, the Start menu is a home-base of sorts, but the desktop and your folders are basically there to store your stuff. When it comes to copying, moving, renaming, deleting, and opening files, Explorer is where it's at. The rest of this chapter includes topics on tweaking Vista's file management features so you can work with your stuff without getting so annoyed.

Why It Takes So Long to Copy Files

Most people first realize that something is wrong with Vista when they try to copy or move files, and they see the little green progress window shown in Figure 2-11. It'd be understandable to see this window on screen for a minute or two if you're copying a lot of data, but should it really take three full minutes to move one small file, or eight minutes to delete another?

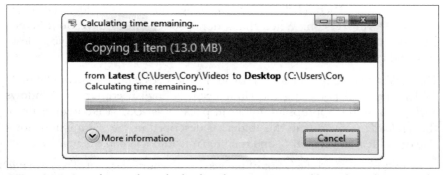

Figure 2-11. Seen this window a lot lately? This tiny "Green Ribbon of Death" is one of the signs that not all is right in the world of Vista

This is one of two "Green Ribbons of Death" in Windows Vista, the other being the larger progress bar—the one dissected in Chapter 6—that appears at the top of the Windows Explorer window in the address bar/path box. So, what's going on?

It turns out that several things can cause Windows Explorer to take a long time copying, moving, or deleting files, and some of them are actually legitimate.

First, Windows Explorer takes time to examine the files and folders you're copying, moving, etc., and checks—ahead of time—to see whether there are any conflicts, such as existing files in the destination folder or security issues that need your attention. That's why you'll see Vista's nifty confirmation window (Figure 2-12) *just once* for 34 conflicts, rather than the 34 individual confirmations you'd have to endure in earlier versions of Windows.

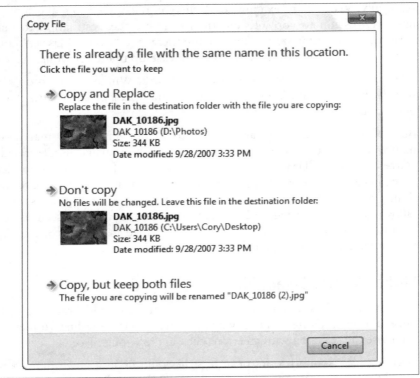

Figure 2-12. This handy new confirmation window lets you deal with all the conflicts at once, rather than having to click through a bunch of windows, but it ends up causing other problems

The confirmation window in Figure 2-12 is actually quite nice because of all the choices you get. If you're copying media files (e.g., photos, videos, PDF documents), you'll see thumbnail previews to aid your decision; you can even right-click the thumbnails directly in this window if you want to work with the files without interrupting the file operation. What's more, you can choose to copy or move the file *without* replacing the original, renaming it instead to avoid the conflict.

The downside is that Explorer must delay your file operation while it prepares the confirmation window; depending on what it encounters along the way, this can take *forever*.

One of the main reasons for the delay is a side effect of User Account Control, the same security "feature" that turns the screen black for an moment before asking your permission to make a change to your system.

Naturally, Vista has to examine each file you're copying to make sure you have permission to copy it, and then examine the destination to make sure you have permission to put the file there. See "Control User Account Control," in Chapter 8, for some ways to ease up the restrictions.

Likewise, if you're copying files over a network, Windows has to do some security reconnaissance, and depending on the speed of your network connection, this can take even longer.

But security checks alone aren't responsible for Vista's abysmal performance in this area; there's also the matter of thumbnails. As described in "Green Ribbon of Death" in Chapter 6, there are a few common problems that can cause Windows Explorer to hang or even crash, and if one of these things hobbles the instance of Explorer you're using, the progress dialog (shown previously in Figure 2-11) can just sit there for what seems like an eternity. Once you've fixed the problems outlined in Chapter 6, the copying, moving, or deleting should go much faster.

Slicker Ways to Select Files

Why drag 17 files individually when you can select and drag them all at once? For one, it's tremendously aggravating to select the first 16 files, and then lose the selection with an errant click in the wrong place.

Selecting files is an art form, or at least it would be in a much more boring world than ours. Here are some slick ways to select multiple files in Windows Explorer:

Rubber bands
> Need to select a cluster of files? Click in an empty area near the first file and then draw a box around the others to select them all in a single swoop, as shown in Figure 2-13.

Keyboard and mouse
> As described in "Who Doesn't Love Keyboard Shortcuts?," earlier in this chapter, you can hold the **Ctrl** key to select files one-by-one, or hold the **Shift** key to select a range of files. Just be careful not to drag the files while holding **Ctrl**, lest you inadvertently create copies of them all.

Keyboard alone
> While holding the **Ctrl** key, move through a list of files with the up and down arrow keys. When the dotted rectangle surrounds a file you want, press the **Space bar** to select it.

> Or, to select a range of files, use the arrow keys to find the first file; then, hold **Shift** while you expand the selection with the arrow keys. Thereafter, you can even use the **Ctrl** key to select and deselect individual items.

Figure 2-13. It's dead simple, but rubber bands—or "selection rectangles," as they like to be called—allow you to select a cluster of files in one quick step

Filespec

In the **Search** box in the top-right of the Explorer window, type a *filespec*—a pattern you choose—to filter the list and show only the matching files. Filespecs typically contain ordinary characters (letters and numbers) along with *wildcards*, like the question mark (?) and the asterisk (*), which represent any single character or any number of characters, respectively.

For instance, type *.txt to show only files with the *.txt* filename extension, or v??.* to show files of any type that start with v and have only three letters in the filename.

In a moment or two, Windows Explorer will show only the files that match your filespec, at which point you can press **Ctrl-A** to select them all. Most of the time, this is a whole lot faster—not to mention more accurate—than trying to select the files by hand. See "Search Tricks," later in this chapter, for more information.

Checkboxes

You like clicking checkboxes? In Windows Explorer, click the **Organize** drop-down, select **Folder and Search Options**, and then turn on the **Use check boxes to select items** option. Click **OK**, and your folder now looks like Figure 2-14; then, click the checkbox next to any file to select it without holding down any keys or worrying about clicking in the wrong place.

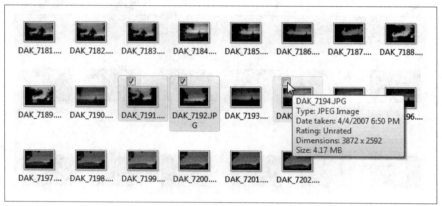

Figure 2-14. Windows Explorer lets you use checkboxes to select items

Take Charge of Drag-Drop

The "desktop metaphor" used as the basis for the interface in Windows Vista revolves around a handful of concepts, one of the most basic being that you can drag an item with the mouse to move it from one place to another.

But when dragging produces inconsistent results, the whole system starts to break down; unfortunately, that's the case in Vista.

Depending on where the item currently lives and where you're trying to put it, a variety of things can happen. The good news is that with an understanding of what's happening, combined with the visual cues you get from Windows Explorer, you can predict what will happen every single time you drag and drop. What's more, you can use some basic tricks to change what happens.

Here are the basic drag-drop rules by which Vista lives:

- If you drag an object from one place to another on the same physical drive (*C:\docs* to *C:\files*), Windows moves the object.

- If you drag an object from one physical drive to another physical drive (*C:\docs* to *D:\files*), Windows copies the object, resulting in two identical files on your PC.

- If you drag an object from one place to another in the same folder, Windows does nothing.
- If you drag an object into the **Recycle Bin**, Windows moves the file into the *Recycle Bin* folder, where it is eventually deleted.
- If you drag an object into a ZIP folder anywhere, Windows copies the file. (See "Zip It Up," later in this chapter.)
- If you drag certain system objects, such as Control Panel icons, anywhere else, Windows makes shortcuts to those items.
- If you drag any file onto an application executable (*.exe*) file, Windows opens the target application and then sends a signal to the application to open the dropped document. See "File Type Associations," in Chapter 3, for details.

That's about it. It used to be that Windows did different things with different types of files, such as creating a shortcut any time you dragged an *.exe* file, but thankfully, those days are over.

Now, here's how to override those rules:

Always copy.   To *copy* an object, hold the **Ctrl** key while dragging. If you press **Ctrl** *before* you click, Windows assumes you're still selecting files (explained in the previous section), so make sure to press it only *after* you've started dragging but before you let go of the mouse button. (The exceptions are system objects, like Control Panel icons, that cannot be copied.)

Duplicate an object.   Hold the **Ctrl** key while dragging an object from one part of a folder to another part of the same folder.

Always move.   To *move* an object, hold the **Shift** key while dragging. Likewise, if you press **Shift** before you click, Windows assumes you're still selecting files, so make sure to press it only after you've started dragging but before you let go. (Of course, system objects and read-only files, like those on a CD, cannot be moved.)

Always create a shortcut.   To create a shortcut to an object under any situation, hold the **Alt** key while dragging.

Choose on the fly.   To choose what happens to dragged files each time *without* having to press any keys, drag your files with the *right mouse button*, and a special menu like the one in Figure 2-15 will appear when you drop the files. This context menu is especially helpful, because it will display only options appropriate to the type of object you're dragging and the place where you've dropped it.

Figure 2-15. Drag files with the right mouse button for more control

To help you predict what will happen, even if you haven't memorized the rules, Windows changes the mouse cursor to indicate what it intends to do. While dragging an item, press and release the **Ctrl**, **Shift**, and **Alt** keys and watch Windows change the cursors in real time. As illustrated by Figure 2-16, you'll see a small plus sign whenever you're copying, a straight arrow when moving, or a curved arrow when creating a shortcut. This visual feedback is very important; it can eliminate a lot of stupid mistakes if you pay attention to it.

There's no way to set the default action for dragging and therefore no way to avoid using keystrokes or the right mouse button to achieve the desired results. Even if there were a way to change the default behavior, you probably wouldn't want to do it; imagine if someone else sat down at your computer and started dragging icons: oh, the horror.

Make a mistake? Press **Ctrl-Z** to undo most types of file operations. If you're not sure what the last file operation was, open Windows Explorer. Then right-click an empty area of the folder and hover the mouse over the **Undo** menu item. Depending on the last action you took, the menu item will read **Undo Copy**, **Undo Move**, **Undo Rename**, or **Undo Delete**. Additionally, if you have the Status bar visible (press the **Alt** key to show the menu and then select **View → Status bar**), Explorer will usually explain what you're about to undo.

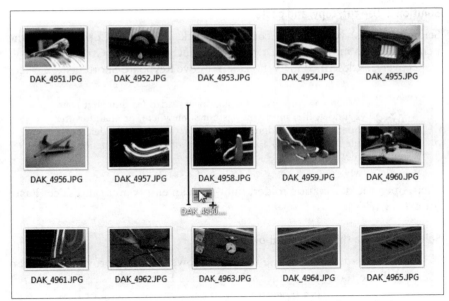

Figure 2-16. Windows Explorer provides visual feedback to let you know what's going to happen when you drop a file

Copy or Move to a Specified Path

Dragging and dropping is generally the quickest and easiest way to copy or move files and folders from one place to another. Typically, though, it helps if the source and destination folders are both visible at the same time. But what if they're not?

Solution 1: Drag patiently

In Windows Explorer, navigate to the source folder. Next, drag one or more items over the tree pane on the left, then hover the mouse cursor over the visible branch of the destination folder, and Explorer will automatically expand the branch. You can also hover near the top or bottom of the Navigation pane to scroll up or down, respectively.

If the destination folder you're looking for is buried several layers deep, you'll have to wait for Explorer to expand each level. This requires a steady hand and a lot of patience.

Solution 2: Use cut, copy, and paste

Select the file(s) you want to copy, right-click, and select **Copy** to copy the items or **Cut** to move them. (Or, to use the keyboard, press **Ctrl-C** or **Ctrl-V**, respectively, as described in "Who Doesn't Love Keyboard Shortcuts?," earlier.

 When you *cut* a file, its icon appears faded (as though it were a hidden file) until you paste it somewhere, or abandon the operation. (Abandoning a *cut* operation does not delete the file, by the way.) Explorer makes no visual distinction for files you *copy*.

Next, open the destination folder, right-click an empty area, and select **Paste** (or press **Ctrl-V**).

Solution 3: Use a third-party add-on

If you're not satisfied with the tools Windows Explorer provides, you can use one of the tools that comes with Creative Element Power Tools (*http://www.creativelement.com/powertools/*). In the Creative Element Power Tools Control Panel, turn on the **Copy or Move files anywhere** tool, and click **Accept**.

Then, right-click any file or folder, select **Move To** or **Copy To**, and then type or point to the destination folder. You can also create new folders on the fly and duplicate paths in the destination folder; the software even remembers the last dozen destinations you specified.

More Ways to Rename Files

Renaming files is just as common as copying or moving, but it can end up being a much more tedious task in Windows Explorer.

In its simplest form, Explorer's rename feature works like this: highlight a file, wait a fraction of a second to avoid double-clicking, then click the filename. When the text field appears, type a new name and then press **Enter** to rename the file. You can also right-click and select **Rename**, or highlight the object and press the **F2** key.

Then, do it 39 more times to rename all 40 files.

Solution 1: Select multiple files in Explorer

If you press **F2** when more than one file is selected in Windows Explorer, only one file—the active file—gets a text field for you to type in. Nothing will happen to the other selected files, at least not yet.

The active file is important, since its name is used as a template to rename the other selected files. If the file marked as active is not the one you want to use, hit **Esc**, and then hold the **Ctrl** key while clicking another file. If the new file was highlighted, it will become deselected—in this case, just **Ctrl**-click the file once more to reselect it. Then, press **F2** again to show the text field.

Rename the active file as desired, and press **Enter** when you're done. The active file keeps its new name, and then Explorer assigns the same name—plus a number, in parenthesis—to all the other files. Table 2-2 shows what happens when you rename files this way.

Table 2-2. What happens when you try to rename multiple files in Explorer

Old filename	New filename
My file.doc (the active file)	*The Penske File.rtf*
Grandma.jpg	*The Penske File (1).jpg*
Readme.1st	*The Penske File (2).1st*
Purchases.mdb	*The Penske File (3).mdb*
Chapter 2 (a folder)	*The Penske File (4)*

Although Explorer doesn't show you a preview of your new filenames, you can undo a multiple rename operation as easily as a single rename operation by pressing **Ctrl-Z** once for each file that was renamed. Want to undo a single rename of 17 files? You'll need to press **Ctrl-Z** 17 times.

Solution 2: Use the Command Prompt

An alternative is to use the ren command (see Chapter 9), either directly from the Command Prompt (*cmd.exe*), or from a batch file or PowerShell script.

First, use the cd command, also explained in Chapter 9, to change the working directory to the folder containing the files you wish to rename. For example, type:

```
cd c:\stuff
```

to change to the *C:\stuff* folder. If the folder name contains a space, enclose it in quotation marks, like this:

```
cd "c:\Progam Files\stuff"
```

Next, use the ren command to rename the file; the general syntax is:

```
ren source destination
```

where both *source* and *destination* can be any combination of permissible characters and wildcards. Two wildcards are allowed: an asterisk (*), which is used to match any number of characters, and a question mark (?), which is used to match only a single character. For example:

Rename a single file
```
ren oldfile.txt newfile.txt
```

Change the extension of all .txt files to .doc
```
ren *.txt *.doc
```

Rename the first part of a filename without changing the extension
```
ren document.* documentation.*
```

Remove the extensions of all files in the folder
```
ren *.* *.
```

Change the first letter of all files in a folder to "b"
```
ren *.* b*.*
```

Add a zero in front of numbered chapter files (note the quotation marks)
```
ren "chapter ??.wpd" "chapter0??.wpd"
```

Rename all files with an "s" in the fourth position so that a "t" appears there instead
```
ren ???s*.* ???t*.*
```

Truncate the filenames of all files in the folder so that only the first four characters are used
```
ren *.* ????.*
```

Now, using wildcards takes a bit of practice and patience. The more you do it, the better intuitive sense you'll have of how to phrase a rename operation. To make things simpler, try issuing several successive ren commands instead of trying to squeeze all your changes into a single step.

If a naming conflict occurs, the ren command never overwrites a file. For example, if you try to rename *Lisa.txt* to *Bart.txt*, and there's already another file called *Bart.txt*, ren just displays an error.

Solution 3: Use a third-party add-on

Got a lot of files to rename? Use Power Rename, part of Creative Element Power Tools (*http://www.creativelement.com/powertools/*). To use the tool, open the Creative Element Power Tools Control Panel, turn on the **Rename files with ease** option, and click **Accept**.

Then, highlight any number of files to rename, right-click, and select **Power Rename**. Or, open the Power Rename utility (Figure 2-17) and drag-drop the files onto the window.

Select the renaming criteria to your right. The first option, **As Specified**, allows you to type a file specification with wildcards, as described previously, but the

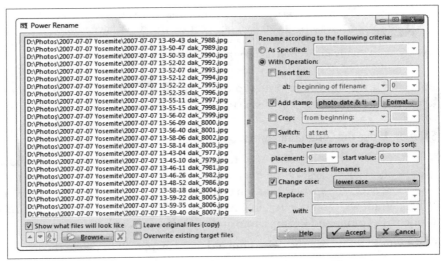

Figure 2-17. Power Rename makes it much easier to rename many files at once

real power lies in **With Operation**, and the operations that follow. For instance, you can insert text anywhere, remove text (crop), search and replace text, add numbering, and even fix numbered codes in files downloaded from the Web.

Turn on the **Show what files will look like** option to see a live preview of the filenames as you adjust the options. When you're done, click **Accept** to rename the files.

Delete In-Use Files

Sometimes Vista won't let you delete a file, which is stupid because it's your PC and you should be able to delete anything you want. So there.

Of course, there are times when Vista does know better than you, and prevents you from deleting files that are currently *in use* to avoid causing crashes or data loss. An in-use file could be a document that's currently open, a program executable that's currently running, or a folder *locked* by a running application.

Most of the time, you can get around this by closing the application or restarting Windows, but it's not always that easy.

For instance, if the program has crashed, you'll need to use Task Manager to end the process; see "What to Do When a Program Crashes," in Chapter 6, for details. Or, if the program is actually a Windows *service*, you'll need to use the Services window (*services.msc*) to stop the service before you'll be allowed to delete the file.

There are times when Windows won't let you delete a file, not because it's in use, but because you don't have *permission*. See "Permissions and Security," in Chapter 8—particularly the section on taking ownership of a file—for details.

But what if the file you're trying to delete is part of a virus? Or what if you know the file isn't open, but Vista still won't let you delete it?

Solution 1: Use the Command Prompt

Windows Vista has a special way to get to the Command Prompt without loading most of the rest of the operating system, not to mention any applications or services (or viruses) that can come along for the ride. See "What to Do When Windows Won't Start," in Chapter 6, for details on getting to the **Safe Mode with Command Prompt**, one of the options in Windows' **F8** menu.

Once you're there, use the del command (see Chapter 9) to delete the file.

When that's done, close the Command Prompt window, or type exit and press **Enter** to restart your PC and load Windows.

Solution 2: Use Wininit.ini

If you don't want to use the Command Prompt, you can use another little-known trick that takes advantage of a feature used by application installers to replace program files.

First, open Windows Explorer and navigate to your *C:\Windows* folder. Double-click the *Wininit.ini* file to open it in Notepad (or any other standard plain-text editor).

If the file isn't there, just create a new empty text file, name it *Wininit.ini*, and type the following line at the top:

    [rename]

(In most cases, the *Wininit.ini* file will exist but will be empty, with the exception of the [rename] line; any other lines you see here would've been added by a recent application installation.)

Under the [rename] section header, type the following line:

    NUL=c:\folder\filename.ext

where c:\folder\filename.ext is the full path and filename of the file you wish to delete. You can specify as many files here as you want, one on each line.

To *replace* a file rather than simply deleting it, the syntax is a little different:

    c:\folder\existing.ext=c:\folder\replacement.ext

where $c:\folder\existing.ext$ is the full path and filename of the file you're trying to replace, and $c:\folder\replacement.ext$ is the full path and filename of the new file to take its place. If the file specified on the right side of the equals sign doesn't exist, then the $existing.ext$ file will be moved/renamed to $c:\folder\replacement.ext$.

When you're done, save the file, close Notepad, and restart Windows. The files will be deleted or replaced as you've specified during the startup procedure.

Zip It Up

The late Phil Katz conceived of the ZIP file format at his mother's kitchen table in 1986, and soon thereafter wrote a little program called PKZip. Although his program, capable of encapsulating and compressing any number of ordinary files and folders into a single archive file, was not the first of its type, it quickly became a standard and ended up revolutionizing the transfer and storage of computer data.

ZIP files work somewhat like folders in that they "contain" files, so it's not surprising that they're represented as folders in Windows Explorer. But a ZIP file is typically smaller than the sum of its contents, thanks to the ZIP compression scheme. (Of course, other standards, like RAR, offer much better compression, but Vista doesn't support .rar files without a third-party utility.)

For example, a folder with 10 spreadsheet documents might consume 8 MB of disk space, but when zipped, might only consume 3 MB (or even less). The level of compression varies with the type of data being compressed; zipped text documents can be as small as 4 or 5% of the size of the original source files, but since movies and images are already compressed, they'll only compress to 95 to 98% of their original size, if that.

 This compression makes ZIP files great for sending over the Internet, since smaller files can be sent faster. The ZIP archive format also has built-in error checking, so if you find that certain files are getting corrupted when you email them or send them through a web site, try zipping them up to "protect" them.

To open a ZIP file, just double-click it. You can extract files from ZIP archives by dragging them out of the ZIP folder window. You can also right-click a ZIP file and select **Extract All**, but you'll have to deal with a more cumbersome wizard interface.

Create a new ZIP file by right-clicking on an empty portion of the desktop or any open folder, and selecting **New → Compressed (zipped) folder**. (The name here is actually misleading, since ZIP archives are actually files and not folders.) Then, add files or folders to the ZIP by simply dragging them onto the icon or the open ZIP window.

Another way to do this is to right-click a folder or a group of files, select **Send To**, and then select **Compressed (zipped) folder**. This is especially convenient, as there's no wizard or other interface to get in the way: if you send the *CompuGlobalHyperMegaNet* folder to a ZIP file, Windows compresses the folder's contents into a new *CompuGlobalHyperMegaNet.zip* file, stored alongside the source folder.

All of this is possible because Windows Vista supports the ZIP format right out of the box. (For years, this wasn't the case because Katz reportedly despised Windows, which may explain why Windows XP, released a year after his death, was the first version of Windows to support ZIP files without a third-party program.)

Unfortunately, there are drawbacks to Windows Explorer's built-in support for ZIP files. For example, it can interfere with searches, as described in "Search Tricks," later in this chapter. It can also interfere with third-party ZIP tools like WinZip (*http://www.winzip.com*), which adds more features and, ironically, better integration with Explorer's own context menus. But the biggest problem is that, by default, Vista displays each ZIP file like a folder, which can make a big mess if you have a folder full of 'em.

Unfortunately, there's no way to get Windows Explorer to treat ZIP files like files without disabling the ZIP feature altogether. But if you want to do it, here's how.

Turn off ZIP support (the easy way)

Download the *vistaunzip.reg* file at *http://www.annoyances.org/exec/download/vistaunzip.reg*, and save it to your desktop. Double-click the *vistaunzip.reg* file, click **Continue** (if prompted), then click **Yes**, and then click **OK** in the final confirmation window. Restart Windows for the change to take effect.

If you want to turn ZIP support back on, download *vistazip.reg* from *http://www.annoyances.org/exec/download/vistazip.reg*, and double-click it as just described.

If you're interested in trying out the Registry hack by hand, see the "Turn Off ZIP Support (the Hard Way)" sidebar, next.

Turn Off ZIP Support (the Hard Way)

If you'd rather disable Vista's built-in ZIP support by hand than have to download files, follow these steps:

1. Open the Registry Editor (see Chapter 3).
2. Expand the branches to `HKEY_CLASSES_ROOT\CLSID`.
3. Delete these two keys in this branch:
   ```
   {E88DCCE0-B7B3-11d1-A9F0-00AA0060FA31}
   {0CD7A5C0-9F37-11CE-AE65-08002B2E1262}
   ```
4. When you're done, close Registry Editor and then restart Windows for the change to take effect.

Customize Drive and Folder Icons

There may come a time when you get a little sick of the generic icons used for drives and folders in Windows Explorer. Now, you've probably figured out that you can create a shortcut to any drive or folder, choose a pretty icon, and place it on the desktop or in another convenient location. Unfortunately, the icon you choose is just for the shortcut; the target object always looks the same.

Here are some ways to give your folders and drives a more custom look.

Solution 1: Choose an icon for a drive

Using the functionality built in to Windows' CD auto-insert notification feature—functionality that allows Windows to determine the name and icon of a CD as soon as it's inserted in the reader (see "Search Tricks," later in this chapter)—there's a simple way to customize the icons of all your drives, including flash drives and USB hard disks:

1. Open a plain-text editor, such as Notepad.
2. Type the following:
   ```
   [autorun]
   icon=filename, number
   ```
   where $filename$ is the name of the file containing the icon, and $number$ is the index of the icon to use (leave $number$ blank or specify 0 [zero] to use the first icon in the file, 1 for the second, and so on).
3. Save the file as *Autorun.inf* and place it in the root directory of the hard disk, flash drive, or CD/DVD you wish to customize.
4. This change will take effect the next time you view it in Windows Explorer; press the **F5** key to refresh the display and read the new icons.

Solution 2: Chose an icon for a folder

You can customize the icon for an individual folder with this procedure:

1. Open a plain-text editor, such as Notepad.

2. Type the following:

   ```
   [.ShellClassInfo]
   IconFile=filename
   IconIndex=number
   ```

   where *filename* is the name of the file containing the icon, and *number* is the index of the icon to use; leave the IconIndex line out or specify 0 (zero) to use the first icon in the file, 1 for the second, and so on. Note the dot (.) in [.ShellClassInfo].

3. Save the file as *desktop.ini* and place it directly in the folder you wish to customize.

 If there's already a file by that name, you can replace it with your version, but it's better to open the existing file and add the [.ShellClassInfo] text to it.

4. Next, open a Command Prompt window (*cmd.exe*), and type the following at the prompt:

   ```
   attrib +s foldername
   ```

   where *foldername* is the full path of the folder containing the *desktop.ini* file (i.e., *C:\docs*). This command turns on the System attribute for the folder (not the *desktop.ini* file), something you can't do in Explorer; see Chapter 9 for details.

5. Close the Command Prompt window when you're done. You'll have to close and reopen the Explorer or single-folder window to see the change (pressing **F5** usually won't do it).

Solution 3: Choose the default icon for all folders

The more global and far-reaching a change is, the more likely it is to be difficult or impossible to accomplish without some serious tinkering in the Registry. An example are the icons used by some of the seemingly hardcoded objects in Windows, such as the icons used for ordinary, generic folders.

1. Open the Registry Editor (see Chapter 3).

2. Expand the branches to HKEY_CLASSES_ROOT\Folder\DefaultIcon (you can also choose a generic drive icon by going to HKEY_CLASSES_ROOT\Drive\DefaultIcon).

3. Double-click the (Default) value in the right pane. This value contains the full path and filename of the file containing the icon, followed by a comma, and then a number specifying the index of the icon to use (0 being the first icon, 1 being the second, and so on). The file you use can be an icon file (*.ico*), a bitmap (*.bmp*), a *.dll* file, an application executable (*.exe*), or any other file containing a valid icon.

 The default icon for folders is %SystemRoot%\System32\ shell32.dll,3, and the default for drives is %SystemRoot%\ System32\shell32.dll,8.

4. When you're done, close the Registry Editor. You may have to log out and then log back in for this change to take effect.

Search Tricks

Most of us rely on the Windows Search tool on a daily basis to find and organize files. It's a tremendously powerful tool, but if you leave its defaults intact, you'll be missing out on a lot of its potential.

Vista's Search tool is easy to use: just click the **Search** box in the upper-right corner of any Windows Explorer window and type a few letters of what you're seeking; the search results will show up below in a few moments.

When you initiate a search, Windows doesn't start looking through all of your folders and files. Rather, it merely runs your query against its own index of files, much like Internet search engines such as Google or Yahoo!. But, just like search engines, Vista's search results can be out of date, to the point of omitting some files or including others that have since been deleted.

The good news is that you can customize Vista's Search feature to include more files, get your results sooner, and even make search results more accurate.

The bad news is that the settings that affect searches are scattered across five different windows, so it's somewhat difficult to see the big picture when choosing search options.

Build a good index

If you want to improve your searches, the best place to start is with the indexing feature itself. In Control Panel, open the Indexing Options window to show the folders in which Windows currently looks for files. Click **Modify** to open the Indexed Locations window shown in Figure 2-18.

Figure 2-18. Use the Indexed Locations window to instruct Windows to include more folders in your searches

Here, place a checkmark next to each folder to include in the index; you can index an entire drive, or use the tiny arrows to expand branches and index only certain subfolders. (If the **Show all locations** button is available at the bottom of the window, click it now to have full reign over your hard disk.)

By default, only your personal files are indexed. But if you plan on hacking up Vista as described elsewhere in this book, you may want to index your entire drive. This will make it easier to find *.exe* files in the *Windows* folder, for instance, but doing so will increase the size of the index, which may slow down the rest of your searches.

For privacy purposes, you may wish to exclude certain folders by clearing their checkboxes. You can further speed up searches by also excluding folders you don't need to search. All the folders you've included or excluded appear in the **Summary of selected locations** section.

Click **OK** when you've selected folders to index, but you're not done yet. Next, click the **Advanced** button to open the Advanced Options window. Most of the options shown here are fairly self-explanatory, but what may not be obvious is that Windows won't index many file types unless you select them by hand in the **File Types** tab, shown in Figure 2-19.

Figure 2-19. Windows won't index many types of files unless you specifically enable indexing for them here

Just place a checkmark next to each file type you want to index; if you're serious about getting complete results, you'll want to check them all. Why? Say you're looking for a DLL file in the *Windows\System32* folder and you decide to use the Search tool to find the file. So, you click the **Search** box and type, say, mapi32.dll. Now, if DLL files aren't indexed, the search results will be empty, erroneously indicating that the file doesn't exist!

Of course, the more file types you index, the larger the index becomes, and the longer your searches might take. One way to mitigate this is to select the **Index Properties Only** option, but this will only take you so far.

You see, the **Filter Description** column shows you exactly how much Vista knows about any particular file; if it says **File Properties filter** or **Null filter**—as it does for DLL files—Windows is able to index the file's name, date, and size, but not much else. Only if it says something more specific, such as **Plain Text filter** for text files, or **Microsoft Office Filter** for Excel spreadsheets, will Windows bother opening the file to index its contents.

So, even if you select the **Index Properties and File Contents** option here, you won't be indexing the contents of that many files.

When you're done, click **OK**, and then close the Indexing Options window. Although the settings will take effect right away, it'll take some time for Windows to rebuild the index to the point where these settings will make any difference in search results. (It could be minutes or days, depending on what you've selected.)

Search outside the index

Vista's search index makes searches much faster, but at a price: the search results are often incomplete. This is particularly true on removable drives; even though you may've instructed Windows to index these drives, it won't do so when they're not connected, and may even purge the index of their contents when you disconnect them.

Not that big a deal, right?

Wrong. When you conduct a search on a location that's supposed to be in the index, yet contains no indexed files, your searches will turn up empty. This means you can be looking at a folder full of files, say, that start with s, but when you type s*.* in the **Search** box, you get nothing.

The solution is to click the **Advanced Search** button under the **Search** box. You don't see **Advanced Search**? When the search is complete, scroll to the bottom of the search results, and under **Did you find what you were searching for?**, click **Advanced Search**. Or, if you don't want to wait for the search to finish, click the **Search Tools** drop-down, select **Search Pane**, and then click **Advanced Search**.

Once the **Advanced Search** pane (Figure 2-20) is open, turn on the **Include non-indexed, hidden, and system files (might be slow)** option, and then watch as Windows populates your window with up-to-date search results.

Unfortunately, there's no way to instruct Windows to automatically search non-indexed files when you're looking at an indexed location, but there are two different workarounds. For one, you can tell Windows to abandon the index altogether; in Control Panel, open **Folder Options**, choose the **Search** tab, and turn on the **Don't use the Index when searching the file system (might be slow)** option.

But a better choice is to simply exclude removable drives and folders from your index, as described earlier in this section. When you search an explicitly excluded folder, Windows automatically skips the index and searches the actual files therein.

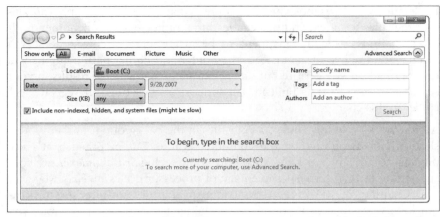

Figure 2-20. Open the Advanced Search pane so you can search outside the index and get more complete search results

Other search tips

Who's in the mood for some advanced search syntax? Here are some helpful shortcuts you can type right in the **Search** box.

To accomplish this:	Type this in the Search box:
Find files containing multiple terms in any order	bottomless peanut bag
Find files containing an exact phrase	"bottomless peanut bag"
Find files with at least one of the search terms	peanuts OR pecans OR cashews
Exclude a search term	peanuts NOT filberts
Combine operators	(peanuts OR filberts) AND (almonds OR hazelnuts) NOT cashews
Look only in filenames, not file contents	name: shiny
Search by filename extension	*.jpg
Show all files in all subfolders	*.*
Find files newer than a certain date	modified: >01/12/1997
Find files in a date range	(modified: >09/20/2002) AND (modified: <12/20/2002)
Find files matching a general date	modified: 2007
Find files of a certain size	(size: >10 MB) AND (size: <20 MB)
Search metadata	author: "Hoban Washburne"
Search music by tag	kind: music artist: ("Carbon Leaf" OR "Nerf Herder")

Note that Boolean operators AND, OR, and NOT must appear in uppercase. Also, as you can see, the AND operator is more or less optional; it's used here mostly for clarity.

By default, Windows looks inside compressed archives like *.zip* and *.cab* files for other files to index, and this can lead to a rather strange phenomenon. If a search finds a file that happens to be inside a *.zip* archive, the search results won't tell you this; instead, the **Folder** and **Folder path** columns will just be blank. If you get tired of seeing extraneous, unlabeled results in your searches, disable Vista's built-in *.zip* support, as described in "Zip It Up," earlier in this chapter.

As you work, Windows indexes your files in the background. In theory, this should happen only when the computer is idle, but in practice, it's not unusual to hear the hard disk thrashing while seeing *SearchIndexer.exe* consuming more than a trivial percentage of processor cycles in Task Manager (see Chapter 5). If you need to complete a processor-intensive task as quickly as possible, or if you just want better performance in a game, you can temporarily stop the search indexer task *without* disabling the search index altogether. Just open the Services window (*services.msc*), find **Windows Search** in the list, right-click and select **Stop**. It will start up again automatically the next time you load Windows, or you can start it manually by right-clicking the service again and selecting **Start**.

CHAPTER 3

The Registry

The Registry is deceptive. At first glance, it's a massive collection of esoteric settings and cryptic codes. But once you get cozy with it, you'll find most of the Registry well-organized, in plain English, and with many of its components illustrating their own structure.

It's also deceptive in its scope. Much of what seems hardcoded in Windows Vista is indeed governed by data in the Registry: delete a certain key, and an icon disappears from the *Computer* folder. But as you dig deeper, you'll find certain things (like parts of the "file types" system) have been jury-rigged to act a certain way despite what's in the Registry.

In essence, the Registry is a database containing all the settings for Windows and most of the applications installed on your system. All of your file type associations—the links between your documents and the applications that created them—are built from Registry data. Your network settings, your hardware settings, each of your applications' customizable toolbars, and even Windows' own Control Panel settings are all stored in the Registry. And the various software components, the building blocks of nearly all your programs (not to mention Windows itself), are "registered" in your Registry.

But who cares? Is the storage mechanism nearly as important as the settings themselves?

The value of diving into the Registry is in discovering the things in the Registry that can *only* be changed by editing it directly. You can fix misbehaving applications, uncover hidden features, and turn off annoying habits of Windows you thought you had to live with. Indeed, a lot of the solutions in this book take advantage of a little Registry hacking.

Now for the obligatory warning. You can irreversibly disable certain components of Windows Vista—or even prevent Windows from loading altogether—by changing certain settings in the Registry. Sure, most modern software is designed to repair broken settings, but it's assured that very few software developers have taken the time to anticipate all the weird things you'll undoubtedly do to your PC. I'm certainly not suggesting that you run and hide, but rather that you employ some of the safeguards described on these pages—such as backing up—before you start hacking the Registry to bits. For instance, take a few moments to create a Registry patch—explained later in this chapter—*before* you change a setting, and you'll thank me later.

The Registry Editor

Most of the changes to the Registry are performed behind the scenes by the applications that you run, as well as by Windows—settings and other information are read from and written to the Registry constantly. But the primary means of editing Registry keys and values directly is the Registry Editor (open the Start menu, type regedit, and then press **Enter**), included with all editions of Windows Vista.

Although the Registry is stored in multiple files on your hard disk, it is represented by a single logical hierarchical structure, similar to the folders on your hard disk. When you open the Registry Editor, you'll see a window divided into two panes (as shown in Figure 3-1). The left side shows a tree with folders, and the right side shows the contents of the currently selected folder. Now, these aren't really folders—this is just a convenient and familiar method of organizing and displaying the information stored in your Registry.

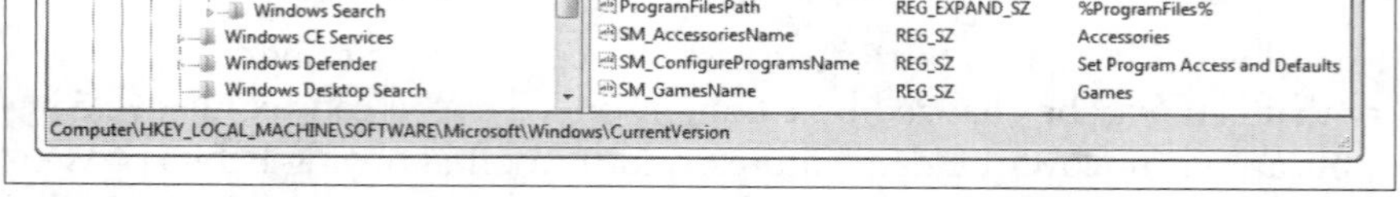

Figure 3-1. The Registry Editor lets you view and change the contents of the Registry

Each folder-like object is called a *key*. Each key can contain other keys, as well as *values*. Values contain the actual information stored in the Registry, while keys are used only to organize the values. Keys are shown only in the left pane; values are shown only in the right pane (unlike Windows Explorer, where folders are shown in both panes).

To display the contents of a key (folder), just click the desired key name on the left, and the values contained therein will be listed in alphabetical order on the right side. To expand a certain branch to show its subkeys, click the tiny arrow to the left of any folder (or double-click the folder name).

Editing the Registry generally involves navigating down through branches to a particular key and then modifying an existing value or creating a new key or value. For instance, this following Registry path:

```
HKEY_CURRENT_USER\Software\Microsoft\Windows
```

points to the location of the Windows key, which you can get to by expanding the HKEY_CURRENT_USER branch, then Software, then Microsoft, and then finally clicking Windows to show its contents on the right.

If you find yourself returning to the same Registry path over and over, use the **Favorites** menu to bookmark the item. Better yet, to view two different Registry locations simultaneously, start a second instance of Registry Editor by typing regedit /m in the Start menu **Search** box and pressing **Enter**.

Once the key is open, you can modify the contents of a value by double-clicking it. See "The Meat of the Registry: Values," later in this chapter, for the skinny on value types and how to edit them.

You can also rename any key or value just like you'd rename a file in Windows Explorer: click twice slowly, right-click and select **Rename**, or highlight and press **F2**. Likewise, you can delete a key or value by highlighting it and pressing the **Del** key or by right-clicking it and selecting **Delete**. (Note that deleting a key will also delete all the values and subkeys it contains.)

You can't drag-drop keys or values here as you can with files in Windows Explorer. Of course, there's very little reason to move a key or value from one place to another in the Registry, as the settings are totally location-dependent. A value in one key will almost always have a different meaning than the same value in a different key.

There are times, however, when you'll need to duplicate a key and all its contents (such as a file type key), which is something you can do with Registry patches, described later in this chapter.

To add a new key or value, select **New** from the **Edit** menu, select what type of object you want to add (Figure 3-2), type a name, and press **Enter**.

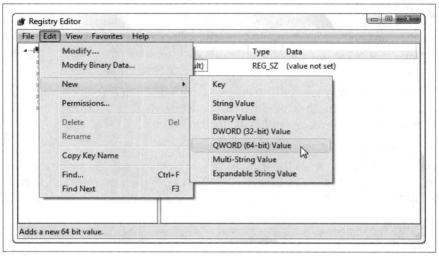

Figure 3-2. Select New from the Edit menu to add a new key or value to any part of the Registry

 You can create a value (or key) almost anywhere in the Registry and by any name and type that suits your whim. However, unless Windows or an application is specifically designed to look for the value, it will be ignored, and your addition will have absolutely no effect.

So far, the Registry Editor should seem pretty straightforward. But you'll find that the hard part is that you can't change something in the Registry until you know *what* to change, and that's what the rest of this chapter is about.

First, the Registry Editor has a Search feature (**Edit → Find** or press **Ctrl-F**), but you'll quickly find that it pretty much sucks. See "Search the Registry," later in this chapter, for search tips, as well as better search tools you can use. There's also "Find the Registry Key That Does...," which is useful if you don't know what to search for. But as I said earlier, the stuff in the Registry is basically location-dependent, which means you need to be acquainted with the structure of the Registry before you'll know where to go to make a specific change.

The Structure of the Registry

There are five primary, or "root," branches, each containing a specific portion of the information stored in the Registry. These root keys can't be deleted, renamed, or moved, because they are the basis for the organization of the Registry. They are:

HKEY_CLASSES_ROOT
> This branch contains the information that comprises your file type associations and the registered software components (called *classes*) used by Windows and many of your applications.
>
> This entire branch is a symbolic link,* or "mirror," of HKEY_LOCAL_MACHINE\SOFTWARE\Classes, but is displayed separately here for convenience and, of course, to confuse you.

HKEY_CURRENT_USER
> This branch simply points to a portion of the HKEY_USERS root key (later in this section) representing the currently logged-in user. This way, any application can read and write settings for the current user without having to know which user is currently logged in.
>
> In each user's branch are the settings for that user, such as Control Panel settings and Explorer preferences. Most applications store user-specific information here as well, such as toolbars, high scores for games, and other personal settings.
>
> The settings for the current user are divided into several categories, such as AppEvents, Control Panel, Identities, Software, and System. The most useful of these branches, Software, contains a branch for almost every application installed on your computer, arranged by manufacturer. Here and in HKEY_LOCAL_MACHINE\SOFTWARE (discussed later) can be found all of your application settings. As though Windows was just another application on your system, you'll find most user-specific Windows settings in HKEY_CURRENT_USER\Software\Microsoft\Windows.

HKEY_LOCAL_MACHINE
> This branch contains information about all of the hardware and software installed on your computer that *isn't* specific to the currently logged-in user. The settings in this branch are the same for all users on your system.

---

* A symbolic link is different from a Windows shortcut you'd find on your hard disk. Information in a linked branch appears twice and can be accessed at two different locations, even though it's stored only once. This means that Find may stop in both places if they contain something you're looking for and, as you might expect, changes in one place will be immediately reflected in the mirrored location.

The sub-branch of most interest here is the SOFTWARE branch, which contains all of the information specific to the applications installed on your computer. Both this branch and the aforementioned HKEY_CURRENT_USER\Software branch are used to store application-specific information. Those settings that are specific to each user (even if your computer has only one user), such as toolbar configurations, are stored in the aforementioned HKEY_CURRENT_USER branch; those settings that are not user-dependent, such as installation folders and lists of installed components, are stored in the HKEY_LOCAL_MACHINE branch. You'll want to look in both places if you're trying to find a particular application setting, because most manufacturers (even Microsoft) aren't especially careful about which branch is used for any given setting.

HKEY_USERS

This branch contains a sub-branch for the currently logged-in user, the name of which is a long string of numbers that looks something like this:

    S-1-5-21-1727987266-1036259444-725315541-500

This number is the SID (security identifier), a unique ID for each user on your system (yours will be different than this one). See Chapter 8 for more information on SIDs.

While it may sound like a good idea to edit the contents of this branch, you should instead use the HKEY_CURRENT_USER branch described earlier, which is a symbolic link (mirror) of this branch:

    HKEY_USERS\S-1-5-21-1727987266-1036259444-725315541-500

No matter which user is logged in, HKEY_CURRENT_USER will point to the appropriate portion of HKEY_USERS.

Because Windows only loads the profile (this portion of the Registry) of the currently logged-in user, only one user branch will ever be shown here. However, there will be a few other branches here, such as *.default* (used when nobody is logged in), and a few other branches that are of little interest to most users.

HKEY_CURRENT_CONFIG

This branch typically contains a small amount of information, most of which is simply symbolic links (mirrors) of other keys in the Registry. There's usually little reason to mess with this branch.

You'll eventually find that everything you'll want to do with the Registry can be done in either HKEY_CURRENT_USER or HKEY_LOCAL_MACHINE.

The Meat of the Registry: Values

Values are where Registry data is actually stored (while keys are simply used to organize values). The Registry uses several *types* of values—eight in all—each appropriate to the type of data it is meant to hold. Each type is known by at least two different names, the common name and the symbolic name (shown in parentheses in Table 3-1).

Table 3-1. Value types visible in the Registry Editor

Value type		Icon used in RegEdit	Can be created in RegEdit?
String (REG_SZ)		ab	Yes
Multistring/string array (REG_MULTI_SZ)		ab	Yes
Expandable string (REG_EXPAND_SZ)		ab	Yes
Binary (REG_BINARY)		011 110	Yes
DWORD 32-Bit (REG_DWORD)		011 110	Yes
DWORD 64-Bit (REG_QWORD)		011 110	Yes
DWORD (REG_DWORD_BIGENDIAN)		011 110	No
Resource List (REG_RESOURCE_LIST, REG_RESOURCE_REQUIREMENTS_LIST, or FULL_RESOURCE_DESCRIPTOR)		ab	No

Although the Registry Editor allows you to view and edit all eight types of values, it is only capable of creating the six most common (and not surprisingly, most useful) types. In practice, you'll typically only create string, binary, and DWORD values.

String values

String values contain *strings* of characters, more commonly known as plain text. Most values of interest to you will end up being string values; they're the easiest to edit and are usually in plain English. To edit a string value, just double-click, type a string of text into the text field (Figure 3-3), and click **OK** when you're done.

Figure 3-3. Edit a string value by typing text into this box

In addition to standard strings, there are two far less common string variants, used for special purposes:

- *Multistring/string array values* contain several strings, concatenated (glued) together and separated by *null* characters. Although the Registry Editor lets you create multistring values, it's impossible to type null characters (character #0 in the ASCII character set) from the keyboard. The only way to place a null character into a Registry value is either through a programming environment (see Chapter 9) or via cut-and-paste from another application.

- *Expandable string values* contain special variables, into which Windows substitutes information before delivering to the owning application. For example, an expandable string value intended to point to a sound file may contain %SystemRoot%\Media\doh.wav. When Windows reads this value from the Registry, it substitutes the full Windows path for the variable, %SystemRoot%; the resulting data then becomes (depending on where Windows is installed) c:\Windows\Media\doh.wav. This way, the value data is correct regardless of the location of the Windows folder.

 If you were to type data intended for an expandable string value into an ordinary string value, the variables wouldn't necessarily be expanded when read by an application.

Binary values

Similar to string values, binary values hold strings of characters. The difference is the way the data is viewed and edited. Instead of a standard text box, binary data is entered with hexadecimal codes in an interface commonly known as a *hex editor*. Each individual character is specified by a two-digit number in base-16 (e.g., 6E is 110 in good-ol' base 10), which allows characters not found on the keyboard to be entered. See Figure 3-4 for an example.

You can type hex codes on the left side or normal ASCII characters on the right, depending on where you click with the mouse.

The purpose of binary values is to hold data that couldn't be easily represented by ordinary string values. As such, binary values are much less likely to contain readable text (despite the example value in Figure 3-4), but rather simply raw data. Of course, the format and purpose of the data in any given binary value depends entirely on the application that created it.

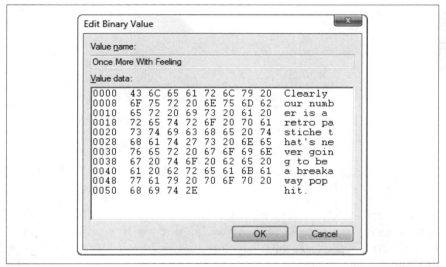

Figure 3-4. Binary values are entered differently from the common string values, but the contents are sometimes nearly as readable

DWORD values

Essentially, a DWORD is a number. Often, the contents of a DWORD value are easy to understand, such as 0 for no and 1 for yes, or 161 for the number of seconds it took you to solve your best game of Sudoku. A DWORD value is used where only numerical digits are allowed, whereas a string or binary value can contain anything.

In the DWORD value editor (Figure 3-5), you can change the base of the number displayed (think back to your grade-school math). For instance, the number 64 in hexadecimal (also known as base 16) is equal to 100 in decimal (base 10).

Type the number in the wrong base, and you'll unwittingly be entering the wrong value. (The **Base** option doesn't matter for any value of 9 or less.)

In most cases, you'll want to select **Decimal** (even though Microsoft didn't bother to make it the default), since decimal notation is what most humans use for ordinary counting numbers. Note that if there's already a number in the **Value data** field, switching the **Base** converts the number in real time, which incidentally is a good way to illustrate the difference between the two settings.

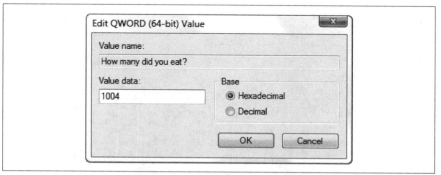

Figure 3-5. DWORD values are just numbers, but they can be represented in decimal or hexadecimal notation

The application that creates each value in the Registry solely determines the particular type and purpose of the value. In other words, no strict rules limit which types are used in which circumstances or how values are named. A programmer may choose to store, say, the high scores for some game in a binary value called High Scores or in a string value called Lard Lad Donuts. All you have to do in your role as Registry hacker is provide the values in the format expected by a given application.

An important thing to notice at this point is the string value named (default) that appears at the top of every key.* The default value cannot be removed or renamed, although its contents can be changed; an empty default value is signified by value not set. The (default) value doesn't necessarily have any special meaning that would differentiate it from any other

---

* In the more simplistic Registry found in Windows 3.1 and Windows NT 3.x, each key had only one value. Starting in Windows 95, a key could contain any number of values; the default value simply took the place of the lone value from previous versions, allowing compatibility with older applications that were written before the change took effect. In fact, many things you'll find in the Registry are designed with such "legacy" support in mind.

value, apart from what might have been assigned by the programmer of the particular application that uses the key.

When Is a Number Not Just a Number?

Sometimes the number stored in a DWORD value is actually made up of several components, all glued together with the binary arithmetic we were supposed to have learned in the seventh grade.

The term "DWORD" is an abbreviation for "Double Word," which means that it can store two 16-bit values (known as "Words" in geekspeak). A 16-bit value is basically a whole number (integer) that can be stored in 16 *bits*, which means it can be no larger than 2^{16}, or 65,536. So, a DWORD value can be used to store two of these, *or* one 32-bit number (up to 2^{32}, or 4,294,967,296), *or even* thirty-two 1-bit numbers (each of which can be 1 or 0).

Windows Vista also supports the 64-bit DWORD value, which is available even if you're using the 32-bit edition of Vista. A 64-bit DWORD—equivalent to a QWORD (Quadruple Word)—can hold sixty-four 1-bit values, four 16-bit values, two 32-bit values, or one 64-bit value (which can be up to about 1.8×10^{19}).

(Strangely, 64- and 32-bit DWORD values are indistinguishable in the Registry Editor except in the DWORD editor (Figure 3-5). Presumably, you'd only want to use a 64-bit value with a 64-bit application, for which you'd need the 64-bit edition of Windows Vista.

So, the question that's probably on your mind is, "Huh? How can this knowledge possibly help me with my love life?"

The answer is that it can't. In fact, it'll probably just make things worse. But it'll be invaluable when you come across a DWORD value that's made up of a bunch of smaller components. For instance, say you flip a switch in some application and you witness a DWORD value change from 16 to 8. What you've uncovered is that the aforementioned switch is stored as the fourth bit (the first being 1, the second being 2, and the third being 4) in this value. (If you're confused, look up "Binary numeral system" in Wikipedia for help with the concept.)

To make things more complicated, there's also the BIGENDIAN variant of the DWORD value (REG_DWORD_BIGENDIAN). This is basically the same as an ordinary 32-bit DWORD, except that the two 16-bit *words* are stored in the opposite order (the larger one coming first). These are rare, but you might run into trouble if you replace one with an ordinary DWORD value.

Registry Tasks and Tools

So, that's it for Registry basics. The real fun begins with the various Registry tools you can use, and what you can do with them.

Search the Registry

The Registry Editor has a simple (to a fault) Search feature, allowing you to search through all the keys and values for text. Just select **Find** from the Registry Editor's **Edit** menu, type the desired text (Figure 3-6), and click **Find Next**.

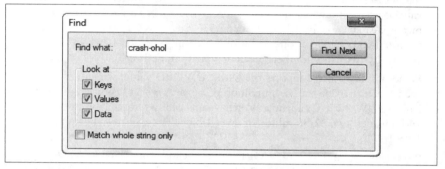

Figure 3-6. Use Registry Editor's Search feature to find text in key names, value names, and value data

The Registry Editor's Search feature is pretty terrible. For one, it's hopelessly slow, and doesn't show a history of past searches. But its biggest drawback is that it only shows one match at a time; you have to click **Find Next** repeatedly to cycle through all the search results, one by one. And if you accidentally double-click **Find Next**, there's no going backward. Finally, there's no search-and-replace feature, but more on that later.

Press **Ctrl-F** or select **Edit → Find** to begin a search at the selected key. (Scroll to the top and select **Computer** beforehand to search the entire Registry.)

In the Find window, make sure that all three options in the **Look at** section are checked, unless you know specifically that what you're looking for is solely a **Key**, a **Value** (value name), or **Data** (value contents). You'll also usually want the **Match whole string only** option turned off, unless you're searching for text that commonly appears in other words; searching for handle might otherwise trigger entries like PersistentHandler and TeachAndLearn.

The Registry Editor stops once it finds the first match to your search term; just press **F3** to continue searching for the next match. If you want to show all the matches at once, use Registry Agent, introduced in the next section.

You may need to employ some tricks to find certain types of things in the Registry, such as:

Context menu items

Context menu items are usually stored in the HKEY_CLASSES_ROOT branch (see "File Type Associations," later in this chapter). When searching for any menu items, keep in mind that most of them have underlined characters to signify keyboard shortcuts, even though, ironically, Windows Vista doesn't display them by default. For instance, the **Datasheet** action associated with Access Form Shortcuts in Microsoft Office 2007 is actually stored as Data&sheet in the Registry. This allows it to be displayed as **Datasheet** if you manage to open the menu with the keyboard (an increasingly difficult task in Windows Vista). The & character in Data&sheet instructs Windows to underline the character that follows it (the s in this case), and since it's present in the Registry value, you'll need to include the & character in your searches; if you don't, the Search tool won't find it.

 Text searches are *not* case-sensitive, so you don't have to worry about capitalization when typing your search terms.

File and folder names

Despite the fact that long filenames (those longer than the archaic 8-dot-3 standard left over from the early days of DOS) had been in wide use on the PC platform for well over a decade before Windows Vista was released, short filenames* still have a role in modern Windows computing, particularly in the Registry. Specifically, a folder path like *C:\Program Files* may be occasionally represented in its short 8.3 form: *C:\PROGRA~1*.

Why, even Microsoft still uses short filenames; a fresh installation of Office 2007 (introduced alongside Windows Vista) placed a reference in the Registry to *C:\PROGRA~1\MICROS~2\Office12\1033\ACCESS12.ACC.*

Unfortunately, this means you need to search for both the long and short versions of a file or folder name if you want to find them all. For example, say you want to move your *Program Files* folder from one drive to another. When you install Windows, any settings pertaining to this folder may be stored in the Registry as *C:\Program Files* or *C:\Progra~1*. Make sure you search for both.

---

* See "Advanced NTFS Settings," in Chapter 5, for more information on short-filename generation.

Now, when searching the Registry for both Program Files and Progra~1, it may occur to you to just search for progra, which will indeed catch both variations. Because this will stumble upon other instances of the word program, try limiting the results by placing a backslash (\) in front of the text (e.g., \progra) to limit the search to only directory names beginning with those letters. Neato.

DLLs, classes, components, extensions, and CLSIDs

Windows and all your applications are constructed from smaller building blocks, sometimes referred to as classes, extensions, or objects. I'll spare you a tirade on COM components, .NET architecture, and a bunch of other developer jargon (sorry). Suffice it to say, the majority of these building blocks are registered in the HKEY_CLASSES_ROOT\CLSID branch of your Registry, and are identified by a 32-digit (16-bit hex) code called a Class ID, or CLSID. CLSIDs are formatted like this:

    {ACOEEBCA-73FA-4EB3-87FF-96E58401FA1F}

Why is this important? It means that you can track down where a class is referenced (in other words, where in Windows it's used) as well as where it's registered, all by searching the Registry for the CLSID.

For instance, configuration data for the aforementioned class is located in:

    HKEY_CLASSES_ROOT\CLSID\{ACOEEBCA-73FA-4EB3-87FF-96E58401FA1F}

If a component isn't working, odds are you can fix the problem, or at least help diagnose it, by fussing with the values in this key. Or, delete the key altogether to effectively unregister the class with Windows. For instance, to turn off Vista's support for "compressed folders" (ZIP files appearing as folders in Windows Explorer), you need to delete two such CLSID branches, as described in Chapter 2.

Windows comes with a utility, *regsvr32.exe*, that you can use to register or unregister DLL files manually. For instance, you can repair a CLSID branch for a specific component by opening a Command Prompt window (in administrator mode; see Chapter 8) and typing regsvr32 "c:\program files\ *my app\some file.dll*" and pressing **Enter**. Or, to remove all the entries used by a DLL, type regsvr32 /u "c:\program files*my app\some file.dll*" and press **Enter**. See "Playing Video," in Chapter 4, for an example of regsvr32 in action.

If a CLSID is found elsewhere (even within another key under HKEY_CLASSES_ROOT\CLSID), it means that the program that owns the key is using said component. Delete the reference, and the link is broken. See Chapters 6 and 8 for some examples.

Search and Replace Registry Data

The Registry Editor has no search-and-replace feature, seemingly with good reason: a single poorly chosen replace operation could make Windows inoperable. But there are times when you do need to replace all occurrences of, say, a folder name like *C:\Program Files\My Program* with another folder name like *D:\My Folder*. Depending on the number of occurrences, such an operation could take hours.

Registry Agent (part of Creative Element Power Tools, available at *http:// www.creativelement.com/powertools*) not only gives you a better way to search the Registry (search results are shown in a list, instead of one at a time), but supports search-and-replace operations as well. Here's how to move an application from one drive to another without having to reinstall it:

1. Open Registry Agent.

2. Type text to search (e.g., `c:\program files\acme`), and click **Find Now**.

3. The results are shown in a list (Figure 3-7) with three columns. The left column shows the location (key) where the text was found; you can click it to open the Registry Editor at that location. The middle and righthand columns show the value name and contents, respectively.

4. Choose the **Replace** tab.

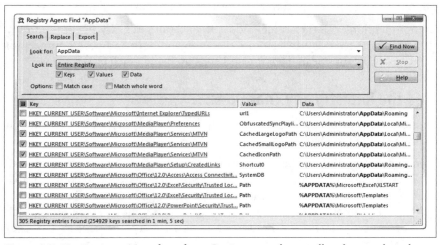

Figure 3-7. Use Registry Agent for a faster Registry search, as well as for search-and-replace operations

Replacing a common word like `Microsoft` in your Registry is a really bad idea. Don't try it at home. I mean it. Ordinary searching with Registry Agent is harmless, but the **Replace** feature can be as dangerous as it is handy if you're not careful.

5. Place a checkmark next to the found items you wish to replace. Use the checkmark at the top of the list to check or uncheck all of them.

6. Type the new text—which will replace the old text in each selected item in the search results—in the **With** field (e.g., d:\new acme).

You don't have to replace the same text you searched. For instance, you can search for c:\program files\acme, and then do a search and replace within these results for anything you like, such as acme by itself, or even portmeirion.

7. Choose which types of text you'd like to replace by checking or unchecking the **Keys**, **Values**, and **Data** options. Note that the **Keys** checkbox is grayed-out (disabled) by default for safety reasons; click **Help** for instructions to lift this restriction.

The Replace tool has no "undo" feature, which means that if you screw up something here, the only way to recover is to restore your Registry from a backup. Want a shortcut? Use the **Export** tab to create a Registry patch (described later in this chapter) containing the selected values, which can be used as a quick and dirty backup.

8. Click the **Replace** button to perform the search and replace.

Even if you don't use the search-and-replace feature, Registry Agent is a pretty slick searching tool, as it overcomes the annoying hunt-and-peck approach of the Registry Editor's Search feature and ends up being much faster, too.

Find the Registry Key That Does...

So, now you know how to change an item in the Registry, but how do you find which item to change?

Sometimes it's obvious. Say you want to reduce the time it takes to load your favorite application, and it occurs to you that maybe you could disable the program's splash screen (the friendly logo you stare at while the program loads, which takes time to load itself). Sure enough, there's a value called ShowSplashScreen in the application's Registry key in HKEY_Current_User\Software. Set it to 1 (one) to turn it on, or 0 (zero) to turn it off.

Zero and one, with regard to Registry settings, typically mean *false* and *true* (or *off* and *on*), respectively. However, sometimes the value name negates this—if the value in the example were instead called DontShowSplashScreen, then a 1 (one) would most likely turn *off* the feature.

Other times it's not so easy. You might see a long, seemingly meaningless series of numbers and letters, or perhaps nothing recognizable at all. Although there are no strict rules as to how values and keys are named or how the data therein is arranged, there's a trick you can use to uncover how a particular setting—any setting—is stored in the Registry.

What's the point? Once you find the Registry value(s) responsible for a particular setting, you can:

Find hidden settings. Not all application settings have tidy little checkboxes in a Preferences dialog window; some things can only be changed in the Registry. By finding out where an application saves its settings, you can uncover others nearby and even learn how they work.

Reproduce settings. By finding the Registry keys and values responsible for one or more settings, you can consolidate them into a Registry patch file (described later in this chapter), and then apply them to any number of other PCs. This is particularly useful for network administrators and software developers.

Enter values not permitted by the software. For instance, say you've configured a virus scanner to scan your system once a week. You'd rather have it perform a scan every 10 days, but the program only lets you choose a multiple of 7. If you find the Registry value responsible, you may be able to enter any arbitrary number.

Fix bugs in software. If an application won't save a particular setting properly in the Registry, you can fix it by hand if you know where it's stored.

Prevent changes to certain settings. Some programs—including Windows Vista itself—have a habit of "forgetting" certain settings, reverting them to their default values for no apparent reason. Once you know where the setting is stored, you can change the permissions (more on that later) to prevent further changes without your consent.

The idea is to take "snapshots" of your entire Registry *before* and *after* you make a change in Windows. By comparing the two snapshots, you can easily see which Registry keys and values were affected. Here's how you do it:

1. Close all applications except the one you wish to examine. Any unnecessary running applications—including those in the system tray/notification area—could write to the Registry at any time, adding unexpected changes.

2. Open the Registry Editor, and select the HKEY_CURRENT_USER branch.

3. Select **Export** from the **Registry** menu. Type User1.reg for the filename, select your desktop or another convenient location to put the file, and click **Save** to export the entire branch to the file.

4. Next, select the HKEY_LOCAL_MACHINE branch and repeat step 3, exporting it instead to *Machine1.reg*.

Although the Registry has five main branches, the others are simply "mirrors," or symbolic links of portions of HKEY_CURRENT_USER and HKEY_LOCAL_MACHINE. See "The Structure of the Registry," earlier in this chapter, for details.

5. Now make the change you want to track.

For instance, say you want to find the value responsible for showing hidden files in Windows Explorer. In this case, you'd go to **Control Panel → Folder Options**, choose the **View** tab, and in the **Advanced Settings** list, turn on the **Hidden Files and Folders** option. Click **OK** when you're done.

6. Immediately—and before doing anything else—switch back to the Registry Editor, and re-export the HKEY_CURRENT_USER and HKEY_LOCAL_MACHINE branches into new files named *User2.reg* and *Machine2.reg*, respectively, as described earlier in steps 2 and 3.

What you now have is a *snapshot* of the entire Registry taken before and after the change was made. It's important that the snapshots be taken immediately before and after the change, so that other trivial settings, such as changes in window positions, aren't included with the changes you care about.

7. All that needs to be done now is to distill the *changed* information into a useful format. Windows comes with the command-line utility File Compare (*fc.exe*), which quite handily highlights the differences between the *before* and *after* files.

There are several Windows-based third-party alternatives that are easier to use or offer more features than *fc.exe*, such as UltraEdit (available at *http://www.ultraedit.com*); even Microsoft Word can do text comparisons (although you'll need to remember to save the results as plain text).

Open a Command Prompt window (type cmd in the Start menu **Search** box and press **Enter**), and then at the Command Prompt, use the cd command (Chapter 9) to change to the directory containing the Registry patches. For instance, if you saved them to your desktop, type:

        cd %userprofile%\desktop

8. To perform the comparison, type the following two lines:

        fc /u user1.reg user2.reg > user.txt
        fc /u machine1.reg machine2.reg > machine.txt

At this point, the File Compare utility scans the two pairs of files and spits out *only* the differences between them. The > character redirects the output, which normally would be displayed right in the Command Prompt window, into new text files: *user.txt* for the changes in HKEY_CURRENT_USER and *machine.txt* for the changes in HKEY_LOCAL_MACHINE.

9. Examine the results. The *user.txt* file should look something like this:

```
Comparing files user1.reg and USER2.REG

***** user1.reg
[HKEY_CURRENT_USER\Software\Microsoft\Windows\CurrentVersion\
            Explorer\Advanced]
"Hidden"=dword:00000001
"ShowCompColor"=dword:00000000
***** USER2.REG
[HKEY_CURRENT_USER\Software\Microsoft\Windows\CurrentVersion\
            Explorer\Advanced]
"Hidden"=dword:00000002
"ShowCompColor"=dword:00000000
*****
```

From this example listing, you can see that the only applicable change was the Hidden value, located deep in the HKEY_CURRENT_USER branch. (There may be some other entries, but if you inspect them, you'll find that they relate only to MRU lists from RegEdit and can be ignored.)*

Note that for the particular setting explained in step 5, no changes were recorded in the HKEY_LOCAL_MACHINE branch, so *machine.txt* ends up with only the message, "FC: No differences encountered". This means that the changes were made only to keys in the HKEY_CURRENT_USER branch.

10. The lines immediately preceding and following the line that changed are also included by FC as an aid in locating the lines in the source files. As luck would have it, one of the surrounding lines in this example happens to be the section header (in brackets), which specifies the full path of the Registry key in which the value is located.

 In this case, the value that changed was located in HKEY_CURRENT_USER\Software\Microsoft\Windows\CurrentVersion\. If you take a peek in that key, you'll find that it contains other settings, some of which aren't included in the Folder Options dialog box. Experiment with some of the more interesting-sounding values, such as CascadePrinters and ShowSuperHidden. Or, search the Web for the value name to see what others have discovered about it.

---

* MRU stands for Most Recently Used. Windows stores the most recent filenames typed into file dialog boxes; from this example, you'll notice several references to the filenames you used to save the Registry snapshots.

If you don't see the line in square brackets, you'll have to do a little more reconnaissance. To find out where the value is located, open one of the source files (*User1.reg*, *User2.reg*, *Machine1.reg*, or *Machine2.reg*) and use your text editor's Search tool to find the line highlighted in step 9. For this example, you'd search *User2.reg* for "Hidden"=dword:00000002 and then make note of the line enclosed in square brackets ([...]) most immediately *above* the changed line. This represents the key containing the Hidden value.

 Sometimes, changing a setting results in a Registry value (or key) being created or deleted, which could mean an entire section may be present in only one of the two snapshots. Depending on the change, you may have to do a little digging, or perhaps try the document comparison feature in your favorite word processor for an easier-to-use comparison summary.

11. This last step is optional. If you want to create a Registry patch that activates the Registry change, you can either convert FC's output to the correct format (described here), or return to Registry Editor and export the appropriate key, as described in "Export and Import Data with Registry Patches," later in this chapter).

Because the FC output is originally derived from Registry patches, it's already close to the correct format. Start by removing all of the lines from *user.txt*, except the *second* version of the *changed* line—this would be the value in its *after* setting, which presumably is the goal. You'll end up with something like this:

```
"Hidden"=dword:00000002
```

Next, paste in the key (in brackets) immediately above the value. (In the case of our example, it was part of the FC output and can simply be left in.) You should end up with text that looks like this:

```
[HKEY_CURRENT_USER\Software\Microsoft\Windows\CurrentVersion\
    Explorer\Advanced]
"Hidden"=dword:00000002
```

Finally, add the text Windows Registry Editor Version 5.00 followed by a blank line at the beginning of the file, like this:

```
Windows Registry Editor Version 5.00

[HKEY_CURRENT_USER\Software\Microsoft\Windows\CurrentVersion\
    Explorer\Advanced]
"Hidden"=dword:00000002
```

When you're done, save this as a new file with the *.reg* filename extension (e.g., *User-final.reg*).

If the settings you've changed also resulted in changes in the `HKEY_LOCAL_MACHINE` branch, simply repeat this step for the *machine.txt* file as well. You can then consolidate both files into one, making sure you have only one instance of the `Windows Registry Editor Version 5.00` line.

For some settings (such as the one in this example), you may want to make two patches: one to turn it on, and one to turn it off. Simply double-click the patch corresponding to the setting you desire.

There are some caveats to this approach, mostly in that the File Compare utility will often pull out more differences than are relevant to the change you wish to make. It's important to look closely at each key in the resulting Registry patch to see whether it's really applicable and necessary.

See Chapter 9 for a way to use Windows Script Host to automate changes to the Registry without using Registry patches.

Create an Interface for a Registry Setting

The whole point of messing around in the Registry is to view and modify settings that are otherwise inaccessible in Explorer, Control Panel, or the hundreds of dialog boxes scattered throughout the operating system. However, there is a way to patch into the interface and add checkboxes and radio buttons that are linked to whatever Registry settings you want.

Why would you want to do this? Perhaps there's a Registry setting you change frequently, or maybe you administer a building full of PCs and there's a feature you want to expose to your users without having them mess around with the Registry themselves.

Start by going to **Control Panel** → **Folder Options** → **View** menu. At first glance, the **Advanced settings** list in this dialog box is presented in a somewhat awkward format, apparently to accommodate the large number of options. However, the less-than-ideal presentation is actually designed to allow customization, permitting Microsoft (or you) to easily add or remove items from the list. See Figure 3-8 for an example of a customized version of this window.

You've probably guessed that Microsoft didn't make this list of options customizable for you. Rather, it was designed to accommodate different settings for different versions of Windows (the actual options present on your PC, for instance, depend on your edition of Vista). But that doesn't mean you can't change it around to suit your needs.

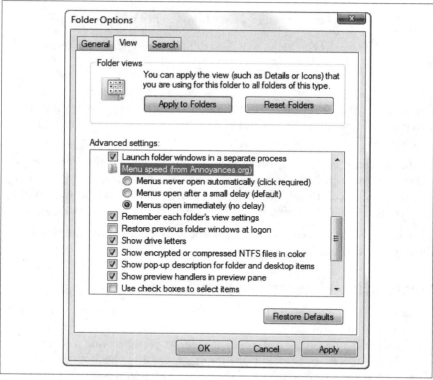

Figure 3-8. The Advanced Folder Options dialog box is a flexible, customizable list of Registry settings

The idea is that you link up a checkbox or radio button to a value—any value you choose—in your Registry. This would, for example, allow you to make certain Registry changes accessible to yourself or others (such as users of other PCs you administer), reducing the need for them to mess around in the Registry. Or, if you're a software developer, you can add your own program's options to this window. Or, maybe you just want easier access to a hidden Microsoft setting you find yourself changing often.

The format is actually quite remarkable, because you don't have to be a programmer to utilize this feature. You can add new options to a certain portion of the Registry and then tie those options to values you choose anywhere else in the Registry. The downside is that it's a little cumbersome to type it all out, and the options are rather limited. Here's how you do it:

1. Open the Registry Editor.

2. Expand the branches to `HKEY_LOCAL_MACHINE\Software\Microsoft\Windows\CurrentVersion\Explorer\Advanced\Folder`.

   Take a look at the keys inside of the `Folder` key. The structure of the hierarchy in the Folder Options window is reproduced here in the Registry, although the list items will appear in a different order than their corresponding Registry entries. This is because the captions in the Folder Options list aren't necessarily the same as the names of the corresponding Registry keys here, yet both collections are sorted alphabetically. For example, the **Remember each folder's view settings** option is represented by the `ClassicViewState` key in the Registry.

3. Take this opportunity to back up the entire branch by highlighting the `Advanced` key and selecting **Export** from the **File** menu. This way, you'll be able to easily restore the defaults without having to reinstall Windows.

4. At this point, you can remove any unwanted entries by deleting the corresponding keys from this branch; the `Text` value in each key should be enough to explain what each key is for.

5. To add a new item, start by simply creating a new subkey in the `Advanced` key. Name the key anything you want, as long as it doesn't conflict with a existing key name. Bonus points for a nice, descriptive key name.

 Some settings are divided into groups, such as **Hidden files and folders**, which contains two radio buttons. You can create a new group using the existing `Hidden` key as a template. Then, add new entries to your group by placing subkeys inside your new group key.

6. The values inside each key determine the properties of the corresponding setting. Feel free to fish around the existing keys for examples.

   Start by adding a new string value to your key named `Text`, and then double-click it to enter the caption of the new entry. When you're done, add another string value named `Type`, and type either `group`, `checkbox`, or `radio` as the value's contents. These two values, plus the others that determine how your new setting looks in the Folder Options window, are explained in Table 3-2.

Table 3-2. Visual properties of Folder Options items

Value name	Datatype	Description of value contents
Type	String	This can be set to either group, checkbox, or radio, representing a folder, checkbox, or radio button, respectively. Checkboxes are square options and can be either on or off. Radio buttons are round options that are linked to other radio buttons in the same folder, in that only one at a time can be selected (you can have multiple groups of radio buttons). And folders, of course, are used to organize the various other options. This parameter is required by all items.
Text	String	This is the actual caption of the option as it will appear in the dialog box. This can be as long as you want (better too descriptive than too vague), but the paradigm dictates that only the first word be capitalized and that there be no period. This parameter is required by all items.
Bitmap	String	This specifies the icon, used for folder items only. If omitted, it's a rather ugly bent arrow. The syntax[a] is $filename, index$, where $filename$ is the full path and filename of the file containing the icon, and $index$ is the icon number (starting with zero), if the file contains more than one icon. To specify the familiar yellow folder, type %SystemRoot%\ system32\Shell32.dll,4 here. This parameter is optional for all folders, and has no effect on checkboxes and radio buttons.
HelpID	String	This is the filename and optionally the help context ID, pointing to the documentation for this item. If the user selects the item and presses the F1 key, this specifies the help note that will appear. The syntax is $filename\#id$, where $filename$ is the name of a .hlp or .chm file, and id is the numeric help context id (commonly used by programmers) of the topic you want to display. Omit id to simply show the index page of the specified help file. This parameter is optional.

[a] The Bitmap value uses the same syntax as the DefaultIcon property for file types, as documented in "File Type Associations," later in this chapter.

7. Next, add values—explained in Table 3-3—to specify what happens when a specific item is turned on or off in the Folder Options window. For radio and checkbox items, you'll need the following values: HKey-Root, RegPath, ValueName, and CheckedValue. (This step isn't necessary if your item is a group.)

Table 3-3. Registry-related properties of Folder Options items

Value name	Datatype	Description of value contents
HKeyRoot	DWORD	This is an eight-digit number representing the root of the Registry path containing the target Registry setting. Use the *hexadecimal* number 80000000 for HKEY_CLASSES_ROOT, 80000001 for HKEY_CURRENT_USER, 80000002 for HKEY_LOCAL_MACHINE, 80000003 for HKEY_USERS, or 80000005 for HKEY_CURRENT_ CONFIG. For some reason, it must be separated from the rest of the Registry path, specified in RegPath, discussed next. This parameter is required for all checkbox and radio items.

Table 3-3. Registry-related properties of Folder Options items (continued)

Value name	Datatype	Description of value contents
RegPath	String	This is the path specifying the location of the target Registry setting, not including the root (see HKeyRoot, earlier). For example, for HKEY_CURRENT_USER\Software\Microsoft\Windows\CurrentVersion, you would only enter Software\Microsoft\Windows\CurrentVersion here. This parameter is required for all checkbox and radio items.
ValueName	String	This is the name of the target Registry value. This value is where the setting data is stored when the option is turned on or off in the Folder Options window. The key containing said value is specified by the RegPath and HKeyRoot parameters, listed earlier. This parameter is required by all checkbox and radio items.
Checked-Value	Should match target value datatype	This holds the data to be stored in the target Registry value (specified by the RegPath and ValueName parameters earlier), when said option is turned *on*. If you're configuring an option to be used on both Windows 9x/Me and Windows Vista/2000 systems, use both the CheckedValueW95 and CheckedValueNT parameters *instead of this value*. This parameter is otherwise required by all checkbox and radio items.
Checked-ValueW95	Should match target value datatype	Use this instead of CheckedValue, above, if you're configuring an option to be used on both Windows 9x/Me and Windows Vista/2000 systems. This value contains the data that will be applied if the system is running Windows 9x/Me. Used in conjunction with CheckedValueNT, discussed next.
Checked-ValueNT	Should match target value datatype	Use this instead of CheckedValue, discussed earlier, if you're configuring an option to be used on both Windows 9x/Me and Windows Vista/2000 systems. This value contains the data that will be applied if the system is running Windows Vista, 2000, or NT. Used in conjunction with CheckedValueW95, later.
UnChecked Value	Should match target value datatype	This holds the data to be stored in the target Registry value, when said option is turned *off*. This value is optional; if omitted, it is assumed to be 0.
Default-Value	Should match target value datatype	This is the default value, used only if the target Registry value does not already exist. As soon as the option in the Folder Options window is turned on or off at least once, this parameter is ignored, and Windows instead reads the state of the target value, comparing it to CheckedValue and UnCheckedValue to determine if the option should appear checked or unchecked. This value is optional; if omitted, it is assumed to be 0.

The value type (String, Binary, DWORD) of the CheckedValue, UnCheckedValue, and DefaultValue parameters all depends on what the target value requires. For example, if the target value you're changing is a DWORD value, then all three of these parameters must also be DWORD values.

8. After you've created keys and entered the appropriate property values, your Registry should look something like Figure 3-9, and the resulting Folder Options dialog box should look like Figure 3-8, shown earlier. If Folder Options is open, you'll have to close it and reopen it for the changes to take effect.

 If you add a setting and it doesn't show up in the Folder Options window (after closing and reopening it), most likely one or more required values are missing.

9. Close the Registry Editor when you're finished.

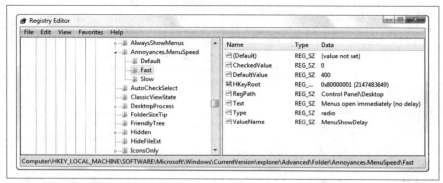

Figure 3-9. Settings that appear in the Advanced Folder Options list are configured in the Registry

When the Folder Options dialog box is first displayed, the current data stored in each target value is compared with the corresponding CheckedValue and UnCheckedValue, and the option in the **Advanced settings** list is set accordingly. In other words, if you did everything right, each option in **Advanced settings** should reflect its own current state. Change a setting and click **OK**, and the corresponding options are written to the Registry.

To reproduce a setting elsewhere in the Windows interface or the interface of another application, you'll first need to find the respective Registry setting as described in "Find the Registry Key That Does...," earlier in this chapter.

Export and Import Data with Registry Patches

Typing in Registry data gets awfully tedious, particularly when the N key breaks on your keyboard. Thankfully, it's not the only way to add keys and values to the Registry.

A Registry patch is a plain-text file with the *.reg* filename extension that contains one or more Registry keys or values. Double-click on a *.reg* file, and Windows runs the Registry Editor, which "applies" the patch to the Registry, meaning that its contents are *merged* with the contents of the Registry.

Patch files are especially handy for backing up small portions of the Registry, distributing Registry settings to other PCs, and duplicating keys.

For example, say you spend an hour or so customizing the toolbars in a particular application used by many employees in your office. Since most programs store their toolbar settings in the Registry, you can use a Registry patch to not only back up the completed toolbar setup—and thus save an hour of reconfiguring should your PC subsequently burst into flames—but to quickly copy the toolbar to all the other PCs in your office.

Or, perhaps you've spent the last six months gradually customizing your file types (covered later in this chapter), only to find that a newly installed application or a Windows upgrade erased all your hard work and reset all your context menus. All you need to do is to make a Registry patch containing all your saved file types, and then reapply it should the need arise.

Create a Registry patch

1. Open the Registry Editor, and select a branch you wish to export.

   The branch can be anywhere from one of the top-level branches to a branch a dozen layers deep. Registry patches include not only the branch you select, but all of the values and subkeys in the branch. Don't select anything more than what you absolutely need.

2. From the **File** menu, select **Export**, type a filename and choose a destination folder, and click **OK**. All of the values and subkeys in the selected branch will then be stored in the patch file. Make sure the filename of the new Registry patch has the *.reg* extension.

Clearly, there's not much to making Registry patches with the Registry Editor. But it gets a little more interesting when you modify them, or even create them from scratch to automate Registry changes.

Edit a Registry patch

Since a Registry patch is just a plain-text file, you can edit it with any decent plain-text editor, or lacking that, Notepad (*notepad.exe*). The contents of the Registry patch will look something like the text shown in Example 3-1.

Example 3-1. Contents of a Registry patch created from HKEY_CLASSES_ROOT\txt

```
Windows Registry Editor Version 5.00

[HKEY_CLASSES_ROOT\.txt]
@="txtfile"
"PerceivedType"="text"
"Content Type"="text/plain"

[HKEY_CLASSES_ROOT\.txt\ShellNew]
"ItemName"="@%SystemRoot%\\system32\\notepad.exe,-470"
"NullFile"=""
```

The first line, `Windows Registry Editor Version 5.00`, tells Windows that this file is a valid Registry patch; don't remove this line. The rest of the Registry patch is a series of key names and values.

Backward Compatibility

Registry patches created in Windows 95, 98, or Me can be imported into the Windows Vista Registry without a problem (that is, not taking into account the screwy settings contained therein).

However, the same is not true the other way around. Patch files made in Windows Vista, XP, 2003, and 2000 are encoded with the Unicode character set, and as you've seen, bear a header indicating the 5.0 version number that will choke the older Registry Editor. To use a Vista-created *.reg* file in Windows 9x/Me, you'll need to deal with both of these issues.

First, replace the `Windows Registry Editor Version 5.00` header line with `REGEDIT4`. Whew, that was hard.

Next, to convert the Unicode *.reg* file into an ASCII-encoded file, those earlier versions of Windows can understand, open the file in Notepad. Then, from the Notepad's **File** menu, select **Save As** and choose a new filename, and from the little **Encoding** drop-down listbox at the bottom of the window, select **ANSI**. Click **Save**, and your patch is now backward-compatible.

The key names appear in brackets (`[...]`) and specify the full path of the key, thus indicating where the values that follow are to be stored. On each subsequent line until the next key section begins, the name of a value is given first (in quotation marks), followed by an equals sign, and then the data stored in the value (also in quotation marks). A value name of @ tells the Registry Editor to place the value data in the (`Default`) value (as shown in the fourth line of the example).

You can go ahead and make changes to anything in the Registry patch file as long as you keep the format intact. Of course, those changes won't take effect in the Registry until the Registry patch is merged back into the Registry, a process described in the next section.

So, why would you want to edit a Registry patch file? Modifying a large number of Registry values often turns out to be much easier with a text editor than with the Registry Editor, since you don't have to open—and then close—each individual value.

 It may be tempting to perform a quick search and replace in the text editor, and then apply your changes back to the Registry. But be careful, as the effect may not be what you expected. If you replace any text in the *name* of a value (to the left of the equals sign) or even the name of a key (the lines in brackets), Registry Editor will create new values and keys with those names when you apply the patch, *leaving the old values and keys intact.* A better choice is to use a tool like Registry Agent (see "Search and Replace Registry Data," earlier in this chapter).

There's no requirement that the keys in a Registry patch file need to have lived next to one another in the Registry, or that they be in any particular order. This means you can combine several separate patch files into one, and use it to restore any number of keys in one step. All it takes is a little copy and paste between side-by-side Notepad windows. The only thing you need to do, besides making sure all the keys and values remain intact, is to remove any extraneous `Windows Registry Editor Version 5.00` header lines.

If you're creating a Registry patch to be used on other PCs, make sure you fix any references to absolute pathnames before you distribute the file. If, for example, your patch file references *D:\Windows\notepad.exe*, it'll cause a problem on any PC where *notepad.exe* is located in *C:\Windows*. The best solution is to use expandable string values, as described earlier in this chapter, along with the appropriate system variables, like this: *%SystemRoot%\notepad.exe*. Now, since expandable string values are stored like Binary values in Registry patch files, such an entry would look like this:

```
"Open"=hex(2):26,00,53,00,79,00,73,00,74,00,65,00,6d,00,52,00,6f,00,6f,\
00,74,00,25,00,5c,00,6e,00,6f,00,74,00,65,00,70,00,61,00,64,00,2e,00,65,00,\
78,00,65,00,00,00
```

Now, as you may've guessed, it's considerably easier to edit expandable string (and binary) values in the Registry Editor than in any text editor, so you'll probably want to make such corrections *before* you export the key to a patch file. If you need to add a binary or expandable string value to a Registry patch file you've already started editing, though, all you have to do is return to the Registry Editor, create a temporary key somewhere, and then create your new value. When you're done, just export the key to a new file, delete the key from the Registry, and then copy and paste the value to your other Registry patch file.

Delete keys and values from a Registry patch

Although the Registry Editor won't ever create a patch that *deletes* Registry keys or values, it's easy enough to make one by hand. To delete a key with a Registry Patch, place a minus sign *before* the key name, like this:

```
-[HKEY_CURRENT_USER\Control Panel\don't load]
```

This patch, when applied, deletes the specified key and all of its values, as well as any subkeys. To delete a single value from a key, place a minus sign *after* the equals sign, like this:

```
[HKEY_CURRENT_USER\Control Panel\don't load]
"desk.cpl"=-
```

Of course, these tricks only work if you have sufficient permission to delete those keys. See "Prevent Changes to a Registry Key," later in this chapter, for more information.

Apply a Registry patch

To copy the stuff from a Registry patch file back into your Registry, you need to apply it. The easiest way is to double-click the file (it doesn't matter if the Registry Editor is running or not).

If you see a UAC prompt at this point, click **Continue**. Then answer **Yes** when asked whether you're sure you want to add the information in the *.reg* file to the Registry, and finally, click **OK** when you see the "Information in *MyPatch.reg* has been successfully entered into the Registry" message. (You can also apply a patch from within the Registry Editor: from the **File** menu, select **Import**, select the patch file to apply, and click **OK**.)

To apply a Registry patch without any other warning messages (except for the UAC prompt; see Chapter 8 to get rid of that), you need to use the command line. Either from an open Command Prompt window or from **Start → Run**, type the following:

    regedit /s c:\folder\mypatch.reg

where $c:\folder\mypatch.reg$ is the full path and filename of the patch file to import. Or, if you want to get rid of the confirmation messages when you double-click a *.reg* file, add the /s switch (as shown here) to the *.reg* file type, as described later in this chapter.

If the Registry Editor is already open and one of the keys modified by a patch that was just applied is currently open, RegEdit should refresh the display automatically to reflect the changes. If it doesn't, press the **F5** key or go to **View → Refresh**.

When you apply a Registry patch, you *merge* the keys and values stored in a patch file with those in the Registry. Any keys and values in the applied patch that don't already exist will be created. If a key or value already exists, only its contents will be changed. It's important to understand that if a key you're updating already contains one or more values, *those values will be left intact* if they're not explicitly modified or deleted by the patch.

See Chapter 9 for another way to automate changes to the Registry from files.

Prevent Changes to a Registry Key

Security has always been one of Microsoft's favorite marketing buzzwords, and never more so than when Windows Vista was introduced. But as it turns out, Vista's security features are quite a bit more useful for protecting your PC from itself than from any alleged intruders.

The permissions system covered in Chapter 8 doesn't just protect files and folders, it restricts who can read and modify Registry entries. This feature is tremendously important, yet most people don't even know it's there. It means you can lock a Registry key to prevent employees from installing software on a company PC, or prevent kids from disabling parental controls on a family PC.

Permissions also let you lock file type associations (covered later in this chapter), preventing other applications from changing them. And by locking certain other keys, you can help protect your PC from viruses and spyware.

Here's how you do it:

1. Open the Registry Editor, and navigate to the key you want to protect.

 You can't protect individual values, but rather only the keys that contain them. This means that if you lock a key to protect one of its values, none of its values can be modified. You can, however, choose whether or not your changes are made to the subkeys of the selected key.

2. Right-click the key, and select **Permissions**. For details on how to use this window, see Chapter 8.

3. Click **Advanced**, and then click **Add**.

 If the **Add** button is disabled (grayed out), you'll have to take ownership of the key, close the Permissions window, and then reopen it before you can make any changes to the permissions of this object. See Chapter 8 for details.

4. In the **Enter the object names to select** field, type Everyone, and then click **OK**. (The "Everyone" user encompasses all user accounts, including those used by Windows processes and individual applications when they access the Registry.)

5. In the next window, "Permission Entry for...", click the checkbox in the **Deny** column, next to the actions you want to prohibit, as in Figure 3-10. See below for examples.

6. When you're done, click **OK** in each of the three open dialog windows. The change will take effect immediately.

Now, you may be tempted to remove **Allow** permissions for a particular user (or even all users), rather than add the **Deny** entry shown here. The problem is that doing so wouldn't prevent an application or Windows from taking ownership or adding the necessary permissions and breaking your lock. Furthermore, it would make it much more difficult to restore the old permissions should you need to remove the lock; using this procedure, all you need to do is remove the Deny rule and you're done.

This works because Windows gives Deny rules priority over Allow rules, which means you can lock a key even if there's another Allow rule that expressly gives a user permission to modify the item.

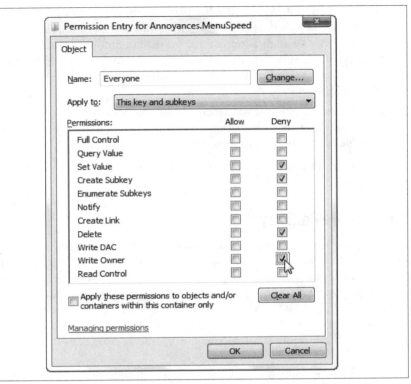

Figure 3-10. Lock a Registry key to prevent applications or Windows from modifying it

So, which keys do you lock, and which actions do you forbid? Here are some examples:

Make a read-only key. To lock a value yet still allow applications and Windows to read it, place a **Deny** checkbox next to **Set Value**, **Delete**, and **Write Owner**, as in Figure 3-10.

Create a complete lock-out. To prevent all applications from reading, modifying, or deleting a value, place a **Deny** checkbox next to **Full Control**.

Keep away ShellNew. To prevent applications from making new keys under the selected key, place a **Deny** checkbox next to **Create Subkey**. For instance, you can do this to file type keys (explained later in this chapter) to prevent applications from adding themselves to Windows Explorer's **New** list.

Enforce security policies. To prevent another user from modifying a security policy (such as those covered in Chapter 8), use the procedure in "Find the Registry Key That Does…," earlier in this chapter, to locate the corresponding key in the Registry. Then, instead of adding a **Deny** rule to the key as described above, remove any permissions that allow anyone other than an administrator to delete, modify, or add subkeys to the key. Make sure that there's still at least one rule for the Administrators group (or at least your own administrator-level account) that affords **Full Control**.

Lock file types. The File Type Doctor utility mentioned in "File Type Associations," later in this chapter, has a feature that uses permissions to lock file types, thus preventing applications from "stealing" them.

See Chapter 8 for more information on the various security systems in Windows Vista.

Back Up the Registry

In a way, the Windows Registry is a weak link in the operating system's stability and robustness. It's remarkably easy to damage, but very difficult to repair. And unless you go to the trouble of making your own backup copy, it's not necessarily easy to replace it if it's damaged (unlike, say, DLLs, which can be pulled right off the Vista CD). A broken Registry—either due to physical corruption or errant data—might cause Windows to behave eratically (or more so than usual) or it may prevent Windows from starting at all.

 The System Protection feature (also known as *System Restore*, and discussed further in Chapter 6) is found in **Control Panel → System → Advanced system settings → System Protection** tab. Windows automatically creates a *restore point* once a day, plus each time you install an application, device driver, or any update from Windows Update. Restore points contain essential Windows system files and Registry settings, although it's not clear how much of the Registry is backed up, nor is it possible to restore all or part of the Registry alone.

So, what's the big problem? Why not just zip up the Registry files or copy them to a CD? The files that contain your Registry data (called *hives*) are constantly being read from and written to, so Windows locks them to ensure they can't be modified, deleted, or even read directly.*

---

* Actually, there is a way around this. You can copy the hive file containing HKEY_CURRENT_USER if you log out and log in as a different user. And you can access all of the hive files if you have a dual-boot setup (see Chapter 1) and you start one of the other operating systems installed on your PC.

This means you have to use a procedure like the following if you want a backup you can create and restore at will. You may want to do this, for instance, just before you install a new program or device driver.

1. Open Registry Editor, and collapse all the branches so only the five main root keys are showing.

2. Highlight HKEY_CURRENT_USER.

3. From the **File** menu, select **Export**.

4. From the **Save as type** list, choose **Registry Hive Files (*.*)**.

5. Type a filename, and give it the .*hive* filename extension (e.g., *hkey_current_user.hive*). RegEdit won't do this for you, nor will Windows recognize the .*hive* extension by default, but it will make the files much easier for you to identify than if they have no extension, which is the default. See "File Type Associations," later in this chapter, to see how to properly register a new file type.

6. Choose a folder to store the backup, and click **Save**.

7. Next, highlight HKEY_LOCAL_MACHINE, and repeat steps 3–6. Make sure to choose a different filename for this branch (e.g., *hkey_local_machine.hive*).

8. To restore either or both of these backups, and replace the current Registry with the data in your backup hive files, select **Import** from the Registry Editor's **File** menu. Select **Registry Hive Files (*.*)** from the unlabeled listbox next to the **File name** field, select the .*hive* file to import, and click **Open**.

There are two things worth noting about this backup procedure. First, it makes use of Registry *hive* files, which are binary files, and the same type of file Windows uses to store the Registry it uses day-to-day. If you were to instead export ordinary Registry patch files—which is what you'd get if **Registration Files (*.reg)** was selected in step 4—then you'd end up with files that couldn't be easily restored back into the Registry. This is because the Registry Editor only *merges* patch files with existing Registry data, which can leave errant data intact, as described in "Export and Import Data with Registry Patches," earlier in this chapter. When the Registry Editor imports hive files, however, it deletes the existing keys from the Registry before bringing in the new (backed-up) data.

 Registry patches can be handy for backing up individual keys, as explained in the upcoming sidebar, "The Local Backup."

The Local Backup

The easiest type of Registry backup to make is the local backup, akin to the local anesthetic. Rather than backing up the entire Registry, you simply back up the portion you'll be working on. If you screw up, you can quickly and easily restore the affected keys without touching anything else.

Say you want to make some changes to the key, `HKEY_CURRENT_USER\Software\Microsoft\Windows\CurrentVersion\Run`, which happens to be responsible for running programs when Windows starts. Just open the Registry Editor, navigate to this key, and select **File → Export**. Type a filename and save the Registry patch file on your Desktop. (See "Export and Import Data with Registry Patches," earlier in this chapter, for more information on this feature.)

Make a mistake and want to restore the backup? Just delete the key(s) you changed, and double-click the Registry patch to load it back in.

Of course, Registry patch files can be hard to keep track of, particularly if you change a setting and only discover two weeks later that it's caused a problem. In this case, you can make an easy-to-find backup right in the Registry.

Before you make any changes to the Registry, make a patch file as just described. Then, rename the key in which you'll be working by adding `.backup` to the end of the key name. For instance, if you want to make a change to:

    HKEY_CURRENT_USER\Software\Microsoft\Windows\CurrentVersion\Run

Highlight the `Run` key, press the **F2** key (or right-click and select **Rename**), and change the name to:

    HKEY_CURRENT_USER\Software\Microsoft\Windows\CurrentVersion\Run.backup

Then, immediately reimport the Registry patch you just made, and delete the *.reg* patch file. You'll end up with two identical keys right next to each other:

    HKEY_CURRENT_USER\Software\Microsoft\Windows\CurrentVersion\Run
    HKEY_CURRENT_USER\Software\Microsoft\Windows\CurrentVersion\Run.backup

At this point, you can go ahead and mess with the `Run` key to your heart's content, and even use the nearby `Run.backup` key as a handy reference. If you ever need to restore your backup—either today or six months from now—just delete the `Run` key and then rename `Run.backup` to `Run`.

See Chapter 2 for a quick way to make a local backup of files you're working on.

Second, notice that only `HKEY_CURRENT_USER` and `HKEY_LOCAL_MACHINE` are backed up here, leaving `HKEY_CLASSES_ROOT`, `HKEY_USERS`, and `HKEY_CURRENT_CONFIG` seemingly unprotected. This is done because the data in `HKEY_CLASSES_ROOT` and `HKEY_USERS` is duplicated in the first two root keys (`HKLM` and `HKCU`, respectively) and `HKEY_CURRENT_CONFIG` is dynamically generated and not stored on the hard disk at all. See "The Structure of the Registry," earlier in this chapter, for details.

Now, other than saving time by not exporting more than you have to, why is it important to know how Windows stores the Registry data? Because if you use a slightly more advanced approach when you back up the Registry, you'll have a backup you can restore *even if Windows won't start*. Here's how you do it:

1. Open a plain-text editor (e.g., Notepad).

2. Type the following into a blank document:

```
if exist C:\Backups\COMPONENTS.OLD del C:\Backups\COMPONENTS.OLD
if exist C:\Backups\SAM.OLD del C:\Backups\SAM.OLD
if exist C:\Backups\SECURITY.OLD del C:\Backups\SECURITY.OLD
if exist C:\Backups\SOFTWARE.OLD del C:\Backups\SOFTWARE.OLD
if exist C:\Backups\SYSTEM.OLD del C:\Backups\SYSTEM.OLD
if exist C:\Backups\NTUSER.OLD del C:\Backups\NTUSER.OLD

ren C:\Backups\COMPONENTS COMPONENTS.OLD
ren C:\Backups\SAM SAM.OLD
ren C:\Backups\SECURITY SECURITY.OLD
ren C:\Backups\SOFTWARE SOFTWARE.OLD
ren C:\Backups\SYSTEM SYSTEM.OLD
ren C:\Backups\NTUSER.DAT NTUSER.OLD

REG SAVE HKLM\COMPONENTS C:\Backups\COMPONENTS
REG SAVE HKLM\SAM C:\Backups\SAM
REG SAVE HKLM\SECURITY C:\Backups\SECURITY
REG SAVE HKLM\SOFTWARE C:\Backups\SOFTWARE
REG SAVE HKLM\SYSTEM C:\Backups\SYSTEM
REG SAVE HKCU C:\Backups\NTUSER.DAT
```

3. Save the file somewhere convenient, such as your desktop, and give it the *.bat* filename extension (e.g., *back up registry.bat*).

4. Open Windows Explorer, open the *Computer* branch, and select drive *C:*. Create a new folder in *C:* named *Backups*. If you want to store the backup hive files in a different location, replace all 24 instances of *C:\Backups* in the listing in step 2 with the full path of your backup folder.

5. To run the backup, just right-click the *back up registry.bat* file and select **Run as administrator**. (See Chapter 8 for an explanation of why you can't just double-click the file to run it.)

> To run this backup automatically every time you start Windows, create a shortcut to the *back up registry.bat* file in your *Startup* folder in your Start menu. Or, if you typically hibernate your PC instead of shutting down, use the Scheduled Tasks feature (Chapter 9) to schedule the backup to run at regular intervals, say, once every three days.

6. At this point, you can be extra compulsive and copy the backed-up hive files to a CD or network drive for safekeeping.

So, what's different about this second procedure? For one, it's automated, using the little-known *REG.exe* command-line Registry tool instead of the Registry Editor to create the hive files. (To learn more about *REG.exe*, open a Command Prompt window, type reg /? and press **Enter**.) Also, it automatically archives the last backup, thus maintaining *two* sets of backup files at all times, a feat accomplished by some simple batch-file commands (see Chapter 9 for more on batch files).

Most importantly, though, it creates five separate hive files from the HKEY_LOCAL_MACHINE branch—one for each sub-branch except HARDWARE, which is dynamically generated—instead of just one. As a result, the backup files you'll end up with are the same as those Windows normally uses to store the Registry on your hard disk.

Windows stores the active hive files—those for HKEY_LOCAL_MACHINE, at least—in the *Windows\System32\Config* folder. The exception is the HKEY_CURRENT_USER branch, stored in the *NTUSER.DAT* file located in the user's home directory (usually *Users\{username}*). See Chapter 8 for more on user accounts.

In your snooping, you might discover the *Windows\System32\config\RegBack* folder. Check the dates of the files in the *RegBack* folder, and sure enough, you'll see that they're recent—perhaps with yesterday's or today's date—backups of your HKEY_LOCAL_MACHINE hive files.

Although Vista indeed regularly creates these backups, they're neither complete (the HKEY_CURRENT_USER branch isn't included) nor as useful as a backup you make yourself. For instance, a problem that prevents Windows from loading is likely to have made its way to the automatic backups, but not the manual backup you made three days ago, just before you installed an application.

All of this means that you can restore your Registry from the backup in a variety of ways. Of course, you can always use **File → Import in Registry Editor**, as described earlier in this section, but that only works if Windows is running. If Windows won't start, though, here's how to restore your Registry from the six hive backups:

1. Insert your Windows Vista setup disc in your drive, and start your PC.

See Chapter 1 if your PC doesn't boot off your CD, or if you only have a "recovery disc" provided by your PC manufacturer.

2. Click **Next** on the first Install Windows screen, and then click **Repair your computer** on the second page.

3. On the System Recovery Options window, select **Microsoft Windows Vista** in the list and then click **Next**.

4. Click **Command Prompt**.

5. In the Command Prompt window that appears, type the following commands to rebuild your Registry from your hive files:

```
REG RESTORE HKLM\COMPONENTS C:\Backups\COMPONENTS
REG RESTORE HKLM\SAM C:\Backups\SAM
REG RESTORE HKLM\SECURITY C:\Backups\SECURITY
REG RESTORE HKLM\SOFTWARE C:\Backups\SOFTWARE
REG RESTORE HKLM\SYSTEM C:\Backups\SYSTEM
REG RESTORE HKCU C:\Backups\NTUSER.DAT
```

 You can omit one or more of these lines if you only want to restore part of the Registry.

6. When you're done, pop out your Vista setup disc and restart your PC.

With any luck, Windows should start normally. If it doesn't, either your most recent backup is defective, or the problem lies elsewhere. If you suspect that an older backup may work where the newer one failed, add the *.OLD* filename extension to each filename in step 5 above, like this:

```
REG RESTORE HKLM\COMPONENTS C:\Backups\COMPONENTS.OLD
```

If Windows still won't start at this point, try reinstalling Windows (see Chapter 1).

Now, there's a chance that the *REG.exe* tool won't work, which might happen if your Registry is sufficiently corrupted or if the *REG.exe* file itself is damaged. In this case, try replacing the active hive files with your backups, like this:

1. Open the Command Prompt as instructed in steps 1–4 above.

2. Type these commands to copy the files:

```
copy C:\Backups\COMPONENTS C:\Windows\System32\Config
copy C:\Backups\SAM C:\Windows\System32\Config
copy C:\Backups\SECURITY C:\Windows\System32\Config
copy C:\Backups\SOFTWARE C:\Windows\System32\Config
copy C:\Backups\SYSTEM C:\Windows\System32\Config
copy C:\Backups\NTUSER.DAT C:\Users\your_user_folder
```

where *your_user_folder* (on the last line) is the name of your user folder, which may or may not be the same as your user name. If you don't know the folder name, type dir c:\users to list all the user folders on your PC. If your user folder name has spaces in it, add quotation marks, like this:

```
copy C:\Backups\NTUSER.DAT "C:\Users\Phillip J. Fry"
```

3. When you're done, pop out your Vista setup disc and restart your PC.

See Chapter 6 for more information on backup software that copies your full Registry along with all of your system files. And check out the "How Else Windows Backs Up the Registry" sidebar, next, for some other features in Windows Vista.

How Else Windows Backs Up the Registry

The aforementioned automatic hive file backups stored in the \Windows\ System32\config\RegBack folder represent just one of several fail-safe systems built in to Windows Vista.

There's also a way to undo a bad hardware driver installation without backing up or restoring the Registry at all. Just open Device Manager, right-click the cranky device, select **Properties**, choose the **Driver** tab, and click **Roll Back Driver**. If that doesn't work, right-click the device and select **Uninstall**. When prompted, confirm that you want to delete the driver files. Then, disconnect and reconnect the device, or restart Windows if reconnecting isn't practical.

You can remove petulant software with the Programs and Features tool in Control Panel, but only if the program's uninstaller behaves itself. Otherwise, search the Web for the program name and the word "uninstall" to see whether there are any special removal tools or procedures for the program you're trying to remove.

Of course, neither of these tools will do you much good if Windows won't start. There's also an entry called **Last Known Good Configuration** in the Vista startup menu (covered in Chapter 1), typically shown if Windows didn't shut down properly last time, or if you press the **F8** key before Windows starts loading. In theory, this feature starts Windows with an earlier collection of hardware drivers and settings taken from the last successful boot. In practice, however, Vista seems to have a hard time defining "good" (with respect to the *Last Known Good* moniker), and is usually unable to find an earlier configuration that either solves the problem or works at all. It's worth trying if you don't have a valid Registry backup, but don't expect miracles.

File Type Associations

File type associations are the links between your documents and the applications that use them. The most apparent use of this feature is that, for example, Windows knows to open Notepad when you double-click a text document on the desktop or show you an online advertisement for anatomical enhancement if you click the link in a spam email message.

One might assume that the aforementioned text file somehow knows it's a Notepad document, but that isn't the case. Instead, Windows determines how to handle a file based solely on the filename extension. The extension is the group of letters—usually three—that follow the period in most filenames. For example, the extension of the file *Readme.txt* is *.txt*, signifying a plain-text file. Likewise, the extension of *Resume.docx* is *.docx*, which means it's a word processor document in the Microsoft Word 2007 file format.

> There are a number of filename extension databases on the Web, which is useful if you encounter a file you can't open and don't recognize. Some of the better resources include *http://wikipedia.org/wiki/List_of_file_formats* and *http://filext. com*. Alternatively, you can double-click the unknown file and when Windows asks you what you want to do (Figure 3-11), select **Use the Web service to find the correct program**, and click **OK**. Just don't be surprised if you don't get a satisfying response.

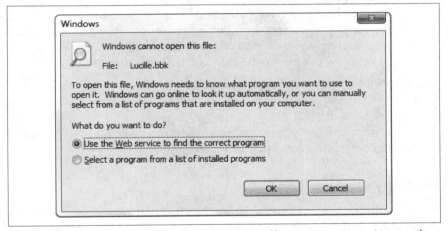

Figure 3-11. If you see this window, the selected file's filename extension isn't currently registered on your PC

It may seem silly that so much of Windows' ability to open files rests on something as easy to break as the filename, but the design does have its advantages. For instance, it's fairly easy to change the program used to open all your digital photos without having to modify all your *.jpg* files to do it.

The biggest flaw in the system is that Windows hides filename extensions by default, which is why Windows Explorer shows only *Readme* instead of *Readme.txt*. Fortunately, this is easy enough to change; just open **Folder Options** in Control Panel (or click **Organize → Folder and Search Options** in Windows Explorer). In the Folder Options window, choose the **View** tab, turn off the **Hide extensions for known file types** option, and click **OK**.

If you have Windows show filename extensions, it's easier to determine what kind of files you're dealing with. Instead of merely a file named *recipe*, you might see *recipe.tif* if it's a scan of a recipe, *recipe.pdf* if it's an Acrobat file with a recipe inside, or *recipe.exe* if it's a Trojan horse you just received via email. Sure, you'll have to open the file to see whether you're making cookies or explosives, but at least you can anticipate which application will appear, and will know whether or not you'll have to convert it to a different format before posting it on your Chocolate Chip Anarchist blog.

Having extensions visible also means you can change Windows' perception of the type of a file by merely renaming its extension. (Note that changing a file's extension doesn't actually change the contents or the format of the file, only how Windows interacts with it.)

Now, Microsoft started hiding filename extensions back in Windows 95 (in a vain attempt to make Windows easier to use), but it's never been handled well. For instance, if you have more than one file, side-by-side, with the same name, having your extensions hidden just makes things more confusing. Rather than *recipe.jpg*, *recipe.wpd*, and *recipe.txt*, you'll just see *recipe*, *recipe*, and *recipe*, with only a miniscule icon to distinguish them.

And since only *registered* filename extensions are hidden, *recipe.pdf* would normally appear as *recipe.pdf* until you install Adobe Acrobat Reader. Once Acrobat registers the *.pdf* file type, the *.pdf* extensions vanish, and the file will be shown merely as *recipe*...unless you elect to make file extensions visible as described above. But what does it mean to register a file type?

Anatomy of a File Type

A registered file type is constructed out of a handful of keys and values in the Registry that Windows reads in real time to handle your documents appropriately. Register a new file type, and Windows will know what to do with files of that type right away.

Usually it's an installer or an application that registers new file types, but anyone (or any program, for that matter) can add new ones or modify existing file type associations. Customizing your PC's file types is one of the most effective ways to save time and reduce annoyances in Windows, but Vista doesn't make it easy, so you've got to know what makes them tick first.

It starts with a single key in HKEY_CLASSES_ROOT, named for a filename extension (including the dot). The (Default) value in that key contains the name of another key that has all the file type's meat in it. For instance, open up the Registry Editor and peer into these keys:

```
HKEY_CLASSES_ROOT\.log
HKEY_CLASSES_ROOT\.scp
HKEY_CLASSES_ROOT\.txt
```

Each one has a (Default) value that contains the word txtfile. Thus, each filename extension *points* to the txtfile file type, which is located in HKEY_CLASSES_ROOT\txtfile. And it's the txtfile key that has all the good stuff. See the "Special File Type Keys" sidebar for some catch-all file types.

Special File Type Keys

There are a few special file type keys in the Registry, each of which work like standard file types, despite having much greater scope. They are:

HKEY_CLASSES_ROOT*

The asterisk (*) Registry key, conveniently placed at the top of the HKEY_CLASSES_ROOT tree in the Registry Editor, defines actions and extensions for all files. If there's a context menu item you'd like to eliminate, odds are it's in the Shell or ShellEx subkeys of the * key.

By adding a new action key to HKEY_CLASSES_ROOT*\Shell, you can add a context menu item for all the files on your PC. For instance, you could add a key named OpenInNotepad, type Open in Notepad into the key's (Default) value, and then add a command key that points to *notepad.exe*, as described later in this section. When you're done, right-click *any file* and select **Open in Notepad** to view the file in a new Notepad window. See "Customize Context Menus for Files," later in this chapter, for details.

HKEY_CLASSES_ROOT\Unknown

This key is used to define the behavior of all files with unregistered file extensions. By default, there's only one file type here, openas, which is responsible for the dialog window in Figure 3-11. You can, of course, add new actions or even change the default action here. For example, you may work with a bunch of different types of documents Windows doesn't recognize, and wish to open them all in your favorite text editor without having to register them all first.

The system Windows uses to keep track of its file types has been around for years and has survived a bunch of different Windows versions. As a result, you'll see a lot of inconsistencies. Sometimes, for instance, the meat of a file type is actually in the *extension* key (e.g., HKEY_CLASSES_ROOT\.scp) rather than the file type key. Because Windows still allows this, some developers still do it this way, and in turn, you'll have to deal with it. Although most file types do follow the structure laid out on these pages, don't be surprised if you see something that doesn't belong *and* still works.

A typical file type key (e.g., HKEY_CLASSES_ROOT\txtfile) has a few values and subkeys, most of which appear in Figure 3-12.

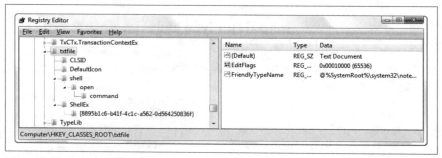

Figure 3-12. A file type key has values and subkeys that determine how Windows treats associated files

First, the (Default) value contains the *name* of the type, the text that appears in Windows Explorer's **Type** column.

If a value named AlwaysShowExt is present in this key, the extension for this file type will be displayed in Explorer, even if you've elected to hide your filename extensions (a setting explained at the beginning of this section). A related value, NeverShowExt, appears in a few file type keys—such as those for Windows Shortcuts (*.lnk* files), Internet Shortcuts (*.url* files), and Explorer Commands (*.scf* files)—and instructs Explorer to always hide the extensions for these files, regardless of your preferences.

You'll also see some other values such as EditFlags, FriendlyTypeName, and InfoTip that are fairly inconsequential, but it's the stuff in the following three subkeys that's responsible for most of the magic:

DefaultIcon

The (Default) value in this key contains the full path and filename of the file containing the icon used for all files of this type. See the next section, "Change the Icon for All Files of a Type," for details.

Shell

Each subkey of Shell corresponds to an item (called an *action*) in the file's context menu. See "Customize Context Menus for Files," later in this chapter, to find out how this branch is structured.

ShellEx

The ShellEx branch lists Windows Explorer *extensions*, add-on programs designed to interact with Explorer and add features. This branch is covered in the "Fix Wonky Shell Extensions" sidebar, later in this chapter.

Once you know where all the essential keys are, you can use Registry Editor or one of the other tools mentioned in the upcoming sections to do just about anything you want with Vista's file types system. When you have everything the way you want it, don't forget to take some steps to protect your customized file types from overzealous application installers, as described in "Lock Your File Types," later in this chapter.

Change the Icon for All Files of a Type

Every file type has a default icon, the icon shown for all files with filename extensions linked to that type. Yet Vista offers no way to choose your own icons—apart from editing the Registry directly—despite the fact that you could do this right in Windows Explorer in previous versions of Windows.

The (Default) value in the DefaultIcon key mentioned in the previous section contains the full path and filename of the file containing the default icon. Often it points right to the application executable that uses the file (e.g., *excel.exe* for *.xls* files), but sometimes it references a *.dll* or *.ico* file containing a bunch of icons. The filename is then followed by a comma and then a number (called the *index*) that indicates *which* icon to use. For example:

```
C:\Program Files\Photoshop\Photoshop.exe,15
```

points to the file *Photoshop.exe*, located in the *C:\Program Files\Photoshop* folder, and references the 16th icon in that file (0 or no number indicating the first icon, 1 indicating the second, and so on).

Occasionally, you may see something like this in the `DefaultIcon` key:

```
%SystemRoot%\system32\wmploc.dll,-731
```

Here, `%SystemRoot%` is a variable that represents the Windows folder (usually *C:\Windows*). When the (Default) value in which this information is stored is an expandable string value (described in "The Meat of the Registry: Values," earlier in this chapter), Windows converts the filename to *C:\Windows\System32\wmploc.dll* before retrieving the icon. You may also sometimes notice a negative value following the filename (-731, in this case) which represents the *resource ID* of the icon to use—as opposed to a positive value indicating the index (position) of the icon as described earlier.

In most cases, you can specify your own icon for a given file type by placing the full path to an *.exe*, *.dll*, *.ico*, or *.bmp* file in the `DefaultIcon` key's (Default) value. (Hint: there are some nice icons in *\Windows\System32\shell32.dll*.) Include a number to indicate which icon to use, or leave out the number to use the first icon in the file. In some cases, Windows Explorer will recognize the change right away, although due to the way Vista caches icons, you may need to restart Windows for your change to fully take effect.

 The easiest way to change an icon for a file type is with a third-party tool like File Type Doctor, discussed in the next section.

The only time when Windows won't pay attention to the icon specified in the `DefaultIcon` key is when an *IconHandler* is defined. IconHandlers generate dynamic icons on the fly (Figure 3-13), typically showing thumbnails of the files' contents in lieu of static icons.

An IconHandler is a program—typically a *.dll* file in the program folder of the application with which the file is associated—that understands the file format. For instance, Adobe Acrobat (version 7.0 and later) makes use of this feature to facilitate thumbnail previews for *.pdf* files in Windows Explorer. For the *.pdf* filename extension, Acrobat's IconHandler could be referenced in any of these Registry keys:

```
HKEY_CLASSES_ROOT\.pdf\ShellEx\IconHandler
HKEY_CLASSES_ROOT\.pdf\ShellEx\{BB2E617C-0920-11D1-9A0B-00C04FC2D6C1}
HKEY_CLASSES_ROOT\AcroExch.Document.7\ShellEx\IconHandler
HKEY_CLASSES_ROOT\AcroExch.Document.7\ShellEx\{BB2E617C-0920-11D1-9A0B-
    00C04FC2D6C1}
HKEY_CLASSES_ROOT\SystemFileAssociations\.pdf\ShellEx\IconHandler
HKEY_CLASSES_ROOT\SystemFileAssociations\.pdf\ShellEx\{BB2E617C-0920-11D1-
    9A0B-00C04FC2D6C1}
HKEY_CLASSES_ROOT\SystemFileAssociations\image\ShellEx\IconHandler
HKEY_CLASSES_ROOT\SystemFileAssociations\image\ShellEx\{BB2E617C-0920-11D1-
    9A0B-00C04FC2D6C1}
```

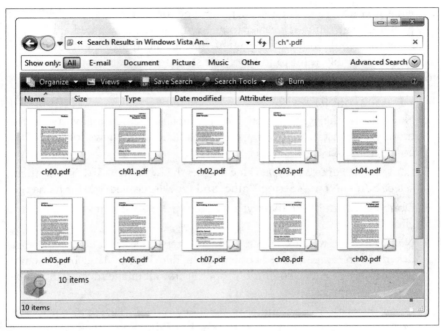

Figure 3-13. If an IconHandler is defined for a file type, Windows generates icons dynamically for each file instead of using the static icon referenced in the DefaultIcon key

As it turns out, Adobe chose the fourth key to register its IconHandler. The (Default) value in that key contains a 38-digit class ID that points to an entry in HKEY_CLASSES_ROOT\CLSID, which in turn contains all the details about the *.dll* file.

If the reference to the IconHandler is contained in one of the keys named IconHandler, the *.dll* is responsible for the dynamically generated icon. But newer programs will use the {BB2E617C-0920-11d1-9A0B-00C04FC2D6C1} key, which facilitates image previews for the Preview pane in Windows Explorer, as well as dynamic icons. See "Expand the Scope of Your File Types," later in this chapter, for more information on the SystemFileAssociations key.

Once you find the reference to the IconHandler, you can delete the key—either the IconHandler key or the {BB2E617C-0920-11d1-9A0B-00C04FC2D6C1} key—to disable the IconHandler and allow Windows Explorer to use the static icon defined in the DefaultIcon key.

But what if you want to fix a broken file type for which icon previews have stopped working? Often it's easier to just reinstall the associated application to repair the IconHandler keys, but if that application is Windows itself, then you'll probably want to follow these steps to reinstate icon previews on your PC:

1. Open the Registry Editor.

2. Navigate to the Registry key for the filename extension you want to modify. For instance, if you want to enable icon previews for TIFF files, go to HKEY_CLASSES_ROOT\.tif.

3. Look for a PerceivedType value inside the .tif key. If it's not there, select **Edit → New → String Value**, and type PerceivedType for its name.

4. Double-click the PerceivedType value, type image for its contents, and click **OK**.

5. Next, navigate to HKEY_CLASSES_ROOT\SystemFileAssociations\image. As described in "Expand the Scope of Your File Types," later in this chapter, this key provides common properties for all image files, such as *.jpg*, *.bmp*, and *.tif* files.

6. Open the ShellEx key, and look for a key named {BB2E617C-0920-11d1-9A0B-00C04FC2D6C1}. If it's not there, select **Edit → New → Key**, and type {BB2E617C-0920-11d1-9A0B-00C04FC2D6C1} for the name of the new key.

7. Open the {BB2E617C-0920-11d1-9A0B-00C04FC2D6C1} key, and double-click the (Default) value. Type {3F30C968-480A-4C6C-862D-EFC0897BB84B} for its contents, and click **OK** when you're done.

> Of the two Class IDs mentioned here, {BB2E617C-0920-11d1-9A0B-00C04FC2D6C1} connects the file type to Windows Explorer's Preview pane, and {3F30C968-480A-4C6C-862D-EFC0897BB84B} points to Windows' own *PhotoMetadataHandler.dll*, the *.dll* file responsible for generating icon previews for all supported photo file formats.

8. The change should take effect immediately; if not, restart Windows to see the new icons.

IconHandlers are most likely to be broken by misbehaving installers for graphics applications, so if you don't want to have to repeat these steps, use the solution in "Lock Your File Types," later in this chapter.

Customize Context Menus for Files

A *context menu* (sometimes called a *shortcut menu*) is the little menu that appears when you use the right mouse button to click on a file, folder, application title bar, or nearly any other object on the screen. Most of the time, this menu includes a list of *actions* appropriate to the object on which you've clicked. In other words, the options available depend on the *context*.

The context menu for files, shown in Figure 3-14, is an assortment of standard actions common to all files (e.g., **Copy**, **Paste**, **Delete**, **Rename**, and **Properties**) plus one or more custom actions depending upon the type of file selected. Each of the custom actions is linked to an application: if you right-click a *.txt* file and select **Open**, Windows launches Notepad (by default) and instructs it to open the selected file. The *default* action—the action that is carried out when you double-click the file—appears in bold text in the context menu, and the rest of the actions are listed below. Among other things, this means you can have *more than one program* associated with a single file type.

In the case of *.html* files, for example, you could add an **Edit** action to open your favorite web page editor, a **View with Firefox** action, and a **View with Internet Explorer** action—all in addition to the default **Open** action.

Sounds great, right? Unfortunately, the File Types window—the tool found in earlier versions of Windows that lets you edit context menus from within Windows Explorer—is completely absent in Windows Vista. In its place is the extremely dumbed-down Set Associations window shown in Figure 3-15. Here, you can only choose default applications for your various file types, and in doing so, obliterate your applications' defaults or any custom context menus you've built (more on that later).

So, you're left with two options if you want to customize your context menus: either hack the Registry or use a third-party program. Given that this is the Registry chapter, let's have some fun digging through keys and values.

As described in "Anatomy of a File Type," earlier in this chapter, there's a Registry key named Shell inside the file type key where all the magic happens. Each subkey of Shell corresponds to a single action in the file's context menu. The text that appears in the context menu (the label) is defined in the action key's (Default) value; if the (Default) value is empty, Windows Explorer just uses the name of the key (e.g., **Open**). Unfortunately, Windows Vista has two competing systems that determine the default actions for your file types; see the upcoming sidebar, "The Evils of UserChoice," for details.

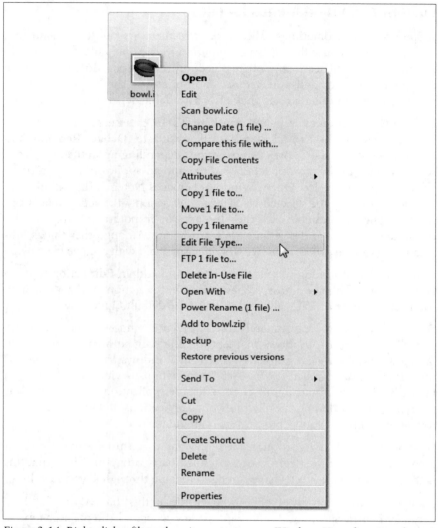

Figure 3-14. Right-click a file to show its context menu; Windows Vista doesn't make it easy to customize the items you see here

Say you right-click a Microsoft Excel document (*.xlsx* file), and at the top of the menu that appears you see **Open** (in bold), **New**, and **Print**. If you open the Registry, you'll see that HKEY_CLASSES_ROOT\.xlsx points to HKEY_CLASSES_ROOT\Excel.Sheet.12, so you proceed to HKEY_CLASSES_ROOT\Excel.Sheet.12\Shell. Inside the Shell key, you'll see three subkeys named—you guessed it —New, Open, and Print. Add a new subkey to Shell, followed by the subkeys described shortly, and you'll get a new entry in the context menu for all files of the selected type.

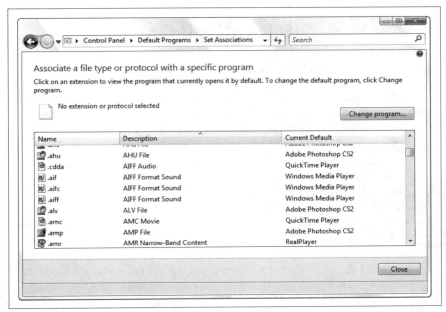

Figure 3-15. The Set Associations window—accessed through Control Panel → Default Programs → Associate a file type or protocol with a program—just plain sucks

See a context menu item you want to get rid of? Just delete the corresponding key here, and it'll disappear immediately. If you don't see the key here, it may be listed in one of five other places:

- Look for a *second* Shell subkey in the *extension* key (e.g., HKEY_CLASSES_ROOT\.xlsx\Shell).

- The ShellEx\ContextMenuHandlers branch, discussed later in this section.

- The * key covered in the "Special File Type Keys" sidebar, earlier in this chapter.

- The nasty UserChoice key described in the upcoming sidebar, "The Evils of UserChoice."

- The SystemFileAssociations branch explained in "Expand the Scope of Your File Types," later in this chapter.

The action shown in bold (usually **Open**) is called the *default*, and is the one carried out when you double-click the file. The (Default) value in the Shell key determines which action is the default; if (Default) is empty and there's more than one action, Windows assumes it's the one named Open. Otherwise, Windows just takes its best guess. You can, of course, change the default by setting the (Default) value to the name of any action key shown here.

The Evils of UserChoice

This is a new addition to Windows Vista, and a nasty one at that. If you right-click a file, select **Open With**, and then select a default application (or if you use Vista's own File Types tool, discussed later in this chapter), Windows doesn't actually change the file type. Instead, Vista creates a new key for the file-name extension in `HKEY_CURRENT_USER\Software\Microsoft\Windows\CurrentVersion\Explorer\FileExts\`, and then in that key, a `UserChoice` key with the full path of the program you've chosen, like this:

```
HKEY_CURRENT_USER\Software\Microsoft\Windows\CurrentVersion\Explorer\
FileExts\.wav\UserChoice
```

The point of the `UserChoice` key is to prevent applications from changing your defaults without your permission; as long as that `UserChoice` key exists, Windows ignores all the actions defined in the ordinary file type key.

Like so many other patchwork features in Windows, the `UserChoice` system just doesn't work that well. For one, any custom context menu items you've defined for a file type vanish if the corresponding extension ever shows up in the `UserChoice` key, with no means of retrieval without you having to manually edit the Registry. And the old trick of reinstalling an application to restore its file types won't work if the `UserChoice` key is involved (unless the installer is smart enough to deal with the `UserChoice` key).

The solution is to open the Registry Editor, navigate to `HKEY_CURRENT_USER\Software\Microsoft\Windows\CurrentVersion\Explorer`, and delete the `FileExts` key altogether. This will eliminate all `UserChoice` keys while leaving your file types intact. Thereafter, refrain from using the **Open With** menu or Control Panel to modify your file types, and your file associations will continue to behave as you expect.

Now, there's another, less obvious facet to the `UserChoice` key, one that may be a possible benefit for PCs with more than one user account. Traditional file types are stored in the `HKEY_CLASSES_ROOT` key, which is a subset of `HKEY_LOCAL_MACHINE`; this means your file types are the same for all users on your PC. But the `UserChoice` keys are buried in `HKEY_CURRENT_USER` branch, allowing each user to to have his or her own set of overrides. Of course, you can still delete your own `FileExts` key without affecting another user's overrides, but any subsequent changes you make to the file types in `HKEY_CLASSES_ROOT` will be put into action for all users right away.

Inside each action key is a subkey named `command` (and perhaps another named `ddeexec`). Inside the `command` key is a (`Default`) value that specifies the full path and filename of the program to run. Right-click an *.xlsx* file and select **Open**, and Windows runs the program listed in HKEY_CLASSES_ROOT\ Excel.Sheet.12\shell\Open\command. For example:

```
"C:\Program Files\Microsoft Office\Office12\EXCEL.EXE" /e
```

The quotes around the full path and filename of the application accommodate the spaces, and tell Windows where the filename ends and the command-line options (such as /e, here) begin. Most of the time, though, the command-line contains a placeholder, %1, for the selected filename, like this:

```
"C:\Program Files\UltraEdit\UEDIT32.EXE" "%1"
```

When Windows opens this program, it passes the full path and filename of the selected file to the program by putting it in place of %1, like this:

```
"C:\Program Files\UltraEdit\UEDIT32.EXE" "C:\Users\Janeane\Desktop\readme.txt"
```

Now, that little option, %1, is the cause of a lot of problems in Windows' file types system, such as:

Application displays "not found" error. The quotation marks are missing around the "%1" and the document you're trying to open has a space in its file- or pathname. Just add the quotes and try again.

Older application displays a "bad command line" error or something similar. Not all programs respond well to the quotation marks around the "%1" parameter. Try taking them out if this happens.

Application doesn't open the file at all. The "%1" parameter is missing altogether, or the application requires a different syntax. For instance, the Mozilla SeaMonkey web browser requires the -url parameter in front of %1, like this:

```
C:\Program Files\Mozilla SeaMonkey\seamonkey.exe -url "%1"
```

If you're not sure what your application needs, check the documentation or search Google for the application name and the words "command line."

Application only opens a document if the application isn't already running. This problem (and the next one) are caused by a background technology called Dynamic Data Exchange, or DDE, that allows Windows programs to communicate with one another. Windows sends a DDE signal to an application that's already running to instruct it to open the document. (If the application isn't already running, Windows launches it just like any other.) The specific DDE commands that the application needs are stored in the ddeexec Registry key, alongside the aforementioned command key (shown previously in Figure 3-12). If the ddeexec key is missing, Windows won't send the signal, and the program won't open your document. You can try rebuilding the ddeexec key if you can find documentation, but it's usually easier to just reinstall the application that owns the key. (Not all programs use DDE; don't bother creating the ddeexec key unless you are having this specific problem.)

Application opens the document twice. The ddeexec key just described often causes more problems than it solves. Sometimes Windows sends the aforementioned DDE message *and* launches another copy of the program, which opens two document windows. If this happens, rename the ddeexec key to ddeexec.backup.

 If an application has stopped responding (in other words, it crashed), it won't respond to Windows' DDE instructions to open your document, nor will Windows open a second copy of the program. To find out whether this is happening, right-click an empty portion of your task bar, select **Task Manager**, and click the **Processes** tab. If the program you're trouble-shooting is there, highlight it and click **End Process**, and then try opening your document again.

At this point, you're probably thinking, "so, I have to type all these Registry keys by hand if I want the least bit of control over my file types?" If so, I laugh at you.

File Type Doctor, part of Creative Element Power Tools (available at *http://www.creativelement.com/powertools/*) and shown in Figure 3-16, lets you customize your context menus, change file type icons, and choose defaults.

In the File Type Doctor window, file types are organized by their names (shown in the righthand column) and by their corresponding filename extensions (shown in the lefthand column); click either column header to sort the list accordingly. The properties of the currently selected file type are shown on the right side of the window.

 You can also right-click any file in Windows Explorer or on your desktop and select **Edit File Type** to customize the file's context menu in File Type Doctor on the fly.

Edit the name of the type—the text that appears in Windows Explorer's **Type** column and in the file's Properties window—by typing in the **Name** textbox at the top-right of the window. Click the **Change** button to choose an icon for all files of this type, or double-click the icon itself (to the left of the **Change** button) to choose from the icons in the default application executable (shown in bold in the **Actions in right-click menu** list).

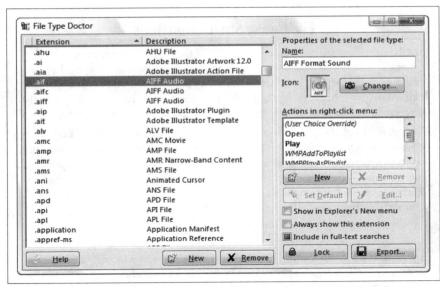

Figure 3-16. File Type Doctor gives you the complete control over your file associations that Vista doesn't

File Type Doctor saves changes automatically as you make them. This makes it easy to test your context menus as you go, but it also means that most changes cannot be easily undone.

The **Actions in right-click menu** list on the right side shows all the context menu items registered for the selected file type. Click **New** to add a new item or click **Edit** (or double-click the item in the list) to modify the associated application and its options.

You can also remove unwanted context menu items by highlighting them here and clicking **Remove**. The list shows everything registered for the selected file type, as well as the *perceived type*, explained in "Expand the Scope of Your File Types," later in this chapter. Shell extensions, explained in the upcoming sidebar,"Fix Wonky Shell Extensions," are shown in *italicized* font; these can be removed but not modified in the traditional sense.

The only items not shown in the **Actions in right-click menu** list are those actions registered for the * file type discussed in the "Special File Type Keys" sidebar, earlier in this chapter. If you're trying to remove clutter from your context menus and you don't see an item you're looking for, try selecting the * **(all files)** entry at the very top of the list of file types.

Fix Wonky Shell Extensions

Shell extensions are programs—usually *.dll* files—that add features to Windows Explorer. When they work, they're great, but when they falter, they can cause poor performance, crashes, and other problems. You can disable shell extensions by unregistering them (deleting their Registry keys) or by simply disconnecting them from their associated file types, as described here.

The `shell` Registry key dissected in "Customize Context Menus for Files," houses the keys responsible for the *static* items in a file's context menu. But context menu shell extensions—ones that can *dyamically* generate context menu items—are located in the `shellex\ContextMenuHandlers` Registry key. Each subkey of `ContextMenuHandlers` usually contains nothing more than a cryptic, 38-character code that looks like this:

    {E88DCCE0-B7B3-11d1-A9F0-00AA0060FA31}

This 32-digit hex code (a.k.a. 16-bit number) is a *Class ID* (or *CLSID* for short) that points to a subkey of the same name in `HKEY_CLASSES_ROOT\CLSID\ {class_id}`. Class IDs are the means by which shell extensions—not to mention components used in all types of software—are registered in Windows and connected to the programs that use them.

In addition to `ContextMenuHandlers`, you'll find these other keys inside the `shellex` key:

`DropHandler`
> Extensions in this branch are activated when you drag files of this type or drop other files *onto* files of this type.

`IconHandler`
> This key points to a program that dynamically generates an icon—usually a preview of the contents of the file—to be used instead of a static icon. See "Change the Icon for All Files of a Type," earlier in this chapter, for details.

`PropertySheetHandlers`
> These extensions add extra pages (tabs) to the window that appears when you right-click a file of this type and select **Properties**.

Of course, the keys in the `shellex` branch aren't always so neatly organized; sometimes you'll find keys named for a Class ID, with another Class ID in its (Default) value. See "Search the Registry," earlier in this chapter, for some tools you can use to help track down Class IDs.

—continued—

File Type Doctor shows context menu shell extensions associated with the selected file type in *italicized* font. Although you can't edit them (you'll need their source code and development software like Visual Studio for that), you can remove their context menus by selecting them and clicking **Remove**. This won't unregister the extension, it'll just disconnect it from the selected file type, and likely fix the problem you're having. (Or, just do it to remove clutter.) You can also right-click a shell extension in File Type Doctor to search the Registry or the Web for its Class ID or other related information to learn more about it.

To list all the shell extensions installed on your PC, use ShellExView, available for free from *http://www.nirsoft.net/utils/shexview.html*.

One of the most useful features of File Type Doctor is the **Lock** feature, described next.

Lock Your File Types

Tech companies used to spend millions trying to get you to buy their products (OK, they still do), but now the race is on to be "the default." Microsoft wants its Live Search web site to be the default search engine in IE, and Google sued Microsoft to try to prevent this before Windows Vista shipped. Companies pay PC manufacturers to preinstall trial versions of their software on all their machines so their products can be the default. And when you install an application on your PC, the installer invariably makes the new program the default for all the file types it supports.

Why is being the default so important? Because people don't change the defaults.

As a result, software companies—Microsoft included—make a habit out of steamrolling over your preferences to promote their own products. Luckily, you have a defense, and it takes place in the Registry.

There are basically two approaches to protecting your file types: you can back them up so they can be restored in case they're ever overwritten, and you can "lock" them, preventing such changes in the first place.

There's actually a third way to protect your file types, by way of Vista's UserChoice feature explained the "The Evils of UserChoice" sidebar, earlier in this chapter. It's not a great solution, but it may be effective in some circumstances.

The easiest way to back up your file types is to create Registry patches as explained in "Export and Import Data with Registry Patches," earlier in this chapter. To make the backup effective, you have to include all the keys laid out in "Anatomy of a File Type," also earlier in this chapter. For instance, if you're backing up the file type for plain-text (*.txt*) files, your Registry patch should include all of these keys:

```
HKEY_CLASSES_ROOT\.txt
HKEY_CLASSES_ROOT\txtfile
HKEY_CLASSES_ROOT\SystemFileAssociations\text
```

That last one—the one in the SystemFileAssociations branch—is described in the next section, "Expand the Scope of Your File Types." And if you want to include other related filename extensions, such as *.log*, *.ini*, and *.csv* (to name a few), you'll want to include those keys as well.

So, if your file type associations for text files ever get wiped out, just double-click your Registry patch backup to restore them.

But a slicker solution is to lock your file types by setting restrictive permissions on the aforementioned keys as described in "Prevent Changes to a Registry Key," earlier in this chapter. That way, no application, no installer, and not even Windows itself can change them unless you unlock them first.

If you want a shortcut, you can use File Type Doctor, introduced in the previous section. Just highlight the file type you want to lock and click the **Lock** button. File Type Doctor will not only protect the selected filename extension and associated file type with one click, but all linked filename extensions as well.

Most programs and installers won't have a problem with locked file types; they'll likely just ignore the error and move on. But it's not beyond the realm of possibility that an application may crash or refuse to continue until it has all the Registry access it needs. In this case, you may need to unlock the affected file types first, so you'll want to back them up as described earlier in this section.

To remove the lock, just select a locked file type (you can click the leftmost column header to group all locked file types together) and click the **Unlock** button.

Expand the Scope of Your File Types

To every rule there's an exception, and in Windows Vista, doubly so. In "Anatomy of a File Type," earlier in this chapter, the basic file types system is laid out, with a collection of keys named for filename extensions (e.g., `HKEY_CLASSES_ROOT\.jpg`) and the corresponding file type keys (such as `HKEY_CLASSES_ROOT\jpegfile`). As it turns out, there's yet another connection in the Registry that affects your file types.

Many extension keys—like `HKEY_CLASSES_ROOT\.jpg`—contain values named `PerceivedType`, which point to subkeys of `HKEY_LOCAL_MACHINE\SOFTWARE\Classes\SystemFileAssociations`. The keys therein work like ordinary file type keys, but they're much broader in scope. Instead of being linked to one or two filename extensions, a *perceived type* key could be linked to dozens.

Say you just installed a new image-resizing utility that you'd like to use with a variety of photo formats. But rather than make it the default for those file types, you decide to add a context menu item for each supported file format (e.g., *.jpg*, *.bmp*, *.png*, and so on). Sure, you can do this for each of the 10 or so graphic formats it supports, but it turns out that all you need to do is add it to this key to affect all your image files at once:

```
HKEY_LOCAL_MACHINE\SOFTWARE\Classes\SystemFileAssociations\image\shell\my_
new_program
```

By default, the `image` key shown here is linked to all filename extensions with a `PerceivedType` set to image, namely *.bmp*, *.dib*, *.emf*, *.gif*, *.ico*, *.jfif*, *.jpe*, *.jpeg*, *.jpg*, *.png*, *.rle*, *.tif*, *.tiff*, *.wdp*, and *.wmf*.

Windows Vista comes with only five perceived type keys (`audio`, `image`, `system`, `text`, and `video`) out of the box, but you can add your own to the `SystemFileAssociations` branch at any time, provided you then link at least one file extension to it by adding a `PerceivedType` value pointing to your new key. The benefit is that you can use this key to add a custom context menu item that affects a large number of different file types at once. The drawback is that it's one more place you'll have to look to track down a misbehaving or unwanted context menu item.

To break the connection between a filename extension and a perceived type, just delete the `PerceivedType` value from the extension key. Or, to link up a file type with an existing `PerceivedType`, create a new string value named `PerceivedType` in the extension key, and set its contents to the name of the matching perceived type key in the `SystemFileAssociations` branch.

File Type Doctor (see "Customize Context Menus for Files," earlier in this chapter) also supports perceived types through its "scope" and "affiliation" features. For instance, if you try to delete a context menu action that's connected through a perceived type, File Type Doctor displays a confirmation box that lists the other filename extensions that will be affected by the change. Likewise, when creating a new action, you can choose the scope; click the **Properties** button next to the **Scope** list to display all the extensions tied to the current selection.

While you're digging around the HKEY_CLASSES_ROOT\SystemFileAssociations branch in the Registry, you may find some file extension keys here as well, like HKEY_CLASSES_ROOT\SystemFileAssociations\.png. These look and work just like the extension keys and file type keys in HKEY_CLASSES_ROOT, discussed earlier in this chapter, but they're used primarily to reference the Windows Explorer extensions that were preinstalled with Windows. Why they're here instead of in HKEY_CLASSES_ROOT with the rest of the extensions is not entirely clear, but what is clear is that the SystemFileAssociations branch is yet another place to look for Registry keys that affect file types.

Customize Windows Explorer's New Menu

If you right-click an empty area of the desktop or any open folder window and select **New**, you'll see special list of registered file types that can be created on the spot. Choose one, and Explorer will create a new (usually empty) file with the appropriate filename extension right there. Not surprisingly, you can edit that list, and even make it do more than just create empty files.

Here's the easiest way to remove unwanted items from Explorer's **New** menu:

1. Install Creative Element Power Tools (introduced earlier in "Customize Context Menus for Files"), turn on the **Edit file type associations** option in the Creative Elements Power Tools Control Panel, and click **Accept**.

2. Right-click an empty area of your desktop, select **New**, and then select one of the entries you'd like to remove.

3. Right-click the new file and select **Edit File Type**.

4. Remove the checkbox next to the **Show in Explorer's New menu** option.

5. The change will take effect immediately; right-click the desktop again and select **New** to check it out.

If you want to do it by hand, you'll need to look in a few different places in the Registry:

1. Open the Registry Editor.

2. Navigate to the key named for the filename extension you'd like to remove from Windows Explorer's **New** menu. For the *.txt* extension, you'd go to HKEY_CLASSES_ROOT\.txt.

3. If you see a subkey here named ShellNew, rename it to Shellnew- (Shellnew followed by a hyphen).

4. Next, look at the (Default) value of the extension key, and then look for a subkey that matches the contents of the (Default) value. Again, for the *.txt* extension, you'd go to HKEY_CLASSES_ROOT\.txt\txtfile.

5. As in step 3, if you see a subkey here named ShellNew, rename it to Shellnew- (Shellnew followed by a hyphen).

6. The change will take effect once you close the Registry Editor; right-click the desktop and select **New** to check it out.

As you can see, it's merely the presence of a ShellNew key that determines whether a file type shows up in Windows Explorer's **New** menu. (Actually, it's a little more complicated than that, but more on that subject later.)

To get a list of all the potential entries to appear in the **New** menu, fire up Registry Agent (see "Search and Replace Registry Data," earlier in this chapter), and search the entire Registry for ShellNew. (If you want to weed out erroneous matches, turn on the **Keys** option, uncheck the **Values** and **Data** options, and then turn on **Match whole word**.)

Now, there are some nifty hacks you can use on the ShellNew keys you choose to leave intact. A standard ShellNew key has only one value (NullFile, described in the upcoming list), but if you add any of the other following values to the ShellNew key, you'll change how Windows Explorer behaves when you select the corresponding items from its **New** menu. All values are string values unless otherwise specified:

Command

If you include the full path and filename of a program executable (*.exe* file), Explorer will launch the program *instead* of creating a new file. Make sure to include the "%1" parameter (see "Customize Context Menus for Files," earlier in this chapter) so the target program knows where to create the new file, like this:

    c:\windows\system32\notepad.exe "%1"

Consult your application's documentation to see whether any other command-line parameters are needed to create the new document; otherwise, the program may just open and complain that it can't find the (as yet nonexistent) file.

Data

Any text stored in this binary value will be placed into the new file. For instance, the Data value for *.rtf* files (in HKEY_CLASSES_ROOT\.rtf\ ShellNew) contains the text, {\rtf1}, which ensures that the new *.rtf* file is readable by whatever program you use to open it. Explorer ignores the `Data` value if either `FileName` or `NullFile` is specified.

`FileName`

This is the full path and filename of a template file—a file to be copied and used for each new document you create—in lieu of creating an empty (zero-byte) file. If you don't include the path, Windows looks in *C:\Users\{your_user_name}\AppData\Roaming\Microsoft\Templates* as well as *C:\Windows\ShellNew* for the template file.

`Handler`

The Class ID (e.g., `{CEEFEA1B-3E29-4EF1-B34C-FEC79C4F70AF}`) of the shell extension used to create the new file. For example, Windows Shortcuts (*.lnk* files) use a handler.

`IconPath`

The full path and filename (plus the icon index) of the icon that appears next to the item in Windows Explorer's **New** menu. If you leave this out, Explorer uses the file type's default icon. See "Change the Icon for All Files of a Type," earlier in this chapter, for the syntax.

`ItemName`

By default, the name of the new file you create is the name of the file type, preceded by the word "New" and followed by the appropriate filename extension; for instance: *New Text Document.txt*. This value determines the name of the new file, but like `MenuText`, described next, it must point to a text resource in a *.dll* file.

`MenuText`

Unfortunately, this is not what it looks like. Yes, it determines the text that appears in Explorer's **New** menu, but you can't just type the text here. Instead, it must be a reference to a text resource in a *.dll* file, such as `@%systemroot%\system32\mspaint.exe,-59414`.

`NullFile`

This instructs Explorer to create an empty (zero-byte) file. If none of these other values are present, you need to include the `NullFile` value, or the file type won't show up in Explorer's **New** menu.

So, how do you keep applications from recreating the `ShellNew` keys and continuously cluttering up Explorer's **New** menu? Adobe Photoshop does this every time it starts, but all it takes is a quick change to the Registry to prevent it from happening again:

1. Open the Registry Editor.

2. Navigate to the extension key you want to permanently exclude from the **New** menu. For Photoshop documents, you'd go to `HKEY_CLASSES_ROOT\.psd`.

3. Delete any ShellNew keys you find here; see the solution spelled out earlier in this section for details.

4. Right-click the extension key (e.g., .psd), and select **Permissions**.

5. In the Permissions window, click the **Advanced** button, and then in the Advanced Security Settings window, click **Add**.

6. Next, in the Select User or Group window, type everyone into the **Enter the object name to select** field, and then click **OK**.

7. Finally, in the Permission Entry window, place a checkmark in the **Deny** column for **Create Subkey**, and then click **OK** when you're finished.

8. Click **OK**, then click **Yes** when asked whether you're sure you want to set a "deny permissions entry," and then click **OK** to close the final window.

9. The change will take effect immediately. Test it out by starting the application; you can press **F5** in the Registry Editor to refresh the view and confirm that no new **ShellNew** subkey has been added.

You can accomplish pretty much the same thing with File Type Doctor's **Lock** feature (covered earlier in "Lock Your File Types"), but that may be overkill if all you want to do is keep unwanted items out of Explorer's **New** menu. See "Prevent Changes to a Registry Key," earlier in this chapter, for other things you can do with Registry permissions.

Fix Internet Shortcuts

Customization is fun, but sometimes all you need to do to a file type is fix it when it breaks. Most of the time you can just reinstall the application that originally created it—unless a UserChoice key is in effect, explained in the "The Evils of UserChoice" sidebar—but that doesn't always work.

One file type that's always getting munged is the *.url* (Internet Shortcut) type, and repairing it can be a little tricky. For one, *.url* files don't launch your web browser directly; instead, they activate a Windows *.dll* that does the launching. In essence, it's a two-step process that employs two different file types; the following sequence of Registry keys shows how it works.

By default, the keys discussed here are all locked to prevent casual changes, a fact that should've prevented them from being corrupted in the first place. (Alas, such things seem to happen anyway.) If Windows won't let you make changes to any of these keys, you'll need to take ownership of them first, as described in "Prevent Changes to a Registry Key," earlier in this chapter, and in Chapter 8.

1. Go to `HKEY_CLASSES_ROOT\.url`, and confirm that the `(Default)` value is set to `InternetShortcut`.

2. Next, go to `HKEY_CLASSES_ROOT\InternetShortcut\Shell\Open\Command`, and make sure the `(Default)` value here is set to:

   `rundll32.exe shdocvw.dll,OpenURL %1`

> This command instructs Windows to crack open the selected Internet Shortcut file, read the URL stored inside (which you can also do with Notepad, by the way), and then launch the program appropriate to the variety of URL. Notice that the default web browser (e.g., Internet Explorer, Firefox, etc.) isn't yet part of the equation.

3. Internet shortcuts also use an "icon handler" by default (explained in "Change the Icon for All Files of a Type," earlier in this chapter), which chooses an icon for each file depending on the type of URL inside. So, this key:

   `HKEY_CLASSES_ROOT\InternetShortcut\ShellEx\IconHandler`

   should be set to `{FBF23B40-E3F0-101B-8488-00AA003E56F8}`. Of course, if you want to disable the icon handler and choose your own static icon instead, just rename the `IconHandler` key to `IconHandler.backup`, and then specify your icon file in the `DefaultIcon` key.

4. Once Windows has determined what type of URL it's dealing with, it executes the **Open** command in the key named for the protocol being used. For instance, the URL *http://www.annoyances.org/* uses the `http://` protocol, so its default application is stored in this Registry key:

   `HKEY_CLASSES_ROOT\http\shell\open\command`

> There are similar keys for the other protocols, like `https://`, `file://`, `ftp://`, `news://`, `nntp://`, `snews://`, `telnet://`, and `mailto:`. (In File Type Doctor, the protocol file types are found at the bottom of the list.) These keys aren't just used for Internet Shortcuts; they control Vista's behavior whenever you try to open a web address by clicking a hyperlink in an email message or typing a URL into the Start menu's **Search** box.

5. The (Default) value of the protocol's command key should be set to the full path and filename of your default web browser. Vista's default is, of course, Internet Explorer:

```
"C:\Program Files\Internet Explorer\iexplore.exe" -nohome
```

Or, if you want Mozilla SeaMonkey to be your default browser, you'd use:

```
C:\Program Files\Mozilla SeaMonkey\seamonkey.exe -url "%1"
```

Or, if you're using Mozilla Firefox:

```
C:\Program Files\Mozilla Firefox\firefox.exe %1
```

See "Customize Context Menus for Files," earlier in this chapter, for details on the command key, command-line parameters, and the sometimes necessary ddeexec key.

6. The change takes effect immediately. Double-click any applicable Internet Shortcut to try out your new settings.

As you can see, there are a lot of Registry keys responsible for something as seemingly simple as opening a web address, and all it takes is one missing key, one misplaced quotation mark, or one mangled class ID to break the whole system. And so it goes with the Registry in Windows Vista.

CHAPTER 4
Working with Media

In the old days, media problems meant using a butter knife to pry a tape out of your VCR. Today, it means tracking down obscure drivers, repairing corrupt media files, hassling with overblown media players, and deciphering incoherent CD burning errors.

Microsoft wants you to think that Vista handles videos, pictures, music, and other media better than any previous version of Windows, and in some ways, it does. For one, Vista's hefty hardware requirements mean that your PC—should it be capable of running Vista—will have the power to handle any media task you throw at it. Windows Explorer recognizes photo, video, and audio files, and displays their embedded information alongside other details, like the file size and date. And Vista recognizes more media file formats and graphics hardware out of the box than, say, Windows XP. But as they say, the devil is in the details, and, as it turns out, in the codecs as well.

Playing Video

Ever encounter a video file Windows won't play? Unlike most other types of files, the filename extension alone doesn't dictate the encoding scheme. All *.jpg* image files use standard JPEG compression, but a given *.mpg* movie file may employ any one of dozens of available compression standards, called *codecs*. Without the proper codec for a video file, you won't be able to play the video or even convert it into another format.

A codec (which stands for *co*mpressor/*dec*ompressor) is software installed on your PC, akin to a device driver, with all the pitfalls and frustrations that implies. Codecs are frequently buggy, causing video distortion or even crashes. Vista only includes codecs for a few common standards; need anything else, and you're on your own. And, of course, the More Information link Media Player shows you when it can't play a video doesn't provide anything one would recognize as useful information.

To play a particular video, you need to install the same codec that was used to create (compress) the video in the first place, regardless of the player application you're using. To determine which codec was used, you'll need a program like GSpot (*http://www.headbands.com/gspot/*) or AVIcodec (*http://avicodec.duby.info*), both of which are free. Just drag-drop the video file onto GSpot (Figure 4-1) or AVIcodec, and the program will display the file's video codec, audio codec, and other statistics.

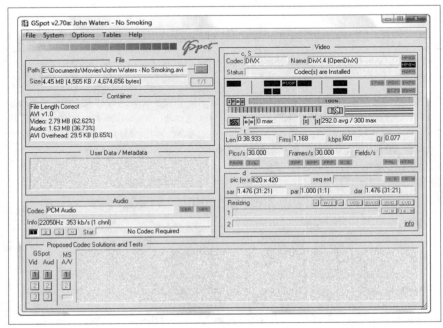

Figure 4-1. Use GSpot to find the software necessary to play a given video clip

The codec utility may indicate that the required codec is already installed. As comforting as that may be, you might still need to download and install the latest version of the codec to play the troublesome video. Otherwise, you may not have all the latest bugs...er, fixes.

If one of these tools can't identify the codec, the file is probably corrupted or encoded with a nonstandard scheme. Provided you're not able to ask whoever created the file for information about the software used, the easiest trick is to open the file in a standard text editor and look for the four-digit *4CC* code near the beginning. Figure 4-2 shows the code buried in a file, DIVX in this case, which indicates that the DivX decompressor is needed to play this video.

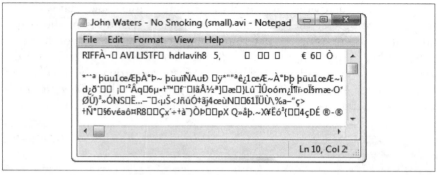

Figure 4-2. A hex editor or text editor will show you the 4CC code embedded in the beginning of most movie files

Armed with the name (or 4CC code) of the codec, proceed to *http://www. fourcc.org/fcccodec.htm*, and download the codec installer from the list. If the 4CC code isn't there, a quick Google search (along with the word "codec") should turn up some useful leads.

Installing and Managing AX Codecs

In an attempt to find the right codec to play a video, you might come across a lone *.ax* file with no installer. This is indeed a codec, albeit not a friendly one.

To install the codec, just copy the *.ax* file to your *Windows**System32* folder. Next, right-click the *.ax* file, select **Properties**, and then click the **Change** button (under the **General** tab). Click **Browse**, navigate to your *Windows*\ *System32* folder, select *regsvr32.exe*, click **Open**, and then click **OK**. Thereafter, you can simply double-click *.ax* files to register them.

Alternatively, you can open a Command Prompt window (*cmd.exe*), type cd \Windows\System32 to change to that folder, and then type regsvr32 FLVSplitter.ax to register the file. (Or, type regsvr32 /u FLVSplitter.ax to unregister/uninstall it.)

If you see a message like "DLLRegisterServer in C:\Windows\System32\ FLVSplitter.ax succeeded," then the new codec is installed and ready to use.

The SLD Active Codec Selector (free, *www.skynet4ever.tk*) is a handy tool you can use to list registered codecs on your PC and even selectively disable codecs you suspect might be causing problems.

Once you've installed the codec, try playing the video again. Keep in mind that there are often multiple versions of a single codec available—sometimes from different vendors—so you may need to install several codecs before you find the one that works.

After a bit of searching, you'll probably figure out how widespread this video codec problem really is. Fortunately, some enterprising individuals have created *codec packages*, large installers that include several, if not dozens, of the codecs that people seem to need most. One good example, known simply as the Vista Codec Package, is available for free from *http://www.jtow.net/users/triess/*.

 Some of these packages are better than others, and depending on what's included (or what isn't), some may cause more problems than they solve. For best results, remove any separate, standalone codecs you've installed before trying out a codec package.

If, after installing an individual codec or codec package, some of your videos no longer play (or their thumbnails no longer show up), there's a little trick you can try before you uninstall and give up. The FFDShow Video Decoder Configuration tool, included with many codec packages and shown in Figure 4-3, helps you troubleshoot specific codec problems.

For instance, on one PC, Vista lost the ability to play back *.avi* files: Media Player crashed each time one was opened, and Windows Explorer displayed an error message whenever it attempted to render thumbnails for the videos. To fix a problem like this, open the FFDShow Video Decoder Configuration tool, select **Codecs** on the left, and then find the codec that's causing the problem in the right pane. Then, in the **Decoder** column, use the dropdown listbox to choose a different decoder from the list. Click **OK** when you're done; the change should take effect immediately.

Repair Broken and Incomplete Videos

There are reasons that Windows Media Player might have trouble playing a video *other* than a missing or broken codec—namely, problems with the video file itself. First, make sure your video file is complete; if you downloaded it from the Web, try clearing your browser cache and downloading the file again.

If you're unable to obtain an intact version of the video, you may be able to repair it with the free MPEG Header Corrector, available at *http://www.vcdhelp.us/html/tutmpegheadercorrector.html*, although this typically only works on true *.mpg* files. Need to repair an *.avi* file? Use DivFix (free, *http://divfix.maxeline.com*).

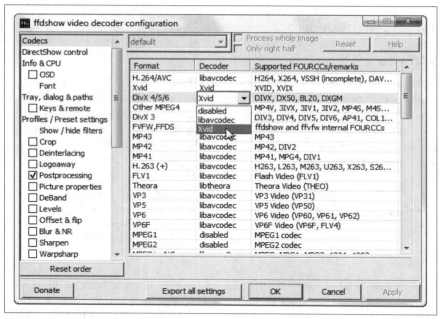

Figure 4-3. When more than one codec is installed for a specific video format, you can choose which one to use with FFDShow Video Decoder Configuration Tool

OK, I know I just said that the filename extension doesn't dictate the codec, but it *does* determine how the video data is organized in the file. See the "Does It Have the Right Extension?" sidebar, next, if you suspect a video file has been misnamed.

Does It Have the Right Extension?

Of course, there's a chance someone gave your file the wrong filename extension; before you attempt to repair that video, make sure it has the correct extension. To check whether that *.mpg* file is really an *.mpg* file, open the file in a text or hex editor. The header (before the aforementioned 4CC code) will read RIFF if it's an *.avi* file, RMF if it's an *.rm* (Real Media) file, MOOV if it's a *.mov* (Apple Quicktime) file, FLV if it's an *.flv* (Flash Video) file, or W.M.F.S.D.K if it's a Microsoft *.asf* or *.wmv* file. If you see no header (only junk), it's likely an *.mpg* file.

See Chapter 3 for more information on file types, and Chapter 2 to find out how to show filename extensions in Windows Explorer. Once extensions are visible, you can change a file's extension merely by renaming the file and typing a new one.

But what if you're in the middle of downloading a video from the Web? Eventually, it'll be intact and playable, but if you want to start playing it before the download is complete, you'll need to employ a few tricks.

First thing to know: Windows Media Player (and many other players) won't play most kinds of videos while they're *in use*; that is, while they're currently being saved by another program (e.g., your browser). The big exception to this rule is streaming video, commonly found in files with the *.asf* or *.wmv* extension (Quicktime *.mov* files, too); by design, these files can be played even while in use by other applications.

To get around this limitation, open the folder containing the file, and create a duplicate of the partially downloaded file. Using the right mouse button, drag the file to an empty area in the same folder, and select **Copy Here** from the menu that appears. Thereafter, you should be able to open the duplicate file with no problems.

 You may have to change the filename extension when playing videos that are in the midst of downloading. For instance, if you're downloading a video with Pando named *skiing.mpg*, the intermediate filename will be *skiing.mpg.downloading*, and thus the filename of the duplicate you create will be *skiing.mpg-Copy.downloading*. Just rename the file to *skiing.mpg-Copy.downloading.mpg* (or simply *skiing.mpg*) and then double-click the file to play it.

With some video formats, particularly *.avi* files, there's a catch: the *index*, essential information about the sequence of frames in the video, is located at the *end* of the file instead of the beginning. Thus an incomplete *.avi* file thus won't have an index, and can't be played at all. The solution is to use a re-indexing utility to rebuild this data and make the file playable. DivFix (free, *http://divfix.maxeline.com*), shown in Figure 4-4, does this quite nicely, but only works on true *.avi* files (discussed earlier in this section). If DivFix can't repair your file, the Windows Media Encoder (free, *http://www.microsoft.com/windows/windowsmedia/forpros/encoder/default.mspx*) is capable of indexing video files, albeit requiring a bit more work to navigate the complex interface.

Fix Other Playback Problems

So, what if your video plays, but just doesn't play well? Problems like stretched or squashed video (too wide or too tall), bad color, and choppy playback can all be caused by buggy or misconfigured video codecs. Just track down and install the latest version of the codec required by the misbehaving video, as described at the beginning of this chapter, and try again. If that doesn't help, there are some other fixes, as follows.

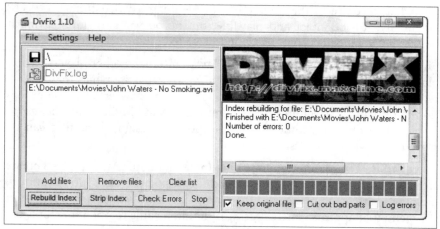

Figure 4-4. Use DivFix to re-index incomplete videos so you can play what you've downloaded so far

Change the aspect ratio. If all your videos seem squashed (too narrow) or stretched out (too wide), you may have to correct your display's aspect ratio setting. Open Windows Media Player, click the **Now Playing** button, and select **More Options**. Choose the **Devices** tab, highlight **Display** in the list, and then click **Properties**. Move the slider until the oval looks like as close to a true circle as possible, and then click **OK**.

On the other hand, if only a single video clip has an incorrect aspect ratio, it may've been encoded that way. To fix the file, you'll have to open the file in a video-editing program that can resize video frames. Although the aforementioned Windows Media Encoder can *crop* frames, it can't stretch or shrink video. To change the aspect ratio of a video clip, use River Past Video Perspective (*http://www.riverpast.com*), Open Video Converter (*http://www.009soft.com*), or a more advanced video application like Adobe Premiere (*http://www.abobe.com*).

The hardest part is the math, but it's not that hard. Most video has a 4:3 aspect ratio, which means the width is four-thirds the height. (HD television and some feature films typically have a 16:9 aspect ratio, while wider "anamorphic" feature films have a 2.39:1 aspect ratio.) If your botched video clip has, say, a resolution of 400×400 (giving you a 1:1 aspect ratio and a square video frame), you can either increase the width to 600 ($400 \times 4/3$) or decrease the height to 300 (400 divided by 4/3). Of the two choices, decreasing the height will usually give you a sharper-looking video, since compressed pixels always look better than stretched pixels.

Synchronize audio and video. Does this happen with all videos, or just one? If only a single video clip is out of sync, then you'll need to repair it using a timeline-based video-editing application like Adobe Premiere (*www.adobe.com*). (Windows Movie Maker, which comes with Vista, won't do.) Drag your video to the timeline, then drag the audio portion of the clip slightly to the left or right until it's synced up with the video. (Naturally, this will take some trial and error, so I hope it's not too boring of a clip.) When you're done, export the project into a new movie file. Consult the documentation that comes with your video application for details.

 If you're watching a DVD and the audio is out of sync, try pausing playback, waiting a few seconds, and then starting up again. Sometimes that's all it takes to get a movie back on track.

If *all* your videos are out of sync, it's usually caused by a problem with your hardware drivers. Go ahead and install the latest drivers for your video card and sound card, and then run Windows Update to make sure you have the latest video-related updates.

If new drivers don't fix the problem, open Windows Media Player, and click the **Now Playing** button. Select **More Options**, and then click the **Performance** tab. Turn on the **Drop frames to keep audio and video synchronized** option, and then click **OK**.

Speed it up or slow it down. Is a video playing too fast or too slow? In Windows Media Player, click the **Now Playing** button, select **Enhancements**, and then select **Play Speed Settings** (Figure 4-5). Adjust the slider until the video plays at the correct speed.

Fix bad color. If some of your videos seem to have messed-up color, open Windows Media Player, click the **Now Playing** button, select **Enhancements**, select **Video Settings**, and then click the **Reset** link. Next, click the little arrows until you see **Color Chooser**, and click the **Reset** link here as well. Now, play a video to try it out; if the colors are still off, you may have to play with the **Video Settings** and **Color Chooser** sliders to fine-tune the color.

If that doesn't do the trick, or if you see colored lines running through your videos, you can usually correct the problem by updating your display drivers.

Figure 4-5. Play any video faster or slower with the Play Speed Settings panel in Windows Media Player

Shed light on blank videos. Ever feel like Sergeant Schultz from *Hogan's Heroes?** You might hear something, but you definitely *see nothing* when you play most videos.

If so, it's likely a video overlay problem.

When you play video, Windows usually paints a special rectangle on your screen, and your video driver is responsible for superimposing the moving video over it. This *overlay* scheme allows your display adapter (video card) to handle the burden of playing the video rather than your CPU, which affords better performance and smoother video. Unfortunately, it can also be the source of problems in some cases, usually manifesting itself as a black rectangle where video should appear.

---

* I would've also accepted Billy Wilder's *Stalag 17* (1953).

First, conduct a little test to see whether you indeed have an overlay problem. Try maximizing or resizing the Windows Media Player window, or cover it with another window and then bring it to the front. If this makes the video play, or if you see pieces of windows left behind in the black rectangle, your video card driver may be to blame. Visit your video card manufacturer's web site and download the latest driver. Also, pay a visit to the company's support web site and look for recommended BIOS settings (see Appendix A).

In previous versions of Windows Media Player, one was able to downgrade Windows' support for video overlays to solve this problem. Unfortunately, Microsoft eliminated this option in Media Player 11, perhaps because Vista's requirements for video hardware are so much heftier than Windows XP's that Microsoft thought it inconceivable that modern video drivers would have any problems playing video.

 To disable video overlays in RealOne Player, go to **Tools →** **Preferences → Hardware → Video card compatibility**. Move the slider to the left until **Enabled optimized video and disable overlays** appears beneath.

Simplify Your Media Players

The Windows Media Player has lots of interesting features and gadgets, most of which just get in the way when all you want to do is play a simple video. Of course, it looks downright minimalistic compared with Real Networks' cumbersome RealPlayer. Fortunately, you have a few choices.

To switch to the simpler Windows Media Player window, just press **Ctrl-2** to switch to Skin Mode. (Or, press **Alt** to show the normally hidden menu, and then select **View → Skin Mode**.) The default skin is "Corporate," but you can choose another skin by clicking **Alt** and selecting **View → Skin Chooser**.

Alternatively, Media Player Classic, available for free at *http://sourceforge.net/ projects/guliverkli/*, can take the place of Windows Media Player, RealPlayer, and QuickTime Player. It has a slimmed-down interface (shown in Figure 4-6), doesn't need to be installed (it's just a standalone *.exe* file), and plays just about any video format. (Really, it's just replacement "shell" that ties into the playback engines that come with the aforementioned media player applications.)

Aside from the streamlined interface and its ability to handle just about any video format, Media Player Classic has several features that make it worth using. For instance, you can play more than one video at once, something Windows Media Player won't let you do. And it's kind enough to show detailed error messages with enough information to solve the problem, such as listing any missing codecs.

Figure 4-6. *Media Player Classic is an alternative to the overblown Windows Media Player and messy RealPlayer applications*

Handling Online Video

Ideally, video should be no different than any other web content, but when was the last time you had trouble viewing static text and still images, or even hearing audio, in web pages? But videos are different, and for several reasons:

- The enormous size of video files forces web publishers to employ a series of tricks, such as nonstandard streaming protocols, dedicated video servers, and special browser plug-ins, to bring video to your desktop.

- The large number of competing formats means that you must have at least a half-dozen browser plug-ins—not to mention all the required codecs, described earlier in this chapter—in order to play most online video.

- The aforementioned plug-ins and codecs must be updated to keep up with the technology.
- Online video publishers—particularly news organizations—often jury-rig their content to make it difficult or impossible to download to your hard disk. This means they rely more heavily on special plug-ins, Java-Script, and other hand-waving, all of which increase the likelihood that you'll run into a problem when you watch their videos.

All of this simply means that playing and downloading online video can be a frustrating experience if you don't know about a few tools and tricks.

First and foremost, make sure you have the latest versions of these four major plug-ins installed in each web browser you use.

Plug-in	Download from	Filename(s) for IE	Filename(s) for Firefox and SeaMonkey
Quicktime	www.quicktime.com	qtplugin.ocx	npqtplugin.dll
			npqtpluginx.dll
RealPlayer	www.real.com	rmoc3260.dll	nppl3260.dll
			nprpjplug.dll
Shockwave Flash	www.adobe.com	flash9.ocx	npswf32.dll
Windows Media Player	www.microsoft.com	wmp.dll	npdsplay.dll
		msdxm.ocx	npwmsdrm.dll

Working with Media

To see a list of plug-ins that are installed in Internet Explorer, open IE, click the **Tools** drop-down, and select **Internet Options**. Choose the **Programs** tab, click **Manage add-ons**, and then from the **Show** drop-down, select **Add-ons that run without requiring permission**. In the **Settings** box, you can also disable any plug-in you suspect might be causing playback problems, or, if you're lucky, you may be able to go to **Control Panel → Programs and Features** to uninstall the plug-in completely.

In Mozilla Firefox (and Mozilla SeaMonkey), just type about:plugins in the address bar and press **Enter** to see a list of installed plug-ins. (Note that plug-ins, used to view embedded content, are indeed different from extensions, which only add features to the browser interface.) Like IE, Mozilla plug-ins can be uninstalled from Control Panel.

You can also try installing the latest version of each of the plug-ins listed here to solve most playback problems with web-based video.

Rewind or Fast-Forward Streaming Video

You've probably encountered a video on the Web that won't let you rewind (without starting over) or fast-forward to skip ahead. It's not such a big deal with 20-second clips, but when you're watching a half-hour broadcast mostly featuring a talking head, it can be infuriating that you can't just skip ahead to the car chase.

Usually, this is a limitation of the video file (or of the player), and not simply an option that can be turned on or off. A lot of streaming video clips have this problem, particularly *.wmv* and *.asf* videos. To rewind or fast-forward these videos, they must be indexed, something you can only do if the video file is stored on your hard disk. If there's a web-based video you want to index, you'll need to download it to your hard disk first—as described in "Download Online Video Clips," later in this chapter.

To index a *.wmv* file, download the free Windows Media Encoder from *http://www.microsoft.com/windows/windowsmedia/forpros/encoder/default.mspx* and open the Windows Media File Editor. Drag-drop the video onto the Editor window, and from the **File** menu, select **Save and Index**. Thereafter, you'll be able to rewind and fast-forward the clip to your heart's content.

Control Video Buffering

Most online video clips are designed to *stream*, allowing you to start watching before your PC has finished downloading. To keep the video playing smoothly, video players often download a few seconds of video ahead of the playback, a technique called *buffering* (or *caching*), and sometimes this means you have to wait. The good news is that you can choose *when* to wait: now, or later.

In Windows Media Player, click the **Now Playing** button, select **More Options**, and then choose the **Performance** tab. Select **Buffer [5] seconds of content**, the second option in the **Network buffering** section.

To shorten the lead time so that videos will start playing sooner, enter a small number, say 3. Depending on the speed of your Internet connection and number of visitors the web server is currently juggling, those 3 seconds of content could take anywhere from 2 seconds to 20 minutes to download. (Obviously, upgrading to a faster Internet connection will minimize the waiting most of the time.)

Unfortunately, entering a small number means that Media Player has to stop playback more often to buffer more content. If you find that Media Player frequently stops playing to buffer more data, raise the buffer number to 10 or 20 seconds. You'll get smoother playback, but you'll have to wait longer before your online videos play.

 The buffering settings discussed here have no effect on video clips stored on your hard disk, nor on video handled by other players (e.g., Flash, Quicktime, and RealOne). To eliminate buffering messages altogether, see "Download Online Video Clips," next.

Download Online Video Clips

Most online video publishers don't make it easy to download video files to your hard disk, and for good reason. For one, they want you to watch their videos only on their own web sites, where they can show you advertising, sell you products and services, or just keep you lingering around their sites a little longer. They also don't want to pay to host videos embedded on *your* web site, nor do they want you to take their copyrighted material and upload it to YouTube. That's all well and good, but who's looking out for *your* needs?

What happens when the publisher takes down a video or moves it to a subscription-based archive before you have a chance to watch it? What if the server is too busy, and your PC isn't able to stream it smoothly? What if you want to save the video to watch later, or if you want to index it (as described earlier in this section) so you can rewind and fast-forward it? What if the video is long, and you want to watch it on your handheld PC or video-enabled iPod? What if you just want to needlessly fill up your hard drive?

Saving online video into a file on your hard disk can be tricky for several reasons, not the least of which is that there are a bunch of different ways video can be delivered on the Web. And, of course, each format has its own download procedure.

 Before you start mucking around, look for the simplest solution. Some sites, such as Google Video, include a download link right on the page. Or, if the video is all by itself, centered in the browser window, and the URL ends with a file-name extension commonly associated with video files (e.g., *.mpg*, *.mov*, *.wmv*), then you can often just save the file by pressing **Ctrl-S**. (Or, go to **Page → Save As** in IE.) Or, if the clip is playing in a separate Windows Media Player or QuickTime window, try saving it there. Of course, most video publishers will disable the **Save As** feature, but it's worth a shot.

The first step is to find out what kind of video file you're dealing with, and the easiest way to do that is to right-click the center of the video frame in the browser window. The context menu that appears should indicate the plug-in being used, most notably, the **About** entry (if there is one). How you proceed depends on the plug-in:

Adobe Flash Player/Macromedia Flash Player

Flash-based videos typically come in two parts: the player module and the video file. The Flash plug-in first loads the player module (an *.swf* file), which in turn downloads and controls the video source (an *.flv* file); the *.flv* file is what you want. (This isn't always the case; if there's no separate *.flv* file, then the video is likely embedded in the main *.swf* file.)

As soon as the player has finished downloading the entire *.flv* file, you can find it in your web browser cache; see the upcoming sidebar, "Pull Files Out of Your Browser Cache," for details.

 Windows Media Player can't play *.flv* files unless you install a special codec, as described in the "Installing and Managing AX Codecs" sidebar, earlier in this chapter. Now, odds are, you won't be able to find a WMP codec that actually works, so you'll need to seek out a dedicated *.flv* file player instead. There are several choices, but the best one is simply called FLV Player, and is available for free from *http:// www.martijndevisser.com*.

If you don't feel like digging through your cache folder, or if the cached file doesn't seem to be playable, you can use one of these handy browser add-ons designed to provide direct links to *.flv* files on the most popular Flash-based video web sites:

Bookmarklet (Firefox, SeaMonkey, or Opera). Go to *http://1024k.de/ bookmarklets/video-bookmarklets.html* and drag the "All-In-One Video Bookmarklet" link from the page onto your browser's Links toolbar. Then, navigate to a video page and click the bookmarklet to open a pop-up window with a download link.

Bookmarklet (Internet Explorer). Since IE7 doesn't support bookmarklets longer than 2,083 characters, you won't be able to use the aforementioned "All-In-One" link. Instead, use the "old" bookmarklets listed at *http://1024k.de/bookmarklets/video-bookmarklets.html*; you'll need to install a bookmarklet for each web site you use (e.g., YouTube, Google Video, etc.).

Greasemonkey User Script (Greasemonkey extension plus Firefox/ SeaMonkey). If you have the Greasemonkey extension (available from *http://greasespot.net*), go to *http://1024k.de/bookmarklets/video-bookmarklets.html*, click the "All-In-One Video Script" link, and then click **Install**. Next, navigate to a video page, and click the yellow bar that appears to display the download link.

Firefox Extension (Firefox only). First, install the VideoDownloader extension from *http://videodownloader.net/*, and then restart Firefox. Next, navigate to a video page, and click the VideoDownloader status bar icon to display a pop-up window with the download link.

Pull Files Out of Your Browser Cache

Web browsers store copies of recently viewed pages and all associated media (images, audio, and video) in a folder on your hard disk, called the *cache*. This improves performance when you're surfing, but also makes it easy to grab copies of media files—such as Flash videos (*.flv* files)—for storage elsewhere.

Internet Explorer's cache folder is *\Users\[username]\AppData\Local\ Microsoft\Windows\Temporary Internet Files*. (In IE, go to **Tools → Internet Options**, click **Settings** in the **Browsing history** section, and then click **View files**.) Sort the list by file type to group all the *.flv* files together, and then drag the file out of the folder or double-click it to play it.

Neither Mozilla Firefox nor Mozilla SeaMonkey assign filename extensions for their cached files, so you'll have to do a little detective work to find a recently viewed *.flv* file. If you're using Mozilla Firefox, open the *Cache* subfolder of *\Users\[username]\AppData\Local\Mozilla\Firefox\Profiles*, and sort the listing by date. If you see a particularly large file with a date sometime in the last few minutes, try adding the *.flv* extension to its filename, and then double-click it to view it. If the video plays (provided you have an FLV player installed), go ahead and drag the file out of the cache; otherwise, undo the rename and try again with a different file.

Apple QuickTime

QuickTime files are typically the easiest videos to deal with. If the video file is playing by itself in the center of the browser window, select **Page → Save As** in Internet Explorer (or **File → Save As** in any other browser). If the video is playing in a standalone QuickTime window, you can select **File → Save As** and save the file right on the spot, but only if you're using QuickTime Pro (the extra-cost upgrade to the free QuickTime player).

Working with Media

If the video is embedded in a web page, you'll need one of these add-ons to yank it out:

Bookmarklet (Internet Explorer, Firefox, SeaMonkey). Go to *http:// plasmasturm.org/code/bookmarklets/* and drag the "unembed" link from the page onto your browser's Links toolbar. Then, navigate to a video page and click the bookmarklet to download the embedded video.

Greasemonkey User Script (Greasemonkey extension plus Firefox/ SeaMonkey). If you have the Greasemonkey extension (available at *http:// greasespot.net*), go to *http://neugierig.org/software/greasemonkey/*, and install the "unembed" user script. This adds a **download** link next to any embedded video; just click the link to download the video file.

Firefox/SeaMonkey Extension (Firefox or SeaMonkey). Get the AdBlock Plus extension from *http://adblockplus.org/*, and then restart your browser. Open the Adblock Plus Preferences window, select **Options**, and turn on the **Show tabs on Flash and Java** option. Thereafter, a small tab will appear just above embedded videos; click the tab to view the URL, highlight the URL text and copy it to the clipboard, and then click **Cancel**. Armed with the URL of the source video file, download the file as described in the upcoming "Download Files Without Viewing Them" sidebar.

Real Player

If the video is embedded in a web page (including a small pop-up web page), try right-clicking the video itself. Select **Play in RealPlayer** to open the clip in a standalone window, and then in Real Player, select **File → Clip Properties → View Clip Info**. Armed with the URL of the file, download it as described in the upcoming "Download Files Without Viewing Them" sidebar.

The file you download likely won't be the video itself, but rather only an *.ram* file, a playlist of sorts that points to one or more videos stored on a server somewhere. Open Notepad and drag the *.ram* file into it to view the URL inside. If the URL begins with http://, you can probably download it normally, again following the routine in the "Download Files Without Viewing Them" sidebar. On the other hand, if the URL begins with rtsp:// (which stands for Real Time Streaming Protocol), you'll need a special program capable of downloading the stream to a file.

Copy the URL (highlight and press **Ctrl-C**) and paste it (**Ctrl-V**) into a program like CoCSoft Stream Down (*http://stream-down.cocsoft.com*), shown in Figure 4-7, or WMRecorder (*http://www.wmrecorder.com*).

Download Files Without Viewing Them

Type a URL into your browser's address bar and hit **Enter**, and the browser will attempt to display the file in its own window or launch the associated player. Only if the file can't be displayed (such as a *.zip* or *.exe*), will you get a standard **Save As** dialog. But what if you want to save (download) a file the browser wants to open, such as a video?

If you're using Mozilla SeaMonkey, this is easy. Instead of pressing the **Enter** key in the address bar, press **Shift-Enter** to save the file instead of opening it. This won't work in Internet Explorer or Firefox, though, so you'll need a slightly trickier method for those browsers.

Open Notepad and paste the URL of the file you want to download. In front of the URL, add this text:

```
<a href="
```

and then after the URL, add this:

```
">download</a>
```

Save the file on your desktop as *download.html*, and then double-click the new file to open it in your browser. Right-click the lone **download** link on the page, and select **Save Target As**.

Alternatively, you can use Bulk Downloader, available at *http://www.creativelement.com/powertools/*. Just choose the **List Manually** tab, paste the URL (or URLs) into the box, and then click **Download**.

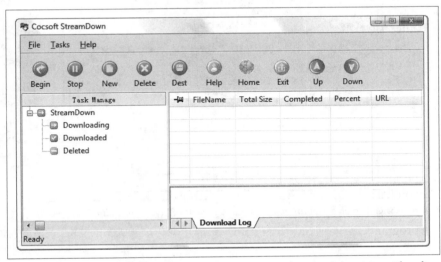

Figure 4-7. Use a program like CoCSoft Stream Down to download streaming video clips to your hard disk

If all goes well, you should have a file on your hard disk in about the same amount of time as it would take to watch the video from start to finish; just double-click the file icon to play the clip.

Windows Media Player

Windows Media Player videos are a pain in the neck because of the wide variety of tricks publishers must use to get the videos to appear in web pages. If you encounter one of these beasts, first try the bookmarklets and extensions for QuickTime videos, listed earlier in this section. If none of those work, you'll need to do some digging to get the URL of the source file.

If the video is playing in a standalone Windows Media Player window, getting the URL is not too hard: from the **File** menu, select **Properties**, and it will be shown in the **Location** field (see Figure 4-8).

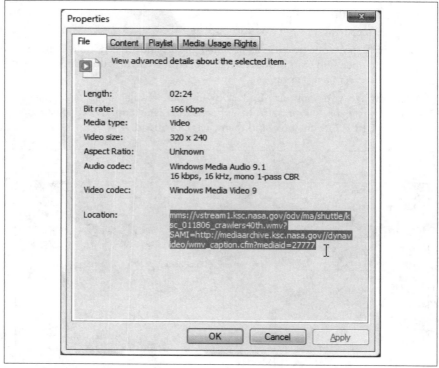

Figure 4-8. Get the URL of an online Windows Media Player video clip

If the video is embedded in a web page, getting the URL is a little trickier. If you're using Firefox or SeaMonkey, right-click an empty area of the web page and select **View Page Info**. Click the **Media** tab, and then scroll down the list until you see the URL of the video, which is often the only entry that isn't an image file (*.jpg*, *.gif*, etc.).

Firefox and SeaMonkey users can also use the AdBlock Plus extension, described in the Apple QuickTime portion of this section, to get the URL of an embedded Media Player video file.

If you're using Internet Explorer, right-click an empty area of the web page and select **View Source** (this works in Firefox and SeaMonkey, too); some familiarity with HTML will make this task much easier. Press **Ctrl-F** and search the code for text that would likely appear in a video clip URL, such as .asf, .asx, .wmv, or rstp:. Somewhere in the code, you'll hopefully find a full (or partial) URL for the source video clip that looks something like rstp://www.some.server/videos/penguin.asx. If you're lucky enough to find the URL, you can proceed to download it by following the instructions for Real Player, previously in this section. Otherwise, you may be out of luck.

Sound and Music

Microsoft revamped the audio subsystem in Windows Vista in order to solve a series of problems it maintains caused stability and quality shortcomings in earlier versions. For one, Microsoft moved most of the code that handles sound out of the drivers and into another echelon of Vista's architecture. In short, this is why your sound doesn't work.

Next, Microsoft redesigned the tools you use to manage sound in Vista, such as the Volume Control and the Sound dialog in Control Panel. This is why you can't find anything.

As a result, manufacturers of sound cards simply discontinued their older products rather than trying to make them Vista-compatible. This is why you have to throw out your old sound card, and why you shouldn't spend too much on a new one.

Get Sound Where There Is None

Sound in Windows Vista is quite a bit more complicated than it needs to be, so troubleshooting sound problems is a real chore. The best way to fix a PC that won't play sound is with a systematic approach.

Start with the obvious. If you're using external speakers, make sure they're plugged in, turned on, and turned up. Try plugging the speakers into an iPod, home stereo, or other audio source to make sure they're actually working.

Using a laptop with integrated speakers? Most laptops have their own independent volume controls, and some are unlucky enough to have two or three. The first type is the old-school walkman-esque dial, usually found right next to the headphone/speaker jack (sometimes these dials only control external audio, but not always). The second type is usually found on the keyboard, accessed by holding the **Fn** key while pressing another key decorated with a speaker icon. The third type is found on newer laptops, in the group of media quick-access buttons. Make your best effort to turn all these controls up.

 Sometimes the push-button volume controls on laptops operate the system volume directly, and sometimes they merely send signals to a Windows application that, in turn, controls the volume. If your laptop's volume controls don't seem to be working, the application with which they communicate may not be installed or running. You can usually download the media access software from the PC manufacturer's web site.

If hardware volume controls are a dead end, open the Vista's Volume Mixer (*sndvol.exe*[*]), and then open the **Device** menu. If there's more than one device listed, make sure the one you want to use has a checkmark next to it. Turn up the **Device** volume control as high as it will go. Also check the subordinate volume controls to the right, one for each open sound-enabled application and one for Windows itself, and make sure they're all turned up.

Next, go to **Control Panel** → **Sound**, and choose the **Playback** tab (Figure 4-9). If, again, there's more than one device listed here, highlight the one you want to use and click the **Set Default** button.

---

[*] Note that it's no longer *sndvol32.exe*, as it was in earlier versions of Windows.

Figure 4-9. More than one sound device on your PC? If so, you may have been setting the volume on the wrong card all this time

Note that a single hardware device, such as a sound card, may be responsible for multiple sound devices shown in Control Panel. For instance, most higher-end audio cards have both analog (headphone jack) and digital (coax or optical/SPDIF) outputs, so make sure the one you're using is set as the default, and is marked with the little green checkmark icon.

With the sound device you want to use highlighted in the Playback window, click the **Properties** button, and choose the **Custom** tab, and make sure the **Digital Output Only** option is turned off. Then choose the **Levels** tab, and make sure all the volume controls here are turned up, and none are muted. (Muted levels have small red symbols on the blue speaker buttons, as shown—albeit in black and white—in Figure 4-10.)

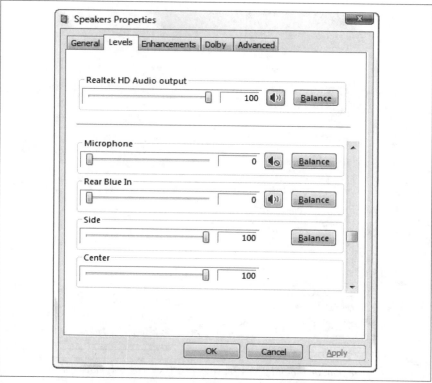

Figure 4-10. The volume controls for your sound card's inputs and outputs are buried in Control Panel, not in the Volume Mixer

Next, choose the **Advanced** tab. Click **Test** to play three tones in the left channel, followed by three in the right (more if you have a 5.1 or 6.1 setup).

- If you don't hear anything, and you don't see an error message at this point, there's likely a problem with your speaker jack, cable, or speakers.

- If you hear only three tones, it means only one stereo channel is working; either the left or right channel (or speaker) is out. The left channel tones decrease in frequency (higher to lower), while the right channel tones increase (lower to higher).

- If you have more than two speakers, but don't hear sound out of all of them, close the Properties window and click **Configure** to show the Speaker Setup page. Follow the prompts to tell Windows how many speakers you have.

- If you hear sound in some applications and not others, it could be the fault of the **Exclusive Mode** options in the Properties window. Try turning off one or both of the options here, click **Apply**, and try again.

- If you hear the tones, but you can't hear music played from an audio CD, the analog audio cable that typically connects CD drives in desktop PCs to sound cards might be missing, or plugged into the wrong connector. (Laptops and newer SATA drives don't usually use these cables.) It's a thin cable with small, plastic, three- or four-conductor plugs, and is found inside your PC case. Unless you're using an add-on sound card, this cable should be plugged into your motherboard; if there's more than one port, try the others until you get sound.

- If you see the message, "Failed to play test tone," it means there's a problem with the driver. Either it's the wrong driver for the device, the driver isn't Vista compatible, or the device itself is not Vista compatible. Solutions are discussed shortly

If you have more than one audio device, and the current default won't produce any sound, try the others, if possible. For instance, if your add-on sound card doesn't work, but the sound outputs on your motherboard do, then you know your sound card is the problem.

 Trying to get the sound adapter built in to your motherboard (desktop or laptop) to work? Check your BIOS settings and make sure the adapter is enabled, as described in Appendix A.

If none of the tools in Control Panel or the Volume Mixer seem to help, it's time to start looking at your sound device. Open **Control Panel → Device Manager** (or launch *devmgmt.msc*), and expand the **Sound, video and game controllers** branch. If your device isn't listed, then Windows hasn't detected it, and hasn't loaded a driver for it. If it's listed, but its icon is covered with a red **X**, then it's just disabled; right-click the device and select **Enable**.

If the device icon is covered with a yellow exclamation point, then there's something wrong with the driver or the device. The first course of action is to right-click the device and select **Uninstall**. Check the **Delete the driver software for this device** option, and click **OK**. When the uninstallation is complete, restart Windows, and Vista should redetect the device and install new drivers by itself. If this doesn't work, visit the sound card manufacturer's web site and download the latest drivers for your card.

Now, if none of your sound devices work, including ones that are supposed to be Vista-compatible, you may have stumbled upon a nasty problem that sometimes affects Vista when it's been installed over an earlier version of Windows. If this is the case with your PC, you should spend some time and remove any remnants of old audio drivers. But be prepared for the possibility that Vista will never produce sound reliably until it has been reinstalled from scratch. To test this hypothesis, try installing another copy of Vista alongside your current installation; see Chapter 1 for details on setting up a dual-boot system.

Get Windows to Listen

Want to transfer those old vinyl LPs to MP3s? Want to use voice dictation software? Want to record video, and need to send the audio track through your sound card? Want to use your PC as a makeshift karaoke machine? Getting Vista to record that sound may not be so easy.

Vista allows more than one audio device, a "feature" that usually makes troubleshooting audio problems needlessly complicated (as evidenced by the previous section). This is particularly true when recording sound, given that Windows can only record from one source at a time.

A single audio device may have two or three audio inputs: an analog (mono) microphone input, an analog stereo "Line-In" or auxiliary input, and sometimes a digital S/PDIF input. And special devices, like voice dictation headsets and TV tuner cards, have their own inputs. All the inputs for all your audio devices are listed in **Control Panel → Sound → Recording** tab, shown in Figure 4-11. (Most desktop sound cards also have internal inputs for CD audio, discussed in the previous section, but these almost never show up in Control Panel.)

To choose the default audio source, highlight the device you want to use and click **Set Default**. Most applications will automatically use the default device to record sound, but some (particularly voice-dictation software) require that you choose a source separately in the application itself.

 If you have a USB audio device, such as a voice-dictation headset, Windows may set it as the default recording *and* playback device each time you plug it in. This will make it look like your sound stops working each time you use the headset; of course, all you have to do is change the default playback device, as described in the previous section.

Next, you'll need to set the recording level (volume) of the device; most of the time, the default level is 0 (off), which won't produce any sound at all. With the device highlighted, click **Properties**, choose the **Levels** tab and move the slider to the right until the level is at least 50. While you're here, choose the **Custom** tab, and make sure the **Do Not Monitor** option is turned off. Click **OK** when you're done.

If you're setting up a voice-dictation microphone, you may have to complete a separate wizard in the software itself to set the input source and its recording level. For instance, if you're using Vista's built-in speech recognition feature, go to **Control Panel → Ease of Access → Speech Recognition Options → Set up microphone**.

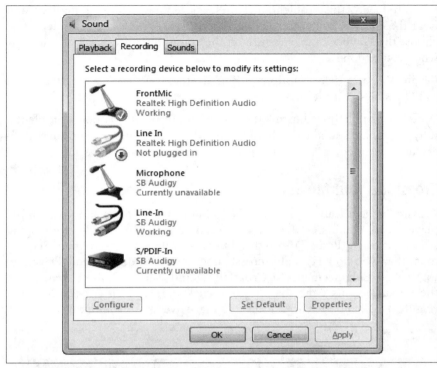

Figure 4-11. Most recording problems are caused by incorrect settings on this Control Panel page

For best results when using voice-dictation software, use a USB microphone/headset instead of the conventional type that plugs directly into your sound card. Not only will the quality and clarity improve, but you'll effectively bypass the often troublesome sound card drivers in favor of a more direct link.

Fix Garbled Music

Your music not sounding its best? The most likely candidate is an "enhancement" in your music player; sometimes these just don't play nice with Vista's audio drivers.

In Windows Media Player, press the **Alt** key to open the menu, and select **View → Enhancements → Graphic Equalizer**. In the Enhancements pane that appears, click the **Turn off** link that appears (if the link says **Turn On**, the equalizer is already turned off). Next, return to the **Enhancements** menu, select **SRS WOW Effects**, and click the **Turn off** link there as well.

If you're having this problem in iTunes, select **View** → **Show Equalizer**, and clear the checkbox next to the **On** option. Next, select **Edit** → **Preferences**, choose the **Playback** tab, and turn off the **Sound Enhancer** option. Click **OK** when you're done.

Or, in WinAmp, select **Options** → **Equalizer**, and if there's a checkbox next to **EQ enabled**, turn it off.

Whether or not this adjustment fixes the problem, this is not a problem a fully functional sound card should have. Make sure you have the latest drivers, and consider replacing the card if nothing else seems to work.

Crossfade Your Music

Crossfading is a feature present in Windows Media Player and other music players that eliminates the gaps between songs by gradually overlapping adjacent tracks. (Radio DJs do this, but they undoubtedly have better equipment than you do.) To enable crossfading, open Windows Media Player, go to **View** → **Enhancements** → **Crossfading and Auto Volume Leveling**. On the Enhancements pane that appears, click the **Turn on Crossfading** link (Figure 4-12), and then adjust the amount of overlap to your liking.

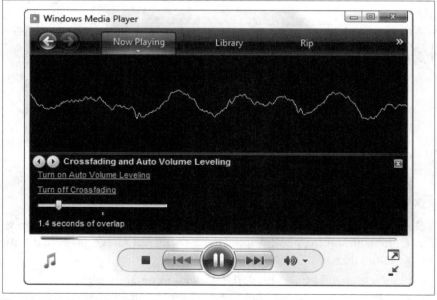

Figure 4-12. Crossfading, which overlaps songs to reduce dead air, works only in certain circumstances

Crossfading only works on data files (such as MP3 or WMA), and then only when the two songs are encoded with the same sampling rate (e.g., 192 Kbps or 256 Kbps). Crossfades won't work if you are playing an ordinary audio CD, or, for some reason, a *data* CD that was originally burned with Windows Media Player.

 Now, it's possible that crossfading is actually working, but you can't tell because your music files have more than a few seconds of silence at the beginning or end. To test the feature, try playing a few songs that don't begin or end in a fade. And try increasing the amount of overlap by moving the crossfade slider to the right.

To enable crossfading in iTunes (which, ironically, is not something you can do with an iPod), select **Edit → Preferences**, choose the **Playback** tab, and turn on the **Crossfade playback** option.

 Crossfading is *really* annoying when you're listening to spoken-word tracks or dialog from movie soundtracks. Try it; you'll see what I mean.

Extract Sound from Video

You'd think that sound and video are easily separable, especially given the fact that they're shown as separate entities in the timeline view in Windows Movie Maker. No such luck, but it is possible with the right software.

The Windows Media Stream Editor, a component of the free Windows Media Encoder (available from *http://www.microsoft.com/windows/windowsmedia/forpros/encoder/default.mspx*), can extract the audio from a *.wmv* video file and save it into a standalone Windows Media Audio (*.wma*) file:

1. First, open the Windows Media Stream Editor and click **Add Source**. Locate a *.wmv* or *.asf* file, and click **Open**.

2. Expand the branches by highlighting the file in the list and pressing the asterisk (*) key, place a checkmark next to the **Audio** entry, and then click **Add**.

3. Then, click **Create File**, specify an output filename, and click **Save**.

4. When you're ready, click **Start** to begin the extraction.

When the process is complete, you'll have a standard *.wma* file; see the next section for ways to convert it to MP3 or any other format.

To yank out the audio track from non-Microsoft video formats, you'll need a different program. A full-blown video editing application like Adobe Premiere (*http://www.adobe.com*) can do this handily, as can Blaze Media Pro (*http://www.blazemp.com*), but if you want to do it for free, try the AoA Audio Extractor (*http://www.aoamedia.com/audioextractor.htm*).

Convert Audio Files

You'd think after all these years, the tech industry would learn its lesson. They put us through the Beta versus VHS battle in the 80s, the Netscape versus Internet Explorer battle in the 90s, and the HD DVD versus Blu-Ray battle in the naughts. On the computer front, the battle of the formats is everywhere, including digital music.

It wasn't always this way. At the beginning of the digital music revolution, it was the compact file size and reasonably good quality of the MP3 file format that popularized portable digital players like the iPod (not to mention P2P file sharing and the like, but that's a different story). But now we have Apple's M4A, M4P, and lossless AAC formats; Microsoft's various versions of the WMA format; OGG Vorbis; Sony's bygone ATRAC; and so on. Granted, most of these formats have risen from the need to copy-protect downloadable music, as well as offer audiophiles better fidelity, but the lack of a single standard is nothing more than a pain in the neck to music lovers everywhere.

Music purchased from Apple's iTunes music store can only be played by Apple iPods (and some Motorola phones). Very few players are compatible with audio files from Microsoft's URGE music store; even some of Microsoft's own Zune players can't play URGE files! And there's no music player that'll play all the commercially available formats.

So, in order to play all the music you have on any particular player, you may have to convert some of it to the proper format, and that's easier said than done.

For one, converting anything other than lossless audio to your desired format will reduce the quality of the music. (Examples of lossless audio include WAV files, Apple's lossless AAC, and, of course, audio CD tracks.) Also, most music purchased online is distributed in protected formats (like iTunes' M4P and Microsoft's protected WMA), and neither Apple nor Microsoft want you converting their content to an unprotected format. But the good news is that where there's a will, there's a way.

Apple's iTunes software, (*http://www.apple.com/itunes/*) is free even if you don't have an iPod or any intention of buying music from the iTunes Music Store, and it can convert songs easily and quickly. It supports MP3 (all bitrates), AAC (*.m4p*, *.m4a*, and *.m4b*), AIFF, lossless AAC, and *.wav* files. Here's how to do it:

1. Start iTunes, and select **Music** from the **Library** section on the left.

2. If all your music isn't already in the iTunes library, drag-drop your music files onto the iTunes window.

> If you move the files into your iTunes music folder *before* dragging them into the iTunes application, iTunes will, by default, organize them into folders based on their embedded tag information. If the files are located elsewhere, they'll be left in their current locations.

3. Next, select **Edit** → **Preferences**, choose the **Advanced** tab, and then choose the **Importing** subtab. Select the file format you want to use from the **Format Using** listbox (i.e., choose MP3 Encoder to convert to the MP3 format), and then select a compression level from the **Setting** listbox. (If you don't know which settings to use, **MP3** at **192kbps** is a good compromise among quality, flexibility, and resulting file size, and the files you create can be played anywhere.) Click **OK** when you're done.

4. Finally, highlight one or more songs in your music library, right-click, and select **Convert Selection to MP3** (or AAC, or whatever). Shortly thereafter, iTunes will place the newly converted file alongside the original—both in the library and in same folder on your hard disk—while leaving the original file intact.

Of course, neither iTunes nor Windows Media Player will let you convert protected files, but they'll both let you burn protected music to an audio CD. Then, all you have to do is rip the CD back into an unprotected format. In fact, NoteBurner (*http://www.noteburner.com*) creates a virtual CD-RW drive on your system specifically for this purpose, allowing you to burn and rip your protected songs without wasting any discs. Unfortunately, the burn-rip process will completely obliterate the embedded tags (meaning that you'll have to retype the track names and other information by hand).

> By default, Windows Media Player adds DRM copy protection to all music files you rip from CDs. To turn this off, open Windows Media Player, select **Tools** → **Options**, choose the **Rip Music** tab, and turn off the **Copy protect music** option.

To convert protected files and preserve your tags, you'll need one of the dozens of different DRM removal tools available, such as Tunebite (*http://www.tunebite.de/*) or MyFairTunes (*http://www.hymn-project.org/*).

Of course, no matter how you do it, there will always be a loss in quality when you're converting from one compressed format to another. The exception is when you convert a protected file to an unprotected file of the same format, such as *.m4p* to *.m4a* or protected *.wma* to unprotected *.wma*, provided the software you use supports lossless conversion.

Fix Music Tags

Most music players, including both Windows Media Player and Apple iTunes, pay no attention to the filenames of your music files, but rather read the information (called *tags*) that are embedded therein. Most audio formats support tags for the artist, track, album, year, genre, and about a hundred other things. To get your music player to display and organize your music properly, the tags in your music files must be correct, and unless all your music came from the same source, some tag cleaning is often in order.

Most music library programs allow you to edit the tags of your music files. Windows Media Player (via the Advanced Tag Editor feature) as well as iTunes (discussed earlier in this chapter) even let you modify the tags of several files at once. You can even edit tags for individual files right in Windows Explorer (see Chapter 2), or multiple files if you install the AudioShell extension (*http://softpointer.com/*).

But what if you have a lot of music files without any tags at all? Try to import those files into a program like iTunes, and you'll just end up with countless tracks labeled "Unknown Artist." The solution is to use the filenames to generate the tags, and for this, you can use Ultra Tag Editor (*http://www.atelio.com/*):

1. Open Ultra Tag Editor, use the tree to navigate to the folder containing your files, and place checkmarks next to the specific files you want to fix.

2. Below, choose the **Ultra Tagger** tab, and then, from the **Action** listbox, select **Generate Tag from Filename** (Figure 4-13).

3. Now, Ultra Tag Editor needs you to tell it where in your songs' filenames to find the artist name, track title, track number, album name, and so on, so you'll need to examine the filename of a typical music file on your hard disk, which might look something like *Artist–Album–Title.mp3*.

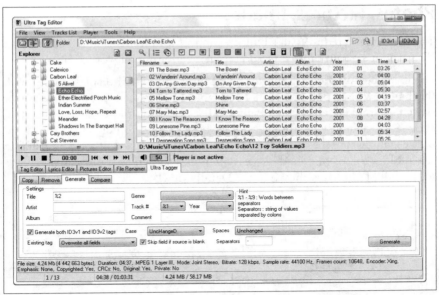

Figure 4-13. Use the Ultra Tag Editor to generate MP3 tags from filenames

Although programs like Ultra Tag Editor are flexible, they do require that your filenames be uniform (i.e., all using the "Artist–Track.mp3" format, for instance). Since you likely have a mish-mash of different filenames, you'll need a program like Power Rename (part of Creative Element Power Tools, *http://www.creativelement.com/powertools/*) to fix up your filenames with ease, without resorting to manually renaming individual files.

First, determine the delimiter used to separate the information in your filenames (a hyphen, -, in this case), and type it into the Delimiters field. Next, type %1 into the field containing the first piece of information (e.g., Artist), %2 into the field containing the second (e.g., Album), %3 for the third (e.g., Title), and so on. (Imagine your files look like %1-%2-%3-%4....mp3).

4. When you're done, click the **Generate** button to preview the new tags, and click **Write Tags** to commit your changes.

Ultra Tag Editor can also go the other direction—that is, to generate filenames based on tags. Better yet, both Windows Media Player and Apple iTunes can organize your music into folders (e.g., *\Music\Artist\Album*) based on the embedded tag information.

Photos, Pictures, Images

To Microsoft's credit, Vista's built-in support for photos is much better than XP's, and it's about time. It would be even better if it all worked properly.

For instance, Windows Explorer has a nifty thumbnail display, along with the handy **Views** pull-down that lets you quickly scale the thumbnails or switch to the **Details** view (Figure 4-14). Now, Explorer is supposed to choose the default view for each folder based on its contents, but the chimpanzee who wrote the code should've been better trained. It's not unusual to see a folder full of Microsoft Access *.mdb* files shown as thumbnails, while a folder full of photos is shown in the **Details** view!

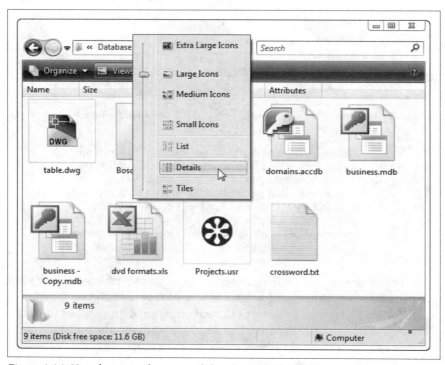

Figure 4-14. Vista has a much-improved thumbnail display but has trouble remembering when to use it

When Explorer gets it wrong, it's easy enough to click the **Views** button to cycle through the various display modes (or click the arrow to choose a view from the list), but it's more effective to change Windows Explorer's *perception* of the folder. Right-click the folder, choose the **Customize** tab (Figure 4-15), and from the **Use this folder type as a template** list, choose one of the five available templates.

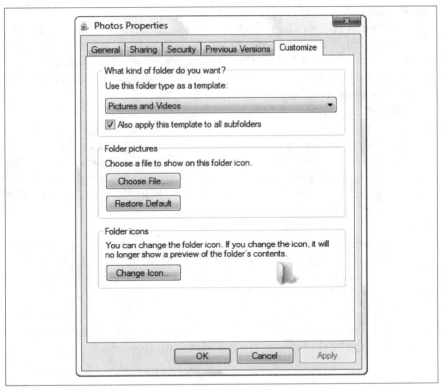

Figure 4-15. Use the Customize tab to choose a display template for the selected folder, but don't forget to customize the template

Here's where it gets a little confusing. First, a *template* is a collection of folder display settings that includes the view (e.g., Large Icons, Details, etc.), the sorting method, and the columns displayed. But you can't change any of these settings here. Nor can you add or remove templates or change the rules Windows uses when it picks a template automatically (hence the problems just outlined).

Next, the templates themselves don't make a whole lot of sense:

All Items
Basically the default view, Explorer uses this template when there's no specific reason to use one of the others. The columns shown by default are **Name**, **Date Modified**, **Type**, and **Size**.

Documents
Used for the *Documents* folder and all of its subfolders, this template is identical to the **All Items** template, except for the addition of the **Tags** column.

Pictures and Videos

A thumbnail display by default, this template is shown for folders containing photo and video files. The columns shown are predominantly for photos, though: **Name**, **Date Taken**, **Tags**, **Size**, and **Rating**. (If you want columns useful for video files, such as **Duration** and **Frame rate**, you'll have to add them yourself.)

Music Details

Shown by default for music files (e.g., MP3 and WMA files), this shows files in **Details** view, making Explorer look somewhat like iTunes' music library listing. The default columns are **Name**, **Artists**, **Album**, **#**, **Genre**, and **Rating**. (Most of the columns get their information from the tags embedded in the music files, as described in "Fix Music Tags," earlier in this chapter.)

Music Icons

This is exactly the same as Music Details, except the files are shown as thumbnails (Large Icons) by default. Why Microsoft felt the need to have two different music templates, yet only a single template for both photos and video files, is anybody's guess.

So, how do you put these to use? The key is to not accept Vista's defaults, but rather to customize each template so that the view Explorer shows you is more likely to be the one you'll want. Here's how you do it:

1. Find a folder with files that are uniquely representative of a certain kind of content, like a bunch of photos or a collection of music files, and open it in a new window.

2. Right-click the folder in the tree to your left, select **Properties**, and then choose the **Customize** tab.

3. Choose a template that most closely matches the contents of the selected folder (i.e., **Pictures and Videos** for a folder containing *.jpg* files).

 The **Also apply this template to all subfolders** option here is particularly handy in that it allows you to customize an entire branch of folders. For instance, you might store all your digital photos in various subfolders of the *Pictures* folder, but this option ensures that they're all shown as thumbnails while preserving the more useful **Details** view for other types of content.

4. Click **OK** to close the Properties window.

5. Use the **Views** drop-down to set a view you find suitable for the files in this folder (e.g., **Large Icons** for photos).

6. Right-click the column headers in the right pane, select **More**, and then place checkmarks next to all the columns you'd like shown. When you're done, click **OK**, and then use your mouse to rearrange and resize the columns to taste.

7. Sort the listing by clicking the appropriate column; click a second time to reverse the sort order.

8. When the folder looks the way you want all folders of this kind to look, click **Organize** and then select **Folder and Search Options**.

9. Choose the **View** tab, click **Apply to Folders**, answer **Yes**, and then click **OK**.

This will save your changes to the active template so that the next folder you view with similar content (at least in theory) will be displayed with the same view settings. This change won't affect any other templates.

 Aside from templates, Windows Explorer can remember the view settings for the 30 or so most recently viewed folders. In Explorer, click **Organize** and then select **Folder and Search Options**. Choose the **View** tab, turn on the **Remember each folder's view settings** option, and then click **OK**. Of course, if you want to make sure your templates are always used, then turn off this option.

Although Vista is very good about remembering your customizations to each of its templates, it's not very good about remembering *which* template to use for a given folder, nor will it reliably choose the appropriate template based on the contents. There are two ways around this.

First, if you don't foresee the need for thumbnails or special columns for music or other media, then you may just as well customize each of the five templates exactly the same way. That is, repeat the nine steps earlier in this section for each template, choosing the same view, sort, and column settings each time. That way, no matter which template Windows picks, you'll get the view you want every single time.

The other way you can help Windows choose templates appropriately is to be diligent about where you store your media files. For instance, if you put all your digital photos in the *Pictures* folder—or, designate the folder where your pictures are stored as the official *Pictures* folder, as described in the next section—then Windows Explorer will be more likely to use the correct template. Of course, it isn't foolproof, but in Windows Vista, what is?

Choose a New Pictures Folder

One way Windows helps you organize your files is to direct different kinds of content to different locations. There's a *Music* folder, a *Videos* folder, a *Saved Games* folder, and a *Pictures* folder. Put all your digital pictures in your *Pictures* folder, for example, and that's where most photo applications will prompt you to open and save your files. And as explained in the previous section, Windows Explorer will be more likely to display your pictures as thumbnails if they're in the *Pictures* folder (or a subfolder thereof). But what if you don't want to put your pictures there?

Since years of digital photos can take up gobs of hard disk space, many people have started storing their pictures (as well as their music) on second hard disks, and it can be a pain to have to manually switch to the new location each time you need to open or save a file.

The solution is to tell Windows where your *Pictures* folder ought to be, a task that requires a quick Registry modification:

1. Open the Registry Editor (described in Chapter 3).

2. Expand the branches to `HKEY_CURRENT_USER\Software\Microsoft\Windows\CurrentVersion\Explorer\User Shell Folders`.

 Also in the **Explorer** branch of the Registry is the `Shell Folders` key. According to Microsoft, the key is no longer used in Vista, although you may want to update it as well for good measure. (You never know which applications may still be reading from it.)

3. Double-click the `My Pictures` value in the right pane, and type (or paste) the full path of the folder you want to use (e.g., `d:\Photos`). (The default here is `%USERPROFILE%\Pictures`, which is an expandable string value that points to the *Pictures* subfolder of your personal profile folder.)

4. Click **OK** and then close the Registry Editor when you're done.

5. Next, open Windows Explorer, open your profile folder (the one matching your user name at the top of the tree), and select the *Pictures* folder inside.

6. Right-click the *desktop.ini* file and select **Copy**. (This file is hidden; see Chapter 2 for details on setting up Windows Explorer to show hidden files.)

7. Navigate to your new pictures folder (e.g., `d:\Photos`), right-click an empty area of the folder, and select **Paste**.

The change should take effect immediately, but you may have to restart any open applications before they'll recognize the new location. (Strictly speaking, the copying of *desktop.ini* in steps 5–7 is optional, but it does help Windows Explorer display the folders properly.) To test the change, open Microsoft Paint (*mspaint.exe*), and select **File → Open**. If the folder that appears is the folder you chose, then you're all done.

You can change the locations of other "special" folders with the same technique. For instance, put the location of your MP3 collection into the My Music value. Or, put the location of your Media Center recordings into the My Video value.

Of course, sometimes you'll have to make a few other changes, depending on the applications you have installed. A classic example is Apple's iTunes software. Now, to Apple's credit, you can change the location of your music folder easily by going to **Edit → Preferences → Advanced** tab, but iTunes will continue to store your music library files in your official *Music* folder. To convince it to put everything in your preferred location, open up the Registry Editor, expand the branches to HKEY_CURRENT_USER\Software\Apple Computer, Inc.\iTunes, double-click the Win2KMyMusicFolder value, and type (or paste) the full path to your new music folder. See Chapter 3 for a way to quickly search the Registry for other occurrences of %USERPROFILE%\Music that might be present, in order to completely commit Windows to the new location.

Get Thumbnails for RAW Photos

Windows understands a bunch of common image and movie formats out of the box, and can produce thumbnails for your files in **Medium**, **Large**, and **Extra Large Icons** views. To get Windows to recognize a new format, though, you need to install the appropriate Windows Imaging Component (WIC) codec.

Once you've set up your digital SLR camera to produce "RAW" images (as opposed to the lesser JPEG or TIFF formats), you can install one of these codecs to get Windows to display thumbnails for your files:

Canon CR2
> *http://www.usa.canon.com/opd/controller?act=OPDSupportVistaAct*

Nikon NEF
> *http://www.nikonimglib.com/nefcodec/*

Olympus ORF
> *http://www.olympus.co.jp/en/support/imsg/digicamera/download/*
> *software/codec/*

Pentax PEF

http://www.pentax.co.jp/english/support/digital/rawcodec_vista.html

Sony SRF

http://support.d-imaging.sony.co.jp/www/cyber-shot/download/raw_driver_e/

If your camera isn't supported, or if the appropriate codec doesn't work, try the free ArcSoft RAW Thumbnail Viewer, available at *http://www.arcsoft.com/products/rawviewer/*. It adds thumbnail support to Vista for RAW formats from Canon, Hasselblad, Kodak, Leica, Mamiya, Nikon, Olympus, Pentax, Ricoh, Samsung, Sigma, and Sony, and even works with Adobe Digital Negative (DNG) files.

The alternative is to use a separate picture viewer with its own thumbnail display, like Google's free Picasa manager (*http://picasa.google.com/*), or commercial products like Adobe Photoshop Elements (*http://www.adobe.com/*) and DxO Optics Pro (*http://dxo.com/*).

To add thumbnail support for new video formats, just install the latest video codecs, covered later in this chapter, and Vista will do the rest.

Get Rid of the Windows Photo Gallery

Like the Windows Picture and Fax Viewer found in Windows XP, Vista's own Windows Photo Gallery application is not easy to get rid of. You can install a new application that makes itself the default for your image files, and in some cases, the Windows Photo Gallery will *still* appear when you double-click image files.

 If you want to use another image viewer without making any changes to your system, there are ways to open images other than double-clicking. For instance, you can drag-drop an image file onto the window of any viewer to open it, or even right-click an image file and select **Open With** to choose another program.

To choose a different application as the default for photos, you may have to disable the Windows Photo Gallery:

1. Open the Registry Editor (described in Chapter 3).
2. Expand the branches to `HKEY_CLASSES_ROOT\SystemFileAssociations\.ico\ShellEx\ContextMenuHandlers\ShellImagePreview`.

3. Highlight the `ShellImagePreview` key, select **File → Export**, type a filename, and click **Save** to back up this Registry key. (See Chapter 3 for details.)

4. Delete the `ShellImagePreview` key and close the Registry Editor when you're done.

If you don't want to mess around in the Registry, you can also do this with Creative Element Power Tools (*http://www.creativelement.com/powertools/*):

1. Open the Creative Element Power Tools Control Panel, turn on the **Edit file type associations** option, click **Accept**, and then close the Control Panel.

2. Right-click any image file and select **Edit File Type**.

3. On the right side, right-click **Windows Photo Gallery Viewer Image Verbs**, and select **Open Registry Editor** here.

4. In the Registry Editor, select **File → Export**, type a filename, and then click **Save** to back up this Registry key. Close the Registry Editor to return to File Type Doctor.

5. With **Windows Photo Gallery Viewer Image Verbs** still highlighted, click the **Remove** button.

To re-enable the Windows Photo Gallery at any time, just double-click the Registry patch you created.

 Microsoft in its infinite wisdom created a new image file format to be released along with Windows Vista, called HD Photo. (I think that makes about 60 formats we now get to deal with.) Unfortunately, very few applications support this format, so if you need to routinely view these files (with the *.hdp* filename extension), you may want to keep Windows Photo Gallery intact for this purpose. Of course, you could always manually edit the *.hdp* file type and add the `ShellImagePreview` key to its `ContextMenuHandlers` key, allowing you to freely disable Windows Photo Gallery for all other formats. See Chapter 3 for details on the structure of file types.

Get Accurate Color Output

Ever notice that the colors in digital photos you view on your PC don't quite match the real thing, or even the colors on the little screen on the back of your digital camera? Or, have you noticed that the colors your printer reproduces don't match those on your monitor?

This is a common problem, and one, unfortunately, without a clear-cut, foolproof solution. The problem is that your monitor, printer, scanner, and digital camera all handle color a little differently. It's up to you to calibrate Windows so that all of these devices know what subtle adjustments they need to make to preserve your colors without botching your photos too badly.

 Before you do anything, make sure your display adapter (video card) is set to the highest color depth it supports. Right-click an empty portion of the desktop, select **Personalize**, and then click **Display Settings**. From the **Colors** drop-down list, select **Highest (32 bit)**. If the **Resolution** slider to the left drops when you do this, see Chapter 5.

First, you'll need to gamma-correct your monitor, which helps ensure that its brightness and color balance are optimized for your setup. Many higher-end monitors have gamma adjustment features, but barring that, you can use the free QuickGamma utility (Figure 4-16), available at *http://quickgamma.de/indexen.html*. (A similar utility also comes with Adobe Photoshop, although the author of QuickGamma claims that it's more accurate.) The process essentially involves adjusting a few controls until two different grayish regions appear indistinguishable when you squint. If you're a perfectionist, you should elect to adjust red, green, and blue values independently.

Next, open Control Panel and then Color Management. Each imaging device on your system should be accompanied by a matching International Color Consortium (ICC) profile, and the Color Management window, shown in Figure 4-17, is where you manage these files.

Start with your monitor; select it from the **Device** list, and then click **Add**. If you're lucky, you'll see a matching profile in the list (having been installed with your driver); otherwise, you'll have to dig up the correct ICC profile from the manufacturer of your monitor and then install it by clicking the **Browse** button here.

 If you have trouble finding ICC profiles from the manufacturers of your monitor, scanner, printer, or camera, try a site like Chromix (*http://www.chromix.com*) or IPhotoICC (*http://www.littlecms.com/iphoto/profiles.htm*). Of course, you can also search Google for your specific product and model, like this: Epson 1520 ICC.

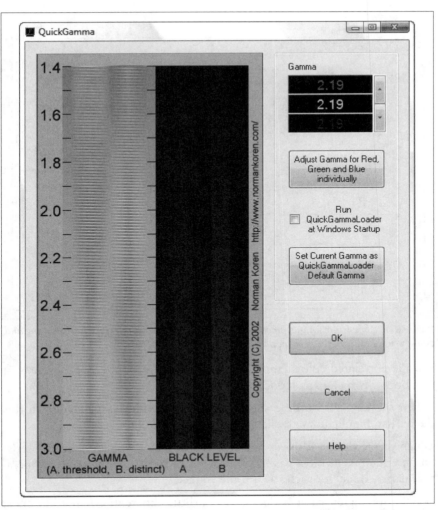

Figure 4-16. Use QuickGamma to adjust your monitor so colors are displayed more accurately

In some cases, you may find more than one ICC profile for your device, each differentiated with a numeric code like D93 or 6500K. These numbers indicate the *color temperature*, a number that describes the color of light emitted by the light source, specifically a theoretical object called a *blackbody radiator*. (In the real world, the closest analog is the sun.) The K numbers indicate temperatures in degrees Kelvin (e.g., 5000K, 6500K, 9300K) while the D numbers indicate standard illuminants (colors of light) corresponding to

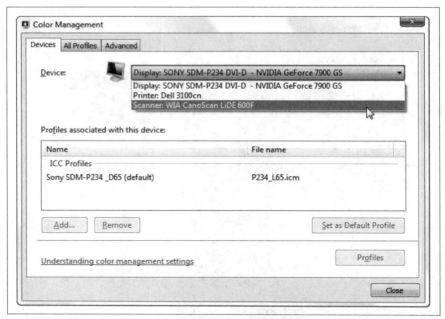

Figure 4-17. The Color Management window is a new, central interface for installing and configuring ICC profiles in Windows Vista

specific correlated color temperatures (CCT). If in doubt, choose 5000K or D50, both of which correspond to "soft daylight."

When the new ICC profile shows up in the **Profiles associated with this device list**, highlight it and click **Set as Default Profile**.

When you're done with your monitor, repeat the process for your printer(s) and scanner(s). In most cases, you'll want to use the same color temperature (D or K value) for each ICC profile you use.

Now, your digital camera does things a little differently. If it's like most cameras, it should store the appropriate ICC information in the EXIF data (discussed in the next section) embedded into each photo file you shoot. And most high-end applications, such as modern versions of Adobe Photoshop, should be capable of reading these tags and putting them to use. But in the unlikely event that your camera is included in the **Device** list, and you have an ICC profile provided by your camera's manufacturer, then you can go ahead and install it just like the others.

Now, playing with gamma correction and color profiles will only take you so far. Variations in ink or toner, as well as paper, can all affect color reproduction on a printer, and the lighting in your room can affect how color looks on your monitor, so you'll have to employ a little trial and error to get the desired results. Professionals use more sophisticated tools, such as colorimeters, to get better color matching, not to mention higher-quality monitors, printers, and scanners. So, don't be surprised if you don't get perfect color every time.

Sort Photos Chronologically

Let me guess. You just had this big party (say, a wedding or commitment ceremony), and you've gotten hundreds of photos from a dozen different people. But when you stick them all in the same folder and sort them by date, they're all out of order.

The **Date Modified** column in Windows Explorer (go to **View → Details** if you don't see it) probably won't reliably sort your photos. If the photographer did any post-processing (e.g., color correction, cropping, retouching) in a program like Photoshop, the file's date will reflect the last time the file was saved, not when the photo was originally shot. Also, file dates and times are typically set when a digital camera saves photos to its memory card, not necessarily when the photos are taken. (The discrepancy occurs because many high-end cameras hold the shots in memory before saving them.)

But aren't you lucky you live in an enlightened age of obsessive photographers and feature-laden gadgets? Embedded in each digital photo is a goldmine of information stored by the camera as part of the EXIF (EXchangeable Image File) format used in *.jpg* files, *.tif* files, and raw formats like Nikon's *.nef* files. EXIF data includes the date and time the photo was taken, the camera settings used (f-stop, exposure, metering mode), the photographer's name (sometimes), and the dimensions of the image. If the camera supports it, even GPS data indicating the exact geographical location of the camera when the photo was shot can be included.

To view EXIF data for a single photo, highlight the image file in Windows Explorer, and then stretch the **Details** pane until it looks like Figure 4-18. If you don't see a **Details** pane, click the **Organize** drop-down and select **Layout → Details Pane**.

Figure 4-18. Windows Explorer shows all the EXIF information embedded in your digital photos, if you know where to look

Of course, you won't find EXIF data in scans of film, nor in digital photos that were modified by software that doesn't support the format. For the record, recent versions of Adobe Photoshop and Paint Shop Pro, and even Vista's measly little Paint program, retain all EXIF data in most circumstances, but many older programs and image converters do not. If in doubt, run a little test before you modify any precious photos: open a photo in your program and save it to a new filename. If the information shows up in Windows Explorer when you highlight the new file, then your software is safe to use.

If you select more than one file, Explorer will only show the data the selected files have in common in the **Details** pane. To view selective EXIF data for a bunch of photos at once, right-click the column header bar in Windows Explorer and select **More**. Place a checkmark next to any new details you'd like to display, and click **OK**. Unfortunately, the details aren't organized at all here; the EXIF data is mixed in with MP3 tags, and other things like **Search ranking** and **Parental rating reason**. But with a little digging, you should be able to find the relevant bits, like **Dimensions**, **Camera model**, and, thankfully, **Date Picture Taken**.

Now, sort the photos chronologically by clicking the **Date Picture Taken** column header. Voilà!

But what if you want to make this sorting more permanent? Use the free Stamp utility (*http://www.snapfiles.com/get/stamp.html*) to rename your files with their EXIF dates. After you do this, your photos will appear in chronological order even when sorted *alphabetically*.

What Stamp doesn't do, unfortunately, is allow you to compensate for the differences among the various cameras' internal clocks. The discrepancies might be as small as three or four minutes among your local guests, or several hours for the party guest who last set up his or her camera in a different time zone. As a result, your photos won't sort properly even *after* you use Stamp, a problem requiring the following three-part fix:

1. First, download the free trial of Creative Element Power Tools (available at *http://www.creativelement.com/powertools/*), and turn on the **Change file dates** and **Rename files with ease** options.

2. Highlight all the photos you want to fix, right-click, and select **Change Date**.

3. Choose the **Date/Time from file metadata** option, select **Date & time photo taken by digital camera** from the list, and then click **Accept**. This will change all the file dates so they exactly match the dates and times the photos were taken.

4. Next, you'll need to determine the discrepancies among your photographers. Pick one photographer to use as the baseline, and then figure out how far off every other photographer is from that baseline. To do this, you'll need to find common points of reference: one or two representative photos of the same instant by each of your photographers. (The more photos you have, the easier this will be.) After a minute or so of studying, you might find that, say, Kathryn's camera was about 3 hours faster than the baseline, while Henry's camera was 6 minutes, 11 seconds slower. (If you're not as compulsive as I am, you don't necessarily need to get it down to the exact second.)

5. To fix the dates, pick a photographer (other than the baseline you chose in step 4), and highlight all of that person's photos. Right-click the files and select **Change Date**.

6. This time, choose the **Relative Date/Time** option and then make your adjustments with the controls below, like the example in Figure 4-19. Click **Accept** when you're done.

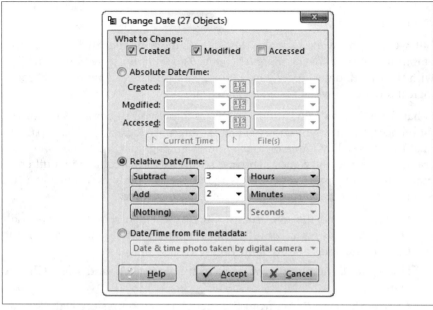

Figure 4-19. Use the Change Date tool to fix discrepancies among the times of different photographers' digital photos

7. Repeat steps 5 and 6 for everyone else's photos. When you're done, the photos should be in perfect order when sorted by **Modified Date** (but not **Date Taken**, at least not yet).

8. To update the EXIF data with your new dates, use AttributeMagic Pro (*http://www.attributemagic.com/*). Select the recently modified files in the main window, use the **Change Dates** feature, and instruct it to set **"date taken" (exif)** to **"modified" (file system)**.

If you don't feel comfortable messing with your photos' valuable EXIF tags, you can alternatively change only the *filenames*, as described next.

At this point, all your photos should appear in chronological order when sorted by modified date *or* date taken, but depending on what you plan to do with your pictures, this may not be enough.

Are you uploading your photos to an online photo sharing/printing service? Or perhaps you're handing them off to someone else to sift through and possibly modify them? If you want to make sure your careful date manipulations remain intact, you may want to tag your filenames as well.

You can do this with Stamp, as described earlier, but only if you've updated the EXIF dates as described in step 8, previously. But if you want to rename your photos *without* changing any EXIF data, you'll need Power Rename (also part of Creative Element Power Tools) to tag the filenames with their *modified dates*. To do this, highlight all the photos, right-click, and select **Power Rename**.

 If you've already renamed the photos with Stamp, place a checkmark next to Power Rename's **Crop** option, select **from beginning**, and type a number representing the amount of text to remove. This will get rid of Stamp's addition to the filename and make room for Power Rename's own **Add stamp** feature.

In Power Rename, place a checkmark next to the **Add stamp** option, select **file date & time**, and then click the **Format** button. From the **Choose a format** list, select **Custom format** and then use the date/time placeholders from the list to assemble a date format conducive to sorting. Your best bet is to start with the year (yy or yyyy), followed by the month, day, hour, minute, and finally, the second, like this:

```
yyyy-mm-dd_hh-mm-ss
```

For example, Power Rename would take a file with the date *August 28, 2005 at 4:53:06 pm* and add this to the beginning of the filename:

```
2005-08-28_16-53-06
```

Click **OK** and then the **Accept** button to rename the files. With all your photos date- and time-corrected and renamed accordingly, they'll appear in chronological order in almost any circumstance.

Media Center Annoyances

If you have the Home Premium or Ultimate edition of Windows Vista, then you also have the Windows Media Center component, which allows you to use your PC and some sort of TV tuner card as a DVR (Digital Video Recorder). Commonly known as a TiVo™ (just as a *novelty flying disc* is commonly known as a Frisbee™), a DVR lets you pause, rewind, and record live television broadcasts.

Of course, you don't have to stick with Media Center. If you don't like the program, if it crashes too often, or if you have only the Home Basic, Business, or Enterprise edition of Vista, you can try any of several alternatives.

Free DVR software includes GB-PVR (*http://www.gbpvr.com*) and MediaPortal (*http://mediaportal.sourceforge.net*). Commercial products, while not necessarily better than their free counterparts, include Meedio (*http://www. meedio.com*), SnapStream BeyondTV (*http://www.snapstream.com*), and SageTV (*http://www.sage.tv*).

Each product has its advantages and disadvantages. When choosing a media center application, the most important consideration is an on-screen interface you like. Aside from that, it should support HD programming and DVD burning, work with a wide variety of remote controls, accept plug-ins or extensions that add functionality (such as news readers and weather forecasters), and not crash.

Watch TV on Your TV

Unless you like watching TV on a 16-inch screen while sitting at your desk, you probably want to hook up your Media Center PC to a real television set. Unfortunately, this is not always as easy as it sounds.

When you connect a TV to your computer (or is it the other way around?), you should see your entire desktop, Start menu, et al., on the big screen. If you see nothing at all, your video card's TV port may be disabled. If you're using a laptop, you may have to press a special keystroke combination to "activate" the TV-out and external VGA ports. On some Dell laptops, for instance, hold the **Fn** key while pressing **F8** to switch between the internal display, the external display, and both; consult your computer's documentation for details. Press these keys repeatedly until you see a picture.

 If you see everything *except* the video rectangle on the big screen, then you have a video overlay problem. See "Fix Other Playback Problems," earlier in this chapter, for details.

Next, make sure you're using the right kind of cable, and with cabling, there's certainly no shortage of possibilities.

The first rule of mating a PC to a TV is to keep it all digital, if you can. If your PC has a DVI port (standard on all new desktop PCs and upscale laptops) and you have a high-definition television set, you can do precisely that.

If your computer doesn't have a DVI port, you'll need to replace your video card with one that does. If you're using a laptop, you'll need a DVI-equipped video card for your ExpressCard slot (or PC Card, if it's an older model), and these can be *very* spendy.

Now, any modern HD television set will either have a DVI or HDMI plug (tired of acronyms yet?). If it's DVI, then it's a simple matter of connecting your PC to your TV with an ordinary DVI monitor cable. HDMI, luckily, is basically the same thing as DVI, albeit with audio, and you can get HDMI-to-DVI adapters readily from small, mom-and-pop computer stores or on eBay.

 As you're setting up your nifty, all-digital home theater PC system, you may hit a roadblock in the form of HDCP (High-bandwith Digital Content Protection). HDCP is a nasty form of copy protection imposed upon high-definition content, such as that from an HD DVD or Blu-Ray drive, or HD cable signal. (For those interested, there's a rant about this in the preface.) An in-depth discussion of HDCP is beyond the scope of this book, but suffice it to say, it may be the reason you're getting a black screen instead of the movie you're trying to play.

If your TV has no digital video inputs—or if they're already being used—your next-best option is to use a DVI-to-composite adapter (also available on eBay). Although your TV's composite inputs are analog (not digital), they do support 16:9 wide format and progressive-scan video, which will still look a lot better than S-Video or (gasp) RCA connectors.

 Many HDTVs have only a single digital (HDMI or DVI) input, which may already be occupied (if you're lucky) by a DVD player with a digital output. If you don't want to settle for an analog connection between your PC and TV, you'll need a HDMI or DVI switch, the best examples of which can be found in some high-end digital home theater receivers.

If your TV is not high-def, or if for whatever reason digital just isn't going to work, then you've got to go analog.

If your PC has a TV-out port, it might accept a standard S-Video plug, or barring that, an ordinary RCA plug. (If it has a proprietary connector, you may need a special adapter from your PC manufacturer—at extra cost, of course.)

If your computer lacks a dedicated TV-out port, see whether your TV has a 15-pin analog VGA port, in which case you can simply use a VGA-to-VGA cable and connect your TV like a monitor. Otherwise, your PC may support TV-out directly through its VGA port (an admittedly uncommon feature), in which case you can get a VGA-to-RCA or VGA-to-S-Video adapter pretty cheaply on eBay.

So, to sum up, here are the connection methods you can try, in order from best to worst.

Computer side	Television side	Signal	16:9 supported?
DVI	DVI or HDMI	Digital	Yes
DVI	composite	Analog	Yes
VGA or DVI-to-VGA	VGA	Analog	Maybe
S-Video	S-Video	Analog	No
RCA	RCA	Analog	No

Once you've got the cabling in order, the next step is to set the resolution on your PC to optimize the picture quality. Set it too low, and it'll look pixelated; set it too high, and you might have overscanning problems (where the video runs off the screen). If in doubt, try a few standard resolutions until you have one that looks good; 1024×768 usually works pretty well. If you still have trouble, use PowerStrip (*http://entechtaiwan.net/util/ps.shtm*) to find the optimal resolution and timing settings for your TV.

Fix Broken TV Listings

A DVR without up-to-date TV listings is nothing more than a playback device; to record your favorite programs, your PC needs to download program data at least once a day. Windows Media Center and other DVR applications do this automatically, but only after you've set them up properly. If you're not getting updated listings, or if your listings are wrong, here are some things you can do to fix the problem.

First, make sure your PC's clock is set correctly: open **Control Panel → Date and Time**, and set the clock if needed. Click **Apply** and then choose the **Internet Time** tab, click **Change settings**, and make sure the **Synchronize with an Internet time server** option is turned on.

Next, your zip code in Media Center might be wrong, thus the program data you're receiving is intended for a different region. Or you may be using an antenna, yet downloading programming data intended for cable or satellite broadcasts. In Media Center, choose **Settings → General → Media Center Setup → Set Up TV Signal**, and follow the prompts. When asked whether you'd like to configure your TV signal automatically, select the **I will manually configure my TV signal** option. On the next page, choose whether your signal comes from cable, satellite, or antenna (terrestrial broadcast), after which you'll be prompted to set up your TV Program Guide. When prompted, type your zip code, and then click **Next** to confirm your choices and download the programming data for your area.

Capture HDTV Programming

So, you've managed to cobble together a pure digital video signal from your PC to your high-definition television, but your broadcast programming still looks like a 20-year-old VHS recording.

Most TV tuners can only receive standard-definition signals. If you want high-def programming, you'll need a few things, starting with a true HDTV tuner card.

In North America, you'll need an ATSC tuner; in Japan, the standard is ARIB, and in Europe, it's DVB. These HD tuner cards will receive terrestrial (over the air) broadcasts, but not necessarily cable or satellite broadcasts. For that, you'll likely need an HD tuner with a cable card slot or a QAM tuner; contact your cable/satellite provider for details.

While the tuner is the most important component, there are other pieces of the HD puzzle. For instance, HD broadcasts use a lot more data, which means you'll need a fast processor (at least 2.4 Ghz or equivalent) for simultaneous capture and playback, required for basic timeshifting of HD programming. And you'll need a larger hard disk, too; while an hour of standard definition (SD) programming typically consumes 1 GB of disk space, that same hour of HD programming will eat up about 10 times as much space. Thus that shiny new 300 GB hard disk will only get you about 25–30 hours of HD storage.

Finally, don't expect just any video card to be capable of displaying high-definition, full-motion video on a high-resolution display. If your HD video plays smoothly in a video, but is jerky when shown full-screen, it's time for a display adapter upgrade.

Of course, it's possible that all your settings are correct, but you're still getting bad data. In this case, you'll need to determine the severity of the problem. If only a single program or a single channel is off, it could be a temporary glitch or last-minute programming change. Try manually downloading the latest programming data to iron out any such discrepancies. From the main Media Center menu, choose **Settings → TV → Guide → Get Latest Guide Listings**.

But if all your program data is off, you'll have to be a bit sneaky about it. The simplest solution is to spoof a different location by entering an adjacent zip code to your own; you may have to try a few different codes to find the one that delivers the data you need. If all else fails, try different DVR software (listed at the beginning of this section), which may get its data from a different source.

CD and DVD Drives

The first CD burner I ever saw was the size of a small microwave oven. It took 68 minutes to fill a 68-minute CD, and it produced more coasters than Six Flags. Suffice it to say, things have improved, although after a few minutes of trying to burn a disc in Vista, you'd be hard pressed to tell.

I'll just come out and say it: the CD/DVD burning feature built into Windows Vista just doesn't work. Sure, I'll get some bafflingly defensive emails from a handful of readers, but if you can show me a CD-R with readable data created by Windows Vista, I'll eat my hat.

In theory, it goes like this:

1. Open Windows Explorer.
2. Place a blank disc in your burner, and close the drawer.
3. Highlight your CD/DVD drive in the tree, and the Burn a Disc window appears. Click **Show formatting options** to show the expanded window in Figure 4-20.

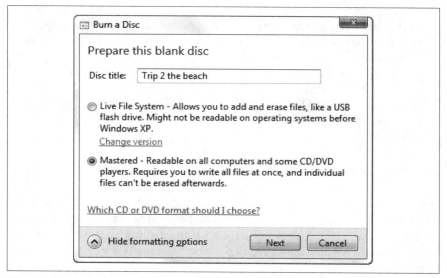

Figure 4-20. Open this window each and every time you make a CD in Vista, or the disc you make may not be readable

4. Select the **Mastered** option and click **Next** to make the Burn a Disc window go away.

 Unless you're absolutely certain you're only going to be using this disc on Vista PCs, don't ever use the **Live File System**. Despite Microsoft's overly optimistic language here, discs formatted with the "Live" filesystem (also known as UDF) won't be readable on older PCs, Macs, or just about anything else. And if you skip steps 3 and 4 here, and instead just start dragging files onto your disc, Windows will use the Live File System without asking. (Naturally, there's no way to change the default.)

5. Drag some files or folders onto your CD/DVD drive.

6. When you're done dragging files, click the **Burn to disc** button (or right-click the CD/DVD drive and select **Burn to disc**), and then follow the prompts.

At this point, Windows Explorer will crash. Or, maybe you'll get lucky, and nothing at all will happen (no CD, no messages, nothing).

If this is happening to you, do yourself a favor and skip the part where you try to diagnose the problem. Instead, just use any other CD/DVD burning software to make your discs, and you'll never look back:

• You can burn ordinary data CDs and data DVDs with Express Burn, available for free from *http://www.nch.com.au/*. If you want more pizzazz, try a commercial solution, such as Roxio Easy Media Creator (*http://www.roxio.com/*), Ashampoo Burning Studio (*http://www.ashampoo.com/*), or Nero (*http://www.nero.com/*).

• You can make audio CDs right in Windows Media Player, as well as Apple iTunes, by creating a custom playlist, and then burning the playlist to a disc.

• You can make DVD movies from your TV recordings from within Windows Media Center.

• To burn discs from ISO image files, as well as create ISO files *from* discs, use ISO Recorder (free; *http://isorecorder.alexfeinman.com*).

With the proper disc burning software, now all that can go wrong is everything else.

Troubleshoot CD and DVD Playback Problems

Not getting the quality and reliability you expect from your audio CDs and video DVDs? Here are some common problems and possible solutions:

Poor audio CD quality

If you hear pops, squeaks, or clicks in your audio CDs, check your source music files to make sure they sound OK. If the tracks are originally from a CD, re-rip any songs that have pops, squeaks, or any quality problems.

Another cause of poor sound quality on audio CDs is a mismatch between the rated speed of your discs and the actual speed at which you burned your music. If you're using 4X-rated CDs in an 24X burner, or vice-versa, you could have problems. Again, higher-quality media is less likely to suffer from this problem, but if all else fails, get slower CDs or a faster burner.

Volume inconsistencies

If your audio CD plays, but the songs all seem to be different volumes, there's not necessarily anything wrong. This is merely a fact of life when you mix audio files from different sources; some songs will naturally be louder than others. The best solution is to use the volume-leveling feature in your media player software.

In Windows Media Player, press the **Alt** key, select **Tools** → **Options**, choose the **Burn** tab, and turn on the **Apply volume leveling across tracks on the CD** option. Or, in iTunes, select **Edit** → **Preferences**, choose the **Advanced** tab and then the **Burning** subtab, and turn on the **Use Sound Check** option.

Smudged DVD subtitles

Illegible subtitles on video DVDs (even store-bought discs) are usually caused by a video resolution that is set too low. If your display is set to 640×480 or 800×600, raise the display resolution to at least 1024×768.

Disc won't play in standalone player

Low-quality discs commonly cause playback problems in standalone CD and DVD players. If the disc won't play, or if the audio quality is bad, try a different brand of disc. Avoid the el-cheapo blank discs in the bargain bin at your local computer store, and instead spend the extra nickel on some brand-name discs (I've found Verbatim discs to be consistently reliable).

Another problem that affects standalone DVD players is that of incompatible disc formats. Some older players can't read movies burned to DVD+R/RW or DVD-R/RW discs, so you may need to buy a new player, or settle for movies played through your PC. (The format that seems to be the most widely supported is DVD+R, although your mileage may vary.)

PC can't read disc

Does Windows Explorer hang when you try to copy files off an old disc? The most common cause of this is simply dust. Try gently wiping the disc with a clean, soft, dry cloth, or barring that, your shirt. (Wipe in a straight line, from the center of the disc out to the edge; don't rub in a circular motion.)

Files missing on a data disc

Can't see all the files you burned to a disc, particularly if you've burned the disc more than once? You may've deleted the old files when you added the latest batch of files. The good news is that—unless you erased a rewritable disc—the "deleted" files are still there, only hidden. To retrieve them, you'll need an application that can create a disk image from a single track, such as ISO Recorder (free, *http://isorecorder. alexfeinman.com*). Once you've created the disc image file, you can either burn it to another disc (by itself), or you can open it with Iso-Buster (*http://www.isobuster.com*) and extract the files by dragging and dropping.

The other possibility is that you're reading the disc with an old CD drive that doesn't support multisession CDs. (Each time you burn files to a disc, you're creating another "session," or track, on that disc.) In this case, there's little you can do to make the earlier sessions readable, short of replacing the drive. Luckily, brand-new CD/DVD readers are cheap and plentiful!

Windows Media Player complains about insufficient space

Assuming your arithmetic skills are up to par, and the total length of all the tracks you're trying to burn to an audio CD doesn't exceed the capacity of the disc, it's possible that it's a hardware problem. If you have more than one CD or DVD drive connected to the same IDE controller, they can fight for system resources. To fix the problem, make sure that your burner is the only CD or DVD writer on the chain; if one drive is connected to the primary IDE controller, make sure the other one is plugged into the *secondary* controller, and that neither is in conflict with another device (such as the hard disk, usually occupying the primary master slot).

None of your discs are readable anywhere

Visit your CD/DVD burner manufacturer's web site and see whether there's a firmware update. Sometimes, a firmware bug will prevent otherwise good discs, written with a good burner, from playing on a perfectly good player. And that's not good.

CHAPTER 5
Performance

Windows Vista is by no means "fast." Running on a high-end PC, at least by the standards of the time of the product's release, Vista seems sluggish and overburdened by its own weight.

This is nothing new. While the above statement may sound like an indictment of Vista, Windows 95 was much worse 12 years earlier on the hardware of *its* time. But put 95 on a PC of today, and it will fly.

Of course, Vista does more with its hardware, right? Well, there's the Glass interface, covered later, which certainly sucks up a lot of processor cycles. And sure, it takes longer to copy or move files than, say, XP, but as explained in Chapter 2, Vista is doing more in the background, which is why you now get a single window warning you of 27 upcoming conflicts rather than 27 individual warnings. And there's the indexing service, also discussed in Chapter 2, which keeps your hard disk busy much of the time. These are all nice toys to have, but how vital are they? Are they more important than a snappy, responsive computer, particularly after you've just laid down a thousand bucks for new hardware?

Perhaps a better question: if you get a new PC with hardware that's twice as fast as your old machine, yet put Vista on it and end up with one that feels *slower* than Windows XP did on the old hardware, is that progress?

Your PC truly spends most of its time—something like 99.9%—waiting for you to do something. That leaves only 0.1% of the time when you really don't want Windows to be doing *anything* other than fulfilling your request. But it's precisely the moment you start a program, move a window across the screen, or apply a filter in Photoshop, that you want your PC to perform; and of course, it's at this moment when Windows has the most work to do.

This is why your PC is full of caching technologies, such as Vista's search indexing service. While your PC is idle, Windows uses that latent power to read through all the documents on your hard disk, making the Windows Explorer's Search feature much more responsive at the moment you actually need a response. Of course, this means that search results are sometimes out of date, but that's the price you pay for speed.

So, it usually comes down to finding a balance; do you want snappy windows or do you want the Glass interface? Do you want quick file searches, or would you rather Windows use that time to defragment your hard disk? Do you want Windows to start up and shut down quickly, or do you want to save power at night by shutting it down completely?

That's what this chapter—and the whole book, really—is about: overcoming the "try to please everybody" approach Microsoft took when it designed Vista, by turning off the stuff you don't need and customizing the stuff you do.

Trim the Fat

Surprise: Windows Vista is not configured for optimal performance right out of the box. Rather, it was built to showcase all the features Microsoft included with the product to help sell it.

Fortunately, there are a bunch of things you can do right now to speed things up without spending a dime.

Tame Mindless Animation and Display Effects

Windows Vista animates almost every visual component that makes up its sparkling new interface. While these affectations may be cute, they create two performance problems. For one, they slow down the motion, causing windows, menus, and listboxes to take longer to open and close, all of which makes your PC feel sluggish. Second, they consume CPU cycles that would otherwise be used to handle processor-intensive tasks like virtual memory and gameplay.

There are settings that affect performance scattered throughout Windows, but the ones that control display effects are the easiest to change, and go the furthest to make Vista feel faster and more responsive.

In Control Panel, open System, and click the **Advanced system settings** link on the left side (or run *SystemPropertiesAdvanced.exe*). In the **Performance** section, click **Settings**. The **Visual Effects** tab, shown in Figure 5-1, contains 20 settings, all explained later.

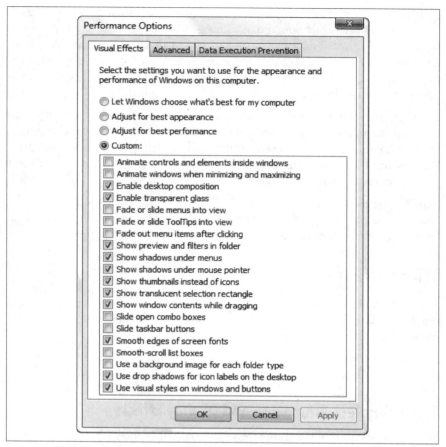

Figure 5-1. The Performance Options window is a good place to start looking for fat to trim

Unfortunately, the four selections above the list are a bit misleading. For example, the **Let Windows choose what's best for my computer** option reverts all settings to the defaults chosen by a marketing committee at Microsoft to best showcase Vista's features. The **Adjust for best appearance** option simply enables all features in the list, while the **Adjust for best performance** option just disables them.

Now, depending on the prowess of your video hardware, some of these settings may make more of a difference than others. And of course, some options may not be present in your edition of Vista.

Animate controls and elements inside windows. Turn this off to nix the slow-fade effect on buttons and tabs in dialog boxes, the cyclic pulsating effect on the default button, and the fading scrollbar arrows. Buttons will still glow blue as you roll over them with the mouse, but they'll do it sans the delay.

Animate windows when minimizing and maximizing. This controls the squeezing and stretching that happens to windows when you minimize, restore, and maximize them. Leave it on to see where a window went when you minimize it, or turn it off to minimize windows without the wait.

 This option also affects the disappearing/reappearing taskbar if you have both the **Auto-hide the taskbar** setting in Taskbar and Start Menu Properties and the **Show window contents while dragging** option (described later) enabled.

Enable desktop composition. This vaguely named option is probably the biggest performance drain you can adjust here, but it's required if you want the glass effect (described next). *Desktop composition* is the behind-the-scenes scheme—run by the Desktop Window Manager (DWM)—that keeps a snapshot of each open window in memory. Turn it off, and Vista draws each window directly to the screen just like XP and earlier versions did. Without it, you can't have the Glass interface or the thumbnail previews on the taskbar and the Alt-Tab window, but the Windows interface will feel snappier and more responsive.

Enable transparent glass. One of the few self-explanatory options here, this option is covered in "Get Glass," later in this chapter.

Fade or slide menus/ToolTips into view. Turn this off to have menus and tool tips "snap" open.

 By default, there's a short delay between the instant you click a menu and the moment the menu actually opens; see "Make Menus More Mindful," later in this chapter, to adjust this.

Show shadows under menus/mouse pointer. This feature has a negligible effect on the performance of most Vista-class PCs, particularly those with fast video cards.

Show thumbnails instead of icons. It takes a lot of processor power to open all the media files in a folder and generate thumbnail images, so this option can potentially have a big effect on your PC's performance (at least while you're using Windows Explorer). Among other things, thumbnail generation is usually responsible for the slowly moving green progress bar in Windows Explorer's address bar, so you should definitely turn this off if you don't care about thumbnails for your images, videos, and PDF files.

 If an installer window appears briefly or if Windows Explorer crashes each time you view a folder full of video files, it means that one of your video codecs is damaged. Turn off the **Show thumbnails instead of icons** option to bypass the problem, or see "Playing Video," in Chapter 4, to fix it.

Show translucent selection rectangle. The translucent selection rectangle—referred to as a "rubber band" in Chapter 2—is what you see when you drag the mouse and make a box to select multiple files in Windows Explorer and on your desktop. It should have no discernable effect on performance, but since it uses alpha channels (an advanced function provided by your display driver), you may want to turn this off if you have any problems using the feature on your PC.

Show window contents while dragging. Turn off this option to show only window outlines when moving and resizing windows; consider it a throwback to the early days of Windows. You probably won't notice much of a performance hit with this feature turned on, unless you're using the Glass interface on a PC with a weak graphics engine (display card). In fact, Vista may seem *more* responsive with this feature enabled, as windows will appear to respond immediately to dragging, as opposed to sitting still until you let go of the mouse button.

Slide open combo boxes. This option controls the animation of drop-down listboxes, similar to the **Fade or slide menus** option described earlier.

Slide taskbar buttons. When you close a window, its button disappears from the taskbar, and the adjacent buttons on the right slide to the left to close the gap. Since this animation doesn't cause any delays, you're unlikely to achieve any performance gains by disabling it. However, I find the taskbar animation rather annoying, and personally prefer to have this one turned off.

Smooth edges of screen fonts. Using a process called anti-aliasing, Windows fills in the jagged edges of larger text on the screen with gray pixels, making the edges appear smooth. Turn off this option to slightly improve the speed at which larger fonts are drawn on the screen, although the speed difference shouldn't be noticeable on faster PCs.

 If you're using a flat-panel display (laptop or otherwise), you may find text slightly more difficult to read if font smoothing is turned on. But before you simply turn it off, try the alternate anti-aliasing method. In Control Panel, open the Personalization page, click **Window Color and Appearance**, and then click **Open classic appearance properties for more color options**. Click **Effects** and then choose between the **Standard** and **Clear Type** smoothing methods; experiment with this setting to see which one looks best on your display.

Smooth-scroll list boxes. Despite the fact that they don't open or close, ordinary listboxes are animated, too. If you've ever noticed a listbox that scrolls slowly, this option is the reason; turn it off to make listboxes scroll faster.

 There's a nearly identical option in Internet Explorer that makes web pages scroll more slowly. In IE, click the **Tools** drop-down, select **Internet Options**, and then choose the **Advanced** tab. At the end of the **Browsing** section, turn off the **Use smooth scrolling** option and click **OK**.

Use a background image for each folder type. Get rid of the watermark picture shown behind certain system folders like Control Panel and *Pictures*, and those folders will open a little more quickly (and the text will likely be more readable, to boot). Strangely, this feature doesn't seem to be present in Vista at all, making this option totally pointless, although your experience may differ.

Use drop shadows for icon labels on the desktop. This setting affects more than just the shadows behind icon captions; it makes the text background transparent. If you're using desktop wallpaper (as opposed to a solid color background), and you turn off this option, small swaths of the current solid background color will show through the captions of your desktop icons.

Use visual styles on windows and buttons. Turn off this setting to make Vista's interface look more or less like Windows 98/2000. It's the same as selecting **Windows Classic style** in the **Window Color and Appearance** page in Control Panel.

That's it for this window; click **Apply** to test your changes, and then **OK** when you're done.

Next, if you've noticed that Windows has been slow to update desktop icons, and you have a lot of them, there is a setting that may help. Right-click an empty area of the desktop, select **View**, and then select **Classic Icons**. Your desktop icons will shrink somewhat, returned to the standard 32×32 pixel size used in earlier versions of Windows. When Windows draws larger icons—**Medium Icons**, the default in Vista—it has to stretch most application icons to the new size, and this can take a little time on slower PCs. (Note that the icons included with Vista all come in larger sizes and don't need stretching.)

Fine-tune video settings

If you're interested in tinkering further with display settings that can affect performance, right-click an empty area of your desktop, select **Personalize**, and then click the **Display Settings** link.

 On older PCs, the speed at which a video card can draw to your screen is somewhat dependent on the current color mode and resolution, as described in "Video Cards (Display Adapters)" in Chapter 6. If your games, or Windows itself, for that matter, are running slowly, try reducing the color depth and resolution. Newer high-end video cards will not show any performance hit when run at higher resolutions or color depths.

In the Display Settings window, click **Advanced Settings** and then choose the **Troubleshoot** tab. Here, the **Change settings** button lets you fine-tune some of the performance features of your display driver, all of which vary with the make, model, and driver version. If the **Change settings** button is grayed-out, look for extra tabs in this window; any tab to the right of **Color Management** is a special feature of your display driver, and can be used to change video settings.

Now, most high-end video cards allow you to modify or disable certain 3D features, such as 8-bit palletized textures, gamma adjustment, zbuffer, and bilinear filter. In most cases, these settings won't have any effect on Windows outside 3D games, with the possible exception of the Flip 3D application (**Winkey+Tab**). But look for other features you can turn off, such as custom shortcut menus, special effects for your windows, or a virtual desktop feature, all of which may slow down your PC when enabled.

Make Menus More Mindful

Ever noticed the half-second or so delay between the instant you move the mouse over a menu item and the moment the menu is opened? By default, Vista waits 400 milliseconds (just under a half-second) before opening menus, but if you eliminate the delay, menus will open instantaneously, and your PC will feel a little more alert.

1. Open the Registry Editor (see Chapter 3).

2. Expand the branches to HKEY_CURRENT_USER\Control Panel\Desktop.

3. Double-click the MenuShowDelay value. If it's not there, go to **Edit → New → String Value**, and type MenuShowDelay for the name of the new value.

4. The numeric value you enter here is the number of milliseconds (thousandths of a second) Windows will wait before opening a menu. Enter 0 (zero) here to eliminate the delay completely.

If you ever have trouble holding your mouse perfectly still, you've probably found it frustrating to navigate menus—particularly those in the Start menu—in Windows Vista. Try typing a very large value (65534 is the maximum) here to stop menus from automatically opening altogether, which should make them easier to use.

5. Click **OK** and close the Registry Editor when you're finished. Log off and then log back in or restart Windows for this change to take effect.

Note that another way to navigate touchy menus is to use the keyboard. In any application, press the **Alt** key by itself to jump to the menu bar (or press **Ctrl-Esc** or the Windows logo key to open the Start menu), and then use the arrow keys to navigate.

Start Windows in Less Time

One of the sure signs of a PC that's been used for more than a few weeks is that it takes a lot longer to start up than when it was new. The longer load time isn't fatigue, nor is it a sign that the PC needs a faster processor; it's a casualty of all the junk that Windows accumulates on a day-to-day basis.

One of the best ways to shorten startup times is to not shut down. Rather, if you put your PC to sleep, as described next in "Start Windows Instantly (Almost)," you can power it back up in just a few seconds.

Several factors can impact the amount of time it takes for your computer to load Windows and display the desktop so you can start working, not the least of which is anything left over from the previous version of Windows. If you installed Vista over, say, Windows XP, then you potentially have years of drivers, add-on services, startup programs, and other stuff clogging up your PC. An upgraded PC can take two to four times as long to start as one on which Vista has been installed clean. (See Chapter 1 for other reasons Vista specifically doesn't like inheriting a predecessor's problems.) Unfortunately, wiping your hard disk and reinstalling is a whole lot easier said than done, so here are some other things you can do to reduce Windows' boot time.

Eliminate unnecessary autostart programs

Probably the most common thing that slows down Windows' loading time is all of the programs that are configured to load at boot time. Not only do they take a while to load, but they commonly eat up processor cycles while they're running, which in turn causes other programs to load more slowly.

There's more running on your PC than the handful of icons in the notification area (tray) suggests, and there are several places where startup programs are specified in addition to the *Startup* folder in your Start menu. Check out "Manage Startup Programs," in Chapter 6, for all the places to look.

Make more free disk space

You may not have enough free disk space for your virtual memory (swap file) to operate comfortably. Windows uses part of your hard disk to store portions of memory; the more disk space you devote to your swap file, the easier it will be for Windows to store data there. See "Optimize Virtual Memory and Cache Settings," later in this chapter, for more information.

The easiest way to create more free disk space is to delete the files on your hard disk that you no longer need; see "If in Doubt, Throw It Out," also later in this chapter, for a safe way to do this.

 See also "Optimize Virtual Memory and Cache Settings" and "A Defragmentation Crash Course," both later in this chapter, for other things you can do to speed up your hard drive and help Windows load more quickly.

Lastly, a new hard disk will give you dramatically more disk space, and a *faster* hard disk can improve boot time considerably. If you're on the fence about replacing that older drive, consider the performance boost as well as the sorely needed space.

Clean out your Temp folder

Sometimes having too many files in Windows' *Temp* folder can not only slow Windows startup, but in extreme cases, can prevent Windows from loading at all. Windows and your applications use this folder to temporarily store data while you're working with documents. When those applications and documents are closed (or when the applications just crash), they often leave the temporary files behind, and they accumulate fast.

By default, Vista has two *Temp* folders:

> *C:\Users\{your_user_name}\AppData\Local\Temp*
> *C:\Windows\Temp*

although the first is used almost exclusively by Windows and your applications. To clear out your old temporary files, open Windows Explorer, navigate to the *Temp* folder, and delete anything more than a day old. (Windows won't let you delete any files that are still in use.)

Another way to clear out the *Temp* folder is to use the Disk Cleanup tool (*cleanmgr.exe*); after selecting your Windows drive from the **Drives** list (usually *C:*), select **Temporary files** in the **Files to delete** list, and click **OK**. Or, if you want your *Temp* folder cleaned automatically, use the **Clear out the Temp folder** tool in Creative Element Power Tools (*http://www.creativelement.com/powertools/*).

 You can change the location of your Temp folder, making it easier to locate and clean out by hand. In Control Panel, open System, click the **Advanced system settings** link, and under the **Advanced** tab, click **Environment Variables**. Underneath the *upper* box, click **New**. Type TEMP for the **Variable name**, put the full path of the folder you'd like to use in the **Variable value** field, and click **OK**. Do the same thing for the TMP variable (no "E" this time), and then click **OK** when you're done. Restart Windows for the change to take effect.

Thin out your fonts

If you have more than 600 fonts installed on your system, it may be negatively impacting on the time it takes to load Windows. If you can survive without 400 different decorative fonts (especially if all you ever use is Times Roman), try temporarily removing them.

If you periodically need a lot of fonts, you might want to try font management software that lets you organize your collection and add or remove fonts easily, such as:

- PigFontViewer (free, *http://www.pigfontviewer.com/*)
- Font Agent Pro (commercial, *http://www.insidersoftware.com/*)
- Suitcase Fusion (commercial, *http://www.extensis.com/*)

Tame antivirus software

Antivirus programs (see Chapter 6) are typically set up to not only load automatically whenever you start Windows, but to check for updates, too. For instance, the otherwise excellent (and free) Avast! Home Edition can completely halt a Vista system for 15–20 seconds while it downloads and installs necessary updates.

While you may not want to stop loading your antivirus software automatically, you can delay it by writing a simple startup script (see Chapter 9) that loads the software after waiting, say, 45 seconds. This way, you can start working while your antivirus program loads in the background.

Add more memory

Vista really isn't happy with less than a gigabyte of memory; 2 GB is better.

Memory prices are always dropping, typically making it remarkably inexpensive to add more RAM to your system, and doing so will *significantly* improve performance across the board. See "Make Your Hardware Perform," later in this chapter, for details.

Networking

Windows polls each active *wired* network connection on your system while it boots your system, and then polls your *wireless* adapter (if you have one) for any networks in range. Each of these steps takes time, so if there are any network adapters on your PC you don't use, you can disable them to speed things up. In the Network and Sharing Center in Control Panel, click **Manage network connections**, and then right-click on each network connection you're not using and select **Disable**.

Next, if you have any permanent mapped network drives (see "Access a Shared Folder Remotely" in Chapter 8) you're not using, open Windows Explorer, right-click any unneeded mapped drives, and select **Disconnect**.

Start Windows Instantly (Almost)

You can optimize Vista all you want, possibly shaving 15 or 20 seconds off your boot time (see the previous topic), or you can approach the problem from a different angle.

All modern PCs support a *Standby* mode that allows you to shut down Windows quickly, and more importantly, start it back up in only a few seconds. Standby is a power-saving mode (known as the S3 sleep state) that maintains power to your system memory and a few other components, while cutting power to your hard disk, monitor, network adapters, and most of the rest of the devices in your PC.

While it looks like it's turned off, a PC in Standby mode still uses some electricity. If you remove the battery from your laptop or unplug your desktop PC while it's in Standby mode, the power to your system memory will be cut, and you will likely lose data (just as though you unplugged it while it was still on).

The *Hibernate* mode (the S4 sleep state) solves the power-off problem by storing an image of your RAM on your hard disk and then shutting down *completely*. This means you can cut power to your desktop PC with a separate power strip or remove the battery from your laptop, and still resume your last Windows session in a fraction of the time it would take to start Windows normally. The downside is that Hibernate takes a little longer to shut down and start up than Standby, and you need a lot more free disk space (at least as much as the amount of RAM in your PC). And then there's the small matter of the Hibernate feature being completely absent from Windows Vista.

 There's a drawback to using any of these sleep states exclusively. Namely, Windows gets cranky when it has had too much sleep: performance worsens, some features stop working properly, and applications are more prone to crashes. The remedy is to shut down and restart Windows periodically, at least once or twice a week (more for heavy use), which, of course, somewhat negates the overall time saved by employing sleep features in the first place. Alternatively, you may choose to avoid sleeping your PC altogether; you'll enjoy a more stable environment, but you'll lose the convenience of the "instant on" feature.

The solicitude of Sleep

Instead, Vista provides only a hybrid of Standby and Hibernate (discussed next) which Microsoft calls *Sleep* mode. Basically, Sleep puts your PC in the S3 power-saving mode just like Standby, but only after saving the stuff in your PC's memory to disk—somewhat like Hibernate—so you won't lose data if you cut power to your PC.

So, Sleep is the best of both worlds, right?

Not so fast. First of all, Sleep doesn't work that well with some modern PCs; cut power to your computer, and Windows may lose the saved state from the last session after all, making it no better than Standby. Second, Sleep doesn't completely shut down your computer, which means that it's still using more electricity than it would if it were truly powered off.

If your Windows session doesn't survive a Sleep, you might not have the hybrid sleep feature enabled. Open the Power Options page in Control Panel, click the **Change plan settings** link under the currently selected plan, and then click the **Change advanced power settings** link. If necessary, click the **Change settings that are currently unavailable** link. Expand the **Sleep** branch, set the **Allow hybrid sleep** option to **On**, and click **OK**.

Conversely, if you'd prefer the quickest possible startup and shutdown, and you're willing to give up the benefits of hibernation, set the **Allow hybrid sleep** option to **Off**. This effectively gives Vista a Standby feature; just don't be surprised when Windows can't resume your previous session because your PC lost power while it was asleep.

Hibernate, for real this time

If you're not happy with Vista's Sleep mode, you can instead use the true *Hibernate* feature that's hidden by default in Windows Vista.

Open a Command Prompt window in administrator mode: open the Start menu, type command in the **Search** box, right-click the **Command Prompt** icon that appears, and select **Run as administrator**. Then, type:

```
powercfg /hibernate on
```

at the prompt and press **Enter**. If the command returns you to the prompt with no message, the change was successful, and you can type exit or close the Command Prompt window. The change takes effect right away (see the "What is hiberfil.sys?" sidebar, next, for evidence), but you'll need to close and reopen any Power Options windows (next) to see the new options.

What is hiberfil.sys?

To avoid some of the drawbacks of Vista's Sleep power-saving mode, you can hibernate your PC. As described in "Start Windows Instantly (Almost)," Hibernate saves a copy of everything in your PC's memory (RAM) onto your hard disk before it shuts down.

Windows uses the file *hiberfil.sys*, stored in the root folder of your hard disk, to hold your hibernation data. Because it must hold everything in memory, its size is the same as the amount of installed system memory. Have 2 GB of RAM? You'll see a 2 GB *hiberfil.sys* file on your hard disk that Windows won't let you delete.

Windows creates the *hiberfil.sys* file automatically when you turn on the Hibernate feature; the only way to delete the file is to turn off Hibernate.

To do this, open a Command Prompt window in administrator mode (see "The solicitude of Sleep," earlier in this chapter, for details) and type this command at the prompt:

```
powercfg /hibernate off
```

Then press **Enter**. If the command returns you to the prompt with no message, the change was successful, and *hiberfil.sys* should be gone.

If *hiberfil.sys* is still there, hibernation may've already been turned off, and the file may be left over from an older version of Windows. Another way to delete the file is to use the Disk Cleanup tool (*cleanmgr.exe*); just select the drive containing the file, place a checkmark next to **Hibernation File Cleaner** in the **Files to delete** list, and click OK.

Put your PC to sleep

The key to using Sleep or Hibernate is to set one of them up as the default action to take when your PC would otherwise be shut down.

Now, regardless of your settings, you can choose to sleep your PC—or for that matter, shut down, restart, or log off—at any time by clicking the tiny arrow next to the red button in your Start menu, as shown in Figure 5-2.

But to change your PC's shutdown settings, open the Power Options page in Control Panel, and click the **Change plan settings** link under the currently selected plan. Next, click the **Change advanced power settings** link to open the Advanced Settings window, and then expand the **Power buttons and lid** branch (Figure 5-3). If necessary, click the **Change settings that are currently unavailable** link (see "Control User Account Control," in Chapter 8, to get rid of this last step).

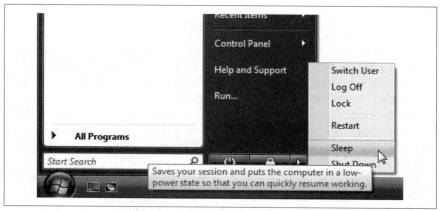

Figure 5-2. Open the Start menu and then click the little arrow to choose how to shut down

Figure 5-3. Power Options' Advanced settings window lets you choose whether your PC goes to sleep or shuts down when you press the power button or close the lid

The options and choices vary depending on your PC's capabilities, but in most cases, you should see at least **Power button action**, which refers to your PC's main power switch, and **Start menu power button**, which refers to the red button next to the **Search** box in your Start menu. You may also see **Sleep button action** if your keyboard or PC has a formal **Sleep** button (which looks like a crescent moon), and **Lid close action** if you're using a laptop.

At most, you'll see four choices under each option: **Do nothing**, **Sleep**, **Hibernate**, and **Shut down**. The **Hibernate** option only appears if hibernation is turned on, as described in the previous section. And if you don't see the **Sleep** option, your BIOS or video driver may not support it.

 By default, the red power button in Vista's Start menu is set to Sleep. While this makes for quick startup and shutdown, it also means that your PC will continue to suck electricity even when it's presumably off. And if your PC isn't fully compatible with Vista's Sleep mode, you may lose data if you cut power to your PC. To prevent this situation, set the **Start menu power button** option to either **Shut down** or **Hibernate**.

Next, scroll up just a bit and expand the **Sleep** branch. Here, you can use the **Sleep after** and **Hibernate after** options to have your PC automatically put itself to sleep after a certain period of inactivity. Think of these settings as a more ecologically friendly—but less entertaining—alternative to the screen saver.

See "Improve Battery Life," later in this chapter, for a way to automatically change your power button and lid settings when you switch between AC and battery power.

Time to wake up

While in Standby, Sleep, or Hibernate mode, your PC waits for you to hit the power button—or optionally press a key or move the mouse—at which point it powers up and resumes your previous Windows session.

All sorts of devices can be used to wake your PC when it's asleep, such as your keyboard, some kinds of mice, network adapters, and modems. But first, you need to turn on a setting in Windows. Open Device Manager, and expand the branch containing the device (e.g., **Keyboards**). Double-click your device, choose the **Power Management** tab, turn on the **Allow this device to wake the computer** option, and click **OK**.

Next, put your PC to sleep and test it out. If you've just enabled wake-up for your keyboard, press the Space bar. Or, if you want to wake up the PC with your mouse, give it a nudge.

If that doesn't do it, you'll need to dive into your BIOS setup screen, discussed in Appendix A. Look for a **Power** or **APM Configuration** category, in which you'll find settings like these:

Power Button Mode. This option lets you choose whether your power switch shuts down your PC or puts it to sleep. Depending on your BIOS, the setting you choose here may or may not be overridden by the similar setting in the Windows Control Panel.

Power On By External Modems. This is also known as "Wake On Ring" (WOR); if you have an internal modem in a PCI or PCIE slot, you can use this feature to call your PC with a telephone to wake it up. (Despite the name, this feature won't work with serial-port or USB modems.)

Power On By PCI/PCIE Devices. Turn on this option to use the "Wake On LAN" (WOL) feature, which lets you send a wake-up signal to your PC from another PC on your local network. Some motherboards also require that you install a jumper or use a specific type of network card, so check your PC's documentation for details.

Power On By PS/2 Keyboard or Mouse. Turn this on if you have an old-style keyboard or mouse that has a round connector. Most PCs should wake up from newer USB keyboards or mice regardless of this setting.

Restore on AC Power Loss. This option lets you decide what happens after you've cut power to your PC. Set this option to **Always On** if you want to turn on your PC with a switch on an external power strip.

As you might've expected, some experimentation may be required at this stage.

When you wake up your PC, Vista may require a password before it resumes your previous session. To turn this off, return to the Advanced Settings window (Figure 5-3), expand the **Additional settings** branch, and set the **Require a password on wakeup** to **No**.

Sleep and Hibernate troubleshooting

For the Standby, Sleep, or Hibernate modes to work properly in Windows Vista, your PC has to cooperate. If it doesn't, you might experience a problem such as:

No sleep. Windows won't go to sleep at all; either nothing happens when you try to stand by, or the system just crashes in the middle of the process.

No wake up. Windows won't wake up after going to sleep, or Windows simply boots normally instead of resuming your previous session.

No more sleep. Windows goes to sleep or hibernates once, but once it wakes up, it won't go back to sleep until you restart it.

Features are unavailable. Some or all of the power management features and settings discussed earlier are grayed-out (disabled) or missing.

Stuff stops working. Some features, like your wireless network, your cordless mouse, or your scanner stop working after waking up, at least until you restart Windows. (Hint: look for new drivers or a firmware update for your device.)

Unfortunately, all of these problems are quite common, mostly because of the inconsistent support for Advanced Configuration and Power Interface (ACPI) in the computer industry. The good news is that there are a few things you can do to help improve your computer's support for APM and ACPI, should you be experiencing any of these problems:

BIOS out of date. Check with the manufacturer of your computer system or motherboard for a BIOS update. Vista requires that your BIOS comply with the ACPI 2.0 specification.

ACPI/APIC not enabled in BIOS. Enter your BIOS setup screen, as described in Appendix A, and make sure the **ACPI APIC support** setting is set to **On** or **Enabled**. If you see a setting referring to **ACPI 2.0** or some later version, try turning it *on* if it's *off*, or vice versa. Reboot your PC when you're done. Depending on how ACPI-compliant your PC is, it may take some trial and error to get Vista to sleep properly.

Hybrid sleep not working. The second most common cause of sleep and hibernation problems, behind an out-of-date BIOS, is a video card (display adapter) driver that doesn't support Vista's *Hybrid Sleep* feature. Check with the manufacturer of your video card for a newer driver, or try turning off Hybrid Sleep, as described in "The solicitude of Sleep," earlier in this section.

Wireless won't connect after waking up. As with the video card, make sure you have the latest driver and firmware for your wireless adapter. Also, try changing the device's power settings: in Device Manager, double-click your wireless network adapter. Choose the **Power Management** tab, and turn off the **Allow the computer to turn off this device to save power** option.

USB devices don't work after waking up. This is a confirmed bug in Windows Vista, one fixed by Microsoft Hotfix #928631, available at *http://support.microsoft.com/kb/928631.*

Out of free disk space. As explained earlier, the Hibernate feature creates an image file on your hard disk equal in size to the amount of installed memory. If you have 2 GB of RAM, then Windows will need 2,147,483,648 bytes of free disk space for the *hiberfil.sys* file. If hibernation doesn't work, or if it's exceedingly slow, try deleting the hibernation file as described in the "What is hiberfil.sys?" sidebar, earlier in this section. Then, defragment your hard disk, and re-enable hibernation.

Trouble recovering from Sleep. Go to *http://www.passmark.com/products/sleeper.htm* and download the free PassMark Sleeper tool to help test your computer's ability to enter and recover from Sleep, Standby, and Hibernate modes.

Keep in mind that you may never get your system to reliably go to sleep and wake up, but if you are able to get this feature working, it can be very convenient.

Shut Down Windows Quickly

Theoretically, when you shut down Windows, your computer should be powered down in less than 15 seconds. The problem is that all of the cleanup Windows tries to do before it considers it "safe" to power the system down can sometimes cause delays. This includes shutting down your open applications, stopping any running services, and writing any pending cache data to the disk.

During the course of using your computer, Windows sometimes postpones writing data to the disk to improve performance. This is called *write caching*, and as a consequence, Windows must take a few seconds before you shut down to make sure all data queued to be written is actually, physically written to the disk before power is lost. See the discussion of removable drives in Chapter 6 for a way to disable this feature.

Of course, the most effective way to speed up shutdown is to not shut down at all. Rather, put your PC to sleep, as described in "Start Windows Instantly (Almost)," earlier in this chapter. That way, you won't have to close your documents, bookmark open web pages, or even quit your games; they'll all still be where you left them when you wake up and resume your previous session.

Of course, it's good for Vista to shut down completely from time to time. If you sleep your PC exclusively, it may mean you'll be operating under the same Windows session for weeks or even months, and that can cause Windows to slow down and become even more unreliable.

When shutting down, Windows attempts to stop all running tasks. If a task—an application, service, or background program—doesn't respond or refuses to shut down, there's a built-in delay before Windows will force the task to end. This delay is called the *timeout*, and it can be shortened if you're experiencing problems or unreasonable delays every time you shut down your system.

1. Open the Registry Editor (see Chapter 3).

2. Expand the branches to HKEY_CURRENT_USER\Control Panel\Desktop.

3. Double-click the WaitToKillAppTimeout value. (If it's not there, select **Edit → New → DWORD Value (32-bit)** and type WaitToKillAppTimeout for the name of the new value.) This number controls the time to wait, in milliseconds, before unresponsive applications are forced to close. The default is 20000 (20 seconds), but you can type any value here; the minimum is 1 millisecond, although it's impractical to use any value smaller than about 2000 (2 seconds) here.

4. Also in this key is the HungAppTimeout value, which does pretty much the same thing as WaitToKillAppTimeout; just enter the same number for both values.

5. Next, you can configure Vista to end hung applications automatically and without asking. Select **Edit → New → DWORD Value (32-bit)** and type AutoEndTasks for the name of the new value. Then, double-click AutoEndTasks and enter 1 (one) to automatically end tasks or 0 (zero) to prompt before ending tasks (the default).

6. Expand the branches to HKEY_LOCAL_MACHINE\SYSTEM\CurrentControlSet\Control.

7. Double-click the WaitToKillServiceTimeout value. This works the same as the WaitToKillAppTimeout value described above, except that it applies to services (managed in *services.msc*) instead of applications.

8. Close the Registry Editor when you're done. You'll have to restart Windows for the change to take effect.

These values also affect the timeouts at times other than just shutting down, such as when you click **End Process** or **End Task** in Task Manager. In most cases, however, these values *won't* affect applications that delay shut down merely because they're waiting for you to save an open document.

Start Applications Faster

One of the things we spend most of our time doing at a PC is waiting for applications to start. Larger applications, particularly, can take what seems like an eternity—OK, 10 to 15 seconds on a fast PC—before they're ready to use. And small programs, even though they load quickly, don't always "pop" on screen as quickly as one would like.

Windows has a lot to do when it loads a program. It has to suck the program file data off your hard disk, something that a clean, optimized drive will handle more quickly (discussed later in this chapter). It also has to make room in your PC's system memory (RAM) for the program, which means your virtual memory settings (see "Optimize Virtual Memory and Cache Settings," later in this chapter) play a significant part, and, of course, more RAM definitely helps.

And then there's the program itself, which must read through all your fonts (the fewer the better), load its own add-on components (DLLs, plug-ins, etc.), and allocate its own section of your hard disk to store temporary files.

But there's also something else at work here, something that isn't strictly necessary. Windows Vista includes an "Application Compatibility" system that checks each program you run against a database of known issues, and warns you if there's a potential problem. This takes time and resources, and is really only useful when you're installing or running older programs not specifically designed for Vista.

Once you've set up your PC and tested it with most of the software you'll be using on a daily basis, you really don't need the Application Compatibility system any more. Turn it off, and that's one less thing Windows needs to do each and every time you start a program.

Open the Start menu, type gpedit.msc into the **Search** box, and press **Enter** to open the Group Policy Object Editor.* Expand the branches to **Local Computer Policy** → **Computer Configuration** → **Administrative Templates** → **Windows Components** → **Application Compatibility**. In the **Application Compatibility** section, double-click the following settings to configure them:

Turn Off Program Compatibility Engine. Set this to **Enabled** to turn off the system that checks each program you run, and allow programs to start more quickly.

The downside is that some of the User Account Control (UAC) features I'll discuss in Chapter 8 may stop working with pre-Vista applications, which may cause those older programs to stop working.

---

* The Group Policy Object Editor (*gpedit.msc*) is only available in the Business and Ultimate editions of Windows Vista; it's not available in Home Basic and Home Premium.

Turn Off Program Compatibility Assistant. The *Assistant* is the window that pops up after you install a program or use it for the first time to inform you that it may not have run correctly. Obviously, this is something you're probably able to determine for yourself, so set this option to **Enabled** to get rid of these prompts.

Remove Program Compatibility Property Page. This gets rid of the **Compatibility** tab in a program's Properties window. If you're setting the other options here to **Enabled**, you might as well set this to **Enabled**, too.

When you're done, close the Group Policy Object Editor and restart Windows for the change to take effect. If one of your programs stops working, you'll need to come back here to re-enable the Application Compatibility engine.

See the "Keeping an Eye on Prefetch" sidebar, later in this chapter, for another feature that can affect application startup times.

Make Your Hardware Perform

There's no end to the tricks you can employ to squeeze more speed out of your PC, but few—apart from the ones in this chapter, hopefully—will end up making that much of a difference. Probably the most effective steps you can take involve your hard disk, discussed later in this chapter.

Paradoxically, this section's first topic involves the Glass interface, a new feature that indeed makes Windows run more slowly. But making Vista perform isn't always about making it run *faster*; rather, performance is as much about the quality of your experience as it is about raw, number-crunching speed.

Disclaimer: Keep in mind that there's a certain point beyond which your computer is going to turn into a money and time pit. The older your system is, the less time and energy you'll want to invest in making it run well, and the more you should start looking to replace it. It's easy to calculate the point of diminishing returns: just compare the estimated cost of an upgrade—both the monetary cost and the amount of time you'll have to commit—with the cost of a new system (minus what you might get for selling or donating your old system). I stress this point a great deal, because I've seen it happen time and time again: people end up spending too much and getting too little in return. A simple hardware upgrade ends up taking days of troubleshooting and configuring, only to result in the discovery that yet something *else* needs to be replaced as well. Taking into account that whatever you end up with will still eventually need to be further upgraded to remain current, it is often more cost effective to replace the entire system and either sell or donate the old parts.

That said, the following sections detail some things you can do to make Windows run faster and/or better.

Get Glass

*Don't tell me the moon is shining; show me
the glint of light on broken glass.*
—Anton Chekhov

We're all suckers for a pretty face. You may or may not think "Aero" Glass, the translucent new interface in Windows Vista, is actually *pretty*, but you can't deny that it's a welcome change from the homely, cartoonish look of XP, and a convenient way to see what's behind the window on top (see Figure 5-4).

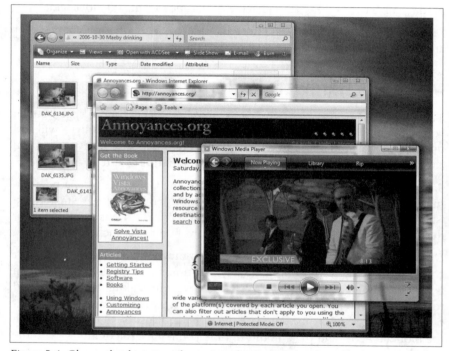

Figure 5-4. Glass—the shiny, translucent interface included with every edition of Vista except Home Basic—is nice to look at, but may be hard to come by on older PCs

Glass also includes some flashy goodies, such as buttons that glow a cool blue when you roll over them with the mouse, live thumbnail previews of running tasks in the taskbar and the **Alt-Tab** window, and the silly Flip3D Rolodex-style task switcher (Winkey+**Tab**).

If you got Windows Vista preinstalled on a new PC, and you're using the Home Premium edition or better, then you're probably already using the

---

Glass interface. But what if you've upgraded an older PC, or have the Home Basic edition of Vista? Or what if Glass simply doesn't work?

The problems with Vista's Glass feature are twofold. First, Glass has somewhat hefty technical requirements, not the least of which is a *fast* video card with at least 64 Mb of video memory (or more for higher resolutions), a Vista-compatible video driver, and a 3D gaming feature called *Pixel Shader 2.0* in hardware. And because Aero Glass guzzles CPU cycles, you'll want a fast processor and a fast video card to enjoy it.

Second, it can be a little tricky to get all the pieces in place so that Vista will even give you the *option* of enabling the Glass interface.

So, without further ado, here's a fairly foolproof procedure to get Glass on your PC.

Part 1: Hardware

The number-one ingredient in a good Glass experience is a fast graphics card with sufficient *video* memory onboard.

A faster card, which you can only get by spending money on a replacement and installing it in your PC, will help offload the burden of the Glass interface, so your CPU is free to handle other tasks. (The exception is if you have a video card with a chip that can be overclocked, akin to "Overclock Your Processor," later in this chapter.) The card must also support a 3D feature called Pixel Shader 2.0 in its hardware (not software), and must be compatible with DirectX 9.

 Modern desktop PCs take PCI-Express (PCIE) cards, and while Glass-capable PCIE cards are common, it can be difficult to find a sufficiently powerful card designed for the AGP slot in an older PC. But if you're not adverse to scrounging on eBay for a used or discontinued card, nVidia's 6800 series of AGP cards are up to the task, and supported by nVidia's frequently updated Vista drivers. If you're looking for top-notch AGP performance, look for a card with the nVidia 6800Ultra chip and 256 Mb of onboard memory.

Video memory may be a different matter. In most cases, video memory is permanently installed on your video card; unlike your PC's system memory, it can't be upgraded unless you replace your card. But if you have a laptop or low-end desktop, your video is likely built into your motherboard, and its video memory is merely a portion of your PC's system memory (which *is* upgradable). This means that it may be possible to allocate more system memory for your video (at the expense of memory Windows can use) by changing a setting or two in your system BIOS. See Appendix A for the appropriate BIOS settings.

So, how much video memory do you need? It depends on your screen's resolution, but a basic rule of thumb is that you need a minimum of about 48 bytes of video memory for each pixel on your screen, as shown in Table 5-1.

Table 5-1. The amount of video memory required to use Glass at common screen resolutions

Resolution	Aspect ratio	# of pixels	Video memory required
800 × 600	4:3	480,000	32 MB
960 × 600	16:10	576,000	32 MB
1024 × 768	4:3	786,432	64 MB
1152 × 864	4:3	995,328	64 MB
1280 × 720	16:9	921,600	64 MB
1280 × 768	5:3	983,040	64 MB
1280 × 800	16:10	1,024,000	64 MB
1280 × 960	4:3	1,228,800	64 MB
1280 × 1024	5:4	1,310,720	64 MB
1360 × 768	16:9	1,044,480	64 MB
1600 × 1024	25:16	1,638,400	128 MB
1600 × 1200	4:3	1,920,000	128 MB
1920 × 1080	16:9	2,073,600	128 MB
1920 × 1200	16:10	2,304,000	128 MB
2560 × 1440	16:9	3,686,400	256 MB
2560 × 1600	16:10	4,096,000	256 MB
2560 × 1920	4:3	4,915,200	256 MB

As you can see, it may be possible to get Glass with as little as 32 MB of video memory on some lower resolutions—and there are those who have achieved this—but depending on your card and its driver, your mileage may vary.

As for your PC, it's a good idea to have at least 1 gigabyte of system memory (RAM). Although you can get away with less—and you may have to if your video memory is being shared with your system memory as described earlier—you may not find the performance acceptable on a PC with less than 512 MB. See the next topic, "Maximize the Windows Performance Rating," for ways to measure whether your processor and hard disk are also up to running Glass.

Part 2: Software

With the hardware elements in place, the next thing to worry about is your video driver. Although Vista comes with drivers for most common display adapters, the best driver you're likely to get is the one provided by the maker of the chip on your video card.

The most common video chips are nVidia GeForce (*http://www.nvidia.com/*) and ATI Radeon (*http://ati.amd.com/*); if you're not sure who makes the video card in your PC, open Device Manager in Control Panel and expand the **Display adapters** branch. Just make sure the driver supports the Windows Display Driver Model; in most cases, the driver must be expressly written for Windows Vista.

Once you're certain you have the latest video driver, follow these steps to enable Glass:

1. Update your *Windows Experience Index*, as described in "Maximize the Windows Performance Rating," later in this chapter, so that Windows can reassess your video subsystem's capabilities. You may need to restart Windows if the Performance Information and Tools window doesn't update your score after a reasonable wait.

2. In Control Panel, open the System page, and click the **Advanced system settings** link on the left side (or run *SystemPropertiesAdvanced.exe*).

3. In the **Performance** section, click the **Settings** button.

4. Turn on the **Enable desktop composition** and **Enable transparent glass** options, and then click **OK** and then **OK** again to close the two windows. (These options may not be present if you're not using the Aero interface.)

5. Back in Control Panel, go to the Personalization page, and click the **Display Settings** link.

If you know how much video memory is on your video card, refer to Table 5-1, earlier in this section, to determine the highest screen resolution you can use with Glass. If needed, adjust the **Resolution** slider to the left to choose a lower value; otherwise, if your card supports it, the resolution should set as high as it goes.

6. From the **Colors** drop-down listbox, select **Highest (32 bit)** and then click **OK**.

7. Back on the Personalization page, click the **Window Color and Appearance** link, and then click the **Open classic appearance properties for more color options** link.

8. From the **Color scheme** list, select **Windows Aero**, and then click **OK**. After a brief delay, the Glass interface should now be active.

9. Again on the Personalization page, click the **Window Color and Appearance** link again, and turn on the **Enable transparency** option if it's not already on.

10. While you're here, use the color blocks to choose a tint for the glass, or click **Show color mixer** for more control. Adjust the **Color intensity** slider to choose the opacity of the glass; move it to the left to make it more transparent, or to the right to make it more opaque.

11. Click **OK** when you're done.

If you still don't have Glass at this point, either your video card or your video driver is to blame. For instance, if the **Windows Aero** entry isn't present in the **Color scheme** list in step 8, or if selecting it shows an error message, then Windows doesn't believe your PC is Glass-capable.

If you're using Vista Home Basic, see the "Part 3a: Vista Home Basic" section, later in this topic.

Part 3: Tweaks

It doesn't take a degree from Art Center to notice that Microsoft took some design cues from the Aqua interface in Mac OS X (not that Apple didn't borrow some of its ideas, too). While Microsoft actually managed to outdo Apple in a few areas—the minimize, maximize, and close buttons spring to mind—the Flip 3D task switcher is no match for Exposé, the Mac's all-at-once task switcher. Luckily, you can mimic Exposé with My Expose, free from *http:// www.annoyances.org/exec/software/myexpose*, and shown in Figure 5-5.

If you find the aforementioned title bar buttons—minimize, maximize, and close—too big (or not big enough), you can resize them. Open the Personalization page in Control Panel, click **Window Color and Appearance**, click **Open classic appearance properties for more color options**, and then click the **Advanced** button. From the **Item** list, select **Active Title Bar**, and then use the **Size** control to the right to shrink or grow the title bar. The preview shows the classic interface only, so take your best guess, and click **OK** to see how it looks.

See "Improve Battery Life," later in this chapter, for another tool you can use with Glass.

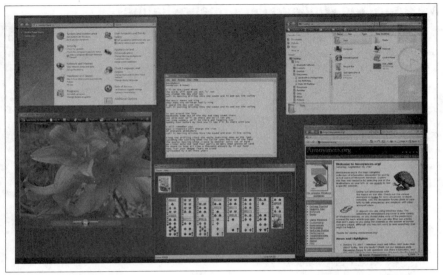

Figure 5-5. My Expose mimics the Exposé all-at-once task switcher from Mac OS X

Part 3a: Vista Home Basic

Vista Home Basic doesn't support the Glass interface, and this is intentional; why else would you pay extra for Vista Home Premium?

Now, there are a number of hacks floating around the Web that promise to bring Glass to Home Basic with nothing more than a change to the Registry. Unfortunately, these were all written for the beta and CTP (Consumer Technology Preview) versions of Vista that made the rounds in 2006. Unfortunately, the Glass interface is simply not present in Home Basic, but that doesn't mean you can't still come close.

Following the steps in "Part 2: Software," the best you can get in Home Basic is the **Windows Vista Basic** scheme, which looks strikingly like Glass, sans the transparency effects.

If that won't cut it, check out Stardock WindowBlinds (demo at *http://www.stardock.com/*). And while there weren't any themes that mimicked Vista Aero Glass exactly at the time of this writing, there were quite a few Vista-esque themes available from *http://www.wincustomize.com/*.

But that's not all. To get the thumbnail previews that float over taskbar buttons in Home Basic, check out Visual Task Tips, free from *http://www.visualtasktips.com/*.

Maximize the Windows Performance Rating

With the introduction of the fancy new Glass interface in Vista (covered in the last section), Microsoft is at last taking display performance seriously in a non-gaming context.

Enter the *Windows Experience Index,* a numeric score that supposedly indicates the baseline performance level of your PC's hardware. To view your PC's current score, open the Performance Information and Tools page in Control Panel (Figure 5-6).

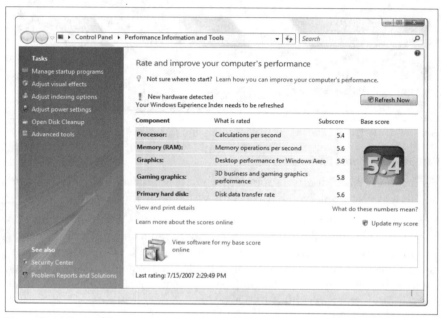

Figure 5-6. The Windows Experience Index is a performance score based on the weakest performer in your PC

Here, you'll see the five performance indexes that Vista calculates:

Processor
This measures your CPU's number-crunching prowess; specifically, how quickly it can compress and decompress data, encryption and decrypt data, compute a hash, and encode a video stream. For perspective, here are benchmarks from a handful of **Processor** scores culled from the Web.

Processor	Processor subscore	Processor	Processor subscore
Dual Intel Xeon 5160 @3.0Ghz	5.9	AMD Athlon 64 X2 4200+ @2.2Ghz	4.9
Intel Core2 Duo 6600 @2.40GHz	5.4	AMD Athlon 64 X2 3800+ @2GHz	4.8
Intel Core2 Duo 6400 @2.13GHz	5.4	Intel T2500 Core Duo @2GHz	4.8
Intel Core2 Duo T7600 @2.33GHz	5.2	AMD Turion 64 X2 Mobile @1.6Ghz	4.7
AMD Athlon 64 X2 5200+ @2.6Ghz	5.1	Intel Pentium 4 @ 2.80GHz	4.1

Want to raise your Processor score without spending any money? Check out "Overclock Your Processor," later in this chapter.

Memory

This measures partly how fast your memory is, but also how much of it your PC has (not including any shared as video memory). Here's how Vista limits the maximum memory benchmark you can attain, regardless of how fast your RAM is.

Amount of RAM	Max. subscore	Amount of RAM	Max. subscore
Less than 256 MB	1.0	513–704 MB	3.5
257–500 MB	2.0	705–960 MB	3.9
501–512 MB	2.9	961 MB–1.5 GB	4.5

Want a higher **Memory** score? Add more RAM. (It'll have the meager side effect of making your PC faster, too.)

Graphics

This value is the one most closely tied to your PC's ability to render the Glass interface (see "Get Glass," earlier in this chapter), and also indicates your PC's ability to play back video. The score is based on the video bandwidth (the speed at which your video card can move data, as well as the amount of video memory you have).

 A video card that doesn't support DirectX 9 automatically earns a score no higher than 1.0. One for which you don't have a Windows Vista Display Driver Model (WDDM) driver can't receive a score higher than 1.9. To use the Glass interface, you must have a **Graphics** score of at least 2.0. Glass should run beautifully on a system ranked at 5.0 or higher. An updated driver will usually raise your **Graphics** score.

Gaming graphics

This measures your video card's 3D prowess, specifically the frames per second it can attain in certain situations.

 Like the **Graphics** benchmark, described previously, there are minimum requirements for certain scores. If your video card doesn't support Direct3D 9, it earns a score no higher than 1.0. If support for Pixel Shader 3.0 is absent, then you won't see a score higher than 4.9, regardless of other factors. If you believe your card is capable of these things, yet your score seems unfairly low, your driver is likely to blame.

Primary hard disk

This measures the transfer rate, the speed at which your PC can read and write information to the drive on which Windows is installed. See the "Hard Disk" section, later in this chapter, for things you can do to increase this score.

Off to the right, you'll see a **Base score** emblazoned on a Windows logo. This score isn't an average of the subscores to the left, but rather an indication of the lowest score—the weakest link in the chain, so to speak.

Don't panic if your **Processor** score is a hair lower than your neighbor's down the street, even though you have a faster CPU. (Because your neighbor is probably worried about your slightly better **Graphics** score, even though his video card cost $40 more than yours.)

Rather, use these scores only to provide quantitative feedback for the upgrades or tweaks you're doing. And keep in mind that these scores, although based on calculations, aren't quite as rigid as they seem. For instance, refresh the index right after booting Windows, and you may see a 0.1 variance from a PC that has been scored after being on all day. Install a new graphics driver, and your **Graphics** subscore may go up a few tenths while **Gaming graphics** dives slightly.

 Click the **View and print details** link to shed some more light on exactly how Vista is calculating your PC's score. You can print the results here, or better yet, highlight everything (**Ctrl-A**), copy the text to the clipboard (**Ctrl-C**), and then paste into Notepad (**Ctrl-V**) to save the results to a file.

Update my score

Click either the **Refresh Now** button on top or the **Update my score** link down below to rescan your system and perform the benchmarks again. But don't be surprised when you don't see any progress bar or other indication that Windows is testing your system; other than periodic sluggishness in the mouse, occasional screen flashes, or increased hard disk activity, you shouldn't notice much of anything happening.

But don't let that fool you: to maximize your scores, make sure you close any running applications (including background tasks like antivirus programs and anything that uses your network), let go of your mouse, and then go get a cup of tea so you avoid doing anything that may interfere with the scoring. It's not unusual for scoring to take 10–30 minutes, even on a fast PC.

If see this error or something similar:

> *Cannot complete the requested operation.*
> *An unknown error has caused WinSAT to fail in an unexpected way.*

it either means you clicked the **Refresh Now** button while Vista was already re-examining your system, or there's a problem with your video driver that's causing the benchmark system to crash. Update your driver, restart Windows, and try again.

Improve Battery Life

Priorities shift when you're not tethered to an AC outlet. Suddenly, processor speed and the glitzy Glass interface just aren't that important when your laptop battery is going to die in 12 minutes. Now, there are things you can do to reduce your laptop's hunger for power, but the best power-saving features are the ones that engage automatically when you're using the battery, but revert to their high-performance settings whenever you plug in.

Start with the obvious: the Power Options page in Control Panel. Here, you'll find at least three plans: **Balanced** (the default), **Power saver**, and **High performance**. It doesn't really matter which one you choose, because each can be configured any way you like.

Click the **Change plan settings** link under the currently selected plan. Next, click the **Change advanced power settings** link to open the Advanced Settings window, and if it's there, click the **Change settings that are currently unavailable** link (see "Control User Account Control," in Chapter 8, to get rid of this last step).

The settings here that will have the most bearing on your battery life are:

Hard disk

Being a mechanical device, your hard disk eats up a lot of power. Set the **Turn off hard disk after** option too low, and you'll spend a lot of time waiting for Windows to wake up your hard disk; set it too high, and you're just wasting power. A setting of 10 or 20 minutes is usually a good compromise.

Processor power management

Your processor can run at different speeds; it runs fast when it's needed, but drops down to a slower speed when your PC is idle. The two settings here let you choose the upper and lower bounds of your processor's speed. Unlike with your hard disk, you never have to wait for your processor to be woken up, so there's very little cost in keeping the **Minimum processor state** setting as low as possible.

 It's worth noting that the **Maximum processor state** is set to only 50% in the **Power saver** plan by default; this means that when this plan is active, your CPU will never run faster than about half its rated speed. Of course, this does save power, but as long as the **Minimum processor state** is set to, say, 5%, you probably won't need to limit your CPU in this way. Of course, processors vary, so experiment with this setting to see how well yours manages its own power consumption.

Search and Indexing

As described in Chapter 2 (and later in this chapter as well), Windows indexes the files on your PC to make searches faster. Of course, this uses your hard disk heavily, so it's best to set the **Power Savings Mode** to **Power Saver** when you're running on a battery.

Display

Use the **Turn off display after** setting as a battery-friendly alternative to a screensaver. Since it takes very little time to wake up modern laptop displays, set this to a small value like 5 minutes. Then set **Adaptive display** to **On** to have Vista automatically (and temporarily) give you a little more time whenever you seem to be frequently waking up your display.

Click **OK** when you're done; the changes take effect immediately.

To switch between power plans, just click the battery status icon in your notification area (tray) and then click the one you want. Or, press Win-key+**X** to show the Windows Mobility Center, where you can also choose the plan you want.

Switch plans automatically

Problem is, you have to switch power plans by hand, and who remembers to do that? Wouldn't it be better to have the plan chosen automatically when you switch between battery and AC power? Vista won't do this, but the free Vista Battery Saver (available at *http://www.codeplex.com/vistabattery*, and shown in Figure 5-7) can.

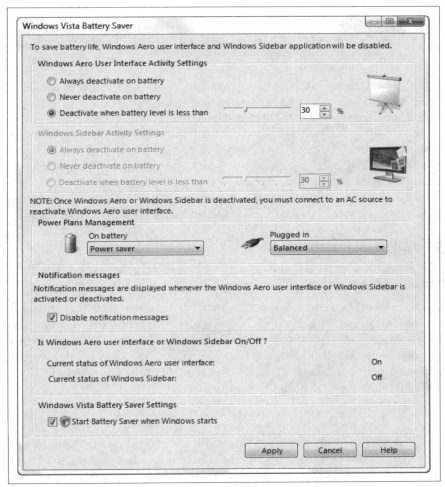

Figure 5-7. Tired of having to change the power plans every time you switch between AC and battery power? Increase your battery life by letting the Vista Battery Saver do it for you

Vista Battery Saver can also turn off the power-hungry Glass interface when you switch battery power, a convenience that has been known to cause huge gains in battery life. Also available is Aerofoil (free from *http://www.silentsoftware.co.uk/*), a program that simply switches off Glass when you're mobile and then turns it back on when you've plugged in.

 Want to know whether your power-saving measures are paying off? Check out the BatTrack tool (free, *http://blogs.microsoft.co.il/files/folders/tamir/entry23412.aspx*), written by the author of Vista Battery Saver, or the BattStat tool (also free, *http://users.rcn.com/tmtalpey/BattStat/*).

What's funny about all this is that in some of Vista's beta-test versions, each entry in the Power Options–Advanced Settings window had two settings: one for **On battery** and the other for **Plugged in**. Microsoft actually removed these settings from the final version, but if you have the Vista Business or Ultimate edition, you can still use them by opening the Group Policy Object Editor (*gpedit.msc*), and expanding the branches to **Computer Configuration → Administrative Templates → System → Power Management**. As it turns out, Vista Battery Saver is much easier to use, but if you don't want to install any third-party software, the Group Policy Object Editor is a workable alternative.

Disable devices, stop services

Don't need that ethernet port right now? Not using your DVD drive? Turn 'em off and save some more power.

Open Device Manager, expand the branches to show your "expendable" devices, and then right-click each one and select **Properties**. Choose the **Power Management** tab, turn on the **Allow the computer to turn off this device to save power** option, and click **OK**. Then, assuming the option was available, right-click the device and select **Disable** (if the option wasn't available, disabling the device won't save any power).

Next, open the Services window (*services.msc*), and stop any unnecessary services (don't touch the ones you don't understand). For instance, if you've installed Apple's iTunes on your PC, you'll see at least two related services here: **Apple Mobile Device** and **iPod Service**. If you have no plans to connect an iPod during the next few hours, right-click each service and select **Stop** to give your PC one less thing to do while you're running on precious battery power.

Cooler or hotter to save power

One of the most significant things you can do to increase battery life is to take your laptop off your lap. Put it on a book, magazine, airline tray table, tennis racket, pasta strainer, or any hard—and preferably ventilated—surface. If the bottom of your laptop is allowed to breathe, it won't get so hot, and the fan won't have to work so hard to keep the processor cool. The harder your fan works—and for that matter, the hotter your CPU gets—the more power is drained from your battery.

If your laptop never seems to get that hot, even when it's on your lap, you may be able to experiment with some more lenient cooling settings. Using your PC's BIOS setup page (see Appendix A) or, optionally, a fan control program like I8kfanGUI (free at *http://www.diefer.de/i8kfan/*), try increasing the allowed temperature of your CPU by a degree or two, and see what happens. With luck, your fan should come on less often and your battery should last a little longer, all without (hopefully) frying your processor.

Manage IRQ Priority

Most components directly attached to your motherboard—including PCI slots, IDE controllers, serial ports, the keyboard port, and even your motherboard's CMOS—have individual IRQs assigned to them. An *interrupt request line*, or *IRQ*, is a numbered hardware line over which a device can interrupt the normal flow of data to the processor, allowing the device to function.

Vista lets you prioritize one or more IRQs (which translate to one or more hardware devices), potentially improving the performance of those devices:

1. Start by opening the System Information utility (*msinfo32.exe*), and navigating to System Summary\Hardware Resources\IRQs to view the IRQs in use on your system, and the devices using them.

2. Next, open the Registry Editor (see Chapter 3), and navigate to HKEY_LOCAL_MACHINE\SYSTEM\CurrentControlSet\Control\PriorityControl.

3. Create a new DWORD value in this key, and call it IRQ#Priority, where # is the IRQ of the device you wish to prioritize (e.g., IRQ13Priority for IRQ 13, which is your numeric processor).

4. Double-click the new value, and enter a number for its priority. Enter 1 for top priority, 2 for second, and so on. Make sure not to enter the same priority number for two entries, and keep it simple by experimenting with only one or two values at first.

5. Close the Registry Editor and reboot your computer when you're done.

Some users have gotten good results prioritizing IRQ 8 (for the system CMOS) and the IRQ corresponding to the video card (found in the first step).

Overclock Your Processor

The processor (CPU) is the highest-profile component in your PC, and indeed, it does a lot of the heavy lifting in it. But processors also become obsolete the fastest, and given how expensive they can be, it's not always a wise place to put your money. That's where overclocking comes in; rather than spending money on a slightly faster chip, you can simply change settings in your PC to squeeze a little extra speed out of the one you currently have. (See the upcoming sidebar, "How Much the CPU Matters," for a little perspective.)

Overclocking is the process of instructing your processor to run at a higher clock speed (MHz) than its rated speed. For example, you may be able to modestly overclock a 2.40 GHz chip to run at 2.48 MHz, or your motherboard may offer overclocking at up to 30% of the rated speed, which would give you more than 3 Ghz on that same old chip.

Supposedly, Intel and other chip makers have taken steps to prevent overclocking (theoretically prompting purchases of faster CPUs instead), but some motherboard manufacturers have found ways to do it anyway.

To overclock your processor (assuming your motherboard supports it), go to your BIOS setup page, as described in Appendix A, and use the controls in the **Overclock Options** category. Make sure you consult the documentation that came with your motherboard or PC for some of the restrictions; for instance, overclocking on your motherboard may be limited by the speed of the installed system memory (RAM).

When you're done, load up Windows and update your *Windows Experience Index*, as described in "Maximize the Windows Performance Rating," earlier in this chapter. Obviously, the **Processor** score should go up as you dial up the overclocking.

Now, over-overclocking a CPU—overclocking past the point where it's stable—can cause it to overheat and crash frequently, and at the extreme, damage the chip beyond repair. Thus, the most important aspect of overclocking your system involves cooling, so make sure you beef up your computer's internal cooling system before you start messing around with overclocking. (Obviously, your options will be limited here if you're using a laptop.)

How Much the CPU Matters

A common misconception is that—with all else being equal—a computer with a processor running at, say, 2.8 GHz, will naturally be faster than a 2.2 GHz system—and the company that just sold you that 2.8 Ghz PC wouldn't have it any other way. Sure, that new system you're drooling over does seem a whole lot faster than your one-year-old machine when you play with it in the gizmo store, but how much is due merely to the processor's clock speed, and how much is determined by other factors?

Naturally, the increased processor speed is an obvious benefit in some specific circumstances, such as when you're applying lens corrections to a few hundred digital photos, creating a PDF from a 200-page document, or playing a particularly processor-intensive game. But in most cases, a faster processor alone won't get you your email any faster, load a web site any sooner, or get your book to the publisher when it's actually due.

If you think about it, your qualitative assessment of your PC's speed is based on its ability to respond immediately to mouse clicks and keystrokes, start applications quickly, open menus and dialog boxes without a delay, start up and shut down Windows quickly, and display graphics and animations smoothly. For the most part, all of these things depend on the amount of system memory (RAM) your PC has, the speed of your hard drive, and the prowess of your video card as much as—if not more than—the speed of your CPU.

Probably the biggest drag on an older PC's performance, and the main reason it may seem so much slower than a new system—not to mention slower than it might've been only last year—is the glut of applications and drivers that have been installed. Any computer that has been around for a year or more will likely suffer a slowdown, a problem that can either be remedied by some of the tricks in the "Hard Disk" section later in this chapter, or by a thorough cleansing and complete reinstallation of the operating system (see "Install Windows Vista" in Chapter 1).

So, if you're wondering how much faster your PC will be if you replace your 2.2 Ghz chip with a 2.4 Ghz chip, the answer is: don't even bother unless someone else is paying for it.

Increase your CPU's speed in stages, if possible; don't start off with the fastest setting, or you may end up with a fried processor and lightly singed eyebrows.

If you feel that your system isn't adequately cooled, don't be afraid to add more fans, but beware: do it wrong, and you could actually make things worse. For instance, you need to consider airflow when installing and orienting fans; if the power supply, for instance, exhausts air through the vent in the back of your PC, it must pull it in through the vent near your processor's heatsink. So, make sure you orient the CPU fan so the airflow is as smooth as possible.

Most fans in modern PCs connect directly to special plugs on your motherboard, and are activated when internal thermometers (thermocouples) detect too high a temperature; these typically do a good job of moderating their cooling duties so that they don't produce too much noise. But you may have to tinker with your BIOS settings to make your PC cooler (which can, by itself, improve performance), even if it means a little more noise from your box.

If you're serious about cooling, there are a number of liquid cooling systems that promise to keep hot systems cool. But they're expensive, they work in large desktop PCs only, and they don't necessarily reduce noise.

Hard Disk

Your hard disk is more than just a storage device; it's used to hold your operating system and to supplement your system's memory. The speed and health of your hard disk is one of the most important factors in your computer's performance, not to mention its reliability and security. Yet it's also the one component that requires the most attention and often is the most neglected. Awww.

The following topics all deal with different aspects of your hard disk and how you can get Windows to use it most effectively. Later in this section, you'll find tips on upgrading and repartitioning your hard disk, to allow you to keep your disk and its data in tip-top shape.

A Defragmentation Crash Course

The best way to ensure maximum performance from your drive is to regularly—weekly or biweekly—defragment it (also called *optimizing*). Figure 5-8 shows how frequent use can cause files to become fragmented (broken up), which can slow access and retrieval of data on the drive, as well as increase the likelihood of lost data. And the fuller the drive, the more serious defragmentation becomes.

Figure 5-8. File fragmentation on your hard disk can hurt performance and decrease reliability

The good news is that Vista defragments your drives automatically; by default, it's scheduled to run at 1:00 a.m. every Wednesday morning from now until the end of time.

PC not on in the middle of the night? Defragmenter will run the next morning while you're working (when the PC is idle, anyway). Or, if you want to run it by hand, open Windows Explorer, right-click your hard disk, select **Properties**, choose the **Tools** tab, and click **Defragment Now** (Figure 5-9).

Disk Defragmenter does its job by rearranging the files on your hard disk to make them contiguous (not broken into pieces). It also defragments the free space by consolidating your files as much as it can. When run automatically, it has no interface to speak of, but rather runs invisibly in the background.

Now for the bad news.

In each successive version of Windows, Microsoft has further buried Disk Defragmenter; in Vista, it's basically invisible. For most Vista users, this is a good thing, but its severely minimalist design prevents just about any advanced tasks.

For instance, there's no way to defragment the swap file (virtual memory), the hibernation file (*hiberfil.sys*), or any other unmovable files. There's no disk map, so you won't know if there's a large file that won't defragment. If you have more than one hard disk (or partition), there's no way to defragment all your drives in one pass unless you schedule it.

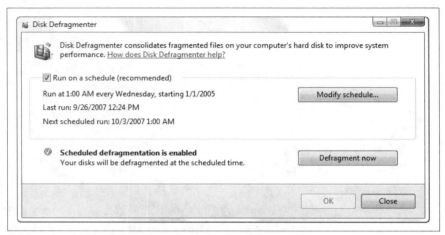

Figure 5-9. The only interface you'll ever see to the mysteriously disappearing Disk Defragmenter tool

Now, to be fair, these are some pretty niche features. If you miss the map, advanced settings, or detailed reporting of the old-school defragmenters, check out PerfectDisk (*http://raxco.com/*, shown in Figure 5-10). It's not free, but there's a time-limited demo on the Raxco web site.

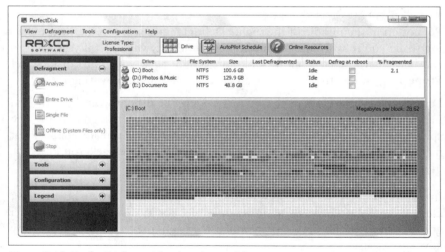

Figure 5-10. PerfectDisk provides the advanced features missing in Vista's own Disk Defragmenter

There's not a whole lot in the way of free defragmenters, but Auslogics Registry Defrag (*http://www.auslogics.com/registry-defrag/*) promises to improve Windows performance by shrinking and optimizing your Registry.

Command-line defragmenter

As it turns out, Vista's own Disk Defragmenter isn't quite as feeble as it first appears. Although it doesn't offer anything close to the usability of Perfect-Disk, there is a little-known command-line version (*defrag.exe*) that gives you just a little more freedom than the one you access through Windows Explorer.

Open a Command Prompt window in administrator mode (right-click the **Command Prompt** icon in the Start menu and select **Run as administrator**), and then type the following at the prompt:

```
defrag -a -v c:
```

and press **Enter** to generate a report like the one in Figure 5-11.

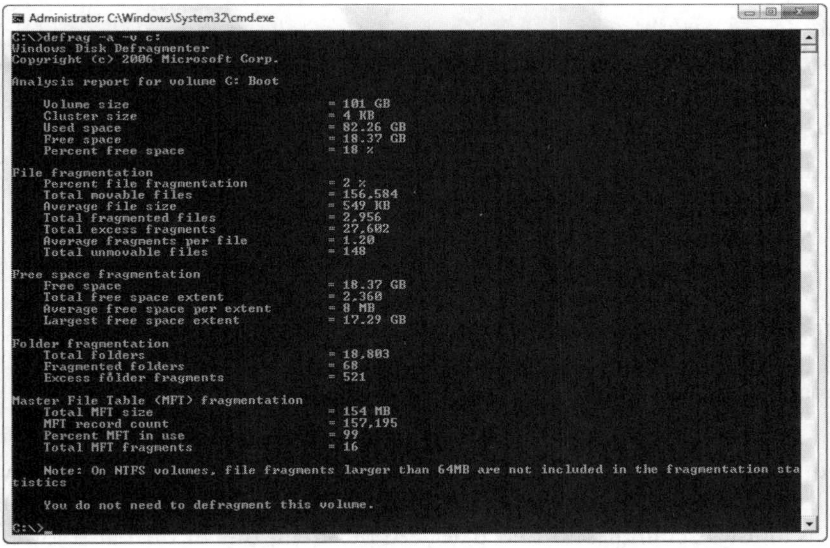

Figure 5-11. Defrag.exe lets you view reports and schedule more thorough defragmenting than the Windows version

To perform a full defragmentation (the default is only a partial defrag), type:

```
defrag -w c:
```

Press **Ctrl-C** at any time to interrupt Defrag. Or, to perform a full defragmentation of all the drives on your PC, while forcing defragmentation on nearly full volumes that would otherwise be skipped, type:

```
defrag -c -w -f
```

For more options, type defrag -? at the prompt and press **Enter**.

Enable automatic boot defragments

Here's a funny little setting in the Registry that seems as though it's supposed to instruct Windows to defragment your hard disk automatically each time it starts:

1. Open the Registry Editor (described in Chapter 3).

2. Expand the branches to HKEY_LOCAL_MACHINE\SOFTWARE\Microsoft\Dfrg\ BootOptimizeFunction.

3. Double-click the Enable value, and type Y for its data (or type N to disable it).

The funny part is that this setting is probably already enabled on your system (it's enabled by default on most Vista systems). Now, have you ever seen Windows run Disk Defragmenter at startup?

The reason you don't see it is because it isn't a full defragment. Instead, it's only a *boot defragment*, which affects only the files registered with Windows' Prefetch feature (see the upcoming "Keeping an Eye on Prefetch" sidebar) and listed in the *Layout.ini* file (not a standard *.ini* file).

You can perform this boot defragment at any time by running the command-line Defrag tool with the undocumented -b option, like this: defrag -b c:.

If in Doubt, Throw It Out

Parkinson's law states that work expands so as to fill the time available for its completion. Along the same lines, it's safe to say that files will quickly expand to fill the amount of available space on your hard drive.

Low disk space doesn't just make it harder to store files; without ample room for virtual memory (discussed later) and temporary files, Windows will slow to a crawl. Less free disk space also increases file fragmentation as Windows scrambles to find places to put data; this in turn also lowers performance. Keeping a healthy amount of free disk space is vital to a well-performing system.

Additionally, removing drivers and applications that are no longer used clears more memory and processor cycles for your other applications, which can substantially improve overall system performance.

Keeping an Eye on Prefetch

Prefetch is a new feature, introduced in Windows Vista, that stores specific data about the applications you run in order to help them start faster. Prefetch is an algorithm that helps anticipate cache misses (times when Windows requests data that isn't stored in the disk cache), and stores that data on the hard disk for easy retrieval.

This data is located in \Windows\Prefetch, and, as the theory goes, periodically clearing out the data in this folder (say, once a month) will improve performance. As new applications are subsequently started, new prefetch data will be created, which may mean slightly reduced performance at first. But with older entries gone, there will be less data to parse, and Windows should be able to locate the data it needs more quickly. Any performance gains you may see will be minor (if you see any at all), but those users wishing to squeeze every last CPU cycle out of their computers will want to try this one.

Note that deleting Prefetch data may increase boot time slightly, but only the next time you boot Windows. Each subsequent boot should proceed normally, since the prefetch data will already be present for the programs Windows loads when it boots.

If you want to disable Prefetch, open your Registry Editor (Chapter 3), navigate to `HKEY_LOCAL_MACHINE\SYSTEM\CurrentControlSet\Control\Session Manager\Memory Management\PrefetchParameters`, and change the `EnablePrefetcher` value to 0. (Other supported values: 1 to Prefetch applications only, 2 to Prefetch boot processes, and 3 to Prefetch both.)

If your PC is low on disk space, try NTFS compression.* Right-click any folder, select **Properties**, click **Advanced**, and turn on the **Compress contents to save disk space** option. Note that this can degrade performance, so you'd be wise to use it only for data that you don't access or modify often.

Even before you install your first application, your hard disk is littered with files from the Windows installation that you most likely don't need. The standard installation of Windows Vista Ultimate Edition places more than 39,000 files, consuming more than two gigabytes of disk space, on your PC.

---

* This feature is only available on NTFS-formatted drives. See "Choose the Right Filesystem," later in this chapter, for details. It's also mutually exclusive of the **Encrypt contents to secure data** option we'll discuss in Chapter 8.

Whether you need a particular file can be subjective; some might consider the 11 MB of *.wav* files that Vista puts in your *C:\Windows\Media* folder to be excessive, while others may scoff at the notion of worrying about such a piddly quantity. (To put things in perspective, this is about the same size as three photos from a 10-megapixel digital camera. It's also slightly more than the total capacity of my first hard disk back in 1983.)

Naturally, it makes sense to be cautious when removing any files from your system. The removal of certain files can cause some applications, or even Windows itself, to stop functioning. It's always good practice to move any questionable files to a metaphorical purgatory folder before committing to their disposal. And I don't have to tell you that backing up your entire hard disk (Chapter 6) before you clean house is very important and not all that difficult.

The easiest way to delete the stuff Windows considers expendable is to run the Disk Cleanup tool (*cleanmgr.exe*), discussed in the "Disable Disk Cleanup" sidebar.

Disable Disk Cleanup

When your PC starts running out of disk space, Windows will prompt you to run the Disk Cleanup Wizard, which presents a list of some of the files you can delete to recover free disk space (the solutions in this book are much more comprehensive).

The disable this annoying warning, open the Registry Editor (see Chapter 3) and expand the branches to `HKEY_CURRENT_USER\Software\Microsoft\Windows\CurrentVersion\Policies\Explorer`. If it's not already there, create a new DWORD value (go to **Edit → New → DWORD value**) called `NoLowDiskSpaceChecks`. Double-click the new value and type 1 for its data. Close the Registry Editor when you're done; the change will take effect immediately.

If in doubt

Before you delete any questionable file, there are several things you can do to get a better idea of what the file contains:

Why not open it? Start by double-clicking a suspicious file to open it in its default application. If you then see the **Open With** dialog box, it means the specific filename extension has not yet been registered. In that case, your best bet is to drag-drop the file into an open Notepad window.

Investigate. Right-click the file, and select **Properties**. If the file has a **Version** tab, it's likely an application, driver, DLL, or other support file.

Choose the **Version** tab to view the manufacturer, copyright date, and possibly the application it accompanies.

Hide it first. If you're not sure if something should be deleted but want to try anyway, move it to another directory first to see whether everything works without it for a week or so. If all is clear, toss it.

Check the date. Check the file's **Last Accessed** date (right-click it and select **Properties**). The more recent the date, the more likely it's still being used. For information on removing a particular application, contact the manufacturer of that application or refer to the application's documentation.

 Windows' System Restore feature can consume up to 15% of the total capacity of your hard disk for restore points and shadow copies. To reduce its usage or turn it off entirely, see "Go Back in Time with Restore Points and Shadow Copies," in Chapter 6.

Optimize Virtual Memory and Cache Settings

One of the most frustrating and irritating things about Windows is the way that it can seize up for several seconds with seemingly random, pointless disk activity. One of the causes of this behavior is the way Windows handles disk virtual memory by default.

Normally, Windows loads drivers and applications into memory until it's full, and then starts to use part of your hard disk to "swap" out information, freeing up more memory for higher-priority tasks. The file that Windows uses for this type of "virtual memory" is the paging file (a.k.a. swap file), *pagefile.sys*, and it is stored in the root folder of your Windows drive.

Because your hard disk is so much slower than your physical memory, the more swapping Windows has to do, the slower your computer gets. This is why adding more memory speeds up your PC: it reduces Windows' appetite for virtual memory. But regardless of the amount of installed physical memory in your system, there are always things you can do to improve virtual memory performance.

Windows' defaults here are rather conservative and can fortunately be modified for better performance. It's important to realize, though, that some experimentation may be required to achieve the best configuration for your setup. Different hardware, software, and work habits require different settings; those with ample hard disks, for instance, can afford to devote more disk space to virtual memory, while others may simply wish to use this procedure to place a cap on the disk space Windows is allowed to consume.

Part 1: Virtual memory settings

One of the reasons the default settings yield such poor performance is that the swap file grows and shrinks with use, quickly becoming very fragmented (as illustrated by Figure 5-8, earlier in this chapter). The first step is to eliminate this problem by setting a constant swap-file size.

Note that making the swap file constant will also result in a more constant amount of free disk space. If your hard disk is getting full, consider this solution to restrict Windows from using up every last bit of free space. (Or better yet, upgrade your hard disk.)

1. In Control Panel, open the System page and click the **Advanced system settings** link (or run *SystemPropertiesAdvanced.exe*).

2. Under the **Advanced** tab, click the **Settings** button in the **Performance** section.

3. On the Performance Options page, choose the **Advanced** tab, and then click **Change** to open the Virtual Memory window shown in Figure 5-12.

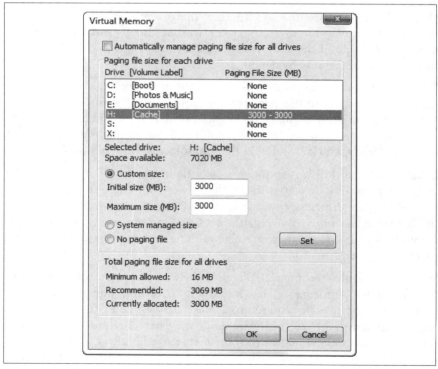

Figure 5-12. Change the way Windows handles virtual memory to improve overall system performance

4. The virtual memory settings are set for each drive in your system independently. If you have only one drive, virtual memory will already be enabled for that drive. If you have more than one drive or partition, virtual memory will be enabled only on the Windows drive by default. Start by selecting the drive that currently holds your paging file (shown in the righthand column) from the **Paging file size for each drive** list.

 Another way to stop Windows from using the hard disk so heavily is to disable virtual memory altogether, but the consequence of short-changing Windows of its resources will easily outweigh any performance gains. A better choice is to move the swap file to a different physical drive than the one on which Windows resides; that way, when Vista accesses virtual memory, it won't suck the life out of your primary drive.

5. To set a constant size for your virtual memory, select **Custom size**, and then type the same value for both **Initial size** and **Maximum size**.

   The size, specified in megabytes, is up to you. If you have the space, it's usually a good idea to allocate two to three times the amount of installed RAM (e.g., 4,096–6,144 MB of virtual memory for 2 GB of physical memory), but you may wish to experiment with different sizes for the one that works best for you.

   Important: after you've made a change for any drive, click **Set** to commit the change before moving on to another drive or clicking **OK**.

6. Press **OK** on each of the three open dialogs.

If you have only resized your swap file, the change will take effect immediately. But if you've added (or removed) a swap file on any drive, you'll need to restart Windows before it uses your new settings.

Part 2: Defragment the paging file

The steps in the previous section eliminate the possibility of your swap file becoming fragmented, but they won't cure an already fragmented one. You'll need to defragment your virtual memory for the best performance, but the good news is that you only need to do it once if you have a constant-size paging file.

There are several ways to defragment your swap file:

Use PerfectDisk. Use an advanced defragmenter like PerfectDisk, discussed in "A Defragmentation Crash Course," earlier in this chapter. Just instruct it to defragment your system files, and it will schedule a defragmentation for the next time you start Windows.

Performance

Use another drive temporarily. If you have more than one partition or hard disk in your system, start by moving your swap file to a different drive letter, as described in the previous section. Then, use the command-line Disk Defragmenter to perform a thorough defragment of your Windows drive, or whatever drive you'd like to use for virtual memory, by typing:

```
defrag -w -f c:
```

and pressing **Enter**. Again, see "A Defragmentation Crash Course," earlier in this chapter, for details. When it's done, move the swap file to its new home, where it will rest nicely in the newly allocated contiguous block of free space.

Turn off virtual memory temporarily. If you don't have a second drive, your other choice is to disable virtual memory altogether by clicking **No paging file** and then **Set** in the Virtual Memory window (see Figure 5-12, earlier). After restarting Windows, run Disk Defragmenter as described previously to set aside a large chunk of contiguous free space. When you're done, go back to the Virtual Memory window, and re-enable the paging file, making sure to set a constant size.

Clear the paging file automatically. See Part 3, next, for another way to reduce fragmentation in your paging file.

Part 3: Clear the paging file on shutdown

It's possible to have Windows delete your paging file each time you shut down Windows. You may want to do this if you have a multiboot system (see Chapter 1), wherein each operating system on your PC has its own virtual memory settings. If the paging file from one OS is present while the other is running, it may cause a conflict and will certainly waste a lot of disk space.

If your paging file becomes corrupted or highly fragmented, Windows may load more slowly (or not at all). Deleting the paging file automatically forces Windows to recreate it each time it starts, which may alleviate this problem. (Naturally, if you've gone to the steps to defragment your paging file, as described earlier in this topic, you probably won't want to use this feature, lest it become fragmented again when it's recreated.)

1. Open the Local Security Policy console (*secpol.msc*). See Chapter 8 for more information on the settings in this window.

2. Expand the **Local Policies** branch and click the **Security Options** folder.

3. In the right pane, double-click the **Shutdown: Clear virtual memory pagefile**.

4. Select **Enabled** and then click **OK**. You'll need to restart Windows for the change to take effect.

Part 4: Advanced settings for the adventurous

Like virtual memory settings, disk cache settings in Windows Vista aren't necessarily optimized for the best performance, but rather for the best compromise between performance and compatibility with older PCs.

 You'll probably need to experiment with different values until you find the ones that work best for your system. Since it's possible to render Windows inoperable with incorrect settings here, you'll want to back up your PC before you begin.

Start by opening the Registry Editor (described in Chapter 3), and expanding the branches to HKEY_LOCAL_MACHINE\SYSTEM\CurrentControlSet\Control\Session Manager\Memory Management. Some of the more interesting values in this key include the following:

DisablePagingExecutive

Values: 0 = disabled (default), 1 = enabled.

Enabling this setting will prevent Windows from paging certain system processes to disk, which effectively will keep more of the operating system in the faster physical memory, in turn making Windows much more responsive.

LargeSystemCache

Values: 0 = standard (default), 1 = large.

By default, Windows uses only 8 MB of memory for the filesystem cache. Enabling this option will allow Windows to use all but 4 MB of your computer's memory for the filesystem cache. This will improve Windows' performance, but potentially at the expense of the performance of some of your more memory-intensive applications.

This option can also be changed by opening the System page in Control Panel: click the **Advanced system settings** link, click **Settings** in the **Performance** section, and then choose the **Advanced** tab. The **Memory usage** section has two settings: **Programs** and **System cache**, which correspond to the 0 and 1 values here.

Other values in this key include PagingFiles, which is more easily set in the Virtual Memory window described in "Part 1: Virtual memory settings" and ClearPageFileAtShutdown, more easily set in the Local Security Settings console, as described in "Part 3: Clear the paging file on shutdown."

Choose the Right Filesystem

The filesystem is the invisible mechanism on your hard disk that is responsible for keeping track of all the data stored on the drive. Think of it as a massive table of contents, matching up each filename with its corresponding data stored somewhere on the disk surface. Vista supports three filesystem types:*

FAT (File Allocation Table, 16-bit)
 FAT is used for all drives under 512 MB, such as flash memory cards and floppy disks. The largest drive supported by the FAT filesystem is 2 GB.

FAT32 (File Allocation Table, 32-bit)
 Designed to overcome the 2 GB partition limit with the FAT system, FAT32 is supported by every version of Windows since Windows 95 OSR2. Today, it's used mostly for flash memory cards larger than 2 GB, and on older PCs running Windows 98 and Windows Me. In addition to the support for larger drives, it also supports smaller file clusters (see the upcoming "Understanding Cluster Sizes" sidebar), so it stores information more efficiently than FAT.

NTFS (NT Filesystem)
 NTFS, designed from the ground up to completely replace FAT/FAT32, is the default filesystem on all Vista PCs. (Specifically, Vista supports NTFS version 3.1.) It offers security features like encryption and permissions (see Chapter 8), compression, and quotas. It's typically faster and more reliable than FAT/FAT32, and supports drives up to 2 terabytes in size.

If Windows Vista is the only operating system on your computer, you should be using NTFS—no question. The only compelling reason to use another filesystem is if you have a dual-boot setup with a very old version of Windows, in which case you'd need to choose a filesystem recognized by all operating systems on your computer. Table 5-2 shows which filesystems are supported by all recent versions of Microsoft Windows.

Table 5-2. Filesystems supported by recent versions of Windows

	FAT	FAT32	NTFS
Windows Vista	✓ (data only)	✓ (data only)	✓ (v3.1)
Windows XP, 2003	✓	✓	✓ (v3.1)
Windows 2000	✓	✓	✓ (v3.0)
Windows Me, 98, and 95 ORS2	✓	✓	

---

* There's actually a fourth type, CDFS, used by CD-ROMs.

Table 5-2. Filesystems supported by recent versions of Windows (continued)

	FAT	FAT32	NTFS
Windows NT 4.0	✓		✓ (v1.2)
Windows 95	✓		

Understanding Cluster Sizes

Clusters are the smallest units into which a hard disk's space can be divided. A hard disk formatted with the traditional FAT system, found in Windows 95 and an ancient operating system called "DOS," can have no more than 65,536 clusters on each drive or partition. This means that the larger the hard disk, the larger the size of each cluster.

The problem with large clusters is that they result in a lot of wasted disk space. Each cluster can store no more than a single file (or a part of a single file); if a file does not consume an entire cluster, the remaining space is wasted. For example, a 2 GB drive would have a cluster size of 32 KB; a 1 KB file on a disk with a 32 KB cluster size will consume 32 KB of disk space; a 33 KB file on the same drive will consume 64 KB of space, and so on. The extra 31 KB left over from the 33 KB file is called *slack space*, and it can't be used by any other files. With thousands of files (especially those tiny shortcuts littered throughout a Windows installation), the amount of wasted slack space on a sizeable hard disk can add up to hundreds of megabytes of wasted space.

The NTFS filesystem used by Vista can handle more than four billion clusters, resulting in much smaller cluster sizes. Now, four billion clusters, at 4 kilobytes each, gives NTFS a maximum partition size of 14.9 terabytes (15,259 GB). Of course, if this drive were commercially available, its manufacturer would contend that 1 terabyte is equal to 1,000,000,000,000 bytes, and market the unit as a 16.4 TB (16,384 GB) drive.

You can see how much space is wasted by any given file by right-clicking on the file icon, selecting **Properties**, and comparing the **Size** value with the **Size on disk** value. The same works for multiple selected files and folders; highlight all the objects in your root directory to see the total amount of wasted space on your drive. To find the current cluster size of your drive, just open the properties sheet for a small file you know will only consume a single cluster (such as a Windows Shortcut); its **Size on disk** will be equal to the size of one cluster.

To find out which filesystem is currently being used by a particular drive on your PC, just right-click the drive in Windows Explorer and select **Properties**. Or, open the Disk Management utility (*diskmgmt.msc*) to see an overview of all of your drives.

Convert your drives to NTFS

If you've upgraded your PC from an earlier version of Windows, there's a chance you're still using the FAT32 filesystem. Assuming you don't need to keep FAT32 for compatibility with other operating systems, you should convert your drive to NTFS. The process is easy, relatively quick, and won't harm your data (although you should back up beforehand just to be safe).

Windows Vista provides the FAT to NTFS Conversion Utility (*convert.exe*) for this purpose. To convert drive *C:*, for example, just open a Command Prompt window (*cmd.exe*) and type:

```
convert c: /fs:ntfs
```

Include the /v option to run in "verbose" mode, which provides more information as it does its job. Type convert /? for other, more esoteric options.

Note that this is a one-way conversion, at least when using the software included with Windows Vista. If you need to convert an NTFS drive to FAT32 for some reason, you'll need a third-party utility such as Disk Director (*http://www.acronis.com/*).

Advanced NTFS Settings

The extra features of the NTFS filesystem discussed in the previous section come at a price, namely a small amount of disk space and performance overhead. The following settings allow you to fine-tune NTFS to squeeze the most performance out of your NTFS drive; experiment with these settings to find the configuration that works best for you.

Start by opening the Registry Editor (Chapter 3) and expanding the branches to HKEY_LOCAL_MACHINE\SYSTEM\CurrentControlSet\Control\Filesystem.

Double-click any one of the following values to change its data. If the value is missing, create it by going to **Edit → New → DWORD Value**, and then typing the name exactly as shown.

NtfsDisable8dot3NameCreation
> Values: 0 = enabled (default), 1 = disabled.
>
> Early versions of Windows and DOS didn't support so-called long filenames, but rather allowed only eight-character filenames followed by three-letter filename extensions. Although Windows 95 and all subsequent versions of Windows more or less eliminated this restriction, an eight-dot-three version of a filename is generated with each file you create to maintain compatibility with older applications. For example, the file *A letter to Mom.wpd* could also be referenced as *alette~1.wpd*. If you don't use older 16-bit programs, you can disable Vista's creation of these 8.3 aliases by changing this value to 1 (the default is zero).

`NtfsDisableLastAccessUpdate`

Values: 0 = enabled (default), 1 = disabled.

Windows keeps a record of the time and date every file and folder on your hard disk was created, as well as when it was last modified and last accessed. You can stop Windows from updating the "last accessed" date for folders every time they're opened by changing the value to 1 (the default is zero), which may improve drive performance. This setting has no effect on files.

`NtfsMftZoneReservation`

Values: 1 = small (default), 2 = medium, 3 = large, 4 = maximum.

The core of the NTFS filesystem is the master file table (MFT), a comprehensive index of every file on the disk (including the MFT itself). Since disk defragmenters can't defragment the MFT (also known as *$mft*), Windows reserves a certain amount of extra space for it to grow, in an effort to reduce its eventual fragmentation. The more fragmented the MFT gets, the more it will hamper overall disk performance.

You can determine the current size and fragmentation level of the MFT on any drive by using the command-line Disk Defragmenter tool (*defrag.exe*) along with the -a parameter, as described in "A Defragmentation Crash Course," earlier in this chapter. The numbers relating to the MFT are shown at the end of the **Volume Information** report. Probably the most interesting statistic here, though, is **Percent MFT in use**. The higher the number, the less space the MFT has to grow (and it will).

 The NtfsMftZoneReservation setting allows you to increase the space reserved for the MFT. Although the default is 1, values of 2 or 3 are probably better for most systems with large hard disks; the maximum value of 4 is good for very large drives with a lot of small files. Specify too small of a value here, and the MFT will become fragmented more quickly as it grows; too large of a value, and it will consume (waste) too much disk space.

The problem is that changing this setting will not have any effect on your drive's current MFT, but rather only influence its future growth. For this reason, the earlier this value is increased in the life of a disk, the better. To defragment or rebuild the MFT on your Windows drive, you'll need to transfer your operating system to a new drive, as described in the next section.

You'll need to restart Windows for any of these changes to take effect.

Transfer Windows to Another Hard Disk

Each new version of Windows consumes something like four times that of its predecessor. That kind of bloat would cause an uproar if the sizes of commercially available hard disks weren't growing at an even faster rate.

Luckily, a new drive is an inexpensive way to improve performance as well as get more space for your stuff. And there are basically two approaches:

Add a second drive. Hard drive manufacturers sell a lot of external USB drives for this purpose. It's the easiest approach, taking only a few minutes to hook up, but it does very little to improve performance. Why run Windows on an aging 60 GB drive, while your photos sit happily on a much faster 500 GB drive?

Replace the primary drive. Use this approach if you want to throw away that old 60 GB drive, and use only the 500 GB drive for Windows *and* all your data. Not only will this give you better performance, you'll have a lot less to worry about if you're running Windows on a new drive rather than one that's seen thousands of hours of use. The downside is that it's more work to completely replace your old drive, and that's what this section is about.

Thanks to improvements in technology, rapidly dropping prices of new hard disks, and a nifty new tool in Windows Vista, it's easier than ever to replace your old hard disk.

The procedure goes like this: first, connect your new drive to your PC alongside your old drive. Then, create an *image* of your old hard disk—a snapshot of every byte of data on the entire drive—and write the image to your new hard disk. Finally, disconnect the old drive and put the new one in its place.

Start by purchasing an SATA/IDE to USB 2.0 Adapter, like the $20 Vantec unit shown in Figure 5-13. Alternatively, you can use an external hard drive enclosure, although a unit like this may be a better investment, as it supports SATA, 3.5 desktop IDE, and 2.5 notebook IDE drives all from the same cable.

Next, plug the drive into the adapter, plug the power supply into the drive, and then plug the adapter into a free USB port on your PC.

Now, I know what you're thinking: why don't I just plug the drive directly into my SATA or IDE controller? While it's true that you can connect your new drive to your motherboard's controller, there are several reasons to use a USB adapter like this one instead. First, it's quick and easy; you don't need to take your PC apart (yet) and you don't have to leave the new drive dangling from the side of your box while you transfer your data.

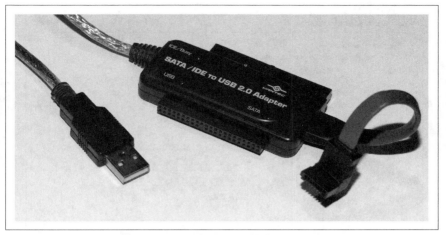

Figure 5-13. Use a handy external USB adapter like this one to hook up your new drive to your PC

Second, it's great for laptops that may not have a way to connect two drives at once. Third, it avoids the nasty problems you'd encounter if your PC tried to boot to the wrong drive in the middle of the procedure. And last but not least, when you're done, you can use the adapter to clear off the old drive. A device like this makes things *so* much easier.

When Windows detects and installs the new drive, it'll show up in **Disk Drives** branch in Device Manager (*devmgmt.msc*). (If it doesn't, see Chapter 6.) As soon as Windows finishes installing the necessary drivers, open Disk Management (*diskmgmt.msc*), right-click the new drive in the lower pane, and select **New Simple Volume**, as shown in Figure 5-14.

On the first page of the New Simple Volume Wizard, click **Next**, and then specify the size of the new partition.

You'll need to make two partitions on the new drive: the primary partition to become your new boot drive, and a secondary partition to temporarily hold the backup of your existing data. The *second* partition needs to be no larger than the capacity of your old hard disk, so set the *primary* partition to the total size of the new drive *minus* the total size of the old drive. For instance, if you're replacing a 60 GB hard disk with a 500 GB hard disk, set the first partition to 440 GB, and use the remaining 60 GB for the second.

So, at the prompt, type a value, in megabytes, for the size of the primary partition (i.e., 440000 for 440 GB) and then click **Next**. Follow the prompts to complete the wizard; make sure to format the drive with the NTFS filesystem, but don't assign a drive letter at this time.

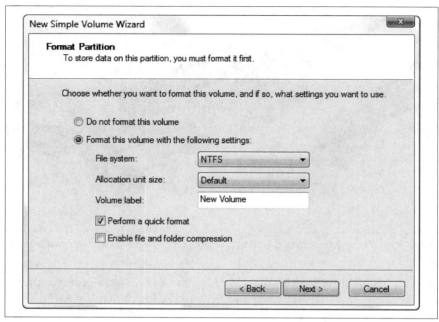

Figure 5-14. Use the Disk Management tool to prepare the new drive

Now, create the second partition in the remaining unused space, and have it consume the rest of the drive. Again, format it as NTFS, but this time, assign a drive letter (your choice).

At this point, you can copy your data to the new drive in either of two ways:

Use Complete PC Backup and Restore. If you have the Business, Ultimate, or Enterprise edition of Vista, you can use the backup software built in to Windows to back up your entire hard disk onto the *second* partition you just created, as described in "Back Up Your Entire System," in Chapter 6.

Then, power down your PC, remove your old drive, connect the new one to your primary controller, and then boot your PC. Follow the instructions in "Recover Your System After a Crash," also in Chapter 6, to restore your backup to the primary partition on the new drive.

When that's done, and you're able to boot Windows with the new drive, use the Disk Management tool to delete the secondary partition and extend the primary partition so that it consumes the whole drive, as described in "Work with Partitions," later in this chapter.

Use third-party disk imaging software. If you're using the Home Basic or Home Premium edition and don't have access to Complete PC Backup and Restore—or if you just want to complete the whole process without having to dig up your Windows installation disc—you can use third-party software instead. Try DriveImage XML (*http://www.runtime.org*) or HDClone Free Edition (*http://www.miray.de*), both free, or use a commercial product like Acronis True Image Home (*http://www.acronis.com*).

Use your disk-imaging software to create an image of your old hard disk, and save it to the secondary partition of the new drive. Then use the same software to restore the image to the new drive's primary partition.

Next, open the Disk Management tool. Delete the secondary partition and extend the primary partition so that it consumes the whole drive, as described in "Work with Partitions," later in this chapter. Then, right-click the sole remaining partition and select **Mark Partition as Active**. Shut down Windows and then unplug both drives. Set the old drive aside and connect the new drive in its place.

Turn on your PC, and Windows should boot to the new drive. If it doesn't, see "What to Do When Windows Won't Start" in Chapter 6.

What to look for in a new hard disk

The speed of your hard disk is a major factor of your system's overall performance, at least as much as its capacity. After all, the faster it's able to find data and transfer it, the quicker Windows will load, the faster your virtual memory will be, and the less time it will take to start applications and copy files.

Money is usually *the* deciding factor when choosing a drive, but with more money, people usually just opt for more gigabytes. If you want the best performance, though, consider these factors to be at least as important:

RPM (revolutions per minute)
    This is the speed at which the disk spins; higher numbers are faster. Cheap drives spin at 5,400 RPM, but you shouldn't settle for anything less than 7,200 RPM. If you're serious about performance, get a more expensive (and harder to find) 10,000 RPM (10k) or 15,000 RPM (15k) drive.

Buffer (measured in megabytes)
    The buffer is memory (RAM) installed in the drive's circuitry that allows it to accept data from your computer faster than it is able to physically write to the disk surface, and to read data from the disk surface faster when your PC isn't necessarily ready for it. A larger buffer is better; don't settle for less than 8 megabytes.

Performance

MTBF (measured in hours)

It doesn't matter how fast a drive is if it dies on you. The higher the MTBF—Mean Time Between Failures—the more reliable the drive is supposed to be. Of course, this isn't a guarantee, but rather merely an indicator of the market for which the drive was designed. Hard disks designed for servers tend to have much higher MTBF ratings than the low-end disks available on most computer-store shelves.

 If you're buying a drive for use in a DVR (Digital Video Recorder) or HTPC (Home Theater PC), it's also wise to seek out the quietest drive you can find. Although manufacturers offer very little in the way of useful, reliable noise data, you can usually cull pretty good feedback from HTPC discussion groups on the Web.

Aside from the specs, you'll also need to consider the *interface*, the connector on the back of the drive that must match the drive controller and cable already in your PC. Here are your choices:

SATA (a.k.a. Serial ATA)

For most Vista users, SATA is probably your best bet. It's faster than IDE (next), supports hot-swapping (connecting and disconnecting while the PC is on), and is easier to hook up (no jumpers or ribbon cables). Look for a SATA 3.0 (also known as SATA II) drive with the NCQ (Native command queuing) feature for the best performance.

The main drawback is that SATA connectors are flimsy and easily broken, so if you'll be hot-swapping your drives, consider instead eSATA (SATA with a stronger connector for external drives) or SCSI (described shortly).

ATA (a.k.a. Parallel ATA or IDE)

This interface is now totally obsolete. Even if you have an older PC with only an IDE controller on the motherboard, it's usually a better idea to get a SATA card ($20–$30) and a SATA drive than to invest in an older IDE drive.

Consider IDE only if you have a laptop that just takes 2.5-inch IDE drives, or if you need to set up a dual-boot system with an older version of Windows that doesn't support SATA.

SCSI/SAS

Ultra320 SCSI is still faster than SATA, and will likely be your only choice if you want a super-fast 15K RPM drive. But given that SCSI controllers are unreasonably expensive, as are SCSI drives, consider this option only if you absolutely need the fastest drive money can buy.

USB/Firewire

If you're buying an external drive—which is great for backups, as I'll explain in Chapter 6—you may be tempted to get a USB drive or enclosure. While USB 2.0 is reasonably fast at 480 mbps, and Firewire 800 is slightly faster at 800 mbps, both of these standards will restrict the speed of your drive. For faster backups and less time spent transferring files, you'd be hard-pressed to beat eSATA (external SATA), which supports speeds up to 2,400 mbps. Most desktop PC and some higher-end laptops include eSATA ports for this purpose, but if your PC doesn't have one, you can get an internal-to-external (SATA-to-eSATA) adapter for just a few dollars, or a standalone eSATA controller for not much more.

Finally, there's the form factor, and this one's easy. Desktop PCs use so-called 3.5-inch drives, while laptops use 2.5-inch drives. If you're getting an external drive, you have a choice between the two; 2.5-inch drives are smaller and lighter-weight, but you get much more speed and capacity for your money with a 3.5-inch drive.

Work with Partitions

Most hard disks are known by a single drive letter, usually *C:*. However, any drive can be divided into several *partitions*, each with its own drive letter.

Most PC manufacturers these days ship partitioned hard disks. In fact, your drive may have one primary partition with all your data, plus another, smaller partition containing your PC's recovery data (to restore your hard disk to the state it was in when you bought it), and sometimes a third *EISA Configuration* partition (discussed later in this chapter). If you decide to nix the other two partitions, you can combine them and finally start using all the space on your drive.

But you also may want to chop up your drive into smaller partitions. For example, if you have a 500 GB hard disk, you may choose to divide it up into four 125 GB partitions, or perhaps a 300 GB partition and two 100 GB partitions. There are a bunch of reasons why you might want to do this:

Organization
Use multiple partitions to further organize your files and make your stuff easier to find. For example, put Windows on one drive, work documents on another, games on another, and music and other media on yet another.

Isolation of system and data
You can use partitions to isolate your programs from your data. For example, place Windows on drive *C:*, your personal documents on drive *D:*, and your virtual memory (swap file) and temporary files on drive *E:*.

This setup gives you the distinct advantage of being able to format your operating system partition and reinstall Windows without touching your personal data, and also makes it easier to back up just your data.

Performance

As illustrated in "A Defragmentation Crash Course," earlier in this chapter, the data on your hard drive can become badly fragmented with use, which hurts performance and increases the chances of data corruption. Because files cannot become fragmented across partition boundaries, you can dramatically reduce fragmentation by separating frequently accessed files, like those in the *Windows* and *Program Files* folders, from frequently updated files, like your virtual memory (swap file) and temporary files, as well as infrequently updated files like photos and music.

Dual-boot

To set up a dual-boot partition, described in Chapter 1, you'll need to create a separate partition for each operating system you install.

Server

If you're setting up a web server (or other type of network file server) or if you're participating in peer-to-peer file sharing, it's a good practice to put the publicly accessible folders on their own partition. This not only helps to secure the operating system from unauthorized access, but allows the OS to be upgraded or replaced without disrupting the shared folders and programs.

The Disk Management nickel tour

Windows Vista comes with several disk partitioning tools, but the most useful is Disk Management, shown in Figure 5-15. You can use Disk Management to view the partitions of any drive on your system, as well as create, delete, and resize partitions, and even change the drive letters for any drives or partitions on your PC. Open the Start menu, and in the **Search** box, type diskmgmt.msc and press **Enter**.

The main Disk Management window is divided into two panes, each of which shows the same information in different ways. (You can change the arrangement of the panes by going to **View** → **Top** or **View** → **Bottom**, but Disk Management won't remember any of your settings for next time.)

The **Graphical View**, shown in the lower pane by default, is easily the most useful, and is the subject of most of the rest of this section. The **Volume List**, shown in the upper pane by default, shows only your hard disk drive letters, and is a subset of the drive list in Windows Explorer. And the **Disk List** is merely a list of the physical disk devices in your PC, somewhat like the **Disk Drives** branch in Device Manager.

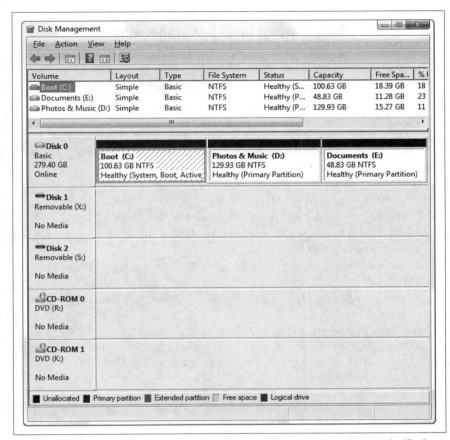

Figure 5-15. Open the Disk Management utility to add or remove partitions, shuffle drive letters, and even change the way volumes are mounted

By default, the boxes in the **Graphical View** representing multiple partitions (volumes) are not displayed proportionally to their size; a 20 GB partition will appear to be roughly the same size as a 100 GB partition. To fix this, go to **View** → **Settings**, choose the **Scaling** tab, and select the **According to capacity, using linear scaling** option in both sections. You can also customize the program's colors with the **Appearance** tab, but unless you follow the steps in the upcoming "Save Settings in Disk Management" sidebar, your changes will be lost as soon as you close the window.

Disk Management takes an active role in making drives available in Windows Explorer. Most of the time, as soon as you insert a flash memory card

Save Settings in Disk Management

The Disk Management tool is actually what Microsoft calls a "snap-in" for the Microsoft Management Console (*mmc.exe*). Other snap-ins include Device Manager, the Services window, and the Group Policy Object Editor.

The *.msc* file you launch to open the Disk Management tool is not actually the program, but rather just a small *console* file, which contains only the settings for the current view. Although you can't save your customizations to *diskmgmt.msc*, you can create a new console file with the snap-ins you need, and customize it to your heart's content:

1. Open the Microsoft Management Console (*mmc.exe*). A new, blank Console Root window will appear in the MMC window.

2. Go to **File → Add/Remove Snap-in**, and then click **Add**.

3. Select **Disk Management** from the **Available Standalone Snap-ins** list, and then click **Add**.

4. From the window that appears, select **This Computer** and then click **Finish**.

5. You can add other snap-ins at this point, or just click **OK** when you're done.

6. If Disk Management is the only snap-in you selected, highlight the Disk Management entry in the tree on the left to show the tool in the center pane. Then go to **View → Customize**, turn off the **Console tree** and **Action pane** options, and click **OK**.

7. Now, you can customize Disk Management as you see fit. For instance, to show only the Graphical View, select **View → Top → Graphical View** and then **View → Bottom → Hidden**.

8. When you're finished customizing, go to **File → Save** to save your custom console view into a new *.msc* file such as *Disk Management.msc*.

The next time you use Disk Management, just open your custom *.msc* file instead of *diskmgmt.msc* to use your customized tool.

into your card reader or pop in a CD or DVD, the new volume appears in Disk Management and Explorer. But sometimes, Disk Management may fail to acknowledge that you've connected a device (say, an external hard disk), and as a result, its drive letter won't appear in Explorer. To force Windows to recognize your drive changes, press the **F5** key or go to **Action → Rescan Disks**, and in a few seconds, the newly connected drive should appear in all windows. If it doesn't, open up Device Manager, and from the **Action** menu there, select **Scan for hardware changes**.

In the **Graphical View**, you'll see different kinds of partitions; here are the most common:

Primary partition

> Most partitions are of this type. If you have more than one partition, the first usable partition (one that can hold data) is almost always a primary. Primary partitions are marked with a dark-blue stripe by default.
>
> The old-school approach is to have only one primary partition, followed by an *extended* partition (discussed next). This is no longer needed for NTFS volumes; in fact, if you're setting up a dual-boot system, each OS must have its own primary partition.

Extended partition

> The extended partition is a holdover from earlier days, and was used when a drive had two or more partitions. It doesn't actually hold data, it merely serves as a container for one or more *logical* drives (discussed next). Extended partitions and logical drives are more or less obsolete today (Vista's Disk Management tool can't even create them), but you may see them on older partitioned drives. The extended partition is, by default, shown as a dark-green outline surrounding any logical drives.

Logical drive

> If you have a drive with an extended partition, each volume inside is called a logical drive. See the notes for primary and extended partitions, earlier, for details. By default, logical drives are identified in light blue.

EISA Configuration

> This is a tiny partition that holds configuration data for the rest of the drive, and it is typically placed at the beginning of the disk. You'll see this on most RAID drives (see Chapter 6) and often on drives installed in mass-produced PCs. Disk Management can't delete EISA Configuration partitions, but Acronis Disk Director (see "Resize and move partitions," later in this chapter) can.

Create and delete partitions

Every hard disk must be partitioned before it can be used, even if that disk only gets a single partition. Here's how to prepare a brand-new hard disk, an unnecessary step when you decide to "Transfer Windows to Another Hard Disk," as explained earlier in this chapter.

First, open Disk Management (*diskmgmt.msc*), and make sure the **Graphical View**, shown by default in the lower pane, is visible. Enlarge the pane and the window if necessary to see all your drives.

To create a new partition, right-click a region of your disk marked **Unallocated**, and select **New Simple Volume**. The steps in the New Simple Volume Wizard are pretty self-explanatory, and basically involve dialing in a size for the new partition (use the maximum if you want to use the whole drive), choosing a drive letter, and picking a filesystem (choose NTFS, as described "Choose the Right Filesystem," earlier in this chapter).

Or, to delete an existing partition, right-click the partition and select **Delete Volume**.

 If you delete a partition, all the data on that volume will be permanently lost. This happens immediately, and there is no undo. Data on other partitions of the same physical drive won't be affected. If you wish to make a partition smaller or larger *without* erasing the data, see the "Resize and move partitions" section, which follows.

In most cases, newly created or deleted partitions will appear (or disappear) in Windows Explorer immediately.

Resize and move partitions

Say you just bought a laptop with an 80 GB hard disk and then discover that Windows Explorer only sees about 70 GB of it. You open Disk Management and discover that there's an extra partition, labeled "Recovery," consuming about 8 GB. How do you get rid of the extra partition and reclaim all that space for your data?

Or, perhaps you've decided to divide a 320 GB hard disk—one that's currently holding an active Windows installation—into two 160 GB partitions. How do you make space for the second partition without deleting the single partition that's currently using the whole disk?

The solution is to resize the partition, which—thanks to some improvements in Disk Manager since Windows XP—is not all that hard to do. And you don't even have to take the data off first. (Of course, despite this confident prose, it's still wise to back up your entire drive before messing with partitions.)

To begin, open Disk Management and expand the Graphical View pane so you can see all your drives.

In the case of the unwanted "Recovery" partition, start by right-clicking it in Disk Management and selecting **Delete Volume**.

You can't undo **Delete Volume**, so make sure you can live without the "Recovery" partition before you proceed. In most cases, it isn't necessary to keep this volume unless you plan on wiping your hard disk and reinstalling Vista *without* the original installation DVD. If you don't have a disc, check with your PC's manufacturer to see whether they can provide you with one.

Once the "Recovery" partition is gone, you'll have a swath of empty space marked **Unallocated** at the end of your drive. (If it's at the beginning, you'll need a tool like Disk Director, discussed in the next section.) Now all you have to do is right-click your primary partition and select **Extend Volume** to resize the remaining partition so that it consumes the unused space.

If you want to do the opposite—that is, make room at the end of the disk for a new partition—just right-click the primary partition and select **Shrink Volume**. After a bit of pondering, Disk Management will show the Shrink dialog (Figure 5-16), which will probably show you less "available shrink space" than you thought you had coming.

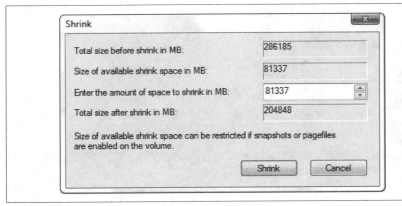

Figure 5-16. Use the Shrink Volume window to make space on your drive for new partitions

Say you have about 150 GB of data on your 500 GB drive, but the Shrink window says you can only reclaim about 75 GB (7,500 MB) of free space. Why so stingy?

It turns out that Windows doesn't necessarily store all your data at the beginning of a partition, but rather scatters it around to help reduce fragmentation. As a result, there may be some data toward the end, serving as a barrier to prevent Disk Management from shrinking your drive past that point.

The solution is to use the command-line Disk Defragmenter tool (*defrag.exe*) with the -w parameter, as described in "A Defragmentation Crash Course," earlier in this chapter. When that's done, return to Disk Management and try **Shrink Volume** once more.

If the **Shrink Volume** feature in Disk Management still won't give you as much space as you need, you'll need a more capable program like Disk Director, covered next.

Alternatives to Disk Management

The Disk Management utility is not your only choice when it comes to repartitioning drives, but as far as the tools included with Windows Vista are concerned, it's the best one.

The other usable alternative is Vista's DiskPart utility (*diskpart.exe*), a way of viewing, adding, and removing partitions from the Command Prompt; see the upcoming sidebar "The DiskPart Command-Line Tool" for a walkthrough.

In the good old days—also known simply as the old days—the only way to resize partitions without deleting the data on them was to use a program called PartitionMagic. But since Symantec bought PartitionMagic and ruined it, the best choice now is Acronis Disk Director (*http://www.acronis.com/*), shown in Figure 5-17.

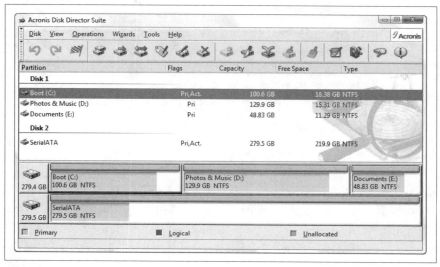

Figure 5-17. To move partitions, delete EISA Configuration volumes, and more, use Acronis Disk Director

The DiskPart Command-Line Tool

DiskPart is essentially the command-line equivalent to the Disk Management tool, and can be useful in certain situations (such as when Windows won't start).

You'll need to run DiskPart in administrator mode (see Chapter 8); one way to do this is to open your Start menu, type diskpart in the **Search** box, and then when **diskpart.exe** appears in the search results, right-click it and select **Run as administrator**.

Once it's running, type help at any time to see a list of commands. To get started, here's how to extend a volume in DiskPart:

1. At the DISKPART> prompt, type:

   `list disk`

   to display all the drives on your computer. Each drive will have a disk number, starting with 0 (zero).

2. Unless you have only one drive, you'll have to tell DiskPart which drive to use, like this:

   `select disk n`

   where *n* represents the number of the disk to modify.

3. Next, at the DISKPART> prompt, type:

   `list volume`

   to display all the volumes on the selected disk. Likewise, each volume has a volume number, starting with 0 (zero).

4. Regardless of the number of volumes on the drive, you'll have to tell DiskPart which one to use, like this:

   `select volume 2`

5. Now that you've selected the partition to expand, go ahead and issue this command:

   `extend`

   to extend the volume. The extend command takes no options and displays no warning message or confirmation. The process begins immediately after you press the **Enter** key, and should take only a few seconds.

6. When it's done, type exit to quit the DiskPart utility.

See Chapter 9 for more information on the Command Prompt.

Among other things, Disk Director lets you move partitions, resize from the left (beginning) or right (end), and delete otherwise undeletable partitions, such as the EISA Configuration volumes discussed earlier in this section.

Unfortunately, Disk Director costs money, and if it's not something you're going to use every day, you may be interested in a free, albeit less convenient, solution. You can use QTParted, the partition editor that comes with Linux. Now, you don't have to install Linux, but rather only boot off a Linux Live CD like the one available at *http://iso.linuxquestions.org/mepis/*. It supports NTFS as well as FAT32, and lets you freely resize partitions without destorying data. (Of course, it's always wise to back up first.)

Different ways to mount a volume

As explained earlier in this section, a hard disk can have one partition or many. Other types of storage devices, such as CD and DVD drives, can only have a single partition. These partitions, regardless of the nature of the physical device on which they're located, are all recognized as *volumes* by the Disk Management tool and by Windows Explorer.

Mounting is the method by which a volume is made accessible to Windows Explorer and all your applications. In most cases, each volume has its own drive letter, such as *C:* or *D:*. But a volume can also be accessed through a folder on any other volume, called a *mount point* (available on NTFS drives only). Finally, there can be volumes on your system that aren't mounted at all, such as those with filesystems Vista doesn't support and those you don't want to show up in Windows Explorer.

You can change how any volume is mounted, except for the *system* volume (the one containing your boot files) and the *boot* volume (the one on which Windows is installed).

To change the drive letter of a hard disk volume, right-click the partition itself in the right side of the Graphical View pane in Disk Management, and select **Change Drive Letter and Paths**.

Or, to change the drive letter of a nonfixed disk, such as your DVD drive or CompactFlash card reader, right-click the disk in the narrow lefthand column, and select **Change Drive Letter and Paths**.

In either case, you can choose a new drive letter (e.g., *H:*) by clicking the **Change** button, shown in Figure 5-18. Click **Remove** if you don't want the drive to show up in Windows Explorer at all. Or, click **Add** to choose an empty folder as a mount point (or pick a drive letter where there is none).

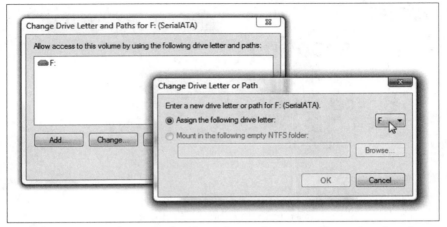

Figure 5-18. You can change the drive letter for any device, as well as mount the volume as a folder on another drive, using the Change Drive Letter and Paths dialog

 If you select **Mount in the following empty NTFS folder**, click **Browse** to point to an existing, empty folder on a hard disk that already has a drive letter. If you were to mount the volume in the folder *C:\backdoor*, then the contents of the newly mounted drive would be accessible in *C:\backdoor*. A folder named *some folder* on the new drive would then appear as *D:\backdoor\some folder*. You can view all of the drives mounted in folders by going to **View → Drive Paths**.

Click **OK** when you're done. For another way to hook up drives and folders, see the "Map a Network Drive" sidebar in Chapter 8.

CHAPTER 6

Troubleshooting

So, what do you find most annoying about Windows Vista?

Is it the name? Maybe the Flip 3D task switcher? Too many sample videos taking up space on your hard disk? Or perhaps it's the softly glowing buttons in the interface that exude self-importance?

At the end of the day, though, it's probably that Windows Explorer keeps crashing. And that Vista can't seem to find a driver for your USB card reader, *again*. And the User Access Control (UAC) prompt that keeps popping up. And the fact that it seems to take forever to copy a handful of files from one place to another. And the fact that Vista won't let you retrieve individual files from a full system backup (or maybe you haven't discovered that last one *yet*).

If these are the reasons you're reading this book, then this chapter is for you. (Actually, the UAC is covered in Chapter 8, but that one drives everyone nuts.)

Troubleshooting is the act of figuring out what's wrong with a program or a piece of hardware, and then fixing it. It used to be that we had error messages to help us, but Microsoft got rid of most of them in Windows Vista; turns out, they weren't that helpful anyway. Now, when something breaks, it simply stops working.

Now, if you remember only two pearls of wisdom from this chapter, let them be these:

- 99% of all computer problems are solved by rebooting. (Restart Windows, turn it off and then back on, press your PC's reset button, whatever.)

- Insanity can be defined as repeating the same actions over and over again, expecting different results. (Or, worse: repeating the same actions over and over again, *knowing* that you'll never get different results.)

Naturally, a corollary to these principles is that rebooting repeatedly will get you nowhere. Herein lies the rub: what do you do during that remaining 1% of the time when rebooting the first time doesn't help?

Unfortunately, troubleshooting a Windows PC involves more than just whining about it. One of the first things you need to do to solve a problem is to find the right words to describe the problem; you'd be surprised at how many people start with something like "it doesn't work." OK, what precisely is it that doesn't work? Did you get an error message? Is there smoke billowing out of the vents? Or did your program simply not do what you expected it to?

Here's a short checklist of questions to ask yourself to get you—or rather, your PC—on the road to recovery:

Is this an isolated incident, or does this problem occur every time?
As much as Microsoft will deny it, crashing is a fact of life on a Windows system, even when you're using Windows Vista (although some clowns will swear up and down that their systems are "rock-solid"). An isolated incident is often just that, and, if nothing else, is a good reminder to save your work often. On the other hand, if a given error message or crash occurs repeatedly at the same time, in the same place, or as a result of the same mouse click, you need to isolate the trigger mechanism if you hope to solve the problem.

When did the problem start happening?
Sudden changes in your computer's behavior are almost never spontaneous; if something suddenly stops working, you can bet that there's a culprit. If the day the problem surfaced is the same day you installed a new application, or the day you asked Windows Update to install a new driver, then you've got yourself a prime suspect.

Is the problem with a specific application or hardware device, or is it Windows' fault?
You can rule out a specific application if the problem occurs in more than one program. You can rule out devices by unplugging them or disabling their drivers in Device Manager. And if you're really motivated, you can rule out your specific Windows installation by installing a second copy of the operating system on a different drive, as described in Chapter 1.

But don't forget that software products are a lot like pharmaceuticals: interactions can cause problems when the products by themselves are harmless.

Am I using the latest version?

Software and hardware manufacturers frequently release updates and fixes, so it's always a good idea to check their web sites for the latest versions of all applications and drivers. See "Dealing with Drivers and Other Tales of Hardware Troubleshooting," later in this chapter, for details.

How likely is it that someone else has encountered the same problem I have?

This is often the most useful question to ask yourself, because the odds are that someone else not only has encountered the same problem (anything from an annoying software quirk to a deafening application crash), but has already discovered a solution and written about it in some online forum. For example, there's a Windows Vista discussion forum at *http://www.annoyances.org* for this specific purpose!

Am I asking the right people?

If you're having trouble connecting to the wireless Internet at the airport, don't call your plumber. On the other hand, the computer store won't be much help with a jammed pressure-balance valve. Again, it comes down to isolating the source of a problem, and this is one of the hardest things to do, particularly when the technical support representative on the phone is insisting that your problem is not *his* problem.

How much is my time worth?

This last tidbit of wisdom comes from years of experience. Some problems require hours and hours of fruitless troubleshooting and needless headaches. In some cases, it makes more sense to replace the product that's giving you trouble than to try to fix it. Keep that in mind when it's four o'clock in the morning and Windows refuses to recognize your $15 flash memory card reader.

Thus endeth the Q&A portion of this evening's programming. Stay tuned for the feature presentation....

Crashes and Error Messages

Once you start peeking under Windows' hood, you'll notice some of the tools that have been included to help the system run smoothly. Some of these tools actually work, but it's important to know which ones to use and which ones are simply gimmicks.

Viruses, Malware, and Spyware

Malware, or *mal*icious soft*ware*, is a class of software designed specifically to wreak havoc on a computer—your computer. Malware includes such nasty entities as viruses, Trojan horses, worms, and spyware.

If you're experiencing frequent crashing, nonsensical error messages, pop-up advertisements (other than when surfing the Web), or slower-than-normal performance, the culprit may be one of the following types of malware (as opposed to a feature authored by Microsoft):

Viruses

A virus is a program or piece of code that "infects" other software by embedding a copy of itself in one or more executable files. When the software runs, so does the embedded virus, thus propagating the "infection." Viruses can replicate themselves, and some (known as *polymorphic* viruses) can even change their virus signatures each time to avoid detection by antivirus software.

Unlike *worms*, defined next, viruses can't infect other computers without assistance from people (a.k.a. you), a topic discussed in detail in the next section. One particular type of virus, a *Trojan horse*, spreads itself by masquerading as a benign application (as opposed to *infecting* an otherwise valid file), such as a screensaver or even, ironically, a virus removal tool.

Worms

A worm* is a special type of virus that can infect a computer without any help from its user, typically through a network or Internet connection. Worms can replicate themselves like ordinary viruses, but do not spread by infecting programs or documents. A classic example is the *W32.Blaster.Worm*, which exploited a bug in Windows XP, causing it to restart repeatedly or simply seize up.

Spyware and adware

Spyware is a little different than the aforementioned viruses and worms, in that its purpose is not necessarily to hobble a computer or destroy data, but rather something much more insidious. Spyware is designed to install itself transparently on your system, spy on you, and then send the data it collects back to an Internet server. This is sometimes done to collect information about unsuspecting users, but most often to serve as a conduit for pop-up advertisements (known as adware).

---

* The term *worm* is said to have its roots in J.R.R. Tolkien, who described dragons in Middle Earth that were powerful enough to lay waste to entire regions. Two such dragons (Scatha and Glaurung) were known as "the Great Worms." The *Great Worm*, a virus written by Robert T. Morris in 1988, was particularly devastating, mostly because of a bug in its own code. (Source: Jargon File 4.2.0.)

Many of these advertisements are pornographic in nature, and will make no exceptions for the age or personal preference of those viewing them. The good news is that this type of attack, whether designed to change your default home page, display pop-up ads, or glean sensitive information from your hard disk, is easily stoppable and clearly preventable.

Aside from the ethical implications, spyware can be particularly troublesome because it's so often very poorly written, and as a result, ends up causing error messages, performance slowdowns, and seemingly random crashing. Plus, it uses your computer's CPU cycles and Internet connection bandwidth to accomplish its goals, leaving fewer resources available for the applications you actually want to use.

Now, it's often difficult to tell one type of malicious program from another, and in some ways, it doesn't matter. But if you understand how these programs work—how they get into your computer, and what they do once they've taken root—you can eliminate them and keep them from coming back.

How malware spreads

Once they've infected a system, viruses and the like can be very difficult to remove. For that reason, your best defense against them is to prevent them from infecting your computer in the first place.

The most useful tool you can use to keep malware off your computer is your cerebral cortex. Just as malware is written to exploit vulnerabilities in computer systems, the *distribution* of malware exploits the stupidity of users.

Malware is typically spread in the following ways:

Email attachments
One of the most common ways viruses make their way into computers is through spam. Attachments are embedded in these junk email messages and sent by the millions to every email address in existence, for unsuspecting recipients to click, open, and execute. But how can people be that dumb, you may ask? Well, consider the filename of a typical Trojan horse:

> *kittens playing with yarn.jpg   .scr*

Since Windows has its filename extensions hidden by default (see Chapter 2), this is how the file looks to most Vista users:

> *kittens playing with yarn.jpg*

In other words, most people wouldn't recognize that this is an *.scr* (screensaver) file and *not* a photo of kittens. (The long space in the filename ensures that it won't be easy to spot, even if extensions are visible.)

And since many spam filters and antivirus programs block *.exe* files, but not *.scr* files—which just happen to be renamed *.exe* files—this innocuous-looking file is more than likely to spawn a nasty virus on someone's computer with nothing more than an innocent double-click.

So, how do you protect yourself from these? First, don't open email attachments you weren't expecting, and manually scan everything else with an up-to-date virus scanner (discussed later in this section). Next, employ a good, passive spam filter (see "Stop Spam" in Chapter 7), and ask your ISP to filter out viruses on the server side.

 Where do these email attachments come from, you may ask? As part of their objective to duplicate and distribute themselves, many viruses hijack your email program and use it to send infected files to everyone in your address book. In nearly all cases, these viruses are designed to work with the email software most people have on their systems, namely Microsoft Outlook and Windows Mail (formerly Outlook Express). If you want to significantly hobble your computer's susceptibility to this type of attack, you'd be wise to use *any other* email software, such as Mozilla Thunderbird (*http://www.mozilla.com*) or stick with web-based email like Gmail (*http://www.gmail.com*) or Windows Live Mail (*http://mail.live.com*).

Infected files

Viruses don't just invade your computer and wreak havoc, they replicate themselves and bury copies of themselves in other files. This means that once your computer has been infected, the virus is likely sitting dormant in any of the applications and even personal documents stored on your hard disk. This not only means that you may be spreading the virus each time you email documents to others, but that others may be unwittingly sharing viruses with you.

One of the most common types of viruses involves *macros*, small scripts (programming code) embedded in documents. By some estimates, roughly three out of every four viruses is actually a macro written for Microsoft Word or Excel. These macros are executed automatically when the documents that contain them are opened, at which point they attach themselves to the global template so that they can infect every document you subsequently open and save. Both Word and Excel have security features that restrict this feature, but these measures are clumsy and most people disable them so they can work on the rest of their documents. In other words, don't rely on the virus protection built in to Microsoft Office to eliminate the threat of these types of viruses.

Peer-to-peer (P2P) file sharing

Napster started the P2P file-sharing craze years ago, but modern file sharing goes far beyond the trading of harmless music files. It's estimated that some 40% of the files available on these P2P networks contain viruses, Trojan horses, and other unwelcome guests, but even these aren't necessarily the biggest cause of concern.

To facilitate the exchange of files, these P2P programs open network ports (Chapter 7) and create gaping holes in your computer's firewall, any of which can be exploited by a variety of worms and intruders. And since people typically leave these programs running all the time (whether they intend to or not), these security holes are constantly open for business.

But wait…there's more! If the constant threat of viruses and Trojan horses isn't enough, many P2P programs themselves come with a broad assortment of spyware and adware, intentionally installed on your system along with the applications themselves. Kazaa, one of the most popular file-sharing clients, is also the biggest perpetrator of this, and the likely culprit if your system has become infected with spyware. (Note that other products like Morpheus, BearShare, Imesh, and Limewire do this, too, just in case you were thinking there was a completely "safe" alternative.)

Web sites

It may sound like the rantings of a conspiracy theorist, but even the act of visiting some web sites can infect your PC with spyware and adware. Not that it can happen transparently, but many people just don't recognize the red flags even when they're staring them in the face. Specifically, these are the "add-ins" employed by some web sites that provide custom cursors, interactive menus, or other eye candy. While loading a web page, you may see a message asking if it's OK to install some ActiveX gadget "necessary" to view the page (e.g., Comet Cursor); here, the answer is simple: no.

Just as many viruses are written to exploit Microsoft Outlook, most spyware and adware targets Microsoft Internet Explorer. By switching to a browser like Firefox, you can eliminate the threat posed by many of these nasty programs. See "Lock Down Internet Explorer," in Chapter 7, for the full story.

Network and Internet connections

Finally, your network connection (both to your LAN and to the Internet) can serve as a conduit for a worm, the special kind of virus that doesn't need your help to infect your system. Obviously, the most effective way to protect your system is to unplug it from the network, but a slightly more realistic solution is to use a firewall. Vista comes with a built-in firewall, although a router provides much better protection. See Chapter 7 for details on both solutions.

How to protect and clean your PC

The most popular and typically the most effective way to rid your computer of malware is to use dedicated antivirus software and antispyware software. These programs rely on their own internal databases of known viruses, worms, Trojans, spyware, and adware, and as such, must be updated regularly (daily or weekly) to be able to detect and eliminate the latest threats.

Vista is the first operating system to include an antispyware tool, known as Windows Defender (found in Control Panel and shown in Figure 6-1). The best part about it is that, left to its own devices, Windows Defender will regularly scan your system and even keep its spyware definitions up to date.

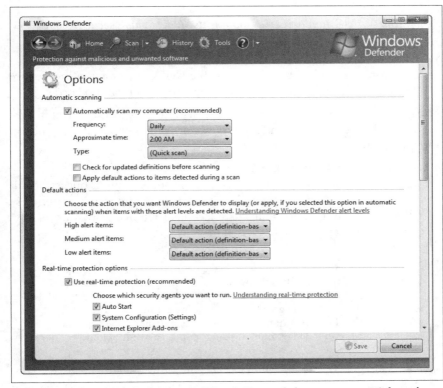

Figure 6-1. Windows Defender is included with Vista to help protect your PC from the myriad of spyware designed to exploit vulnerabilities in Windows

But Vista still doesn't come with an antivirus tool, mostly to appease the companies that make money selling aftermarket antivirus software (which is ironic, since the best tools are free). Following is a list of the more popular antivirus products.

Avast Home Edition (http://www.avast.com)
Freeware, with a slick interface and good feature set.

Avira AntiVir Classic (http://www.free-av.com)
Freeware, with frequent updates, but only average detection rates.

AVG Anti-Virus (http://free.grisoft.com)
Freeware, a popular yet poor-performing antivirus solution.

Kaspersky Antivirus Personal (http://www.kaspersky.com)
Very highly regarded solution with an excellent detection record.

McAfee VirusScan (http://www.mcafee.com)
Trusted and well-established all-around virus scanner with an intuitive interface and few limitations.

Panda Anti-Virus Titanium & Platinum (http://www.pandasecurity.com)
Lesser-known but capable antivirus software.

Symantec Norton AntiVirus (http://www.symantec.com)
Mediocre, slow antivirus software with a well-known name—but beware of its expensive subscription plan to keep virus definitions updated.

Antispyware software is a more complex field, and as a result, you'll have the best luck using multiple tools in addition to Windows Defender. The top antispyware products include:

Ad-Aware Personal Edition (http://www.lavasoft.de)
Ad-Aware is one of the oldest antispyware tools around, but its definitions are still updated frequently. The personal edition is free and very slick, although it's not usually as effective at removing spyware as Spybot or Spysweeper, both discussed next.

When using Ad-Aware, make sure you click **Check for updates now** before running a scan. Also, to turn off the awful, jarring sound Ad-Aware plays when it has found spyware, click the gear icon to open the Settings window, click the **Tweak** button, open the **Misc Settings** category, and turn off the **Play sound if scan produced a result** option.

Spybot - Search & Destroy (http://www.spybot.info)
Not quite as nice to look at as Ad-Aware, Spybot (Figure 6-2) excels at purging hard-to-remove spyware. And while both Ad-Aware and Spybot remove tracking cookies (see "Surf Anonymously" in Chapter 7) from Internet Explorer, Spybot supports Firefox as well.

Spy Sweeper (http://www.webroot.com)
This highly regarded antispyware tool, while not free like the first two, is still a welcome addition to any spyware-fighter's toolbox, and can often remove malware that the others miss.

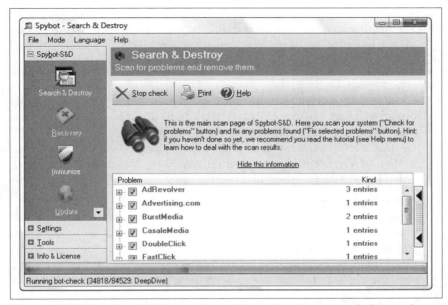

Figure 6-2. Spybot - Search & Destroy is one of several antispyware tools that can be used in conjunction with Windows Defender to help keep your PC malware-free

So, armed with proper antivirus and antispyware software, there are four things you should do to protect your computer from malware:

- Place a router between your computer and your Internet connection, as described in Chapter 7.
- Scan your system for viruses regularly, and don't rely entirely on your antivirus program's auto-protect feature (see the next section). Run a full system scan at least every two weeks.
- Scan your system for spyware regularly, at least once or twice a month. Do it more often if you download and install a lot of software.
- Use your head! See the previous section for ways that malware spreads, and the next section for some of the things you can do to reduce your exposure to viruses, spyware, adware, and other malware.

The perils of auto-protect

Antivirus software is a double-edged sword. Sure, viruses can be a genuine threat, and for many of us, antivirus software is an essential safeguard. But antivirus software can also be a real pain in the neck.

The most basic, innocuous function of an antivirus program is to scan files on demand. When you start a virus scanner and tell it to scan a file or a disk full of files, you're performing a useful task. The problem is that most of us don't remember or want to take the time to routinely perform scans, so we rely on the so-called "auto-protect" feature, where the virus scanner runs all the time. This can cause several problems:

Performance hit
> Loading the auto-protect software at Windows startup can increase boot time; also, because each and every application (and document) you open must first be scanned, load times can increase. Plus, a virus scanner that's always running consumes memory and processor cycles, even though you're not likely to spend most of your time downloading new, and potentially hazardous, files for it to scan.

Browser and email monitoring
> Some antivirus auto-protect features include web browser and email plug-ins, which scan all files downloaded and received as attachments, respectively. In addition to the performance hit, these plug-ins sometimes don't work properly, inadvertently causing all sorts of problems with the applications you use to open these files.

Annoying and obtrusive messages
> The constant barrage of virus warning messages can be annoying, to say the least. For instance, if your antivirus software automatically scans your incoming email, you may be forced to click through a dozen or so messages warning you of virus-laden attachments, even though your spam filter will likely delete them before you ever see them. And nearly every antivirus program makes a big show each time it receives definition updates; while it's nice to know the software is doing its job, it would also be nice to have it do it *quietly*.

False sense of security
> Most importantly, having the auto-protect feature installed can give you a false sense of security ("Sure, I'll open it—I have antivirus software!"), reducing the chances that you'll take the precautions listed elsewhere in this section and increasing the likelihood that your computer will become infected. Even if you are diligent about scanning files manually, no antivirus program is foolproof, and is certainly no substitute for common sense.

Now, if you take the proper precautions, your exposure to viruses will be minimal, if not nil, and you will have very little need for the auto-protect feature of your antivirus software. Naturally, whether you disable your antivirus software's auto-protect feature is up to you, but if you keep the following practices in mind, you should be able to effectively eliminate your computer's susceptibility to viruses.

If you don't download any documents or applications from the Internet, if you're not connected to a local network, if you have a firewalled connection to the Internet, and the only type of software you install is off-the-shelf commercial products, your odds of getting a virus are pretty much zero.

Viruses can only reside in certain types of files, including application (*.exe* and *.scr*) files, document files made in applications that use macros (such as Microsoft Word), Windows script files (*.vbs*), and some types of application support files (*.dll*, *.vbx*, *.vxd*, etc.). And because ZIP files (described in Chapter 2) can contain any of the aforementioned files, they're also susceptible.

 Conventional wisdom holds that plain-text email messages, text files (*.txt*), image files (*.jpg*, *.gif*, *.bmp*, etc.), video clips (*.mpg*, *.avi*, etc.) and most other types of files are benign in that they simply are not capable of being virus carriers. However, things aren't always as they seem. Case in point: the *Bloodhound.Exploit.13* Trojan horse (discovered in 2004) involved certain JPG files and a flaw in Internet Explorer (and most other Microsoft products). The bug has since been fixed, but it's not likely to be the last.

Actually, it is possible to embed small amounts of binary data into image files, which means, theoretically, that an image could contain a virus. However, such data would have to be manually extracted before it could be executed; a virus embedded in an image file would never be able to spontaneously infect your system.

You've heard it before, and here it is again: don't open email attachments sent to you from people you don't know, especially if they are Word documents or *.exe* files. If someone sends you an attachment and you're tempted to open it, scan it manually beforehand, and then *refrain from opening it*. Most antivirus software adds a context-menu item to all files, allowing you to scan any given file by right-clicking on it and selecting **Scan** (or something similar).

If you're on a network, your PC is only as secure as the least-secure PC on the network. If it's a home network, make sure everyone who uses machines on that network understands the concepts outlined here. If it's a corporate network, there's no accounting for the stupidity of your coworkers, so you may choose to leave the auto-protect antivirus software in place.

What to Do When Windows Won't Start

Unfortunately, Windows' inability to load itself is a common problem, usually occurring without an error message or any obvious way to resolve it. Sometimes you'll just get a black screen after the startup logo, or your computer may even restart itself instead of displaying the desktop. Of the many causes to this problem, many deal with hardware drivers, conflicts, or file corruption—all of which are discussed elsewhere in this chapter.

But when Windows won't start, how do you fix the problem? There's no Windows Explorer to delete files, no Internet to research solutions, no Device Manager to check and uncheck boxes, and no *Solitaire* to while away the time. You have only this book and the sound of your breath wafting over your keyboard like an evening breeze over a dead mongoose.

Luckily, Microsoft has provided an out—actually, about a dozen of them. Gone is the frustratingly limited *Recovery Console* found in Windows 2000 and XP; in its place are a handful of useful "recovery tools" on the Vista setup disc, and several alternative ways to get into Windows that are already on your hard disk (discussed later in this chapter).

Grab your Vista DVD

The best tools are on your Windows Vista setup disc, the location of which has probably escaped your mind. If you don't have one, and Vista came preinstalled on your PC, you may have a "recovery partition" as described in Chapter 5; otherwise, contact your PC manufacturer and request the original Vista DVD (after all, you paid for it when you bought the machine).

Pop the Vista disc in the drive and turn on your computer. (If your PC won't boot off the disc, see Chapter 1.) When you see the "Install Now" page, click the **Repair your computer** link at the bottom to get to the System Recovery Options window shown in Figure 6-3.

Here's how these options work:

Startup Repair
> This is the first step you should take when Vista won't start. This tool repairs your hard disk's master boot record (MBR) and partition boot sector. If Vista still won't start after using **Startup Repair**, read on.

System Restore
> This reverts your Windows installation to an earlier incarnation, which is useful if a recent driver installation has prevented Windows from booting. But beware, depending on the age of the most recent restore point, this may do nothing, or may go back too far. Use this option only if you don't have a more recent backup (discussed next). See "Go Back in Time with Restore Points and Shadow Copies," later in this chapter, for details.

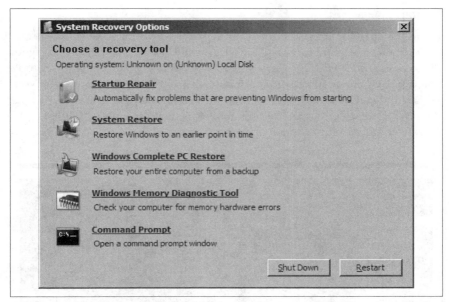

Figure 6-3. These recovery tools, available on your Vista setup disc, allow you to repair your installation in the event that Windows won't start

Windows Complete PC Restore

Use this option to wipe your hard disk clean and restore a backup you made with the Backup and Restore Center that comes with the Business and Ultimate editions of Windows Vista. (Sorry, Home Basic and Home Premium users—apparently your data is not that valuable.) See "Recover Your System After a Crash," later in this chapter.

 The fact that the Windows Complete PC Restore feature wipes your hard disk clean is a strong case for having your personal data on a separate partition from Windows, as explained in "Work with Partitions" in Chapter 5.

Windows Memory Diagnostic Tool

This examines your PC's system memory (RAM) for errors; see "Test for Bad Memory (RAM)," later in this chapter. Unlike the other tools here, this one makes no changes to your hard disk, so it's safe to use at any time.

Command Prompt

Use this tool to open a Command Prompt window, from which you can copy, delete, or rename files that may be preventing Windows from loading. Also available is the Safe Mode with Command Prompt, discussed later in this section. See Chapter 9 for details on the Command Prompt, including an overview of the commands you can type at the prompt.

Use the F8 menu

It's a pity that the recovery tools on the Vista disc aren't available without the disc itself. If you can't find the Windows DVD (or CD disc 1), or your PC manufacturer was too stingy to give you one, there are some lesser tools you can use that are already on your hard disk. Just after you power up your PC (and after it displays its own logo or POST screen), but before you see the Windows logo, press the **F8** key on your keyboard to invoke the **Advanced Boot Options** menu shown in Figure 6-4.

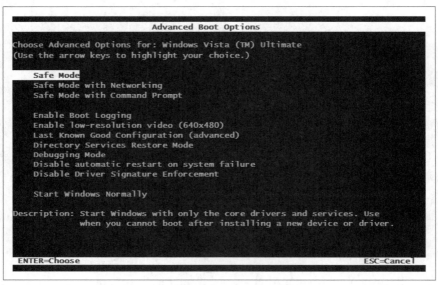

```
                         Advanced Boot Options

Choose Advanced Options for: Windows Vista (TM) Ultimate
(Use the arrow keys to highlight your choice.)

    Safe Mode
    Safe Mode with Networking
    Safe Mode with Command Prompt

    Enable Boot Logging
    Enable low-resolution video (640x480)
    Last Known Good Configuration (advanced)
    Directory Services Restore Mode
    Debugging Mode
    Disable automatic restart on system failure
    Disable Driver Signature Enforcement

    Start Windows Normally

Description: Start Windows with only the core drivers and services. Use
             when you cannot boot after installing a new device or driver.


ENTER=Choose                                             ESC=Cancel
```

Figure 6-4. Press F8 just before you see the Windows logo to display this menu, from which you have access to several tools to help you get into Windows when it won't load normally

If you can't get to the **F8** menu, then your PC isn't even trying to load Windows. At this point, you should use the **Startup Repair** option on your Vista setup disc, followed by the other choices on the System Recovery Options window. If those don't work, or if you don't have the original Vista disc, then your best bet is to remove your hard disk from your PC and hook it up to another computer using the special USB tool extolled in "Transfer Windows to Another Hard Disk" in Chapter 5. There, you should be able to determine the problem, or—worst case scenario—try to recover whatever data you can, as described in "Recover Your System After a Crash," later in this chapter.

From the **F8** menu, you'll have these choices:

Safe Mode

This forces Windows to start up in a hobbled, semi-functional mode, useful for troubleshooting or removing software or hardware drivers that otherwise prevent Windows from booting normally. Use the next option, **Safe Mode with Networking**, instead of **Safe Mode**, unless it turns out that your network drivers are the ones responsible for breaking Windows.

Safe Mode with Networking

This is the same as Safe Mode, except that Windows loads your network drivers. This is vitally important if you want Internet access when you get into Windows (useful for researching your problem).

Safe Mode with Command Prompt

Instead of loading Windows and your desktop, all you'll see is a Command Prompt window, sort of like the one you can get to from the System Recovery Options window (Figure 6-3, earlier). See Chapter 9 for help with the Command Prompt. To fix file errors on your hard disk from the Command Prompt, see "Check Your Drive for Errors with Chkdsk," later in this chapter.

The Safe Mode with Command Prompt option is a good choice if you suspect that a recent driver installation is to blame for Windows' inability to start. Once the Command Prompt appears, type `devmgt.msc` at the prompt and press **Enter** to start Device Manager. Then, find the driver in the Device Manager window, right-click the entry, and select **Disable**. Close Device Manager and restart Windows when you're done.

To get out of the Command Prompt cleanly and restart Windows, type `exit` at the prompt and press **Enter**. If typing `exit` closes the Command Prompt window but leaves Windows running, press **Ctrl-Alt-Del** and then click the tiny arrow next to the red button at the bottom of the screen.

Enable Boot Logging

This starts Windows normally, except that a log of every step is recorded into the *ntbtlog.txt* file, located in your *Windows* folder. If Windows won't start, all you need to do is attempt to start Windows with the **Enable Boot Logging** option at least once. Then, reboot your PC, press **F8** again, and choose one of the Safe Mode tools above (preferably, **Safe Mode with Networking**). When you're back in Windows, read the log with Notepad; the last entry in the log is most likely the cause of the problem.

Enable low-resolution video (640×480)

This starts Windows normally, but in VGA mode (640×480 resolution at 16 colors). This helps you troubleshoot bad video drivers or incorrect video settings by allowing you to boot Windows with the most compatible (and ugliest) display mode there is.

Last Known Good Configuration (advanced)

This starts Windows with the last set of drivers and Registry settings known to work. Use this if a recent Registry change or hardware installation has caused a problem that prevents Windows from starting. See "Go Back in Time with Restore Points and Shadow Copies," later in this chapter, for details.

Directory Services Restore Mode

Don't bother with this unless the PC is a Windows NT domain controller.

Debugging Mode

This option, typically of no use to end-users, sends debug information to your serial port to be recorded by another computer.

Disable automatic restart on system failure

Unlike the previous eight entries here, this option merely changes a setting so you can determine why Windows won't start. By default, if Vista crashes while it's loading (see "Blue Screen of Death," later in this chapter), it reboots your PC so fast, you can't read the error message on that infamous blue screen. Choose **Disable automatic restart on system failure** if you want to read the message and then reboot by hand.

Disable Driver Signature Enforcement

By default, the 64-bit edition of Windows Vista won't allow you to install any device drivers that haven't been digitally signed (a bureaucratic requirement to get the Microsoft certification logo on a product's packaging). In theory, you should be able to choose **Disable Driver Signature Enforcement** to allow your PC to install nonsigned drivers, but in practice, this never works. Instead, boot Windows normally, open a Command Prompt window (in administrator mode; see Chapter 8), and type the following:

```
bcdedit.exe -set loadoptions DDISABLE_INTEGRITY_CHECKS
```

and then press **Enter**. Close the Command Prompt and restart Windows for the change to take effect. If that doesn't help, you may have to forgo supporting a specific device until the manufacturer makes a signed, native (64-bit) driver available.

Repair your computer (not shown in Figure 6-4)

You may see this option if your PC came with Vista preinstalled and your PC manufacturer was too cheap to include a real Windows installation disc. See "Recover Your System After a Crash," later in this chapter, for details.

Start Windows Normally

Use this self-explanatory option to continue booting Windows normally, as though you never had invoked the **F8** menu.

With these tools (and the referenced sections in this book), you should have everything you need to get Windows running again. At the point you discover the grim fact that your repair mission has turned into a *recovery* mission, see "Recover Your System After a Crash," later in this chapter.

Manage Startup Programs

The *Startup* folder in the Start menu is where most people go if they want Windows to start an application automatically when it boots. Just drag a shortcut to the program into the folder, and Windows will do the rest.

Or, if there's a program you don't want Windows to load—either because it's causing an error message or because Vista is booting too slowly—just right-click the shortcut in the *Startup* folder and select **Delete**.

Trouble is, there are many ways to configure startup programs, and if you're trying to solve a problem or just reduce boot times, you need to look at them all:

Startup folders

There are actually two of these on your hard disk, but shortcuts in both places show up in the **Startup** menu (under **All Programs** in your Start menu). If you have a lot of cleanup to do, you'll find it's easier to open Windows Explorer than to repeatedly open the Start menu. First, your personal *Startup* folder is located here:

C:\Users\{username}\AppData\Roaming\Microsoft\Windows\Start Menu\Programs\Startup

and programs listed therein will load automatically when you first log in to your user account. Next, the "All Users" *Startup* folder here:

C:\ProgramData\Microsoft\Windows\Start Menu\Programs\Startup

lists the programs to load automatically when *anyone* logs into your PC.

Registry

There are several places in the Registry (see Chapter 3) in which startup programs are specified. Installers add their programs to these keys for several reasons: to prevent tinkering, for more flexibility, or—in the case of viruses, Trojan horses, and spyware—to hide from plain view.

These keys contain startup programs for the current user (er, you):

```
HKEY_CURRENT_USER\SOFTWARE\Microsoft\Windows\CurrentVersion\Run
HKEY_CURRENT_USER\SOFTWARE\Microsoft\Windows\CurrentVersion\RunOnce
```

These keys contain startup programs for all users:

```
HKEY_LOCAL_MACHINE\SOFTWARE\Microsoft\Windows\CurrentVersion\Run
HKEY_LOCAL_MACHINE\SOFTWARE\Microsoft\Windows\CurrentVersion\RunOnce
```

The naming of the keys should be self-explanatory. Programs referenced in either of the Run keys listed previously are run every time Windows starts, and are where you'll find most of your startup programs. An entry referenced in one of the RunOnce keys is run only once and then removed from the key.

 If you find yourself returning to the two **Run** keys frequently, use Registry Editor's **Favorites** menu to create shortcuts to each location, and name them accordingly (e.g., HKCU-Run and HKLM-Run).

Services

The Services window (*services.msc*) lists dozens of programs especially designed to run in the background in Windows Vista. The advantage that services have over the other startup methods here is that they remain active, even when no user is currently logged in. That way, for example, your web server can continue to serve web pages when the Welcome/Login screen is displayed.

By default, some services are configured to start automatically with Windows and others are not, and this distinction is made in the **Startup Type** column. Double-click any service and change the **Startup type** option to **Automatic** to have it start with Windows, or **Disabled** if you never want it to start automatically. You can even group all the automatic services together by clicking the **Startup Type** column to sort the list.

 Changing the Startup type for a service won't load (start) or unload (stop) the service. Use the **Start** and **Stop** buttons on the toolbar of the Services window, or double-click a service and click **Start** or **Stop**.

So, you've decided to scour your system for superfluous or dangerous startup programs, and you've encountered one you don't recognize. Before you pull the plug on a particular entry, follow these steps to find out what it's for:

1. First, determine the name of the file involved. If it's a Registry entry, the filename (and usually the full path) is shown in the right column in the Run/RunOnce key. For *Startup* folder items, right-click the shortcut icon and select **Properties** to uncover the program filename. Or, if it's a service, double-click the service and look at the **Path to executable** line under the **General** tab.

2. Once you have the program filename, open Windows Explorer and navigate to the file's location. (If the pathname wasn't included, type the filename into Explorer's **Search** box, and be sure to look beyond the index (see Chapter 2).

   Right-click the program executable, select **Properties**, and choose the **Version** tab. The manufacturer name, and sometimes the product name, will be listed here. If there's no **Version** tab, it means the file has no version information, a symptom typically indicative of a virus or some form of malware (see "Viruses, Malware, and Spyware," earlier in this chapter).

3. If the file itself doesn't explain its own purpose, fire up a web browser and search Google for the filename. In nearly all cases, you'll find a web site that describes what it's for, and in the case of malware, how to remove it.

4. Still stumped? Some malware installers create new, random filenames for their startup programs specifically so you can't easily identify them. If you have a hunch that an entry doesn't belong, try temporarily relocating it.

   If it's a shortcut in your *Startup* folder, move the shortcut to a temporary folder rather than deleting it, which allows for easy retrieval if it turns out to be necessary.

 For entries in your Registry, create a Registry patch (see Chapter 3) to back up the key, and then simply delete the offending entry. Now, as a test, click another key in the Registry tree, and then flip back to the **Run** key where you just made your change. Is the entry still gone? If not, you may be dealing with malware that knows how to repair itself, and you'll likely have to use one of the tools listed in "Viruses, Malware, and Spyware," earlier in this chapter.

5. Restart your system, and look for abnormalities (as well as normalities). If all is well, you can probably discard the removed entries.

If you don't feel like looking in all these places separately, but you also don't feel comfortable ignoring them, open the Performance Information and Tools page in Control Panel and click the **Manage Startup Programs** link on the left to open the Windows Defender Software Explorer. You can also try a program like Startup Control Panel, available for free from *http://www. mlin.net/StartupCPL.shtml*. Among other things, it has a "Recycle Bin" of sorts that lets you easily recover recently axed Startup programs.

Check Your Drive for Errors with Chkdsk

The Chkdsk utility—*chkdsk.exe*, pronounced "check disk" for those who enjoy pronouncing program executable filenames—scans your hard disk for errors and optionally fixes any it finds. To run Chkdsk, open a Command Prompt window (*cmd.exe*), type chkdsk at the prompt, and press **Enter**.

> File errors—one of the problems Chkdsk can detect and fix —are also capable of preventing Windows from booting. If Windows won't start, use the **Safe Mode with Command Prompt** startup option discussed in "What to Do When Windows Won't Start," earlier in this chapter.

When you run Chkdsk without any options, you'll get a report that looks something like this:

```
The type of the file system is NTFS.
Volume label is SHOEBOX.

WARNING!  F parameter not specified.
Running CHKDSK in read-only mode.

CHKDSK is verifying files (stage 1 of 3)...
  156352 file records processed.
File verification completed.
  433 large file records processed.
  0 bad file records processed.
  2 EA records processed.
  54 reparse records processed.
CHKDSK is verifying indexes (stage 2 of 3)...
  586626 index entries processed.
Index verification completed.
  5 unindexed files processed.
CHKDSK is verifying security descriptors (stage 3 of 3)...
  156352 security descriptors processed.
Security descriptor verification completed.
  18159 data files processed.
CHKDSK is verifying Usn Journal...
  36020056 USN bytes processed.
Usn Journal verification completed.
```

```
Windows has checked the file system and found no problems.

105520148 KB total disk space.
 58674344 KB in 134061 files.
    60396 KB in 18160 indexes.
        0 KB in bad sectors.
   320208 KB in use by the system.
    65536 KB occupied by the log file.
 46465200 KB available on disk.

     4096 bytes in each allocation unit.
 26380037 total allocation units on disk.
 11616300 allocation units available on disk.
```

You can interrupt Chkdsk at any time by pressing **Ctrl-C**.

If Chkdsk finds any errors, it'll say so in its report. However, as suggested by the WARNING! F parameter message in the report, it won't fix any problems it finds unless you specifically instruct it to do so with the /f parameter, like this:

```
chkdsk /f
```

The following terms describe most of the different types of problems that Chkdsk might report:

Lost clusters
> These are pieces of data that are no longer associated with any existing files. They just need to be cleaned up.

Bad sectors
> Bad sectors are actually physical flaws on the disk surface. Use the /r option, explained shortly, to attempt to recover data stored on bad sectors. Note that recovery of such data is not guaranteed (unless you have a backup somewhere).

 You may have one or more bad sectors if you see gibberish when you view the contents of a directory (with the dir command), or if Windows crashes or freezes every time you attempt to access a certain file. Of course, this may also be the work of the "Green Ribbon of Death," covered later in this chapter.

Cross-linked files
> If a single piece of data has been claimed by two or more files, those files are said to be *cross-linked*.

Invalid file dates or times
> Chkdsk also scans for file dates and times that it considers "invalid," such as missing dates or those before January 1, 1980.

By default, Chkdsk will only scan the current drive (shown in the prompt—C:> for drive C:). To scan a different drive, include the drive letter as one of the command-line options, like this: chkdsk d: /f.

The other important options available to Chkdsk are the following:

/r The /r parameter is essentially the same as /f, except that it also scans for—and recovers data from—bad sectors, as described earlier. This just takes longer, and probably isn't necessary unless /f is insufficient.

/b When Chkdsk finds a bad sector (as the result of an /r scan), it effectively "fences off" the region so Windows can never store data there again. Use the /b parameter to recheck those regions in the hopes that they can be used once again. For obvious reasons, this is usually not a good idea, and is pretty much a big waste of time.

/x Include this option to force Windows to dismount the volume before scanning the drive, a useful step for drives with shared folders (see Chapter 8). If you don't include /x, and the drive is in use, Chkdsk usually has to schedule a scan during the next boot. The /x parameter implies the /f option.

There are also the /i and /c options, which are used only to skip certain checks in order to complete the scan more quickly; there's usually no reason to use them.

To run Chkdsk from Windows Explorer, right-click any drive, select **Properties**, choose the **Tools** tab, and click **Check Now**. Here, the **Automatically fix file system errors** option corresponds to the /f parameter, and the **Scan for and attempt recovery of bad sectors** option corresponds to the /r parameter. Unfortunately, this way, you don't get the detailed report. And when Windows won't start, the Command Prompt interface is basically your only choice.

Dirty drives and automatic scans

When a volume is marked "dirty," Windows scans it with Chkdsk automatically during the boot process. A drive can become dirty if it's in use when Windows crashes, or Chkdsk schedules a scan when you attempt to check a disk that is in use. A drive not considered dirty is marked "clean" (no surprise there).

You can use the Fsutil (*Fsutil.exe*) utility to manage dirty drives. Open a Command Prompt window and type fsutil (without any arguments) to display a list of commands that can be used with the tool. As you might have expected, the dirty command is the one that's most relevant here. Here's how it works:

To see whether drive *G:* is currently marked as dirty, type:

```
fsutil dirty query g:
```

To mark drive *H:* as dirty, so it will be scanned by Chkdsk the next time Windows starts, type:

```
fsutil dirty set h:
```

 Fsutil has been found to be unreliable when used on FAT or FAT32 drives, so you may wish to use it only on more modern NTFS disks. (See "Choose the Right Filesystem" in Chapter 5.)

Another utility, Chkntfs, is used to choose whether or not Windows runs Chkdsk automatically at Windows startup, regardless of the so-called cleanliness of the drive. (It is not used to check NTFS drives, as its name implies, however.) Here's how it works:

To display a dirty/clean report about any drive (say, drive *G:*), type:

```
chkntfs g:
```

To *exclude* drive *H:* from being checked when Windows starts (which is not the default), type:

```
chkntfs /x h:
```

To *include* (un-exclude) drive *H:* in the drives to be checked when Windows starts, type:

```
chkntfs /c h:
```

To force Windows to check drive *H:* the next time Windows starts, type:

```
chkntfs /c h:
fsutil dirty set h:
```

To include all drives on your system, thereby restoring Vista's defaults, type:

```
chkntfs /d
```

Finally, when Windows detects a dirty drive, it starts a timed countdown (10 seconds by default), allowing you to skip Chkdsk by pressing a key. To change the duration of this countdown to, say, five seconds, type:

```
chkntfs /t:5
```

 The Registry location of the timeout setting is stored in the AutoChkTimeOut value in the HKEY_LOCAL_MACHINE\SYSTEM\ CurrentControlSet\Control\Session Manager key.

You'll have to restart Windows for any of these changes to take effect.

What to Do When a Program Crashes

Error messages are passé. When a program crashes, Windows doesn't necessarily tell you that it has crashed. Rather, the program simply "stops responding." This means that you can't click any of the controls in its interface, save your open document, nor (most importantly) close and reopen it easily. Sure, Windows usually lets you move it around the screen, and sometimes even click the **Close** button, but that's about it. But these are also symptoms of an application that's simply busy, caught up in the last task you asked it to perform.

Either way, triggered by your first attempt to use a crashed or busy program, Windows turns the whole window a pale version of itself while trying to communicate with it. If you want to know whether a program has reached this state *without* triggering it with a click, just try moving the mouse over the edges of the window; if the mouse cursor doesn't change to the familiar "resize" arrows (and given that it's a resizable window), the program has probably stopped responding.

So, how do you tell the difference between a crashed program and a busy one? Well, Vista can't even do that reliably, instead showing you a window that looks like the one in Figure 6-5 when you try to close it. The solution is to be patient and use your best instincts.

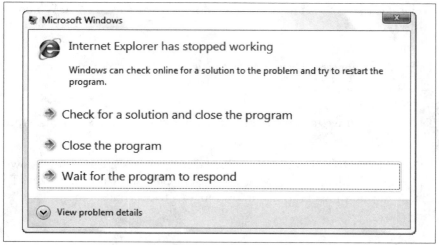

Figure 6-5. When you see this message, it means that Windows doesn't know whether the program you're trying to use has crashed, or is simply busy

But patience only gets you so far. After waiting an intolerable length of time, say, three to four seconds, one has to wonder whether the program will ever start responding. If you're through waiting, you can go ahead and elect to close the program, a strategy that works some of the time.

If an application window is visible, it's easy enough to click the small × button on the application title bar to close it. But if it's minimized, or if the main window isn't responding at all, right-click the program's button on the taskbar and select **Close**.

If closing doesn't help, or if, after closing a window, you can't open another one, then it's time to pay a visit to Task Manager, shown in Figure 6-6.

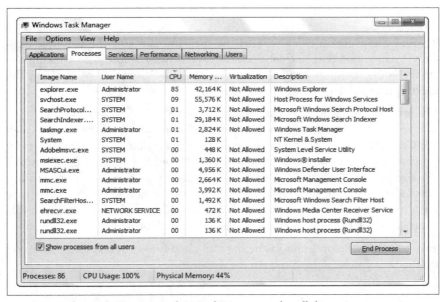

Figure 6-6. Choose the Processes tab in Task Manager to list all the programs running on your PC, a necessary step if one of them has crashed and you need to close it (the hard way)

There are three ways to start Task Manager:

Taskbar
Right-click an empty area of the taskbar and select **Task Manager**.

Keyboard
Press the **Shift-Ctrl-Esc** keys together.

Three-finger salute
If the taskbar and keyboard methods don't work, then Windows itself is crashed or busy. In this case, press **Ctrl-Alt-Del** to blank the screen and show a special administrative menu, at which point you can click **Task Manager** to launch it.

Although the **Applications** tab is inviting and easy to understand, it's not too helpful for this purpose. Choose the **Processes** tab, turn on the **Show processes from all users** option at the bottom (if it's there), and then locate the crashed program in the list.

 There's a funky bug in Vista's Task Manager, but fortunately, it's one that's easy to fix. If your Task Manager appears with no title bar, menu, or tabs, just double-click the thin gray border around the main list to bring them back. If that doesn't help, or if your mouse is unavailable, open the Registry Editor, navigate to `HKEY_CURRENT_USER\Software\Microsoft\Windows NT\CurrentVersion\TaskManager` and delete the `TaskManager` key.

To find the program to close, sort the list. You can sort the list alphabetically by filename (e.g., *explorer.exe* for Windows Explorer) by clicking the **Image Name** column header. Or, sort by application title by clicking the **Description** header.

But for most hung applications—also known as "frozen" or "locked up"— it'll be most entertaining to sort by exactly *how* busy the program is. Click the **CPU** column header twice (so its little arrow is pointing down) to sort by processor usage (a percentage from 0 to 99), and the crashed program will usually leap to the top of the list. For instance, if Windows Explorer has crashed—unfortunately, such a common occurrence in Vista that a new term was invented for it, explained in "Green Ribbon of Death," later in this chapter—its CPU usage will usually be in the high 80s!

Just highlight the program in the list and click **End Process**. Only after you do this will you be able to reopen the application.

 Vista comes with another tool you can use to examine the running processes: just open Windows Defender in Control Panel, click the **Tools** button at the top of the window, and then click the **Software Explorer** link. From the **Category** list, choose **Currently Running Programs**, and then select any task in the list to see its details on the right. It's not as powerful as the Task Manager (it won't let you close Microsoft applications, for instance), but it does offer more details in the righthand pane, such as the executable file size, version, and other details.

See "Shut Down Windows Quickly," in Chapter 5, to configure how long Windows waits for a busy application to respond before it considers it crashed.

Programs commonly running in the background

Windows is basically just a collection of components, and at any given time, some of those components may be loaded into memory and listed as running processes in Task Manager. In fact, you'll probably see more programs running than you expected, especially after you turn on Task Manager's **Show processes from all users** option.

If you see a program you don't recognize, don't panic; it's not necessarily malware, but then again, it's not necessary legitimate. See Table 6-1 for a list of those items commonly found on most Windows Vista systems.

Table 6-1. Processes you should expect to find running on your system

Process	Description
csrss.exe	Called the Client Server Runtime Process, csrss.exe is an essential Windows component, as it handles the user-mode portion of the Win32 subsystem. It is also a common target for viruses, so if this process appears to be consuming a lot of CPU cycles on your system, you should update and run your antivirus software.
explorer.exe	This is simply Windows Explorer, which is responsible for your desktop and Start menu. If this program crashes or is closed, Windows will usually start it again automatically. If you see more than one instance of explorer.exe, it means that each folder window is being launched as a separate process (see Chapter 2 for details).
lsass.exe	This is the Local Security Authority subsystem, responsible for authenticating users on your system.
rundll32.exe	This program, the purpose of which is to launch a function in a DLL as though it were a separate program, is used for about a million different things in Windows.
services.exe	This is the Windows NT Service Control Manager, and works similarly to svchost.exe, described shortly. The difference is that services.exe runs services that are processes, and svchost.exe runs services that are DLLs.
smss.exe	Called the Windows NT Session Manager, smss.exe is an essential Windows component. Among other things, it runs programs listed in the HKEY_ LOCAL_MACHINE\ SYSTEM\CurrentControlSet\Control\Session Manager key in the Registry.
spoolsv.exe	This handles printing and print spooling (queuing).
svchost.exe	This is the application responsible for launching most services (listed in services.msc). See the upcoming "What Is Svchost?" sidebar for details. See also services.exe.
System	This is the System process, an essential Windows component.
System Idle Process	The "idle" process is a 16k loop, used to occupy all CPU cycles not consumed by other running processes. The higher the number in the CPU column (99% being the maximum), the less your processor is being used by the currently running programs.
winlogon.exe	This process manages security-related user interactions, such as logon and logoff requests, locking or unlocking the machine, changing the password, and the remote Registry service.
wmiprvse.exe	This is responsible for WMI (Windows Management Instrumentation) support in Windows Vista, also known as WBEM. Like csrss.exe, above, wmiprvse.exe is a common target for viruses, so if this process appears to be consuming a lot of CPU cycles on your system, you should update and run your antivirus software.

Troubleshooting

Naturally, you shouldn't interfere with the components Windows requires to operate while you're looking for errant programs or programs you can get along without. And just because something isn't listed here doesn't mean it isn't required by your system, so use caution when ending a process with which you're unfamiliar.

What Is Svchost?

Svchost.exe and *services.exe* are responsible for launching the processes associated with the behind-the-scenes programs controlled by the Services window (*services.msc*).

A single instance of *svchost.exe* may be responsible for a single service or several. You should never interfere with any instances of *svchost.exe* or *services.exe* you might see listed in Task Manager. Instead, use the Services window to start or stop a service or choose whether or not a service is started automatically when Windows starts.

If you're using Windows Vista Professional edition, you can use the TaskList utility (*tasklist.exe*) to see which services are handled by any given instance of *svchost.exe*. Just open a Command Prompt window (*cmd.exe*), and type:

```
tasklist /svc
```

Then, match up the numbers in the **PID** column of TaskList's output with those in the **PID** column of Task Manager's **Processes** tab.

See "Manage Startup Programs," earlier in this chapter, for tips on researching and identifying processes and programs you don't recognize.

Stop notifying Microsoft

There's something comforting about Windows inviting you to share details about your last application crash with Microsoft engineers—people who, presumably, can use that information to help solve the problem. But if a warm, fuzzy feeling isn't as high of a priority as getting back to work after a crash, you may choose to turn off the error reporting feature.

In Control Panel, open the Problem Reports and Solutions page. On the left side, click the **Change settings** link, and then on the next page, click the **Advanced settings** link. Finally, on the "Advanced settings for problem reporting" page (Figure 6-7), select **Off**, and then click **OK**.

But turning off problem reporting doesn't mean you necessarily have to sever all connections with Microsoft's automated support system, only that

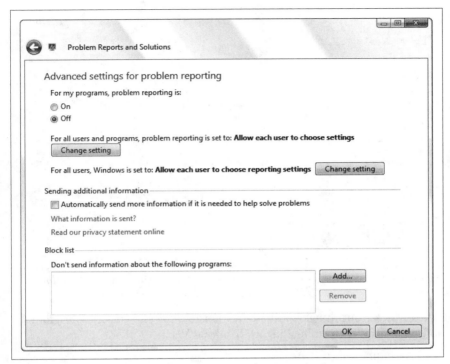

Figure 6-7. You can choose whether or not to notify Microsoft whenever a program crashes

you don't have to do it the instant a program crashes. There's still a way to get some satisfaction.

Back in the Problem Reports and Solutions page, click the **See problems to check** link to open a history of unreported application crashes (Figure 6-8). Here, place a checkmark next to any crash on which you'd like to follow up (or use the **Select all** option), and then click **Check for solutions**.

See "Blue Screen of Death," later in this chapter, for another (rather nasty) type of crash that doesn't necessary follow any of the same rules of the crashes discussed here.

What to Do When a Program Won't Start

Ever double-click an icon on your desktop, only to see the mouse cursor momentarily turn into the little spinning circle before it reverts to the arrow pointer, with no newly opened application in sight? This is typically what happens when a program won't start, and this is not necessarily Windows' fault.

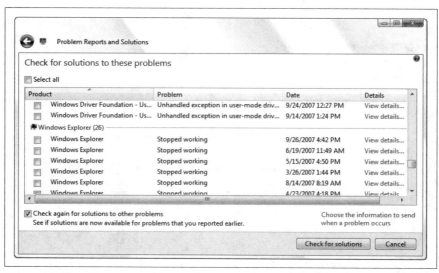

Figure 6-8. Vista shows you a history of recent crashes, and gives you the opportunity to share that information with Microsoft at a time that's convenient for you

One of these four things is usually responsible for preventing a program (or software installer) from loading in Windows Vista:

User Account Control (UAC)
As explained in Chapter 8, Vista's UAC feature is designed to prevent malicious or poorly written applications from harming your PC. Unfortunately, a program not specifically written for Vista won't be aware of UAC, and as a result, may close when UAC prevents it from doing something like writing to its own folder in *Program Files*. The solution is to run the program in administrator mode; see "Control User Account Control," in Chapter 8, for details.

Not written for Vista
Some programs—particularly those that interact with the operating system or rely on features only available in certain versions of Windows—won't load if your version of Windows isn't on their preapproved list. (This also applies to setup programs.) To get around this, right-click any *.exe* file (or a shortcut to any *.exe* file), select **Properties**, and choose the **Compatibility** tab. Turn on the **Run this program in compatibility mode for** option, and from the list immediately underneath, choose a Windows version you know to be supported by your software. Click **OK** and then try running the program again. Note that just because the program now thinks it's running under, say, Windows XP with Service Pack 2, doesn't mean the program will actually function correctly in Windows Vista. But much of the time, a little spoofing is all it takes.

Missing file or setting

Most applications require a laundry list of different support files—not to mention a few dozen Registry settings to be in place—for them to function. If the program worked at one point, but no longer does, it might need nothing more than to be reinstalled. (This is particularly true of programs that were installed on a previous version of Windows, and were simply left intact when you upgraded to Vista.)

It's a piece of junk

OK, maybe this is too harsh, but don't discount the possibility that there's simply a bug in the software that is preventing it from running. Check the software publisher's web site for an update, patch, or other workaround.

Software is an ever-evolving landscape, so don't be surprised if you have to eventually retire an old favorite because it just won't run anymore. Of course, your favorite is likely someone else's, too, so it's worth a quick web search to see whether anyone else has come up with a trick to get your program running on Vista.

Green Ribbon of Death

Don't you just love it when something is so notorious for a particular shortcoming that a new term is invented to describe it? It happened with the *Blue Screen of Death*, described in the next section. It happened with the *Spinning Beach Ball of Death* in Mac OS X. And it happened with the *odd-number curse*, referring to every other *Star Trek* film.

Now it has happened with Vista's own *Green Ribbon of Death*, shown in Figure 6-9.

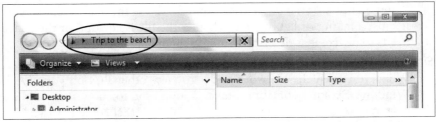

Figure 6-9. The Green Ribbon of Death, the harbinger of a Windows Explorer window that has crashed

The green ribbon is basically a progress bar, a screen element Microsoft has sadly gone to great pains to excise from Windows Vista. But this particular progress bar is the harbinger of death for the active Windows Explorer window, which, unfortunately, is not uncommon in Vista.

The green progress bar inches across Windows Explorer's address bar as Windows attempts to assemble a list of files to show for the current folder. Most of the time, it's only visible for a few seconds, if it shows up at all. The problem occurs when it doesn't go away, at which point Windows Explorer stops cooperating when you try to view another folder or cancel the progress by clicking the little red × button next to the address bar.

What's worse, if you try to open another Windows Explorer window, that one is likely to malfunction, too, *even if you closed the first one*! The solution, temporary as it may be, is to close the seized *explorer.exe* process in Task Manager, as described in "What to Do When a Program Crashes," earlier in this chapter. But if you want to stop the Green Ribbon of Death from visiting you again, you'll have to take matters into your own hands.

There are basically four things that cause this problem:

Broken thumbnails

This is the most common cause of this problem, and also the easiest to fix. Each time you view a folder containing photos (JPG, TIF files) or movies (AVI, MPG, WMV files), Windows Explorer opens each one to extract and build thumbnail previews for the file icons. If even one file in the folder is corrupted, or if one of the files makes use of a corrupted *codec* on your system, Windows Explorer crashes.

To fix this problem, you need to do two things. First, figure out which file is crashing Explorer. Of course, since you can't view the folder in Explorer without it crashing, you'll have to turn off the thumbnails feature first. On the System page in Control Panel, click **Advanced system settings**, and then in the **Performance** box, click **Settings**. Turn off the **Show thumbnails instead of icons** option, and click **OK**.

Next, open the folder and then test each of your media files. The video that won't play or the photo that won't display is the likely culprit. Now it's just a matter of figuring out whether the file is corrupt, or the codec needs to be fixed, as described in the beginning of Chapter 4.

Slow network access

When you open the Network folder to view other PCs on your LAN, Windows Explorer sometimes takes a long time to show them all. See Chapters 7 and 8, specifically "Stop Sharing Scheduled Tasks," in Chapter 8, for help troubleshooting network connections and shared folders.

Searching when files are changing

If you're searching a folder, especially if you're using the **Include non-indexed** option as described in Chapter 2, and another program is writing files to that folder, the search results may repeatedly appear and disappear while you stare at the green progress bar. To solve this problem, close the **Search** window (or select a real folder in the tree) while programs are saving files to your hard disk.

Copying files

Vista is hopelessly slow at copying files in certain situations, two in fact. (More on this in Chapter 2.)

First, Vista's UAC feature forces Windows Explorer to evaluate the security impact of each file you copy, and this has far-reaching consequences, particularly when you're copying files over a network. See "Control User Account Control," in Chapter 8, for more information.

And second, Vista notoriously has trouble copying files to and from USB devices. So, if you copy a folder full of images from your USB card reader directly to your external USB hard disk, or move document files from a USB memory key to a shared network folder, Windows Explorer may crash. There's no easy fix to this one, but you can work around it by copying files to your desktop first.

As explained above, you need to use Task Manager to close a crashed Windows Explorer window. But if you want to be able to close a crashed window and leave any other Explorer windows (and the desktop) intact, you'll need to make a change in Control Panel. Open Folder Options and choose the **View** tab. In the **Advanced settings** list, turn on the **Launch folder windows in a separate process** option, and then click **OK**. From now on, when you see the Green Ribbon of Death, it'll only mean death for one of your Windows Explorer windows, not all of them.

Blue Screen of Death

The Blue Screen of Death (BSoD) is aptly named. It's blue, it fills the screen, and it means death for whatever you were working on before it appeared. Microsoft refers to BSoD errors as "Stop Messages," a euphemism for the types of crashes that are serious enough to bring down the entire system.

 A single error is no cause for concern. Only if a BSoD error happens a few times, or repeatedly, do you need to pursue any of the solutions listed here.

By default, Windows restarts your computer as soon as the BSoD appears, leaving almost no time to read the error message before it vanishes. To change this, open the System page in Control Panel and click the **Advanced system settings** link on the left side. In the **Startup and Recovery** box, click **Settings**, turn off the **Automatically restart** option, and click **OK**.

Or, if Windows won't start, and you need to read the BSoD error message, use the **Disable automatic restart on system failure** option, as described in "What to Do When Windows Won't Start," earlier in this chapter.

Alphabetical list of BSoD errors

There are a whole bunch of possible BSoD messages; probably more than a hundred. However, only about 20 happen frequently enough that they might imply that an actual problem exists. More than likely, you've seen at least one of the following stop messages on your own system:

Attempted Write To Readonly Memory (stop code 0X000000BE)
 A faulty driver or service is typically responsible for this error, as is outdated firmware. If the name of a file or service is specified, try uninstalling the software (or rolling back the driver if it's an upgrade).

Bad Pool Caller (stop code 0X000000C2)
 Causes and remedies are similar to "Attempted Write To Readonly Memory." Additionally, this error might also be the result of a defective hardware device.

 If you encounter this message while upgrading to Windows Vista (see Chapter 1), it may mean that one or more devices in your system are not compatible with Vista. Try disconnecting unnecessary devices, or at least look for updated drivers and firmware. Also, disable any antivirus software you may have running.

Data Bus Error (stop code 0X0000002E)
 This can be caused by defective memory (see "Test for Bad Memory (RAM)," later in this chapter), including system RAM, the Level 2 cache, or even the memory on your video card. Other causes of this error include serious hard disk corruption, buggy hardware drivers, or physical damage to the motherboard.

Driver IRQL Not Less Or Equal (stop code 0X000000D1)
 Drivers programmed to access improper hardware addresses typically cause this error. Causes and remedies are similar to "Attempted Write To Readonly Memory (stop code 0X000000BE)," earlier in this list.

Driver Power State Failure (stop code 0X0000009F)
 This error is caused by an incompatibility between your computer's power management and one or more installed drivers or services, typically when

the computer enters the Hibernate state (discussed at length in Chapter 5). If the name of a file or service is specified, try uninstalling the software (or rolling back the driver if it's an upgrade). Or, try disabling Windows' support for power management.

Driver Unloaded Without Cancelling Pending Operations (stop code 0X000000CE)

Causes and remedies are similar to "Attempted Write To Readonly Memory (stop code 0X000000BE)," earlier in this section.

Driver Used Excessive PTEs (stop code 0X000000D8)

Causes and remedies are similar to "No More System PTEs (stop code 0X0000003F)," later in this section.

Hardware Interrupt Storm (stop code 0X000000F2)

This error occurs when a hardware device (such as a USB or SCSI controller) fails to release an IRQ, a condition typically caused by a buggy driver or firmware. This error can also appear if two devices are incorrectly assigned the same IRQ (discussed later in this chapter).

Inaccessible Boot Device (stop code 0X0000007B)

You may see this error during Windows startup if Windows cannot read data from the system or boot partitions (described in Chapter 1). Faulty disk controller drivers are often to blame, but this problem can also be caused by hard disk errors, or even a corrupted *boot.ini* file (also described in Chapter 1).

If all is well with your drivers and your drive, and you haven't been messing with the *boot.ini* file (such as while installing multiple operating systems), check your system BIOS settings (described in Appendix A).

If you encounter this message while upgrading to Windows Vista (see Chapter 1), it may mean that one or more devices in your system are not compatible with Vista. Try disconnecting unnecessary devices, or at least look for updated drivers and firmware. Also, disable any antivirus software you may have running.

Kernel Data Inpage Error (stop code 0X0000007A)

This error implies a problem with virtual memory (discussed in Chapter 5), most often in the case that Windows wasn't able to read data from—or write data to—the swap file. Possible causes include bad sectors, a virus, improper SCSI termination, bad memory, or physical damage to the motherboard.

Kernel Stack Inpage Error (stop code 0X00000077)

Causes and remedies are similar to the previous entry, "Kernel Data Inpage Error (stop code 0X0000007A)."

Kmode Exception Not Handled (stop code 0X0000001E)

A faulty driver or service is sometimes responsible for this error, as are memory and IRQ conflicts, and faulty firmware. If the name of a file or service is specified, try uninstalling the software (or rolling back the driver if it's an upgrade).

If the *Win32k.sys* file is mentioned in the message, the cause may be third-party remote control software (discussed in Chapter 7).

This error can also be caused if you run out of disk space while installing an application or if you run out of memory while using a buggy application with a memory leak.

Mismatched Hal (stop code 0X00000079)

The currently installed Hardware Abstraction Layer (HAL) must match the type of computer on which Windows Vista is installed, or you may see this error. For example, if you use a HAL intended for a dual-processor system on a single-processor motherboard, Windows may not start. The best way to correct problems with the HAL is to reinstall Windows Vista.

This error can also be caused by out-of-date *Ntoskrnl.exe* or *Hal.dll* files, so if you've recently attempted to repair these files on your system, look for backups of the original versions.

No More System PTEs (stop code 0X0000003F)

Page Table Entries (PTEs) are used to map RAM as it is divided into page frames by the Virtual Memory Manager (VMM). This error usually means that Windows has run out of PTEs.

Aside from the usual assortment of faulty drivers and services that can cause all sorts of problems, this error can also occur if you're using multiple monitors.

If you find that you're experiencing this error often, you can increase Windows' allocation of PTEs with this procedure:

1. Open the Registry Editor (discussed in Chapter 3).

2. Then expand the branches to `HKEY_LOCAL_MACHINE\SYSTEM\CurrentControlSet\Control\Session Manager\Memory Management`.

3. Double-click the `PagedPoolSize` value, enter 0 for its value data, and click **OK**.

4. Next, double-click the `SystemPages` value. If you're using multiple monitors, enter a value of 36000 here. Otherwise, enter 40000 if you have 128 MB of system RAM or less, or 110000 if you have more than 128 MB of RAM.

5. Click **OK** and then close the Registry Editor when you're done. The change will take effect when you restart Windows.

NTFS File System (stop code 0X00000024)

This is caused by an problem reported by *Ntfs.sys*, the driver responsible for reading and writing NTFS volumes (see Chapter 5). If you're using the FAT32 filesystem, you may see a similar message (with stop code 0X00000023).

Causes include a faulty IDE or SCSI controller, improper SCSI termination, an overly aggressive virus scanner, or errors on the disk (try testing it with Chkdsk).

To investigate further, open the Event Viewer (*eventvwr.msc*), and look for error messages related to **SCSI** or **FASTFAT** (in the **System** category), or **Autochk** (in the **Application** category).

Page Fault In Nonpaged Area (stop code 0X00000050)

Causes and remedies are similar to "Attempted Write To Readonly Memory (stop code 0X000000BE)," earlier in this list.

Status Image Checksum Mismatch (stop code 0Xc0000221)

Possible causes for this error include a damaged swap file (see the discussion of virtual memory in Chapter 5), or a corrupted driver. See "Attempted Write To Readonly Memory (stop code 0X000000BE)," earlier in this section, for additional causes and remedies.

Status System Process Terminated (stop code 0Xc000021A)

This error indicates a problem with either *Winlogon.exe* or the Client Server Runtime Subsystem (CSRSS). It can also be caused if a user with administrator privileges has modified the permissions (see Chapter 8) of certain system files such that Windows cannot read them. To fix the problem, you'll have to install a second copy of Windows Vista (see "Set Up a Dual-Boot System" in Chapter 1), and then repair the file permissions from there.

Thread Stuck In Device Driver (stop code 0X000000EA)

Also known as the infamous "infinite loop" problem, this nasty bug has about a hundred different causes. What's actually happening is that your video driver has essentially entered an infinite loop because your video adapter has locked up. Microsoft has posted a solution on its web site that involves disabling certain aspects of video acceleration, but I've never encountered an instance where this worked. Instead, try the following:

- Try upgrading your computer's power supply. A power supply of poor quality or insufficient wattage will be unable to provide adequate power to all your computer's components, and may result in a "brown out" of sorts in your system. Note that newer, more power-hungry video adapters are *more* susceptible to this problem. See "Don't Overlook the Power Supply," later in this chapter.

- Make sure you have the latest driver for your video card. If you already have the latest driver, try "rolling back" to an older driver to see whether that solves the problem.

- Make sure you have the latest driver for your sound card, if applicable. Also, make sure your sound card is not in a slot immediately adjacent to your video card, lest the resulting interference or heat disrupt the operation of either card.

- Make sure your video card is properly seated in its AGP or PCI slot. If it's a PCI card, try moving it to a different slot.

- Inspect your video card and motherboard for physical damage.

- Try messing with some of your system's BIOS settings, especially those concerning your AGP slot or video subsystem, as described in Appendix A. For example, if your AGP slot is set to 2x mode, and your video adapter only supports 1x AGP mode, then you'll want to change the setting accordingly.

- Make sure your computer—and your video card—are adequately cooled. Overheating can cause your video card's chipset to lock up.

- Check with the manufacturer of your motherboard for newer drivers for your motherboard chipset.

  For example, the "infinite loop" problem is common among motherboards with VIA chipsets and nVidia-based video cards. Visit the VIA web site (*http://www.viaarena.com/?PageID=64*) for updated drivers and additional solutions.

- Try replacing your system's driver for the Processor-to-AGP Controller. Open Device Manager (*devmgmt.msc*), expand the **System devices** branch, and double-click the entry corresponding to your Processor-to-AGP Controller. Choose the **Driver** tab, and click **Update Driver** to choose a new driver. Unless you can get a newer driver from the manufacturer of your motherboard chipset, try installing the generic "PCI standard PCI-to-PCI bridge" driver shown in the Hardware Update Wizard.

- If your motherboard has an on-board Ethernet adapter, try disabling the **PXE Resume/Remote Wake Up** option in your system BIOS (see Appendix A).

- If you're using a dual-processor motherboard, Windows Vista is probably loading a HAL (Hardware Abstraction Layer) for an MPS (Multiple Processor System). Such HALs support the I/O APIC (Advanced Programmable Interrupt Controller), a method of accommodating more than 15 IRQs in a single system. Unfortunately, APIC can cause problems with AGP-based video cards. Try changing your HAL to "Standard PC" to see whether that solves the problem.

Unexpected Kernel Mode Trap (stop code 0X0000007F)

Typical causes of this error include defective memory, physical damage to the motherboard, and excessive processor heat due to overclocking (running the CPU faster than its specified clock speed).

Unmountable Boot Volume (stop code 0X000000ED)

This means that Windows was unable to mount the boot volume, which, if you have more than one drive, is the drive containing Windows (see Chapter 1 for more information on the boot and system volumes). This can be caused by using the wrong cable with a high-throughput IDE controller (more than 33 MB/second); try an 80-pin cable instead of the standard 40-pin cable. See also "Inaccessible Boot Device (stop code 0X0000007B)," earlier in this list.

Dealing with Drivers and Other Tales of Hardware Troubleshooting

A driver is the software that allows Windows and all of your applications to work with a hardware device, such as a printer or video card. That way, for example, your word processor doesn't need to be preprogrammed with the details of all available printers (as in the early days of PCs). Instead, Windows manages a central database of drivers, silently directing the communication among all your applications and whatever drivers are required to complete the task at hand.

Problems arise when a driver is buggy or outdated, or one of the files that comprise a driver is missing or corrupted. Outdated drivers designed either for a previous version of Windows or a previous version of the device can create problems. Additionally, manufacturers must continually update their drivers to fix incompatibilities and bugs that surface after the product is released. It's usually a good idea to make sure you have the latest drivers installed in your system when troubleshooting a problem. Furthermore, newer drivers sometimes offer improved performance, added features and settings, better stability and reliability, and better compatibility with other software and drivers installed in your system.

The other thing to be aware of is that some drivers may just not be the correct ones for your system. For example, when installing Windows, the setup routine may have incorrectly detected your video card or monitor and hence installed the wrong driver (or even a *generic* driver). A common symptom for this is if Windows does not allow you to display as many colors or use as high a resolution as the card supports. Make sure that Device Manager (*devmgmt.msc*) lists the actual devices, by name, that you have installed in your system.

Device drivers worth investigating include those for your video card, monitor, motherboard chipset, network adapter, and any USB devices you may have. If you're not sure of the exact manufacturer or model number of a device installed inside your computer, take off the cover of your computer and look, or refer to the invoice or documentation that came with your system.

How to Add Hardware

Windows Vista comes with a huge assortment of drivers for hardware available at the time of its release, but as time passes, more third-party devices are released, requiring drivers of their own. The first rule is to never use the disc that comes with a device, but rather go straight to the manufacturer's web site for the latest version.

That said, hardware installation in Vista is pretty straightforward...that is, when it works. When it doesn't, Vista is no help.

Now, you've probably discovered the Add Hardware wizard in Control Panel, and while it seems inviting enough, it's a trap!

Any modern hardware that's working properly will identify itself to Windows as soon as you connect it—or in some cases, as soon as you boot Windows—at which point Windows will do the rest. Never try to do it the other way around; it will always end in tears.

When to use the Add Hardware wizard

There is one reason—and one reason only—to use the Add Hardware wizard, and that is to find out whether Windows comes with a driver for a specific piece of hardware before you try to install it (or even before you purchase it). Here's how this works:

1. Double-click the **Add Hardware** icon in Control Panel, and click **Next** on the first page.

2. On the next page, choose the second option, **Install the hardware that I manually select from a list (Advanced)**, and click **Next**.

3. Chose the category of the device, or just select **Show All Devices** if you're feeling lazy, and click **Next**.

4. The next page is essentially a list of every hardware device driver included with Windows Vista. Choose a manufacturer from the list on the left, and then the specific model number from the list on the right.

If the driver you seek is not listed and you don't see a driver for a similar device that might be usable, you'll have to obtain a driver from the manufacturer.

How to update a driver

In nearly all cases, Device Manager (*devmgmt.msc*, also in Control Panel) will show an entry for the device you're installing, whether it's working or not. If the device isn't working, it either pops open automatically with a teensy, yellow exclamation point over its icon, or shows up in the **Unknown Devices** branch, as shown in Figure 6-10.

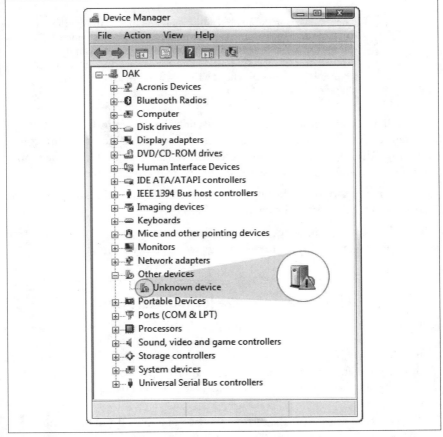

Figure 6-10. Here are two signs that Windows isn't loading the driver for your device

These are often symptoms of a driver problem, and this can be fixed. (Of course, it may also be an errant BIOS setting, as described in Appendix A, or a problem with the hardware itself...but usually, it's the driver.)

To see what driver a device is currently using, double-click the device in Device Manager and choose the **Driver** tab. An easy (but certainly not foolproof) way to tell whether you're using the driver that came with Windows Vista is to look at the driver date—it should be June 21, 2006 (for the initial release, that is)—and its version number should be 6.0.6000.xxxxx. If not, it probably came from another source, such as from a driver disk, from the Web, from Windows Update, or from a previous installation of Windows. Drivers with newer dates are usually—but not always—more recent, but the date alone is not a reliable indicator.

 Click the **Driver Details** button to view the files in use by the driver. Sometimes a driver won't load merely because one of the files listed here is missing or broken—a problem updating the driver, discussed next, doesn't always fix. Instead, uninstall and reinstall the device, as described later in this chapter.

To install a new driver for a device, right-click the device in Device Manager and select **Update Driver Software**. When prompted, point to the folder containing the latest and greatest driver you've just obtained from the manufacturer's web site and, if necessary, extracted from the ZIP file.

Or, to start over, right-click the device and select **Uninstall**. Then, from the **Action** menu, select **Scan for hardware changes**.

When troubleshooting a device, don't forget to update the firmware, too; see the "Firmware: Software for Your Hardware" sidebar, next.

Firmware: Software for Your Hardware

User-upgradable firmware is a feature found in many modern devices. Firmware is software stored in the device itself, used to control most hardware functions. Although it's not possible to, say, increase a hard disk's capacity by upgrading its firmware, it is possible to improve performance and fix bugs in devices like wireless routers, DVD recorders, motherboards, and even digital cameras.

The beauty of firmware is that if you purchase a peripheral and the manufacturer subsequently improves the product, you can usually update the firmware to upgrade the product.

When a device isn't working or a driver won't install, go to the hardware manufacturer's web site and look for a firmware update. Since there's no standard method of upgrading firmware, be sure to get the firmware upgrade utility from the web site as well.

What to do when Windows can't find a driver

There's a bug in Windows Vista that makes it seem like it has amnesia. You plug in a device—even one you've used before—and after quite a long time of thinking about it, Vista complains that it can't find the driver. This is particularly disconcerting when it's a common device like a hard disk or a USB card reader. Fortunately, it's fairly easy to fix.

The problem is that Vista maintains a cache of its driver locations, and for reasons that aren't entirely clear, Vista won't abandon the cache when it becomes corrupted. Such is the case here.

To clear the driver cache, open Windows Explorer, and navigate to the *C:\ Windows\inf* folder. If you see a file named *INFCACHE.1*, delete it immediately. If Windows won't let you delete the file, see "Delete In-Use Files" in Chapter 2.

When you've excised the file, try uninstalling and then reinstalling the misbehaving device to reinstall the driver. For real this time.

Stop Plug and Play from detecting devices

One of the problems with Plug and Play (PnP) is its tendency to detect and load drivers for devices you don't want to use. Although there is no way to prevent Windows' PnP feature from detecting and installing drivers for some devices, you can disable most devices that may be causing conflicts.

To disable a device and prevent Windows from detecting it again, right-click it in Device Manager (*devmgmt.msc*), and select **Disable**. A red × then appears over the device's icon to signify that it has been disabled. You can later re-enable the device by right-clicking and selecting **Enable**.

Uninstall drivers for devices you no longer use

By default, Device Manager doesn't show devices that aren't connected to your computer, even if the drivers for those devices are installed and loaded. But why would you want to do this?

When you disconnect or remove a device from your system without first right-clicking its entry in Device Manager and selecting **Uninstall**, its driver will remain installed on your system. The only way to remove it is to either reattach the device, or show hidden devices.

Now, in Device Manager, you can select **Show hidden devices** from the **View** menu, but all this will add to the listing are non-PnP devices. To have Device Manager show *all* hidden devices, follow these steps:

1. Open the System page in Control Panel, and then click the **Advanced system settings** link on the left.
2. Click the **Environment Variables** button.
3. In the lower **System variables** section, click **New**.
4. Type devmgr_show_nonpresent_devices for the **Variable name**, and enter 1 for the **Variable value**. Click **OK** when you're done, and click **OK** to close the System Properties window.
5. If Device Manager is open, close and reopen it.
6. In Device Manager, select **Show hidden devices** from the **View** menu.

Hidden devices (sometimes called *ghosted* devices) now appear in Device Manager with grayed-out icons. Other than the fact that they represent non-present hardware, these hidden entries should behave normally, in that you can uninstall them, change their properties, or update their drivers.

Interpret Device Manager Errors

From time to time, Device Manager will report a problem with one of your devices by marking it with a yellow exclamation mark (!) or a red ×. Double-click the device name, and you'll likely see one of the following errors:

This device is not configured correctly (Code 1). This is a driver problem; click **Update Driver** to install a new driver.

Windows could not load the driver for this device… (Code 2). Again, try installing a new driver. If that doesn't work, contact the manufacturer of your motherboard for a BIOS update.

The driver for this device may be bad, or your system may be running low on memory or other resources (Code 3). Try removing the device (right-click and select **Uninstall**), restarting Windows, and then reinstalling the driver.

This device is not working properly because one of its drivers may be bad, or your registry may be bad (Code 4). Of course, try updating the drivers. (Laughably, Microsoft suggests running *Scanregw.exe*, a program designed for Windows Me and not included in Windows Vista, to fix this error.) If a new driver doesn't fix the problem, try the solution for Code 3, just discussed.

The driver for this device requested a resource that Windows does not know how to handle (Code 5). Remove the device (right-click and select **Uninstall**) and then run the Add New Hardware wizard from Control Panel.

Another device is using the resources this device needs (Code 6). You'll see this error if you've installed a device that doesn't support PnP.

The drivers for this device need to be reinstalled (Code 7). Click **Update Driver** to reinstall the drivers. Duh.

This device is not working properly because Windows cannot load... (Code 8). This may indicate a missing or damaged *.inf* file, located in the *\Windows\INF* folder, which may make it difficult to reinstall the driver for this device. If the **Reinstall Device** button doesn't work (or isn't there), and installing drivers provided by the manufacturer fails, you may have to run Windows setup again.

This device is not working properly because the BIOS in your computer is reporting the resources for the device incorrectly (Code 9). This indicates a problem with your motherboard's support for ACPI power management (discussed in Chapter 5). Contact the manufacturer of your motherboard for a BIOS update. Next, try removing the device (right-click and select **Uninstall**) and then restarting Windows.

This device is either not present, not working properly, or does not have all the drivers installed (Code 10). If the device is a PCI or ISA card inserted in your computer, make sure it's firmly seated in its slot. Otherwise, make sure it's plugged in and powered up. If it's an external device, try turning it off and then on again. Then, of course, try removing the drivers (right-click and select **Uninstall**) and then run the Add New Hardware wizard from Control Panel.

Windows stopped responding while attempting to start this device, and therefore will never attempt to start this device again (Code 11). Windows may disable devices that prevent it from loading. To re-enable this device, right-click the device name and select **Uninstall**, and then restart Windows.

This device cannot find any free {type} resources to use (Code 12). See the solution for error code 6.

This device is either not present, not working properly, or does not have all the drivers installed (Code 13). See the solution for error code 10.

This device cannot work properly until you restart your computer (Code 14). Do I need to tell you what to do here?

This device is causing a resource conflict (Code 15). See the solution for error code 10.

Windows could not identify all the resources this device uses (Code 16). Right-click the device, select **Properties**, and then choose the **Resources** tab. You may have to fill in some information provided by your hardware documentation. See also the solution for error code 10.

The driver information file {name} is telling this child device to use a resource that the parent device does not have or recognize (Code 17). You'll need to obtain and install newer drivers for this device.

The drivers for this device need to be reinstalled (Code 18). See the solution for error code 7.

Your registry may be bad (Code 19). This extremely helpful message will appear if there is any corrupt data in your Registry pertaining to this device. Note that if you restart Windows, it may revert to an earlier copy of your Registry, which you may nor may not want to happen. See Chapter 3 for help with backing up your Registry.

Windows could not load one of the drivers for this device (Code 20). The driver you're using is likely designed for an earlier version of Windows; contact the manufacturer of the device for a driver written for Windows Vista.

Windows is removing this device (Code 21). This temporary message will appear immediately after you've attempted to uninstall a device. Close the Properties window, wait a minute or two, and then try again. If it doesn't go away, try restarting Windows.

This device is disabled (Code 22, version 1). This means you've manually disabled the device by right-clicking and selecting **Disable**. Click **Enable Device** to re-enable the device. If you can't enable the device, try removing it (right-click and select **Uninstall**) and then restarting Windows.

This device is not started (Code 22, version 2). Some devices can be stopped, either manually or via their drivers. Click **Start Device** to re-enable the device. If this persists, look for updated drivers, and see whether the device has any power management features you can disable.

This display adapter is functioning correctly (Code 23). Despite the fact that the message states the device is functioning correctly, there's obviously a problem. This typically occurs in systems with two display adapters (video cards), wherein one doesn't fully support being installed in a system with two display adapters. Try updating the drivers for both cards, and look for an updated BIOS for either card.

This device is either not present, not working properly, or does not have all the drivers installed (Code 24). See the solution for error code 10.

Windows is in the process of setting up this device (Code 25 and Code 26). You'll see this if Windows is waiting until the next time it starts to complete the installation of the drivers for this device. Restart Windows to use the device. Note that you may have to restart twice. If that doesn't help, remove the device (right-click and select **Uninstall**), restart Windows one more time, and then try again.

Windows can't specify the resources for this device (Code 27). See the solution for error code 16.

The drivers for this device are not installed (Code 28). Click **Reinstall Driver** to install the drivers currently on your system, or obtain new drivers from the manufacturer of the device.

This device is disabled because the BIOS for the device did not give it any resources (Code 29). This message appears for devices on your motherboard—such as on-board hard disk controllers, network adapters, or video adapters—that have been disabled in your computer's BIOS setup. See Appendix A for more information. (Note that this error may also appear for the device's *firmware* if it's not on your motherboard; in this case, refer to the hardware documentation.)

This device is using an Interrupt Request (IRQ) resource that is in use by another device and cannot be shared (Code 30). See the solution for error code 10.

This device is not working properly because {device} is not working properly (Code 31). This means that the device is dependent on another device. For instance, this message may appear for a joystick (game) port that is physically installed on a sound card that's having problems. To fix this error, troubleshoot the hardware on which this device is dependent.

Windows cannot install the drivers for this device because it cannot access the drive or network location that has the setup files on it (Code 32). First, restart your computer. If that doesn't fix the problem, copy said drivers directly to your hard disk, and try installing them again.

This device isn't responding to its driver (Code 33). This may indicate a problem with the hardware, or simply a bad driver. Start by removing the device (right-click and select **Uninstall**), restarting Windows, and then reinstalling the drivers. If that doesn't help, you may have a dead device on your hands.

Currently, this hardware device is not connected to the computer (Code 45). This message will appear for any hidden or ghosted device, shown when you select **View** → **Show Hidden Devices** in Device Manager. This means the driver is installed, but the hardware has been physically disconnected or removed.

Go Back in Time with Restore Points and Shadow Copies

The System Restore service runs invisibly in the background, routinely backing up drivers, important system files, and certain Registry settings so that at some point, you can roll back some or all of your computer's configuration to an earlier time. Plus, if you're using the Business, Ultimate, or Enterprise edition of Vista, you can extend this feature to include your personal documents, forming what are called *shadow copies*.

 Windows maintains your PC's restore points somewhat like the Recycle Bin; old data is deleted invisibly in the background to make room for new restore points. For this reason, never rely solely on restore points to provide backups of your documents.

There are several different ways to access restore points, each with its own purpose and scope:

Roll Back Driver

In Device Manager (*devmgmt.msc*), expand a category, right-click a device, and select **Properties**. Choose the **Driver** tab, and then click **Roll Back Driver** to replace the current driver with an earlier version. If the **Roll Back Driver** button is grayed out, then either you've loaded no earlier version of this driver, or the System Restore feature isn't operational (discussed later in this section). What's nice about this feature is that the scope of the change is crystal clear; when you click **Roll Back Driver**, only the driver files and settings for the current device are affected.

System Restore

To open the System Restore wizard, open the Start menu, type `rstrui` and press **Enter**. Click **Next** on the first page to show a list of the recent restore points, and then select an entry and click **Next** to revert your PC's system files and configuration to an earlier state. (If you don't see any restore points, read on to see how to enable this feature.)

It's best to think of this feature as neither an uninstall tool nor a time machine, but rather something in between. Windows makes a restore point when you install hardware drivers, when you install software (most of the time), and occasionally at regular intervals. (You can also create restore points manually in the System Protection window, described later in this section.) But it's never made clear what exactly changes when you restore a restore point, making this a potentially dangerous tool. The good news is that you can return to the System Restore wizard and undo your last change should something go wrong (assuming you can boot Windows thereafter).

If all you're trying to do is uninstall software, you should do so through the Programs and Features page in Control Panel. Likewise, to uninstall a hardware driver, open Device Manager (*devmgmt.msc*), right-click the device, and select **Uninstall**. With these features, at least the scope of your change will be easily predictable.

Last Known Good Configuration

If a recent driver or software installation has prevented Windows from loading, press **F8** just after your PC powers up (see "What to Do When Windows Won't Start," earlier in this chapter), and from the Advanced Boot Options menu that appears, select **Last Known Good Configuration (advanced)**.

If you're lucky, the effect is more or less the same as choosing a recent restore point in the System Restore wizard, allowing you to subsequently start Windows. But in practice, this feature often has no effect, either because the scope of the change isn't great enough to fix whatever problem you're having, or because Vista wasn't set up to create restore points in the first place (more on that shortly).

Previous Versions

Right-click a document you've been working on recently, select **Properties**, and choose the **Previous Versions** tab. What you see in the **File versions** list here depends on several factors.

First, if you've used the Back Up Files wizard described in "Back Up Your Entire System," later in this chapter, and that backup included the file you right-clicked, you should see at least one entry marked **Backup** in the **Location** column. (Thus the usefulness of this feature relies on the scheduled backup system that comes with every edition of Vista except Home Basic.)

Next, if you have the Business, Ultimate, or Enterprise edition of Vista, and the file is on a drive protected by System Restore, you should see at least one entry marked **Shadow copy** in the **Location** column.

The Previous Versions feature relies on administrative (hidden) shares of your drives; if you've disabled them as described in "Turn Off Administrative Shares," in Chapter 8, the **File Versions** list won't appear. Furthermore, Windows will never save previous versions of encrypted files (also covered in Chapter 8).

To roll back a file to an earlier version, select the backup or shadow copy you want, and click **Restore**. Better yet, click **Copy** (available for shadow copies only) and restore the old version without overwriting the new one. If you want to preserve the new one when restoring a backup, you'll either need to make a copy of the file before you click **Restore**, or you'll need to restore the backed-up file manually (explained later in this chapter).

The biggest problem with the System Restore and Previous Versions features is that they often don't work. If they're not properly set up, the restore points on which they rely don't get made.

To fully enable restore points, start by opening the System Protection window. Open the Start menu, type SystemPropertiesProtection, and press **Enter**. (Or, open the System page in Control Panel, click the **Advanced system settings** link on the left, and choose the **System Protection** tab.) Here, place a checkbox next to drive C: and any other drive for which you want to create restore points, and then click **Apply**. Unless those checkmarks were already present, take this opportunity to save a restore point by clicking **Create**.

Next, open the Services window (*services.msc*), and find the **Volume Shadow Copy** entry in the list. If it doesn't say **Started** in the **Status** column, double-click the entry, and from the **Startup type** list, select **Automatic**. Click **Start** to get the service running, and then click **OK**. Do the same for the **Microsoft Software Shadow Copy Provider** service as well.

Lastly, check your PC for utilities that may not be fully compatible with Vista's restore points. For instance, some Registry "cleaners," like TuneUp Utilities and CCleaner, have been known to interfere with restore points (among other things). And Diskeeper 2007 (defragmenter software) and earlier versions were known to erase shadow copy data (Diskeeper 2008 fixes this problem). If you're having trouble getting shadow copies to work, try disabling any "fix-it" utilities on your PC until you track down the culprit.

Choose how space is allocated for restore points

Restore points can consume as much as 15% of your hard disk's total capacity; on a 320 GB drive, that means up to 48 GB can be sucked up by previous versions of your files, hardware drivers, and other detritus.

To find out how much space restore points are currently taking up, open a Command Prompt window in administrator mode (see Chapter 8), type this command:

```
vssadmin list shadowstorage
```

and press **Enter** to produce a report that looks like this:

```
vssadmin 1.1 - Volume Shadow Copy Service administrative command-line tool
(C) Copyright 2001-2005 Microsoft Corp.

Shadow Copy Storage association
    For volume: (C:)\\?\Volume{3b5ab54e-c86b-11cb-a2d6-306f6f6e7963}\
    Shadow Copy Storage volume: (C:)\\?\Volume{3b5ab54e-c86b-11cb-a2d6-
        306f6f6e7963}\
    Used Shadow Copy Storage space: 11.706 GB
    Allocated Shadow Copy Storage space: 12.286 GB
    Maximum Shadow Copy Storage space: 13.83 GB
```

Here, restore points and shadow copies consume about 12 GB. The files themselves are stored in the *System Volume Information* folder, which is hidden in Windows Explorer unless you turn off the **Hide protected operating system files** option covered in Chapter 2. (Regardless of the setting, Windows will never let you view the files therein directly.)

Whether the amount of space restore points consume on your hard disk is too much or not enough is up to you, but either way, it's easy enough to change. At the Command Prompt, type:

```
vssadmin resize shadowstorage /for=C: /on=C: /maxsize=5GB
```

(Replace *C:* with the drive you want to adjust, and *5GB* with the actual amount of space you wish to allocate.) If you want to release the limit for shadow copy storage, omit the `maxsize` parameter, like this:

```
vssadmin resize shadowstorage /for=C: /on=C:
```

Now, you may have noticed that you need to indicate the drive letter twice. This permits a nifty little hack: it turns out you can allocate space on one drive to hold the shadow data from another drive. For instance, type:

```
vssadmin add shadowstorage /for=C: /on=D:
```

to have the shadow data for drive *C:* stored on drive *D:*. (If *C:* is your primary Windows drive, putting your shadow data on *D:* should improve performance.) To rescind this order, delete the shadow storage "association" with this command:

```
vssadmin delete shadowstorage /for=C: /on=D:
```

You can also delete shadow copy data without changing the associations:

```
vssadmin delete shadows /for=C: /all
```

Or, if you have a lot of drives and you want to clear the shadow data for all of them at once, use this WSH script (see Chapter 9):

```
Set oWMI=GetObject("winmgmts:{impersonationLevel=impersonate}!\\.\root\
    cimv2")
Set cVolumes = oWMI.ExecQuery("Select * From Win32_ShadowCopy")
For Each oVolume in cVolumes
```

Troubleshooting

```
    oVolume.Delete
Next
```

See "Quick, On-the-Fly Backups," later in this chapter, for a quick and dirty alternative to shadow copies.

Test for Bad Memory (RAM)

Bad memory can manifest itself in anything from frequent error messages and crashes to your system simply not starting. Errors in your computer's memory (RAM) aren't always consistent, either; they can be intermittent and can get worse over time.

Problems due to using the wrong kind of memory are not uncommon; to find out which type of memory you should use, consult the documentation that accompanies your computer or motherboard. If you have no such literature, check the web site of the computer or motherboard manufacturer and find out for sure before you just jam something in there. Odds are, your friend's old memory modules not only won't work in your system, but they're probably responsible for that burning smell, too.

The first thing you should do is pull out each memory module and make sure there isn't any dust or other obstruction between the pins and your motherboard (use a dry tissue or lens-cleaning paper; don't use any liquids or solvents). Look for broken or bent sockets, metal filings or other obstructions, and, of course, any smoke or burn marks. Make sure all your modules are seated properly; they should snap into place and should be level and firm (don't break them testing their firmness, of course).

If all that is in order, there are three ways to determine whether your RAM is actually faulty. The first way is to rely on your PC to do it for you; see Appendix A for the BIOS setting that disables "quick start," which is necessary to perform a full memory test each time you boot your PC.

The second is to use the **Windows Memory Diagnostic Tool**, mentioned in "What to Do When Windows Won't Start," earlier in this chapter.

The third method of testing for bad memory is to go to your local computer store and just buy more. It may only be necessary to buy a single additional module, because most likely only one module in your system is actually faulty (make sure you get the right kind). Next, systematically replace each module in your computer with the one you've just acquired, and test the system by turning it on. If the problem seems to be resolved, you've most likely found the culprit—throw it out immediately. If the system still crashes, try replacing the *next* module with the new one, and repeat the process. If you replace all the memory in your system and the problem persists, there may be more than one faulty memory module, or the problem may lie elsewhere, such as a bad CPU or motherboard (or you may even find that you're not using the correct memory in the first place).

You can, of course, also take this opportunity to add more memory to your system (possibly replacing all your existing modules). Adding memory is one of the best ways to improve overall system performance; see the "How to Buy Memory" sidebar, next, for more information.

How to Buy Memory

There are no two ways about it: the more memory, the better (at least up to a point). Adding more memory to a computer will almost always result in better performance, and will help reduce crashes as well. Windows loads drivers, applications, and documents into memory until it's full; once there's no more memory available, Windows starts pulling large chunks of information out of memory and storing them on your hard disk to make room for the applications that need memory more urgently. Because your hard disk is substantially slower than memory, this "swapping" noticeably slows down your system. The more memory you have, the less frequently Windows will use your hard disk in this way, and the faster your system will be. (See "Optimize Virtual Memory and Cache Settings," in Chapter 5, for more information on this mechanism.)

The nice thing about memory is that it is a cheap and easy way to improve performance. When Windows 3.x was first released, 32 MB of RAM cost around a thousand dollars. The same quantity of memory (and a faster variety) available at the release of Windows Vista costs less than a ticket to the movies.

The type of memory you should get depends solely on what your motherboard demands—refer to the documentation that came with your motherboard or computer system for details. There are many different brands of memory, and some are simply known for better reliability and stability. Some motherboards require more expensive varieties (and some even demand certain brands), so do your research before you buy.

That simply leaves one thing to think about: quantity. In short, get as much memory as you can afford. Like everything else, though, there is a point of diminishing returns. 1 GB (1,024 MB) is probably the lowest amount you should tolerate on a Windows Vista system.

Lastly, memory comes in individual modules, which are inserted into slots on your motherboard. The higher the capacity of each module, the fewer you'll need—the fewer modules you use, the more slots you'll leave open for a future upgrade. Sometimes, however, lower-capacity modules can be a better deal (costing fewer dollars per megabyte).

Don't Overlook the Power Supply

Every time I encounter a problem that seems to have no reasonable explanation (on a desktop PC, that is), the culprit has been the power supply. I'm beginning to think it's a conspiracy.

Say, all of a sudden, one of your storage devices (hard disk, tape drive, etc.) starts malfunctioning, either sporadically or completely. You try removing and reinstalling the drivers (if any), you replace all the cables, and you take out all the other devices. You may even completely replace the device with a brand-new one—and it still doesn't work. Odds are your power supply needs to be replaced.

Your computer's power supply runs all of your internal devices, as well as some of your external ones (i.e., the keyboard, the mouse, and most USB devices). If your power supply isn't able to provide adequate power to all your hardware, one or more of those devices will suffer.

The power supplies found in most computers are extremely cheap, a fact that ends up being the cause of most power supply problems. This means that it doesn't make too much sense to replace one cheap unit with another cheap unit, even if the replacement has a higher wattage rating.

Power supplies are rated by the amount of power they can provide (in watts); most computers come with 200–300W supplies, but many power users end up needing 350–400W. The problem with power ratings, however, is that most of those cheap power supplies don't hold up under the load. A cheap 400W unit may drop under 300W when you start connecting devices, but better supplies can supply more than enough power for even the most demanding systems, and will continue to provide reliable operations for years to come. A well-made power supply will also be heavy and have multiple fans, as well as being a bit more expensive than the $20 landfill fodder lining most store shelves.

Possible exceptions are portable computers, which may not have user-replaceable power supplies. However, the need for increased power is generally only applicable to a desktop system that can accommodate several additional internal devices, so the matter is pretty much moot.

Fix USB Power Management Issues

Power management is a common cause of USB problems; if Windows is able to shut down your USB controller to save power, it sometimes won't be able to power it back up again, which will prevent some USB devices (especially scanners) from working.

To prevent Windows from "managing" power to your USB controller or devices, follow these steps:

1. Open Device Manager (*devmgmt.msc*).

2. Expand the **Universal Serial Bus controllers** branch.

3. Double-click the **USB Root Hub** device, and choose the **Power Management** tab.

4. Turn off the **Allow the computer to turn off this device to save power** option, and click **OK** when you're done.

See "Start Windows Instantly (Almost)," in Chapter 5, for other power management issues.

Fix Printer Problems

A lot of people are having trouble printing in Vista, but nearly all their problems can be narrowed down to two areas: cables and drivers.

If you're experiencing poor printing speed, errors, or garbled output, eliminate any USB hubs you might be using, and plug your printer directly into your PC. If you're out of USB ports, consider connecting your printer directly to your network; see "Use a Print Server Without Software" in Chapter 8.

As for drivers, the problem that plagues many printers is that the drivers provided by the printer manufacturer try to do too much, and as a result, bog down your system (and your printing) with extraneous programs and dialog boxes. If Windows Vista supports your printer out of the box, consider abandoning the fancy drivers that came with your printer in favor of the plain-vanilla ones Microsoft provides.

Otherwise, many common printer problems involve incorrect paper: use laser paper for laser printers, and inkjet paper for inkjet printers—avoid the "multipurpose" junk. Also, the ink cartridges in inkjet printers are usually cheaply made and therefore are one of the first things to fail; simply installing a new ink cartridge will fix many printing problems. Better yet, discard your disposable inkjet printer and replace it with a nice, fast, color laser printer.

Preventive Maintenance and Data Recovery

Face it: some sort of data loss is inevitable. Whether it's a single lost file or a dead hard disk—whether it's tomorrow or 12 years from now—it will happen. On that happy note, there is plenty you can do about it.

First and foremost, there's no better method of disaster recovery than having a good backup copy of all your data. Any stolen or damaged hardware is easily replaced, but the data stored on your hard disk is not. Unfortunately, hindsight is 20/20, and if you didn't back up, there's not much you can do about it after the fact; even if your computer equipment is insured with Lloyds of London, once your data is gone, it's gone. Thus, a little preventative maintenance is in order.

Patch Windows with Windows Update

If software manufacturers waited until their products were completely bug-free before releasing them, then we'd all still be using typewriters.

Windows Vista has a fairly automated update system, wherein patches to the operating system that Microsoft considers important are made available on its web site, and, by default, automatically downloaded and installed on your PC.

Just open Windows Update in Control Panel, and click the **Check for updates** link on the left to compile a list of the updates you haven't yet installed. This is a fairly straightforward procedure, but largely unnecessary because Windows does it for you. Or is it necessary after all?

Right out of the box, Vista asks you how you'd like to handle updates. Microsoft recommends the **Install updates automatically** option, and even goes so far as to alert you through Security Center (see Chapter 7) if you've selected any other option (or none at all). But if you go this route, you're setting yourself up to have your PC indiscriminately hijacked by Microsoft whenever it needs to install an update. That means annoying pop-up reminders to restart Windows while you're trying to get your work done, or worse: a long delay when you need to shut down in a hurry.

Of course, the other end of the spectrum is **Never check for updates**, which some Windows users swear by. Sure, you never get the frequent bug fixes for Internet Explorer, but that's not such a big deal if you're a Firefox user.

But the **Download updates but let me choose whether to install them** option is the best of both worlds. This way, you can pick and choose your updates, and more importantly, install them only when it's convenient for you.

The hardware drivers delivered along with the other Windows updates are a mixed bag, at best. Sometimes the driver install fails, and other times, it succeeds and then breaks the device. Update a driver only when you're already using a Microsoft driver (see "How to Add Hardware," earlier in this chapter), and to be safe, only if the device isn't working. Fortunately, drivers installed through Windows Update can be "rolled back," but who wants to roll back drivers when you don't have to?

If, for some reason, you need to uninstall an update, you can do so sometimes. In Control Panel, open Programs and Features, and then click the **View installed updates** link on the left. Highlight any update in the list and click **Uninstall** to get rid of it.

If you're using Microsoft Office or another high-profile Microsoft product, you can update those products along with Windows. To do this, open Windows Update, click the **Change settings** link, and turn on the **Use Microsoft Update** option.

Quick, On-the-Fly Backups

In its simplest form, a backup is simply a copy of your data. Now, a full system backup, as described in the next topic, is obviously valuable, but often too involved of a procedure to practice frequently enough to be entirely effective.

While you might perform a full backup once a week or once a month, you can do a quick backup of your most important files several times a day. No special software or hardware is required, and, best of all, it takes only a few seconds.

The following two solutions are remarkably simple, but the idea is sound, and if you make a habit of making these quick, on-the-fly backups, it will save you hours of work.

Solution 1: Simple copy

The next time you've put a few hours into a document, open the folder in Explorer, and make a duplicate of the file by dragging it to another part of the same folder with the right mouse button and selecting **Copy Here**.

Then, if you screw up a file you're working on, if it gets accidentally deleted, or if it gets corrupted by a system crash, you'll have a fresh backup right in the same folder.

Solution 2: Simple ZIP

At the end of the day (or even several times a day), just right-click the folder of a project on which you've been working, select **Send To**, and then select **Compressed (zipped) Folder**. A new *.zip* file containing compressed versions of all of its contents will appear next to the folder in a few seconds.

If you then need to retrieve a file from the backed-up folder, just double-click the new *.zip* file.

 If you've disabled Windows Vista's built-in support for ZIP files, and have instead installed a third-party utility, such as WinZip (*http://www.winzip.com*), the procedure may be slightly different. In the case of WinZip, all you'd have to do is right-click the folder and select **Add to** *foldername.zip*.

See "Zip It Up," in Chapter 2, for the scoop on this ubiquitous format.

Back Up Your Entire System

There are more ways to back up your data than to store it in the first place. The sole purpose of a backup is to have a duplicate of every single piece of data on your hard disk that can be easily retrieved in the event of a catastrophe (or even just an accidental deletion). Imagine if your computer were stolen and you had to restore a backup to a brand-new computer. Could you do it? If the answer is no, you're not backed up.

You need to be able to complete a backup easily and often, to store the backup in a safe place (away from the computer) and to retrieve all your data at any time without incident. If it's too difficult or time-consuming, odds are you won't do it—so make it easy for yourself.

A bare-minimum backup could be little more than a single CD or USB memory key with your last three or four important documents on it. It's better than nothing, and it does protect your most recent work, but what about your email, your web browser bookmarks, your digital photos, and the thousands of documents you've written over the past six years?

I know what you're thinking, because I've heard it a thousand times: *nothing on my computer is really that important, so it's really not worth the time to back up*. OK, assume that's true—how long would it take you to reinstall Windows and all your applications, install all your drivers, reconfigure all your hardware, and customize all your toolbars? If you have a full backup of your system, the answer is not only "not long," but "no problemo" as well.

Ideally, you should be able to back up your entire hard disk on a single piece of media. We won't even entertain the idea of CDs (you'd need 57 of them to back up a full 40 GB hard disk), nor DVDs (you'd need nine standard or five dual-layer discs). ZIP drives are a joke, and USB memory keys are too slow and too small. Tapes are so far beyond passé, most Vista-compatible backup software doesn't even support tape drives.

The only choice for backing up a modern PC is a removable hard disk. Shortly after the initial release of Vista, a 500 GB 3.5-inch hard disk cost about $100, with a decent external enclosure adding only $30. (If you're not a do-it-yourselfer, prebuilt solutions are about 50% more.)

There are basically three software-based backup technologies included with Windows Vista:

Back Up Files

The *Back Up Files* wizard attempts to make it easy to back up your personal data onto any drive—removable or otherwise—and restore individual files as needed. Just open the Backup and Restore Center (Figure 6-11) and click the **Back up files** button.

Unfortunately, this feature is severely limited. For one, you can't choose which files to back up, but rather only which *types* of files to back up (and there's not much latitude there, either). Next, the Back Up Files wizard tool won't back up your system files, your Registry, or anything else you'd need to quickly rebuild your PC in the event of a catastrophe; for that, you'll need the *Complete PC Backup and Restore* tool (discussed next) or third-party backup software (such as that included with some external hard disk products).

But what's most frustrating about Back Up Files is how easily it trips up. The first time you use the Back Up Files wizard, it asks you to choose a destination, select files to back up, and—in all editions except Home Basic—schedule future backups. Thereafter, clicking **Back up files** will start a backup immediately, and without any prompts. But if Windows can't find the previous backup archives—you've deleted them, switched media, etc.—Windows won't ask you to make it right; the backup will just fail. To fix the problem, click the **Change settings** link, click **Change backup settings**, and specify a new location to save the backup. (Never mind if you don't want to choose a different destination; just change it and then change it back.)

 The automatic backup provided by the Back Up Files wizard is an essential ingredient to the Previous Versions feature discussed in "Go Back in Time with Restore Points and Shadow Copies," earlier in this chapter.

The Back Up Files wizard is included with all editions of Windows Vista.

Complete PC Backup and Restore

If you have the Business, Ultimate, or Enterprise edition of Windows Vista, you have access to the handy *Complete PC Backup and Restore* feature. This tool copies every last byte on your hard disk to the destination of your choice, making it possible to restore your PC easily in the event of a hard disk crash or other catastrophe. Just open the Backup and Restore Center (Figure 6-11), click the **Back up computer** button, and follow the prompts to create image files of each of your hard disks.

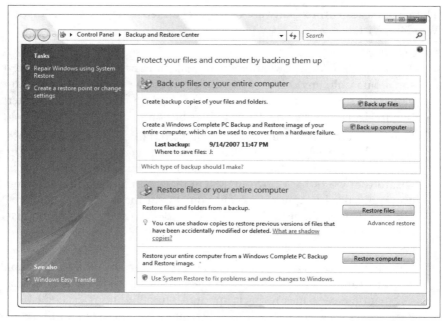

Figure 6-11. The Backup and Restore Center, showing the Back Up Files wizard that everybody gets, plus the Complete PC Backup and Restore tool only included with higher-end editions of Vista

But as though Microsoft had plotted some cruel joke, you can't restore individual files from Complete PC backups, at least not without a little hack demonstrated later in this section. (Microsoft's advice, if you can believe it, is to back up your data *twice*—once with Complete PC Backup and once with the Back Up Files wizard—if you want complete protection *and* the luxury of restoring individual files.)

Shadow Copies/Previous Versions

The *Shadow Copies* feature, also known as *previous versions*, is only available in the Business, Ultimate, and Enterprise editions of Vista. It's an extension of the System Restore feature, which stores older versions of system files and hardware drivers in case Windows won't start as the result of a recent change. See "Go Back in Time with Restore Points and Shadow Copies," earlier in this chapter, for details.

Truth be told, there's a fourth means of automated backup supported by Vista; see the upcoming sidebar, "Protect Your Data with RAID," for the scoop.

Restore a Complete PC Backup

A saving grace of Vista's Complete PC Backup and Restore is how simple it is. True, a few more features and interactivity would've been nice (such as the ability to restore individual files), but at least it works as advertised.

 Restoring a Complete PC Backup involves erasing your hard disk and replacing all your data with the data in the backup. This means any data on your hard disk created or modified since your last backup will be sucked into oblivion, so you'll likely only want to use this feature if your hard disk crashes. If you're restoring from within Windows, consider making another, newer backup on different media before you restore the older archive.

There are two ways to restore a backup made by the Complete PC Backup tool. The first method, useful when you're rebuilding your PC with a new hard disk or when Windows won't start, is outlined in "Recover Your System After a Crash," later in this chapter. The other method—the one Vista doesn't support out of the box—is explained next.

Restore individual files from a Complete PC Backup

The most egregious limitation of the Complete PC Backup tool is that Microsoft made no provision for restoring individual files from backup archives. Their solution? Create a second backup with the lesser Back Up Files wizard and use it to restore individual files. Never mind that your backups will take twice as long to complete, consume much more disk space, and provide individual file restoration only for personal documents. Why Microsoft didn't simply provide the following tools is anybody's guess.

Protect Your Data with RAID

RAID, or *Redundant Array of Inexpensive Disks*, is a collection of two or more hard drives that your PC (and Windows) treats as a single volume. Save your data once, and it's invisibly stored on two different physical disks simultaneously. If one of your drives fails, just swap it out for a new one and keep working while your RAID subsystem rebuilds the new drive in the background.

RAID comes in several varieties, but not all offer this vital redundancy. *Raid 1* is the most common, safeguarding your PC by "mirroring" your data on your multiple drives. *Raid 0*, on the other hand, spreads your data across multiple drives to improve performance (called *striping*), yet offers no data redundancy. *Raid 5* works similarly to Raid 0, but adds a "parity" mechanism to safeguard your data, and requires at least three drives. Finally, *Raid 10* offers true mirroring (like Raid 1) and striping (like Raid 0)—the best of both worlds—but requires four drives for the full effect. Raid 1 is the easiest to implement and is the least expensive way to get data protection from RAID.

The first ingredient you need is a SATA RAID controller, one either built in to your motherboard, or, barring that, an add-on RAID card. Next, you need two SATA hard disks of the same capacity, preferably the same brand and model, too.

To get started, plug your drives into ports 0 and 1, respectively, unless your documentation says otherwise. (Some controllers have dedicated RAID plugs.) To make room, you may need to relegate any other SATA devices, such as DVD drives, to higher-numbered ports. To set up the drives, enter your PC's BIOS setup screen (see Appendix A), and make sure all of the SATA ports you're using are enabled. Next, disable any unused SATA ports (some RAID controllers mistake unused ports for missing drives), and then turn on the RAID feature if it's not already on. Save your settings and reboot when you're done.

After the BIOS setup prompt but before Windows begins to load, look for a message from your RAID controller, and then press the required keystroke (e.g., **Ctrl-I** for the Intel Matrix Storage Manager) to enter your RAID configuration utility. Use this screen to select drives and build your array. (Since this step may erase any data on your drives, make sure they're fully backed up before you proceed.)

When you're done, you can install Windows (see Chapter 1) or restore your backup (if applicable) on the array as though it were only a single drive. Once you're back in Windows, install the RAID management software so you can monitor the health of your array.

There is one thing to gain by running both a Complete PC Backup and a backup with the Back Up Files wizard: *shadow copies*. If you have plenty of disk space to spare, create a second partition (see Chapter 5). Then use Back Up Files to schedule routine backups of your personal documents on the new parition. Once this is underway, you'll be able to use the Previous Versions feature, as described in "Go Back in Time with Restore Points and Shadow Copies," earlier in this chapter.

Complete PC Backup creates its backups in the form of virtual hard disk image (*.vhd*) files, the very same files used by Microsoft Virtual PC and Virtual Server to store data for virtual machines. Not only does this allow Vista's Complete PC Restore tool to rebuild a hard disk from a backup, but it means that you can open a window to the past, so to speak, and operate a virtual PC off your backup. It also means you can restore individual files... with the right software.

First, download the latest version of Virtual Server 2005, freely available at *http://www.microsoft.com/virtualserver/*. (Nevermind the version number; the latest release at the time of this writing, R2 SP1, works just fine with Vista.) Get either the 32-bit or 64-bit version, depending on your edition of Vista, and save the *setup.exe* file in a new folder named *virtualserver* on your desktop.

When the download is complete, open a Command Prompt window in administrator mode (see Chapter 8) and use the cd command (Chapter 9) to make the new folder the active folder, like this:

```
cd \users\username\desktop\virtualserver
```

where *username* is your username. Now, if you wish, you can install the entire Virtual Server application, but it's not necessary for the purposes of this solution. Instead, all you need are a handful of files. Start by extracting the *.msi* installer file by typing this command at the prompt:

```
setup /c /t .
```

Make sure to put spaces between the parameters, and don't forget the lone dot at the end. Next, type this command to install the VHDMount utility from the archive:

```
msiexec /i "Virtual Server 2005 Install.msi" /qn ADDLOCAL=VHDMount
```

Note that VHDMount is case-sensitive, so type the command exactly as shown. When that's done, close the Command Prompt window. If you like, you can delete both *setup.exe* and *Virtual Server 2005 Install.msi*, although it may be wise to hold on to *setup.exe* in case Microsoft decides to discontinue the product, or worse, start charging for it.

The installer puts the VHDMount utility in the *Program Files\Microsoft Virtual Server\Vhdmount* folder. But since it's a Command Prompt program, there's one more thing to do to make it more easily accessible: download the *vhdmount.reg* Registry patch file from *http://annoyances.org/downloads/vhdmount.reg*, or type the following into Notepad and save it as *vhdmount.reg*:

```
Windows Registry Editor Version 5.00

[HKEY_CLASSES_ROOT\.vhd]
@="Virtual.Machine.HD"

[HKEY_LOCAL_MACHINE\SOFTWARE\Classes\Virtual.Machine.HD\shell]
@="Mount"

[HKEY_LOCAL_MACHINE\SOFTWARE\Classes\Virtual.Machine.HD\shell\Mount\command]
@="\"C:\\Program Files\\Microsoft Virtual Server\\Vhdmount\\vhdmount.exe\"
/p \"%1\""

[HKEY_CLASSES_ROOT\Virtual.Machine.HD\Shell\Unmount-commit]
@="Unmount (commit changes)"

[HKEY_CLASSES_ROOT\Virtual.Machine.HD\Shell\Unmount-commit\command]
@="\"C:\\Program Files\\Microsoft Virtual Server\\Vhdmount\\vhdmount.exe\"
/u /c \"%1\""

[HKEY_CLASSES_ROOT\Virtual.Machine.HD\Shell\Unmount-discard]
@="Unmount (discard changes)"

[HKEY_CLASSES_ROOT\Virtual.Machine.HD\Shell\Unmount-discard\command]
@="\"C:\\Program Files\\Microsoft Virtual Server\\Vhdmount\\vhdmount.exe\"
/u /d \"%1\""
```

If your *Program Files* folder is on a different drive than *C:*, edit the *vhdmount.reg* file and change both occurrences of the *VHDMount* folder path to the correct location. Double-click the *vhdmount.reg* file and answer **Yes** to merge it with your Registry.

In theory, the aforementioned components are all you need, but in practice, the VHDMount utility may not work until you also install the full Microsoft Virtual PC package (not the same as Virtual Server). You can get Virtual PC 2007 for free from *http://www.microsoft.com/virtualpc/*. You don't have to use the program, only have it present on your system.

Now that all the pieces are in place, open Windows Explorer and navigate to the folder containing your backup. If you're using an external hard disk assigned to *J:* as your backup drive, your *.vhd* files are in *J:\ WindowsImageBackup\{computername}\Backup {date}*, where *{computername}* is the name of your PC and *{date}* is the date of your last backup.

Right-click a *.vhd* file and select **Mount**. A Command Prompt window will appear briefly with a message; leave it alone while it does its job. If you see any Found New Hardware messages, click **Locate and install driver software (recommended)** and follow the prompts.

 To confirm that all the drivers are in place, open Device Manager (*devmgmt.msc*). In the **Disk drives** category, you should see an **MS Virtual Service SCSI Disk Device** entry. You should also see a **Microsoft Virtual Server Storage Devices** category, with at least one entry by the same name. If they're not there, look in the **Other devices** category for any **Unknown device** entries. See "What to do when Windows can't find a driver," earlier in this chapter, for help getting these drivers installed.

With all the drivers in place, you should see a new drive in Windows Explorer, from which you can restore any individual files from your backup by just dragging and dropping. If it's not there, open Disk Manager (*diskmgmt.msc*, discussed in Chapter 5), and if you see a drive in the lower pane with no drive letter, right-click **Change Drive Letter and Paths** and assign an unused drive letter to the virtual drive.

When you're done with the backup, return to the folder containing your *.vhd* files, right-click the one you've mounted, and select **Unmount (discard changes)**. (Only use the other option, **commit changes**, if you made changes to the virtual drive that you want to keep.) The drive should disappear from Windows Explorer immediately.

Recover Your System After a Crash

The purpose of backing up is to give you the opportunity to restore your system to its original state if something nasty should happen to your hard disk, whether it be theft, fire, malfunction, termites, or just your own clumsiness. You'd be surprised at how many people back up their systems without having any idea how to restore it later should the need arise. The backup doesn't do you any good if you can't get at your files later, so it's important to take steps to make sure you can restore your system *from scratch* if necessary.

So, assume your hard disk is completely dead, totally empty, or missing, and you now need to restore your PC onto an empty volume.

If you have the Business, Ultimate, or Enterprise edition of Windows Vista, you can use the Complete PC Backup and Restore tool for this purpose, as described in "Back Up Your Entire System," earlier in this chapter. To restore a Complete PC backup, boot off your Vista setup disc (see Chapter 1), and when you see the Install Now page, click the **Repair your computer** link and then click **Windows Complete PC Restore**, as shown earlier in Figure 6-3.

 So, what do you do if you don't have a genuine, bootable Vista installation CD, but rather only a proprietary "Recovery" disc or partition provided by your PC manufacturer? In this case, you'll need to first use your PC's Recovery feature to rebuild your default Windows installation. When that's done, restart your PC and press **F8** to open the **Advanced Boot Options** menu described in "What to Do When Windows Won't Start," and depicted in Figure 6-4, earlier in this chapter. Use the arrow keys to select the **Repair Your Computer** option and then follow the prompts. When the System Recovery Options page appears, click **Windows Complete PC Restore**.

(If you don't see the aforementioned **Repair Your Computer** option, your PC manufacturer screwed up; at this point, you should contact the company and demand a genuine Windows install disc.)

Otherwise, if you have the Home Premium or Home Basic edition, you may have more work cut out for you. Assuming you've used the Back Up Files wizard described earlier in this chapter, you'll need to install Windows or use your PC's recovery disc before you can restore any of your files. (You'll also need to install each of your applications if you want to subsequently open your documents.) Once you're back in Windows, open the Backup and Restore Center (shown previously in Figure 6-11), click the **Restore files** button, and follow the prompts.

But what if your hard disk isn't empty? Say Windows got hosed and won't start, or perhaps you just lost half your data files. Unless your backup is from this morning, you won't necessarily want to erase all your recent files and replace them with whatever is in your backup archive. In this case, you can place a parallel installation of Vista on your drive, as described in "Fresh install on a dirty drive" in Chapter 1. Or, you can install a new drive, restore your Complete PC backup onto it, and then hook up your old drive and copy your recent data onto it. (The latter solution has the advantage of allowing you to format or discard the damaged drive.)

CHAPTER 7

Networking and Internet

Pop quiz: how do you compromise your PC's security, stability, and performance in about 10 seconds, without installing any new software? If you guessed, "sledgehammer," you're wrong—that takes only two seconds.

Of course, the correct answer is "connect it to a network." You get bonus points if you added, "leave Vista's security settings intact."

It's fair to say that Windows Vista is more secure than any previous (network-capable) version of Windows, but unfortunately, that's not quite as earth-shattering as it sounds. Sure, Vista's Windows Firewall isn't booby-trapped to prevent file sharing or time synchronization like it was in XP, but the defaults in Vista still leave most of your PC vulnerable to anyone who knows where to look.

Use this chapter plus Chapter 8 to connect your PC to a local network and the Internet without having to worry that Vista isn't doing its job of keeping your data safe.

Build Your Network

As far as Vista is concerned, your connection to the Internet is no different than your connection to other PCs in your home or office. It's this fact that makes Windows all at once easy to network and frustrating to troubleshoot and secure.

Terminology Primer

To start building a network, you should understand a few basic networking concepts:

The distinction between local and remote resources

A *local resource* is an object—a folder on your hard disk or a printer physically connected to your PC—that's accessible without a network connection. A *remote resource* is one that resides on another computer to which yours is connected over a network. For example, a web page at *www.annoyances.org* is a remote file, but an HTML file on your own hard disk is a local file, even though they may appear indistinguishable in a browser. Vista tries to blur the line, a strategy that sometimes works and other times causes problems: for instance, different security restrictions and drag-drop rules apply to remote files and folders than to local ones, and the subtlety can be a pain in one's keister.

LAN versus WAN

LAN is shorthand for *Local Area Network*, a small assemblage of PCs in a home or small office connected with cables or wireless signals. Likewise, WAN stands for *Wide Area Network*, or a network formed by connecting computers over large distances (e.g., the Internet).

Ethernet

Ethernet is the wired technology upon which the vast majority of local area networks is built. Any PC capable of handling Vista is likely to have a built-in Ethernet adapter (also called a NIC, or Network Interface Card).

 A standard Ethernet connection is capable of moving data up to 10 megabits per second (Mbps; see "Bandwidth," later in this list), a Fast Ethernet connection (sometimes marked "10/100") can move data at 100 Mbps, and a Gigabit connection can move data at up to 1000 Mbps.

WiFi

WiFi is a trendy shorthand term for wireless networking based on the 802.11*x* standards. The early favorite was 802.11b, but with a leisurely maximum speed of only 11 Mbps, it was quickly obsoleted by 802.11g (54 Mbps). Further tweaking has given us multichannel 802.11g and the overhyped 802.11n standards, both of which promise even faster speeds and greater range. Of course, all of these advertised specs assume laboratory-perfect conditions, so unless you're interested in building a vacuum chamber for your wireless equipment, you'll likely get about a third of the quoted speed of your equipment (and less, the poorer the reception gets).

A further caveat is that you need matched equipment to get the best performance: your laptop must have an 'n' radio to get the most out of an 'n' network. Luckily, each of these standards (with the exception of 802.11a) is backward-compatible with earlier incarnations, so an older 'g' laptop will still work on a newer 'n' network, albeit at the slower 'g' speed. Of course, with typical DSL and cable Internet speeds at only 1–3 Mbps, a faster WiFi signal will do nothing to get you your email any faster.

Bluetooth

Bluetooth is a wireless networking "standard" (the term must be used loosely here). Bluetooth will never supplant WiFi, nor is it meant to. Rather, it's an inexpensive, low-power technology and is commonly used in high-end cell phones, handheld PDAs, and some laptops. Most people get their first taste of Bluetooth with wireless cell phone headsets or cordless mice and keyboards, but it does much more than that (at least in theory). See "Get Bluetooth to Work," later in this chapter, if you feel like wasting an afternoon installing and reinstalling Bluetooth drivers.

Bandwidth

Bandwidth is the capacity of a network connection to move information (the size of the pipe, so to speak). Bandwidth is measured in Kbps (kilobits per second) for slow connections, Mbps (megabits per second) for faster connections such as DSL, cable, or Ethernet LAN connections, and Gbps (gigabits per second) for the kinds of connections used by huge corporations and Internet providers.

 Bandwidth is a shared resource. If a network connection is capable of transferring data at, say, 1.5 Mbps, and two users simultaneously download large files, each will only have roughly 0.75 Mbps (or 768 Kbps) of bandwidth at their disposal.

Ethernet-based local networks can transfer data at up to 1,000 Mbps. High-speed T1, DSL, and cable modem connections typically transfer data up to 1.0 to 6.0 Mbps, while the fastest analog modems communicate at a glacial 56 Kbps, or 0.056 Mbps.

To translate a bandwidth measurement into more practical terms, you'll need to convert bits to bytes. There are 8 bits to a byte, so you can determine the theoretical maximum data transfer rate of a connection by simply dividing by 8. For example, a 384 Kbps connection transfers 384/8 = 48 kilobytes of data per second, which should allow you to transfer a 1 megabyte file in a little more than 20 seconds. However, there is more going on than just data transfer (such as error correction), so actual performance will always be slower than the theoretical maximum.

Protocols

A protocol is the language, so to speak, that your computer uses to communicate with other computers on a network. Now, the days of configuring individual network protocols are long past, having died out with the Windows 95/98 generation. As long as your stuff speaks TCP/IP, it'll work, provided you don't mind occasionally typing in numeric IP addresses.

TCP/IP

TCP/IP is a protocol, or more accurately, a collection of protocols, used in all Internet communications and by most modern LANs. For those of you excited by acronyms, the TCP/IP specification includes TCP (Transmission Control Protocol), IP (Internet Protocol), UDP (User Datagram Protocol), and ICMP (Internet Control Message Protocol).

The amazing thing about TCP/IP, and the reason that it serves as the foundation of every connection to the Internet, is that data is broken up into *packets* before it's sent on its way. The packets then travel to their destinations independently, possibly arriving in a different order than they were originally sent. The receiving computer then reassembles the packets (in the correct order) back into data.

TCP Ports

TCP/IP data moves in and out of your PC through *ports*, virtual doors opened by the software that uses your network connection. For example, your email program uses port 25 to send email (using the SMTP protocol) and port 110 to retrieve email (using the POP3 protocol), while your web browser downloads pages through port 80 (using the HTTP protocol). Other commonly used ports are listed in Appendix B.

 Windows and some applications typically leave more ports open than you probably need, potentially making your PC vulnerable to spyware, pop ups, viruses, intruders, and other annoyances. See "Secure Your Networked PC," later in this chapter, for the solution.

IP addresses

An IP address is a set of four numbers (e.g., 207.46.230.218) that corresponds to a single computer or device on a TCP/IP-based network. Each element of the address can range from 0 to 255, providing 256^4 or nearly 4.3 billion possible combinations. On the Internet, dedicated machines called *domain name servers* are used to translate named hosts, such as *www.microsoft.com*, to their respective numerical IP addresses and back again.

 No two computers on a single network can have the same IP address, but a single computer can have multiple IP addresses (one for each network to which it's connected). A router, discussed later in this chapter, does allow multiple PCs to share a single Internet connection (and thus a single IP address), but only by creating a separate network (LAN) and acting as a gateway between them.

To connect two different networks to each other, while still maintaining two separate sets of IP addresses, you'll need either a *bridge* or a *router*. Provided that you install two network adapters in your PC, Windows can act as an impromptu bridge; just highlight two connections in your Network Connections window (discussed later in this chapter), right-click, and select **Bridge Connections**. A router, of course, is a better choice because it works even if your PC is off, and includes firewall protection to boot.

Firewalls, and why you need one

A firewall can be used to restrict unauthorized access to your system by intruders, close backdoors opened by viruses and other malicious applications, and eliminate wasted bandwidth by blocking certain types of network traffic.

A firewall is a layer of protection that permits or denies network communication based on a predefined set of rules. These rules are typically based on the TCP port through which the data is sent, the IP address from which the data originated, and the IP address to which the data is destined.

The problem is that an improperly configured firewall can cause more problems than it ends up preventing. Windows includes a rudimentary firewall feature, described later in this chapter, but software-based firewalls simply don't work as well as hardware firewalls like those found in routers.

Switches, access points, and routers

A *switch* allows you to connect more than two computers together—using cables—to form a local network (see Figure 7-1, later in this chapter). (Note that a *hub* does pretty much the same thing as a switch, but much less efficiently.) Without a hub or switch, the best you could do is connect two computers to each other with a *crossover* cable (discussed later in this chapter).

A wireless access point is essentially a switch (or a hub) for a wireless network, allowing you to connect multiple computers wirelessly. Without an access point, you could only connect two computers wirelessly in "ad hoc" mode (more on that later, too).

Finally, a *router* is a device that connects two networks, and *routes* traffic between them. For example, a router can connect a peer-to-peer workgroup to the Internet, allowing you to share a single Internet connection with all the computers in your office (see "Share an Internet Connection," later in this chapter, for details). Most routers also double as switches, just as *wireless routers* double as wireless access points. Plus, any modern router (wireless or otherwise) will have a built-in firewall (typically superior to a software firewall that runs on your computer), so you can basically get everything you need in one inexpensive package.

The good news is that Vista comes with everything you need to take advantage of all of these standards, and use them to access the Internet or share files and devices with other PCs on your network. The bad news is that it's almost never as easy to get it working properly as the industry would lead you to believe.

To Wire or Not to Wire

Wiring is a pain, but it works. Wireless is convenient, but flaky. Luckily, you don't have to just stick with one system, nor have it all planned out ahead of time.

For best results, wire your nonmobile desktop system to your router/switch/hub when it's nearby. Cables aren't affected by poor reception, security codes, or interference, and they provide full speed all the time.

Plug one end of an Ethernet cable into your router or DSL/cable modem, and the other end into your PC, and you're done; Vista will set up the connection and get you on the Net in less than two seconds, no questions asked. And unless a small rodent chews its way through said cable, it'll keep working until you unplug it.

 If you see a prompt that entices you to **Connect to a network**, resist the urge if you're using cables; even though it doesn't explicitly say it, the window that appears when you click this link is only for connecting to wireless networks.

Wiring can vary in complexity and cost, depending on your needs, budget, and office layout. (See the upcoming "Cabling Tips" sidebar for additional help.) For example, if you have two or more desktop computers in the same room, wiring is a simple matter of adding a switch and one category-5 *patch* cable for each machine, as shown in Figure 7-1. More PCs require a switch with more ports, or possibly multiple switches connected together, and of course, more cables.

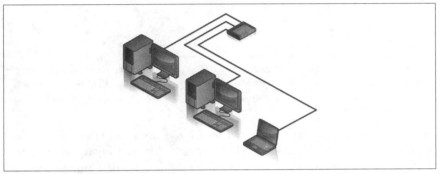

Figure 7-1. An example of a wired peer-to-peer network (LAN) comprised of three computers connected with a switch (or hub); the printer is connected to one of the PCs, which shares it with the others

If you only have two computers, you can eliminate the switch and simply connect them with an inexpensive category-5 *crossover* cable, as shown in Figure 7-2. Total cost: $3.99.

Figure 7-2. A quick and dirty hubless workgroup; given its limitations, however, it's best suited as a temporary solution

Most of the time, it doesn't make sense to use cables to connect a laptop to your network unless its wireless doesn't work. (Of course, if you're using a docking station, plugging in is more practical, but that's up to you.) Wireless, of course, is slicker than using cables, and works anywhere within range of the router; no drilling holes in walls so you can feed cables to all parts of your home or office. Figure 7-3 shows a typical wireless network with four computers (three PCs and one PDA).

Networking and Internet

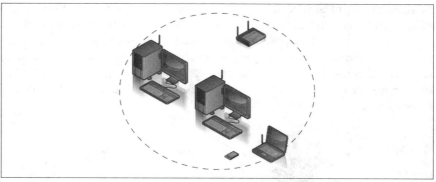

Figure 7-3. A wireless router acts as both a wireless access point and a switch, allowing you to connect any number of computers —and even WiFi-enabled PDAs—to form a wireless LAN (WiFi antennas are typically internal, and are shown here only for illustrative purposes)

Wireless needs more setup than cables (if you do it right) and is less reliable than Ethernet. Windows needs at least 5–10 seconds to connect to a previously configured wireless network (more for the first time), and may drop your connection as you move around.

Speed may or may not be a factor in your decision. WiFi is not nearly as fast as wired Ethernet; common 802.11g wireless connections (rated at 54 Mbps) transfer data at about 20–30 Mbps, and this speed drops rapidly as reception worsens. The fastest Ethernet connections move data at 1,000 Mbps (1 Gbps), reception notwithstanding. Of course, the difference is moot if you're only doing Internet (typical broadband is only about 1–3 Mbps), but if you need to transfer files between PCs in your workgroup, wired Ethernet will do it in a fraction of the time.

So, what if you want the convenience of wireless, but the speed and reliability of cables? The short answer is to wait about five years for the technology to improve, and then pick up the latest Annoyances book to learn why you'll need to wait another five years. The even shorter answer is to simply connect your WiFi-equipped laptop to your network with a cable when your wireless gets cranky or you need to transfer files. Luckily, a properly configured network should have no trouble handling both wired and wireless PCs. Figure 7-4 shows a common peer-to-peer network setup with two wired desktop computers and a wireless connection to a laptop.

Cabling Tips

Within a second or two of connecting both ends of a network cable, the corresponding lights on your hardware should light up. Lights should be visible right on the network adapter, whether it's in the back of your desktop computer or in the side of your laptop. (Note that some devices use multicolor LEDs that appear green if the connection is correct, and red if it's wrong.) Flashing lights usually mean data is being transferred.

Connect all your cables while your switch and any other equipment are turned on and while Windows is running. That way, you'll see the corresponding lights go on, indicating that the switch, router, or NIC has detected the new connection. Note that the lights only confirm that the cabling is correct; they won't tell you whether the drivers and protocols are correctly installed.

Use only category-5 (Cat-5) *patch* cables, except for a few very specific situations that require category-5 *crossover* cables. Use a crossover cable to connect two computers directly (without a hub, switch, or router) or to connect two switches. In some cases where a DSL/cable modem connects directly to a computer with a patch cable, a crossover cable may be required to connect either of these devices to a hub or switch (naturally, consult the documentation to be sure). Either way, if the lights go on, you're using the right kind of cable.

When measuring for cables, always add several extra feet to each cable; too long is better than too short. Also, bad cables are not uncommon, so have a few extras around in case any of those lights don't light up.

Shop around when looking for cables. Most of the huge mega-computer stores charge too much for cables; you can often find longer, better cables at a fraction of the price (sans the fancy packaging) by shopping at smaller mom-and-pop computer stores.

Finally, if your cables are to pass through walls, you may want to install category-5 wall jacks for the tidiest appearance. Note that these accessories can be expensive and cumbersome to wire properly, and are typically unnecessary for all but the most compulsive neat-freaks among us. <Grin>

There's one crucial aspect of wireless networking that simply doesn't exist on a wired network: intruders. By default, most wireless routers have no security features enabled, meaning that any WiFi-enabled computer within range can connect to your workgroup and use your Internet connection. See "Set Up a Wireless Router," next, and "Sniff Out WiFi Hotspots," later in this chapter, for help securing your wireless network and connecting to someone else's unsecured wireless network, respectively.

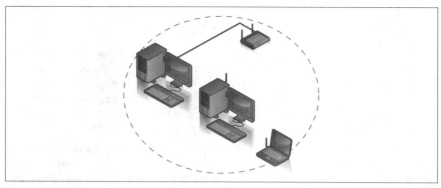

Figure 7-4. You can mix and match wired and wireless devices with a wireless router; these three computers are on the same network, despite the different means of connection

Set Up a Wireless Router

If you've read other solutions in this chapter, you've probably seen routers mentioned several times (if not, drop back to the "Terminology Primer" section to read up).

A router allows you to connect your computer (or your workgroup) to the Internet, while simultaneously protecting you with its built-in firewall. A *wireless* router does the same thing, but also adds a wireless *access point*, which allows you to connect any number of WiFi devices to each other and to the Internet.

A typical WiFi setup was shown in Figure 7-3 (see, no wires), but you'll probably want something closer to the setup shown later in Figure 7-20, in which a wireless router provides Internet access to all your computers. Here's how to set this up and configure the security measures that *should've* been enabled out of the box:

1. Plug your DSL or cable modem (or whatever broadband connection you're using) into your router's WAN or Internet port.

2. Use an Ethernet cable to connect at least one PC to one of the numbered ports on your router, even if you eventually want to use that PC wirelessly.

3. Dispense with the software that comes with your router. Instead, open a web browser on the wired PC and type the IP address of your router into the address bar. In most cases, this is 192.168.1.1, but your router may be different; refer to your router's documentation for details. (You may also need to log in with a username and password at this point, also listed in said documentation, at least in theory.) If you can't connect to your router, and you're sure your PC's network card is working, see the "Can't Connect To Your Router?" sidebar, next.

Can't Connect To Your Router?

If you can't load your router's setup page, and you're certain you're using the correct IP address, the most likely cause is that your PC and your router are not on the same *subnet*. The subnet is the range of addresses governed by the first three components of the IP address, and Windows likes the default 192.168.1.*x* subnet.

This means that the first three numbers of your computer's IP address must mach the first three numbers of your router's IP address, while the fourth number must be different. For instance, if your router's address is 192.168.0.1, then you might not be able to connect to it until you either change your PC's address to 192.168.0.*x* (where *x* is any number larger than zero) *or* change your router's address to 192.168.1.1 to connect to the router.

Now, in theory, Vista should do all of this for you when you use the **Obtain an IP address automatically** option described later in this chapter, but this is notorious for not working when the subnets don't match. If you suspect this is the problem, try setting a static IP address on your PC, at least temporarily, until you can connect to your router and reconfigure it to use the 192.168.1.*x* subnet.

4. Once you get your connection to your router working, you'll see your router's setup page, which should look vaguely like the one in Figure 7-5. Of course, your router's setup page will almost certainly look different, but most of the same settings will still be there.

5. Choose your connection type from the list. If your Internet connection requires a username and password, select **PPPoE**. If your ISP has provided an IP address for your connection, select **Static IP**. Otherwise, choose **Automatic Configuration - DHCP**.

6. If you've selected **PPPoE** or **Static IP** in the previous step, you'll probably need to enter the IP addresses of your ISP's DNS servers (your ISP should provide these numbers for you).

7. Click **Apply** or **Save Settings** at the bottom of the page when you're done.

8. At this point, you should have Internet access; go ahead and test it by opening a second browser window (**Ctrl-N**) and visiting any web site.

9. Take this opportunity to visit the router manufacturer's web site and look for an update to the router firmware; if there's a newer version, download and install it right away.

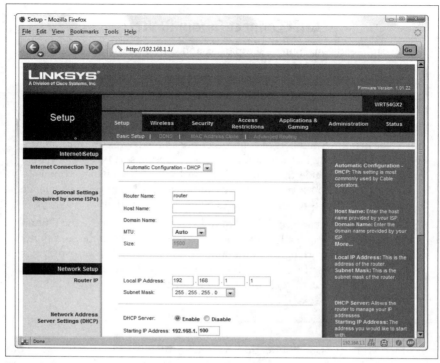

Figure 7-5. Most routers use a web-based setup, meaning that you can configure your router from any computer, running on any platform, as long as it has a web browser

Firmware updates typically fix bugs and improve performance, and substantial updates may add support for newer encryption protocols like WPA2 (discussed later), so don't skip this step!

10. Next, go to your router's *wireless* setup page, like the one shown in Figure 7-6—you can get there with either a link in the main menu or a tab across the top of the page—and choose a new name (SSID) for your wireless network. (Note that the SSID should not be confused with the Windows network name used in Chapter 8.)

The only way Vista distinguishes one configured network from another is the SSID, so choose a *unique* name for your network. If you were to use a generic name like "wireless" or leave the default name (e.g., "link-sys") intact, you might run into a problem later on. For instance, if a neighbor has a WiFi network with the same name, you might not be able to see your own network. Or, if your home network has the same

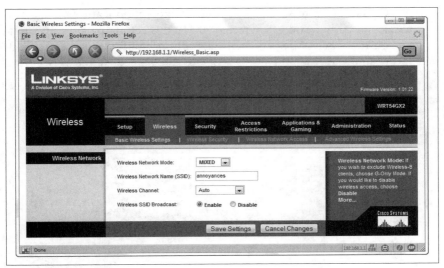

Figure 7-6. Use your router's wireless setup page to configure the security settings for your wireless network

name as the one at work, yet both have different encryption settings (set later in this section), Windows may not recognize both networks as unique without a lot of hassle.

When choosing an SSID, you should also avoid names that give away your location, such as your street address or the name of your business. An intruder—or WiFi leech, for that matter—might exploit that extra information to boost his or her own signal or, worse, break into your network.

11. Next, check to see whether the **Wireless SSID Broadcast** option is turned on or off, and make sure it's set the way you want it.

 Opinions differ on whether turning off SSID broadcast is a good or bad idea. Your SSID is a backdoor to your wireless network; if you broadcast your SSID, you expose one more piece of information someone could use to connect to your network. If it's hidden (and you've chosen a unique name), you make it that much harder for someone to break in. On the other hand, a hidden SSID doesn't necessarily guarantee an invisible network; in fact, certain settings in Windows can be exploited to expose your hidden SSID, as described in the next section, "Sniff Out WiFi Hotspots." So, don't rely solely on a hidden SSID to protect your wireless network.

When you're done here, click **Apply** or **Save Settings**.

12. Next, you'll want to set up your router's encryption feature for the best wireless security. You can typically get to this setting by clicking a button on the wireless page named **Encryption**, **WEP**, or—in the case of the example in Figure 7-6—a separate tab named **Wireless Security**. Figure 7-7 shows a typical wireless encryption setup page.

Figure 7-7. Configure your wireless router's encryption settings to prevent others from connecting to your wireless network without your permission

Now, Vista understands several different types of wireless encryption, all used to prevent intruders from connecting to or spying on your wireless network unless they have your secret encryption key. Of course, some are better than others; see the upcoming "Choosing the Right Encryption Scheme: WEP, WPA, or WPA2?" sidebar for details.

13. Once you've enabled wireless encryption, you'll need to choose a *key* or *passphrase*.

With WPA or WPA2, you type a word or a phrase into your router's setup page, and then type the *same* word or phrase into Windows to connect, as described in "Sniff Out WiFi Hotspots," next. (In Figure 7-7, I chose "Beware of the Leopard!" as my passphrase.) The stronger the passphrase you enter, the more secure your wireless network will be. A WPA passphrase can be 8–63 characters (bytes) long, but the 802.11i standard recommends a passphrase at least 20 characters long to deter practical attacks.

Choosing the Right Encryption Scheme: WEP, WPA, or WPA2?

Encrypting your wireless network accomplishes two things: it helps keep out leeches who would otherwise use your WiFi for free Internet, and it helps prevent intruders from breaking into your system to snoop around your PC.

Of course, most wireless routers have encryption turned off by default, so any choice you make is better than none at all. The three prevailing standards for wireless encryption—all supported by Vista out of the box—are:

WEP

Wired Equivalent Privacy (or Wireless Encryption Protocol) is the original protection scheme included with early wireless routers, and it is also the weakest. With the right software, an intruder can easily break into a WEP-protected network in a few minutes using the *Related-key attack*. Use WEP only if you have older PCs or devices that don't support *WPA*, described next.

WPA

WiFi Protected Access was established as a stopgap measure to remedy the vulnerabilities in WEP. If you have any Windows XP machines on your network, they'll need Service Pack 2 to connect to a WPA-encrypted network.

WPA2/PSK

Also known as 802.11i or PSK for *Pre-Shared Key*, WPA2 is the completed form of WPA, and is considered the strongest nonproprietary encryption scheme for 802.11x wireless networks. Any wireless products certified after March 2006 are supposed to fully support WPA2. WPA2 is supported under Windows XP if the WPA2/WPS IE update (available at *http://support.microsoft.com/kb/893357*) is installed. Macs will need AirPort 4.2 or later to use WPA.

Those using WPA or WPA2 will have a choice between the *Personal* and *Enterprise* varieties. As enticing as Enterprise may sound, it requires a RADIUS server typically used only in large companies, making Personal the proper choice for most home and small-business networks.

Next, your router may support the *AES (Advanced Encryption Standard)* or *TKIP (Temporal Key Integrity Protocol)* encryption algorithms, or both. Of the two, AES is stronger, but it is supported only by WPA2. If you experience connection problems with AES, wherein certain web sites won't load, try switching to TKIP (or vice-versa). If your router allows it, select AES and TKIP to make troubleshooting easier, and then choose one algorithm or the other in Windows.

So, for best wireless security, choose WPA2-Personal with AES and TKIP.

With WEP, your router may have you type a passphrase, but it's only used to generate a *key*. WEP keys are hexadecimal strings of numbers (0–9) and letters (A–F), and are either 10 or 26 digits long (for 64- or 128-bit security, respectively). You then type the hex key—not the passphrase—into Windows to connect.

 Before you save your changes here, make things easy on yourself and take this opportunity to record your passphrase or key. Highlight the key (if there's more than one, use the first key, **Key 1**) and press **Ctrl-C** to copy it to the clipboard. Then, open your favorite text editor (e.g., Notepad), and press **Ctrl-V** to paste it into a new, empty document. Save the file on your desktop (or a USB memory key to set up other PCs); this will allow you to easily paste it into various dialog boxes later on, which is easier than having to type it.

14. Click **Apply** or **Save Settings** at the bottom of the page when you're done.

15. Unplug the cable connecting your PC to your router, and then attempt a wireless connection, as described in the next section, "Sniff Out WiFi Hotspots." See the upcoming "Router Placement 101" sidebar for ways to improve reception (and thus the performance of your wireless network).

 If you employ encryption using these settings, but you subsequently can't connect to it wirelessly, it most likely means that you've entered the encryption key incorrectly on your PC. To fix the problem, you'll have to reconnect your PC to your router with a cable and modify the settings as described here. If that doesn't help, make sure you've installed the latest firmware on your router and the latest wireless drivers on your PC. As a final resort, reset the router as described in your router's documentation, and start over.

While it's important to employ as many security features on your wireless network as you can, you shouldn't rely entirely on them to protect your sensitive data. When you're done here, make sure you set a password for your Windows user account, and keep a watchful eye on precisely what resources you're sharing, both as described in Chapter 8.

Router Placement 101

The tiny WiFi transceiver in your laptop should be capable of picking up any wireless network within about 100 feet, perhaps a little more if you have newer equipment. If indoors, this typically includes no more than about two or three walls, and perhaps one floor or ceiling. But the placement of your wireless router and the arrangement of natural obstacles near it will have a significant effect on the strength and range of your WiFi signal.

Assuming you're using a setup like the one pictured later in Figure 7-20, your router will need to be within spitting distance of your DSL or cable modem. But provided that the cable from your modem to your router is long enough, you should have a little leeway there.

Your router should be out in the open; don't put it under your desk, in a drawer, or behind a metal file cabinet. If you're feeding more than one computer, it should be placed in a central location, if possible. Use the signal strength indicator (Figure 7-10) to test various configurations. Consider cabling stationary computers so that you can optimize the placement of the router for your portable ones.

The 802.11b, g, and n standards operate over the 2.4 Ghz band, which is also inhabited by cordless phones and microwave ovens. (The black sheep of the family, 802.11a, solves this problem by using the 5 Ghz band, but its short range and limited compatibility make it an unpopular choice.) This means that you'll get better results if you move the router away from any cordless-phone base stations, televisions, radios, or TV dinners.

If, after adjusting the placement of your router, you still need more range than it seems to be able to provide, consider either a repeater (range extender) or an aftermarket antenna for your router. There are even a number of do-it-yourself antenna projects for both the router and client (e.g., laptop), including the creative use of a Pringles™ can.

Sniff Out WiFi Hotspots

The centerpiece of Windows' built-in wireless networking is the "Connect to a network" window shown in Figure 7-8, which basically serves as a WiFi *sniffer*.

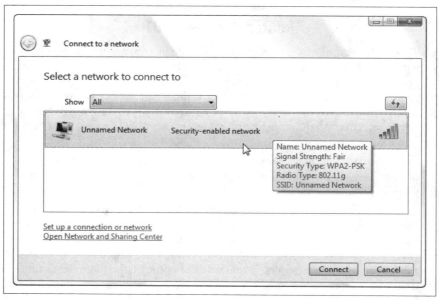

Figure 7-8. The "Connect to a network" window in Windows Vista lets you sniff out and connect to any WiFi hotspots in range

 To display the "Connect to a network" window, open the Start menu and click **Connect To** (if it's there). Or, click the network icon to the right of the notification area (tray) and then click the **Connect to a network** link. Or, if you're in Control Panel, open the **Network and Sharing Center**, and click the **Connect to a network** link on the Tasks pane on the left side. (Note that this window is not needed at all if you're connecting your PC to a network with a cable.)

A WiFi sniffer is a program (or device) that scans for and lists the WiFi networks within range. This is where the SSID Broadcast setting in the previous section, "Set Up a Wireless Router," comes into play: as long as your router is broadcasting your SSID, any sniffer within range will see it.

Just highlight an entry in the list and click **Connect**. Now, if a network is identified as a **Security-enabled network**, you'll need its encryption passphrase or key to connect to it. Provided it's your own network, you can just paste the passphrase from step 13 of "Set Up a Wireless Router," earlier in this chapter; otherwise, you'll have to get it from the administrator of that particular hotspot. Naturally, you won't need a key for non-encrypted networks, only the patience to click through the security warning Vista displays every time you try.

If you connect successfully, Vista will give you the opportunity to **Save this network**. To see a list of saved networks, open the Manage Wireless Networks window, discussed in the next section, "Troubleshoot Wireless Networks."

Things are a little different if you've disabled your router's SSID broadcast option. For one, your WiFi network will either show up as **Unnamed Network** in the sniffer window, or it won't show up at all. But more importantly, you may have to go a different route to connect to your hidden network (particularly if there's more than one "unnamed" network in range).

On the "Connect to a network" page, click the **Set up a connection or network** link on the bottom. Then, select **Manually connect to a wireless network** in the list, and click **Next** to open the page shown in Figure 7-9.

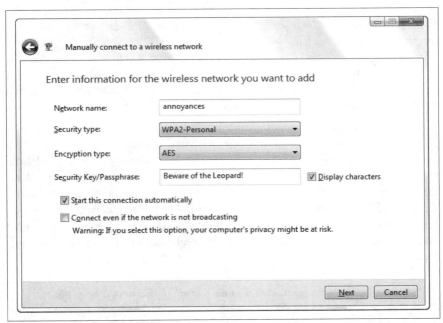

Figure 7-9. To connect to a wireless network that isn't broadcasting its SSID, go to this page to hand-enter the SSID and encryption key

In the **Network name** field, type the SSID exactly as it appears in your router setup page, and then choose the **Security type** (e.g., WEP, WPA2) that matches the one used by your router.

Next comes the encryption key or passphrase. Now, despite the fact that it clearly says **Passphrase** here, Windows Vista will only accept a passphrase if you're using WPA or WPA2 encryption; with WEP, you're only allowed to type the formal 10- or 26-digit WEP encryption key in the **Security Key/ Passphrase** field. So, turn on the **Display characters** option so you can see what you're doing, and then paste (press **Ctrl-V**) the key from step 13 of "Set Up a Wireless Router," earlier in this chapter.

Below, turn on the **Start this connection automatically** option, and then pause while you try to figure out what Microsoft means when it warns you that "Your computer's privacy might be at risk" if you turn on the **Connect even if the network is not broadcasting** option.

Give up? It turns out that Microsoft's stated position—one not explained anywhere on this window, but rather only published online at *http:// www.microsoft.com/technet/network/wifi/hiddennet.mspx*—is that if you turn off your router's SSID broadcast feature, bad things can happen.

It works like this: when connecting to a normal, broadcasting network, Windows waits until it sees a network you've already set up before it attempts to connect. But when you turn *off* SSID broadcast to hide your wireless network, Windows *continually* sends out a signal with the hidden SSID until it finds your network. And as you may have guessed, someone wrote a program that "listens" for a PC that's trying to connect to a hidden network and records any SSIDs it encounters.

Now, in order for someone to discover your network's hidden SSID, the hacker must be within range of your PC when it's on, and listening at the moment it attempts to connect to your wireless network. If you're already connected at home or if you're surfing the Web at the coffee shop, Windows won't send out any signals. But more importantly, if someone discovers your SSID, she still won't be able to connect to your network as long as you've enabled encryption. As it is, a hidden SSID won't adequately protect your network if it's the sole security measure, and that's what Microsoft means by its vague warning.

 The aforementioned **Connect even if the network is not broadcasting** option is a new feature in Windows Vista. If you have any older PCs on your network running, say, Windows XP, there is no such option unless you install the Wireless Client Update at *http://support.microsoft.com/?kbid=917021*.

So, to connect to your home network with a hidden SSID, you have four choices:

- Take Microsoft's advice and configure your wireless router to broadcast its SSID. Rely on encryption, explained in "Set Up a Wireless Router," earlier in this chapter, and authentication, described in Chapter 8, to protect your privacy. Then, connect to your network as described earlier in this section.

- Turn *off* your router's **SSID Broadcast** setting and enable the **Connect even if the network is not broadcasting** option. This way, your PC will automatically connect to your hidden network whenever it's in range, but you'll run the risk of exposing your "secret" SSID. If you do this, make sure you encrypt your network and that you employ authentication (Chapter 8) in full force.

- Turn *off* your router's **SSID Broadcast** setting, but don't use the **Connect even if the network is not broadcasting** option. But beware: it's a trap!

  Here's the problem: since your network is not broadcasting, Windows won't ever connect to it automatically. So, you need to connect by hand, but how?

  When you click **Next** on this page, Vista saves the network you've just set up in the Manage Wireless Networks window (discussed in the next section), but there's no **Connect** button there. Don't try using the "Manually connect to a wireless network" window either, as it'll just ask you to set up another new network. And since your network isn't broadcasting, it won't show up in the "Connect to a network" window, at least not yet.

  The solution is to wait. *Eventually*, the "Connect to a network" window will list your hidden network, assuming it's in range. (It knows when it's in range, by the way, because it continually polls the airwaves for the network, using the process described earlier in this section that supposedly compromises your privacy.) If you don't see your new network entry after a few minutes, close all open network windows and then reopen the "Connect to a network" window; if that doesn't help, restart Windows and try again.

  If your hidden network entry never shows up, you'll need to either turn on the **SSID Broadcast** option in your router (the first bullet point in this list) or use the **Connect even if the network is not broadcasting** option (the second bullet point).

- Your final option is to abandon wireless altogether and use a cable. Cables are a pain, but intruders won't be able to break into your wireless-less network without cables of their own. And that's about as secure as it gets.

Back on Earth, or more specifically, the "Manually connect to a wireless network" window, click **Next** when you're done toiling with these settings. If you see a message at this point that reads, "A network called *xxx* already exists," see the next section, "Troubleshoot Network Connections." Otherwise, Vista should tell you that it has "successfully added" your network.

If you used the **Start this connection automatically** option on the last page, Vista should be connecting as you read these words, and you can just click **Close** here. Otherwise, click **Connect to** to return to the "Connect to a network" window, select your new network, and click **Connect**. Of course, if it's a hidden network as described earlier, it won't show up there, so you'll have to click **Change connection settings** and then turn on the **Connect even if the network is not broadcasting** option in order to connect.

If Vista won't connect, see "Troubleshoot Wireless Networks," next.

Troubleshoot Wireless Networks

WiFi tends to be temperamental, not to mention annoying and tear-your-hair-out frustrating. So, what do you do when you can't connect to a wireless network you've just set up?

Your instinct might be to attempt to connect again through the "Connect to a network" window. Or, if you're connecting to a network with a hidden SSID (described in the previous section), you may click the **Set up a connection or network** link to attempt to enter all the information about your network *again*. Of course, Vista will either let you complete setting up this network only to have it not work, or complain that a network by that name already exists. Arrgghhh.

Instead, you should go directly to the little-known Manage Wireless Networks window (Figure 7-10) via a tiny link by the same name on the left of the Network and Sharing Center window.

Here, you'll see all the wireless networks you've ever saved or set up manually, whether they're in range or not. Double-click a network in the list to show the Wireless Network Properties window (Figure 7-11). All the options here are described in "Sniff Out WiFi Hotspots," earlier in this chapter.

Here's how to solve some of the more common wireless connection problems:

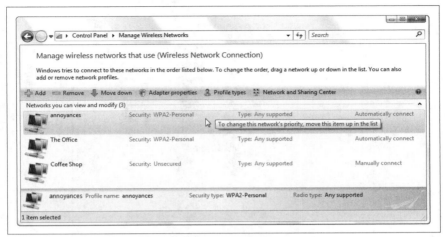

Figure 7-10. Use the Manage Wireless Networks window to fix broken wireless connections or delete wireless networks you no longer use

Windows cannot connect to xxx. This can be caused by a variety of problems, but Windows won't tell you which one. The most likely cause, at least when you're connecting to an encrypted network, is that you entered the wrong WPA passphrase or WEP key. If the network is hidden, you may have typed the wrong SSID (or if there's more than one hidden network in range, you may have selected the wrong one).

If you ask Windows to diagnose the problem, it'll probably suggest a weak signal, but that's unlikely if the network is showing up in your list with at least two signal-strength bars. More likely, it's not a real network (perhaps someone else's laptop errantly set to accept incoming connections), or it's using MAC address filtering, as described in "Lock Out Unauthorized PCs," next.

Non-broadcasting network won't show up. If you see an entry named **Unnamed Network**, select it, click **Connect**, and fill out the details of the hidden network. But if you've already set up this network and it *still* isn't showing up, then you've encountered a nasty little problem in Windows Vista. See "Sniff Out WiFi Hotspots," earlier in this chapter, for help dealing with networks that have the **SSID broadcast** feature turned off.

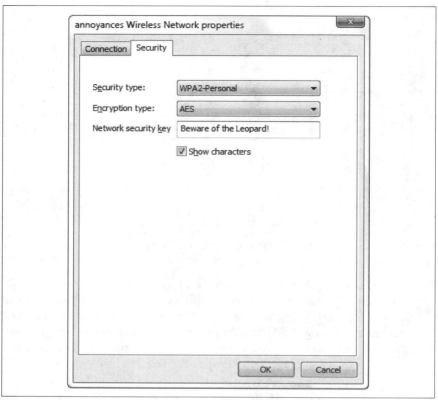

Figure 7-11. Open the Properties window for a wireless network you've saved to change the connection options or modify the encryption passphrase/key

Broadcasting (non-hidden) network won't show up. If you're mixing old and new equipment, make sure none of it is set to work only with its own kind. For instance, many 802.11g routers have a setting that either permits them to talk to older 802.11b devices, or restricts them so only g-class devices can connect. If this is the case, make sure your router and all your devices are set to work with the widest range of standards.

Also, make sure both your router and your other equipment are communicating on the same channel (channel 6, 2.437 Ghz, is the typical default).

Windows tries to connect to the neighbor's network first. Open the Manage Wireless Networks window and delete the entry for your neighbor's network if it's there. Next, double-click the entry for your own network to show the Properties window, turn on the **Connect automatically**

when this network is in range option and turn *off* the **Connect to a more preferred network if available** option (unless it's grayed out). Click **OK**, and then drag your network to the top of the list (or use the **Move up** button just above the list).

Now, if your network isn't in this list, then you haven't set it up yet. Close the Manage Wireless Networks window, and then follow the instructions in "Sniff Out WiFi Hotspots," earlier in this chapter, to connect to it, and be sure to use the **Save this network** option when you're done.

After disconnecting, Windows immediately tries to reconnect. Just click **Disconnect** again; Windows rarely does this more than two or three times. If the problem persists, open the Manage Wireless Networks window and delete the entry for this network.

A network called xxx already exists. You'll see this error if you try to set up a new wireless network with the same SSID as one already saved on your PC. If you've already used the **Manually connect to a wireless network** option to set up your network, don't go back to that if it doesn't connect. Instead, open the Manage Wireless Networks window and double-click the network to modify that entry's settings.

On the other hand, if you're setting up a new network that coincidentally has the same SSID as a *different* wireless network you've set up previously, see the next topic.

Handle two networks with the same SSID. Windows distinguishes one network from another by its SSID; in other words, its name. Say you've named your home network *wirelessnetwork*, and you've got it working. Then, you take your PC to work and learn that the SSID there is also called *wirelessnetwork*. When Windows sees *wirelessnetwork*, it tries to connect with the encryption passphrase it already knows, and not surprisingly, fails.

The best solution to this problem is to rename your home network to something more unique, but this won't help if both networks are administrated by other people. In this case, you have to make some changes. First, open the Manage Wireless Networks window, right-click the network you have saved, and click **Rename**; this changes the name of the network entry while leaving the SSID intact. Next, double-click the saved network, turn off the **Connect automatically when this network is in range** option, and click **OK**. With that out of the way, you should be able to connect to the new network by the same name *and* save its encryption settings for next time.

If you frequently connect to different wireless networks, use the Network and Sharing Center (shown in Figure 7-12 and discussed in Chapter 8) to quickly switch between *Public* and *Private* modes.

Windows loses its wireless connection when the phone rings. If you're using a cordless telephone, it's likely the older 2.4 Ghz variety. 802.11b/g/n wireless networks operate on the same frequency, so move the cordless base station away from the router. For best results, replace your old phone with a new WiFi-friendly 5.8 Ghz model.

Windows connects, but the Internet doesn't work. If you seem to be getting a solid wireless connection, but you can't load any web pages or check your email, open the Network and Sharing Center, shown in Figure 7-12. Now, this window is mostly a "home base" of sorts that provides links to the other networking tools discussed in this chapter and the sharing tools discussed in Chapter 8, but the **Access** line right in the middle of the window is a quick way to diagnose this particular problem.

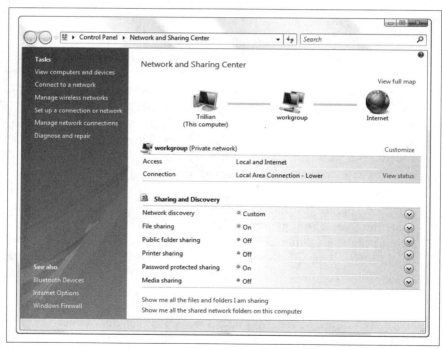

Figure 7-12. The Network and Sharing Center shows the status of your LAN connection, your Internet connection, and your sharing options, and provides links to most of Windows' networking tools

If it says **Local and Internet** on the **Access** line, then the problem is likely not with Windows, but rather with your Internet connection. Check your router status and restart your DSL/cable modem, if applicable. If you're on a public network, you might need to sign in or pay a subscription fee for full Internet services, a fact that might be clear from the first page your browser loads or perhaps suggested by the SSID. Of course, if other PCs on the network have Internet access, then try restarting your PC and temporarily disabling any firewall software that may be interfering.

But if you don't see **Local and Internet** here, but rather **Local only** or something similar, it means Windows wasn't able to get a valid IP address. This can happen if you're connected to an ad-hoc network (basically just another PC) instead of a true hotspot, but odds are that you need to mess around with your PC's TCP/IP settings as described in "Troubleshoot Network Connections," later in this chapter.

Everything works until you enable encryption. Open your router's configuration page and determine the current firmware version, which is usually shown on the home page or the Status page. Then, visit your router manufacturer's web site and see whether there's a newer firmware available; if so, download it and use your router's firmware upgrade feature to ensure you have the latest bugs and bug fixes. Likewise, make sure you're using the latest drivers for your wireless equipment on your PC.

If that doesn't help, it's likely that either your router or your wireless adapter in your PC is not fully 802.11i-compliant. This means you'll have to downgrade your encryption to one of the weaker standards explained in the "Choosing the Right Encryption Scheme: WEP, WPA, or WPA2?" sidebar, earlier in this chapter, and try again.

Beyond SSIDs and encryption, a wireless connection is not much different than a wired connection. See "Troubleshoot Network Connections," later in this chapter, for help fine-tuning TCP/IP addresses, a particularly useful tool when you have a mix of different computers and devices on your network.

Lock Out Unauthorized PCs

You've got encryption. You've got a hidden SSID. You've set up a password on all your shared folders (see Chapter 8). You're probably thinking that your biggest problem is that nobody seems capable of remembering any of their passwords, but it may be quite the opposite.

All of these security schemes rely on *preshared* information: anyone with your WPA2 passphrase, your SSID, and your Windows password can connect to your wireless network and possibly even read the files on your hard disk.

The system is built upon secrecy, and all it takes is a breach of that secrecy for the whole system to break down.

For example, say you've got a small business with 20 employees, and someone gets fired. Or, perhaps you live in an apartment building with shared wireless, and someone moves out. Either way, the person who has left the system may still have the wireless passphrase (and, in the case of the small business, a common Windows password), and may still be able to get into your network.

What do you do? For one, you can change the password and then have everyone remaining on the network update their PCs and try to remember the new password. But the ex-employee might sneak a peek at the new password when he comes back to clean out his desk. Or, that ex-tenant might have a friend who still lives in the building and is willing to share the new password. In short, a network that relies *only* on passwords to keep out intruders is still vulnerable.

The solution for home networks and small businesses—any outfit without the means to install an authentication server typically available only to large companies—is to use *MAC address filtering*.

A MAC (Media Access Control) address is a (more or less) unique ID for each network adapter on your PC, or—from the point of view of your router—a unique ID for each connection on your network. You can configure your router to allow only specific MAC addresses to connect to your network, and in so doing, turn away anyone else whether he or she knows your WPA2 passphrase or not.

A typical Wireless MAC Filter page is shown in Figure 7-13. Here, turn on the **Permit only PCs listed to access the wireless network** option, and then type or paste the MAC address of your PCs' wireless adapters into the boxes. Click **Save Settings** when you're done.

To get your PC's MAC address—which has nothing to do with Macintosh computers, by the way—open the Network and Sharing Center in Control Panel, and then click the **View status** link next to the **Connection** area in the middle of the window. Finally, click the **Details** button to show the Network Connection Details window shown in Figure 7-14; the six-segment **Physical Address** is the MAC address for this adapter.

Figure 7-13. Use your router's wireless MAC address filtering to keep out unauthorized PCs

To show the MAC addresses for all the network adapters on your PC at once, open a Command Prompt window and type ipconfig /all. Or, for a more abbreviated view, type getmac at the prompt. (Note that only the MAC address of your wireless adapter matters here.)

You'll need to enter the MAC address of each and every PC that connects to your network wirelessly; leave one off, and it won't be able to connect (and the person using the PC won't know why). Don't worry about any PCs connected to your network with cables; they won't be affected.

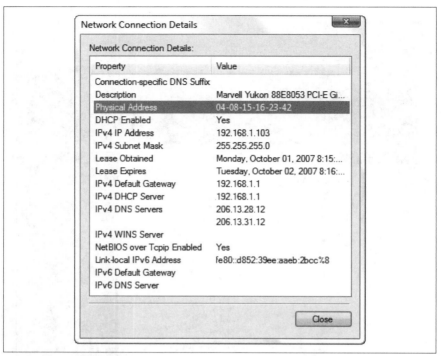

Figure 7-14. The MAC address of your wireless adapter is the "Physical Address" listed in the Network Connection Details window

Now, MAC address filtering is a useful solution, but it's not foolproof. For one, anyone with access to your router setup page can make changes to the approved list, so you'll want to change your router's administrative password if you haven't done so already; you're asking for trouble if you leave the default password in place (e.g., "admin" for Linksys routers). Next, turn off your router's **Remote Administration** option to ensure that only those connected to your private network have access. Finally, consider the potential weakness in MAC address filtering explained in the upcoming "Why MAC Address Filtering Is Not Perfect" sidebar.

With MAC address filtering in place, all you have to do is create a new entry for each new PC you want to allow to connect wirelessly. And of course, you'll need to remove entries for PCs you want to de-authorize. For this reason, it's useful to keep a record of the MAC addresses of all the PCs on your network in say, a text file, somewhere safe.

If you're worried about others on your local network breaking into your PC and reading your files, see "Turn Off Administrative Shares," in Chapter 8, for another backdoor you can close.

Why MAC Address Filtering Is Not Perfect

MAC addresses—which are different for each device on your network—may seem to be the perfect way to keep out intruders, but there's a catch. Since you can change the MAC address on most modern hardware, someone could theoretically connect to a filtered network by spoofing the MAC address.

This makes the MAC address somewhat like a password, right?

Not exactly. First, no two devices on a network can have the same MAC address, so if your PC is connected, and someone else tries to break in by spoofing your MAC address, the attempt will fail. Second, each PC has its own MAC address and its own entry on your router's MAC address filter page; this means that an administrator can remove a compromised entry without affecting any other PCs. (This is in contrast to the single WPA-Personal passphrase or WEP encryption key that everyone on the network shares.)

The real problem is that, like the hidden SSID dilemma explained earlier in this chapter in "Sniff Out WiFi Hotspots," a savvy intruder can use monitoring software to grab MAC addresses out of the air and use them to connect.

Think it's difficult to change the MAC address? Think again. You can use Mac Makeup, available for free from *http://www.gorlani.com/publicprj/ macmakeup/macmakeup.asp*, or MadMACs, free from *http://www.irongeek. com/i.php?page=security/madmacs-mac-spoofer*, to change your wireless adapter's MAC address in a few moments.

You can also change your MAC address—without any special software—by editing the Registry. Open Registry Editor (Chapter 3) and expand the branches to HKEY_LOCAL_MACHINE\SYSTEM\CurrentControlSet\Control\Class\ {4D36E972-E325-11CE-BFC1-08002BE10318}. Press **Ctrl-F**, type DriverDesc in the box, and click **Find Next**. Press **F3** to cycle through the subkeys here (e.g., 0001, 0002, etc.) until you hit the one where the DriverDesc value matches the name of your wireless adapter. Once you stumble upon the correct key, select **Edit → New → String Value**, and name the value NetworkAddress. Double-click the new value, type the MAC address you want to use in the **Value data** field (without any hyphens, like this: 040815162342), and click **OK**. To put the new address into effect, use the Network Connections window to disable and then re-enable your network adapter (or restart Windows).

Of course, there are plenty of legitimate reasons to change one's MAC address, such as troubleshooting or conflict management. Even your router probably has a way to change its MAC address—via the **MAC Address Clone** feature—to match your PC's address so remote servers that have been configured to permit access from your PC won't reject your router.

All this means that there's no such thing as an impentetrable wireless network. If you really care about security, abandon wireless and stick with cables.

Connect to a Public Wireless Network

The point of wireless networking is not necessarily to do away with a few feet of cables, but to make a network do things it could never do before. For instance, if you have a portable computer equipped with wireless, you should be able to walk into any airport, coffee shop, hotel, or college dormitory and connect to the Internet in a matter of seconds. In more populated areas, it's not uncommon to walk down the street and have your pick of WiFi networks. (See the sidebar "The Ethics of WiFi," next, for an extra consideration.)

The Ethics of WiFi

Once you get the technical details out of the way, the one remaining hurdle when considering using someone else's Internet connection is a question of ethics. There are countless personal wireless networks around the globe and most of them, you'll find, are unsecured. This means that you can literally walk down the street in a populated area and probably find a working wireless Internet connection before you reach the end of the block. Some will have been left open intentionally, but most will be unsecured merely because their owners don't have the benefit of the "Set Up a Wireless Router" procedure found earlier in this chapter.

Now, just because you *can* connect to these networks, does it mean you *should*? Are you taking advantage of someone else's ignorance by breaking into his private network, or are you simply making use of a public resource that you'd be equally eager to share?

I'm not about to try to solve this dilemma in these short pages; I only wish to raise the question, and to suggest that if you do ever decide to utilize someone else's wireless network, that you not do any harm. Think about your impact, both on the bandwidth of the foreign network and the privacy of those who operate it. And then tread lightly.

As described in "Sniff Out WiFi Hotspots," earlier in this chapter, you can connect to any unsecured wireless network that Vista's built-in WiFi sniffer is able to detect. (The exceptions, of course, are those networks requiring a paid subscription or account access, but that's a different story.) This applies to networks you'll encounter while you're on the road, as well as those that are in range of your home or office.

The problem is that by connecting to these networks, you're exposing your computer to the full array of viruses, hackers, and other dangers present on any network.* The solution is to take steps to protect your computer (or workgroup), and the steps necessary depend on the scenario.

Scenario 1: Single-serving Internet

Say you've just sat yourself down at a sidewalk cafe and pulled out your laptop. (This scenario also applies to hotel rooms, airports, and coffee shops.) You boot up Windows, open the "Connect to a network" window as described previously in "Sniff Out WiFi Hotspots," find a local network, and connect for 20-or-so minutes to check your email. When you're done, you'll likely never use this network again.

Now, if you typically use your laptop when connected to your own private network, protected by your wireless router's firewall, you'll want to take some extra steps to secure your PC *before* you connect elsewhere. Since you won't have your router with you on the road, and thus won't have any dedicated firewall hardware, you'll want to employ the built-in Windows Firewall software (or a third-party firewall solution), as described later in this chapter. This will provide minimal protection, but certainly nothing you'd want to live with for the long haul.

Scenario 2: The long haul

Say you just moved into an apartment complex (or have a small business in an office building) that provides free wireless Internet. Naturally, you would never want to connect your computer or workgroup to this wireless free-for-all without some sort of reliable, long-term firewall protecting you from the rest of the riff-raff. Now, since this is not your own, private Internet connection, you can't just plug in a router to facilitate your firewall. But you can add another device, a *wireless bridge*, in order to build an "island" of sorts, in a sea otherwise filled with peril.

A bridge connects two networks; in this case, you're bridging the public network to your private, secure network, as shown in Figure 7-15. Between them is the wireless bridge and your router (which protects your private network with its built-in firewall). The two dotted areas represent the scope of the two different WiFi networks in effect: your own private, encrypted wireless network is shown on the left, and the public network is illustrated on the right. (Your bridge and router actually form a tiny, third network, complete with its own IP space separate from those in either of the two wireless networks.)

---

* This may be reason enough to keep strangers out of your own WiFi network; see "Set Up a Wireless Router," earlier in this chapter, for help securing your network.

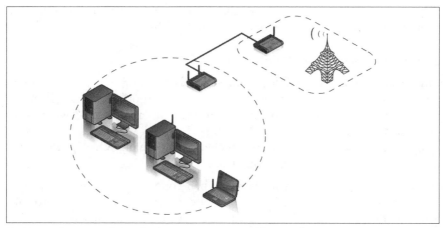

Figure 7-15. Use a wireless bridge in conjunction with a wireless router to protect your workgroup when connecting to a public Internet connection

Here's how you set it up:

1. Use the "Connect to a network" window as described earlier in "Sniff Out WiFi Hotspots" to find the name (SSID) of the public wireless network to which you'd like to connect. Connect to the network temporarily to confirm that it actually works.

2. Obtain a wireless bridge, and follow the procedure laid out in its documentation to set it up with the public wireless network you want to use, a process that typically involves plugging the bridge directly into your PC with an Ethernet cable.

3. While the bridge is still connected to your PC, obtain the *local* IP address of your bridge; it'll be something like 192.168.1.1 or 192.168.0.1. (You won't need the bridge's *remote* IP address assigned to it by the public network.)

4. When you're done setting up the bridge, unplug it from your PC and connect it directly to the WAN port of your wireless router. (This is the port into which you'd normally plug a DSL or cable modem.)

5. Connect your PC to your router and use a web browser to open up your router's setup page, as described in "Set Up a Wireless Router," earlier in this chapter.

6. Configure your wireless router so that it has a **Connection Type** of **Static IP**. (Refer to your router's documentation for the specific details on this and the next few settings.)

7. In the router setup, set the **Gateway** address to the IP address of your bridge that you obtained in step 3.

8. Then, still on the router setup page, set the static IP address of the Internet connection (as the router sees it) to a fictitious IP address in the same *subnet* as your bridge. This means that the *first three numbers* of both IP addresses should be the same, but the fourth should be different. That is, if your bridge's address is 192.168.1.1, then you could set the IP address of your Internet connection to something like 192.168.1.2 or 192.168.1.73.

 Don't confuse these addresses with the IP addresses used on your private network. The local IP address of your bridge and the IP address for your Internet connection that you enter here form the tiny, third network mentioned at the beginning of this section. Alternatively, you could set your router to obtain its IP address automatically (back in step 6), a strategy that may or may not work depending on how cooperative your bridge is.

9. Finally, set the DNS server addresses in your router setup to the IP addresses of your Internet Service Provider's DNS servers.

   If you don't know which ISP is responsible for the public network you're trying to connect to, try connecting directly with your PC once more. Open a web browser, type *http://www.annoyances.org/ip* in the address bar, and press **Enter**; this will show the true IP address of your Internet connection. Then, open a Command Prompt window and type nslookup *ip_address*, where *ip_address* is the set of four numbers reported by Annoyances.org. This gives you the name of your ISP, plus some extra stuff. So, you might see something like dsl456.eastcoast.superisp.net, which means your ISP is superisp.net. Then, it's only a matter of visiting the ISP's web site (e.g., *http://www.superisp.net/*) and determining its DNS server addresses from its online documentation.

10. Complete the setup of your router as explained in "Set Up a Wireless Router," earlier in this chapter, and make sure to enable wireless encryption and any other security settings at your disposal.

This should do it. The bridge will funnel the public Internet connection into your router, and your router will funnel it to the computers in your workgroup. The router acts like a firewall, provided that you connect all your computers directly to your own, personal WiFi network, and not the public, unsecured one.

Among other things, your bridge/router combination will serve as a repeater (a.k.a. range extender), and should boost the signal strength and might even improve performance over connecting your PCs directly to the public network.

Networking and Internet

Add Wireless Support to Any Device

As soon as you have your wireless network up and running, you'll probably be inclined to do away with as many cables as you can. This feeling is normal; there's no need to seek psychiatric help or psychic guidance.

Here's how to add support for wireless networking to nearly any computer or device:

Desktop computer

Add a wireless PCI card just as you would an Ethernet NIC (network interface card). When shopping for a WiFi NIC, look for a card with an adjustable, external antenna (versus merely a nub); and make sure to get one certified for Windows Vista. Alternatively, you can use a USB-based WiFi adapter and avoid having to take apart your PC; the downside is that these tend to be less reliable than internal adapters.

Laptop computer

WiFi PC Cards have been available for some time, but if you have a modern laptop, you most likely have a better choice. For about the same price as the aforementioned PC Card, an *internal* Mini-PCI adapter will typically offer better range (thanks to the internal antenna likely already present in your laptop) without the clumsy protrusion of a PC Card. (See the "Handheld PDA" entry, later in this section, for information on using Bluetooth with your laptop.) Another solution is explained in the upcoming "Quick and Dirty WiFi Piggyback" sidebar.

Printer

Although you can connect a printer to a WiFi-equipped PC and share it with the rest of your network (as explained in Chapter 8), a better choice is to connect your printer directly to your wireless network. Among other things, this means you don't have to connect any cables to your laptop to print a document,[*] no specific PC must be turned on to access the printer, and you have the option of placing the printer in a more convenient location. To do this, you'll need a wireless print server that plugs into the back of your printer. Then, simply install the software that comes with your print server to create a virtual printer port on your PC, to which your printer's drivers connect and send documents. (See Chapter 8 for a way to print to a network printer without installing any special software.)

---

[*] A number of years ago, printer manufacturers started including infrared ports on some printers, allowing laptops with infrared ports to print to them wirelessly. This was never much of a success, which probably explains why it's now nearly impossible to find a laptop (or printer, for that matter) with an infrared port.

Quick and Dirty WiFi Piggyback

Say you and a partner are staying in a hotel, and each of you has a laptop. The hotel, of course, charges for wireless, and you don't feel like ponying up the extra dough for two connections, nor do you feel like taking turns.

Or, perhaps a friend visits your home or office and wants to check her email with her laptop. What if you don't want to share your wireless encryption passphrase with any passerby who asks for it? Or, what if the laptop doesn't have wireless?

Assume you have a sample wireless network like the one illustrated in Figures 7-3 or 7-4. You can, of course, plug any PC (provided that it has an Ethernet port) directly into your wireless router with an ordinary category-5 patch cable, and give it instant access to the Internet. But what if the router isn't in a convenient location?

Fortunately, any Windows PC can act as a gateway, funneling Internet access to any computer to which it is physically connected, using Windows' built-in Internet Connection Sharing feature (discussed later in this chapter). All you need to do is connect this new laptop directly to your own desktop or laptop PC, and this typically requires only a single cable.

If the visitor's laptop has an Ethernet port, and your PC has an unused Ethernet port (likely if you're on a *wireless* network), just connect the two computers with a category-5 *crossover* cable, and you've got yourself something like the wired network shown later in Figure 7-19. Just activate Internet Connection Sharing on your PC, and the guest PC will have Internet access.

You wouldn't want to use this as a long-term solution, but it works well enough for a quick email download, takes only a few minutes and a $4 cable, and doesn't compromise your network's security (much).

 Wireless print servers tend to be a bit flaky. Since most printers don't need to be portable, consider a wired print server for more reliable printing. Just plug the device into your router with an Ethernet cable, and then plug your printer into the device.

DVR, video game console, or other media device
   If your device has an Ethernet port, just add a wireless bridge (sometimes called a wireless game adapter) and cut the cords for good. Or, if your device has a USB port for this purpose, you may be able to plug in an off-the-shelf USB WiFi adapter if your device supports it.

Handheld PDA

As introduced in the beginning of this chapter, there are two prevailing wireless technologies: WiFi and Bluetooth. While some handhelds come with built-in WiFi, a larger percentage support Bluetooth (and only a select few play for both teams). Although only WiFi-equipped handhelds can connect to the WiFi networks discussed throughout this chapter, you'll need Bluetooth support if you want to connect to the Internet with your Bluetooth-equipped cell phone. (The same goes for laptops; get an inexpensive Bluetooth USB dongle to connect your Windows PC to your cell phone wirelessly and surf the Web from the park or even the train!)

Now, some higher-end PDAs come with WiFi or Bluetooth support built in, while others have special expansion cards that provide connectivity. You can get a WiFi SecureDigital (SD) card or a Bluetooth SD card that will fit in many PalmOS and PocketPC handhelds, but if you have only one SD slot, you'll have to remove your memory card. If you need the wireless support, you may prefer to replace your PDA with one that has WiFi or Bluetooth (or both) built in, and do away with the awkward protrusion of the expansion card.

Digital camera

Some high-end digital cameras now have WiFi options, allowing you to send your photos to the hard disk in a nearby computer wirelessly, either in batches or immediately after you take them. Unfortunately, this only works in the studio (as opposed to outdoors), where you'd be in range of your wireless router. At the time of this writing, there are no wireless cards you can conveniently insert in place of your digital film, but it shouldn't be long.

Video camera (webcam)

Get a WiFi-enabled Internet video camera, and place it anywhere within range of your network. Then, use your PC to view a live video feed wirelessly. Or, use it in its server mode, and let anyone in the world see how much coffee is left in your coffee pot. (See Chapter 9 for a simple WSH script that works with webcams.)

Home theater

Several companies sell WiFi music and video players that connect directly to your stereo or TV. The better ones have HDMI plugs to support HD video, allowing you to play downloaded movies on your home theater in all their glory.

There's virtually no limit to the number of devices you can make wireless, provided that they support some form of networking already. If all else fails, a wireless bridge, as illustrated in "Connect to a Public Wireless Network," earlier in this chapter, should allow you to connect just about anything to your wireless network.

Get Bluetooth to Work

Bluetooth holds a lot of promise. For one, you can do things like connect your laptop wirelessly to a Bluetooth GPS receiver for portable navigation, or to your cell phone for cordless address-book synchronization. You can use your Bluetooth cell phone as a portable wireless modem and surf the Web on the go, or transfer photos you took with your cell phone to your PC without touching a cable. There are even tiny remote-controlled toy cars—like the Sony Ericcson CAR-100—that you can drive with your Bluetooth phone (truly illustrating the noble role of technology in our lives).

The problem is that Bluetooth standards are poorly implemented in most devices; don't be surprised if you can't exchange a simple address book entry between your Bluetooth-capable PDA and your cell phone, even if they're the same brand. Even Vista's built-in Bluetooth stack only works with certain types of Bluetooth transceivers, and then only under a full moon.

Usually the biggest stumbling block is getting Vista to recognize and use the Bluetooth transceiver in your PC. You can tell whether Vista is aware of—and has loaded a proper driver for—your Bluetooth hardware if there's a **Bluetooth Devices** icon in your Control Panel (**Classic View**, please).

Most PC-based Bluetooth adapters are either tiny cards wired inside some laptops or lipstick-sized USB dongles that plug in to the back of your PC. But just because the manufacturer of that adapter claims compatibility with Vista doesn't mean you'll see the Bluetooth icon in Control Panel. The problem is that only some Bluetooth adapters use Microsoft's *Bluetooth stack*, the set of drivers and utilities that allows your programs to talk to your Bluetooth devices. Many adapters instead use either the Toshiba Bluetooth stack or the Broadcom Bluetooth stack; good luck trying to find out which stack your adapter uses simply by reading the packaging.

To determine the missing pieces on your PC, open Device Manager in Control Panel. If all is well, you'll see a **Bluetooth Radios** category, under which you'll find an entry for your adapter and another for **Microsoft Bluetooth Enumerator**. If you don't see the Microsoft driver, or if your adapter appears in the **Unknown Devices** category, you have three choices: hunt down a native Vista driver, be content with your device's proprietary software (if it works), or discard your adapter and spend $20 on a newer one.

Networking and Internet

Don't bother trying to brute-force install a driver right here in Device Manager. If you manage to install the proper software, Device Manager will identify your Bluetooth adapter and install the driver automatically. Otherwise, the best you'll get with a manually loaded driver is an icon in the **Bluetooth Radios** category covered by a yellow exclamation mark and the error "Device cannot start." Before you try to install one of the Bluetooth stacks listed here, unload any drivers already on your PC by right-clicking the entry for your Bluetooth radio in Device Manager and clicking **Delete**.

Inspect the software that comes with your Bluetooth adapter (even if it won't install on Vista), or check the manufacturer's web site to find out what kind of chip your adapter uses. If you have a Toshiba Bluetooth adapter, you can get the Toshiba stack at:

http://aps.toshiba-tro.de/bluetooth/pages/toshiba/general-information-pc-stack.html

Or, if you have an adapter that uses a Broadcom or Widcomm Bluetooth chip, you can get the Broadcom stack at:

http://www.broadcom.com/products/bluetooth_update.php

or the Broadcom Vista update at:

http://update.broadcom.com/downloads/btwinitialupdate.exe

Once you get that **Bluetooth Devices** icon to appear in Control Panel, go ahead and click it (or run *bthprops.cpl*) to open the Bluetooth Devices window shown in Figure 7-16. There's a lot of stuff here, but for the most part, only two of the tabs are useful when connecting to other devices: **Devices** and **COM Ports**.

The **Devices** tab lists your phone, PDA, GPS, and any other Bluetooth-devices *you've already paired* with your PC. (Use the **Hardware** tab to list your PC's internal Bluetooth radio.) It won't show all the Bluetooth devices in range, like the "Connect to a network" window discussed elsewhere in this chapter. Rather, click **Add** and then turn on the **My device is set up and ready to be found** option. Make your device "discoverable," and then click **Next** here to find it.

Most PC software communicates over Bluetooth airwaves via virtual COM ports that Windows opens on your PC (just like the ones you plugged your mouse into in the 1980s, except invisible). Click the **COM Ports** tab to see which ports have been claimed by the devices listed in the **Devices** tab; any software you use to talk to your Bluetooth device will either autodetect this

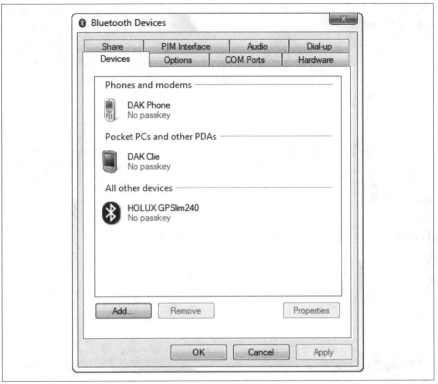

Figure 7-16. The elusive Bluetooth Devices window makes an appearance in Control Panel only if you've installed native Vista drivers for your Bluetooth radio

information or ask you to specify the COM port to use. If you don't see at least one COM port associated with your device, return to the **Devices** tab, highlight the device in question, click **Properties**, and choose the **Services** tab to see what the device is capable of.

There's no **Edit** or **Properties** button on the COM ports page, so you'll need to open Device Manager if you want to change any settings. In Device Manager, expand the **Ports (COM & LPT)** category, and then double-click a **Standard Serial over Bluetooth link** entry and select the **Port Settings** tab to configure it.

You'll notice there's no **Connect** or **Disconnect** button anywhere in the Bluetooth Devices window. While the absence of these features can be inconvenient, they're not strictly needed because Windows connects automatically whenever an application tries to use one of those virtual COM ports.

To disconnect, just turn off the other device, or (if your PC has one), turn off your PC's wireless radio switch.

If you have trouble getting your software to talk to your Bluetooth device, make sure it's using the same COM port identified in the Bluetooth Devices window. If it doesn't ask for a COM port, check the software publisher's web site for an update or see whether an additional driver is needed.

Finally, don't be afraid to try a different software product, which can be helpful in determining whether the problem lies with your device, with Microsoft's Bluetooth stack, or with the software you're trying to use. One nifty little program is called MeHere (free from *http://mehere.glenmurphy.com/*), which uses your Bluetooth GPS to navigate a live Google Maps window, and guess what...it works with Vista!

Troubleshoot Network Connections

Whether you're connected wirelessly or with a cable, Vista needs certain details to be squared away, or nothing will work right. With that in mind, you should get to know the Network Connections window shown in Figure 7-17.

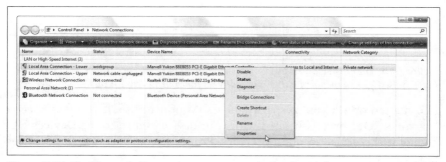

Figure 7-17. Use Network Connections to manage the hardware that connects your PC to your network

In versions of Windows before Vista, the Network Connections window was the central interface for all network settings. With the introduction of the Network and Sharing Center—from which you can open Network Connections by clicking the **Manage network connections** link—this is no longer entirely true. But it's still the best way to fine-tune your TCP/IP settings and fix many networking problems. If you haven't done so already, open the **Views** drop-down and select **Details** to show the pertinent information.

Here you'll see the status of all your network adapters—both wireless and wired—at a glance. The **Status** column tells you which connections, if any, are connected, albeit with some inconsistencies. Wireless and Bluetooth adapters that are not in use say **Not connected**, but Ethernet (wired) adapters say **Network cable unplugged**. In either case, any adapter currently in use (connected) is marked only with Vista's current *network name*.

 Don't let the *network name* throw you. It's not the SSID of the wireless network you're using (see "Sniff Out WiFi Hotspots," earlier in this chapter), nor is it the workgroup name used for sharing folders and printers (explained in Chapter 8), nor does it have anything to do with your Internet connection. Rather, it's a name you can enter by clicking the **Customize** link in the Network and Sharing center, used to make it easy to switch between public and private networks. See Chapter 8 for details.

Also important is the **Connectivity** column, which shows exactly what each adapter is providing (e.g., **Access to Local and Internet**).

But the main reason to use this window is to change TCP/IP settings. Right-click the connection you're using and select **Properties**. Then, select **Internet Protocol Version 4 (TCP/IPv4)** from the list and click the **Properties** button to open the Properties window shown in Figure 7-18.

In most cases, selecting the **Obtain an IP address automatically** and **Obtain DNS server address automatically** options will suffice. This works because your router, if you have one, automatically assigns a unique IP address to each new PC it sees using Dynamic Host Configuration Protocol (DHCP).

But sometimes DHCP doesn't cooperate as well as it should; either a PC is given the wrong IP address or no address at all. Or, for a variety of reasons (such as enabling remote control, discussed later in this chapter), you need a PC to always have the same IP address. To do this, you need to pull your PC out of the DHCP arena and assign it a *static* (nonchanging) IP address:

1. If you have a router, open its configuration page in a web browser (usually *http://192.168.1.1* or *http://192.168.0.1*), and navigate to the DHCP client table. This shows all the PCs connected to your network (both wired and wireless) controlled by DHCP, along with their dynamically assigned IP addresses. (In most cases, PCs with static addresses will be absent from this list.)

2. Open the Internet Protocol Version 4 (TCP/IPv4) Properties window as described at the beginning of this section, and select **Use the following IP address**.

Figure 7-18. You may have to manually configure TCP/IP properties to get your PC noticed on your network

3. For the IP address, type the address you want to use (e.g., `192.168.1.107`).

 Often, networks don't work because Windows and your router are unable to negotiate the correct addresses automatically. The first three numbers in each PC's IP address (e.g., 192.168.1.*xxx*) must exactly match the first three numbers in the IP address of your router—usually 192.168.1.1 or 192.168.0.1—which you can get from your router's documentation. The last number (e.g., 100, 101, 102) must be different for each PC.

4. For the **Subnet mask**, type `255.255.255.0`.

5. For the **Default gateway**, type the IP address of your router (usually `192.168.1.1` or `192.168.0.1`).

6. For the **Preferred DNS server** and the **Alternate DNS server**, type the IP addresses of your ISP's primary and secondary DNS servers, respectively.

   If you don't know the DNS addresses, contact your ISP. If you're on a public network or you're using a friend's ISP, open a web browser, type *http://www.annoyances.org/ip* in the address bar, and press **Enter** to show the true IP address of your Internet connection. Then, open a Command Prompt window and type nslookup *ip_address*, where *ip_address* is the set of four numbers reported by Annoyances.org. This should give you the name of your ISP, plus some extra stuff. So, you might see something like dsl456.eastcoast.superisp.net, which means your ISP is superisp.net. Then, it's only a matter of visiting the ISP's web site (e.g., *http://www.superisp.net/*) and determining its DNS server addresses from its online documentation.

7. Click **OK** in both boxes when you're done.

These static IP numbers, provided you've typed them correctly, will help ensure that all the PCs on your network can communicate reliably with one another. You don't have to set static IP addresses on all the PCs on your network, but it may help settle a cranky network, particularly one with computers running several different operating systems (Linux, Mac OS X, older versions of Windows, etc.).

Return to the Network Connections window when you're done, and look at the **Status** column entry for the connection you've just modified. If it says **Acquiring network address**, it means Windows is in the process of establishing a connection; if you see this for more than, say, 10 seconds, you've probably done something wrong. If the status is **Limited or no connectivity**, it means that a connection has been established, but your IP address is incorrect.

If, at this point, your network appears to be functioning, you can proceed to set up the various services you need, such as file and printer sharing (described in Chapter 8) and Internet Connection Sharing (described later in this chapter). Otherwise, look through the following checklist for possible solutions:

Restart
> Heed the advice at the beginning of Chapter 6: restarting your computer will fix 99% of all problems. This is never truer than when diagnosing a networking problem.

Bad cables?
> Make sure the green light is on next to each cable you've plugged in. If not, try replacing one or more of the cables, especially if they're old or their connectors are worn.

Networking and Internet

Blinkenlights

When you transfer data across a network connection, each network card and the hub (if you have one) should have an "activity" light that flashes. Some devices have separate lights for receiving and transmitting data, while others have only a single light for all incoming and outgoing communication. Activity lights tend to flash intermittently and irregularly; if they flash regularly, it could be a sign of a problem with one of the devices.

No dupes

Make sure no two computers on your network are attempting to use the same IP address or computer name (set in **Control Panel** → **System** → **Advanced system settings** → **Computer Name** tab, and discussed in Chapter 8).

Drivers

Make sure you have the latest drivers for each network adapter on your PC, and remove any proprietary network software that may have come with your network hardware.

Firmware

Nearly all network hardware (adapters, routers, print servers, etc.) has user-upgradable firmware. Check the manufacturer's web site for the latest firmware if you're experiencing any network problems.

Device Manager

Some problems are caused by improper hardware settings, usually attributed to the network adapter itself. Open Device Manager and double-click the icon for your troublesome adapter (or right-click it in the Network Connections window, select **Properties**, and then click **Configure**). Choose the **Advanced** tab, and thumb through the **Property** list on the left, looking for possible problems. If you don't understand a particular setting, look it up in the documentation or on Google.

Can't "see" another PC

This is a nasty problem, one with several different causes and often no clear-cut solution. First, open the Services window (*services.msc*), find the **Computer Browser** service, and make sure its **Status** is **Started** and its **Startup Type** is **Automatic** (if it isn't, double-click the service to change its settings). Next, try the Ping utility, described in "Test an IP Address," to determine whether your PC can actually see another PC on your network. If the Ping test fails, try pinging your router (if you have one) from each computer to see which PC's connection isn't working. If Ping is successful, proceed to Chapter 8 for help with file sharing.

Add new network connections

You may have noticed that there's no obvious way to add a new connection to the Network Connections window. By default, the Network Connections window only shows your installed hardware, which means you can add a new network adapter, and it will show up in this list.

But the Network Connections window also supports *virtual* connections, such as dial-up (analog modem) connections and broadband (PPPoE) connections. To add one of these, open the Network and Sharing Center and click the **Set up a connection or network** link, as described in "Internet Me," later in this chapter. Of course, you'll have to return to the Network Connections window if you want to modify or delete one of these virtual connections.

If you ever use more than one network connection at once, see the next sidebar, "Prioritize Network Connections," for a way to get the desired results.

Prioritize Network Connections

There's a little-known setting you can play with that may solve problems if you have more than one network adapter on your PC. Say you connect wirelessly at home most of the time, but when you transfer a lot of files from one PC to another, you prefer to use a cable for greater speed.

Except in specific cases, Windows Vista will only use one network adapter at a time. So, if you're connected wirelessly *and* with a cable, you'll want to choose which connection Windows prioritizes.

In the Network Connections window, press the **Alt** key to temporarily show the menu, and then from the **Advanced** menu, select **Advanced Settings**. Pick the fastest connection, and use the up arrow to move it to the top of the list.

While you're here, choose the **Provider Order** tab, and make sure the **Microsoft Windows Network** entry appears at the top of the list.

Click **OK** when you're done; the change will take effect immediately.

Test an IP Address

One surefire way to test a connection is to use the Ping utility, which essentially sends small packets of information to another computer on your network, and reports on its success (if any).

Open the Start menu, type `cmd`, and press **Enter** to open the Command Prompt. At the prompt, type `ping` *address*, where *address* is the IP address of another computer or perhaps your router. For example, from the computer at 192.168.1.102, you'd type:

```
ping 192.168.1.101
```

If the connection is working, the Ping transaction will be successful, and you'll get a result that looks like this:

```
Pinging 192.168.0.1 with 32 bytes of data:
Reply from 192.168.0.1: bytes=32 time=24ms TTL=53
Reply from 192.168.0.1: bytes=32 time=16ms TTL=53
```

To be fair, this test only works if *both* connections are working, and if the network is functional. If you get this result:

```
Pinging 192.168.0.1 with 32 bytes of data:
Request timed out.
Request timed out.
```

it means that Ping never got a response from the other computer. A failed Ping can mean that the adapter on your local PC is misconfigured, or that the target machine isn't up and running.

You can also test your Internet connection by pinging a host outside your local subnet, like this one:

```
ping 64.233.187.99
```

Now, if you get a reply from 64.233.187.99, but *no reply* when you ping a host name, like this:

```
ping google.com
```

it means that your DNS nameservers—the machines at your ISP that translate host names to their IP addresses and back—are misconfigured or possibly down. In this case, follow the steps in "Troubleshoot Network Connections," earlier in this chapter, to enter the correct DNS addresses.

Internet Me

Connecting to the Web is much easier than it used to be, so much so that Windows basically takes this for granted. In fact, I'm going to make this really easy for you: if you have broadband (typically via DSL or cable), and you're not using a router, get one right now and hook it up. Once you set up your router (see "Set Up a Wireless Router," earlier in this chapter), connect your Vista PC to the router either wirelessly or with a cable, and you're online. That's it.

Now, if have broadband but you can't use a router for some reason, or if you're (gasp) still using dial-up, then you need to configure Vista to connect to the Internet for you. Of course, the procedure depends on the type of connection you're setting up:

Broadband with a static IP address

Follow the steps in "Troubleshoot Network Connections," earlier in this chapter, to set up your Ethernet adapter to use your Internet connection's static IP address.

Broadband with a username and password (PPPoE)

Point-to-Point Protocol over Ethernet (PPPoE) is used to establish temporary, dynamic-IP connections over high-speed Internet connections. If your Internet connection has a dynamic IP address, it means your ISP assigns you a different IP address every time you connect to the Internet. The PPPoE protocol facilitates this connection by sending your username and password to your provider.

 Never use the proprietary software provided by your ISP to connect via PPPoE; use the procedure explained here instead for best results.

To set up a PPPoE connection, follow these steps:

1. Open the Network and Sharing Center, and click the **Set up a connection or network link** on the left.

2. Select **Connect to the Internet**, and click **Next**.

3. Click **Broadband (PPPoE)**.

4. Type the **User name** and **Password** provided by your ISP, and turn on the **Remember this password** option.

5. Type a name for the connection (anything you like); click **Connect**.

Later on, if you need to connect manually or make changes to the connection, use the Network Connections window, as described in "Troubleshoot Network Connections," earlier in this chapter.

Dial-up (analog modem) connection

Sure it's obsolete, but it's cheap, and if there's no broadband around, it may be your only choice. Here's how to set it up:

1. Open the Network and Sharing Center and click the **Set up a connection or network link** on the left.

2. Select **Set up a dial-up connection**, and click **Next**.

3. Type the **Dial-up phone number** and **User name** and **Password** provided by your ISP, and turn on the **Remember this password** option.

4. Type a name for the connection (anything you like), and click **Create**.

5. To connect, click the **Manage network connections** link, and then double-click your new connection.

See the "Live with PPPoE" sidebar, next, for tips that also apply to dial-up connections.

Live with PPPoE

PPPoE can be a pain on a day-to-day basis, mostly because Windows is responsible for the dialing. Here are some ways to make it a little more seamless:

Connect on demand. To have Windows connect automatically whenever the connection is needed, open the Network Connections window, right-click the connection icon and select **Set as Default Connection**. Then, go to **Control Panel → Internet Options**, choose the **Connections** tab, and select the **Always dial my default connection** option.

Connect automatically. To have Windows connect automatically when you first start your computer, drag the connection from the Network Connections window to your *Startup* folder.

Connect without asking. To skip the Connect dialog that asks for your username and password each time, open the Network Connections window, right-click the connection, and select **Properties** (or click the **Properties** in the Connect window itself). Choose the **Options** tab, turn off the **Prompt for name and password, certificate, etc.** option, and click **OK**.

Share a PPPoE connection. If you're using PPPoE in conjunction with Internet Connection Sharing, discussed later in this chapter, and you've found that some web pages won't load on the client computers, see "Fix your shared Internet connection with a new MTU," later in this chapter.

Of course, the best way to live with PPPoE is to get a router and let it handle the connection. It'll do a much better job than Windows will, plus it provides a superb firewall and a very convenient means of sharing an Internet connection among several PCs.

Share an Internet Connection

When including an Internet connection, you have several choices. The old-school approach, shown in Figure 7-19, involves a single computer connected directly to the Internet (via broadband, dial-up, or whatever). That PC then serves as a *gateway* (thanks to Internet Connection Sharing, discussed shortly) and shares the Internet connection with the other computers on the LAN.

There are several downsides to Internet connection sharing. For one, it can be temperamental and frustrating to set up. Performance and security leave a lot to be desired, and it tends to be slow. Also, one computer (the gateway) must always be on for the others to have Internet access, and that computer must have two network adapters.

The preferred method is to use a wireless router, as shown in Figure 7-20.

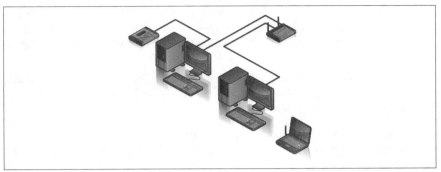

Figure 7-19. A simple workgroup with three computers, one of which has a shared Internet connection

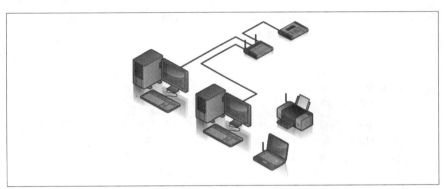

Figure 7-20. A wireless router not only makes it easy to share an Internet connection, it offers better security and more flexibility than the old-school approach shown in Figure 7-19; all of these computers, wired and wireless, have equal access to the Internet—note the wireless print server

The router is a sole unit (the little box with two antennas in Figure 7-20) that plays a whole bunch of valuable roles on your network:

- A switch, which connects all the PCs on your network to one another.

- A wireless access point, which serves as a base station for your wireless PCs and devices, and connects them to the rest of your network.

- A router, which *bridges* your local network to the Internet and provides Internet access to all the computers on your LAN. Plus, if you're using a broadband connection that requires a username and password (e.g., PPPoE), the router will log in automatically for you, and keep you logged in.

- A DHCP server, which automatically assigns IP addresses to computers in your local network (typically starting with 192.168.1.100, where 192.168.1.1 is the router itself), allowing them to coexist peacefully on your network.

- A firewall, preventing any and all communication from the outside world, except that which you specifically allow. (This is done through your router's port-forwarding feature.)

You'll see routers discussed throughout this chapter. If you don't yet have one, do yourself a favor and pick one up. They're cheap, and as shown here, do quite a lot. Even if you only have a single PC (no local network to speak of), the firewall feature of a router provides excellent security, and far better protection than Windows' built-in firewall.

Now, if you don't have a router, the alternative is to use the Internet Connection Sharing (ICS) feature built into Windows, along with a bunch of cables. To get ICS to work, you'll need the following:

- At least two computers, each with an Ethernet adapter properly installed and functioning. ICS can be used with both conventional and wireless networks.

- One of the computers must have an Internet connection properly set up, as described in "Internet Me," earlier in this chapter.

- If you're sharing a broadband (DSL or cable) connection, the PC with the Internet connection must have *two* Ethernet cards installed. See Figure 7-19, earlier, for a diagram of this setup.

 If your Internet connection is accessed through a router or you've allocated multiple IP addresses, you don't need ICS.

The first step in setting up ICS is to configure the host, the computer with the Internet connection that will be shared:

1. In the Network and Sharing Center, click the **Manage network connections** link. If you haven't already done so, open the **Views** drop-down and select **Details**.

2. Here, you should have at least two connections listed: one providing your Internet, and the other providing access to your LAN. If they're not there, your network is not ready. (For clarity, rename the two connections to "Internet Connection" and "Local Area Connection," respectively.)

3. Right-click the connection providing your Internet, and select **Proper-ties**. This is either an Ethernet adapter plugged into your DSL or cable modem, or, if you're using PPPoE, your broadband connection.

4. This step is optional, but may be required if there are any PCs on your network running Windows 98 or older versions: follow the steps in "Troubleshoot Network Connections," earlier in this chapter, to set the IP address of the host to 192.168.0.1.

5. Choose the **Sharing** tab, and turn on the **Allow other network users to connect through this computer's Internet connection** option, as shown in Figure 7-21.

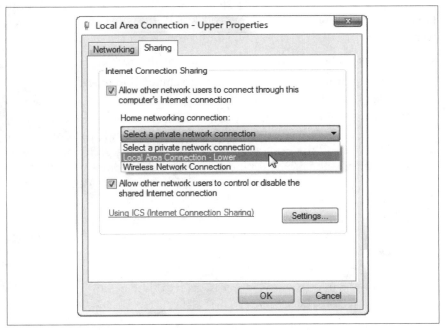

Figure 7-21. Any Internet connection can be shared with other computers in your workgroup

6. Click **OK** when you're done. Verify that Internet Connection Sharing is enabled; it should say "Enabled, Shared" in the **Status** column of the Network Connections window.

That's it! The change will take effect immediately, and you won't have to do anything special on the client PCs. Verify that the Internet connection still works on the host by attempting to open a web page, and then try it on each of the clients.

Fix your shared Internet connection with a new MTU

There are some circumstances when a shared Internet connection doesn't quite work as it's supposed to. The problem, where some web pages load and some do not, affects client computers that access a shared Internet connection facilitated by PPPoE.

Although all web sites will be accessible on the host computer, certain web sites will never load successfully from any of the client machines. If you don't know what "hosts" or "clients" are with regard to ICS, you'll want to review the previous section before you proceed. Also, see "Broadband with a username and password (PPPoE)," earlier in this chapter for more information on PPPoE connections. Note that this applies to Windows' built-in PPPoE support, as well as PPPoE provided by third-party software and even some routers.

The following solution is intended to fix this specific problem.

1. Sit down in front of one of your client machines, and type:

   ```
   PING -f -l 1500 192.168.0.1
   ```

   This assumes that 192.168.0.1 is the IP address of the host computer (or router); substitute the correct address if it's different. If you don't know the IP address of the host computer, open a Command Prompt window (*cmd.exe*) on the host, and type ipconfig at the prompt. (If a router is providing your Internet connection, consult the router documentation for details on obtaining its IP address.)

2. You'll probably get an error message indicating that it must be fragmented. (If not, then this solution doesn't apply to you.) Next, type the following:

   ```
   ping -f -l 1492 192.168.0.1
   ```

   If that results in the same error message, try this instead:

   ```
   ping -f -l 1480 192.168.0.1
   ```

   If you still get an error, try:

   ```
   ping -f -l 1454 192.168.0.1
   ```

   The numbers in each of these examples (1500, 1492, 1480, and 1454) are values for the Maximum Transmission Unit (MTU). Continue issuing this command with lower and lower MTU numbers until you get normal ping responses instead of an error message. The highest MTU value that does not result in an error is the correct one for your network. It's not unheard of for an MTU as low as 576 to be required, although Microsoft recommends no value less than 1,400 for Windows XP.

3. Once you've found an MTU that works for you, open the Registry Editor (see Chapter 3) on the *client* machine.

4. Expand the branches to HKEY_LOCAL_MACHINE\SYSTEM\CurrentControlSet\ Services\Tcpip\Parameters\Interfaces.

   There should be several subkeys under the Interfaces key; most likely, you'll find three. View each key's contents, and find the one that corresponds to your primary network adapter; it will be the one with more values than the other two, and will have an IP address value set to the IP address of the machine.

5. Once you've found the correct subkey, create a new DWORD value in it by selecting **New** and then **DWORD Value** from the **Edit** menu. Name the value MTU.

6. Double-click the new value, choose the **Decimal** option, type the MTU value you determined earlier in this procedure, and click **OK**.

7. Close the Registry Editor when you're done; you'll need to restart Windows for this change take effect.

8. Repeat steps 3–7 for each client machine on your network (but not the host).

In most cases, this should solve the problem. However, on some systems, you may need to set the MTU in another registry location as well. If you've found that a lower MTU value is what you need, but the above procedure didn't work, try this as well:

1. Navigate to HKEY_LOCAL_MACHINE\System\CurrentControlSet\Services\ Ndiswan\Parameters\Protocols\0. If any keys in this Registry path aren't there, just create them by going to **Edit → New → Key**.

2. Once you're in the key, create a new DWORD value called ProtocolType and give it a **Decimal** value of 2048.

3. Then, create a new DWORD value called PPPProtocolType and give it a **Decimal** value of 33.

4. Finally, create a new DWORD value called ProtocolMTU and give it a **Decimal** value of the MTU you determined above.

5. Close the Registry Editor and restart your system when you're done.

Test Your Throughput

Throughput is the practical measurement of bandwidth: the quantity of data you can transmit over a connection in a given period of time.

The simplest way to measure your throughput is to visit one of the many bandwidth-measuring web sites, such as Broadbandreports.com (*http:// www.dslreports.com/stest/*) or Bandwidth Place (*http://bandwidthplace.com/ speedtest/*).

For the most accurate results, make sure you close all superfluous programs before running the test. In addition to calculating your bandwidth and reporting the results, these services typically ask for your zip code and connection type to compile statistics on typical connection speeds in your area. The results should look something like Figure 7-22.

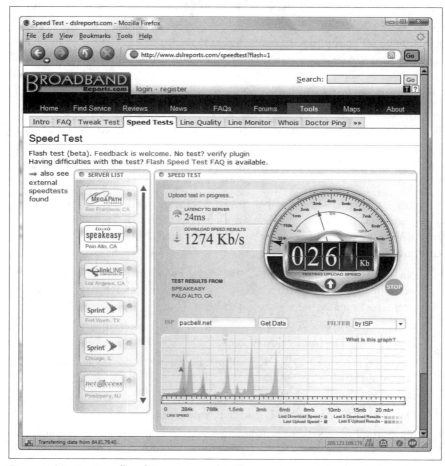

Figure 7-22. Use Broadband Reports' speed test page to measure the speed of your Internet connection

Now, according to the results in Figure 7-22, the download speed is a respectable 1,267 Kbps, which means, in practical terms, that it should take about 6.5 seconds to download a 1 MB file under ideal conditions.

However, ideal conditions are rare; real-life transfers are often much slower, due to overburdened servers and busy networks. Since your connection speed (or lack thereof) is most noticeable during file downloads (compared with web surfing or emailing), you can overcome some of these conditions by using a download manager, as described later in this chapter.

So, what do you do if your connection seems too slow? First, close all open windows, and turn off all background programs (such as the ones that show up in the System Tray in the lower-right corner of the screen, near the clock). Do the same for any other PCs using your Internet connection. Next, examine the lights on your router or broadband modem; if they're flashing, it means that some program is still running on your PC, possibly consuming bandwidth. This is a possible sign that a virus, worm, Trojan horse, or some sort of spyware (covered in Chapter 6) has made its way onto your PC.

Of course, it's also possible that you're hitting the upper limit of your broadband connection. But whether or not an upgrade from your ISP is worth the money depends on the bandwidth you're getting now and the amount of cash your ISP is demanding for the faster service. If your connection measures more than 1 Mbps (1,024 Kbps), it's unlikely you'll notice a huge difference in real-world speed with a faster connection unless you download a lot of large files (such as music). On the other hand, more expensive connections sometimes offer substantially higher upload speeds, which may be worth the added cost if you spend a lot of time sending files to web servers, or even if you want to host a web site on your PC.

Do-it-yourself bandwidth test

One of the simplest ways to measure the throughput is to transfer a binary file (such as a *.jpg* or *.zip* file) from your computer to another location and then back again, recording the time it takes to complete the transfer each way. Just divide the file size by the transfer time to get the throughput, typically in kilobytes or megabytes per second.

When testing the speed between two PCs on your local network (for instance, when comparing the speed of your wireless network with that of cables), you might be inclined to drag and drop the files in Windows Explorer, a process discussed at length in Chapter 8. Sure, it's a good real-world test, but Windows—and Vista in particular—adds a lot of overhead to this process, so it won't be a true test of raw throughput. If you're feeling adventurous, try using FTP: just set up an FTP server on one PC, either using Windows' built-in IIS service or a third-party freeware alternative, and then connect to that PC with a basic FTP client.

Do Download Accelerators Really Work?

There are a number of "download accelerator" software products available, all of which promise to speed up the transfer of files downloaded to your computer. As you might've guessed, none of them are actually capable of increasing the bandwidth or throughput of your Internet connection. Rather, they employ download *managers* that compensate for inefficiencies in the download process.

These programs work by downloading a file in pieces, via multiple concurrent download streams (not unlike the TCP/IP protocol that powers the transfer explained at the beginning of this chapter). While two concurrent downloads would each be allotted half the bandwidth normally consumed by a single download, this boundary only applies when your Internet connection is the bottleneck. In practice, download managers do use a larger percentage of your available bandwidth, and as a result, do tend to shorten download times, particularly for large files.

The problem is that any speed advantage you notice may be offset by the annoying and cumbersome interfaces these programs add to the mix: numerous dialog boxes and unnecessary prompts, not to mention bloated manager applications that take too long to load before they even get started. But in the end, the convenience afforded by some of these programs' extra features may make them worth the hassle.

Here are a few of the better download managers available, all free:

- Download Express (*http://www.metaproducts.com*)
- Free Download Manager (*http://www.freedownloadmanager.org*)
- Fresh Download (*http://www.freshdevices.com*)

 Be aware that some download accelerators contain spyware (see Chapter 6), so use caution when trying an unproven product.

Of these tools, probably the slickest is Download Express, shown in Figure 7-23. If you use Download Express, there are two changes you should make. If you're an Internet Explorer user, open Download Express, click **Advanced**, and then choose the **Integration** tab. Turn on the **Use alternative integration method** option and click **OK**; you'll need to exit and relaunch Internet Explorer for the change to take effect. Or, if you're a Firefox or SeaMonkey user, install the MetaProducts Integration extension, available at *http://metaproducts.com/*.

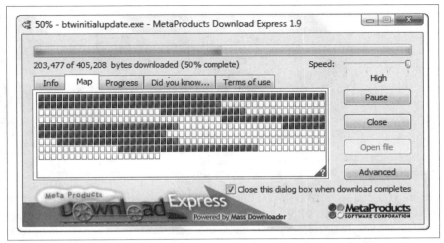

Figure 7-23. Download Express can speed up downloads without forcing you to fill out a page of options every time

The real advantage of products like these is not so much in the speed increase, but in the perks. Some programs also can resume aborted downloads, find alternative servers from which to download your files, and schedule downloads for off-peak times.

Set Up Virtual Private Networking

Virtual Private Networking (VPN) is a system involving a workgroup of two or more computers connected by an Internet connection rather than a physical cable. In theory, VPN provides the security and privacy of a closed environment, without the astronomical cost of a private wide-area network.

 Need privacy on a public wireless network? Set up a VPN to transfer data between PCs securely. For another way to get privacy on a public network, see "Connect to a Public Wireless Network," earlier in this chapter.

The technology used in VPN—either the Point-to-Point Tunneling Protocol (PPTP) or the Layer Two Tunneling Protocol (L2TP)—allows you to create a private "tunnel" across the Internet connection. With a VPN, you can accomplish tasks previously available only over a LAN, such as file and printer sharing, user authentication, and even networked games. Figure 7-24 illustrates a typical scenario with a tunnel connecting a single computer to a remote workgroup.

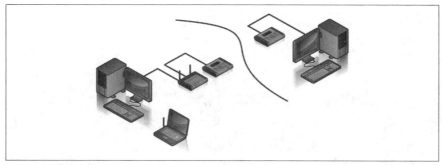

Figure 7-24. Form a virtual private workgroup through a tunnel across the Internet

Before you can set up VPN, you need a *tunnel server*. If you're connecting to a large company, the VPN administrator will provide the necessary settings (and software, if necessary) to establish a connection. Otherwise, you can use a Vista PC as a tunnel server by following these instructions.

Part 1: Set up the tunnel server

Although there's no mention of it in Vista's Help and Support, Windows Vista can indeed serve as a VPN server; you don't need any extra software.

Here's how you do it:

1. Open the Network and Sharing Center, and click the **Manage network connections** link on the left.

2. Press the **Alt** key to show the menu, and then select **File → New Incoming Connection**.

3. On the "Who may connect to this computer?" page shown in Figure 7-25, place a checkmark next to each user account you wish to use as a login for VPN clients. Unless you're using this VPN connection yourself, you'll probably want to click **Add someone** to create a separate user account for others to use (otherwise, you'll have to share your own username and password with those who will be connecting). Click **Next** when you're done.

4. On the next page, turn on the **Through the Internet** option, and then click **Next**.

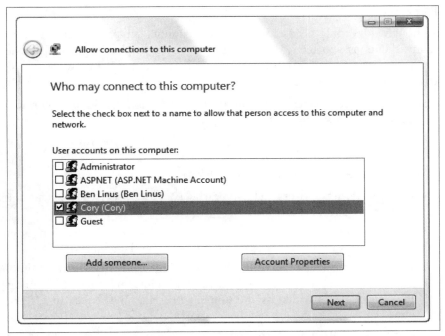

Figure 7-25. This page lets you choose who can connect to your PC and join your network over a secure VPN connection; click "Add someone" to create a new account on the fly

5. On the next page, highlight **Internet Protocol Version 4 (TCP/IPv4)** and click **Properties**. Turn on the **Allow callers to access my local area network** option, and then specify how you'd like to assign IP addresses to incoming connections; you can optionally assign a range of addresses here.

   Click **OK** and then **Next** when you're done, and then click **Allow access** to complete the wizard.

6. If you're using a router on the server end, you'll need to set up Port Forwarding to route VPN traffic to the IP address for your tunnel server. VPN over PPTP uses port 1723, and IPSec uses 500, 50, and 51. See "Control Your PC Remotely," later in this chapter, for details, and see Appendix B for more information on TCP/IP Ports.

Next, set up at least one other PC as a VPN client to connect the two.

Part 2: Set up the VPN client

Although there only needs to be one VPN tunnel server, you can have as many clients as you like (that is, until you reach the limit specified in the tunnel server's configuration). Here's how to connect a Windows Vista PC to an existing VPN network:

1. Open the Network and Sharing Center, and click the **Set up a connection or network link** on the left.

2. Select **Connect to a workplace** (you may have to scroll through the list to see it), and then click **Next**.

3. Click **Use my Internet connection (VPN)**.

4. In the **Internet address** field, type the IP address (157.54.0.1) or the host name (sally.mydomain.net).

5. Next, choose a name for the new connection (it can be anything you want), type it into the **Destination name** field, and click **Next**.

6. On the next page, type your user name and password on the tunnel server; this is either the login for a valid Windows user account on that PC, or a login provided by the tunnel server's administrator (if it's not you).

7. Turn on the **Remember this password** option, and click **Connect** (or **Create**, if you opted not to connect on the last page).

 As soon as you're connected, you should have access to the additional resources shared on the remote network; see Chapter 8 for details on accessing shared folders and printers. Later on, you can connect by double-clicking the VPN connection in the Network Connections window.

8. If you connect to the Internet through a router, you'll most likely need to turn on the IPSec option in your router's setup to get VPN to work. See "Set Up a Wireless Router," earlier in this chapter, or refer to your router's documentation for details.

For additional tips on working with VPN connections, such as how to bypass the Connect dialog, see the "Live with PPPoE" sidebar in the "Internet Me" section, earlier in this chapter.

Control Your PC Remotely

A network is good for much more than simply transferring data. Although Windows does let you transfer files to and from other computers in Windows Explorer (see Chapter 8), it's a far cry from actually sitting in front of the PC on the other end.

Enter the Remote Desktop feature, included with the Windows Vista Business and Ultimate editions (lesser editions can only use the feeble Remote Assistance feature described later in this section). Remote Desktop lets you view and interact with the desktop of a PC in a window, as though you were sitting in front of it.

There are almost limitless uses to this technology; a few examples include:

- Do you travel frequently, yet prefer to use a desktop (non-portable) computer at home? Rather than duplicating all your programs, documents, and settings on a second laptop, just use Remote Desktop to connect to your home PC from the road, and access your applications and data as though you're sitting at your own desk.

- Do you need to access your work documents and programs while you're at home, or access your home documents and programs while you're at work? Use Remote Desktop together with VPN (see the previous section, "Set Up Virtual Private Networking") to bridge the link and stop worrying about carrying so much stuff back and forth to work every day.

- Are you the person whom family members and friends call with their computer problems? Instead of spending hours on the phone, trying to explain to them how to fix their computers, just connect with Remote Desktop and fix the problem yourself in minutes.

- Do you administer several computers in different locations? Rather than having to go to the other side of the building (or the other side of the state) to access another employee's PC, use Remote Desktop and get it done in a fraction of the time.

- Are you a software developer? If you need to test your software on different operating systems or platforms, it simply isn't practical to use a multiboot computer;* you'll just spend all your time rebooting. Instead, set up a second (or even third) computer with the necessary test environments, and then control them remotely right from your development machine.

Networking and Internet

---

* See Chapter 1 for information on setting up more than one operating system on a single PC.

Well, now that this chapter has descended into an advertisement for Remote Desktop, here are some of the disadvantages. First of all, you'll need a relatively fast connection to use any remote control software like Remote Desktop, since a lot of data is transferred to update the screen image. For example, a direct Ethernet (LAN) connection will provide nearly instantaneous responsiveness, while a DSL or cable connection will be more sluggish.

Next, Remote Desktop isn't included with Windows Vista Home (Basic or Premium), and won't work with Macs or Linux PCs, so you'll need one of the alternatives mentioned later. The good news is that you can control any Windows XP or Windows 2000 PC with Remote Desktop.

Part 1: Enable the Remote Desktop server

Allowing others to connect to a computer with Remote Desktop is relatively easy. Use these steps to set up your own PC, or read them over the phone if you're trying to connect to someone else's PC:

1. Open Control Panel, go to System, and then click the **Remote settings** link on the left side.

2. Vista offers two levels of access. If you know you'll be using Windows Vista to access this PC, select **Allow connections only from computers running Remote Desktop with Network Level Authentication**. Or, if you'll need to access this PC from an older Windows XP or Windows 2000 machine, use the **Allow connections from computers running any version of Remote Desktop** option.

 Network Level Authentication (NLA) is also known as Terminal Services Client 6.0. To use NLA with Windows XP or Windows Server 2003, install the update available at *http:// support.microsoft.com/kb/925876*.

3. By default, all active administrator-level users can connect to your PC when Remote Desktop is enabled. If you wish to grant access to a lesser user account, click **Select Users**. (See Chapter 8 for more information on user accounts.)

4. Click **OK** when you're done; the change will take effect immediately.

5. Next, if you're using a router, you'll have to set up your router's *port forwarding* feature to permit the incoming connection. (This step, of course, is not necessary if you're connecting from another PC on your local network.)

6. To do this, you'll first need to assign a static IP address to your PC, as described in "Troubleshoot Network Connections," earlier in this chapter.

7. Next, open your router's setup page as described in "Set Up a Wireless Router," and navigate to the "Port Range Forwarding" page, which should look something like the one in Figure 7-26. Here, fill out the first blank line as follows:

Application
This is just a description; type Remote Desktop here.

Start
Type 3389, the TCP port number used by Remote Desktop. (See Appendix B for more information on TCP/IP Ports.)

End
Type 3389 here, too.

Protocol
Choose TCP.

IP Address
Enter the static IP address you chose for your PC.

Enable
Place a checkmark in this box to permit this service.

Click **Save Settings** when you're done.

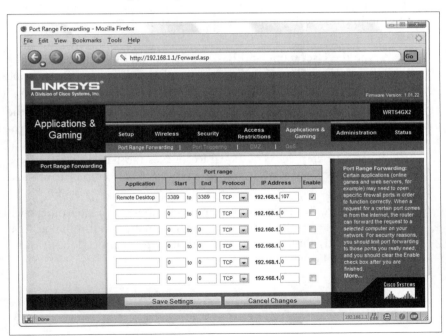

Figure 7-26. To control a PC across an Internet connection, you'll need to permit the incoming signal by going to your router's Port Range Forwarding page

8. If you're connecting to this PC from another PC on your network, all you need is this PC's computer name. In Control Panel, open System and then click the **Change settings** link in the middle of the page; use the name under **Full computer name** (not **Computer description**).

Or, to access this PC from another PC elsewhere on the Internet, you'll need the true IP address of this PC's Internet connection. Just open a web browser, navigate to *http://annoyances.org/ip/*, and record the number displayed.

Part 2: Connect to a remote computer

Once you've set up a machine to accept remote connections, follow these steps on the *client* side to connect to that computer remotely:

1. Start Remote Desktop Connection (*mstsc.exe*).

2. The default Remote Desktop Connection dialog is very simple, with only a single field. This typically will not be adequate, however, so click **Options** to display the full dialog, shown in Figure 7-27.

3. If you're connecting to another computer in your workgroup, type the name of the computer in the **Computer** field, or, if you're connecting to another computer on the Internet, type its IP address here. Use the information you got in the final step of Part 1 earlier in this section.

4. Next, type the **User name** and **Password** of a valid user account on the remote computer. (The **Domain** field is only used if you're connecting to a computer in a Windows Server domain; leave it blank otherwise.)

5. The rest of the options in this dialog are optional. The settings in the **Display** and **Experience** tabs deal with performance issues, and the **Programs** tab lets you start programs on the remote computer automatically when you connect. The **Local Resources** tab has similar options, plus a **Local devices** section, which lets you share remote drives and printers.

6. If you plan on reconnecting to the remote computer at a later time, click **Save As** to create an *.rdp* file with all the information in this dialog. You can subsequently double-click the file to initiate a connection, or right-click and select **Edit** to change its settings.

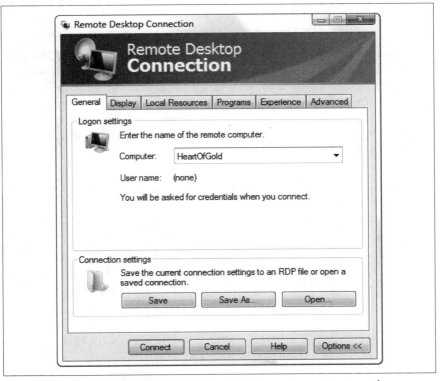

Figure 7-27. Use Remote Desktop Connection to initiate a connection to another computer and view and interact with its desktop as though you're sitting in front of it

 If the remote PC you're connecting to uses a dynamic IP address, it won't do much good to save the connection settings. See the upcoming Remote Desktop tips for workarounds if you need to access this PC consistently.

7. Click **Connect** to initiate a connection to the remote computer. If all is well, a window will appear with an image of the desktop of the remote computer. You can interact with this desktop by pointing, clicking, and dragging, just as though you are sitting in front of it.

8. Simply close the window or open the remote Start menu and select **Disconnect** to close the connection. Or, for better security and to relinquish control to someone sitting at the remote PC, select **Log Off** instead.

Tips for Remote Desktop

Here are some ways to improve your experience with Remote Desktop:

Shut down remotely. You'll see in the remote Start menu that the **Shut down** button is gone, with **Disconnect** in its place. This is obviously done intentionally, since a shut-down computer will not accept remote connections, but it does make it more difficult to actually shut down or restart the remote PC. To shut down a remote computer, click an empty area of the desktop and press **Alt-F4**. Or, open a Command Prompt window and type:

```
shutdown -s -t 5
```

where 5 is the number of seconds to wait before shutting down; specify 0 here to shut down immediately.

Want an audience? When you connect to a remote PC, anyone currently logged in to that computer will be unceremoniously logged out to make way for your remote connection. This poses a problem if you wish to use the remote PC while its owner watches. The Remote Assistance feature, described in the "Using Remote Assistance" sidebar, next, as well as VNC, described below, both overcome this limitation.

Using Remote Assistance

The Remote Assistance feature is optional, but can make it easier for less experienced users to transmit the required information to the person who will be accessing her computer remotely, including the IP address and user account.

On the PC to be controlled, open Control Panel, go to System, and then click the **Remote settings** link on the left side. Turn on the **Allow Remote Assistance invitations to be sent from this computer** option, and then click the **Remote Assistance** link in this window to open the Remote Assistance dialog (or launch `rcimlby -launchra`).

Here, you have the option of using Windows Messenger (Microsoft Live/Passport account required) or your default email program (set in **Control Panel → Internet Options → Programs** tab) to send the invitation. When asked to type a personal message, just leave it blank. You can also choose a special password for the person connecting to your computer, which is useful if you don't want to give the remote user your normal password.

Since these "invitations" can be a security hazard, there are two safeguards in place to automatically disable the feature after a specified amount of time. In the **Remote** tab of the System Properties window, click **Advanced** to disable the feature completely after a few days. Plus, when sending an invitation, you can configure it only to expire an hour or two after being sent.

Keep it windowed. While you can have your Remote Desktop session fill your screen, it makes things simpler to have it in a window you move around. To do this, set the resolution of the remote desktop lower than the resolution of the *local* desktop. For example, if you're using a computer with a display resolution of 1280×1024, use the **Display** tab of the Remote Desktop Connection Properties window to set the remote desktop to no more than 1024×768. (Note that this setting will have no effect on the remote computer's normal desktop size.)

Share files, too. As nice as it would be to drag files into (and out of) the Remote Desktop window to transfer them, the Remote Desktop feature doesn't include any provision for it. Instead, you'll need to use more traditional means of transferring files. If the remote computer is on your own LAN, you can drag and drop files right in Windows Explorer, as described in Chapter 8. Otherwise, if you're connected to the remote computer over the Internet, you'll either need to set up VPN to mimic a workgroup (described earlier in this chapter) in order to access that PC's shared folder, or use FTP.

Control Vista Home, Macs, Unix, etc. Remote Desktop Connection is not your only choice when it comes to controlling a computer remotely. Although there are several commercial alternatives available, one of the best is a free program called VNC. There are actually several derivations of VNC floating around the Web, but one of the best is TightVNC, available at *http://www.tightvnc.com/*. Among other things, VNC has the advantage of a very small "viewer" executable that doesn't even need to be installed on the client PC, and there's a version available for almost every platform (even Palm OS). It also lets both the person sitting in front of the PC and the person controlling it remotely view the desktop and even interact simultaneously.

 Remote Desktop, when enabled, will remain enabled even if the computer is restarted. But third-party programs must be specially configured to start automatically with Windows in case the computer crashes or the power goes out. VNC, for instance, has an option to be started as a "service" (accessible in *services.msc*), which is much more reliable than a mere icon in the Start menu's *Startup* folder.

Punch through any firewall. If you run into a problem getting Remote Desktop or VNC working through a firewall, proxy, or router, or you simply need to get a connection up and running fast, try GoToMyPC (*http://www.gotomypc.com*). It's a web-based service that tends to work when the others fail. Short sessions are free; longer sessions require a paid subscription.

Manage the Nameserver (DNS) Cache

As mentioned a few times elsewhere in this chapter, a nameserver (or DNS) is a machine that translates IP addresses to domain names and back again. For example, when you type *http://www.oreilly.com* into your web browser's address bar, Windows sends a request to your service provider's nameserver, and the nameserver responds with something like 209.204.146.22, and your browser can contact the web server and download the requested page.

Each time such a DNS (Domain Naming System) lookup is performed, the information is stored in the DNS cache so Windows doesn't have to query the nameserver every time you access a page on that site. The DNS cache is emptied when you shut down Windows, which is why it can take a little longer to find web sites just after you've booted up.

The following two solutions allow you to change the way Windows interacts with its DNS cache, and will affect all applications that access the Internet (not just your web browser).

Part 1: Increase the size of the DNS cache

A larger DNS cache will mean fewer trips to the nameserver and faster overall performance:

1. Open the Registry Editor (see Chapter 3).
2. Expand the branches to HKEY_LOCAL_MACHINE\SYSTEM\CurrentControlSet\ Services\Dnscache\Parameters.
3. Add the following four DWORD values by going to **Edit → New → DWORD Value**. Then, enter the numeric values specified by double-clicking and selecting the **Decimal** option:
   - CacheHashTableBucketSize, set to 1
   - CacheHashTableSize, set tot 384
   - MaxCacheEntryTtlLimit, set to 64000
   - MaxSOACacheEntryTtlLimit, set to 301

   Remember, these are **Decimal** values (not **Hexadecimal** values).
4. Close the Registry Editor when you're done. You'll have to restart Windows for this change to take effect.

Part 2: Add a permanent entry to the DNS cache

When you add a permanent entry to the DNS cache, it will always override the information provided by the nameserver. Here are a few reasons why you might want to do this:

It's a quick and dirty workaround. If a nameserver gives the wrong address for a domain or provides no information at all, you can still access the domain if it's listed as a permanent entry.

It puts a stopper in spyware. A permanent entry with intentionally incorrect information will block requests sent to the corresponding servers. This can be an effective way to prevent some web sites from tracking you, some "spyware" software from recording your personal information, and even stop some pop-up ads when you visit web pages. A list of known "tracking" hosts can be downloaded from *http://www.accs-net.com/hosts/*.

It improves lookup performance. If you frequently access a particular server, and you know its IP address isn't likely to change anytime soon, you can add a permanent entry to eliminate the initial delay as Windows looks it up. For example, add an entry for your mail server to decrease the time it takes to check for mail.

It's a shortcut for the lazy. If you frequently access a remote server without a domain name (rather than only by its IP address), you can configure a custom domain name, for your use only, to be used as a kind of "shortcut" to the server.

 Providing incorrect information here can prevent you from accessing certain remote servers. Use care when modifying the permanent DNS entry table.

Here's how to create and modify the list of permanent DNS entries:

1. Open Explorer and navigate to the *C:\Windows\System32\Drivers\etc* folder.

2. Look for a file called *hosts* (no filename extension). If it's not there, create it by going to **File → New → Text Document**, and typing hosts for the filename.

3. The *hosts* file is just a plain-text file; open it in your favorite text editor (or Notepad).

4. A standard entry looks like this:

```
207.46.230.218   www.microsoft.com
```

The first part is the IP address, and the second part (separated by a tab or several spaces) is the domain name.

Keep in mind that variations like *www.microsoft.com* and *microsoft.com* aren't necessarily the same server, and represent different DNS entries. You'll need to add a separate *hosts* entry for each variation if you want to access them all, like this:

```
207.46.230.218   www.microsoft.com
207.46.230.218   microsoft.com
```

Using this syntax, add an entry for each domain you wish to hardcode into Windows' DNS table. Note that these addresses affect your machine only; other machines, such as those in your workgroup or others on the Internet, will not be affected.

5. You may also see some lines that begin with the # character. These are comments, and they are ignored by Windows.

6. Save the *hosts* file when you're done. The change should take effect immediately.

Secure Your Networked PC

Security is a very real concern for any computer connected to a network or the Internet. There are three main categories of security threats:

A deliberate, targeted attack through your Internet connection
  Ironically, this is the type of attack most people fear, but realistically, it's the least likely to occur, at least where home and small-office networks are concerned. It's possible for a so-called hacker to obtain access to your computer, either through your Internet connection or from another computer on your local network; it's just not terribly likely that such a hacker will bother.

 Of course, the same is not true when it comes to wireless networks. Since intruders have something obvious to gain—namely, free Internet—and since wireless networks can be easy to break into if they're not secured properly, this is a real concern. See "Set Up a Wireless Router," earlier in this chapter, for details. See also "Connect to a Public Wireless Network" (earlier in this chapter as well) for ways to protect your computer and your workgroup if you're using someone else's Internet connection.

An automated invasion by a virus, worm, Trojan horse, or robot

A *virus* is simply a computer program that is designed to duplicate itself with the purpose of infecting as many computers as possible. If your computer is infected by a virus, it may use your network connection to infect other computers; likewise, if another computer on your network is infected, your computer is vulnerable to infection. The same goes for Internet connections, although the method of transport in this case is typically an infected email message. (See Chapter 6 for complete coverage of viruses, worms, Trojan horses, and spyware.)

There also exist so-called *robots*, programs that are designed to scan large groups of IP addresses, looking for vulnerabilities. The motive for such a program can be anything from exploitation of credit card numbers or other sensitive information to the creation of a "zombie," a PC that has been hijacked for the purpose of distributing spam, viruses, or extreme right-wing propaganda.

Finally, a *Trojan horse* is a program that works somewhat like a virus, except that its specific purpose is to create vulnerabilities in your computer that can subsequently be exploited by a hacker or robot. For example, a program might open a port on your computer (see Appendix B) and then communicate with a remote system to announce its presence.

A deliberate attack by a person sitting at your computer

A person who sits down at your computer can easily gain access to sensitive information, including your documents, email, and even various passwords stored by your web browser. An intruder can be anyone, from the jerk who has just stolen your laptop, to a coworker casually walking by your unattended desk, to your eight-year-old niece. Naturally, it's up to you to determine the actual likelihood of such a threat and to take the appropriate measures (such as password-protecting your screen saver, or hiding your keyboard in the closet). Several examples are discussed in Chapter 8.

Defending your computer (and your network) against these attacks essentially involves fixing the vulnerabilities they exploit.

Close Vista's Backdoors

Windows Vista includes several features that will enable you to implement a reasonable level of security without purchasing additional software or hardware. Unfortunately, few of these features are in effect by default.

The following steps will help you close some of these "backdoors":

Sharing Wizard bad. One of the main reasons to set up a workgroup is to share files and printers with other computers. But it's wise to share only those folders that need to be shared, and disable sharing for all others. A feature called Simple File Sharing, which might allow anyone, anywhere, to access your personal files without your knowledge, is turned on by default. In Control Panel, open Folder Options, choose the **View** tab, and turn *off* the **Use Sharing Wizard (Recommended)** option. See Chapter 8 for details on sharing resources and protecting your shared resources.

UPnP bad. Another feature, called Universal Plug-and-Play (UPnP), can open additional vulnerabilities on your system. UPnP could more aptly be called *Network Plug and Play*, since it only deals with network devices. UPnP is a collection of standards that allow such devices to announce their presence to UPnP servers on your network, much in the same way as your PnP sound card announces its presence to Windows when you boot your system.

Windows supports UPnP out of the box, which, on the surface, sounds like a good idea. However, UPnP is a service that most users don't need, and unless you specifically need to connect to a UPnP device on your network, you should disable UPnP on your system *immediately*. Leaving a service like UPnP running unnecessarily exposes your system to several security threats.

To disable UPnP, open the Services window (*services.msc*). Find the **SSDP Discovery Service** in the list and double-click it. Click **Stop** to stop the service and change the **Startup type** to **Disabled** to prevent it from loading the next time Windows starts. Click **OK** and then do the same for the **UPnP Device Host**. Close the Services window when you're done.

Remote Desktop good, but only when you need it. The Remote Desktop feature, described in "Control Your PC Remotely," earlier in this chapter, is enabled by default in the Windows Vista Business and Ultimate editions. Unless you specifically need this feature, it should be disabled. In Control Panel, open System and then click the **Remote settings** link on the left. In the **Remote** tab of the System Properties window, turn off the **Allow Remote Assistance connections to this computer** option, and select the **Don't allow connections to this computer** option, beneath it.

Passwords good. Make sure each and every user account on your system has a unique password. Even though you may not be concerned about security among users, unprotected accounts can be exploited by an attack over a network. See Chapter 8 for details.

Firewall good, sometimes. Set up a firewall, as described in the next section, to further protect your computer by strictly controlling network traffic into and out of your computer.

Open ports bad. Finally, look for vulnerabilities in your system by scanning for open ports, as discussed later in this chapter.

The Security Center and the Firewall

The Windows Security Center, shown in Figure 7-28, is a central page in Control Panel used to keep tabs on the Windows Firewall, Windows Defender, User Account Control, and automatic updating. It also monitors your antivirus software, but for *purely political and marketing reasons*, Windows Vista includes no antivirus functionality of its own.

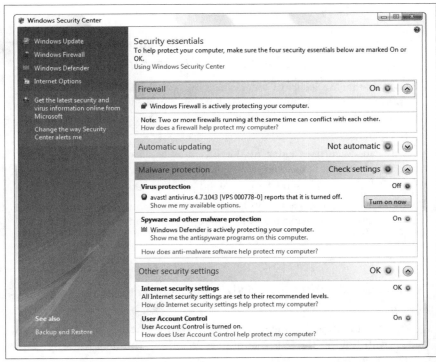

Figure 7-28. The Windows Security Center goes a long way to make Windows appear safer

There are two problems with the Windows Security Center. First, its alerts can be particularly repetitive and annoying (this is intentional). Second, it doesn't actually do that much to protect your PC (unfortunately, this is also intentional).

Above all, the Security Center is a monitoring tool. If it sees that a particular feature is turned on (whether or not it's doing its job), the Security Center is happy, and you won't see any options in that section. Otherwise, you'll have the option of fixing the "problem" by clicking a big, friendly button (e.g., **Turn on now**). Or, to stop monitoring a specific feature, click the **Show me my available options** link.

 Click the **Change the way Security Center alerts me** link to the left to choose what happens when the Security Center finds a problem. To effectively turn off the Windows Security Center (or more accurately, take away its only power), click **Don't notify me and don't display the icon** here. Or, if you feel that's too severe, click **Don't notify me, but display the icon**; that way, you'll know if there's a problem, but Security Center won't interrupt you to tell you. See the "Disable the Security Center" sidebar, next, for another solution.

Disable the Security Center

If you find that the Security Center is hassling you with unnecessary scans and warning messages, despite the fact that you've asked it not to, your only resort may be to disable it completely. Here's how to do it:

1. Open the Services window (*services.msc*).
2. Locate **Security Center** in the list, double-click it, and change the **Startup type** to **Disabled**.
3. Click **OK** and close the Services window when you're done.

Note that this doesn't actually disable the firewall, antivirus, or automatic update features you may have employed, only the "monitoring" effects of the Windows Security Center.

Click the colored ribbons to expand or collapse each section:

Firewall

You can't actually change any firewall settings here; click the **Windows Firewall** link on the left to configure Windows' built-in firewall feature, discussed in the next section.

Automatic updating

The Automatic Updates feature is responsible for periodically contacting Microsoft to see whether new updates to Windows (and optionally, other installed Microsoft products) are available. Open Windows Update in Control Panel to change this setting.

In its most automated mode (Microsoft's recommended setting), Windows downloads and installs so-called "high priority" updates automatically. But a better option is **Download updates but let me choose whether to install them** for a variety of reasons explained in "Patch Windows with Windows Update" in Chapter 6.

Malware protection

This section actually monitors two areas: **Virus protection**, which is the only feature not included with Windows Vista, and **Spyware and other malware protection**, which is handled by Windows Defender (and turned on by default). See Chapter 6 for effective ways to protect your system against viruses, spyware, and the like.

The Security Center has been known to initiate virus scans unnecessarily, including—for some users—every time Windows starts. Even if you already have Security Center-aware antivirus software installed, you may wish to disable monitoring for this reason. Click the **Show me my available options** link and then click **I have an antivirus program that I'll monitor myself**, and the antivirus status will change to **Not monitored**.

Other security settings

This section also includes two entries: **Internet security settings** (despite the name, these only apply to Internet Explorer; click the **Internet Options** link on the left to change them) and **User Account Control** (see Chapter 8).

Now, if you're the forgetful type, it's best to leave all of the alerts and warnings in the Windows Security Center intact. But if you're annoyed by all the messages, and have taken the time to secure your PC yourself, then you may feel safe scaling back the Security Center's reach.

Set Up the Windows Firewall

A firewall is a layer of protection that permits or denies network communication based on a predefined set of rules. These rules restrict communication so that only certain applications are permitted to use your network connection. This effectively closes some backdoors to your computer that otherwise might be exploited by hackers, certain types of viruses, and other malicious applications.

For the most part, you can leave Windows Firewall alone and never touch it. Unlike the early firewall debacle that came with Windows XP, the one in Vista is not booby-trapped to prevent file sharing or the Internet time feature.

In fact, it's pretty unobtrusive, bothering you only if it detects a program it hasn't seen before.

 The biggest problem with Windows Firewall is that it doesn't protect your PC nearly as much as people think it does, nor does it offer the same kind of protection as a router or hardware-based firewall. While it's better than having no firewall, Windows Firewall can provide a false sense of security.

One of the main reasons a router is so effective is that it provides a layer of abstraction between your network and the outside world. Consider a single packet of incoming data: if your PC is connected directly to the source of the threat (no router), all that packet has to do is sneak in through one of Windows Firewall's many exceptions (explained later), and it's home free. But with a router, that incoming packet hits a wall once it reaches your network; unless you enable the *port forwarding* feature described in "Control Your PC Remotely," earlier in this chapter, that packet will have nowhere to go.

To illustrate the another difference between the security offered by the Windows Firewall versus that afforded by a router, consider Figure 7-29. The larger dotted rectangle shows what's protected by your router's firewall, and the smaller rectangle shows what's protected by Windows. In addition to the larger scope of the router's protection, it's also much less likely to be compromised than a software-based solution like the Windows Firewall.

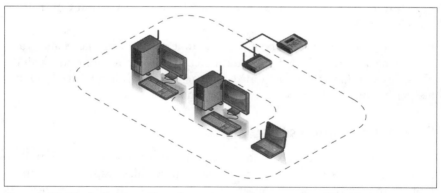

Figure 7-29. The larger dotted box shows the scope of protection offered by a router; the smaller box shows the scope of the Windows Firewall

Now, assuming you've bought the previous argument, you might think that more firewall is better—that using Windows Firewall along with a router will protect your system better than a router alone. The problem with this approach is that, again referring to Figure 7-29, Windows Firewall somewhat isolates your PC from the other computers in your workgroup. This can be good, in that viruses and other spyware on other PCs on your network will have a harder time infecting your PC (a particularly useful feature when you're surfing on a public network), or it can be bad, in that the Windows Firewall can break features you use every day.

 If you're on the road, and not behind the protective veil of your router's firewall, you should always use Windows Firewall or some other software-based firewall to help protect your PC from other PCs lurking on any public networks you might use.

By default, Windows Firewall is enabled for all network connections on your PC; you can turn it off or on in the main Windows Firewall page in Control Panel. To turn it on or off for a specific network connection, open the Windows Firewall Settings window, choose the **Advanced** tab, and remove the checkmarks next to the connections you don't want to protect.

Poke holes in the firewall

On a day-to-day basis, the Windows Firewall creates new rules on the fly as it needs them. When it detects that a program it hasn't seen before wants to open a port, it'll ask your permission. Whether you choose to grant or deny the request, Windows Firewall makes a new rule, and that rule remains in effect indefinitely, or until you change it.

But there are times when the firewall blocks connections without asking, mostly because of its default settings. If you suspect that Windows Firewall is preventing an application from working, open the Windows Firewall window in Control Panel, click the **Turn Windows Firewall on or off** link on the left, select **Off** (Figure 7-30), and click **OK**. If the program starts working, then Windows Firewall is the culprit; otherwise, the problem lies elsewhere.

If it turns out that Windows Firewall is to blame, all you need to do is create a new rule to permit your application to do what it needs to do.

Networking and Internet

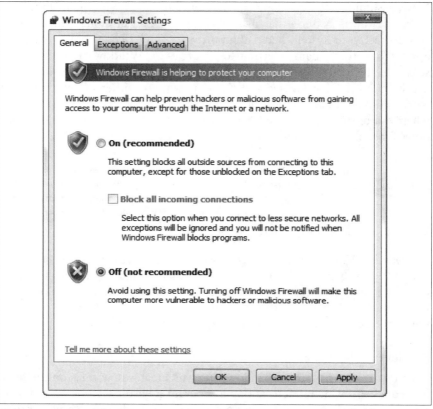

Figure 7-30. Turn off Windows Firewall temporarily to see whether it is indeed causing the problem

Don't head to the Windows Firewall window in Control Panel; that tool is extremely limited, in that it only lets you create simple *exceptions* (rules) that either give a single application free reign, or open a port that any application can use (never both at the same time). Instead, use the Windows Firewall with Advanced Security tool, described next.

1. Open the Start menu, type `wf.msc` in the **Search** box and press **Enter** to open the Windows Firewall with Advanced Security window, shown in Figure 7-31.

2. Click the **Inbound Rules** category in the left pane, and then click **New Rule** in the right pane to show the New Inbound Rule Wizard (Figure 7-32).

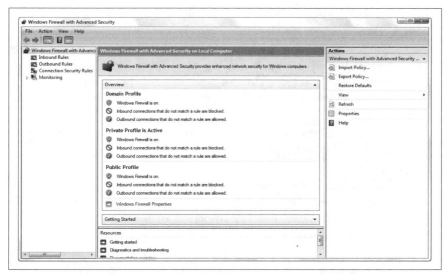

Figure 7-31. The secret Windows Firewall with Advanced Security window lets you fine-tune inbound rules, enable outbound rules, and even log firewall activity

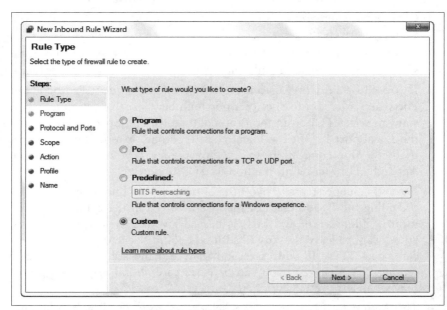

Figure 7-32. The New Inbound Rule Wizard gives you much more control than the feeble Windows Firewall window in Control Panel

3. For the **Rule Type**, choose one of the following:

Program

Use this to give a specific application free reign over your Internet connection. This is the easiest way to fix an application that has been broken by Windows Firewall's restrictions, but it can be risky if you're not exactly sure how that application will use its new freedom.

Port

This option exposes a TCP/IP port (see Appendix B) that can be used (read *exploited*) by any application.

Predefined

Choose this if you want to create a rule for a built-in Windows service. Note that this selection doesn't start or stop the service, it only instructs Windows Firewall to permit or block it; use the Services window (*services.msc*) to enable or disable Windows services.

Custom

Use **Custom** if you want to make a rule that involves both a specific application and a specific port simultaneously, something you can't do with the Windows Firewall window in Control Panel.

4. Click **Next** when you're done; what happens next depends on the type of rule you're creating.

If you chose **Program** or **Custom** in step 3, the subsequent **Program** step lets you associate the rule with all programs, or a specific *.exe* file.

If you chose **Port** or **Custom** in step 3, the subsequent **Protocol and Ports** step asks you to specify a port number. Most of the time, you'll want to select **TCP** from the **Protocol type** list and **Specific Ports** from the **Local port** list. Below **Local port**, type one or more port numbers used by the connection to be governed by your new rule; see Appendix B for more information on TCP/IP ports.

5. Next, the **Scope** step gives you the opportunity to fine-tune the rule by providing the IP addresses of the PCs involved in the connection. The local IP address (the top box) is basically your PC, so in most cases, you'll want to leave the **Any IP address** default selected. But below, you can select **These IP addresses** and then add the addresses of specific remote PCs; that way, you can be extra careful and, say, open a port only when a trusted PC wants to connect.

6. The **Action** step is more or less self-explanatory. By default, Windows Firewall blocks all inbound data except when a rule instructs it to let the data through, so typically you'll want to choose **Allow the connection** here.

7. The **Profile** step lets you choose when this rule is in effect; this is covered in more detail shortly.

8. Finally, use the **Name** and **Description** fields to label your new rule so you can find it easily in the list later on.

9. Click **Finish** when you're done.

The new exception will take effect immediately, at which point you can test the new exception. You may have to experiment with different firewall rules until your software or service works properly.

In most of the pages in the Windows Firewall with Advanced Security window, settings are divided into three "profiles," used at different times depending on the type of network Windows thinks you're using at the moment:

Private Profile
The settings in this profile are automatically put into effect when you choose **Home** or **Work** when Windows asks you to select a network location. This is typical of a home or small-office network, protected by a router, and with folder and printer sharing (explained in Chapter 8).

Public Profile
This is the profile used when you choose **Public location**, such as when you connect wirelessly to a public hotspot.

Domain Profile
This firewall profile is active when your PC is part of a corporate network with a domain controller.

By default, the general settings in each of these profiles is more or less the same, but the inbound and outbound rules are typically different. To change the settings shown on the summary page in Figure 7-31, click the **Windows Firewall Properties** link, and choose the tab corresponding to the profile you want to configure, as shown in Figure 7-33.

Here, you can make a pretty substantive change: from the **Outbound connections** list, select **Block** to give Windows Firewall control over data flowing in both directions (rather than just inbound data). This option won't necessarily be trouble-free until you take the time to customize the outbound rules in the main window. But it can, for instance, let you contain a virus outbreak on a PC without completely severing the network connection you may need in order to make repairs.

Click the **Customize** button in the **Logging** section to have Windows Firewall keep a log of data it blocks in a text file you choose. Although logging enables you to see exactly what the firewall is doing behind the scenes, the real value is in troubleshooting. For instance, if you know Windows Firewall is interfering with a specific application, but you want to know exactly what the application is trying to do before you grant it permission, check the log.

Networking and Internet

Figure 7-33. Click the Windows Firewall Properties link to choose whether or not to block Inbound and Outbound connections, change notification options, and enable logging

Alternatives to Windows Firewall

Windows Firewall that comes with Vista is much better than the XP version, but it still may not provide the ease-of-use or flexibility of a third-party program. Here are some alternative solutions:

- Agnitum Outpost (*http://www.agnitum.com*)
- Kerio Personal Firewall (*http://www.kerio.com*)
- Vista Firewall Control (*http://www.sphinx-soft.com*)

 Be careful, however, when installing and configuring a third-party firewall solution, including the ones discussed here. Overly strict firewall rules may break some software on your system. Worse yet, overly lenient rules may not protect your computer adequately and only give you a false sense of security. Check out the PC Flank Leaktest at *http://www.pcflank.com/* if you want to test your firewall.

If all you need to do is block a specific program, you can use Windows Defender. Just open Windows Defender in Control Panel, click the **Tools** button at the top of the window, and then click the **Software Explorer** link. From the **Category** list, choose **Network Connected Programs**, and then select the application you want to block in the list (it must be currently running and making use of the connection). Then, click either **End Process** or **Block Incoming Connections**, depending on what you want to do. (Strangely, it won't let you block Microsoft programs, but I suppose every company is entitled to a little vanity.)

No matter which firewall solution you choose, however, you'll most likely still need to take the time to configure custom rules using a similar procedure to the one described earlier in this section.

Scan Your System for Open Ports

Each open network port on your computer is a potential security vulnerability, and Vista's tendency to leave more ports open than it needs is a common cause for concern. Fortunately, there's a way to scan your computer for open ports so you know which holes to patch.

Start by opening a Command Prompt window (*cmd.exe*). Then, run the Active Connections utility by typing:

```
netstat /a /o
```

The /a option tells netstat to show all open ports; without it, only ports participating in active connections would appear. And the /o option shows the owning process of each port (explained shortly). The report will be displayed in the Command Prompt window, and will look something like this:

```
Active Connections
```

Proto	Local Address	Foreign Address	State	PID
TCP	annoy:pop3	localhost:4219	TIME_WAIT	0
TCP	annoy:3613	javascript-of-unknown:0	LISTENING	1100
TCP	annoy:3613	localhost:3614	ESTABLISHED	1100
TCP	annoy:3614	localhost:3613	ESTABLISHED	1100
UDP	annoy:1035	*:*		1588
UDP	annoy:1036	*:*		1588
UDP	annoy:1037	*:*		1588
UDP	annoy:1038	*:*		1588
UDP	annoy:1039	*:*		1588

 The width of the Command Prompt window is typically limited to 80 characters, causing some pretty ugly word-wrapping. To send the report to a text file (say, *report.txt*) for easier viewing, type netstat /a /o > report.txt at the prompt.

The Active Connections utility displays its information in these five columns:

Proto
> This will either be TCP or UDP, representing the protocol being used (see Appendix B).

Local Address
> This column has two components, separated by a colon. The first part is the computer name, which will typically be the name of your computer. The second part will either be a port number or the name of a service. See Appendix B for help deciphering the port numbers that appear here and in the Foreign Address column, detailed next.

Foreign Address
> For active connections, this will be the name or IP address of the remote machine, followed by a colon, and then the port number being used. For inactive connections (showing only the open ports), you'll typically see only *:*.

State
> This shows the state of the connection (TCP ports only). For example, for server processes, you'll usually see LISTENING here, signifying that the process has opened the port and is waiting for an incoming connection.
>
> For connections originating from your computer, such as a web browser downloading a page or an active Telnet session, you'll see ESTABLISHED here.

PID
> This is the Process Identifier of the application or service that is responsible for opening the port.
>
> To find out more about a particular PID, open Task Manager (launch *taskmgr.exe* or right-click an empty area of your taskbar and select **Task Manager**), and choose the **Processes** tab. If you don't see a column labeled **PID**, go to **View** → **Select Columns**, turn on the **PID (Process Identifier)** option, and click **OK**. Finally, turn on the **Show processes from all users** option at the bottom of the Windows Task Manager window. You can then sort the listing by PID by clicking the **PID** column header. The corresponding program filename is shown in the **Image Name** column.
>
> If you have the Business or Ultimate edition of Vista, you have the added luxury of being able to use the Reliability and Performance Monitor tool (*perfmon.exe*, shown in Figure 7-34) to view a live list of applications using your network connection, complete with the aforementioned PID, bytes sent and received, and even the foreign address to which they're

connected. You can even sort by network usage and find the processes most responsible for hogging your connection.

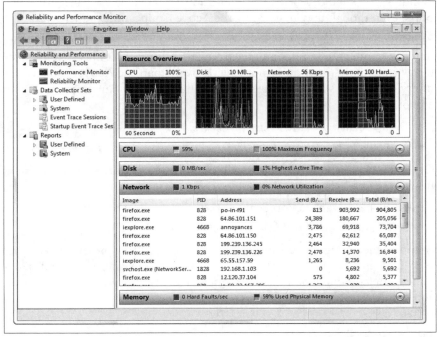

Figure 7-34. Click the Network section in the Reliability and Performance Monitor to view a list of all the programs using your network connection

This means that you can use the Active Connections Utility in conjunction with the Windows Task Manager, as described here, to look up the program responsible for opening any network port on your computer.

Don't be alarmed if you see a lot of open ports. Just make sure you track down each one, making sure it doesn't pose a security threat.

You may see *svchost.exe* listed in the Windows Task Manager, and reported by the Active Connections utility as being responsible for one or more open ports. This program is merely used to start the services listed in the Services window (*services.msc*). For an example of a service Vista runs by default, but shouldn't for security reasons, see the discussion of Universal Plug-and-Play in "Close Vista's Backdoors," earlier in this chapter.

Use an external port scanner

If you're using a firewall, such as the Windows Firewall feature built in to Windows, it should block communication to most of the currently open ports, even though they're listed by the Active Connections utility.

For this reason, you may prefer to use an external port scanner, a program that can connect to your computer through an Internet connection to check for all open ports, and do it more aggressively than the Active Connections utility. Here are some example utilities that you can run from your own computer:

- Nmap Security Scanner (*http://insecure.org/*)
- AATools Port Scanner (*http://www.glocksoft.com/port_scanner.htm*)

Or, using one of these web sites will allow you to perform port scans right from your web browser:

- PC Flank Advanced Port Scanner (*http://www.pcflank.com*)
- Open Ports Tool (*http://www.yougetsignal.com/openPortsTool/*)

Among other things, you can use these services to test the effectiveness of your firewall. If a port scanner cannot detect any open ports, cannot determine your computer name, and cannot detect any running services, then you're in good shape!

Web and Email

The Web makes our world simultaneously bigger and smaller; it's hard to imagine computing—or even a meal—without a web browser within reach. It's also hard to forget everything that comes along for the ride, such as pop ups, spam, and the constant reminders that "your privacy may be at risk."

Lock Down Internet Explorer

Over the years, Microsoft has fixed dozens of security holes in Internet Explorer, and if you've been using the Windows Update feature regularly, you already have the latest and greatest fixes installed. But the larger issue is IE's underlying design—and its cozy connection with the underlying operating system—which permits any web site to install software on your PC. At first, web site designers used this capability sparingly, mostly to install widgets and small helper programs to add trivial features to their pages. But it didn't take long for unscrupulous hackers and greedy corporate executives to learn how to exploit Internet Explorer's open nature, which is why we now have spyware, adware, browser hijackers, pop ups, and other nasty surprises. Despite these problems, Microsoft has too much corporate strategy tied up in this design to change it now, which leaves you with two choices: hobble Internet Explorer by turning off the most dangerous features, or use a different browser (or both).

If you want to stick with Internet Explorer for now, open Control Panel and then Internet Options (or in IE, open the **Tools** drop-down and select **Internet Options**). Choose the **Security** tab, and turn on the **Enable Protected Mode** option if it's not already enabled. Then select the **Internet** "zone" globe icon at the top, and then click **Custom Level** below to open the Security Settings dialog box shown in Figure 7-35.

Figure 7-35. Use the Security Settings window to turn off some of the more dangerous Internet Explorer features

Next, go down the list, and set the options as follows. (Note that your list may differ slightly as the result of recent updates from Microsoft.)

Option	Set to...
.NET Framework → Loose XAML	Disable
.NET Framework → XAML browser applications	Disable (!)
.NET Framework → XPS documents	Disable
.NET Framework-related → Run components not signed with Authenticode	Disable (!)
.NET Framework-related → Run components signed with Authenticode	Disable
ActiveX controls → Allow previously unused ActiveX controls to run...	Disable
ActiveX controls → Allow scriptlets	Disable
ActiveX controls → Automatic prompting for ActiveX controls	Disable
ActiveX controls → Binary and script behaviors	Administrator approved
ActiveX controls → Display video and animation on a web page that does not use external media player	Disable
ActiveX controls → Download signed ActiveX controls	Disable (!)
ActiveX controls → Download unsigned ActiveX controls	Disable (!)
ActiveX controls → Initialize and script ActiveX controls not marked as safe	Disable (!)
ActiveX controls → Run ActiveX controls and plug-ins	Administrator approved
ActiveX controls → Script ActiveX controls marked safe for scripting	Disable
Downloads → Automatic prompting for file downloads	Disable
Downloads → File download	Enable
Downloads → Font download	Prompt
Enable .NET Framework setup	Disable
Java VM → Java permissions	High safety
Miscellaneous → Access data sources across domains	Disable
Miscellaneous → Allow META REFRESH	Enable
Miscellaneous → Allow scripting of Internet Explorer Web browser control	Disable
Miscellaneous → Allow script-initiated windows without size or position constraints	Disable
Miscellaneous → Allow Web pages to use restricted protocols for active content	Disable
Miscellaneous → Allow web sites to open windows without address or status bars	Disable
Miscellaneous → Display mixed content	Prompt
Miscellaneous → Don't prompt for client certificate selection...	Disable
Miscellaneous → Drag and drop or copy and paste files	Enable
Miscellaneous → Include Local directory path when uploading files to a server	Disable (!)
Miscellaneous → Installation of desktop items	Disable (!)
Miscellaneous → Launching applications and unsafe files	Disable (!)

Option	Set to...
Miscellaneous → Launching programs and files in an IFRAME	Disable
Miscellaneous → Navigate sub-frames across different domains	Prompt
Miscellaneous → Open files based on content, not file extension	Enable
Miscellaneous → Software channel permissions	High safety
Miscellaneous → Submit nonencrypted form data	Enable
Miscellaneous → Use Phishing Filter	Enable (!)
Miscellaneous → Use Pop-up Blocker	Enable (!)
Miscellaneous → Userdata persistence	Enable
Miscellaneous → Web sites in less privileged web content zone can navigate...	Enable
Scripting → Active Scripting	Prompt
Scripting → Allow Programmatic clipboard access	Disable (!)
Scripting → Allow status bar updates via script	Disable
Scripting → Allow web sites to prompt for information using scripted windows	Disable
Scripting → Scripting of Java applets	Enable
User Authentication → Logon	Anonymous logon

Click **OK** when you're done changing security settings. Next, click the **Trusted sites** (green checkmark) icon, click the **Sites** button, and turn off the **Require server verification (https:) for all sites in this zone** option. Type the following URLs into the **Add this Web site to the zone** field, clicking the **Add** button after each one:

```
http://*.update.microsoft.com
https://*.update.microsoft.com
http://*.windowsupdate.com
http://*.windowsupdate.microsoft.com
```

These four URLs permit the Windows Update feature to continue working unencumbered by your new security settings. The asterisks are wildcards allowing these rules to apply to variants, such as *http://download. windowsupdate.com*. Feel free to add the domains for other web sites you trust, and then click **OK** when you're done.

Now that you see what's required to make Internet Explorer safer (albeit not bulletproof), you might be tempted to dump IE entirely in favor of a design that doesn't put your PC at risk. Mozilla Firefox, available for free from *http:// www.mozilla.com/*, is an open source, standards-compliant web browser that is faster, much safer, and more feature-rich than Internet Explorer. It does a better job of blocking pop ups, has a more customizable interface, and can be enhanced with powerful extensions (see "Improve Any Web Site" for an example). If you want to disable IE altogether, see the "Turn Off Internet Explorer" sidebar, next.

Networking and Internet

> ## Turn Off Internet Explorer
>
> Thanks to a court settlement several years ago, you can completely block Internet Explorer on your PC, a particularly effective tactic if you're setting up a PC for someone else and you don't want to have to come back six months later to cleanse it of spyware.
>
> In Control Panel, open **Default Programs**, and then click the **Set program access and computer defaults** link. In the window that appears, choose the **Custom** option, and then click the little double-arrow icon on the right side to expand the category. In the **Choose a default Web browser** section, make sure your favorite web browser is selected, and then turn off the **Enable access to this program** checkbox next to Internet Explorer.
>
> When you're done, click **OK**; the change will take effect immediately. The IE icons will disappear, and you'll get an error if you try to launch *iexplore.exe*.

Change Internet Shortcut Icons

If you're a fan of desktop icons, you've probably grown accustomed to right-clicking a new shortcut, selecting **Properties**, and then clicking the **Change Icon** button to choose a new icon for it. Pity this doesn't work on Vista's Internet Shortcuts.

Not surprisingly, Microsoft likes its IE logo, and it doesn't want you to change it. Good thing we don't care what Microsoft wants.

It turns out that this problem is the result of an intentional change introduced in Internet Explorer 7; while Microsoft insists that "this behavior is by design," it offers a hotfix update at *http://support.microsoft.com/kb/935779* that does indeed fix the problem.

 At the time of this writing, you can't download this hotfix directly from the Microsoft web site. Rather, Microsoft will only let you have it if you pick up a telephone and call (the U.S. number is 1-800-936-4900) to request that hotfix 935779 be sent to you via email. If you can't get it that way, you can also download it from *http://annoyances.org/935779* until it has been made more easily available via the Windows Update service.

If Microsoft's hotfix doesn't solve the problem, try the following solution:

1. Open the Registry Editor (see Chapter 3).
2. Expand the branches to HKEY_CLASSES_ROOT\InternetShortcut\ShellEx.

3. Look for a subkey of ShellEx called IconHandler; if it's not there, right-click the ShellEx key, select **New** → **Key**, and type IconHandler for the name of the new key.

4. If the key already exists, it might be locked (as described in Chapter 3), so you'll need to unlock it before you make any changes.

   Right-click the IconHandler key and select **Permissions**. On the Permissions for IconHandler window, click **Advanced**, and then choose the **Owner** tab. From the **Change owner to** list, select your username (or select **Administrators**) and turn on the **Replace owner on subcontainers and objects** option. Click **OK** and then **OK** again to close both windows.

   Right-click the IconHandler key and select **Permissions** again. From the **Group or user names** list, select your username (or, again, select **Administrators**), place a checkmark in the **Allow** column next to **Full Control**, and then click **OK**.

5. Next, highlight the IconHandler key and double-click the (Default) value in the right pane.

6. Type {FBF23B40-E3F0-101B-8488-00AA003E56F8} into the **Value** data field, and click **OK**.

7. Click **OK** and then close the Registry Editor. If the change doesn't take effect immediately, restart Windows.

There's a quirk that prevents some Internet Shortcut icons from working. The INI file format upon which *.URL* files are based has a limit on the length of any line of text in the file. If a URL is too long, it wraps around to the next line and disrupts the icon (and of course, doesn't work as intended). To fix an Internet Shortcut broken in this way, open it in Notepad and shorten the URL. See "Email Long URLs," later in this chapter, for tips.

Now, if you actually turned to this page to change the default icon used for *all* Internet Shortcuts, then follow these steps:

1. Open the Registry Editor (see Chapter 3).

2. Expand the branches to HKEY_CLASSES_ROOT\http\DefaultIcon.

3. This key is locked (as described in Chapter 3) by default, so before you can make any changes, you'll need to unlock it. Right-click the DefaultIcon key and select **Permissions**.

   On the Permissions for DefaultIcon window, click **Advanced**, and then choose the **Owner** tab. From the **Change owner to** list, select your username (or select **Administrators**) and turn on the **Replace owner on**

subcontainers and objects option. Click **OK** and then **OK** again to close both windows.

Right-click the `DefaultIcon` key *again* and select **Permissions**. From the **Group or user names** list, select your username (or, again, select **Administrators**), place a checkmark in the **Allow** column next to **Full Control**, and then click **OK**.

4. Now that you've unlocked the key, highlight it and then double-click the (`Default`) value in the right pane.

5. Type (or paste) the full path and filename of the icon you want to use, followed by a comma and a zero:

   ```
   c:\icons\maeby.ico,0
   ```

6. Click **OK** and then close the Registry Editor. If the change doesn't take effect immediately, restart Windows.

See Chapter 3 for more information on file types, including ways to lock your changes so you won't have to do this again.

Live with Firefox in an IE World

Ever found a web site that won't let you in because you're using Firefox or some other browser instead of Internet Explorer? The problem is the *user agent* string, a text "signature" your browser sends to every web site you visit that identifies the browser name and version, and even the operating system version you're using. For example, the user agent string for Internet Explorer 7.0 on the Windows Vista Ultimate edition looks like this:

```
Mozilla/4.0 (compatible; MSIE 7.0; Windows NT 6.0; SLCC1; .NET CLR 2.0.50727;
Media Center PC 5.0; .NET CLR 3.0.04506; Tablet PC 2.0; .NET CLR 1.1.4322)
```

On the other hand, Firefox 2.0 looks like this to web sites you visit:

```
Mozilla/5.0 (Windows; U; Windows NT 6.0; en-US; rv:1.8.1.6) Gecko/20070725
Firefox/2.0.0.6
```

If you use Firefox (or any non-IE browser, for that matter), you'll occasionally encounter a web site that won't cooperate. The problem is usually caused either by lazy developers who haven't made their web sites standards-compliant, or corporate licensing restrictions that forbid developers from supporting any non-Microsoft products. The good news is, you can fool 'em all!

The User Agent Switcher Extension for SeaMonkey and Firefox, (available for free from *http://chrispederick.com/work/useragentswitcher/*), allows Mozilla browsers to masquerade as any other browser, including Internet Explorer, good ol' Netscape 4, and even Opera. When you stumble upon an IE-only web site, just go to **Tools → User Agent Switcher** and pick a browser, as shown in Figure 7-36.

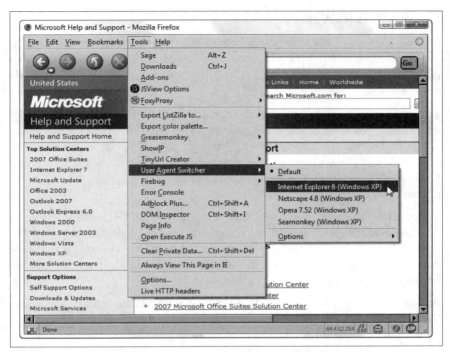

Figure 7-36. The User Agent Switcher can masquerade as IE to gain entry to sites that don't expressly support Firefox

Click **Options** to edit the browser list; you can even type in a custom user agent string and spoof a different version of Windows. What fun!

Of course, dressing up your browser as Internet Explorer doesn't necessarily mean the site will work like it's supposed to. Often, these sites require Internet Explorer because they employ proprietary IE features, such as the ActiveX add-ons that can open the door to spyware (see "Lock Down Internet Explorer," earlier in this chapter). In these cases, you must either view the page in IE or abandon the site. If you take the former course of action, you'll appreciate the IE View extension for Firefox and SeaMonkey (freely available from *http://ieview.mozdev.org/*). When you encounter a site that won't work properly in Firefox, just right-click an empty area of the page and select **View This Page in IE** or right-click any link on the page and select **Open Link Target in IE**.

When you find a site that doesn't work in Firefox or SeaMonkey, send the webmaster a note and request the site be made standards-compliant. A single email probably won't change the site owner's mind, but enough complaints may convince the webmaster to rethink the decision to support only Internet Explorer.

Networking and Internet

Fix Symbols in Web Pages

Ever view a page with strange symbols in the text, particularly where you'd expect to see hyphens or apostrophes? Although it may look like a font or language problem, it's more than likely that you just have the wrong code page selected.

The code page is the mapping of characters your browser uses to render text, and it must match the code page that was used to create the site. Usually your browser picks the correct one automatically, but if you've previously changed the code page (or if another web site switched code pages on you), or if the web site doesn't specify the correct code page, the site won't display properly.

In Internet Explorer, open the **Page** drop-down, and select **Encoding** → **Auto-Select**. If there's already a checkmark next to **Auto-Select**, or if that doesn't help, go to **Encoding** → **More**, and choose the nationality that best matches the document you're viewing. The default code page for sites in English is **Western European (Windows)**.

In Firefox and SeaMonkey, go to **View** → **Character Encoding**, and select **Western (ISO-8859-1)** for sites in English, or another nationalization that more closely matches the site you're viewing. If you find yourself returning to this menu often, go to **View** → **Character Encoding** → **Customize** to choose which code pages are displayed in the top-level menu. With either browser, some trial-and-error may be necessary before the site displays correctly.

Fix Broken Pictures in Web Pages

There are a bunch of things that can cause this problem, not the least of which is a web server that's down or a page that's out of date. But if several different sites are missing photos, try the following fixes.

First, clear your browser cache to remove any corrupt data that your browser might be using to display pages. In Internet Explorer, open the **Tools** drop-down, select **Internet Options**, and in the **Temporary Internet files** section, click **Delete Files**. Check the **Delete all offline content** box and click **OK**. If you're using Firefox, go to **Tools** → **Options**, choose the **Privacy** category, and click the **Clear** button next to **Cache**. Or, in SeaMonkey, go to **Edit** → **Preferences**, choose the **Advanced** → **Cache** category, and click the **Clear Cache** button.

Some improperly configured firewall software, particularly Norton Internet Security and Norton Personal Firewall, can interfere with images in some web sites. Temporarily disable your firewall; if that helps, consult the firewall's documentation (specifically relating to the anti-hotlinking features) to help fix the problem. (Note that neither Windows Firewall nor most firewall-enabled routers typically exhibit this problem.)

Ad-blockers may also be suppressing content you want to see. By design, ad-blockers block images, animations, inline frames, and other content served up by certain sites, but your ad-blocker might be blocking more than just the ads. Many sites also pull non-ad content from these same servers, sometimes for economic or technical reasons, but primarily in an attempt to thwart ad-blockers. Either way, turn off your ad-blocking software to see whether that solves the problem.

Finally, bad proxy settings can break all sorts of things in web sites. If you're surfing from work, your employer may require you to go through a proxy server; turn it off and see whether the problem stops. Likewise, if you're surfing from home and you're using a proxy server (as described in "Surf Anonymously," later in this chapter), you may have to turn it off to view sites reliably. In Internet Explorer, open the **Tools** drop-down, select **Internet Options**, choose the **Connections** tab, and click the **LAN Settings** button to configure your proxy server. In Firefox, go to **Tools → Options**, choose the **General** category, and click **Connection Settings**. Or, in SeaMonkey, go to **Edit → Preferences** and choose the **Advanced → Proxies** category.

Improve Any Web Site

Web sites aren't as untouchable as they may seem. In the early days of the Web, if you frequented a web site with some annoying quirks or features that didn't quite work right, you just had to grit your teeth and live with it. But Greasemonkey has changed all that.

Greasemonkey is a free extension (available at *http://www.greasespot.net/*) for the Firefox web browser that lets you add custom JavaScript code to any web page. The code then runs automatically as though it were part of the page itself and alters its appearance or changes its behavior accordingly.

 There's also a version for SeaMonkey at *http://xsidebar.mozdev.org/modifiedmisc.html*. If you're using Internet Explorer, try Trixie (*http://www.bhelpuri.net/Trixie*), which runs Greasemonkey user scripts on IE. Keep in mind that most Greasemonkey user scripts are written for—and tested with—Greasemonkey on Firefox, so there's no guarantee that they'll work as well (or at all) with Trixie and IE.

By itself, Greasemonkey doesn't do much. To bring it to life, you must install user scripts that you download or write yourself. Most user scripts are designed to add features to individual web sites, but some are written to fix bugs. Visit *http://userscripts.org/*, and you'll find enough gems to keep you entertained for some time.

The easiest way to find a user script is to search *userscripts.org* for the site you want to grease up. For instance, there were 35 scripts for Google Maps at the time of this writing, including one that changes the input field to a multiline textbox, making it easier to copy and paste street addresses, and another that lets you quickly zoom to a specific region on the map by drawing a rectangle right on the page.

Or, in the eBay section, you'll find a script that makes it easy to show only the complaints in an eBay member's feedback profile (Figure 7-37), something eBay won't let you do. (See my book, *eBay Hacks,* Second Edition—also from O'Reilly—for more tricks like this.)

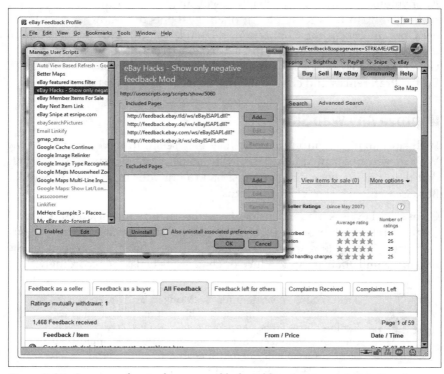

Figure 7-37. Greasemonkey is also responsible for adding the Complaints Left and Complaints Received tabs to this eBay page

When you've found a user script you want, right-click the link to the script and select **Install User Script**. Or, click the link to display and examine the script in the browser, and if you like what you see, go to **Tools → Install User Script**. The script will be active immediately, but you'll have to reload any applicable pages to see the results.

Not all scripts are site-specific. The "Linkifier" script turns anything that looks like a URL—on any page—into an active link you can click. Similar scripts do the same thing for email addresses and even UPS and FedEx tracking numbers. The best part, though, is that with some knowledge of JavaScript, you can write your own user scripts and customize the Web to your heart's content! To get started authoring user scripts, visit *http://diveintogreasemonkey.org/* and pick up a copy of O'Reilly's *Greasemonkey Hacks* by Mark Pilgrim.

Put an End to Pop Ups

Pop-up ads are everywhere, but alas, I suspect anti-pop-up laws would be about as effective as antispam laws. But that doesn't mean you can't take matters into your own hands and stop the madness (more or less). In the old days, all you'd have to do is install a third-party pop-up blocker, and you'd be set. Today, all major browsers come with built-in pop-up blockers (though some are better than others). The problem is that pop ups are no longer limited to web sites, which means your anti-pop-up arsenal must grow to keep up.

Although web-based pop ups are blocked by default in Internet Explorer, you may want to make it more aggressive to block more pop ups. Open the **Tools** drop-down, and select **Pop-up Blocker → Pop-up Blocker Settings**. From the **Filter level** list, select **High: Block all pop-ups**, and then click **OK**.

Of course, some sites use pop-up windows for legitimate purposes, so you may decide to exclude sites from the blocker from time to time to allow their pop ups to work. Return to the Pop-up Blocker Settings window, type (or paste) the URL of the site into the **Address of Web site to allow** box, click **Add**, and click **OK**.

You can also allow pop ups on a case-by-case basis by clicking the yellow information bar when it appears. And if you've selected the **High: Block all pop-ups** filter level as described above, you can also press **Ctrl-Alt** when clicking links to temporarily allow pop ups.

Firefox also blocks pop ups by default. To permit pop ups from certain sites, go to **Tools** → **Options**, choose the **Web Features** category, and click **Allowed Sites** next to **Block Popup Windows**. Or, in SeaMonkey, go to **Tools** → **Popup Manager** → **Allow Popups From This Site**, and click the **Add** button to exclude the current site from being blocked.

Firefox and SeaMonkey also give you more control than IE over JavaScript, the programming language used to facilitate most pop ups and add some other annoying traits to web sites. In Firefox, go to **Tools** → **Options**, choose the **Web Features** category, and click the **Advanced** button next to **Enable Javascript**. Or, in SeaMonkey, go to **Edit** → **Preferences** → **Advanced** → **Scripts & Plugins**. In either browser, you can prevent sites from moving or resizing windows, changing the text in the status bar, and more, by simply turning off the respective options. See "Improve Any Web Site," earlier in this chapter, for other ways to make sites less annoying.

So, now you're blocking pop ups, but ad windows are still showing up? If you see pop ups when you're not surfing the Web, your PC may be infected with spyware, software designed to display advertisements and sometimes even monitor your surfing habits. (Of course, the software you're using, such as Windows Messenger, may be showing you its own ads, but that's a different problem.) Spyware, adware, and other types of malware (malicious software) come from some web sites (see "Lock Down Internet Explorer," earlier in this chapter) and also piggy-back on some downloadable applications, commonly P2P file-sharing programs and, strangely, many weather-forecasting desktop applications. See Chapter 6 for various malware removal techniques.

Solve the Blank Form Mystery

When was the last time you filled out a form on a web page and clicked **Submit**, only to be told there's something wrong with what you've entered? You do as you're told and click the **Back** button to return to the previous page, but now the form is completely empty.

This is caused by a bug in your web browser, not the web site. All versions of Internet Explorer, and older releases of Netscape (versions 4.x and earlier) exhibit this bug. Browsers based on the Mozilla engine, such as Firefox and SeaMonkey, are better at saving form information, except under certain circumstances. For instance, if a form is generated on the fly, Mozilla browsers usually can't save the text you've typed into it.

To date, no browser handles form data in previously visited pages perfectly, but there are a few workarounds.

For one, most web site designers are aware of the bug, and have built their web sites accordingly. So, if you submit a form, and need to go back and change what you've typed, don't press your browser's **Back** button. Rather, look for a **Back** button or **Edit** button *right on the page*, and click it to safely modify your text.

Next, make a habit of performing an impromptu backup before you submit any form. For instance, if you've written a long message, click in the text box, press **Ctrl-A** to highlight all the text, press **Ctrl-C** to copy it, open Notepad, and press **Ctrl-V** to paste. (Repeat these steps for each long field in the form.) If you're later returned to an empty form, simply paste your text back into the fields and try again.

Finally, Mozilla SeaMonkey can prefill most types of web forms. Just before submitting a form, select **Edit → Save Form Info**. Then, if the form is blank when you return (or if you encounter a new form requiring similar data), select **Edit → Fill in Form** to restore your data.

Stop Annoying Animations

It seems like everywhere you go on the Web, something is pulsating, flying across the screen, or playing music. So, how do you make this online circus stop?

In most cases, pressing the **Esc** key stops the animations, but this is temporary and only works with animated *.gif* image files. If you want to permanently disable *.gif* animations altogether in Internet Explorer, open the **Tools** drop-down, select **Internet Options**, click the **Advanced** tab, and turn off the **Play animations in web pages** option. You can also turn off sounds and videos with similar settings in the same section. Click **OK** when you're done.

In Firefox and SeaMonkey, type about:config into the address bar to show the staggering list of all available fine-tuning options for these browsers. Find **image.animation_mode** in the list (type something like anim in the **Filter** field to locate it quickly), double-click the option, and type none in the **Enter String Value** box. If you don't want to completely disable animations, you can type once here instead (normal is the default) to let sites play all animations only once, but never repeat (loop) them. Click **OK** when you're done.

Other types of animations require different strategies. To turn off Flash animations in Internet Explorer, you must uninstall the Flash player using Macromedia's elusive uninstaller tool, available at *http://www.macromedia.com/support/flashplayer/* (search the knowledgebase for "uninstall").

Networking and Internet

But in Mozilla Firefox and SeaMonkey, you can use the powerful Adblock Plus extension, available for free at *http://adblockplus.org/*, to selectively hide animations. Once installed, restart your browser, and then go to **Tools →️ Adblock Plus**. Open the **Options** menu, and if the **Show tabs on Flash and Java** entry doesn't have a checkmark next to it, select it and then click **OK**. Thereafter, a little tab labeled **Block** will protrude from any Flash animation on a page (see Figure 7-38); just click the **Block** tab to show the address of the ad, and then click **OK** to begin blocking that particular Flash animation.

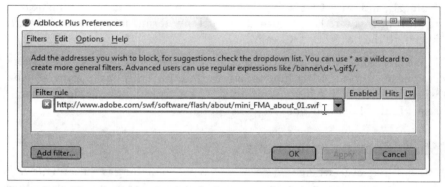

Figure 7-38. The tabs feature in AdBlock Plus is a quick way to get the address of an embedded web object, as well as a means of eliminating annoying animations from a web page

Adblock Plus supports wildcards so that, for instance, you can block all Flash animations from a particular server, rather than having to do it manually for each one. The next time you click a **Block** tab, you'll see the address of the *.swf* file, like this:

```
http://advertising.server/ads/chipmunk.swf
```

Just replace the filename with an asterisk (*), like this:

```
http://advertising.server/ads/*
```

to block all the files from the */ads/* folder on that server. Adblock Plus will continue to hide these animations until you manually remove the corresponding rule from the Adblock Plus Preferences window.

Now, if the animation, video, or sound is coming from an embedded Java applet, and you don't have the luxury of an ad blocker, you can turn off Java support altogether. In Internet Explorer, go to **Tools →️ Internet Options**, click the **Security** tab, click **Custom Level**, and in the **JavaVM** section, select

Disable Java, and then click **OK** in both boxes. In Firefox, go to **Tools** → **Options**, choose the **Web Features** category, turn off the **Enable Java** option, and click **OK**. Or, in SeaMonkey, go to **Edit Preferences**, highlight the **Advanced** category, turn off the **Enable Java** option, and click **OK**.

JavaScript, not to be confused with Java, is often used to create flyovers (where a button or icon changes when you move the mouse over it) as well as cursor trails (the flying bits that follow your mouse pointer). Now, because so many sites rely heavily on JavaScript, it isn't a good idea to turn it off just to purge these sorts of animations. In most cases, you can curb annoying JavaScript behavior with an appropriate *user script*, as described in "Improve Any Web Site," earlier in this chapter. If you're using Firefox or SeaMonkey along with Adblock Plus, you can use the "Blockable items" window (press **Ctrl-Shift-B**) to block one or more of a specific site's external JavaScript source files.

Opt Out of Tabbed Browsing

Some people like tabs because they can be used to reduce screen clutter, but if you don't specifically want to use them (for instance, if you like to view pages side-by-side), tabs are just a nuisance.

Fortunately, it's easy to do away with tabs in Internet Explorer. Just open the **Tools** drop-down, select **Internet Options**, and choose the **General** tab. In the **Tabs** section, click **Settings**, and turn off the **Enable Tabbed Browsing** option. Click **OK** and then **OK** again, and then close any open Internet Explorer windows for the change to take effect.

If you're using Firefox or SeaMonkey, turning off tabbed browsing is a little more involved. To disable all tabs in Firefox or SeaMonkey permanently, install the free TabKiller extension available at *https://addons.mozilla.org/addon/1938*, and then restart Firefox. Thereafter, Firefox will ignore any attempts to open new tabs, instead opening such links directly. (To have Firefox open such links in new windows, go to **Tools** → **Extensions**, highlight **TabKiller**, click **Options**, turn on the **Open new windows instead of new tabs** option, and click **OK**.)

On the other side of the fence are those who despise the pile-up of windows, and are happy to put up with tabs to keep the browser window tidy. If you fall into this category (and you're a Firefox user), install the Switch Windows Mode extension, free from *https://addons.mozilla.org/addon/3881*, or the This Window extension, free from *http://www.mrchucho.net/downloads/thiswindow.xpi*.

Networking and Internet

If you don't want to turn off tabbed browsing or mess with add-ons, you can use keystrokes to control what happens when you click links:

Internet Explorer
> Hold **Ctrl** when clicking a link to open it in a new tab, or **Shift** to open it in a separate window. If you have IE's pop-up blocker set to the highest filter level, you can also press **Ctrl-Alt** to temporarily allow pop ups from the site.

Firefox
> Like IE, hold **Ctrl** when clicking a link to open it in a new tab, or **Shift** to open it in a separate window. You can also hold **Alt** to save the link target on your hard disk.

SeaMonkey
> Hold **Ctrl** when clicking a link to open it in a new window, or **Shift** to save the link target on your hard disk.

In any browser, you can also right-click a link and select **Open in New Window** or **Open in New Tab** to control tabs from the comfort of your index finger.

Surf Anonymously

Web sites you visit know more about you than you probably realize. Along with the browser signature (see "Live with Firefox in an IE World," earlier in this chapter), your browser sends your PC's Internet IP address to every web site it visits, and from that, a web site can extract some pretty interesting things. (See the upcoming "What Can They Find Out About You?" sidebar for the nitty gritty.)

Use a proxy server to mask your IP address (and yes, your state) from the web sites you visit. As the name implies, a proxy server stands between your browser and the sites you surf, in effect "hiding" you from prying sites. Once you set up a proxy server, all information you send and receive with your browser goes through that server (email and other programs must be configured separately to use the proxy). Most large companies use their own proxy servers to help protect the data on company PCs from prying eyes, but you don't have to work at a big company to get the same protection.

Start by visiting *http://annoyances.org/ip* to view your IP address as web sites see it. Then, go to *http://www.proxy4free.com/*, click **page 1**, and find any server marked "anonymous." Highlight its IP address and press **Ctrl-C** to copy it to the clipboard; also note the **Port** shown in the adjacent column. Next, configure your browser to use that proxy server.

What Can They Find Out About You?

Your IP address is sent to every web site you visit. While no one can determine your exact street address directly from your IP address, there are ways to infer this information with elaborate tracking schemes. Think of your IP address as a serial number, a unique identifier some web sites can use to identify you when you visit.

For instance, let's say you make a purchase from an online store that sells toasters. As soon as you pay for that fancy new four-slicer, the store records your name, street address, credit card information, *and your IP address*. Provided the toaster store keeps your private information private, you've got nothing to worry about. But can you say the same thing for the other site you just used to sign up for a free plasma TV?

This is where advertising comes in. Most ads on many web sites originate from only a handful of companies, and those companies track who's looking at their ads, even when you don't click them. If you view a page at a news web site that displays a banner ad hosted by, say, *adknowledge.com* or *targetnet.com*, and then you sign up to win a free TV on another site that has another ad from the *same agency*, that ad server knows you've visited both sites. What's more, if the ad agency is in cahoots with the people who are giving away the TV, they have your email address, street address, shoe size, and anything else you typed into the sweepstakes sign-up page.

Now, most folks have dynamic IP addresses, which change every time they start a connection, but a single IP can remain active all day (or with a router, for weeks at a time), which means your IP address can be used to track quite a bit of your online activity. And with a geolocation tool like *http://www.yougetsignal.com/*, anyone can find your approximate location. What's more, many unscrupulous sites use so-called tracking cookies to do the same thing—namely, tag your PC with a unique serial number that can be read as you visit many different sites.

So, how can you stop the snooping? Most antispyware software (see Chapter 6) is designed to scan your system and delete any tracking cookies it finds, but you may want to take it one step further and configure your browser to not accept any cookies from these sites. You can get a list of known tracking sites from *http://www3.ca.com/securityadvisor/pest/ browse.aspx?cat=Tracking%20Cookie*. (If this feels like overkill, block only those sites responsible for the cookies your antispyware software finds on your PC.) To block cookies in Internet Explorer, go to **Tools → Internet Options**, choose the **Privacy** tab, and click **Sites**. In Firefox, go to **Tools → Options**, choose the **Privacy** category, expand the **Cookies** section, and then click **Exceptions**. Or, in SeaMonkey, go to **Tools → Cookie Manager → Manage Stored Cookies**.

—continued—

Networking and Internet

Next, install ad-blocking software such as the Adblock extension described in "Stop Annoying Animations," earlier in this chapter, and use a proxy server to mask your IP address.

 Wondering whether you can trust the proxy service not to use your IP and other info for nefarious purposes? The truth is that there's no reason to trust an anonymous proxy any more than the sites from which you're hiding. For practical purposes, you should only use one of these proxies when you specifically need to surf anonymously, and avoid logging in to your bank's web site while connected to a proxy.

If you're using Internet Explorer, open the **Tools** drop-down, select **Internet Options**, choose the **Connections** tab, and click **LAN Settings**. Turn on the **Use a proxy server for your LAN** option, and then paste (press **Ctrl-V**) the IP address you got at *proxy4free.com* into the **Address** field. Type the port number (usually 80 or 8080) into the **Port** field, and click **OK** when you're done.

 If you find yourself using proxies often, you may want to reduce the number of trips you make to Internet Explorer's LAN Settings window. Click the **Advanced** button, and in the **Exceptions** box, type the addresses of web sites you want to connect to directly (no proxy).

Settings made in the Internet Options window affect Internet Explorer only, so you'll have to use a slightly different procedure for other browsers. If you're using Firefox, go to **Tools → Options**, choose the **General** category, choose the **Connection Settings** tab, and select **Manual proxy configuration**. If you're using SeaMonkey, go to **Edit → Preferences → Advanced → Proxies**, and select **Manual proxy configuration**.

Now, go back to *http://annoyances.org/ip* and notice that your IP has changed! (If you can't load the page, the proxy server is down; just choose another proxy server from *proxy4free.com*, and try again.) From here on, every site you visit will see your proxy server's IP address instead of yours until you disable the proxy.

Every byte of data you send and receive with your web browser will be sent through the proxy server. Unless you know—and trust—whoever is hosting that server, you should always disable the proxy before sending sensitive information (e.g., your home address, credit cards, etc.).

If you don't want to go to the trouble of setting up a proxy server whenever you visit sketchy web sites, there are alternatives. One solution is to use a free, single-serving proxy web site, such as Proxify (*http://proxify.com/*), The Cloak (*http://www.the-cloak.com/*), and the Private Surfing box in the upper-right corner at Anonymizer (*http://www.anonymizer.com/*). Just type or paste the URL of the site you want to visit into the text box on any of these pages, and press **Enter**. The proxy site will load up the page, allowing you to surf anonymously for this session. Click the links in the page to continue surfing anonymously, or use your browser's address bar, bookmarks, or Internet Shortcuts to return to the normal, non-proxy surfing.

Anonymizer also has a free Privacy Toolbar (for Internet Explorer only), which does pretty much the same thing as the web-based Anonymizer, albeit with a slicker interface.

If you're using Firefox, check out the excellent FoxyProxy add-on, available for free from *http://foxyproxy.mozdev.org/*. Among other things, FoxyProxy makes to easy to switch between proxy servers (or none at all), and even lets you set up rules (called patterns) to automatically enable a specific proxy when you visit certain web sites.

If you want more flexibility than web-based proxies can offer, and don't mind paying for it, try Anonymizer's Anonymous Surfing tool, the Anonymous Browsing Toolbar 3.3 (*http://www.amplusnet.com/*), or Hide the IP (*http://www.hide-the-ip.com/*). These products, in the form of software you install on your PC, perform pretty much the same function as the web-based proxies mentioned above, albeit with more features and speed. All things considered, these software-based proxies are probably marginally safer than anonymous proxies, and less of a hassle than web-based proxies.

Now, you might be thinking, why not just use a router? Well, routers—discussed in Chapter 6—offer terrific firewall production and indeed act as a layer between your PC and the rest of the Web. But when you surf from behind a router, web sites still see your *router's* IP address, and thus are still able to collect all the same information about you and your geographical location.

See "Lock Out Unauthorized PCs," earlier in this chapter, for a way to spoof the MAC address of your PC (or your router).

Change the Default Email Reader

Just because email is ubiquitous doesn't mean it's irrelevant which email software you use. Sure, Microsoft would love it if you used the Windows Mail application that comes with Vista, or better yet, the Windows Live Mail web site that's tied to its online corporate marketing strategy. And it wants you to use Microsoft Office and Internet Explorer, rather than Open-Office and Firefox. If Microsoft had its way, you'd be brushing your teeth with Microsoft Toothpaste. The good news is that you can have it your way; Sinatra would be proud.

The most ceremonious place to start is the **Email** link at the top of your Start menu. Right-click the **Start** button, select **Properties**, and choose the **Start Menu** tab. Make sure the **Start menu** option is selected, and click the **Customize** button. From the **E-mail link** list, pick the email program you want to use. (See below if your favorite program or web site isn't in the list.)

But changing the Start menu entry doesn't affect the *default* email program, the one that opens when you send a file from an application or click a *mailto:* link in a web page. In Control Panel, open **Default Programs**, and then click the **Set program access and computer defaults** link. In the window that appears, choose the **Custom** option, and then click the little double-arrow icon on the right side to expand the category. In the **Choose a default e-mail program** section, select your favorite email program.

 If your program doesn't appear in the Set Program Access and Computer Defaults window, but the **Use my current e-mail program** entry is selected, your favorite email program may already be set as the default, despite the fact that it isn't mentioned by name here. To test it, open the Start menu, and in the **Search** box, type `mailto:test` and see what happens.

If your favorite email reader isn't showing up in either of the aforementioned lists, it doesn't mean that Microsoft specifically excluded it. (Of course, neither did Microsoft make it easy to browse for a new entry, but that's a different story.) Rather, it simply means that your application or web site isn't properly registered with Windows.

The easy way to fix the problem is to check the software publisher's web site for an update and get it if there is one, and then reinstall your email application.

If that doesn't help, or if the email program you want to use is actually a web site, you can edit the list by hand, which, of course, requires a visit to the Windows Registry:

1. Open the Registry Editor (see Chapter 3).

2. Expand the branches to HKEY_LOCAL_MACHINE\SOFTWARE\Clients\Mail.

3. Here, you'll find a separate subkey for each program currently registered on your PC; to remove an entry from the list, just delete the corresponding key here.

   Adding entries is a little more involved. Rather than filling out everything by hand, get the template from *http://www.annoyances.org/downloads/ gmail.reg* and save it to your desktop. Double-click the *gmail.reg* patch file to merge it with your Registry, and then return to the Registry Editor to have a look at the new entry, located at HKEY_LOCAL_MACHINE\SOFTWARE\ Clients\Mail\Gmail.

4. You can rename the Gmail key to whatever you like, but to change the title that appears in the Windows list of registered email programs, double-click the (Default) value on the right side.

5. Next, go to HKEY_LOCAL_MACHINE\SOFTWARE\Clients\Mail\Gmail\shell\ open\command, and double-click the (Default) value there to change the address of the program.

   If it's an application on your hard disk, type (or paste) the full path and filename of the program's *.exe* file (i.e., *C:\Program Files\AcmeMail\ acme.exe*). Or, if it's a web site, type the *.exe* filename of your browser followed by the appropriate parameter and then the URL of your site, like this:

        iexplore.exe -nohome http://gmail.com

   or, for Mozilla Firefox, type:

        c:\program files\firefox\firefox.exe http://gmail.com

   or, for Mozilla SeaMonkey, type:

        c:\program files\mozilla\mozilla.exe -url http://gmail.com

   (Note the -nohome and -url parameters for Internet Explorer and Sea-Monkey, respectively, and the fact that Firefox doesn't need one.)

Networking and Internet

6. You're not done yet; to set up your new Registry entry to respond correctly to mailto: links you click in web pages, navigate to `HKEY_LOCAL_MACHINE\SOFTWARE\Clients\Mail\Gmail\Protocols\mailto\shell\open\command`, and double-click the (Default) value to the right.

Just like the command key you set in step 5, type the path of the application or the path of your browser plus the web site address. But this time, also include the %1 parameter so that Windows can pass the email address you clicked to your email program. You'll need to check the documentation for your program or web site for the correct command-line syntax, but for programs it should look something like this:

```
c:\Program Files\Eudora\Eudora.exe /m %1
```

or for a web site (like GMail), type:

```
iexplore.exe -nohome
        https://mail.google.com/mail/?view=cm&tearoff=1&fs=1&to=%1
```

Naturally, substitute your favorite browser for IE in this example, but note that the only difference between this and the syntax in the previous step is the URL to use, which now includes &to=%1, among other things. If your web site doesn't provide the necessary URL, just search Google for the word mailto and the name of your web site (or application), and you should get the information you need.

When you're done, test your changes by clicking the **Email** entry in your Start menu, and then follow-up by clicking a *mailto:* link in any web page.

Stop Spam

Of the 873 messages in your inbox this morning, I bet only about 5 were actually for you (thinning hair and waning sex drive notwithstanding). So, how do you do away with the other 868 messages that are sure to be delivered again tomorrow?

Unfortunately, there is no perfect solution. Either you live with some junk mail in your inbox, or you employ a spam filter that occasionally deletes valid messages. But there are things you can do to mitigate the problem and reduce your exposure to spam.

First, don't post your email address on web sites, public forums, or in the backs of computer books. If you've already done this, you're already on every spam list on the planet. Also, be wary of phishing emails (see the upcoming "Don't Phall for Phishing" sidebar), another source (and scourge) of spam.

Don't Phall for Phishing

"Hmmm, a talking moose wants my credit card number. Sounds fair..."

—Homer Simpson

So, you get this message from eBay telling you that your account will be suspended if you don't update your information, and then you get a nearly identical message from Wells Fargo. I'm sure the urgent tone of the messages might be more disconcerting if you actually had accounts at those institutions.

Of course, those messages aren't from eBay or Wells Fargo; they're spam. But unlike come-ons for weight loss and real estate schemes, this spam tries to trick you into revealing personal information through a practice called *phishing* (not to be confused with the musical group Phish).

Phishing messages have become such a problem that *even Microsoft* has snapped into action and included a Phishing Filter with Internet Explorer 7.0. The filter, which is enabled by default, warns you if you visit a site it suspects to be fraudulent, and even lets you report a phishing web site so others can be warned. (From the **Tools** drop-down in IE, select **Phishing Filter** for options.) But for the IE's Phishing Filter to work, you need to have automatic updates enabled, as described in "The Security Center and the Firewall," earlier in this chapter.

But no filter is foolproof. To avoid this trap, you need to recognize the red flags. First, no reputable company will ever ask you to "verify" your information, and while many sites ask you to log in to access your account, never do so after following a link in an email. Instead, use a trusted bookmark or just type the URL into your browser's address bar by hand. If you're not comfortable simply discarding the message, contact the company and ask whether the email is legitimate.

Second, inspect any URLs in the message. Pass your mouse pointer over the link and the address should pop up (assuming your email program supports this). Odds are, you won't see something like *http://www.ebay.com*, but rather a long arcane URL with lots of symbols or a numeric web address like *http://168.143.113.54*. This is a sure sign the link points to a fake web site.

Next, if you've configured your browser to save your login information, you'll know you're not looking at the real site if your browser does fill out the form for you; browsers save passwords for specific URLs, and your PC can tell the real thing even if you can't.

To further scrutinize a suspicious email, right-click the message body and select **View Source** to view the HTML source code of the message. Search for http and you'll find the real URLs tied to the links in the message.

Now, some email messages have embedded pictures (as opposed to attachments); when you view one of these messages, your email program fetches the picture from the server, and that server records the event. (And voilà, the sender has confirmed that you've read the message.) If you turn off image fetching, those servers are never notified, and you'll find yourself on fewer spam lists:

Microsoft Windows Mail

Go to **Tools → Options**, choose the **Security** tab, and under **Download Images**, turn on the **Block images and other external content in HTML e-mail** option.

Microsoft Outlook 2007

Go to **Tools → Trust Center**, choose the **Automatic Download** category on the left, and then in the right pane, turn on the **Don't download pictures automatically in HTML e-mail messages or RSS items** option.

Eudora

Go to **Tools → Options**, choose the **Display** category on the left, and then turn off the **Automatically download HTML graphics** option.

Mozilla Thunderbird

Go to **Tools → Options**, choose the **Advanced Privacy** category, and select the **Block loading of remote images in mail messages** option.

Gmail

By default, inline images aren't displayed in Gmail messages. Instead, you'll see a green stripe at the top of the message; just click the **Display images below** link if you need to see them, or the **Always display images** link if you trust the sender. Now, if you click the **Always display images** link by accident, you can rescind your permission by clicking **Show details** and then **Don't display from now on**.

Windows Live Mail (a.k.a. MSN Hotmail)

At the top of any Live Mail page, click **Options**. Choose the **Mail** category on the left, click **Mail Display Settings**, and then under **Display Internet content**, select **Automatically suppress Internet content in messages**.

Next, install an independent, passive spam filter—one that marks potential spam instead of deleting it—like SpamPal (free, *http://spampal.org/*). Then configure your email program's filter to send all email containing the text ****Spam**** in the subject line to the **Junk** or **Trash** mailbox. That way, you can get the spam out of your face, but later peruse your junk mail for valid messages before it's gone for good. Now, most email programs (e.g., Outlook,

Thunderbird, and Eudora) have built-in spam filters that can likewise route spam into the trash. But programs like SpamPal are more configurable and update their spam lists and definitions frequently. Note: SpamPal works with any POP3- or IMAP4-based email program, which means it doesn't work with AOL, or web-based mail systems like Gmail.

All spam filters rely on up-to-date lists and definitions to block spam effectively, so make sure they are kept up-to-date. If you're using Outlook, you can get spam filter updates with Microsoft Update: open Windows Update in Control Panel, click **Settings**, and turn on the **Use Microsoft Update** option. (For older versions of Office, you can get updates manually from *http://office.microsoft.com/en-us/officeupdate/*.) Some other email programs, like Eudora, include updates only with subsequent versions of the software; check your documentation for details.

If your spam situation is particularly bad, and passive spam filters aren't cutting it, there are more drastic options. First, contact your ISP and request that it employ a server-based spam filter such as Postini (*http://postini.com/*). Server-side filters delete spam en route to your inbox, so you don't even have to download it. The downside: some valid mail may never make it to your inbox.

You can also employ a more aggressive interactive spam filter, such as Cloudmark Desktop (*http://www.cloudmark.com/*), which won't allow any email to reach your inbox unless the sender is on an approved-senders list. (Many ISPs and some web-based email providers offer this type of service to their customers as well.) If a non-approved sender tries to send you a message, the program sends back an email requesting that the sender fill out a web form. This not only trips up spam (which is sent by machines), it lets you reject humans with whom you'd rather not correspond. Of course, you can also easily add any sender to your approved list, but that in itself introduces extra work. This approach can turn a flood of spam into a trickle, but it won't ever let valid automated messages through, such as newsletters, registration codes you paid for, or order confirmation emails from online merchants. And spoofed messages, wherein the sender is made to look like someone likely to be on your approved list (such as other people in your domain), won't be stopped by these types of filters.

 If you're running an online business, think twice before you deploy one of these aggressive spam filters. The last thing you want is a spam filter deleting your customers' emails! And eBay users take note: spam filters are the number-one cause of negative feedback for both buyers and sellers.

If you're already getting tons of spam, perhaps now is the time to change your email address. Get your own domain name and create a bunch of different addresses for different purposes, such as *shopping@mydomain.com* for online shopping, *auctions@mydomain.com* for buying and selling on eBay, *subscriptions@mydomain.com* for newsletters, and *personal@mydomain.com* for correspondence with friends and family, and have them all go to the same inbox. That way, if one of your addresses makes its way onto a spam list, you can take down the address without disrupting the email to your other accounts. Better yet, create a new email address for every site you visit, such as *amazon@mydomain.com*, *ebay@mydomain.com*, *nytimes@mydomain.com*, and *annoyances@mydomain.com*. That way, if an address starts getting spam, you'll know who sold you out.

 Do you receive email at more than one address? Use your email program's **Filters** feature to sort through your incoming mail and even mark individual messages so that when you can reply, the correct return address is automatically used.

Send Large Files

Clogging a friend's inbox with 20 megabytes of email attachments is a great way to get your friend to configure a spam filter that automatically dumps all your email in the trash.

If all you need to send is a few photos, emailing them is fine…as long you shrink them down first. Your 8-megapixel digital camera creates 4 Mb files, but your friends don't need full-resolution photos unless they're going to print them. So, use your photo editor to make them all smaller before you email them; the total size of all the files you send should never be more than 400–500 Kb.

Need your recipients to be able to print the photos? There's a plethora of free photo-sharing web sites designed for this purpose, but few let visitors download high-resolution pictures. The better ones that do include Picasa (*http://picasa.google.com/*), PhotoBucket (*http://photobucket.com/*), Image-Shack (*http://imageshack.us/*), and PutFile (*http://www.putfile.com/*). Just upload your photos to the site and then send the URL the site provides to as many recipients as you like, without fear of email attachment clog.

To send other types of files, such as documents or ZIP files, you need a slightly different tack. Since photo-sharing web sites can make money when visitors order prints, they're only too happy to host your photos, but few sites will be interested in hosting that 50 Mb database file you need to send to a colleague.

Now, if you have your own web space (often provided free by your ISP), you can FTP your files to the server, and then send your friends an address like this:

http://www.{my-isp.net}/~{myusername}/{quarterlyanalysis.zip}

where *{my-isp.net}* is your ISP's web site, *{myusername}* is your user account, and *{quarterlyanalysis.zip}* is the name of a file you want to share.

Unfortunately, your ISP probably isn't interested in helping you host—and have all your friends download—gigabytes of your data. If you don't have web space, or if your ISP restricts the types or size of files you can upload to it, try a site like YouSendIt (*http://www.yousendit.com/*). You can upload any type of file (up to 100 Mb in size) to YouSendIt's servers, and they'll automatically email your recipients a link to your files. The service is free, but your files are deleted after 7 days or 25 downloads, whichever occurs first. Other sites, like MegaUpload (*http://megaupload.com/*) and RapidShare (*http://rapidshare.com/*) tend to permit more downloads, but the countdown timers and less-than-wholesome advertising that accompanies them may put off some of your more prudish associates.

Email Long URLs

Ahh, the evils of word wrap. The basic terminal display used to read early email messages was only 80 characters wide, and while few people still use terminals to read email, the standard lives on. Today, if you send someone a message with a long URL, it'll be broken apart by his or her email program to conform to that 30-year-old standard.

Since email vendors have yet to fix this glitch, and your recipients will likely have no idea what to do when they receive your message with pieces of a URL spanning several lines, shrink the URL before you send it. For example, TinyURL (*http://tinyurl.com/*), can take any horrendously long URL, such as:

http://maps.google.com/maps?ll=37.826870,-122.422682&spn=0.
007197,0.009112&t=k&hl=en

and turn it into a tidy, easy-to-email URL like this:

http://tinyurl.com/cfpmc

TinyURL is fast and free, and the URLs it makes never expire. Also available is SnipURL (*http://www.snipurl.com*), which does pretty much the same thing, but adds tracking features.

Find yourself making TinyURLs often? Just go to *http://tinyurl.com/#toolbar*, and drag the **TinyURL!** link onto any browser's **Links** toolbar. Thereafter, just click the button to create a TinyURL from the current page.

If you use Firefox, try TinyURL Creator (*https://addons.mozilla.org/en-US/firefox/addon/126?id=126*, or better yet, *http://tinyurl.com/574q9*). To use the tool, right-click an empty area of the current page and select **Create Tiny URL for this Page**. A shortened URL is created on the spot and copied to your clipboard for your immediate use. A similar tool, Maxthon (free from *http://www.maxthon.com*), works with Internet Explorer and SnipURL.

So, what do you do when someone sends you a long URL? Well, you can highlight it, copy it to the clipboard (**Ctrl-C**), and then paste it into Notepad (**Ctrl-V**), where you can then proceed to carefully reassemble the URL onto one line. (Take care to remove extraneous characters, such as spaces and punctuation, while leaving the stuff that belongs intact.) Then, copy it again and paste it back into your web browser's address bar. But if you're using Firefox or SeaMonkey, you can streamline this process with the free Open Long URL extension (*https://addons.mozilla.org/addon/132*). Install the extension, restart your browser, and then select **File → Open Long URL**. Paste the long, broken URL into the box, click **OK**, and the extension will reassemble the URL for you and open the page. See? Much easier than fixing our email software.

CHAPTER 8

Users and Security

Microsoft tried something new with user accounts in Windows Vista. In the past, the purpose of having separate accounts was to make it easy for more than one person to use a single PC: each user got his or her own desktop, documents, settings, and even a password to keep private things private. But in Vista, user accounts also help your PC protect itself from...well, *you*.

User Account Control (UAC) is the name of the system that displays the "Windows needs your permission to continue" message whenever you try to make a change to your system. On one hand, having to watch the screen go black while you wait for the UAC prompt to appear every time you open Device Manager can be tremendously annoying. On the other hand, the system is designed to let you know whenever a change is being made to your system, which (in theory) makes it harder for spyware and viruses to do their dirty work. See "Control User Account Control," later in this chapter, for the scoop.

Otherwise, User Accounts are the primary means of protecting your data, even if you're the only person who uses your PC. The user accounts system allows you to encrypt your data, so it can't be read by someone who doesn't know your password, and it makes it possible to securely share your files with those on your network who do. And it means you can share your PC with your kids without having to stare at their "Astronaut on a Surfboard" desktop wallpaper.

Manage User Accounts

There are actually three different User Accounts dialogs in Windows Vista, each with a completely different design and "intended audience," so to speak. The problem is that each tool has a few options not found in the other, so no single window can be used exclusively to handle all your tasks.

User Accounts

The primary user accounts interface, found at **Control Panel → User Accounts** and shown in Figure 8-1, is the one that most users see. It's large, friendly, and unfortunately, somewhat cumbersome.

Figure 8-1. You can add, delete, or modify user accounts in the User Accounts dialog, but not much else

Adding, customizing, and removing user accounts is extremely easy, and for the most part, self-explanatory in this window, and that is admirable. But sometimes you'll need one of the alternate dialogs, listed next, to accomplish some of the more advanced tasks, such as managing groups and configuring Windows to log in a password-protected account automatically.

> The standard User Accounts window is the only place you can choose a user's picture, shown in both the login dialog and at the top of Vista's Start menu (see "Massage the Start Menu" in Chapter 2). It's also the only place you can choose between the Welcome screen and the standard Login screen, as discussed in "Hide the List of User Accounts," later in this chapter.

User Accounts 2

Some additional settings, discussed later in this chapter, can be changed only with the alternate User Accounts window, which, incidentally, is identical to the sole User Accounts tool in Windows 2000. To open the old-style User Accounts dialog (Figure 8-2), open the Start menu, type `control userpasswords2` in the **Search** box, and click **OK**.

Figure 8-2. The "other" User Accounts dialog can do many things that are otherwise impossible in the standard User Accounts window

Like the primary User Accounts window, you can add new users, as well as rename or remove existing accounts. But here, you have more control over a user's permissions and restrictions. You can access accounts that would otherwise be hidden in the User Accounts window, such as the Administrator account (see "Log In As the Administrator," later in this chapter) and the IUSR account used by the IIS web server. See "Hide the List of User Accounts," also later in this chapter, for another use of this dialog.

Use the alternate User Accounts dialog and the Local Users and Groups window (discussed next) with caution, as both allow you to disable all accounts with administrator privileges. If this happens, the computer will be completely inaccessible by any administrator, and you'll probably have to reinstall just to log in.

Local Users and Groups

The third way to manage user accounts in Windows is to use the Local Users and Groups policy editor, shown in Figure 8-3; open the Start menu, type lusrmgr.msc in the **Search** box, and press **Enter**. The Local Users and Groups window (LUaG) is actually a Microsoft Management Console (*mmc.exe*) snap-in, like the Disk Management utility (see Chapter 1) and the Windows Firewall with Advanced Security window (Chapter 7), and therefore can be accessed remotely if necessary. Figure 8-3 shows the LUaG dialog in all its glory.

Figure 8-3. The Local Users and Groups window gives you the most control over user accounts, but at the expense of a rather sparse and intimidating Registry Editor-like interface

LUaG is where you manage groups, set the automatic expiration of passwords, and change the location of a user's home directory. Just double-click any entry in the **Users** or **Groups** categories to change their properties. Or, right-click in an empty area of the right pane to add a new user or group.

A *group* is a collection of users that can be referenced with a single name. Groups can be useful when you wish to make a folder accessible to several users (as described later in this chapter); instead of having to specify each one individually, all you would need to do is specify the group. Note that once the group has been set up here, you can use the User Accounts 2 dialog (described earlier) to assign new or existing members to that group.

What can be confusing is finding the right place to accomplish a specific task regarding user accounts. Table 8-1 shows a bunch of different tasks and where to go to accomplish them.

Table 8-1. The various places user-account tasks can be performed

Task	User Accounts	User Accounts 2	Local Users and Groups
Add groups			✓
Add users	✓	✓	✓
Assign a user to a group		✓	✓
Assign a user to multiple groups			✓
Change a user's account name	✓		
Change a user's description		✓	✓
Change a user's home profile folder			✓
Change a user's password	✓	✓	
Change a user's picture	✓		
Choose a logon script			✓
Copy a user's profile folder	✓		
Disable a user or group account without removing it			✓
Export a list of users/groups to a text file			✓
Find Administrator accounts without passwords	✓		
Manage network user names and passwords	✓	✓	
Modify groups			✓
Password reset disk	✓		
Prevent forgotten passwords	✓		
Remove almost any user	✓	✓	✓
Remove any user		✓	✓
Rename certain users	✓	✓	✓
Remove a user's password	✓		
Require Ctrl-Alt-Del to log on		✓	
Set password expiration			✓
Turn on/off Administrator account			✓
Turn on/off Guest account	✓		✓
Turn on/off login window		✓	
Turn on/off User Account Control (UAC)	✓		
Turn on/off Welcome screen	✓		
Use Fast User Switching	✓		
View members of groups			✓

Users and Security

For the most part, adding, removing, and modifying user accounts is a fairly self-explanatory process, so I won't go into every excruciating detail here.

Security Identifiers (SIDs)

Every user on your machine has a unique Security Identifier (SID), which is used in conjunction with most of the features discussed in this chapter, such as permissions and encryption, as well as some of the solutions in other chapters in this book. For example, your personal settings in the Registry (Chapter 3) are stored in a branch that looks something like this:

```
HKEY_USERS\S-1-5-21-1727987266-1036259444-725315541-500
```

The numeric portion is your SID, and is composed of the following elements:

```
S-r-i-sa-xxxxxxxxxx-yyyyyyyyyy-zzzzzzzzz-uid
```

where S stands for security identifier, r is the revision level and is always set to 1, i is the identifier authority, and $sa\text{-}xxxxxxxxxx\text{-}yyyyyyyyyy\text{-}zzzzzzzzz$ is the subauthority. Finally, uid is the user id.

For example, the identifier authority (i) can tell you something about the type of user to which an SID corresponds:

- S-1-0...is an unknown group or a group with no members.
- S-1-1...is the "world" group that includes all users.
- S-1-2...is a local user logged into "terminal."
- S-1-3...is the creator of an object (file, folder, etc.).
- S-1-4...is a non-unique user identifier.
- S-1-5...is a standard user account.

Aside from some of the solutions that use SIDs, they can be an issue if you clone your machine, at which time you may have to change your SID. Microsoft's System Preparation Tool (SysPrep) can be used to do this.

Permissions and Security

Setting the permissions for a file or folder allows you to permit some users to read or change your files while restricting access to others. Problem is, if you rely on Vista's defaults, *anyone* will be able to read your files and *no one* will be able to change them.

So, before you start messing with permissions, you'll need to turn off Simple File Sharing. Open Control Panel and then Folder Options, choose the **View** tab, and turn off the **Use Sharing Wizard** option at the end of the **Advanced Settings** list. Click **OK** when you're done.

Note that permissions can only be used on files and folders stored on NTFS volumes (see the discussion of NTFS in Chapter 5).

Set Permissions for a File or Folder

Shockingly, Microsoft actually took default permissions seriously when designing Windows Vista. In previous versions of Windows, everyone with an account on your PC had access to every file on your hard disk; if you wanted to protect your private data, you had to take matters into your own hands. In Vista, defaults are set to protect your private data from other users, and to protect Windows operating system files from all users.

Of course, no progress is without its price. Some of Vista's defaults are so restrictive that they can break certain software not expressly written for Vista, as described in "Control User Account Control," later in this chapter.

To give someone access to your files, or to further restrict access, you'll need to mess with his or her permissions. Of course, it gets a little confusing when you realize that there are two different Permissions windows for any given object (file, folder, printer, etc.).

Object permissions
> Right-click any file, folder, drive, Registry key, or printer, select **Properties**, and choose the **Security** tab to view or change the permissions for the selected object(s). These settings affect how the object is accessed by users on your machine (including you).

Share permissions
> Right-click any file, folder, drive, or printer, select **Properties**, choose the **Sharing** tab, click **Advanced Sharing**, and then click the **Permissions** button to view or change the share permissions for the selected object(s). These settings affect whether users on other PCs on your network can read or write to your shared files or print to your shared printers.

Fortunately, all Permissions windows look and work the same; the only difference is their scope. Figure 8-4 shows a typical Permissions window.

Typically, a single entry, "Everyone," will appear at the top of the list. In the example in Figure 8-4, only five single users are shown here. Any user not in the list will not be allowed to view or modify the object.

Permissions protect files from other user accounts only. If you walk away from your PC while you're logged in, for example, someone else sitting down at your keyboard will have full access to all your files, regardless of permissions or even encryption. This is why—when your PC is in a public place, anyway—it's a good idea to use the "**On resume, display logon screen**" option in the Screen Saver Settings window.

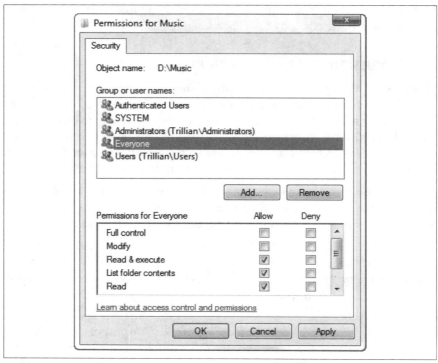

Figure 8-4. The standard Permissions window allows you to permit or deny access to other users on your computer or in your workgroup

Select any user in the list, and then use the checkboxes in the list below to modify the permissions for that user. In this example, members of the Everyone group are allowed to read the selected file, but not allowed to write to it. Although this window only shows the permissions for one user or group at a time, you can click **Advanced** to see a better overview, as shown in Figure 8-5.

In some cases, when you attempt to remove or modify permissions in the standard Permissions window (Figure 8-4), Windows will complain about the fact that the object is *inheriting* permissions. The reason is the **Inherit from parent** option in the Advanced Security Settings dialog shown in Figure 8-5.

Inheritance and ownership

Inheritance can be confusing at first, but it does save time in the long run. Essentially, if you set the permissions of a folder, those permissions will propagate to all of the files and subfolders contained therein (although Windows will usually ask you whether or not you want this to happen).

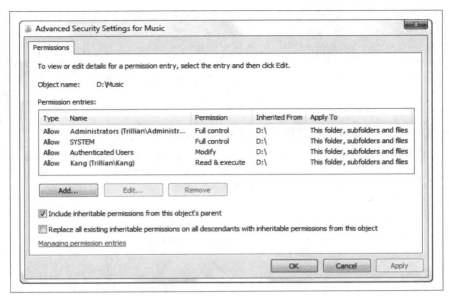

Figure 8-5. Open the Advanced Security Settings window to see all users and permissions for an object at once

When the permissions for a "parent" folder trickle down to a "child" folder or file, that child object is said to "inherit" the permissions of its parent folder. Furthermore, the child's inherited permissions are locked, at least until you turn off the aforementioned **Inherit from parent** option.

The **Auditing** tab in the Advanced Security Settings window allows you to log access activity relating to the selected object. Before auditing will work, you'll need to set up an auditing policy by opening the Group Policy window (*gpedit.msc*). Then, navigate to Computer Configuration\Windows Settings\Security Settings\Local Policies\Audit Policy, and double-click any entry in the right pane (such as **Audit logon events** or **Audit privilege use**) to instruct Windows to start keeping track of those events. Later on, open the Event Viewer (*eventvwr.msc*) to view the corresponding logs. Note that settings in the **Auditing** tab also obey the inheritance scheme just discussed.

The **Owner** tab is used to assume *ownership* of one or more objects, and can be the source of a lot of frustration when wrestling with permissions. One of the means by which Vista maintains its lock on important operating system files and Registry keys is through ownership; by default, all these system-level objects are owned by a user named "Creator Owner." (See the upcoming sidebar, "What's the Creator Owner Account?," for details.) To make any changes to these objects, you must first assume ownership by selecting your own name in the list, turning on the **Replace owner on subcontainers and objects** option, and clicking **OK** in all the open Permissions windows. Only then can you reopen the main Permissions window to set the appropriate permissions, after which you can make your changes; there are several examples of this procedure throughout this book, particularly in Chapters 3 and 7.

What's the Creator Owner Account?

From time to time, you'll see a reference to *Creator Owner* in the Permissions window, but if you try to find the account by that name in one of the user account tools described at the beginning of this chapter, you'll come up empty handed.

Why? Because *Creator Owner* is not an account.

Rather, it's a generic moniker that protects an object by ensuring that only the object's owner can modify it.

Say a user on your PC creates an Excel spreadsheet and puts it in a shared folder. Then, another user logs in to the same PC and opens the document. In some cases, and depending on the file's permissions, the second user won't be able to make changes and save the file until he assumes ownership of it.

The subtleties of this scheme can be complex and rather confusing, but luckily, they aren't particularly important. When that second user clicks the **Owner** tab in the Advanced Security Settings window, the **Current owner** may be *Creator Owner* rather than the actual username of the person who created the file. No matter; the new user just selects his own username from the list and clicks **OK**.

Probably the most you'll see of the *Creator Owner* entry is when you try to modify a Registry key and Windows won't let you until you assume ownership, close all the Permissions windows, and then reopen them to give yourself permission to make the change. See "Prevent Changes to a Registry Key," in Chapter 3, for one such example.

Another time when you'd use the **Owner** tab is when you need to share documents between two Windows installations on the same PC (see "Set Up a Dual-Boot System" in Chapter 1); in most cases, Windows won't let you access such files until you "take ownership" using the **Owner** tab of this window.

For another way to manage ownership of files and folders, see the "Take Ownership from the Command Line" sidebar, next.

Take Ownership from the Command Line

It's a real pain to dig down through all those windows to take ownership of a file, only to have to close them all, and then reopen them to subsequently change the permissions. If you're comfortable with the Command Prompt or you need a way to take ownership from script (see Chapter 9), there are a few useful tools included with Vista for this purpose.

To assume ownership of a file or folder, use the `takeown` command. Open a Command Prompt window, and at the prompt, type:

```
takeown /f "c:\full_path\myfile.ext"
```

where `c:\full_path\myfile.ext` is the full path and filename to take ownership of. Add the `/r` option—only if you're specifying a folder name—to also take ownership of all the folders and files contained therein. Type `takeown /?` for more options.

Next, to set Full Access permissions on the file or folder, use the `cacls` command, like this:

```
cacls "c:\full_path\myfile.ext" /G your_username:F
```

where *your_username* is, obviously, your username.

And for those familiar with Unix, there's a chown (change ownership) command-line utility (written for NT but works in Vista) available for free at *http://www.thep.physik.uni-mainz.de/~frink/nt.html*.

Finally, the **Effective Permissions** tab is a troubleshooting tool that lets you view the selected object's permissions as they pertain to a single user. This is most useful when dealing with groups of users.

Add new users to the Permissions window

Typically, a single entry, **Everyone**, will appear at the top of the **Group or user names** list in the Permissions window. (Here, **Everyone** literally means all users and groups in perpetuity.) More than likely, though, you'll want to eliminate the **Everyone** entry and add only those users (such as yourself) whom you need to specifically grant access to your stuff.

Start by deleting any unwanted users by selecting them and clicking **Remove**. Then, click **Add** to open the Select Users or Groups window, as shown in Figure 8-6.

The first time you use this tool, you'll probably expect to see a list of all the users on your PC; unfortunately, Microsoft in its infinite wisdom decided it would be easier for you to type each user's account name by hand.

Users and Security

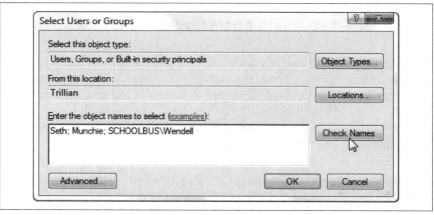

Figure 8-6. New users and groups are added to a Permissions list with this rather confusing dialog

To add a user, type one or more names in the **Enter the object names to select** field; separate multiple names with semicolons.

> In the example in Figure 8-6, notice that the third entry, *SCHOOLBUS\Wendell*, is unlike the others. While *Seth* and *Munchie* are users on the PC (or in the corporate domain to which this computer belongs), this third entry shows how you'd specify a user account on a different machine; in this case, the user *Wendell* on the computer *SCHOOLBUS* is to be added. The only time you'd likely need to do this is if *Wendell* needed to access your shared files remotely (discussed later in this chapter), and you didn't want to create an account for *Wendell* on your own PC.

So, why, in the Select User or Groups window, can you not actually *select* a user or group? Why aren't all the user and group names on your PC listed in here? Why all the typing? The reason is that this window was originally designed to accommodate a company-wide network with thousands of users, and since Microsoft hasn't made a single change to this interface in at least seven years, you'll need to go elsewhere to get a list of users. To see the users on your own PC, open the User Accounts window in Control Panel, or use one of the other tools explained at the beginning of this chapter. Or, if you're part of a corporate domain, you can click **Advanced** to search for users on your network.

When you click **OK**, Windows will verify the user and group names you've entered, and if all is well, will add them to the Permissions window. Mistype a name, and you won't be allowed to leave. (To verify your entries without closing the window, click **Check Names**.)

When you've added a new user to the Permissions window (shown previously in Figure 8-4), highlight the user, and selectively click the checkmarks in the **Allow** or **Deny** columns.

 Deny entries take precedence over any **Allow** entries. Say a user named *Surly* is part of a group named *Duff*. If you deny read access to the *Duff* group, and then allow read access to the *Surly* account, *Surly* still won't be able to read the files.

Depending on the type of object you've selected, you may see any number of different types of entries here, such as **Full Control**, **Read**, **Write** and **Modify**. After playing with the checkmarks, you'll notice that there is quite a bit of redundancy in this list; for example, **Modify** is an umbrella term that includes **Read & Execute**, **Read**, and **Write**.

For more control over permissions, click **Advanced** to show the Advanced Security Settings window (shown earlier in Figure 8-5), select the user with whom you want to work, and click **Edit**. The Permission Entry window shown in Figure 8-7 allows you to fine-tune permissions and allow only those permissions that are absolutely necessary for the object. When settings most permissions day-to-day, you won't ever need to use this tool.

When you're done choosing permissions, click **OK**. If you're modifying the permissions for a folder, Windows may or may not prompt you to have your changes propagated to all subfolders and files.

How permissions affect software

In most cases, you'll want to set permissions to protect your files and folders from unauthorized access. But some permissions are necessary to get certain programs to work.

For example, if you're writing a CGI or ASP program for the IIS web server (see Chapter 9), you'll need to set the permissions of your files to give the *Internet Guest Account* full access. The *Internet Guest Account* user account name is based on the machine name: for a system named *SERVER*, you'd enter SERVER\IUSR_SERVER into the Select Users or Groups dialog (as shown earlier in Figure 8-6).

Vista uses this scheme as part of the UAC feature discussed in "Control User Account Control," later in this chapter, which is why software not written especially for Vista won't know that it's not allowed to write files to your PC's *Program Files* folder.

Of course, you can also use overly restrictive permissions to your advantage and prevent changes to certain Registry keys, as described in "Lock Your File Types" in Chapter 3.

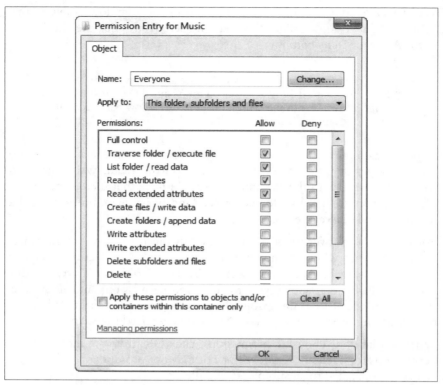

Figure 8-7. The Permission Entry window lets you fine-tune permissions

Protect Your Files with Encryption

Encryption effectively adds another layer of protection for your especially sensitive data, ensuring that a file can only be viewed by its creator (well, sort of). If any other user—even someone with administrator privileges—attempts to view the file, she will see only gibberish.

When a file is marked for encryption, the encryption and decryption of the file are handled by Windows invisibly in the background when its creator writes and views the file, respectively. The problem is that Windows Vista's on-the-fly encryption can be somewhat unpredictable, and security is one place where you don't want there to be any guesswork.

Encryption is a feature of the NTFS filesystem (discussed in "Choose the Right Filesystem" in Chapter 5) and is not available with any other filesystem. This means that if you copy an encrypted file onto, say, a memory card, USB key, or CD, the file will become unencrypted, since none of those drives support NTFS.

Encrypt an Entire Drive with BitLocker

Vista's file and folder encryption is a handy way to protect sensitive data, but mixing encrypted data and unencrypted data on the same drive can lead to unpredictable results, as described in this section. But if you have the Ultimate or Enterprise edition of Vista, you'll also have the luxury of using the BitLocker drive encryption feature.

BitLocker works by placing all the data on your drive into a single, enormous archive file, and then accessing the file invisibly like a virtual hard disk. You can access the files on a BitLocker-encrypted drive through Windows Explorer as though it were any other drive, while Windows handles the encryption and decryption in the background. The BitLocker approach has the significant advantage of encrypting Windows and all your system files, thereby preventing a hacker from cracking your password and breaking into your account, thus rendering your individual file encryption worthless.

Before you try to use BitLocker, fire up Windows Update and click the **View Update History** link to see whether you have the "BitLocker and EFS enhancements" update from 1/31/2007 or 2/28/2007 (or both). If not, click the **Check for updates** link, and in the **Windows Ultimate Extras** section, place a checkmark next to any BitLocker updates that appear.

Next, open the BitLocker Drive Encryption page in Control Panel. If you see an error explaining that a "TPM was not found," see whether there's a BIOS update available for your PC, as described in Appendix A, that supports TPM.

TPM, or *Trusted Platform Module*, is a chip on your motherboard that's used to store the BitLocker encryption key, allowing you to boot off an encrypted drive. If your BIOS doesn't support TPM, you can use an ordinary removable USB flash drive for this purpose. Open the Group Policy Object Editor (click **Start** and type gpedit.msc), and then expand the branches to Computer Configuration\Administrative Templates\Windows Components\BitLocker Drive Encryption. On the right, double-click the **Control Panel Setup: Enable advanced startup options** entry, click **Enabled**, turn on the **Allow BitLocker without a compatible TPM** option, and then click **OK**.

In order for you to use BitLocker, your hard disk must have at least two partitions (see Chapter 5): one for your operating system, and another "active" partition—of at least 1.5 Gb in size—used to boot your PC. If your drive isn't currently set up this way, start the BitLocker Drive Preparation Tool (*\Program Files\BitLocker\BdeHdCfg.exe*) and follow the prompts. When your drive is ready, open the BitLocker Drive Encryption page in Control Panel and click **Turn on BitLocker**.

Hint: If you don't have Vista Ultimate, you can do pretty much the same thing with either FreeOTFE (*http://www.freeotfe.org/*) or TrueCrypt (*http://www.truecrypt.org/*), both of which are free and compatible with all editions of Vista.

Here's how to encrypt a file:

1. Right-click one or more files in Windows Explorer and select **Properties.**
2. Under the **General** tab, click the **Advanced** button.
3. Turn on the **Encrypt contents to secure data** option, click **OK**, and click **OK** again.

See "Add Encrypt/Decrypt commands to context menus," later in this section, for a quicker way to encrypt and decrypt files.

4. If you encrypt a folder that contains files or other folders, Windows will ask you whether or not you want those contents to be encrypted as well. In most cases, you'll want to answer **Yes**. If you decline, the folder's current contents will remain unencrypted, and only newly created files will be encrypted. See "The ins and outs of folder encryption," later in this chapter, for details.

After a file has been encrypted, you can continue to use it normally. You'll never have to manually decrypt an encrypted file in order to view it.

Encrypting a file may not guarantee that it remains encrypted forever. For example, some applications, when editing and saving files, will delete the original file and then recreate it in the same place. If the application is unaware of encryption, the protection will be lost. The workaround is to encrypt the folder containing the file rather than the file itself.

If you change the ownership of a file (as described in "Set Permissions for a File or Folder," earlier in this chapter) and the file is encrypted, the encryption will remain active for the *original* owner and creator of the file, even though that user no longer technically "owns" the file.

Since all users need to access files in certain folders, such as the \Windows and \Windows\System folders, Windows won't let you encrypt files and system folders or the root directories of any drives.

Compression, another feature of the NTFS filesystem, reduces the amount of space consumed by a file or folder. The rules that apply to compression are more or less the same as those that apply to encryption. But you cannot simultaneously use encryption and compression on any object; turn on one option in the Properties window, and Windows will turn the other off. See "If in Doubt, Throw It Out," in Chapter 5, for more information.

Highlight encrypted files in Windows Explorer

By default, Windows Explorer visually differentiates encrypted files, which can be a very handy way to keep track of the scope of your encryption. In Control Panel, open Folder Options, choose **View** tab, and turn on the **Show encrypted or compressed NTFS files in color** option to use this feature, or turn it off if you want all your filenames to be printed in black text. Click **OK** when you're done.

By default, the names of encrypted files appear in green, while those of compressed files appear in blue (except for icons on the desktop). Note that files can't be simultaneously compressed and encrypted (as mentioned in the previous section), so you'll never see any turquoise, teal, or aquamarine filenames.

Actually, that's not entirely true. You can customize the color Windows uses to highlight encrypted filenames by editing the Registry:

1. Open the Registry Editor (see Chapter 3).

2. Expand the branches to: `HKEY_CURRENT_USER\Software\Microsoft\Windows\CurrentVersion\Explorer`.

3. Create a new binary value by going to **Edit → New → Binary Value**, and type `AltEncryptionColor` for the name of the new value.

4. Double-click the new **AltEncryptionColor** value, and then type a code to indicate the color you'd like to use, following this pattern:

   `RR GG BB 00`

   The RGB hex code used here follows the same scheme as RGB codes in HTML web pages (except for the two trailing zeros), which means you can use any common color mixer to generate the hex codes for you. For an excellent, free web-based color mixer, go to *http://colormixers.com/mixers/cmr*. Or, if you have Adobe Photoshop, you can match an existing color with the eyedropper tool and grab the code from the # field in the color mixer window.

   For example, to get a nice aquamarine color, you'd type this:

   `00 B4 C5 00`

   Here, the first `00` indicates no red, the `B4` is the hex code for 180 (out of 255; roughly 70% green), the `C5` is the hex code for 197 (about 77% blue), and then the last two zeros are for good measure. Or, to get the default green color, type:

   `00 80 40 00`

   By the way, don't type the spaces; Registry Editor will do it for you.

5. Likewise, you can customize the color used for compressed filenames by creating a new binary value named AltColor in this same key, and filling its value data with whatever RGB code you like.

6. Close the Registry Editor when you're done. The change will take effect the next time you log in.

Allow others to access your encrypted files

By default, only you can read your own encrypted files. But what if you want someone else to have access to a file, yet keep your password to yourself and maintain the file's encrypted state?

Right-click a file or folder you've already encrypted, select **Properties**, and under the **General** tab, click the **Advanced** button. Click the **Details** button to open the User Access window shown in Figure 8-8.

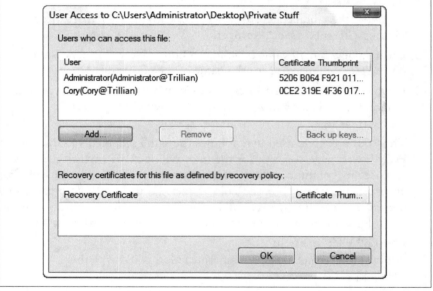

Figure 8-8. This elusive window lets you share an encrypted file with another user while keeping your password secret and the file's encryption intact

If the **Details** button is grayed out (disabled) in the Advanced Attributes window, it means that encryption isn't yet active for the selected file or folder. If you just turned on the **Encrypt contents to secure data** option, you need to click **OK** here and in the main Properties window, then come back here before you can click **Details**.

To permit another user to access your files, click **Add** to show the Encrypting File System window.

Now, you won't necessarily see all the user accounts on your PC here, only those that already have security certificates. If you don't see the account you want to include here, you'll need to log in to that account and encrypt at least one file or folder.

If the user doesn't have an account on your PC, you can either create one, or you can install the user's own certificate on your PC by hand. To do this, ask the user to send you the certificate from her PC. Then, open the Start menu on your PC, type certmgr.msc, and press **Enter** to fire up the Certificate Manager. Expand the **Personal** branch and then select the **Certificates** folder. From the **Action** menu, select **All Tasks → Import**, and then complete the Certificate Import Wizard by following the prompts.

Note that the **Expiration Date** shown here represents the date the user's security certificate expires, and has nothing to do with the permissions you're setting up. No hurry, though; you've got at least 100 years.

View someone else's encrypted files

So, how do you access someone else's encrypted files *without* that person's permission? (This is an important question to ask if you care about the security of your own data.) If you try to view someone's encrypted files, you'll get an "Access is Denied" error message, as shown in Figure 8-9.

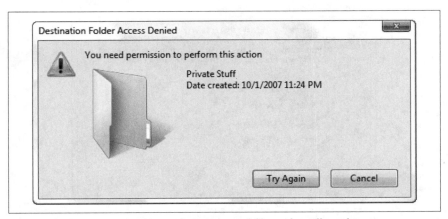

Figure 8-9. Try to access someone else's encrypted file, and you'll get this error

Not even administrators can view files encrypted by other users. However, any administrator can change any other user's password, and then subsequently log in to that user's account and view (or unencrypt) any of his protected files. This means that your files won't be totally secure unless you're the only administrator on the machine.

There is a little-known side effect to this fact: if the owner of encrypted files deletes his or her encryption keys, neither the user nor any administrator will be able to read the encrypted files until the key is reinstalled. See "Back up your encryption certificates," later in this chapter, for more information.

The ins and outs of folder encryption

You can also encrypt a folder and all of its contents using the procedure for files shown earlier. It gets a little more complicated, though, when you mix and match encrypted and unencrypted files and folders, and it can be difficult to predict what happens to the folders' contents.

Now, if a file in an encrypted folder is moved into an *unencrypted* folder, the file becomes unencrypted. The exception is when you've specifically encrypted the file itself; in this case, the file remains encrypted, no matter where you put it. Whenever you try to encrypt a file located in an unencrypted folder, Windows warns you and gives you the option to encrypt the folder as well (shown in Figure 8-10).

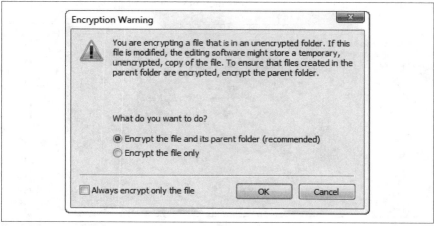

Figure 8-10. Windows displays this warning if you encrypt a file located in an unencrypted folder

Be especially careful here, as the default is to encrypt the containing (parent) folder in addition to the selected file, which can be counterintuitive if you're accustomed to warnings that only deal with child objects. Check the **Always encrypt only the file** option if you never want to see this warning again.

If you ever inadvertently encrypt your desktop (by encrypting an item on your desktop, and then accepting the default in this box), the only way to unencrypt it is to open Windows Explorer, and unencrypt the source desktop folder (usually *Users**[your username]**Desktop*).

If an unencrypted file is placed in an encrypted folder, the file will become encrypted, too. The catch is when one user encrypts a folder and *another user* places a file in that folder; in this case, the file is encrypted for the *creator of the file*, which means that the owner of the folder, the one who originally implemented the encryption, will not be able to read the file.

On the other hand, if the user places a file in a folder, and a different user comes along and encrypts the folder thereafter, only the user who implemented the encryption will be able to read the file, even though the file is officially "owned" by that first user.

Add Encrypt/Decrypt commands to context menus

If you find yourself frequently encrypting and decrypting files, having to repeatedly open the Properties window can be a pain. Instead, follow these steps to add **Encrypt** and **Decrypt** commands to the context menus for every file and folder:

1. Open the Registry Editor (see Chapter 3).

2. Expand the branches to `HKEY_LOCAL_MACHINE\SOFTWARE\Microsoft\Windows\CurrentVersion\Explorer\Advanced`.

3. Create a new DWORD value by going to **Edit → New → DWORD (32-bit) Value**, and type `EncryptionContextMenu` for the name of the new value.

4. Double-click the new `EncryptionContextMenu` value, enter 1 for the **Value data**, and click **OK**.

5. Close the Registry Editor when you're done. The change will take effect immediately.

6. To use this new trick, right-click any unencrypted file in Explorer or on your desktop, and select **Encrypt**. Or, right-click an already encrypted file, and select **Decrypt**.

If at least one of the selected items is a folder, you'll have the option of encrypting only the folder or all the folders contained therein. If encrypting any individual files, you'll also be asked if you wish to encrypt only the file or the parent folder as well.

Back up your encryption certificates

Think of your encryption certificate as the combination to a safe. Forget the combination, and you can't open the safe. Likewise, lose your certificate, and you won't be able to open your encrypted files.

Windows Vista's encryption system employs symmetric key cryptography, which uses the same key to encrypt and decrypt data. Windows generates a unique key for each user, so that no user can decrypt another user's data.*

The first time you use encryption on your PC, Vista creates a new encryption certificate for you (if you don't already have one) and prompts you to back up your certificate with the window shown in Figure 8-11.

Whether or not you take Windows up on its offer, you can use one of the two included tools to manage your encryption certificates:

Certificate Manager

Open your Start menu, type certmgr.msc, and press **Enter** to fire up the Certificate Manager. Expand the **Personal** branch and select the **Certificates** folder to view the certificates installed on your PC. The one used for NTFS encryption is labeled **Encrypting File System** in the **Intended Purposes** column. View any certificate by double-clicking it.

You can back up a certificate by highlighting it and then selecting **All Tasks → Export** from the **Action** menu. Just save the file to a USB memory key or CD so it's safe in the event that your hard disk crashes and you need to install a second copy of Windows to access your data. (This is the same thing that happens if you click **Back up now (recommended)** when you see the prompt in Figure 8-11.)

If you need to, you can install a backed-up encryption certificate on any PC—and thus read the files encrypted with it—by importing it as described in "Allow others to access your encrypted files," earlier in this chapter.

---

* The classic example of cryptographic keys is how Julius Caesar encoded messages to his allies. Each letter in the message was shifted by three: A became D, B became E, C became F, and so on. Only someone who knew to shift the letters *back* by three could decode the messages. Cryptographic keys work the same way, except they're slightly more complicated.

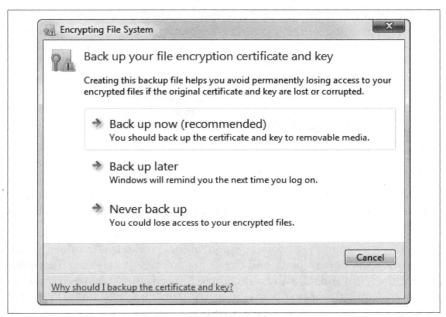

Figure 8-11. The first time you use encryption on your PC, you'll be prompted to back up your encryption certificate (key) so you can access your protected files even if you reinstall Windows

NTFS Encryption Utility

The NTFS Encryption Utility (*cipher.exe*) lets you encrypt or decrypt files and manage certificates from the Command Prompt, but it's not included with all editions of Windows. It does have the added benefit of being able to perform some tricks that the Certificate Manager, just discussed, cannot.

Open a Command Prompt window (*cmd.exe*) and type cipher without any arguments to display the encryption status for all the files in the current folder. (Use the cd command discussed in Chapter 9 to change to a different working folder.) Encrypted files will be marked with an E; all others will marked with a U.

To encrypt a file, type cipher /e *filename*, where *filename* is the name of the file or folder (include the full path if it's in a different folder). Likewise, type cipher /d *filename* to turn off encryption for the item.

To back up your certificate, type cipher /r:*filename* at the prompt, where *filename* is the prefix of the output filename (without an extension). Cipher asks for a password, and then generates two separate files based on the specified filename. For example, if you type cipher /r: julius, you'll end up with two files: *julius.pfx*, which contains the

Encrypting File System (EFS) recovery agent key and certificate, and *julius.cer*, which contains the EFS recovery agent certificate only (without the key). Double-click either file in Windows Explorer to import the certificate or key, or use the Certificate Manager.

 Worried that your key got in the wrong hands? You can generate a new key at any time by typing `cipher /k` (without any other options). Then, type `cipher /u` to update the encrypted files on your system with the new key.

Secure your drive's free space

Normally, when you delete a file, only the file's entry in the filesystem table is deleted; the actual data contained in the file remains in the folder until it is overwritten with another file.

Cipher, discussed in the previous section, allows you to *wipe* a folder, which only means that it goes black and cleans out any recently deleted files, overwriting the leftover data with random bits. This effectively makes it impossible to subsequently recover deleted data with an "undelete" utility. Think of the wipe feature as a virtual paper shredder.

To wipe a folder, open a Command Prompt window and type `cipher /w:` *foldername*, where *foldername* is the full path of any folder on the drive to wipe. Although Cipher requires the path of a folder, it actually wipes all the free space on the drive. This means that the commands `cipher /w:c:\` `Romulus` and `cipher /w:c:\Remus` have exactly the same result.

 Set up Cipher to wipe folders containing sensitive data at regular intervals (or when Windows starts) to automatically protect deleted data. See Chapter 9 for information on the Scheduled Tasks feature and WSH scripts, both of which can be used to automate Cipher.

Note that Cipher's /w option does not harm existing data, nor does it affect any files currently stored in the Recycle Bin. It also works on unencrypted folders and encrypted folders alike.

Control User Account Control

For years, Windows-based PCs have been under siege by viruses, spyware, and adware, concepts introduced in Chapter 6. User Account Control, or UAC, is Microsoft's response to this scourge in Windows Vista.

It works like this: Windows Vista, like its predecessors, supports different "levels" of user accounts, some with administrator rights—necessary to install software and configure the system—and others with lesser privileges. But Vista doesn't give administrators carte blanche like Windows XP and 2000. Instead, an administrator (you, for instance) operates in a more-restrictive *standard* user account mode most of the time. Only when you make a change that supposedly affects other users on your PC (whether there are any or not), like installing a new hardware driver or changing Windows Firewall settings, does Vista request your permission with the UAC prompt like the one in Figure 8-12.

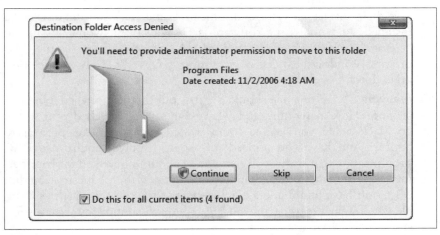

Figure 8-12. Every time you (or a program) tries to make a change to your system, Windows shows you this annoying prompt

If you click **Continue**, Windows permits the action, and thereafter, it's smooth sailing. Or, click **Cancel**, and Windows forbids the request. As with any preventive measure, there are costs and benefits to Vista's UAC.

First, the good:

It can make Windows safer. In theory, nothing bad can happen to your PC without your approval. This means so-called *drive-by installations* from nasty web sites you view in Internet Explorer, the source of some spyware and adware, are a thing of the past (in theory). (Of course, you can also deal with this by changing a few settings, as described in "Lock Down Internet Explorer" in Chapter 7.)

It can make Windows more stable. Provided you take a few extra steps, UAC makes it harder for incompetent users to damage a PC by deleting or replacing files, making unauthorized changes to the Registry, and screwing up network settings.

It can make Windows easier to administer. It's possible to require a password at each UAC prompt, meaning a PC's administrator doesn't have to create a separate account to make changes. The PC's day-to-day user doesn't know the password and can't make changes, but the administrator can sit down and fix a problem in minutes, without even logging out.

Now for the bad:

It breaks some programs. UAC may break software not expressly written for Vista and the UAC feature. For instance, any program that attempts to write files to the *Program Files* folder (even its own application folder) will be denied access; this is why lots of older applications can't save their settings on Vista, and some programs can't start up or even be installed. And unless the software is UAC-aware, it won't attempt to "elevate" itself to the administrator level, and you'll never see the UAC prompt; Windows just denies it. In short, you won't know why the program doesn't work.

It's annoying. (OK, this one should be first, but that just seemed a bit self-serving.) How many times today have you sat and watched your screen go black while you waited...and waited...for the UAC prompt to appear? And have you noticed that some features require *two* UAC prompts: one that warns you that you're about to be asked for your permission, and the other that actually makes the request? Couldn't Microsoft have found a less cumbersome way to do this, such as a single window that elevates the current session to administrator status for, say, the next 20 minutes?

It's easily defeated. The UAC feature can be disabled with a single setting; it's only a matter of time before some hacker figures out how to do this without you knowing about it. And if you install software that registers a Windows service (managed with *services.msc*), that service could be used to carry out administrator-level requests by any program, even one run under the lowly *standard* user account.

Nobody reads prompts anyway. It's only a matter of time before an average PC user becomes accustomed to the prompt and gets into the habit of clicking **Continue** without reading the message. Even if it were an otherwise flawless system, there's no system in place to make sure the user knows what he is doing.

When designing Windows Vista, Microsoft tried to please everybody by making UAC strict enough to prevent certain mischief, yet lenient enough that it wouldn't be such a nuisance that you'd want to turn it off. Of course, the result is a system that is either too much or not enough for most people. The solution, of course, is to customize it.

Fix a program broken by UAC

So, you've got a program that won't install on Vista, or perhaps it won't remember its settings. The problem is likely that UAC is preventing the application (or the installer) from doing what it was designed to do. And since the application isn't UAC-aware, it doesn't request "elevation," the step necessary to tell Windows that it's time for the UAC prompt. The result? Vista prevents the change and keeps its mouth shut, and the application doesn't work.

The solution is to elevate the application by hand. You can't do this while it's running, but, as shown in Figure 8-13, you can do it when you start the application. Just right-click the application's icon on your desktop or Start menu (or the program's *.exe* file), and select **Run as administrator**.

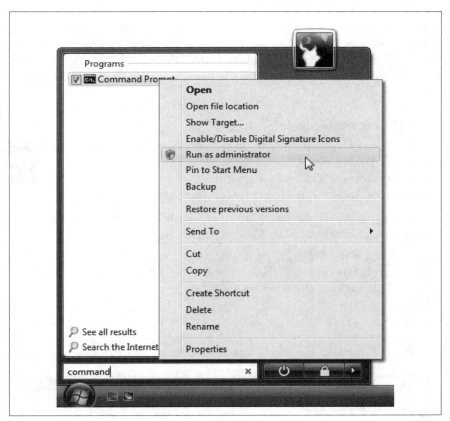

Figure 8-13. Right-click a program icon and select "Run as administrator" to temporarily elevate a program so it's no longer restricted by Vista's security system

This time, you'll see the UAC prompt, and assuming you click **Continue**, Windows will elevate the application and it should work as designed.

Users and Security

If you don't see the **Run as administrator** option, it means that the icon you've clicked isn't a standard Windows shortcut. In this case, just open Windows Explorer, navigate to the program's application folder (usually found under *C:\ Program Files*), and right-click the main *.exe* file. Of course, Windows won't show the **Run as administrator** option when you right-click documents, so be sure you only do this with the main application icon.

This trick also works for application installers, but beware: if the installer needs this workaround, the application is likely to need it, too. Before you install, check the software publisher's web site for an update or a new version that's compatible with Vista.

If the program won't run unless you use the **Run as administrator** feature, you may want to make the change more permanent. Right-click the program icon (or *.exe* file), select **Properties**, and choose the **Compatibility** tab. In the **Privilege Level** box, turn on the **Run this program as an administrator** option, and click **OK**.

Turn off User Account Control

The easiest way to turn off UAC is through the User Accounts window in Control Panel. On the "Make changes to your user account" page, click the **Turn User Account Control on or off** link, and then turn off the **Use User Account Control (UAC) to help protect your computer** option.

But turning off UAC altogether isn't necessarily the best choice if you just want to get rid of the incessant UAC prompts.

If you're using the Ultimate or Business editions of Vista, open the Start menu **Search** box, type secpol.msc, and press **Enter** to display the Local Security Policy editor, shown in Figure 8-14.

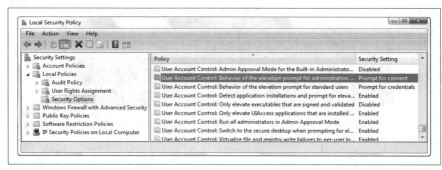

Figure 8-14. Use the Local Security Policy editor to get rid of the UAC prompts without disabling UAC altogether

---

Expand the **Local Policies** branch and click the **Security Options** folder. In the right pane, double-click the **User Account Control: Behavior of the elevation prompt for administrators in Admin Approval Mode** setting. Here you have three choices:

Elevate without prompting. This is the best choice if you want to skip the UAC window altogether.

 Even though this option gets rid of the UAC prompts, it does not disable UAC. This means that applications that aren't UAC-aware won't request elevation, and thus Vista will still block any changes it considers dangerous.

Prompt for credentials. Use this to toughen security on your PC by requiring a password each time. The UAC prompt still appears, but the user can't click **Continue** if she doesn't know the password.

If you're an administrator who's setting up this PC for someone else to use, your best course of action is to give that person a *standard* account. Then, in the Local Security Policy editor, set the **User Account Control: Behavior of the elevation prompt for standard users** option to **Prompt for credentials**.

Prompt for consent. This is the default in Windows Vista. The UAC prompt appears every time an application requests administrator-level access, but all you have to do is click **Continue** to permit the action.

As you've probably noticed, there are at least nine different settings for UAC here, and while most are fairly self-explanatory, there are a few that deserve special attention.

If you're using the built-in Administrator account described in "Log In As the Administrator," later in this chapter, then you won't ever see UAC prompts by default. You can change this with the **User Account Control: Admin Approval Mode for the Built-in Administrator account** setting.

Windows Vista tries to automatically elevate most software installers to administrator-level, which may not be such a great idea if you want to cut your odds of a spyware infestation on your PC. If you've turned off the UAC prompt as described above, then set the **User Account Control: Detect application installations and prompt for elevation** option to **Disabled**. Otherwise, if you've chosen to leave UAC prompts intact, you may want to set the **User Account Control: Only elevate executables that are signed and validated** option to **Enabled**.

Finally, see the "File and Registry Virtualization Explained" sidebar, next, for details on the **User Account Control: Virtualizes file and registry write**

Users and Security

failures to per-user locations setting, and an explanation of something else that can break UAC-unaware programs.

File and Registry Virtualization Explained

As described in this chapter's "Control User Account Control" section, Vista's UAC feature is designed to prevent changes to operating system folders like *Program Files*, as well as protected areas of the Registry. If a program wasn't designed with UAC in mind, it won't request elevation to administrator-level access, and its attempt to, say, write to its own application folder in *Program Files* will fail.

Microsoft had to come up with a compromise that would allow some of these older programs to work.

That compromise is *virtualization*, a system that redirects older (*legacy*, as Microsoft puts it) applications to special, protected areas of your hard disk and Registry. So, if a program with an auto-update feature tries to write files to *C:\Program Files\Acme Update\newversion.dll*, Windows will instead send it to *C:\Users\{your_username}\AppData\Local\VirtualStore\Program Files\ Acme Update\newversion.dll*.

Likewise, if a program tries to make a change to the Registry, in the HKEY_LOCAL_ MACHINE\Software\Acme key, the change will be made instead to the HKEY_ CURRENT_USER\Software\Classes\VirtualStore\MACHINE\Software\Acme key.

By default, your *Program Files* and *Windows* folders, and most of their subfolders, are protected, as well as almost all of the HKEY_LOCAL_MACHINE\ Software branch in the Registry. UAC does not protect a user's own folder *C: \Users\{your_username}*, nor does it lock out changes to the HKEY_CURRENT_ USER\Software branch of the Registry.

To turn virtualization off, set the **User Account Control: Virtualizes file and registry write failures to per-user locations** option in the Local Security Policy editor to **Disabled**. But keep in mind that turning off virtualization won't, in itself, permit older applications to write in these protected areas; instead, it will cause more of your older programs to stop functioning, since Windows will no longer give them a safe place to play.

To see which of your running programs are subject to virtualization, right-click an empty area of your taskbar and select **Task Manager**. Choose the **Processes** tab, and then go to **View → Select Columns**. Turn on the **Virtualization** column, and then click **OK**. Now, in the **Processes** list, you'll see that some programs—particularly the older ones—have virtualization set to **Enabled**, as do *explorer.exe* and *iexplore.exe* (because of the danger of add-ons). UAC-aware programs will have virtualization set to **Disabled**, and programs already running as the administrator will have it set to **Not Allowed**.

Logon and Profile Options

Here's the dilemma: you've set up multiple user accounts on a machine, and you've gone the extra mile to ensure that your data is properly protected by configuring permissions and employing encryption. Now you find Windows so locked-down that you can't do anything without having to enter a password first. Fortunately, you can streamline the logon process to suit your needs and tolerance for cumbersome logon procedures, or use some lesser-known features to lock it down even further.

Hide the List of User Accounts

The friendly Welcome screen is the default interface you see when you log on to Windows Vista.

Back in the old days, we didn't have any fancy pictures to click; we actually had to type our usernames *and* passwords to log on. In the snow. Uphill, both ways.

If you long for those simpler times, or perhaps if you just realize that it's wise *not* to show a list of all the user accounts on a PC, you can opt for a more retro-style login box.

Unfortunately, Microsoft removed the bare-bones, "classic" Windows NT-style logon window that was present even in Windows XP, but there is an alternative. To get a login screen with both username and password fields, albeit with a look reminiscent of Vista's Welcome screen, follow these steps:

1. Open the Start menu **Search** box, type secpol.msc, and press **Enter** to display the Local Security Policy editor. (This tool is only available in the Windows Vista Business and Ultimate editions.)

2. Expand the **Local Policies** branch and click the **Security Options** folder.

3. In the right pane, double-click the **Interactive logon: Do not display last user name** option, select **Enabled**, and click **OK**.

4. Close the Local Security Policy window when you're done; the change will take effect the next time you log in.

Keep in mind that if your goal is to hide the list of user accounts from everyone but you, then this is only part of the solution. Sure, this hides the user list from passersby, but anyone with an administrator account on the PC could log in and open the User Accounts window to view other users on the system. (Of course, anyone could also re-enable the Welcome screen, or even create new accounts.) So, to keep your user list hidden, use standard user accounts for all other users.

Users and Security

Log In Automatically

If you assign a password to your account, or if you add a second user account in Control Panel, Vista will show you the Welcome screen when Windows first starts.

But it's never a good idea to have any accounts on your system set up without passwords, not so much because someone could break in to your computer while sitting at your desk, but because if you're connected to a network or the Internet, an account—any account—without a password is a big security hole. See "Close Vista's Backdoors," in Chapter 7, for more information.

The problem with setting up a password, however, is that Windows will then prompt you for the password every time you turn on your computer, which can be a pain if you're the only person who uses the machine. Fortunately, there is a rather easy way to password-protect your computer and not be bothered with the Welcome screen.

1. Open the alternate User Accounts window (described at the beginning of this chapter) by opening the Start menu, typing control userpasswords2 in the **Search** box, and pressing **Enter**.

2. Select from the list the username you'd like to be your primary login, and then turn off the **Users must enter a username and password to use this computer** option.

3. The Automatically Log On dialog will appear, prompting you to enter (and confirm) the password for the selected user.

4. Click **OK** when you're done. The change will take effect the next time you restart your computer.

Note that these steps won't affect your ability to log out and then log in to another user account (see the next topic if that's what you're after). Furthermore, this is not a temporary setting; if you log out and then log back in, you'll be logged in automatically the next time you restart Windows.

Prevent users from bypassing the automatic login

Automatic logins are also good for machines you wish to use in public environments (typically called "kiosks"), but you'll want to take steps to ensure that a visitor can't log in to a more privileged account. There are two ways for a user to skip the automatic login and log in to another user account:

- Hold the **Shift** key while Windows is logging in.
- Once Windows has logged in, log out by selecting **Log Off** from the Start menu or pressing **Ctrl-Alt-Del** and selecting **Log Off**.

To eliminate both of these backdoors, follow these steps:

1. Open the Registry Editor (discussed in Chapter 3).
2. Expand the branches to `HKEY_LOCAL_MACHINE\SOFTWARE\Microsoft\Windows NT\CurrentVersion\Winlogon`. (Note the `Windows NT` branch here, as opposed to the more common `Windows` branch.)
3. Create a new string value here by going to **Edit → New → String Value**, and name the new value `IgnoreShiftOverride`. Double-click the new value, type 1 for its value data, and click **OK**. (This disables the **Shift** key during the automatic login.)
4. Next, create a new DWORD value in this same key by going to **Edit → New → DWORD (32-bit) Value**, and name the new value `ForceAutoLogon`. Double-click the new value, type 1 for its value data, and click **OK**. (This automatically logs back in if the user tries to log out.)
5. Close the Registry Editor when you're done. The change will take effect immediately.

To remove either or both of these restrictions, just delete the corresponding Registry values.

Limit automatic logins

It's possible to limit the automatic login feature, so that the Log On dialog (or Welcome screen) reappears after a specified number of boots:

1. Open the Registry Editor (discussed in Chapter 3).
2. Expand the branches to `HKEY_LOCAL_MACHINE\SOFTWARE\Microsoft\Windows NT\CurrentVersion\Winlogon`. (Note the `Windows NT` branch here, as opposed to the more common `Windows` branch.)
3. Create a new DWORD value here by going to **Edit → New → DWORD (32-bit) Value**, and type `AutoLogonCount` for the name of the new value.
4. Double-click the new `AutoLogonCount` value, and type the number of system boots for which you'd like the automatic login to remain active.

Every successive time Windows starts, it will decrease this value by one. When the value is zero, the username and password entered at the beginning of this topic are forgotten, and the `AutoLogonCount` value is removed.

Force passwords to expire

Treat your password like your toothbrush.
Don't let anybody else use it, and get a new
one every six months.
—Clifford Stoll

If you have the Business or Ultimate edition of Vista, you can have Windows force you to routinely change your password.

Open the Local Users and Groups manager (in the Start menu **Search** box, type lusrmgr.msc), and then open the **Users** folder. Double-click your username, turn off the **Password never expires** option, and click **OK**. (Do the same for any other accounts here, if needed.) When you're done, close the Local Users and Groups manager.

Next, open the Local Security Policy editor (in the Start menu, type secpol. msc) and expand the branches to Account Policies\Password Policy. On the right, double-click **Maximum password age** and enter the amount of time before Windows expires your password. (To take Cliff Stoll's advice, enter 182 days.) Close the Local Security Policy editor; the change takes effect the next time you log in.

Reset a Forgotten Administrator Password

Forgot your password? No problem. There are two ways to get into your PC: the easy way and the hard way.

If there are any other administrator-level accounts on your PC, the easy way is to log in to one of those accounts, open the User Accounts page in Control Panel, and change your password there.

If yours is the only administrator account, you'll have to reset your password the hard way. (This won't work if your drive is protected by BitLocker Drive Encryption, described earlier in this chapter.) Start by downloading the free Trinity Rescue Kit from *http://www.trinityhome.org/*, and burn the ISO image to a blank CD.

Next, boot your PC with the Trinity Rescue Kit disc, which is essentially a bootable Linux CD. At the prompt, type

```
winpass -u username
```

where *username* is your login name. The software will then search your hard disk for Windows installations, display a list of any it finds, and ask you to choose one.

At this point you'll be asked to either provide a new password or type merely * (asterisk) to choose a blank password. Confirm that you wish to change the password, and you'll be sent back to the terminal prompt when it's done.

Now, restart your PC to log in to your newly unlocked Windows account.

Prevent Users from Shutting Down

Among the restrictions you may want to impose on others who use your computer is that of shutting down Windows. For instance, if you're logging in remotely, as described in "Control Your PC Remotely" in Chapter 7, you'll want to make sure that your PC is always on. Or, if you're setting up a system to be used by the public, you won't want to allow anyone to shut down or reboot the system in an effort to compromise it. Here's how to do it:

1. Open the Registry Editor (discussed in Chapter 3).

2. Expand the branches to `HKEY_CURRENT_USER\Software\Microsoft\Windows\CurrentVersion\Policies\Explorer`.

3. Create a new DWORD value by going to **Edit → New → DWORD (32-bit) Value**, and type `NoClose` for its name.

4. Double-click the new `NoClose` value and type 1 for its data.

5. Close the Registry Editor when you're done. You'll need to restart Windows for this change to take effect.

Keep in mind that this isn't a bulletproof solution. For instance, anyone will be able to shut down Windows by pressing **Ctrl-Alt-Del** and clicking **Shut Down** there. Also, someone with ready access to your computer's on/off switch, reset button, or power cord will be able to circumvent this restriction. At the very least, though, it'll provide some reasonable assurance that your PC will remain powered on.

Log In As the Administrator

When you first install Windows Vista, Setup walks you through the process of setting up a user account for yourself by asking for your name and then having you choose a picture. One of the requirements of the username is that it not be "Administrator."

The account named *Administrator* is a built-in account, mostly as a holdover from earlier versions of Windows. For more intents and purposes, it's pretty much the same as any other administrator-level account, except that it *can* have the name "Administrator." So, what's the point?

Users and Security

Truth is, there's not much point for most users. But if you have a network with PCs running older versions of Windows, like XP or 2000, and any of them are using the Administrator account, you may need enable the Administrator account on your own PC to overcome a peculiarity in the way that Windows handles usernames and passwords for folders shared over a network.

Or, maybe you just like the name.

Either way, here's how you do it:

1. Open the Start menu, type `lusrmgr.msc` in the **Search** box, and press **Enter** to start the Local Users and Groups tool described at the beginning of this chapter.

2. In the left pane, select **Users**.

3. In the middle pane, double-click **Administrator**.

4. Turn off the **Account is disabled** option, and click **OK**.

5. Right-click **Administrator** and select **Set Password**.

6. Choose a password for the new account, type it into both boxes, and click **OK**.

7. Close the Local Users and Groups window when you're done.

8. Log out of your current session, and then log in as Administrator. If the Administrator account doesn't show up on the Welcome screen, you may need to follow the steps in "Hide the List of User Accounts," earlier in this chapter. But once you log in as Administrator a few times, it should start appearing on the standard Welcome screen.

Despite the fact that the Administrator account is turned off by default, it's perfectly acceptable to use it as your primary login. You may wish to do this for no other reason than you've simply gotten tired of seeing your name in huge, blazing letters in the Start menu.

 Two caveats: first, in each successive version of Windows since Windows 2000, Microsoft has gone to greater lengths to discourage use of the Administrator account, which may complicate your efforts to upgrade to Vista's successor. Second, one of the reasons Microsoft has tried to get rid of the Administrator account is that having a common username (and Administrator would be the most common) might be seen as a security risk, and it could make it easier for someone to break in to your PC.

If you've already started using the Administrator account, and you want to change the name of your account without creating and breaking in a brand-new account, then you can rename it. If you're using Windows Vista Business or Ultimate, open the Local Security Policy window (*secpol.msc*), go to **Local Policies → Security Options**, and double-click the **Accounts: Rename administrator account** entry in the right pane.

If you're using Vista Home Basic and you don't have access to the Local Users and Groups window, you can enable the Administrator account from the Command Prompt. First, open a Command Prompt window in administrator mode (explained earlier in this chapter) and at the prompt, type:

```
net user Administrator/active:yes
```

and press **Enter**. Close the Command Prompt window and follow step 8, previously, to complete the process.

If all you want is a more generic-sounding username, see "Rename Your Profile Folder," later in this chapter.

Customize the Welcome Screen Background

Unless you've opted to log in automatically (described earlier), you'll see the Welcome screen every time you turn on your PC (not to mention every time you shut down). Why not dress it up a bit with some custom wallpaper?

Open Windows Explorer and navigate to your *Windows\System32* folder. Take ownership of the *imageres.dll* file, as described in "Inheritance and ownership," earlier in this chapter, and then set the permissions to **Full Control** for your user account. When that's done, create two copies of the file in the *Windows\System32* folder, naming them *imageres-new.dll* and *imageres-old.dll*.

Next, download and install the XN Resource Editor, freely available at *http://www.wilsonc.demon.co.uk/d10resourceeditor.htm*. Open the XN tool and select **View → Options**. From the **Choose which parser to use** list, select **XN Resource Editor internal resource parser**, and click **OK**.

Then from the **File** menu, select **Open**, find *imageres-new.dll*, and open the file. On the left, you'll see the various graphical and user-interface resources in the file organized into a collapsible tree; expand the **IMAGE** branch and then open one of the numbered folders therein. Inside each numbered folder is a single entry representing a different resolution of the stock Welcome screen background image. Select an entry to view the image along with its dimensions (shown in the gray box at the top of the window). Choose the version corresponding to your PC's current display resolution; if you don't know the current resolution, open the Personalize page in Control Panel and click the **Display Settings** link.

Users and Security

You can edit the image right in XN Resource Editor, but you'll likely want to grab a photo from somewhere else. Any portrait-oriented photo will do, provided it has exactly the same pixel dimensions as the one it's replacing. If your photo is too big, use your favorite image editor to shrink and crop it to size; if it's too small, just pad it with black space. When you're ready, just copy your new image to the clipboard (**Ctrl-C**), and then return to XN and press **Ctrl-V** to paste it over the selected image. (Resist the urge to use any of the options in the **Resource** menu, lest you render the file unusable.) Save the file and close XN when you're done.

The last step is to replace the *imageres.dll* file with the one you've modified, but since it's in use, Windows won't let you touch it. To get around this, restart Windows, press **F8** to show the Advanced Boot Options menu (as described in "What to Do When Windows Won't Start," in Chapter 6), and select **Safe Mode with Command Prompt**. When the Command Prompt appears, click inside the window and type:

```
copy imageres-new.dll imageres.dll
```

When prompted, answer **Y** to confirm that you'd like to replace the file. When you're done, type exit to close the Command Prompt. (If Windows doesn't restart at this point, press **Ctrl-Alt-Del**, click the arrow next to the red button on the bottom-right of the screen, and select **Restart**.)

When the Welcome screen appears, your new wallpaper should be plastered all over the background. If it isn't, you likely updated the wrong dimension, or you weren't successful in replacing the original *imageres.dll* file.

 If Windows won't start, or if you don't like your change, you can restore the original file by returning to the Safe Mode with Command Prompt, as just described, and typing copy imageres-old.dll imageres.dll.

Customize the Default Profile for New Users

Have a lot of user accounts to create, and don't want to waste hours customizing each one? Here's a simple way to customize a single account and then use it as the default for all new user accounts on your PC.

1. From an administrator-level account, use the User Accounts window in Control Panel to create a new account on your PC.

2. Log off and then log on to the new account.

3. Make all the changes you like. See Chapter 2 for some Windows Explorer settings that might be useful in this situation.

4. When you're done, log off and then log back in to your normal, administrator-level account.

5. If you haven't done so already, use the Folder Options window in Control Panel to show hidden files and folders in Windows Explorer, as explained in Chapter 2.

6. Next, open the System window in Control Panel and click the **Advanced system settings** link on the left side.

7. Under the **Advanced** tab, in the **User Profiles** section, click **Settings**.

8. Highlight the user account you just created and customized, and click **Copy To**.

9. In the Copy To window, click **Browse**, select the *C:\Users\Default User* folder, and click **OK**.

10. Click **OK** and then answer **Yes** to initiate the copy. Windows will delete the contents of the *Default User* folder, replacing them with the ones you've just customized.

When it's done, the new settings you've created will be in place to be used as the template for new user accounts. If you like, you can go ahead and delete the temporary account you created in the first step.

Rename Your Profile Folder

If you've ever uploaded a file to a web site or used a peer-to-peer file sharing program (see Chapter 6), you've probably noticed that it's possible in some circumstances for others to see the full path of the files you're sharing. (This doesn't apply to the file sharing system discussed later in this chapter, thankfully.)

This means that if you upload the file *personal.doc* to a web site, the web site might be able to record that the full path of the file is actually:

C:\Users\Guy Q. Incognito\Documents\Some stuff of mine\personal.doc

And there it is: your full name.

Now, you can't fix this by renaming your account with the User Accounts window in Control Panel. But you can change the location of your profile folder *without* renaming your account; here's how:

1. Open Windows Explorer, and navigate to *C:\Users*. Create a new, empty folder here. This will be your new home folder, so name it whatever you like.

2. Next, use the User Accounts window in Control Panel to create a new, temporary, administrator account on your PC.

Users and Security

3. Log off and then log on to the new account.

4. Open the System window in Control Panel and click the **Advanced system settings** link on the left side.

5. Under the **Advanced** tab, in the **User Profiles** section, click **Settings**.

6. Highlight your user account (the old one you want to move) and click **Copy To**.

7. In the Copy To window, click **Browse**, select the folder in *C:\Users* you created in the first step, and click **OK**.

8. Click **OK** again and then answer **Yes** to initiate the copy.

9. Now, use the Folder Options window in Control Panel to show hidden files and folders in Windows Explorer, as explained in Chapter 2.

10. Open Windows Explorer, and navigate to your old home folder (e.g., *C:\Users/Guy Q. Incognito*).

11. Press **Ctrl-A** to select everything in your home folder, and then, holding the **Ctrl** button, drag the selected files into the new location. When Windows asks whether you want to replace a file that already exists, turn on the **Do this for the next *x* conflicts** option, and then click **Don't copy**.

12. When it's done, open the Start menu, type `lusrmgr.msc` in the **Search** box, and press **Enter** to start the Local Users and Groups tool described at the beginning of this chapter.

13. In the left pane, select **Users**.

14. In the middle pane, double-click your username, and then choose the **Profile** tab.

15. In the **Home folder** section, select **Local path**, and in the **Local path** field, type or paste the full path of the new folder you created in step 2. (Ignore the **User profile** section at the top of this window.)

16. Click **OK** and then close the Local Users and Groups window when you're done.

17. Log out of the temporary account and log back in to your real account.

18. Once you've confirmed everything is working, open Windows Explorer again and delete the old home folder from *C:\Users*.

Change the Locations of Personal Folders

Every user account on your system has its own home folder, stored, by default, in *C:\Users*. In this folder are such special user folders as *Desktop*, *Send To*, *Start Menu*, *Documents*, and *Application Data*, among others.

Files placed in the *Desktop* folder appear as icons on the user's desktop, shortcuts placed in the *Start Menu* folder appear as Start menu items, and so on. This arrangement lets each user have her own desktop, Start menu, etc.

There's also an *All Users* folder, used, for example, to store icons that appear on all users' desktops. Likewise, the *Default User* folder is a template of sorts, containing files and settings copied for each newly created user. All in all, the use of these folders is pretty self-explanatory.

 See "Back Up the Registry," in Chapter 3, for more information on the *NTUSER.DAT* file found in each user folder.

You can change the default locations for any user's special folders, but the process is different for different folder types:

Home folder
> To change the location of any user's home folder, open the Local Users and Groups window (*lusrmgr.msc*, described at the beginning of this chapter). Open the **Users** category, double-click a user, and choose the **Profile** tab.

Documents, Send To, etc.
> To change the location of any system folder in a user's home folder, such as the *Documents* folder or the *Send To* folder, you must be logged in as that user. Start TweakUI, open the **My Computer** category branch, select **Special Folders**, and choose the folder to relocate from the **Folder** list. Note that this only changes the place that Windows looks for the associated files; you'll have to create the folder and place the appropriate files in it yourself.
>
> For folders not listed in TweakUI, you'll need to edit the Registry. Most user folders are specified in these two Registry keys:
>
> ```
> HKEY_CURRENT_USER\Software\Microsoft\Windows\CurrentVersion\
>         Explorer\Shell Folders
> HKEY_CURRENT_USER\Software\Microsoft\Windows\CurrentVersion\
>         Explorer\User Shell Folders
> ```
>
> One of the exceptions is the *Application Data* folder, which is defined by the `DefaultDir` value in:
>
> ```
> HKEY_CURRENT_USER\Software\Microsoft\Windows\CurrentVersion\
>         ProfileReconciliation\AppData
> ```
>
> You'll need to log out and then log back in for any of these changes to take effect.

Users and Security

Program Files

The *Program Files* and *Common Files* folders (shared by all users) are both defined in:

HKEY_LOCAL_MACHINE\SOFTWARE\Microsoft\Windows\CurrentVersion

For *Program Files*, you'll need to change both the ProgramFilesDir and ProgramFilesPath values; for *Common Files*, just change the CommonFilesDir value.

 When relocating system folders, keep in mind that there can be hundreds of references to them throughout the Registry, especially *Program Files* and *Common Files*. You'll probably need to use a program like Registry Search and Replace (available at *http://www.annoyances.org*) to easily get them all.

Share Files and Printers

There are so many things you can do with even a basic network; just a few of them are described in Chapter 7. But one of the best uses for the connection between the PCs in your office or home is to exchange data.

In Windows Vista, this is a two-step process. First, you share a folder on one PC, and then someone on another PC reads or even modifies the files in that shared folder. Windows uses the user account system discussed throughout this chapter to protect your shared data from prying eyes, and the permission system to give you the power to determine exactly what others can and can't do with your shared files.

Civilized, isn't it?

Sharing folders is for more than just sending stuff from one PC to another, too. Multiple users can collaborate on a project by working on the same files, and avoid having several versions of each document floating around. (There are limits, of course; for instance, you can't modify a Word document if someone else currently has it open. But database programs like Microsoft Access let multiple users read and write to the same file simultaneously under certain circumstances.)

Naturally the PC hosting the shared folder must be powered on for others to be able to access the folder, but the person who shared the files doesn't necessarily have to be logged in.

But here's the rub: the defaults in Windows Vista could allow anyone on your network to read your files, yet permit nobody to modify them. It's just a matter of knowing where the vulnerabilities are and which buttons to click.

Whenever you share a folder, you are essentially opening a backdoor to your computer, potentially allowing access to sensitive data. It's important to keep security in mind at all times, especially if you're connected to the Internet. Otherwise, you may be unwittingly exposing your personal data to intruders looking for anything they can use and abuse. Furthermore, a nonsecure system is more vulnerable to viruses, Trojan horses, and other malicious programs. This doesn't mean that you shouldn't use file sharing, just that you'll want to use some common sense if you do.

Share a Folder

Sharing resources is easy, but you'll need to take care of a few things first.

Before you share any resources on your PC, your account must have a password. If you haven't done so already, open the User Accounts window in Control Panel and click **Create a password**.

Now, any user account on your PC could be used as a backdoor to gain access to your data, which is why every account should have a password. To have Windows enforce passwords for your administrator-level accounts, open Parental Controls in Control Panel. If you see a yellow box that says **One or more administrator accounts do not have a password**, click the box. On the Ensure Administrator Passwords page, turn on the **Force all administrator accounts to set a password at logon** option, and then click **OK**.

Next, open the Network and Sharing Center in Control Panel, shown in Figure 8-15, and make sure the network type (just above **Access**) is set to **Private network**. If it isn't, or if the **File sharing** option below is **Off**, click the **Customize** link on the right side, select **Private**, and then click **Next**. When you're done, **Network discovery** should be set to either **On** or **Custom**, and **File sharing** should be **On**.

Vista's default sharing mechanism leaves a lot to be desired, so go ahead and change it. In Control Panel, open Folder Options, and choose the **View** tab. At the bottom of the **Advanced settings** list, turn off the **Use Sharing Wizard** option and then click **OK**.

Finally, if you don't already know it, determine the name of your PC, as described in the upcoming "What's My PC's Name?" sidebar.

Now you're ready to share.

Figure 8-15. The Network and Sharing Center window must be set to "Private network" before you can share any folders or printers

---

What's My PC's Name?

Your PC's name is the name others see when they access your shared folders over the network, so make it a good one.

In Control Panel, open System, click the **Advanced system settings** link on the left, and then choose the **Computer Name** tab. Ignore the **Computer description** field and instead look at the **Full computer name** entry immediately beneath it: this is your PC's name.

Each computer on your local network must have a different name, but they all must have the same **Workgroup** name. If you need to rename your PC or modify the Workgroup name, click the **Change** button (don't use the **Network ID** button).

When you're done, you may have to restart Windows for any changes to take effect.

To share a folder with others on your network, simply right-click its icon and select **Share** (or select **Properties** and choose the **Sharing** tab), and then click **Advanced Sharing** (Figure 8-16).

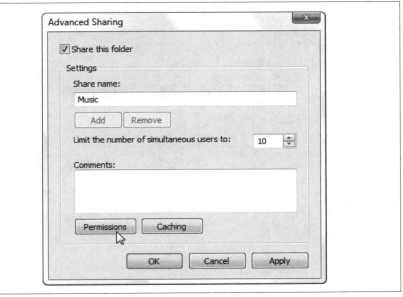

Figure 8-16. Use the Advanced Sharing window to safely share your folders and allow other users to modify the files therein (at your discretion)

Turn on the **Share this folder** option to start sharing the selected folder and all of its contents. The **Share name** is the name under which the folder will be accessed from other computers; although the name can be anything, it usually makes sense to leave the default, which is the same as the name of the folder.

A drive can be shared as easily as any folder, but it's not necessarily a good idea. First of all, conventional wisdom holds that you should only share folders you want made public, and keep everything else unshared. Second, Windows may already be sharing your *entire drive* without your knowledge, and it's in your best interest to stop it. See "Turn Off Administrative Shares," later in this chapter, for details.

But wait! You're not done yet. Click the **Permissions** button to open the Permissions window shown in Figure 8-17. Here, notice that the *Everyone* group (which is indeed everyone) has **Read** access, yet nobody has **Change** or **Full Control** access. This is probably not what you want.

So, highlight the **Everyone** entry in the **Group or user names** box and click **Remove**. Then, click **Add**, type your own username in the **Enter the object names to select** box, and click **OK**.

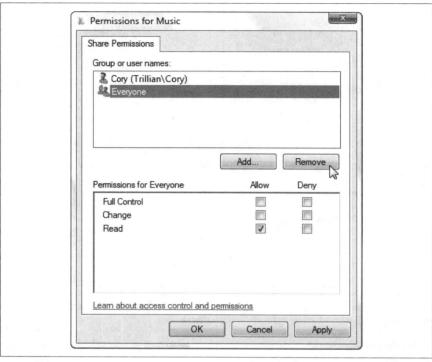

Figure 8-17. To protect your data, you should set the permissions for every folder you share

Next, highlight the name you just added in the **Group or user names** box, and below, click the checkbox in the **Allow** column for each right you'd like to grant. If you want a remote user to be able to read, write, and delete files in the folder, click the **Allow** checkbox next to **Full Control**.

Now, this means that anyone who tries to access your shared folder will need both your username and your password. If you don't want to share this information with anyone else on your network, you'll need to make another user account on your PC.

Say across the hall in your home, your daughter has a PC on your network and her username is *Willow*. If you create an account on your own PC named *Willow* and assign it the same password your daughter uses, she'll be able to access the files in this folder without a login at all. (See the next section if you have two PCs with the same username, yet different passwords.)

So, once you've created the new account, return to the Permissions window (Figure 8-17), click **Add**, type the name of the new account (e.g., Willow), and click **OK**.

When you're done adding users, click **OK** and then **OK** again to close the Advanced Sharing and Properties windows, respectively. Voilà; a tiny two-person insignia appears on the folder's icon, which means the folder is shared and ready to be used.

Access a Shared Folder Remotely

As soon as a folder or drive has been shared, it can be accessed from another PC on your local network. Just open Windows Explorer and navigate to the *Network* folder in the tree.

The *Network* folder will show all the PCs (discoverable PCs, that is) on your local network. If it doesn't, press **F5** to refresh the window; if you see the green progress bar moving slowly from left to right at the top of the window, be patient.

Or not. If the PC you want isn't in the list, you don't have to sit around and wait for it to magically appear. Just click the address bar, erase the text that's there, type two backslashes (\\) followed by the PC's name (as in Figure 8-18), and press **Enter**.

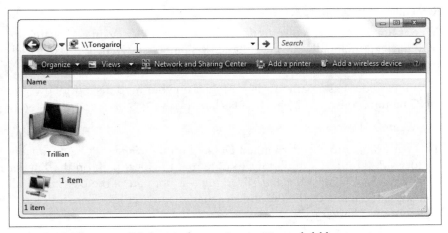

Figure 8-18. If a remote PC doesn't show up in your Network folder, type two backslashes in Windows Explorer's address bar, followed by the remote PC's name

One reason why another PC may not show up in the *Network* folder is if it's not in the same *Workgroup* as your PC; see the "What's My PC's Name?" sidebar, in the previous section, for details. Of course, there are other reasons why a PC may not show up; it may not be turned on, it may not be connected to the network, it may not be discoverable (see the previous section), or your network may be down. See Chapter 7 for network troubleshooting topics.

Users and Security

Once you see the remote PC in the *Network* folder, double-click it to see its shared resources. Here, you should see an entry for each shared folder and printer on that PC; just open the resource to see what's inside, and then access those files as though they were on your own hard disk.

Force a Login Box for a Remote Folder

If there's an account on a remote machine with the same username as the one you're using, Vista won't give you the opportunity to log in as a different user, even if it's necessary to access the resource.

To get around this, click the shared folder and select **Map Network Drive** and then click the **different user name** link. Fill out the fields, and click **OK** and then **Finish** when you're ready.

At this point, you'll see a new drive letter appear in Windows Explorer, which you can use to access the remote folder. Unfortunately, this is the only way to force a login box to appear.

Remember remote shared folders

It's not uncommon to return to the same remote folder again and again. So, why navigate manually through the slow-as-molasses *Network* folder each time?

A remote folder has a path just like a folder on your hard disk; it follows the UNC naming convention, which looks like this:

> *Xander**Desktop*

This path points to a folder named *Desktop* on the *Xander* PC (presumably Xander's desktop). It's important to note that the local path on the Xander PC—namely, *C:\Users\Alexander\Desktop*—is not part of the UNC path; all you see is the name of the PC and the share name, set in "Share a Folder," earlier in this chapter.

Open the *Zeppo* folder on Xander's desktop, and the path changes to:

> *Xander**Desktop**Zeppo*

Not only does this mean that you can quickly get to a remote path by typing, but it means that you can create shortcuts to remote paths to get back even quicker. Just drag the icon on the left side of Windows Explorer's address bar onto your desktop to create the shortcut.

Of course, if Xander ever renames his PC, or if he ever stops sharing the *Desktop* folder, then the shortcut will stop working.

Another way to access frequently used remote shares is with the old-school drive-mapping approach explained in the "Map a Network Drive" sidebar, next.

Map a Network Drive

In most cases, you'll want to access remote folders through the *Network* folder, as described in "Access a Shared Folder Remotely," earlier in this chapter. However, there's another system in place in Windows Vista, included mostly as a holdover from years past.

In Windows Explorer, navigate to the *Network* folder. Open a remote PC, right-click a shared folder, and select **Map Network Drive**. In the window that appears, select a free drive letter from the list, turn on the **Reconnect at logon** option (if you think you'll use this again), and click **Finish** when you're done.

A new drive will appear in the Computer branch of the folder tree in Windows Explorer, and you can use it to get to the files contained therein.

There are a few reasons why you might want to do this. First, the feature is there to provide compatibility with old—and I mean *old*—applications that don't understand UNC paths (e.g., *Xander**Desktop*). Of course, you may encounter a new program that doesn't work reliably with UNC paths, and this is a perfectly cromulent workaround.

Second, network drives make for shorter paths. Map drive *N:* to *Xander*\ *Desktop*, and the file *Xander**Desktop**carrots.xlsx* can now be found at *N:*\ *carrots.xlsx*. The latter is certainly easier to type, which is a real concern when working with the Command Prompt.

Turn Off Administrative Shares

In a world where we must concern ourselves with spyware, phishing emails, and clowns trying to break in to our wireless networks, it's almost reassuring when Windows itself is the security threat. Well, not so much reassuring as *infuriating*.

It turns out that every copy of Vista has a backdoor that could permit someone else to read any file on your PC, and that vulnerability exists on Windows 2000 and XP PCs, too.

Users and Security

By default, every hard disk on your PC is shared. That's right, the whole thing.

What's worse is that the shares are hidden, which means they don't show up in the *Network* folder in Windows Explorer, and thus most users don't know their drives are being shared.

You can hide any network share by adding the $ character to the end of the share name, like this: Desktop$. Then, to access the share, type the UNC path into Windows Explorer's address bar (e.g., \\Xander\Desktop$) and press **Enter** to open it.

To test your PC, open Windows Explorer and type the name of your own PC into the address bar, followed by the administrative share name for drive C:, like this:

> *your_pc_name*\c$

and then press **Enter**. If you see the contents of your hard disk, then administrative shares are enabled on your PC.

Now, it's not just a matter of unsharing the drives; you've got to disable the mechanism that shares them automatically each time your PC starts. If administrative shares are enabled on your PC, here's how to turn them off:

1. Open the Registry Editor (see Chapter 3).

2. Expand the branches to HKEY_LOCAL_MACHINE\SYSTEM\CurrentControlSet\ Services\lanmanserver\parameters.

3. In the right pane, double-click the AutoShareServer value, type 0 in the **Value data** field, and click **OK**. (If AutoShareServer isn't there, go to **Edit → New → DWORD (32-bit) Value** to create a new DWORD value by that name.)

4. Next, double-click the AutoShareWks value, type 0 in the **Value data** field, and click **OK**. (Again, create the value if it's not there.)

5. Close the Registry Editor when you're done.

6. Next, open the Start menu, type compmgmt.msc into the **Search** box and press **Enter** to fire up the Computer Management tool.

7. Expand the **System Tools** branch on the left, then expand **Shared Folders** underneath that, and then click the **Shares** folder.

   Here, you'll see a list of all the shared folders on your PC, whether they're hidden or not. Even if you're not hunting down administrative shares, this is a handy tool to keep tabs on your shared resources.

8. To manually remove the administrative shares, right-click each one (e.g., **C$**, **D$**, **E$**) and select **Stop Sharing**. Answer **Yes** to both prompts.

Go ahead and remove any hidden share you want (anything with a dollar-sign suffix in the name), with the following three exceptions:

- **IPC$**, which stands for Inter-Process Communication, is used for remote administration of your computer, something very few people need outside of a corporate environment. Although it has been proven that the *IPC$* share can be exploited, the only way to disable it permanently is to turn off file sharing altogether. You can stop sharing IPC$ temporarily, but Windows will recreate the share the next time you restart.

- **print$** is used to exchange printer driver files when you share a printer. You should leave this share intact.

- **wwwroot$** will be present if Microsoft's Internet Information Server (IIS) software is installed. Leave this share intact if you want to use your computer as a web server or a web software development platform.

9. When you're done, restart Windows, then reopen the Computer Management tool to make sure the administrative shares are gone for good.

The preceeding solution is sometimes met with skepticism among those who don't see administrative shares as a security threat. After all, these hidden shares are there for legitimate reasons; namely, to allow network administrators to install software, run Disk Defragmenter, access the Registry, or perform other maintenance on a PC remotely.

Administrative shares are required for the Previous Versions feature to work, as described in "Go Back in Time with Restore Points and Shadow Copies," in Chapter 6. Turn off administrative shares, and the **Previous Versions** tab of any file's Properties window will be empty.

If you're on the fence, go to another PC on your network and perform a little experiment. Type the UNC path from the beginning of this section into Windows Explorer's address bar, and press **Enter** to see what happens.

Now, consider that user accounts in Vista don't have passwords by default, and remember that Windows passwords can be cracked with a variety of methods, and you'll see the problem. Unless your PC is in a corporate environment and you need to use remote administration, you have nothing to gain by leaving this backdoor open—and everything to lose.

Share a Printer

As soon as you share a printer, anyone on your local network can print to it.

Sharing a printer is, for the most part, just like sharing a folder. The difference is that security and permissions aren't particularly important. What's more, Windows Vista sometimes lets you connect to a remote printer even if it isn't shared, and Vista even often connects shared printers automatically.

Here's how to do it by hand. In Control Panel, open the *Printers* folder. Right-click the printer you want to share, and select **Sharing**. Turn on the **Share this printer** option (see Figure 8-19) and click **OK**.

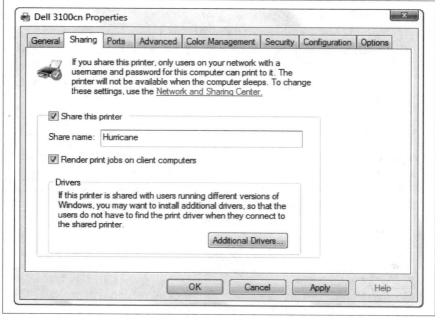

Figure 8-19. You can share a printer in much the same way as sharing a folder

Before other PCs on your network can print, they must be set up. Again, Vista sometimes does this automatically, but if not, here's how to do it by hand:

1. Open Windows Explorer and navigate to the *Network* folder.

2. Double-click the PC to which the printer is physically connected. (If the printer is a network printer and not connected to any PC, see "Use a Print Server Without Software," next.)

3. In the PC's *Network* folder, open the *Printers* folder.

4. Double-click the printer to install the driver on your PC.

5. Open the *Printers* folder in Control Panel to see whether the new printer has shown up. Right-click the printer, select **Properties**, and under the **General** tab, click **Print Test Page** to try it out.

If you have a lot of PCs on your network (or a lot of printers) and you're not sure where each one is connected, there's another way to set up a remote printer:

1. Open the *Printers* folder in Control Panel, and click the **Add a printer** button on the toolbar.

2. In the Add Printer window, click **Add a network, wireless or Bluetooth printer**.

3. Wait while Windows searches for "available printers."

   When the printer you want appears in the list, highlight it, click **Next**, and then follow the prompts to complete the wizard.

4. If your printer never shows up, click **The printer that I want isn't listed**. On this next page, you can type the UNC path by hand, as described earlier in this chapter, or you can select **Browse for a printer** to show the old tool used in earlier versions of Windows. The browse window is a nonstandard collapsible tree, from which you'll need to navigate to the remote printer you wish to install. Navigation is a little different here than in Explorer; instead of the usual plus signs, you'll have to double-click branches to expand them. When you've found the printer, highlight it and click **Next**.

5. If the printer still doesn't show up, go back to the PC to which it's connected and troubleshoot the problem there.

 It's important to realize that some printers can't be shared over a network, which is usually a limitation of the printer's driver, and an intentional one at that.

Note that the host computer, the one to which the printer is physically attached, must be turned on and connected to the network in order to allow other computers to print. You can overcome this limitation by using a print server device, which connects most types of printers directly to your network.

Use a Print Server Without Software

A print server lets you plug most types of printers directly into your network, something otherwise only high-end network printers can do.

A print server gets you two things. One, anyone on your network can print without requiring that a specific PC be turned on and connected; this is particularly useful on a wireless network, where nobody wants to have to feed a printer cable to a PC each time someone needs to print. Second, adding a print server means you can put the printer anywhere; it no longer has to be right next to a PC.

Problem is, most print servers come with software you're supposed to install on every PC. This can be a pain, and the software is often buggy.

The good news is that most of the time, you don't need the software at all, provided you do the setup by hand:

1. First, connect your print server to your printer and turn everything on.

2. Next, connect your print server to your network. If it's a wireless print server, you may need to hook it up to your PC first to enter the SSID and encryption information; consult the documentation for details.

3. Determine your print server's IP address.

   The address might be a static default address, which would be mentioned in the documentation.

   Otherwise, your router's DHCP system will automatically assign it an IP address. To find out, open your router setup page, and view the DHCP Client Table, as described in "Troubleshoot Network Connections" in Chapter 7. Here, you'll see the IP address your print server is currently using.

4. Open a web browser, type the print server's IP address into the address bar, and press **Enter**.

5. On the print server setup page, turn off DHCP and specify a static IP address. Make sure you pick an address no PC on your network is likely to use; for instance, if your PCs are currently at 192.168.1.101, 192.168.1.102, and so on, choose something out-of-the-way like 192.168.1.177 for your print server, and then save the settings. Check the print server's documentation if you need further help with this step.

6. Next, add the printer to a PC. Open the *Printers* folder in Control Panel, and then click the **Add a printer** button on the toolbar.

7. In the Add Printer window, click **Add a network, wireless or Bluetooth printer**.

8. Don't wait for Windows to search for available printers; instead, click **The printer that I want isn't listed** right away.

9. On the next page, select **Add a printer using a TCP/IP address or hostname** and click **Next**.

10. In the **Hostname or IP address** field, type the static IP address of your print server you chose in step 5. Windows fills in the **Port name** automatically as you type; click **Next** when you're done.

11. If you see the **Additional Port Information Required** page, select **Standard** for the **Device Type**, then **Generic Network Card**, and then click **Next**.

12. Next, Windows will attempt to talk to the printer, but it will likely need your help in choosing the manufacturer and model.

13. Click **Next** and then finish the wizard when you're done.

Nearly all print servers work this way, but you may find that some units (likely the one you just bought) have trouble remembering their settings. Obviously, a print server that forgets its static IP address won't be much use with an operating system like Vista that requires a consistent IP address for reliable printing. If this happens to you, check the manufacturer's web site for a firmware upgrade that may fix the problem, and then try again.

Stop Sharing Scheduled Tasks

As explained earlier in this section, you can access the shared printers and folders—as well as the Scheduled Tasks folder—of any other computer in your network. The problem is that sharing Scheduled Tasks slows network browsing considerably. Follow these steps on every PC in your workgroup to stop sharing Scheduled Tasks and increase your network performance considerably:

1. Open the Registry Editor (see Chapter 3).

2. Expand the branches to `HKEY_LOCAL_MACHINE\SOFTWARE\Microsoft\Windows\CurrentVersion\Explorer\RemoteComputer\NameSpace`.

3. Under the `NameSpace` key, you'll see at least two keys named for Class IDs. The (`default`) value inside each key will tell you what the key is for.

   Find the key for "Scheduled Tasks" (it will be `{D6277990-4C6A-11CF-8D87-00AA0060F5BF}`), and delete it.

4. Close the Registry Editor when you're done.

The change will take effect immediately, and you'll notice that Windows is now much more responsive when browsing shared folders.

CHAPTER 9

Scripting and Automation

It's sometimes hard to escape feeling like an automaton—an extension of your computer, rather than the other way around. What percentage of the time you spend at your PC is used carrying out repetitive, mundane tasks? Your motor memory has likely enabled you to do things like rename multiple files quickly by hand, or open your database application, email client, and web browser each morning when you sit down at your desk—pretty quickly, and all without thinking about it. But if you do stop and think, your PC, not you, should be handling all this nonsense, leaving you to handle the creative end.

One of the best ways to reduce your involvement in repetitive tasks—and thus the time and effort required to perform them—is to employ some form of scripting or Command Prompt automation. Whether you need to back up important files once a week, generate custom web pages once every three seconds, or close errant processes only occasionally, there's almost certainly a better and faster way to do it than the way you're doing it now.

Enter *scripts*, very simple programs you can write with nothing more than Notepad and a few minutes looking up syntax. Scripts are plain-text files that can be written and executed without a special development environment and/or compiler. (A compiler is a program that translates editable program source code into application executables, such as *.exe* and *.dll* files.) Scripts are *interpreted* rather than compiled, which means that another program reads and executes the commands in the script, line-by-line. While you wouldn't want to use a word processor made from scripts, you'll find that they're ideal for quick and dirty tasks, such as simple file operations, managing network connections, and even starting several programs with a single click of a button.

Microsoft hasn't gone out of its way to publicize these features, but they can be immensely useful. Windows Vista supports three technologies that offer scripting: Command Prompt (DOS) batch files, the Windows Script Host (WSH), and Windows PowerShell scripts. All three types have their strengths and limitations, and you may decide to use different ones for different purposes:

Command Prompt (DOS) batch files
Batch files are the oldest scripts and probably the easiest to write on a PC, but they're severely limited in what they can do. Batch files, not to mention the Command Prompt itself, are handy for copying or renaming files based on wildcard character specifications, for instance. But they can't interact with Windows programs, and have no knowledge of running processes, security policies, or any of your other favorite Vista buzzwords. On the plus side, you can run a batch file on any PC made after 1982, regardless of the version of Windows being used, and the DOS commands used therein can also be used to recover your PC in the event it won't start (see "What to Do When Windows Won't Start," in Chapter 6).

Windows Script Host scripts
WSH scripts are more flexible and powerful than batch files, and offer better user interaction. WSH scripts are Windows-based, and can take advantage of Windows services, such as printing, networking, and Registry access. WSH scripts work on any PC running Windows 98 or later, or Windows 95 and Windows NT 4.0 after installing an add-on. Unfortunately, these days they're seen as a system vulnerability, to the point of being blocked by some modern antivirus software, and despite having been around for about a decade, they're still pretty feeble when compared to the kind of scripting found on Unix/Linux systems.

Windows PowerShell scripts
Designed to address the shortcomings of WSH scripts, Microsoft's PowerShell (also known as MSH, or the Monad Shell) is somewhat the ideal scripting solution. PowerShell is more or less a replacement for the Command Prompt, and its scripting feature is only part of the package. In some cases, even a single line entered by hand at the PowerShell prompt can do more than a complex batch file or WSH script. But since PowerShell is not installed by default in Vista, you can't ever assume it's there, thus making it more useful as a personal tool than as a platform for scripts to distribute to other PCs.

Which scripting platform you choose should depend on your comfort level and familiarity with the language, as well as the task.

Windows Script Host

The Windows Script Host is the engine responsible for running scripts. Rather than a tangible, interactive application like the Command Prompt or Windows PowerShell (both discussed in more detail later in this chapter), WSH is simply an extensible collection of support files. In theory, WSH is language-independent, meaning that it can be extended to support any modern scripting language, such as Perl and Python. Of course, you can install and run Perl on your PC and then run Perl scripts completely independently of WSH, but the concept of WSH integration means that your Perl scripts would have access to all the WSH objects and services described later in this chapter. Regardless, most WSH scripts end up being written in VBScript.

VBScript is based on another Microsoft programming language, Visual Basic (VB), which, in turn, is loosely based on Beginner's All-purpose Symbolic Instruction Code (BASIC). If you're at all familiar with BASIC, taught in grade school since the 70s, the fundamentals of VBScript won't be much of a challenge. VBScript is used primarily in this chapter because it's easy to learn; it supports easy access to the features we need, like Registry access and file operations; and its cousin, VB, is one of the most widely used programming environments in the world.

So, where does WSH end and the VBScript language begin? From the point of view of the person running the script, WSH starts when you double-click a script file, at which point it automatically chooses an appropriate language interpreter based on the script filename extension. From the point of view of the developer, WSH provides special functionality to all languages through the use of objects (see "Object References," later in this chapter); that way, each WSH-supported language needn't bother providing functionality for advanced functions, such as Registry access and filesystem operations.

Build a VBScript Script

A *script* is simply a list of commands placed one after another and stored in a text file. Script commands are like building blocks: the more commands and programming techniques you learn, the broader your palette will be for making useful scripts. Some of the simpler building blocks will be used in this section of the chapter to illustrate the way scripts are built. For more advanced topics, skip ahead to subsequent sections of this chapter.

To run a script, just double-click on the script file icon; you'll probably never need to run the Scripting Host program (*wscript.exe*) directly.

There are actually two WSH script interpreters (engines) included with Vista. *WScript.exe* is a native Windows interpreter and is used in most cases. *CScript.exe* is a console interpreter, and is used when you want the script output to be sent to the console (Command Prompt). You can use *CScript.exe* at any time by right-clicking a script file and selecting **Open with Command Prompt**.

When the Scripting Host runs the script, the commands are executed in order, one by one. You can leave a Notepad window open to make changes and additions while you test the script; big screens are especially handy for this sort of thing.

You can quickly open an existing script file for editing by right-clicking and selecting **Edit**. This will, by default, open Notepad, although you might want to associate the **Edit** action for *.vbs* files with a more powerful text editor (see "File Type Associations" in Chapter 3).

The process of putting a script together essentially involves typing commands and then running the scripts to test them. Following are the background concepts necessary to complete many tasks with scripts:

- Using variables to store and manipulate information
- Asking for and displaying information with the `InputBox` and `MsgBox` commands
- Creating interactive scripts with conditional statements
- Using loops to repeat a series of commands
- Making building blocks with subroutines and functions
- Extending scripts with object references

Use Variables to Store and Manipulate Information

The use of variables is essential when some interaction is required by a script. A variable can be assigned a value, which is subsequently used or simply recalled later in the script. For example, the following two commands:

```
MyName = "joe user"
MyShoeSize = 12
```

set two different variables to two different values. The first variable, `MyName`, is assigned to a text string, while the second, `MyShoeSize`, is set to a numeric value.

You can also assign variables in terms of other variables:

```
MyIQ = MyShoeSize + 7
```

which, when placed after the two preceding lines, would result in the variable $MyIQ$ having a value of 19 (12 plus 7). When a variable name appears on the left side of an equals sign, its value is being manipulated. When it appears on the right side of an equals sign or within some other command, its value is simply being read. You can carry out more complex mathematical operations using various combinations of parentheses and the standard operators (+, -, *, /, and ^ for addition, subtraction, multiplication, division, and exponentiation, respectively).

Give Your Scripts an Interface with the InputBox and MsgBox Commands

Some scripts are ideally suited to run in the background and perform a sequence of tasks, and then simply exit when those tasks are complete. Others require some sort of user interaction, either in the form of asking the user for input or informing the user when something has gone wrong. For example, this command:

```
MyName = InputBox("Please enter your name.")
```

will display a prompt on the screen when the script is run, asking for some text to be typed. When you enter some text and click **OK**, the script places the text you've typed into the variable $MyName$ and continues on to the next command.

Now, collecting and rearranging information does no good without the ability to spit out a result. The versatile $MsgBox$ function allows you to display a simple message, as follows:

```
MsgBox "Hello, Hello Again."
```

Combining the principles covered so far, consider the following code:

```
MyAge = InputBox("Please type your age.")
NewAge = MyAge + 5
MsgBox "In 5 years, you will be " & NewAge & "."
```

The first line does two things: it first asks the user to type something, and then assigns the typed text to the variable $MyAge$. The second line creates a new variable, $NewAge$, assigns the user's input to it, and adds five. Note the lack of any error checking in this example: if one enters something other than a number, this code will cause a WSH error, and the script will end early. The third line then uses the & operator to concatenate (glue together) a text string to the $NewAge$ variable and displays the result in a message box.

Notice that plain text is always enclosed in quotation marks, but variable names are not. If you were to enclose the NewAge variable in quotation marks, the script would simply print out the text NewAge instead of whatever value is stored in the variable.

The MsgBox statement can also be used like this:

```
Response = MsgBox("Here's My Message", 17, "Message Title")
```

which allows it to be used for not only displaying a message, but recording the response as well. The 17 is the sum of a few different values, which specify the options used to customize the message box. Figure 9-1 shows two sample message boxes, each with different buttons and icons.

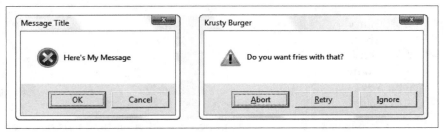

Figure 9-1. Various options can be combined to produce a variety of message boxes

To choose the buttons that are displayed by the MsgBox function, specify:

0 for OK
1 for OK & Cancel
2 for Abort, Retry, & Ignore
3 for Yes, No, & Cancel
4 for Yes & No
5 for Retry & Cancel

To choose the icon that is displayed, specify:

16 for a red × (error)
32 for a question mark (query)
48 for an exclamation mark (warning)
64 for a blue "I" (information)

Additionally, you can add:

256 to give the second button the focus (dotted lines)
512 to give the third button the focus
4096 to make the message box "system modal" (i.e., all applications are suspended until the user responds to the message box)

So, to have a message box with the **Yes** and **No** buttons, to have the question mark icon, and to have **No** be the default, you would specify a value of 4 + 32 + 256 = 292. The two message boxes in Figure 9-1 have values of 17 (that's **OK**, **Cancel**, and the × icon) and 292, respectively. Note that it's good practice *not* to add the values together (like I did in the first example with 17), but rather to leave them separated, like this:

```
Response = MsgBox("Here's My Message", 16 + 1, "Message Title")
```

This way, it's easier to understand and modify later on.

When the user responds to the message box, the `Response` variable will be set to:

1 if the user clicked OK
2 for Cancel
3 for Abort
4 for Retry
5 for Ignore
6 for Yes
7 for No

The next step is to write code that can perform different functions based on this recorded response. See the next topic, "Creating Interactive Scripts with Conditional Statements," for details on using the results from a `MsgBox` statement to determine what happens next in a script.

Creating Interactive Scripts with Conditional Statements

Conditional statements allow you to redirect the flow depending on a condition you determine, such as the value of a variable. Take, for example, the following script:

```
Response = MsgBox("Do you want to continue?", 32 + 4, "Next Step")
If Response = 7 Then WScript.Quit
MsgBox "You asked for it..."
```

The first statement uses the `MsgBox` function, described in the previous topic, to ask a question. The value of 32 + 4 specifies **Yes** and **No** buttons, as well as the question mark icon. If the user chooses **Yes**, the value of the `Response` variable is set to 6; if **No** is chosen, `Response` is set to 7.

The next statement uses the vital `If...Then` structure to test the value of the `Response` variable. If it's equal to 7 (meaning the user clicked **No**), then the script exits immediately (using the `WScript.Quit` statement). Otherwise, script execution continues to the next command.

Here's another example using a slightly more complex version of the `If` statement:

```
MyShoeSize = InputBox("Please type your shoe size.")
MyIQ = InputBox("Please type your IQ.")
If MyShoeSize > MyIQ Then
  MsgBox "You need to read more."
Else
  MsgBox "You need larger shoes."
End If
```

One of the nice things about VBScript is that most of the commands are in plain English; you should be able to follow the flow of the program by just reading through the commands. Before you run the previous script, try to predict what will happen for different values entered at each of the two InputBox statements.

This script uses the If...Then structure to redirect output depending on the two values entered at runtime (when the script is actually being executed). It should be evident that the first message is displayed if the value of MyShoeSize is larger than the value of MyIQ. In all other cases (including when both values are equal), the second message is displayed. Note also the use of End If, which is required if the If...Then structure spans more than one line, as it does in this example.

The If...Then structure can have as many elements as you need. For example:

```
Crashes = InputBox("How many times a day does Windows crash?")
If Crashes <= 3 Then
  MsgBox "You lucky sod..."
ElseIf Crashes = 4 or Crashes = 5 Then
  MsgBox "The national average: good for you!"
Else
  MsgBox "Take two aspirin and call me in the morning."
End If
```

accommodates three different ranges of answers to the question posed by the first line of code (thanks to the ElseIf line). Note also the use of or on the fourth line; you could also use and here, or a combination of the two. Use parentheses to group conditions in more complex statements.

Using Loops, Using Loops, Using Loops

Another useful structure is the For...Next loop, which allows you to repeat a series of commands a specified number of times:

```
SomeNumber = InputBox("How many lumps do you want?")
TotalLumps = ""
For i = 1 To SomeNumber
  TotalLumps = TotalLumps & "lump "
Next

Rem -- The next line displays the result --
MsgBox TotalLumps
```

The For...Next loop repeats everything between the two statements by incrementing the value of the variable i until it equals the value of the variable SomeNumber. Each time WSH goes through the loop, another "lump" is added to the variable, TotalLumps. When the loop is finished, the contents of the TotalLumps variable are displayed.

Notice the use of the concatenation operator (&) in the middle of the loop, which adds a new lump to the variable. Those new to programming might be put off by the fact that we have the TotalLumps variable on both sides of the equals sign.[*] This works because the scripting host evaluates everything on the right side of the equals sign (adds it all up) and then assigns it to the variable on the left side.

Note also the TotalLumps="" statement before the For...Next loop; this empties the variable before we start adding stuff to it. Otherwise, whatever might be assigned to that variable before the loop would still be kept around—something we didn't anticipate or want. It's good programming practice to prepare for as many different situations as can be imagined.

Also good practice is the use of spaces, indentations, and remarks to make the code easier to read without affecting the execution of the script. The Rem command is used to include remarks (comments that are ignored when the script is run), allowing you to label any part of the script with pertinent information. In place of the Rem command, you can also use a single apostrophe ('), which—unlike Rem—can be placed on the same line as another command, like this:

```
MsgBox TotalLumps    'display the result
```

As you write these scripts, think about the formatting as you would in writing a word-processor document; scripts that are easier to read are easier to debug and much more pleasant to revisit six months later.

Make Building Blocks with Subroutines and Functions

A *subroutine* allows you to encapsulate a bit of code inside a single command, making it easy to repeat that command as many different times as you want as though it were a built-in command. Simply include the entire subroutine anywhere in a script, and then type the name of the subroutine elsewhere in the script to execute the subroutine.

---

[*] In traditional algebra, you couldn't have a statement like this; it would be like saying $x=x+1$, which has no solution. However, this is not an equation; it's an instruction that you want carried out. Besides, you're supposed to have forgotten algebra years ago.

A *function* is essentially the same as a subroutine, except that it has a result, called a *return value*. Both subroutines and functions accept input variables, listed in parentheses after the respective Sub and Function statements.

To those who are familiar with macros in a word processor, subroutines are similar. In fact, Microsoft Word, Excel, and Access (in Office 95 and later) save their macros as VBScript subroutines.

Consider Example 9-1, which compares the contents of two text files. At the heart of this example are the two structures at the end of the script, although their specific position in the script is not important. WSH separates all subroutines and functions before executing the script; they won't be executed unless they're called, and the variables used therein are unrelated to variables used elsewhere in the main script. Whenever it encounters the name of a subroutine or function in the script body, it executes it as though it were a separate script. Try to follow the execution of the script, command by command.

Example 9-1. Using functions and subroutines

```
Filename1 = InputBox("Enter the first filename")
Filename2 = InputBox("Enter the second filename")

If Not FileExists(Filename1) Then
  MsgBox Filename1 & " does not exist."
ElseIf Not FileExists(Filename2) Then
  MsgBox Filename2 & " does not exist."
Else
  Call RunProgram("command /c fc " & filename1 & _
            " " & filename2 & " > c:\Users\username\Desktop\temp.txt", True)
  Call RunProgram("notepad c:\Users\username\Desktop\temp.txt", False)
End If

Function FileExists(Filename)
  Set FileObject = CreateObject("Scripting.FileSystemObject")
  FileExists = FileObject.FileExists(Filename)
End Function

Sub RunProgram(Filename, Wait)
  Set WshShell = WScript.CreateObject("WScript.Shell")
  RetVal = WshShell.Run(Filename, Wait)
End Sub
```

One of the most important aspects of both subroutines and functions is that they can accept one or more input variables, called *parameters* or *arguments*. The parameters that a subroutine can accept are listed in parentheses after the subroutine definition and are separated by commas (if there's more than one).

Then, using the Call statement, the values you wish to pass to the subroutine (which are placed in the parameter variables when the script is run) are listed in parentheses.

This way, the same subroutine or function can be called repeatedly, each time with one or more different variables. Functions (such as FileExists in this example) also can return a single variable (usually dependent on the outcome of some operation).

The first structure defines the FileExists function (discussed later in this chapter), which is passed a filename and returns a value of True (-1) if the file exists, and False (0) if it does not. The FileExists function is called twice, once for each filename entered when the script is run (Filename1 and Filename2). The If...Then structures (see "Creating Interactive Scripts with Conditional Statements," earlier in this chapter) first call the function, then redirect the flow based on the return value (result).

The second structure defines the RunProgram subroutine, also called from the script two times. RunProgram simply runs the program filename passed to it; since it's a subroutine and not a function, there is no return value. In theory, you could use functions exclusively, and simply ignore the return values of those functions that don't use them; the benefit of subroutines, though, is that you don't have to think about handling a return value at all.

 In FileExists and RunProgram, Filename is a variable (shown in parentheses) in which passed data is placed so it can be used inside the subroutine or function. It's considered a local variable, i.e., it has no value outside of the subroutine or function.

The most important consequence of this design—the separation of the code into subroutines and functions—is that it makes it easy to reuse portions of code. Experienced programmers will intentionally separate code into useful subroutines that can be copied and pasted to other scripts. Just think of programming as building something out of Lego™ blocks; the smaller the blocks, the more versatile they become.

It's worth mentioning that, in the case of subroutines, the Call statement is not strictly necessary. For example, the line:

    Call RunProgram("notepad c:\temp.txt", False)

is equivalent to:

    RunProgram "notepad c:\temp.txt", False

Note that without the Call keyword, the parentheses around the arguments are omitted. Personally, I like using Call; it makes references to my custom subroutines more distinct and easier to find, but others might prefer the simpler form.

The solutions in the subsequent topics are presented as either subroutines or functions. I've used subroutines for code that performs an action, such as copying a file or writing information to the Registry. When a result is expected, such as reading information from the Registry or finding the date of a file, a function is used instead.

You should be able to place the subroutines and functions directly into your scripts and call them with a single command. It's up to you to put the pieces together (and to modify them) to accomplish whatever tasks you have in mind.

Object References

There are some operations that can be performed with the Windows Script Host regardless of the language being used. These operations, such as accessing the filesystem, are made possible by extending the language with *objects*. For the time being, consider an object to be simply a context that is referred to when certain commands are carried out.

Admittedly, this can make executing some tasks rather difficult and convoluted, but it is necessary given the modular architecture of WSH. For example, many scripts require a line similar to the following (using VBScript syntax in this case):

```
Set WshShell = WScript.CreateObject("WScript.Shell")
```

which creates and initializes the WshShell object. WshShell is not a visible object like a file or other component of Windows, but rather a required reference used to accomplish many tasks with WSH, such as running programs, creating Windows shortcuts, and retrieving system information.

If you're unfamiliar with object references, your best bet is to simply type them as shown and worry about how they actually work when you're more comfortable with the language. The subsequent topics include many solutions that take advantage of objects, such as WScript.Shell, which has many uses, and Scripting.FileSystemObject, used for accessing files, folders, and drives.

How to Run Applications

This code is used to run a program, which can be a DOS program, a Windows application, an Internet or *mailto* URL, or anything else you might normally type in the Start menu's Run command or Explorer's address bar. Place this subroutine in your scripts:

```
Sub RunProgram(Filename, Wait)
   Set WshShell = WScript.CreateObject("WScript.Shell")
   RetVal = WshShell.Run(Filename, Wait)
End Sub
```

and call the routine like this:

```
Call RunProgram("c:\windows\notepad.exe", True)
```

You can replace True with False if you don't want to wait for the program to finish before the next script command is executed.

See the next sidebar, "Scripting and the UAC," for important security considerations.

Scripting and the UAC

When writing scripts for use in Vista, you've always got to think about security and the User Access Control (UAC) feature, both discussed in Chapter 8. For instance, with Vista set to its defaults, any applications you launch with a script will be run under the standard (limited) user account. If your script needs to open applications and issue commands (such as the Registry functions covered in the next section) as the administrator, then your script needs to be run under the administrator account. As explained in Chapter 8, you can set *wscript.exe* to always run in administrator mode, but this would cause all scripts to run under the administrator account, and would open up a nasty vulnerability on your PC. So, what to do?

Unfortunately, you can't right-click a *.vbs* file and select **Run as administrator**, as you can with executables (*.exe* files). But you can get around this limitation in a few different ways.

First, you can write a one-line batch file (discussed later in this chapter) that does nothing more than launch your script. Then, to run the script in administrator mode, right-click the *batch file* and select **Run as administrator**.

Or, to run all your scripts in administrator mode *without* making your system vulnerable, make a copy of the *wscript.exe* file called something like *wscript_admin.exe*. Right-click the *wscript_admin.exe* file, select **Properties**, choose the **Compatibility** tab, and then turn on the **Run this program as an administrator** option. Next, add a new file type (see Chapter 3) for *.vbsa* files and associate its **Open** action with the *wscript_admin.exe* file. Thereafter, just rename the filename extension of any *.vbs* file to *.vbsa* to run the script as an administrator.

How to Access the Registry

The following code is used to write, read, and delete information in the Registry. Include the following three routines in your script:

```
Sub RegistryWrite(KeyName, ValueName, ValueData, ValueType)
  ValueType = UCase(ValueType)
  If ValueType <> "REG_DWORD" and ValueType <> "REG_BINARY" Then _
                                        ValueType = "REG_SZ"
  Set WshShell = WScript.CreateObject("WScript.Shell")
  WshShell.RegWrite KeyName & "\" & ValueName, ValueData, ValueType
End Sub

Function RegistryRead(KeyName, ValueName)
  Set WshShell = WScript.CreateObject("WScript.Shell")
  RegistryRead = WSHShell.RegRead(KeyName & "\" & ValueName)
End Function

Sub RegistryDelete(KeyName, ValueName)
  Set WshShell = WScript.CreateObject("WScript.Shell")
  WshShell.RegWrite KeyName & "\" & ValueName, ""
  WshShell.RegDelete KeyName & "\" & ValueName
End Sub
```

Using these three routines, you can accomplish nearly all Registry tasks. To create a Registry key, type this (note that all HKEY... roots must appear in uppercase):

```
Call RegistryWrite("HKEY_LOCAL_MACHINE\Software\My Key", "", "", "")
```

To assign data to a Registry value:

```
Call RegistryWrite("HKEY_LOCAL_MACHINE\Software\My Key", "My Value", _
                                        "Some Data", "")
```

Leave "My Value" blank to set the (Default) value. To read the data stored in a given value:

```
Variable = RegistryRead("HKEY_LOCAL_MACHINE\Software\My Key", "My Value")
```

Leave "My Value" blank to read the (Default) value. To delete a key:

```
Call RegistryDelete("HKEY_LOCAL_MACHINE\Software\My Key", "")
```

To delete a value:

```
Call RegistryDelete("HKEY_LOCAL_MACHINE\Software\My Key", "My Value")
```

To delete the (Default) value in a key, we just set the value to nothing:

```
Call RegistryWrite("HKEY_LOCAL_MACHINE\Software\My Key", "", "", "")
```

You'll notice that, in the RegistryDelete subroutine, there's a RegWrite statement. This is necessary to ensure that the key or value that you're trying to delete actually exists. If you *don't* include this statement and you try to delete a nonexistent key or value from the Registry, the Windows Script Host will give an error to the effect that "The system cannot find the file specified." (A helpful Microsoft error message, as always.) This way, the subroutine will create the key or value entry to be deleted if it doesn't already exist.

As part of a security/safety feature present in Windows Vista (and XP, 2000, and 2003), you won't be able to delete a key that contains subkeys (this is not true of Windows 9x/Me) using the `RegistryDelete` routine. See "Export and Import Data with Registry Patches," in Chapter 3, for a workaround.

See Chapter 3 for more information on Registry keys and values, tools, and tricks.

How to Manipulate Files

One of the myths surrounding the Windows Script Host, and VBScript in particular, is that there's no provision for accessing the filesystem (copying, deleting, and writing to files). This assumption is based on the fact that VBScript, when used in web pages, is not permitted to access the filesystem for obvious security reasons.

The following routines, all of which rely on the `FileSystemObject` object, should provide most necessary file operations. The names I've chosen for these functions and subroutines are based on what they act upon and what they're used for; for example, the `FolderCopy` subroutine is used to copy a folder, and the `FileCopy` subroutine is used to copy a file.

The following two functions return properties of drives—whether a specific drive letter exists and how much free space a specified drive has, respectively:

```
Function DriveExists(DriveLetter)
  Set FileObject = CreateObject("Scripting.FileSystemObject")
  DriveExists = FileObject.DriveExists(DriveLetter)
End Function

Function DriveFreeSpace(DriveLetter)
  If Left(DriveLetter,1) <> ":" Then DriveLetter = DriveLetter & ":"
  Set FileObject = CreateObject("Scripting.FileSystemObject")
  Set DriveHandle = _
              FileObject.GetDrive(FileObject.GetDriveName(DriveLetter))
  DriveFreeSpace = DriveHandle.FreeSpace
End Function
```

These next seven subroutines and functions are used to manipulate folders. The functions are used to retrieve information about a folder, and the subroutines are used to perform actions on a folder. The arguments should all be full folder names (e.g., *C:\Users\Lurlene\Desktop*). Note that the `FolderSize` function returns the combined size of all the contents of a folder, including all subfolders, and may take a few seconds to return a result for large folders. You may want to use the `FolderExists` function before any others to prevent errors:

```
Sub FolderCopy(Source, Destination)
  Set FileObject = CreateObject("Scripting.FileSystemObject")
  FileObject.CopyFolder Source, Destination
End Sub

Function FolderCreate(Foldername)
  Set FileObject = CreateObject("Scripting.FileSystemObject")
  Set Result = FileObject.CreateFolder(FolderName)
  If Result.Path = "" Then
    FolderCreate = False    'failure
  Else
    FolderCreate = True     'success
  End If
End Function

Sub FolderDelete(Foldername)
  Set FileObject = CreateObject("Scripting.FileSystemObject")
  FileObject.DeleteFolder(Foldername)
End Sub

Function FolderExists(Foldername)
  Set FileObject = CreateObject("Scripting.FileSystemObject")
  FolderExists = FileObject.FolderExists(Foldername)
End Function

Sub FolderMove(Source, Destination)
  Set FileObject = CreateObject("Scripting.FileSystemObject")
  FileObject.MoveFolder Source, Destination
End Sub

Function FolderSize(Foldername)
  Set FileObject = CreateObject("Scripting.FileSystemObject")
  Set FolderHandle = FileObject.GetFolder(Foldername)
  FolderSize = FolderHandle.Size
End Function

Function FolderParent(Foldername)
  Set FileObject = CreateObject("Scripting.FileSystemObject")
  FolderParent = FileObject.GetParentFolderName(Foldername)
End Function
```

These next seven subroutines and functions are used to manipulate files, and are similar to the folder counterparts listed above. And likewise, the functions are used to retrieve information about a file, and the subroutines are used to perform actions on a file. The arguments should all be fully qualified filenames (e.g., C:\Windows\notepad.exe). You may want to use the FileExists function before any others to prevent errors:

```
Sub FileCopy(Source, Destination)
  Set FileObject = CreateObject("Scripting.FileSystemObject")
  FileObject.CopyFile Source, Destination
End Sub
```

```
Function FileDate(Filename)
  Set FileObject = CreateObject("Scripting.FileSystemObject")
  Set FileHandle = FileObject.GetFile(Filename)
  GetFileDate = FileHandle.DateCreated
End Function

Sub FileDelete(Filename)
  Set FileObject = CreateObject("Scripting.FileSystemObject")
  FileObject.DeleteFile(Filename)
End Sub

Function FileExists(Filename)
  Set FileObject = CreateObject("Scripting.FileSystemObject")
  FileExists = FileObject.FileExists(Filename)
End Function

Function FileExtension(Filename)
  Set FileObject = CreateObject("Scripting.FileSystemObject")
  GetFileExtension = FileObject.GetExtensionName(Filename)
End Function

Sub FileMove(Source, Destination)
  Set FileObject = CreateObject("Scripting.FileSystemObject")
  FileObject.MoveFile Source, Destination
End Sub

Function FileSize(Filename)
  Set FileObject = CreateObject("Scripting.FileSystemObject")
  Set FileHandle = FileObject.GetFile(Filename)
  FileSize = FileHandle.Size
End Function
```

This next two functions can be used on either files or folders and allow you to retrieve and set file attributes (*Archive*, *Read-Only*, *System*, and *Hidden*), respectively.

File attributes are specified numerically: Read-Only = 1, Hidden = 2, System = 4, and Archive = 32. So, to set the Hidden and System attributes for a file, the Attrib parameter would be set to 6 (or 2 + 4). To read a file's attributes, the same constants are used, but only individually. For example, to see whether a file had, say, the System attribute turned on, you would use this statement:

```
If GetAttributes("c:\somefile.txt",4) = True Then Msgbox "This is a system
File."
```

And the routines are:

```
Function GetAttributes(Filename, Attrib)
  Set FileObject = CreateObject("Scripting.FileSystemObject")
  Set FileHandle = FileObject.GetFile(Filename)
  If FileHandle.Attributes And Attrib Then
    GetAttributes = True
```

```
    Else
        GetAttributes = False
    End If
End Function

Sub SetAttributes(Filename, Attrib)
    Set FileObject = CreateObject("Scripting.FileSystemObject")
    Set FileHandle = FileObject.GetFile(Filename)
    FileHandle.Attributes = Attrib
End Sub
```

The following four functions are used to obtain the locations of special Windows folders, or, in the case of GetTempFilename, to obtain the full path and filename of a newly generated temporary filename. (The file returned by GetTempFilename is guaranteed not to exist, so you can use it for the purposes of temporary storage without fear of conflicting with another open application.)

For example, to get the full path of the current user's *Desktop* folder, you would use something like MyDesktopFolder = GetSpecialFolder("Desktop"). The folders accessible with this function include *AllUsersDesktop*, *AllUsersStartMenu*, *AllUsersPrograms*, *AllUsersStartup*, *Desktop*, *Favorites*, *Fonts*, *MyDocuments*, *NetHood*, *PrintHood*, *Programs*, *Recent*, *SendTo*, *StartMenu*, *Startup*, and *Templates*. See "Wacky Script Ideas," later in this chapter, for further examples.

```
Function GetSpecialFolder(Foldername)
    set WshShell = WScript.CreateObject("WScript.Shell")
    GetSpecialFolder = WshShell.SpecialFolders(Foldername)
End Function

Function GetSystemFolder( )
    Set FileObject = CreateObject("Scripting.FileSystemObject")
    GetSystemFolder = FileObject.GetSpecialFolder(1) & "\"
End Function

Function GetTempFilename( )
    Set FileObject = CreateObject("Scripting.FileSystemObject")
    GetTempFile = FileObject.GetSpecialFolder(2) & "\" _
                & FileObject.GetTempName
End Function

Function GetWindowsFolder( )
    Set FileObject = CreateObject("Scripting.FileSystemObject")
    GetWindowsFolder = FileObject.GetSpecialFolder(0) & "\"
End Function
```

While the previous functions and subroutines are used to manipulate files, the following two manipulate the *contents* of files. The ReadFromFile function will transfer the contents of any file into a variable (naturally, this is most useful with plain-text files). Likewise, the `WriteToFile` subroutine will transfer the contents of a variable (specified as `Text`) into a file. If the file doesn't exist, it will be created; if the file already exists, the text will be appended to the end of the file:

```
Function ReadFromFile(Filename)
  Const ForReading = 1, ForWriting = 2, ForAppending = 8
  Set FileObject = CreateObject("Scripting.FileSystemObject")
  Set FileHandle = FileObject.OpenTextFile(Filename, ForReading)
  Buffer=""
  Do Until FileHandle.AtEndOfStream
    Buffer = Buffer & FileHandle.ReadLine & vbCrLf
  Loop
  FileHandle.Close
  ReadFromFile = Buffer
End Function

Sub WriteToFile(Filename, Text)
  Const ForReading = 1, ForWriting = 2, ForAppending = 8
  Set FileObject = CreateObject("Scripting.FileSystemObject")
  If FileObject.FileExists(Filename) Then
    Set FileHandle = FileObject.OpenTextFile(Filename, _
                                      ForAppending)
    FileHandle.Write vbCrLf
  Else
    Set FileHandle = FileObject.CreateTextFile(Filename)
  End If
  FileHandle.Write Text
  FileHandle.Close
End Sub
```

The use of all of the "file operations" subroutines and functions listed in the preceding section should be fairly self-explanatory, and they all work similarly. For example, the `FolderExists` function and the `FileExists` function are both nearly identical, except that `FileExists` checks for the existence of a single file, while `FolderExists` checks for the existence of a folder (and can be used to see whether a path refers to a folder or a file).

 See the "Rename Files with Search and Replace" example script, later in this chapter, for additional examples, as well as a method for obtaining a list of all the files in a given folder.

How to Create Windows Shortcuts and Internet Shortcuts

Include the following subroutine in your script to allow easy creation of Internet Shortcuts (*.url*) and Windows Shortcuts (*.lnk*):

```
Sub Shortcut(LinkFile, CommandLine)
  Set WshShell = WScript.CreateObject("WScript.Shell")
  If LCase(Right(LinkFile, 4)) <> ".lnk" And _
       LCase(Right(LinkFile, 4)) <>".url" Then _
       LinkFile = LinkFile & ".LNK"
  Set ShortcutHandle = WshShell.CreateShortcut(LinkFile)
  ShortcutHandle.TargetPath = CommandLine
  ShortcutHandle.Save
End Sub
```

To create a shortcut to a program or file, use the following statement:

```
Call Shortcut("C:\Users\username\AppData\Roaming\Microsoft\Windows\
              SendTo\Notepad.lnk", _"Notepad.exe")
```

To create a shortcut to an Internet address:

```
Call Shortcut("D:\Prjects\Important\Annoyances.url", _
              "http://www.annoyances.org/")
```

If the first parameter, LinkFile, ends in *.lnk* (case doesn't matter), the Shortcut subroutine automatically creates a standard Windows shortcut; if LinkFile ends in *.url*, however, an Internet Shortcut file is created. Note the If...Then structure in the routine, which automatically adds the *.lnk* filename extension if no proper extension is found.

> The LCase function, which transforms the contents of any variable to lowercase, is vital here, as it completely compensates for *.URL*, *.url*, *.Url*, and any other case mismatches in the specified filename.

If you specify a nonexistent folder in the path for the new shortcut file, an "Unspecified Error" will occur. You may want to use the FolderExists function, detailed in the "How to Manipulate Files" topic earlier in this chapter, to supplement this routine and eliminate the possibility of this error.

How to Use the Network

WSH has a few limited networking functions built in that can be used for mapping network drives and connecting to network printers. For advanced network functionality (such as communication and network traffic monitoring), check out PowerShell, discussed later in this chapter. For more information on networking, see Chapter 7.

The following routines provide access to some of the more useful network-related functions in VBScript.

The following function checks a given drive letter to see whether it has already been mapped. It returns True (-1) if the drive letter has been mapped, False (0) if it hasn't:

```
Function AlreadyMapped(DriveLetter)
  Set WshShell = WScript.CreateObject("WScript.Shell")
  Set WshNetwork = WScript.CreateObject("WScript.Network")
  Set AllDrives = WshNetwork.EnumNetworkDrives( )

  If Left(DriveLetter,1) <> ":" then DriveLetter = DriveLetter & ":"
  ConnectedFlag = False
  For i = 0 To AllDrives.Count - 1 Step 2
    If AllDrives.Item(i) = UCase(DriveLetter) Then ConnectedFlag = True
  Next

  AlreadyMapped = ConnectedFlag
End Function
```

This subroutine maps a drive letter to any valid remote path:

```
Sub MapNetDrive(DriveLetter, RemotePath)
  Set WshShell = WScript.CreateObject("WScript.Shell")
  Set WshNetwork = WScript.CreateObject("WScript.Network")
  WShNetwork.MapNetworkDrive DriveLetter, RemotePath
End Sub
```

This subroutine maps an unused printer port (e.g., *LPT3*) to any valid remote network printer:

```
Sub MapNetPrinter(Port, RemotePath)
  Set WshShell = WScript.CreateObject("WScript.Shell")
  Set WshNetwork = WScript.CreateObject("WScript.Network")
  WshNetwork.AddPrinterConnection Port, RemotePath
End Sub
```

These subroutines remove the mapping for previously mapped drive letters and network printers, respectively:

```
Sub UnMapNetDrive(DriveLetter)
  Set WshShell = WScript.CreateObject("WScript.Shell")
  Set WshNetwork = WScript.CreateObject("WScript.Network")
  WShNetwork.RemoveNetworkDrive DriveLetter
End Sub

Sub UnMapNetPrinter(Port)
  Set WshShell = WScript.CreateObject("WScript.Shell")
  Set WshNetwork = WScript.CreateObject("WScript.Network")
  WshNetwork.RemovePrinterConnection Port
End Sub
```

This next script serves as an example for these subroutines. It's used to map a network drive if it's not already mapped, or to disconnect a currently mapped drive. The AlreadyMapped, MapNetDrive, and UnMapNetDrive routines are required.

```
DriveLetter = "N:"
RemotePath = "\\server\c"

If AlreadyMapped(DriveLetter) then
   Call UnMapNetDrive(DriveLetter)
   Msgbox "Drive " & DriveLetter & " disconnected."
Else
   Call MapNetDrive(DriveLetter, RemotePath)
   Msgbox "Drive " & DriveLetter & " connected."
End if
```

This script requires no user interaction once it has been executed and displays only a single confirmation message when it's done. The first two lines contain the drive letter and network path to be mapped together. Then, the AlreadyMapped function is used to determine whether the drive mapping already exists. The script then maps or disconnects the drive, depending on what's needed; it's a quick and easy toggle that Windows itself just doesn't provide.

How to Control Internet Explorer

Because VBScript owes its existence, in part, to Internet Explorer (IE), it seems only fair that there would be some integration between WSH and IE. The key is the IE *object* and the properties and methods associated with it.

Note that the code in this section is not presented as a subroutine, mostly because all of the subsequent statements that reference the IEObject object (such as IEObject.Document.Write) would fail if the initial Set statement was isolated in its own routine.

Begin with the following lines in your script, which start the IE application, initialize an object to reference, and open a blank IE window:

```
Set IEObject = CreateObject("InternetExplorer.Application")
If Err.number <> 0 Then
   MsgBox "There was a problem starting Internet Explorer."
   wScript.Quit
End If
IEObject.Left = 75
IEObject.Top = 75
IEObject.Width = 400
IEObject.Height = 300
IEObject.Menubar = 0
IEObject.Toolbar = 0
IEObject.Navigate "About:Blank"
IEObject.Visible=1
Do while IEObject.Busy
   Rem -- wait for window to open --
Loop
```

Note the error checking at the beginning, which quits if there's a problem loading IE. The subsequent commands customize the window to our needs; the Left, Top, Width, and Height properties are all in pixels; for the MenuBar and Toolbar properties, 0 means hidden and 1 means visible. Lastly, the Navigate property specifies the URL to load; in this case, specify "About: Blank" to show a blank page.

Once the IEObject.Visible=1 command is issued, the window appears, and the real fun begins. (OK, perhaps "fun" is too strong of a word.) The following lines send HTML code to the active IE window, and form a simple web page:

```
IEObject.Document.Write "<html>"
IEObject.Document.Write "<h1>Hello World</h1>"
IEObject.Document.Write "<p>"
IEObject.Document.Write "<i>Aren't we sick of that phrase yet?</i>"
IEObject.Document.Write "</html>"
```

This has nearly limitless possibilities, not the least of which is a more elegant way to display information than the MsgBox command, a much more sophisticated way of gathering information than the InputBox command (using fill-out forms), and a way to display an ongoing log of a script's activities without interrupting script flow. To clear the page at any time, simply issue another IEObject.Navigate "About:Blank" command.

Note that the IE window stays open after the script completes; use the IEObject.Quit command to close the window during script execution.

How to Use Command-Line Parameters

A *command-line parameter* is a bit of text specified after the filename of a script when it is executed from a Command Prompt (see the following examples). This function converts a single command-line parameter into a variable:

```
Function CommandLine(Number)
  Set Arguments = WScript.Arguments
  If Number <= Arguments.Count Then
    CommandLine = Arguments(Number - 1)
  Else
    CommandLine = ""
  End If
End Function
```

For example, to display the second command-line parameter passed to a script, issue the following statement:

```
MsgBox CommandLine(2)
```

Although the command line may seem to be an antiquated concept, it's still very much a part of Windows. When you double-click on a *.vbs* file, for example, Windows actually executes the following command:

```
wscript.exe filename.vbs
```

where *filename.vbs* (the file that was double-clicked) is the command-line parameter for *wscript.exe*, telling it which script to run. (See "File Type Associations," in Chapter 3, for the nitty-gritty.) Scripts also accept command-line parameters, which are entered like this:

```
wscript.exe filename.vbs param1 param2
```

The two additional parameters (you can have as many as you like), *param1* and *param2*, are both passed to the script as command-line parameters, and can be retrieved during runtime by referencing CommandLine(1) and CommandLine(2), respectively.

One of the most common uses of command-line parameters in scripts is to accept filenames, and there are two circumstances when this is most useful:

- Drag one or more items onto the script file icon. Note that this didn't work in some earlier versions of Windows, as scripts were considered to be documents instead of programs.

- Place the script in your *Send To* folder. Then, right-click one or more items in Explorer, select **Send To**, and then select the name of the script. You can also place a shortcut to the script in your *Send To* folder, which eliminates the *.vbs* filename extension that would otherwise appear in Explorer's **Send To** menu.

In either case, when Windows executes the script, the names of the input file(s) are accessible as command-line parameters, one for each filename. The following example script displays the names of all the files and folders drag-dropped on the script icon:

```
Report = ""
Set Arguments = WScript.Arguments
For i = 1 to Arguments.Count
   Report = Report + Arguments(i - 1) + vbCrLf
Next
Msgbox Report
```

The script starts off by clearing the Report variable, and then borrows some code from the CommandLine function listed earlier* to initialize the Arguments object and determine the number of dropped files. Next, a For...Next

---

* It's actually possible to use the CommandLine function here instead, but doing so would make the script more cumbersome. And exactly who are you going to impress with a cumbersome script?

structure runs through the arguments, adding each one to the Report variable, followed by a linefeed (using vbCrLf, a handy built-in constant containing carriage-return and linefeed characters). Note that the Arguments array is zero-based (the first item is Arguments(0), the second is Arguments(1), and so on), so the (i - 1) part is needed to compensate. Lastly, a Msgbox command is used to display the list of dropped files.

How to Manage Windows Services

Windows Vista Services, such as the IIS web server service, the FTP daemon service, or the Remote Desktop service, can be managed with the Services window (*services.msc*). Rudimentary service control is also possible with WSH scripts. The following routine allows you to start and stop any service, or just see whether a service is running:

```
Function Service(ServiceName, Action)
  Const SERVICE_STOPPED = 1
  Const SERVICE_RUNNING = 4
  Set WshShell = WScript.CreateObject("WScript.Shell")
  Set EnvObject = WshShell.Environment("PROCESS")
  ComputerName = EnvObject("COMPUTERNAME")
  Set ComputerObject = GetObject("WinNT://" & ComputerName & ",computer")
  Set ServiceObject = ComputerObject.GetObject("Service",ServiceName)
  If Action = True and ServiceObject.Status = SERVICE_STOPPED Then
    ServiceObject.Start
  ElseIf Action = 0 and ServiceObject.Status = SERVICE_RUNNING Then
    ServiceObject.Stop
  End If
  If ServiceObject.Status = SERVICE_RUNNING Then
    Service = True
  Else
    Service = False
  End If
End Function
```

This general-purpose routine accepts two parameters: ServiceName and Action. ServiceName is a single word that represents the service you wish to control, and Action is either True to start the service, False to stop it, or (1) to see whether it's running or not. To find the service name for a given service, open the Services window (*services.msc*) and double-click the service in question. The name is listed at the top of the **General** tab; for example, the service name for the IIS service is IISADMIN, the name for the FTP service is MSFTPSVC, and the name for the Remote Desktop (a.k.a. Terminal Services, discussed in Chapter 7) service is TermService.

So, to start the FTP service, you would type:

```
Result = Service("MSFTPSVC", True)
```

or, to stop the service, you would type:

```
Result = Service("MSFTPSVC", False)
```

Either way, the function returns True (-1) if your action resulted in the service being started, or False (0) if your action resulted in the service being stopped. To simply query the service, without starting or stopping it, specify (1) or any other positive number for Action, like this:

```
Result = Service("MSFTPSVC", 1)
```

Including this routine in your script would allow you to start and stop a service with a single click (rather than having to wade through the Services window). Or, using these script routines in conjunction with the Task Scheduler (explained later in this chapter), for example, you could schedule your web server service to operate only during certain hours of the day.

How to Write CGI Scripts for Web Servers

WSH scripts have the potential to produce simple, yet quite capable CGI (Common Gateway Interface) applications: programs that are run by web servers to generate dynamic web content. For example, a CGI program can process data entered in web-based fill-out forms, or read data from files and produce web content on the fly. Although a full discussion of web server implementation and CGI programming is *way* beyond the scope of this book, there are some extra steps and additional commands necessary to write CGI programs with WSH scripts.

The first step is to set up your web server software to execute WSH scripts. There's a variety of different web server software packages (such as Apache, freely available at *http://www.apache.org*, and IIS, which comes with Windows), and naturally the configuration varies with each package. The following procedure shows how to set up IIS and configure it to execute WSH scripts as CGI programs:

1. If IIS is not currently installed, open **Control Panel → Programs and Features**, click **Turn Windows features on or off**, and then turn on the Internet Information Services option.

2. Start the IIS Snap-In (*\Windows\system32\inetsrv\iis.msc*), and then expand the branches to Internet Information Services\My Computer\Web Sites\Default Web Site. The files and folders that make up your web site are shown here (note that your setup may be different).

3. Scripts to be executed cannot be placed in ordinary folders; otherwise, the web server will simply display their contents instead of running them. So, they must be placed in a *virtual directory* with executable permissions; if you've already set up such a folder, skip to the next step.

Otherwise, right-click on **Default Web** in the left pane, select **Add Virtual Directory**, and follow the prompts. The **Alias** option is the folder name that appears in the URL when the script is referenced from a browser (described subsequently), and the **Directory** option is the full path of the physical folder on your hard disk containing your script. Finally, when asked about **Access Permissions**, make sure to turn on the **Execute** option.

4. Once you have a virtual directory configured, right-click the folder, click **Properties**, choose the **Virtual Directory** tab, and then click **Configuration**.

 For a CGI program to work, its output must be sent to the "console," a text-based display that works like the Command Prompt. For this reason, the *CScript.exe* script interpreter (engine), mentioned near the beginning of this chapter, must be used instead of the standard *WScript.exe* Windows-based interpreter.

5. Click **Add**, and type the following:

```
c:\windows\system32\cscript.exe "%s" "%s"
```

in the **Executable** field (change the path to match your system, if necessary), and type `.vbs` in the **Extension** field (make sure to include the dot).

Naturally, the filename extension will be different for JavaScript or Perl script files. Or, if you like, you can even make up a new filename extension for use with your VBScript CGI scripts (such as *.vbsc* or *.vbcgi*), as long as what you type doesn't conflict with another entry in the list.

6. The **All Verbs**, **Script engine**, and **Check that file exists** options should all be selected. Click **OK**, and then **OK** again when you're done.

The next step is to write a CGI script and place it in your executable folder. CGI scripts can use any of the commands and routines discussed elsewhere in this chapter, except, of course, for those that create dialog windows, such as `MsgBox` and `InputBox`.

The key to a CGI script, though, is the `WScript.Echo` command, which is used to send your text output to the web server. Here's an example of a simple four-line script that generates a basic HTML-formatted[*] web page:

```
WScript.Echo "<html>"
WScript.Echo "<body>"
WScript.Echo "<h1>Here Comes the Metric System!</h1>"
WScript.Echo "<body></html>"
```

---

[*] A discussion of HTML (HyperText Markup Language) is beyond the scope of this book, but there are many adequate HTML references on the Web.

To run the script, first save it in the executable folder you configured earlier. If the IISAdmin service is not currently running, start it now (via *services.msc*). Then, open a web browser, and type this URL into the address bar:

```
http://localhost/foldername/script.vbs
```

where *foldername* is the Alias you chose for the executable folder, and *script.vbs* is the filename of the script. If all goes well, you should see our message, "Here Comes the Metric System!" right in the browser window. If it doesn't work, check the permissions of the script file and executable folder (right-click, select **Properties**, and choose the **Security** tab). See Chapter 8 for more information on user accounts, ownership, and file permissions.

With IIS installed and active, your PC is a web server, which means you can just as easily call the script from a remote computer, as long as you're connected to a network or to the Internet, and you know the IP address or URL of your machine (visit *http://www.annoyances.org/ip* to find your computer's IP address). For example, if your IP address is 207.46.230.218, you'd simply type http://207.46.230.218/foldername/script.vbs. (If you have a router, this won't work until you mess with your router's *port range forwarding* feature, as described in "Control Your PC Remotely" in Chapter 7.)

Naturally, you'll probably want to generate dynamic (rather than static) content with your CGI script. Here's a script that displays the current date and time in the browser window:

```
WScript.Echo "<html><body>"
WScript.Echo "Today's date is: " & Date
WScript.Echo "and the current time is: " & Time
WScript.Echo "<body></html>"
```

For those familiar with writing CGI programs, you may be concerned that there are no HTTP headers included here. Although the CGI specification requires that a CGI program produce its own HTTP headers (such as Content-type: text/html), IIS automatically generates the headers based on the type of content it *thinks* you're sending (text/html for HTML or text/plain for plain text, for example). This not only means that any headers you include (with WScript.Echo) will simply appear as part of the generated page, but that you can't add your own headers. Drat.

If you need to obtain the value of a browser environment variable in your script, include this function:

```
Function Environment(EnviroName)
    Set WshShell = Wscript.CreateObject("Wscript.Shell")
    Set EnvHandle = WshShell.Environment("Process")
    Environment = EnvHandle(EnviroName)
End Function
```

For example, you display the user's web browser version with this short script:

```
WScript.Echo "Your browser's signature is:"
WScript.Echo Environment("HTTP_USER_AGENT")
```

Some other useful environment variables include QUERY_STRING (for retrieving form input or any text after a question mark in the URL) and HTTP_COOKIE (for reading HTTP cookies).

You can, of course, use other routines in your CGI scripts. For example, here's a script that displays the contents of a text file, using the ReadFromFile function (see "How to Manipulate Files," earlier in this chapter):

```
OrderNum = "234323"
WScript.Echo "Here is your order (number " & OrderNum & "):"
WScript.Echo "<p>"
WScript.Echo "<img src=""/pictures/smiley.jpg""><br>"
WScript.Echo ReadFromFile("d:\data\orders\" & OrderNum & ".txt")
```

Note the use of HTML to include an image in the output. Although many HTML tags require quotation marks, adding a quotation mark in the middle of a line would cause WSH to confuse it with the beginning and trailing quotes. To tell VBScript to treat a quotation mark as a character to print, just put two of them together (as shown on the "smiley" line).

Decipher Script Errors

One of the general disadvantages of scripts is that they are typically created with a plain-text editor, rather than a rich debugging environment used with more sophisticated programming languages (see "Find a Better Editor," later in this chapter). Because Notepad isn't specifically designed to understand VBScript, it can't offer any assistance with syntax (grammar) or errors while you're editing. Therefore, you must wait until you run the script to see whether there are any problems. If WSH encounters an error, it will display a message similar to that shown in Figure 9-2.

Surprisingly, this sparse message box actually provides enough information to resolve most problems. Naturally, the first field, **Script**, shows the script filename in which the error occurred. This is especially useful if the script was run from a scheduled task or from your *Startup* folder, and you might otherwise not know which script caused the error.

The **Line Number** and **Column** fields show exactly where in the script the error occurred, and include blank lines and remarks. If you're using Notepad, select **Status Bar** from the **View** menu to display the line number at which the insertion point (text cursor) is resting. Or, select **Go To** from Notepad's **Edit** menu to quickly jump to any line. Better yet, switch to a better text

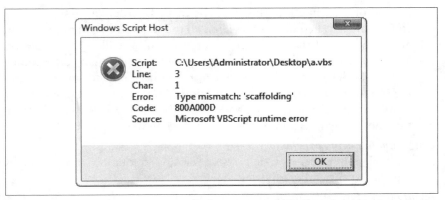

Figure 9-2. The Windows Script Host displays a message like this whenever it encounters an error

editor (discussed later in this chapter) that has more debugging tools, such as numbered lines.

The **Category** field describes—more than anything else—what it was doing when it encountered the error. A *compilation error* occurs when WSH is first reading the file and making sure all of the commands are correctly entered; you'll see this if you forgot a parenthesis or quotation mark, misspelled a command, or left out some other important keyword. A *runtime error*, on the other hand, is an error encountered while the script was being executed; this is caused by errors that WSH doesn't know are errors until it actually tries them, such as trying to read from a file that doesn't exist or trying to calculate the square root of a negative number.

Lastly, the **Description** field shows a brief explanation of the error encountered. Sometimes it's helpful, but most of the time it's either too vague or too cryptic to be of much help. This is where programming experience comes in handy for interpreting these messages and figuring out what caused them. The following are a few of the more common error descriptions and what they mean:

Expected ')'

Compilation error: you left out a closing parenthesis, such as at the end of an InputBox statement. Note that sometimes you can have nested parentheses (e.g., x=1+(6+7*(3-4))), and you need to make sure you have an equal number of open and close parentheses.

Expected 'End'

Compilation error: you left out a closing statement for a structure, such as If, Sub, or For. Make sure you include End If, End Sub, and Next, respectively. Note that WSH might report that the error occurred on line 37 of a 35-line file; this happens because in looking for a closing statement, WSH continues to search all the way to the end of the script, at which time, if the statement was not found, it will report the error. You'll have to look through the entire script for the unpaired beginning statement. See the topics on flow control earlier in this chapter ("Creating Interactive Scripts with Conditional Statements," "Using Loops, Using Loops, Using Loops," and "Make Building Blocks with Subroutines and Functions") for more information on these commands.

Unterminated string constant
Compilation error: you left out a closing quotation mark, usually required at the end of a "string of text."

Invalid procedure call or argument
Runtime error: this usually means that a subroutine or function has been called with one or more improper parameters. This can occur, for example, if you try to do something WSH isn't capable of, such as calculating the square root of a negative number.

Type mismatch: '[undefined]'
Runtime error: this means you've tried to use a command or function that VBScript doesn't recognize. You'll get this error whenever you try to use a VB command that doesn't exist in VBScript.

Object doesn't support this property or method
Runtime error: because it can be difficult to find documentation on the various objects used in VBScript, you're likely to encounter this error frequently. It means that you've tried to refer to a property or method of an object (such as WScript) that doesn't exist (such as WScript.Dingus).

The system cannot find the file specified
Runtime error: this error, obviously reporting that you've tried to access a file on your hard disk that doesn't exist, also appears when you try to delete a Registry key that doesn't exist. See "How to Access the Registry," earlier in this chapter, for a Registry function that solves this problem.

ActiveX component can't create object
Runtime error: you'll get this when you try to use the Set statement, as described throughout this chapter, and for whatever reason, WSH isn't familiar with the object you're trying to initialize. Typically, objects are extensions to WSH, some of which come with Windows Vista, some of which are installed through Add or Remove Programs, and some of which come with third-party programs. The resolution usually involves installing the missing component (which usually can be found on the Web), but depends entirely upon the specific object reported by the error.

If you plan on distributing your scripts, you'll want to take steps to eliminate any error messages that may pop up. See the "How to Manipulate Files" example script, earlier in this chapter, for more information on error trapping and the On Error Resume Next statement.

Find a Better Editor

Notepad is a very rudimentary text editor. Although it does the job, it doesn't go any further than making it possible to write and save VBScript. It has no toolbar, no syntax highlighting, no visible line numbers, and no macro feature. If you find yourself writing VBScript files often, you'll want to use a better editor. Now, Windows also comes with WordPad, although it doesn't do much more than Notepad in helping to write scripts, and it has that creepy Microsoft Word–like interface.

One direction to go is simply to use a better plain-text editor, such as UltraEdit-32 (*http://www.ultraedit.com*). It has many features prized by programmers, such as column selections, visible line numbers, a terrific multi-file search and replace, and many other goodies. However, it's still just a text editor and therefore doesn't provide any VBScript-specific assistance.

The good news is that there are several excellent (but mostly not free) dedicated VBScript editors, such as:

Adersoft VbsEdit (http://www.vbsedit.com/)
   Supports breakpoints, watches, and other VBScript debugging tools.

CodeLobster Handy Code Editor (http://www.codelobster.com/)
   Offers autocomplete, code collapsing, and HTML code conversion.

iTripoli Admin ScriptEditor (http://www.itripoli.com/)
   Can create self-contained executable packages for scripts.

JanSoft Backedit (http://jansfreeware.com/)
   A free tool with integrated Internet Explorer, syntax highlighting, and autocompletion.

Sapien PrimalScript (http://www.primalscript.com/)
   Features include syntax checking, parenthesis matching, class browser, and more.

Further Study

Given that writing scripts for the Windows Script Host is a language-dependent endeavor, the most helpful reference material will be specific to the particular language you're using. Microsoft's support web site for all its scripting technologies, including WSH, can be found at *http://msdn.microsoft.com/scripting/*. In addition to documentation on VBScript and JScript, you can download updates to the WSH engine. Note that if you distribute scripts to other machines, you'll need to be careful about supporting features found only in newer releases of WSH.

Before committing to VBScript for a project, you may want to do some research on other supported languages listed here. Due to VBScript's heritage in web pages, security concerns have resulted in some limitations in the VBScript language, such as its inability to access the clipboard or link to external *.dll* files.

Given that JavaScript (which actually has nothing whatsoever to do with Sun Microsystems' Java™ programming language) was created by Netscape, you can find a lot of background information at *http://en-wikipedia.org/wiki/Javascript*. Keep in mind, however, that JScript is Microsoft's bastardized version of JavaScript and therefore not exactly the same language.

The Practical Extract and Report Language (Perl) is probably the most powerful and flexible scripting language available for WSH at the time of this writing. It's traditionally very popular among the Unix crowd and has gained tremendous popularity for its use in writing CGI programs for web servers. Unfortunately, Windows Vista doesn't come with the Perl engine; you'll have to obtain a separate Perl add-on module from *http://www.activestate.com*. More information is available at *http://www.perl.com*.

Make a Startup Script

The process of making a startup script—a script that is executed automatically when Windows starts—is quite simple. Essentially, you create an ordinary WSH script and then take steps to have it executed when Windows starts. There are a few different ways to do this:

Use the Startup folder. Put a shortcut to the script in your *Startup* folder (usually *C:\Users\[username]\AppData\Roaming\Microsoft\Windows\Start Menu\Programs\Startup*). This is by far the easiest to implement, but also the most fragile, because it's equally easy to disable.

If there is more than one user account on a computer, and you want the script to be executed regardless of the currently logged-in user, you can use the "All Users" *Startup* folder (usually *C:\Users\All Users\Microsoft\Windows\Start Menu\Programs\Startup*) instead.

Use the Registry. Open the Registry Editor (discussed in Chapter 3) and expand the branches to HKEY_CURRENT_USER\Software\Microsoft\ Windows\CurrentVersion\Run. Select **New** and then **String Value** from the **Edit** menu, and type startup script. Double-click the new Startup Script value, type the name of your script (e.g., c:\scripts\myscript. vbs), and click **OK**. Although it's a bit harder to implement, this setup is a little more buried, and thus more difficult for unwitting users to mess up than items placed in the *Startup* folder.

Many viruses and spyware install themselves in this Registry key precisely because it's so transparent. See Chapter 6 for tips on how to remove malware from this key.

Likewise, you can implement this solution for all users rather than just the current user by adding the Registry value to HKEY_LOCAL_MACHINE\ Software\Microsoft\Windows\CurrentVersion\Run instead.

Use the Group Policy Editor. This is probably the coolest solution, as it gives you the most control over precisely when the script is run, and it's the only way to facilitate a shutdown or logoff script as well. Open the Group Policy Editor (*gpedit.msc*), and expand the branches to Computer Configuration\Windows Settings\Scripts (Startup/Shutdown). Double-click the **Startup** entry on the right side, and then click **Add**. Click **Browse** to locate a script file, and click **OK** when you're done. The script will be run every time you start your computer, but before the logon or Welcome screen appears (and before scripts specified in the Registry or Start menu are ever run).

Likewise, double-click the **Shutdown** entry to specify a script to be run every time your computer shuts down.

Now, there's a similar setting called Scripts (Logon/Logoff), located in the User Configuration branch. Like everything in the User Configuration branch, these settings apply only to the currently logged-on user (as opposed to all users). If you specify your startup script here (under Logon), instead of under Computer Configuration, the script will run *after* you log in. And, of course, a script specified under Logoff will be run when you log off, whether or not you actually shut down the computer.

A startup script can contain a list of programs that you want to run in a specific order when Windows starts, such as connecting to the Internet and then checking your email. (Neither Explorer's *Startup* folder nor the Registry allow you to choose the order in which programs are run.) But there are other, less apparent uses for a startup script, such as for security or remote administration.

For example, say you've discovered malware that has infected some or all of the computers on a network. By writing a script that eliminates the malware by deleting key files or running a removal utility and setting it up as a startup script, you can effectively eliminate it from each computer.

But with scripts, you can take it even further: utilize a single script stored on a single computer that is run, over the network, on all computers. This way, you can make changes to the script once and have those changes propagated to all computers effortlessly. So, if you place the script *Startup.vbs* on a machine called *Server* in a folder called *C:\scripts* (drive C: would be shared as "C"), then each client machine should be configured to automatically execute \\server\c\scripts\startup.vbs (using one of the previous methods). The beauty of this is that when you don't want the script to do anything, you can simply leave it intact yet empty. If you find that you need to, say, make a Registry change or copy a group of files onto each computer, just type the appropriate commands into the script and turn on (or reboot) all the client computers. This can turn some administration tasks into very short work.

Wacky Script Ideas

The point of scripting is that instead of using a canned application to perform a certain task, you can easily and quickly throw together a script that does exactly what you need. That said, you may need some inspiration to get you cooking.

The following examples use many of the custom subroutines and functions outlined earlier in this book, but for brevity and sanity, they won't be repeated in the forthcoming snippets of code.

Quick and Dirty Backup Tool

The script in Example 9-2 starts by prompting you for the name of a folder to back up and checks whether it exists. If not, it gives you an opportunity to either type another folder name or exit. Once you've entered a valid folder name, the script creates a backup of the entire folder on a removable drive (set with the TargetDrive variable), such as a USB memory key or flash card.

Example 9-2. Quick and dirty backup tool

```
On Error Resume Next
TargetDrive = "K"
Accepted = False
Do Until Accepted
  MyFolder = InputBox("Please enter the name of the folder_
      you want to back up.")
  If Not FolderExists(MyFolder) Then
    Answer = MsgBox("The folder you typed doesn't exist._
        Try again?", 36, "")
    If Answer = 7 Then WScript.Quit
  Else
    Accepted = True
  End If
Loop

Answer = MsgBox("Please get drive " & TargetDrive & ": ready.", 33, "")
If FolderSize(MyFolder) > DriveFreeSpace(TargetDrive) Then
  MsgBox "The folder you specified won't fit on this drive.", 16
  WScript.Quit
End If

If FolderCreate(TargetDrive & ":\Backup\") = False Then
  MsgBox "There was a problem writing to drive " & TargetDrive & ":.", 16
  WScript.Quit
End If

Call FolderCopy(MyFolder, TargetDrive & ":\Backup\")

If Right(MyFolder, 1) <> "\" Then MyFolder = MyFolder & "\"
Call WriteToFile(MyFolder & "backuplog.txt",_
            "Last backed up: " & Now)
```

This script uses several MsgBox prompts and, if used unaltered, will probably irritate just about anybody. (Hint: think about who will be using the scripts you write when you decide how much error checking and prompting is appropriate.) However, it also shows part of the power of interactive scripting: a little intelligent planning and error trapping can keep your scripts running smoothly, interrupting you only when necessary. For instance, note the use of the FolderExists function at the beginning of the script; rather than risking encountering an error, the script checks for a potential problem (a missing file) and then takes the necessary steps to resolve it. If the folder doesn't exist and the user doesn't want to try again, the user can exit; always give your users a choice to get out if they want.

Because the script implements some degree of error checking, the line On Error Resume Next appears at the beginning of the script. This statement instructs WSH to simply ignore any errors it finds. This doesn't automatically *resolve* any errors; it just eliminates the error message that would otherwise appear in the event of an error, allowing the script to skip problems and continue uninterrupted. This way, you're only bothered with the errors that concern you.

This example also uses the Do...Loop loop structure (which is similar to the For...Next loop, documented earlier in this chapter) at the beginning of the script. The code inside such a loop is repeated until a specific condition is met; in this case, the loop will repeat until the Accepted variable has a value of True (notice that it's set to False at the beginning of the script). The If... Then structures ensure that the Accepted variable is only set to True if the folder actually exists.

The second part of the script compares the total size of the folder and all its contents with the amount of free space on the target drive. You could expand the script, so that if the diskette is not sufficient to store the folder, the user is given the opportunity to insert another diskette and try again. You'd need to use a similar Do...Loop, as described earlier.

Once the script has gone through all of the tests (eliminating the possibility of most errors), the FolderCopy subroutine copies the folder to the floppy. Finally, the WriteToFile subroutine records in a logfile that the folder was backed up. Note also the preceding line that adds a backslash (\) to the end of the MyFolder variable; this way, you can pass a valid filename (the folder name followed by a backslash and then the filename) to the WriteToFile subroutine.

This script requires the following subroutines, which are found earlier in this book: DriveFreeSpace, FolderCopy, FolderCreate, FolderExists, FolderSize, and WriteToFile.

Internet Fishtank

Nothing exemplifies the power of the Internet more than an Internet-enabled fishtank. This, essentially, is a web page with a dynamic picture of the contents of a fishtank. There are several ways to do this, but the following shows that it can be done with nothing more than a script, a webcam,* and a common FTP account.

These listings assume that the camera program and all images it creates are stored in the folder *C:\camera*. Start with the script shown in Example 9-3.

---

* See "Add Wireless Support to Any Device," in Chapter 7, for information on wireless webcams.

Example 9-3. Internet fishtank script

```
On Error Resume Next

ImageFile = "c:\camera\fish.jpg"
Call FileDelete(ImageFile)
Call RunProgram("c:\camera\camera.exe " & ImageFile, True)
If Not FileExists(ImageFile) Then WScript.Quit

Call RunProgram ("ftp -n -s:c:\camera\ftpscript.txt myhost.com", False)
```

The script starts by suppressing all error messages, as described in the previous example. The subsequent lines use the snapshot utility that comes with nearly all cheap webcams to snap a still photo and save it to a *.jpg* image file. Note also the line that deletes the old file before the photo is taken, and the line thereafter that checks for the existence of the file before proceeding (in case something went wrong); this way, the script never sends the same photo twice. The inclusion of True in the RunProgram line instructs the script to wait for the *camera.exe* program to complete before the script continues, necessary for a script like this to work. You could alternatively incorporate a Do...Loop loop instead of the simple If statement to repeatedly check for the file over the course of several seconds.

The last line then runs the FTP utility that comes with Windows Vista to transfer the JPG file to a web server (available for free from nearly all Internet service providers). Normally, FTP is an interactive program, requiring that the user type commands into the console, but the -n and -s options shown here eliminate the need for user interaction. Replace myhost.com with the name of the server containing your web account. Example 9-4 shows the FTP script used by the WSH script in Example 9-3; type it into a plain-text file and save it as *ftpscript.txt*.

Example 9-4. FTP script for use with Internet-fishtank script

```
user mylogin
pass mypassword
bin
cd public_html
put c:\camera\fish.jpg
bye
```

The FTP script, like a batch file, is simply a text file containing the commands (in order) that you'd otherwise type manually into the FTP console window. Naturally, you'll want to replace the specifics, like mylogin and mypassword, with your own login and password, respectively, and public_html with the directory containing your public HTML files. Note that all commands must be typed lowercase. Type FTP -? at the Command Prompt for more command-line parameters.

Next, you'll want to set up a scheduled task to repeatedly run the script; the interval (five seconds, five minutes, etc.) depends on your needs and the capabilities of your system. Lastly, if you haven't already done it, create a web page that references the *fish.jpg* photo; just visit the page to view a current picture of your fishtank, from anywhere in the world. You can even include JavaScript code in the page to automatically reload itself and update the picture after a certain delay.

This script requires the following subroutines, found earlier in this book: FileDelete, FileExists, and RunProgram.

Quick SendTo Shortcut Creator

Explorer's **SendTo** menu contains a list of programs and shortcuts to which any selected file can be sent. The idea is to list programs that could be used with any type of file, such as an email program or file viewer, without having to specifically set up file associations for each supported file type. The following script (Example 9-5) allows you to right-click on any application executable (*.exe* file), folder, or drive and create a shortcut in the *SendTo* folder on the spot.

Example 9-5. SendTo shortcut creator

```
SendToFolder = GetSpecialFolder("SendTo")
Call Shortcut("SendToFolder\Notepad.lnk", CommandLine(1))
```

Whenever you can, you should try to make your scripts "smart." If you wanted to be lazy, all you'd need is the second line of this script, which creates a shortcut based on the command-line parameter (see "How to Use Command-Line Parameters," earlier in this chapter, for details). However, the first line uses the GetSpecialFolder function to obtain the location of the *SendTo* folder from the Registry, which is handy if there's more than one user account (each with its own *SendTo* folder), if you intend to use this script on more than one computer, or if you don't want to have to modify the script when Microsoft changes the location of the *SendTo* folder in the next version of Windows (which it did for Vista, dontcha know).

Once the script has been written, you'll need to associate it with all file types. See "File Type Associations," in Chapter 3, for details on using the "*" file type (located in HKEY_CLASSES_ROOT*).

This script requires the following subroutines, found earlier in this book: CommandLine, GetSpecialFolder, and Shortcut.

Rename Files with Search and Replace

Although Explorer lets you rename more than one file at a time (as described in Chapter 2), it's not terribly flexible or intuitive. The Command Prompt provides a decent multiple-file renaming tool, but it's not always convenient. Example 9-6 shows a script that will rename all the files in a given folder based on rules you choose.

Example 9-6. File-renaming script

```
On Error Resume Next
FolderName = InputBox("Enter the name of the folder:")
If Not FolderExists(FolderName) Then WScript.Quit
SearchText = InputBox("Type the text to look for:")
ReplaceText = InputBox("Type the text with which to replace" _
                                      & SearchText & ":")
If SearchText = "" or ReplaceText = "" Then WScript.Quit

Set FileObject = CreateObject("Scripting.FileSystemObject")
Set FolderObject = FileObject.GetFolder(FolderName)
Set FilesObject = FolderObject.Files

FileCount = 0
For Each Filename in FilesObject
  If InStr(Filename.Name,SearchText) Then
    Filename.Name = Replace(Filename.Name,SearchText,ReplaceText)
    FileCount = FileCount + 1
  End If
Next

If FileCount > 0 Then
  MsgBox FileCount & " files were renamed."
Else
  MsgBox "No filenames containing " & SearchText & " were found."
End If
```

The first section of code is responsible for asking for input, including the folder name, the text to look for, and the text with which to replace it. The next three lines set the appropriate objects (for further documentation on these objects, check *http://msdn.microsoft.com/scripting/*).

The For...Next structure that follows does the real work: this particular example uses a special form of the loop intended to cycle through all the elements of an *object collection*. In this case, the collection contains the filenames of all the files in the specified folder. The Replace function (built into VBScript) then does the search and replace for each individual filename. Lastly, the FileCount variable tallies the number of files renamed, the result of which is displayed in the final code section.

Now, it may take some experience to understand the extensive use of objects in this example, but for the time being, just typing it in will serve as a good example that can be used in other circumstances. This script requires the FolderExists subroutine, found earlier in this book.

Note that a far more powerful file-renaming utility, Power Rename (part of Creative Element Power Tools), is available for Windows Vista (download it from *http://www.creativelement.com/powertools/*).

Command Prompt Scripting

If you don't quite have a grasp on the concept of DOS or the Command Prompt, here's a quick primer on this useful but oft-forgotten interface.

The Command Prompt in Windows XP is based on MS-DOS (Microsoft Disk Operating System), the operating system used by the first PCs and the basis for many versions of Windows, including 95 and 98, up until Windows Me. As explained in Chapter 1, however, the Windows XP/2000/NT platform has been designed from the ground up to be completely independent of DOS.

Fortunately, the DOS-like Command Prompt is still available from within Windows. You can open the **Command Prompt** by clicking its icon in the **All Programs** portion of your Start menu, or by typing cmd into the Start menu **Search** box and pressing **Enter**.

Windows Vista also includes the Command Prompt application found in Windows 9x/Me (*command.com*), but given its poor support for long filenames and other limitations, you shouldn't ever use it. Use either the native Windows Command Prompt (*cmd.exe*), or the Windows PowerShell, discussed later in this chapter.

When you open a Command Prompt window, you'll see a window that looks like the one shown in Figure 9-3. The cursor indicates the command line (where commands are typed), and the prompt usually shows the current working directory (here, *C:\Users\Cory\AppData\Local*), followed by a caret (>).

To run a program or execute a command, just type the name of the program or command at the command line (also called the "C" prompt because it usually looks like **C:\>**), and press **Enter**.

Some Command Prompt applications simply display information and then exit immediately. For example, Figure 9-3 shows some output from the Active Connections utility (*netstat.exe*) discussed in "Scan Your System for Open Ports" in Chapter 7.

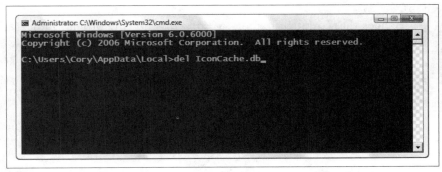

Figure 9-3. The Command Prompt is the old-school way to get things done

DOS Commands

You should know the following basic DOS commands to be able to complete some of the solutions in this book and get by in the world of Windows.

> The commands shown here are in constant width, and any parameters (the information you supply to the command) are in *constant width italic*. Optional parameters are shown in [square brackets]. It doesn't matter which case you use when you type them in the Command Prompt (DOS, like Windows, is not case-sensitive). If there is more than one parameter, each is separated by a space.

attrib *attributes filename*

> Changes the attributes of a file or folder. The four attributes are R for *read only*, S for *system*, A for *archive*, and H for *hidden*.
>
> In Explorer, you can right-click a file or group of files and select **Properties** to change the attributes; attrib is the DOS counterpart to this functionality. In addition, attrib lets you change the S (system) attribute, something Explorer doesn't let you do.* Here are some examples:

attrib +h *myfile.txt*

> This turns *on* the H parameter for the file *myfile.txt*, making the file hidden.

attrib -r *"another file.doc"*-

> This turns *off* the R (read-only) parameter for the file *another file.doc* (note the use of quotation marks because of the space in the filename).
>
> Type attrib /? for additional options.

---

* The **Change file attributes** tool in Creative Element Power Tools (*http://www.creativelement.com/powertools/*) lets you quickly add or remove any of the four standard attributes by right-clicking.

cd *foldername*

Changes the working directory to *foldername*. If the prompt indicates you are in *C:\Windows* and you want to enter the *C:\Windows\ System32* folder, type cd system32. You can also switch to any folder on your hard disk by including the full path of the folder. Type cd .. to go to the parent folder. Type cd by itself to display the current directory.

To switch to another drive, just type the drive letter, followed by a colon (:). For example, type a: to switch to the floppy drive.

cls

Clear the display and empty the buffer (the history of output accessible with the scroll bar).

copy *filename destination*

Copies a file to another directory or drive, specified by *destination*. This is the same as dragging and dropping files in Explorer, except that you use the keyboard instead of the mouse. For example, to copy the file *myfile.txt* (located in the current working directory) to another drive, type copy myfile.txt g:\. Type copy /? for additional options.

del *filename*

Deletes a file. For example, to delete the file *myfile.txt*, type del myfile. txt. This is not exactly the same as deleting a file in Windows, because the file will *not* be stored in the Recycle Bin. The advantage of the DOS variant is that you can more easily and quickly delete a group of files, such as all the files with the *.tmp* extension: del *.tmp. Type del /? for additional options.

dir *name*

Displays a listing of all the files and directories in the current working directory. Use cd to change to a different directory, or type dir c:\ files to display the contents of *C:\Files* without having to first use the cd command. Type dir /p to pause the display after each page, useful for very long listings (or just enlarge the window). You can also specify wildcards to filter the results; type dir *.tmp to display only files with the *.tmp* filename extension. Type dir /? for additional options.

echo *text*

Displays the text, *text*, on the screen. See "Variables and the Environment," later in this chapter.

exit

Closes the Command Prompt window. In most situations, you can just click the close button ✕ on the upper-right corner of the window, but the exit command works just as well.

md *foldername*

This command creates a new directory (md=make directory) with the name *foldername*. The command will have no effect if there's already a directory or file with the same name.

move *filename destination*

Is the same as copy, except that the file is moved instead of copied. Type move /? for additional options. (Unlike dragging and dropping in Windows Explorer, this command moves files unconditionally.)

rd *foldername*

This command deletes an empty directory (rd=remove directory) with the name *foldername*. The command will have no effect if the directory is not empty. To delete a directory and all of its contents, use deltree.

ren *oldfilename newfilename*

Renames a file to *newfilename*. This is especially useful, because you can use the ren command to rename more than one file at once—something Explorer doesn't let you do. For example, to rename *hisfile.txt* to *herfile.txt*, type ren hisfile.txt herfile.txt. To change the extensions of all the files in the current working directory from *.txt* to *.doc*, type ren *.txt *.doc. Type ren /? for additional options.

set [*variable*=[*string*]]

When used without any arguments, displays a list of active environment variables (described in "Variables and the Environment," later in this chapter). The set command is also used to assign data to environment variables.

type *filename*

Displays the contents of a text file. Type type *filename* | more to display the file and pause between each page of information rather than displaying the whole file at once.

Using Long Filenames in the Command Prompt

Given the nature of long filenames (they can have spaces), there are times that typing them on the command line can cause a problem. The workaround is to enclose the filename in quotation marks.

Say you wish to rename a file named *my stuff.txt* to *her stuff.doc*. Instinctively, you might type:

```
ren my stuff.txt her stuff.doc
```

However, this won't work, since the ren command sees only that you've typed *four* parameters: my, stuff.txt, her, and stuff.doc. Instead, you'll need to use quotation marks, like this:

```
ren "my stuff.txt" "her stuff.doc"
```

Now, this isn't always the case. For example, say you want to use the cd command to change the current working directory to *Program Files*, like this:

```
cd Program Files
```

Here, the Command Prompt is smart enough to interpret this correctly, and no quotation marks are needed.

Tip for you lazy types: you can often leave off the final quote, and it'll still work.

Batch Files

When it comes to quick and dirty scripting, it's hard to beat DOS batch files. Batch files, similar to WSH scripts (discussed earlier in this chapter), are plain-text files with the *.bat* or *.cmd* filename extension. However, rather than relying on a complex, unfamiliar scripting language, batch files simply consist of one or more DOS commands, typed one after another.

One of the problems with Windows-based scripting is that it tries to control a graphical environment with a command-based language. Because DOS is a command-based interface, DOS-based scripting (batch files) is a natural extension of the environment.

Consider the following four DOS commands:

```
c:
cd \windows\temp
attrib -r *.tmp
del *.tmp
```

If you type these commands into a plain-text editor, such as Notepad, save them into a *.bat* file, and then execute the batch file by double-clicking or typing its name at the Command Prompt, it will have the same effect as if the commands were manually typed consecutively at the prompt. Obviously, this can be a tremendous time saver if you find yourself entering the same commands repeatedly.

 When you run a batch file, each command in the file will be displayed (echoed) on the screen before it's executed, which can be unsightly for the more compulsive among us. To turn off the echoing of any given command, precede it with the @ character. To turn off the printing of all commands in a batch file, place the command @echo off at the beginning of the batch file.

To run a batch file, double-click its icon in Explorer or, if it's in the current working directory (folder), you can type its name at the Command Prompt. You'll want to put more frequently used, general-purpose batch files in a folder specified in the system path (see the upcoming sidebar, "The Path Less Travelled"), so that they can be executed regardless of the current working directory.

Although batch files can run Windows programs (just type notepad to launch Notepad), it's preferable to run Windows programs with WSH scripts, because they'll be able to run without having to first load a Command Prompt window.

In addition to the standard DOS commands, most of which are documented earlier, batch files use a couple of extra statements to fill the holes. Variables, conditional statements, and for...next loops are all implemented with statements that are ordinarily not much use outside of batch files.

The next few section cover the concepts used to turn a task or a string of DOS commands into a capable batch file.

Variables and the Environment

The use of variables in batch files can be somewhat confusing. All variables used in a batch file (with the exception of command-line parameters) are stored in the *environment*—an area of memory that is created when you first boot and kept around until the computer is turned off. The environment variable space is discussed in more detail in the upcoming sidebar, "The Path Less Travelled."

To view the contents of the environment, type set without any arguments. To set a variable to a particular value, type this command:

```
set VariableName=Some Data
```

The Path Less Travelled

Although it isn't really emphasized as much as it was in the heyday of DOS and Windows 3.x, the system path is still an important setting in Windows Vista. It can be helpful as well as detrimental, depending on how it's used.

The system path is simply a list of folder names kept in memory during an entire Windows session. If a folder name is listed in your system path, you'll be able to run a program contained in that folder *without* having to specify its location. The path is one of several *environment variables* that are kept in memory from Windows startup until you shut down. In early versions of Windows, the path was set with a line in the now-obsolete *Autoexec.bat* file; now, all environment variables are set by going to **Control Panel** → **System** → **Advanced System Settings** → **Environment Variables**.

By default, the Path system variable (shown in the lower box), contains the following folders:

```
%SystemRoot%
%SystemRoot%\system32
%SystemRoot%\system32\Wbem
```

The %SystemRoot% element represents the Windows folder (usually *C:\Windows*); see the discussion of expanded string variables in Chapter 3 for details.

One of the consequences of this design is that if two different versions of the same executable file (any *.exe*, *.dll*, or *.ocx* file, for instance) are placed in two different folders in the path, only one of the available versions of the file—and not necessarily the most recent one—may be in use at any given time.

How do you escape this trap? First, remove any unnecessary directories from your path variable. Next, if you suspect a conflict with a specific file, try searching your hard disk for the filename; if you see more than one copy of the file in the search results, it could potentially cause a conflict. Compare the versions of the files (right-click, select **Properties**, and click the **Details** tab), and delete (or temporarily rename, to be on the safe side) all versions but the most recent. Then move the newest file to your *\Windows\System32* folder if it's not already there.

Unlike VBScript, the SET command is required and no quotation marks are used when setting the value of a variable. To remove the variable from memory, you set its value to nothing, like this:

```
set VariableName=
```

To then display the contents of the variable, use the echo command, as follows:

```
echo %VariableName%
```

Here, the percent signs (%) on both ends of the variable name are mandatory; otherwise, the echo command would take the argument literally and display the name of the variable rather than the data it contains. What's confusing is that in some cases, variables need no percent signs; sometimes they need one, two at the beginning, or one on each end. More on this later.

Flow Control

Batch files have a very rudimentary, but easy-to-understand flow-control structure. The following example exhibits the use of the goto command:

```
@echo off
echo  Griff
echo  Asa
goto LaterOn
echo  0x
:LaterOn
echo  Etch
```

The :LaterOn line (note the mandatory colon prefix) is called a label, which is used as a target for the goto command. If you follow the flow of the script, you should expect the following output:

```
Griff
Asa
Etch
```

because the goto command has caused the printing of 0x to be skipped. The label can appear before or after the goto line in a batch file, and you can have multiple goto commands and multiple labels.

Command-Line Parameters

Suppose you executed a batch file called *Demo.bat* by typing the following at the Command Prompt:

```
Demo file1.txt file2.txt
```

Both file1.txt and file2.txt are command-line parameters and are automatically stored in two variables, %1 and %2, respectively, when the batch file is run.

The implication is that you could run a batch file that would then act with the filenames or options that have been passed to it. "How to Use Command-Line Parameters," earlier in this chapter, shows how command-line parameters are used with WSH scripts.

The following two-line example uses command-line parameters and the FC utility to compare two text files. A similar example using the Windows Script Host, shown in "Make Building Blocks with Subroutines and Functions," takes 22 lines to accomplish approximately the same task:

```
fc %1 %2 >c:\windows\temp\output.txt
notepad c:\windows\temp\output.txt
```

Save this batch file as *compare.bat*, and execute it like this:

```
compare c:\windows\tips.txt c:\windows\faq.txt
```

which will compare the two files, *tips.txt* and *faq.txt* (both located in your Windows folder), save the output to a temporary file, and then display the output by opening the file in Notepad. Note that the > character on the first line *redirects* the output of the FC program to the *output.txt* file, which would otherwise be displayed on the screen. The second line then opens the *output.txt* file in Notepad for easy viewing.

There are ways, other than typing, to take advantage of command-line parameters. If you place a shortcut to a batch file (say, *Demo.bat*) in your *SendTo* folder, then right-click on a file in Explorer, select **Send To** and then **Demo**, the *Demo.bat* batch file will be executed with the file you've selected as the first command-line parameter. Likewise, if you drag-drop any file onto the batch-file icon in Explorer, the dropped file will be used as the command-line parameter.*

Batch files have a limit of nine command-line parameters (%1 through %9), although there's a way to have more if you need them. Say you need to accept 12 parameters at the command line; your batch file should start by acting on the first parameter. Then, you would issue the shift command, which eliminates the first parameter, putting the second in its place. %2 becomes %1, %3 becomes %2, and so on. Just repeat the process until there are no parameters left. Here's an example of this process:

```
:StartOfLoop
if "%1"=="" exit
del %1
shift
goto StartOfLoop
```

---

* If you drop more than one file on a batch-file icon, their order as arguments will be seemingly random, theoretically mirroring their ordering in your hard disk's file table.

Save these commands into *MultiDel.bat*. Now, this simple batch file deletes one or more filenames with a single command; it's used like this:

```
MultiDel file1.txt another.doc third.log
```

by cycling through the command-line parameters one by one using shift. It repeats the same two lines (del %1 and shift) until the %1 variable is empty (see "Conditional Statements," next, for the use of the if statement), at which point the batch file ends (using the exit command).

Conditional Statements

There are three versions of the if statement, which allow you to compare values and check the existence of files. The first version, which is usually used to test the value of a variable, is used as follows:

```
if "%1"=="help" goto SkipIt
```

Note the use of quotation marks around the variable name and the help text, as well as the double equals signs, all of which are necessary here. Notice also there's no then keyword, which those of you who are familiar with VBScript might expect. If the batch file finds that the two sides are equal, it executes everything on the right side of the statement; in this case, it issues the goto command.

The second use of the IF command is to test the existence of a file:

```
if exist c:\windows\tips.txt goto SkipIt
```

If the file *C:\Windows\tips.txt* exists, the goto command will be executed. Similarly, you can you can test for the absence of a file, as follows:

```
if not exist c:\autoexec.bat goto SkipIt
```

The third use of the if command is to test the outcome of the previous command, as follows:

```
if errorlevel 0 goto SkipIt
```

If there was any problem with the statement immediately before this line, the errorlevel (which is similar to a system-defined variable) will be set to some nonzero number. The if statement shown here tests for any errorlevel that is greater than zero; if there was no error, execution will simply continue to the next command.

Here's a revised version of the file-compare example first shown in the "Command-Line Parameters" section, earlier in this chapter:

```
if "%1"=="" goto problem
if "%2"=="" goto problem
if not exist %1 goto problem
if not exist %2 goto problem
```

```
fc %1 %2 >c:\windows\temp\output.txt
if errorlevel 0 goto problem
if not exist c:\windows\temp\output.txt goto problem
notepad c:\windows\temp\output.txt
exit
:problem
echo "There's a problem; deal with it."
```

This batch file is essentially the same as the original two-line example shown earlier, except that some error-checking if statements have been added to make the batch file a little more robust. If you neglect to enter one or both command-line parameters, or if the files you specify as command-line parameters don't exist, the batch file will display the error message. An even more useful version might have multiple error messages that more accurately describe the specific problem that was encountered.

Loops

Batch files have a very simple looping mechanism, based loosely on the for...next loop used in other programming languages. The main difference is that the batch file for loop doesn't increment a variable regularly, but rather cycles it through a list of values. Its syntax is as follows:

```
for %%i in ("Abe","Monty","Jasper") do echo %%i
```

Here, the variable syntax gets even more confusing; the reference to the i variable when used in conjunction with the for...in...do statement gets two percent signs in front of the variable name and none after. Note also that only single-letter variables can be used here.

If you execute this batch file, you'll get the following output:

```
Abe
Monty
Jasper
```

Note also the use of the quotation marks; although they aren't strictly necessary, they're helpful if one or more of the values in the list has a comma in it.

To simulate a more traditional For...Next statement in a batch file, type the following:

```
for %%i in (1,2,3,4,5) do echo %%i
```

Simulating Subroutines

Batch files have no support for named subroutines (as described in "Make Building Blocks with Subroutines and Functions," earlier in this chapter). However, you can simulate subroutines by creating several batch files: one *main* file and one or more *subordinate* files (each of which can accept command-line parameters). You probably wouldn't want to use this if performance is an issue.

This is useful in cases like the for...in...do statement (described in the proceeding section), which can only loop a single command.

In one batch file, called *WriteIt.bat*, type:

```
if "%1"=="" exit
if exist %1.txt del %1.txt
echo This is a text > %1.txt
```

Then, in another batch file, called *Main.bat*, type the following:

```
for %%i in ("Kang","Kodos","Serak") do call WriteIt.bat %%i
```

The single-line *Main.bat* batch file uses the call command to run the other batch file, *WriteIt.bat*, three times. You could omit the call command, but doing so would cause the whole process to end after the subordinate batch file was run the first time. Don't ask me why.

When this pair of batch files is run, you should end up with three files, *Kang.txt*, *Kodos.txt*, and *Serak.txt*, all containing the text, "This is a text." The if statement and the for...in...do loop are explained in earlier sections.

Get to the Command Prompt Quickly

If you find yourself using the Command Prompt frequently, you'll probably benefit from the following solution. Instead of having to use the cd command to change to a given folder, you can simply open a Command Prompt window on the fly in Explorer, already rooted in the selected folder.

1. Open the Registry Editor (see Chapter 3).
2. Expand the branches to HKEY_CLASSES_ROOT\Directory\shell. (See "File Type Associations," in Chapter 3, for details on the structure of this branch.)
3. Create a new key by going to **Edit** → **New** → **Key**, and type cmd for the name of this new key.

4. Double-click the (default) value in the new cmd key, and type the following for its contents:

```
Open Command &Prompt Here
```

5. Next, create a new key here by going to **Edit** → **New** → **Key**, and type command for the name of the new key.

6. Double-click the (default) value in the new command key, and type the following for its contents:

```
cmd.exe /k "cd %L && ver"
```

This line launches the *cmd.exe* application, and then, using the /k parameter, instructs it to carry out these two commands:

```
cd %1
ver
```

which change the working directory to the folder that has been right-clicked, and then displays the Windows version, respectively.

7. Close the Registry Editor when you're done; the change will take effect immediately. Just right-click any folder and select **Open Command Prompt Here** to open a Command Prompt window at the selected folder.

A simpler (and somewhat slicker) solution is to use Creative Element Power Tools (*http://www.creativelement.com/powertools/*). Once you turn on the **Open a Command Prompt in any folder** option, you can right-click any folder icon or the background of any open folder window (or the desktop), and select **Command Prompt** to open a new Command Prompt window rooted at the selected folder. The tool can also be configured to open the Windows PowerShell (covered next), or any third-party Command Prompt application.

Windows PowerShell

Windows PowerShell, known prior to its official release as the Monad* Shell (MSH), is an advanced replacement for the good ol' Command Prompt. Although it uses many familiar DOS commands (sort of), it introduces some Unix-like functionality to the Windows platform while borrowing some of

---

* "Monad" literally means "one" or "single," but was likely chosen by Microsoft as the codename for PowerShell to evoke *monadism*, Gottfried Leibniz's philosophy that the physical and metaphysical universe exists because of a divine "harmony" between fundamental elements he called monads. To say the comparison is presumptuous on Microsoft's part is an understatement, but a noble goal nonetheless.

the Windows-aware features found in WSH scripts, like printing, security, and process control.

Windows PowerShell 1.0 was released more or less concurrently with Windows Vista, but it's not included in the default Vista installation. You can download PowerShell for free from *http://www.microsoft.com/powershell/*, but Microsoft has hinted that it'll be included with future versions of Windows.

At first glance, PowerShell (Figure 9-4) looks like an ordinary Command Prompt window, with the main distinguishing feature being the text PS preceding the prompt. As you may have guessed, you type a command at the prompt and press **Enter** to excecute the command. But the commands you can type—and how they interact with each other—are what really set PowerShell apart.

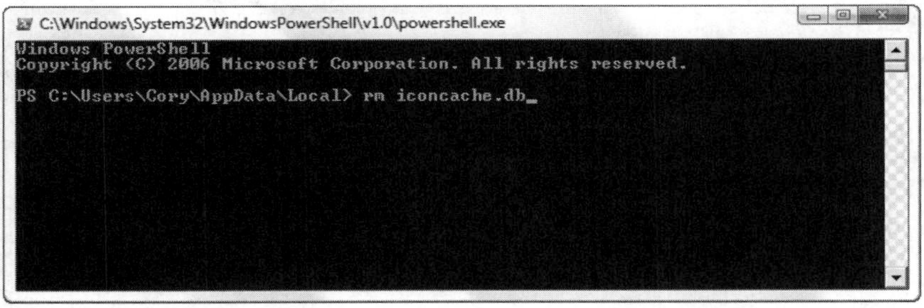

Figure 9-4. Microsoft PowerShell, a free, powerful alternative to the Command Prompt, also supports scripting

CmdLets and Aliases

PowerShell's built-in commands are called *CmdLets* for reasons that aren't entirely clear, and the CmdLets all have long, rather inconvenient names like Copy-Item, ConvertFrom-SecureString, and Invoke-Expression. The good news is that most of the commands have short versions, called *aliases*, that just happen to coincide with familiar DOS and Unix command names. For instance, instead of typing Copy-Item, you can type copy (as in DOS) or cp (à la Unix) to copy files from one place to another; if nothing else, this dualism is an important advantage over the conventional Command Prompt.

Table 9-1 shows a list of common, basic PowerShell commands, and their DOS and Unix counterparts.

Table 9-1. Common DOS and Unix commands and their PowerShell equivalents

DOS	Unix	PowerShell	Description
cd	cd	Set-Location	Change the working directory (folder)
cls	clear	Clear-Host	Clear the screen
copy	cp	Copy-Item	Copy a file or object from one place to another
del, rd	rm, rmdir	Remove-Item	Delete a file, directory (folder), or object
dir	ls	Get-ChildItem	Display the contents of the current directory or object
help	man	Get-Help	Display a list of commands or details about the specified command
md	mkdir	New-Item	Create a directory (folder) or object
move	mv	Move-Item	Move a file, directory (folder), or object to a new location
ren	mv	Rename-Item	Change the name of a file or object
type	cat	Get-Content	Display the contents of a file or object

What's more enticing is that you can make your own aliases. For example, if you find yourself frequently using the Get-Culture command (which retrieves the language in use by Windows), you could shorten it like this:

    Set-Alias -Name *lang* -Value *Get-Culture*

so that you could thereafter type only lang to display the current language. The Set-Alias command also lets you change (overwrite) any of the built-in aliases.

> The Set-Alias command only creates aliases for bare commands; you can't bury your favorite command-line parameters in an alias. To replace a complex, multipart command with a single word you can type at the prompt, use PowerShell variables, discussed later.

Of course, once you close the current PowerShell window, your custom alias will be forgotten. So, to save your custom aliases from session to session, add your Set-Alias commands to your PowerShell profile file. Of course, you probably don't have a profile yet, so type:

    New-Item -type file -force $profile

to create one. Then type:

    notepad $profile

to open the newly created profile for editing.

PowerShell has about 130 commands, most of which are documented in the *UserGuide.rtf* file included with the package. There's also a simple online help system, via the help command, that displays a list of available commands (in a not-so-helpful format), or if invoked with the name of a command, displays the syntax and explanation of the command. To see all the available information about a command, include the -full parameter, like this:

```
help Get-Item -full
```

While using the online help, you'll soon discover the needlessly complex SYNTAX section, which lists all the parameters supported by a single command. For instance, the syntax line for the Copy-Item command (copy to you and me) consumes four lines, and is about as easy to read as the computer output in the *Matrix* movies.* But rest assured, it's more or less the same as its DOS counterpart; in other words, this command:

```
copy c:\stuff\myfile.txt d:\misc
```

still works as you'd expect.

Pipelines

So, if PowerShell looks like the Command Prompt, and most of the commands you know and love work the same, then what's the point?

Without drowning you in technical jargon, what sets PowerShell Cmdlets apart from their Command Prompt counterparts is that they work better with *piping*, a means of redirecting the output of one command so that it's used as the input for another. For example, this two-part command:

```
get-process m* | stop-process
```

works because the get-process Cmdlet sends (through the *pipe*) its output (a list of running processes that start with the letter m) as a *structured object*. In turn, the stop-process Cmdlet receives this object and uses it as a list of processes to stop. In lesser Command Prompts, this information is passed between commands (piped) as plain text, which means you need to use a variety of tools (like grep in Unix) to format the output so the receiving command can process it. (Imagine what this would all sound like if I had left in the jargon.)

Unfortunately, this particular aspect of PowerShell is a little more hype than dope. For one, the example command above (taken from Microsoft's own documentation) is pointless, since the following simpler command works just as well:

```
stop-process m*
```

Of course, the downside of this object-oriented model is that the various data is all *typed*, and can't be easily converted from one type to another.

---

* Too geeky? Naaah....

That is, you can't easily pipe output to a command that hasn't been specifically designed to receive it. In good ol' Unix and DOS, you can pipe anything to anything. For instance, this PowerShell command:

```
help | help
```

which I expected would send a list of Cmdlets generated by help *back to* help, which in turn would spit out a detailed explanation of each Cmdlet, did not work at all. Perhaps this is a silly example, but it sure would've made my job easier.

What does work well is the passing of filenames from one Cmdlet to another. Here's a sophisticated series of commands that illustrates this:

```
Get-ChildItem 'H:\MediaCenterPC\My Music' -rec | where { -not $_.
PSIsContainer -and $_.Extension -match "wma|mp3" } | Measure-Object -
property length -sum -min -max -ave
```

This amalgam of three Cmdlets does the following:

- Retrieves a list of filenames in the *H:\MediaCenterPC\My Music* folder and all its subfolders (thanks to the -rec option), and passes the list to...

- the where (Where-Object) Cmdlet, which filters out any files that don't have the *.wma* or *.mp3* filename extensions, and then passes the modified list to...

- the Measure-Object Cmdlet, which outputs detailed information about the music files in the list.

And you could keep going like this, including a command that take the output from Measure-Object to process, store, or display it in some fashion. The syntax may look a little messy to the uninitiated, but it would be much more difficult to do this sort of thing in WSH and nearly impossible in a batch file.

PowerShell Variables

PowerShell variables work much like variables in other scripting languages (see "Use Variables to Store and Manipulate Information," earlier in this chapter): they hold data. A variable name starts with a dollar sign and what follows can be any string of characters. But what makes variables in Power-Shell particularly useful is that they can capture the output of Cmdlets, and then be put in place of static information in subsequent Cmdlets, like this:

```
$url = "http://www.nytimes.com/services/xml/rss/nyt/Science.xml"
$content = [xml](new-object System.Net.WebClient).DownloadString($url)
$content.rss.channel.item | select title -first 8
```

The first line fills the $url variable with the address of a web site (specifically, an RSS feed for the purposes of this example). The next line downloads the file at the $url address and sends it to the $content variable. And the last line uses a pipe (discussed earlier) to first process the news feed and then show only the first eight headlines.

You can also assign a variable to a command, or more importantly, a series of commands, like this:

```
$showtemp = Get-ChildItem 'C:\Users\Administrator\AppData\Local\Temp' -rec
```

then, to execute the command (complete with all the juicy command-line parameters), just type:

```
$showtemp
```

and (in this case), you'll see a listing of all the files in your *Temp* folder.

Variables can also be used with object references, just like in WSH scripts (see "Object References," earlier in this chapter). PowerShell even makes use of some of the same objects as WSH, like this one:

```
$WshShell = New-Object -ComObject WScript.Shell
```

This means you can use this object to do things like access the Registry or create shortcuts. For instance, once the $WshShell object has been initialized, try this:

```
$lnk = $WshShell.CreateShortcut("$Home\Desktop\Solitaire.lnk")
$lnk.TargetPath = "%ProgramFiles%\Microsoft Games\Solitaire\Solitaire.exe"
$lnk.Save( )
```

which creates another object reference, $lnk, applies characteristics to it, and then saves it to a file. Note some subtleties:

- The preset $Home variable conveniently contains the full path of the current user's home folder.

- The quotation marks are significant in that if you were to substitute the "double" quotes with 'single' quotes, PowerShell would not interpret your variables, but rather leave them literally as you've typed them.

- The %ProgramFiles% *environment* variable—a separate entity from PowerShell variables—is explained in "Variables and the Environment," earlier in this chapter.

See the PowerShell documentation for more ins and outs of variables and object references.

PowerShell Scripts

Like the WSH scripts or DOS batch files, a PowerShell script is just a text file with a list of commands. Just type the commands into a Notepad window or other text editor, and save it to a file with the *.ps1* filename extension.

Unfortunately, you can't run PowerShell scripts until you jump through a few hoops to disable some of the security safeguards. The first step is to check the execution policy by typing:

    Get-ExecutionPolicy

If the reply you get is Restricted (the default), then you need to type this command to allow script execution:

    Set-ExecutionPolicy RemoteSigned

To run a script from an open PowerShell window, type the name of the script file, complete with its path and filename extension, like this:

    $home\Desktop\MakeShortcut.ps1

Unlike the Command Prompt, you can't leave off the path if the script is in the same folder as the working folder. For instance, this doesn't work:

    MakeShortcut.ps1

but this does:

    .\MakeShortcut.ps1

The single dot (.) represents the current folder, and is necessary when launching scripts from the PowerShell command line.

Also, and presumably for security reasons, you can't run PowerShell scripts by double-clicking them until you make a change to your system. To enable script launching, right-click a *.ps1* file, select **Open With → Choose Default Program**, click **Select a program from a list of installed programs**, and then click **OK**. Click **Browse**, locate the PowerShell executable (usually *C:\Windows\System32\WindowsPowerShell\v1.0\powershell.exe*), and click **OK**.

 By default, the PowerShell window closes when it's done executing a script, but you can change this by modifying the file type (see Chapter 3) and adding the -NoExit option to the *powershell.exe* command line.

Thereafter, you can double-click any *.ps1* file to run the script.

Automate Scripts with the Task Scheduler

Vista's Task Scheduler is fairly simple, allowing you to schedule any program or—more importantly in the context of this chapter—any script to run at a specific time or regular intervals.

To open Task Scheduler, open your Start menu, type `taskschd.msc /s` in the **Search** box, and press **Enter**. (Omit the `/s` parameter to jump to the Task Scheduler Library instead of showing the summary page by default.) The Task Scheduler tool in Windows Vista (Figure 9-5) is complex and somewhat unfriendly, which is surprising since it replaces the simpler (and more feeble) *Scheduled Tasks* folder in earlier versions of Windows.

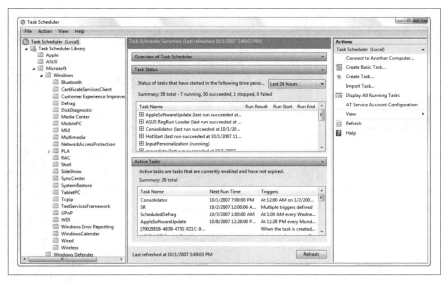

Figure 9-5. Use Task Scheduler to run programs or scripts at certain times or regular intervals, or to change schedules other programs may have set up without your knowledge

What's nice about Task Scheduler is that it's actually a technology that is somewhat well integrated into the operating system. Any application can create a schedule for itself, and you can plainly see those that are in effect simply by opening Task Scheduler and selecting the `Task Scheduler Library` folder. For the more forgetful among us, you can use it to schedule backups once a week, remind you to stand up and stretch once an hour, or even fire up Media Center when your favorite TV show is about to air.

To create a new schedule, click the **Create Basic Task** link in the **Actions** pane to your right, and then answer the questions as follows:

Create a Basic Task
> Type the name of the task to appear in your task library; the description is optional.

Trigger
> Choose when to run the task: **Daily**, **Weekly**, **Monthly**, **One time**, **When the computer starts**, **When I log on**, or **When a specific event is logged**.

Daily, Weekly, etc.
> Specify your criteria for the trigger you chose. For instance, if you selected **Daily**, you'll be asked what time of day to carry out the task, and for how many days in a row.

Action
> Here's where you specify what to do. If you want Task Scheduler to run a script, select **Start a program**, click **Next**, and then specify the full path and filename of the script to run.

Finish
> This one speaks for itself.

Or, if you don't like wizards, you can click the **Create Task** link instead to jump right to the Properties window shown in Figure 9-6. Here, only two pieces of information are required: the **Name** (under the **General** tab) and at least one action (under the **Actions** tab). But if you want Task Scheduler to ever run your task, you need to add your criteria (**Daily**, **Weekly**, etc.) under the **Triggers** tab. Click **OK** when you're done.

The Task Scheduler Library is a little confusing, especially if you're used to the *Scheduled Tasks* folder in earlier versions of Windows. Only on the Summary page—select **Task Scheduler (Local)** in the folder pane on the left—are all your active tasks shown in one place, and it's at the bottom of the window.

 In the **Actions** pane on the right, click the **View** link and then select **Show Hidden Tasks** to make sure you're seeing everything Task Scheduler is doing.

In the Active Tasks pane, you can double-click any task to jump to its entry in the hierarchical library, or click the tiny arrow next to the **Task Scheduler Library** folder on your left to expand the branches and browse the categories. Once you're in the library, highlight a task to view its details in the pane below, or double-click it to edit its properties.

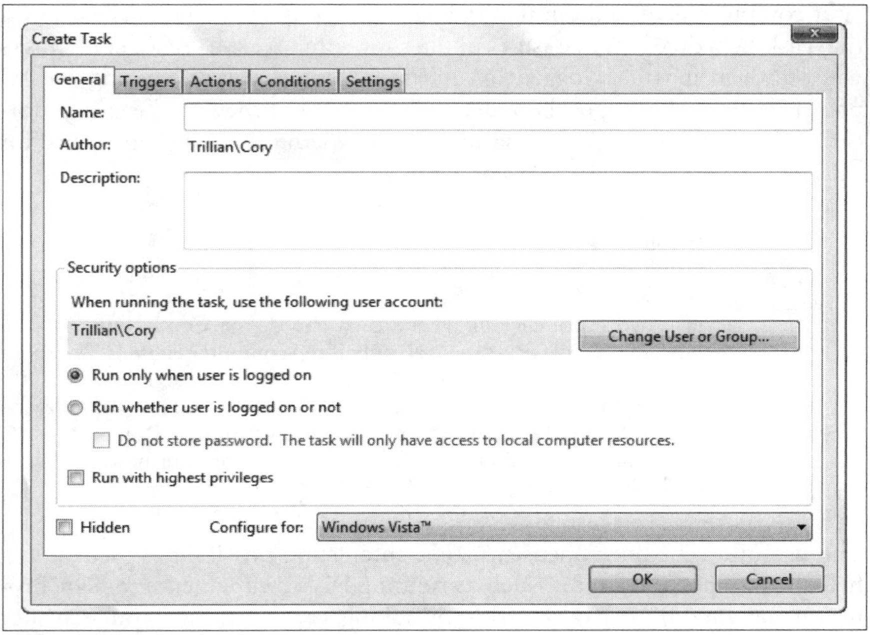

Figure 9-6. The Create Task window is another way to enter the scheduling details of a task, particularly useful if you're not fond of step-by-step wizards

You can also create a new task on the fly from the Command Prompt (or the Address Bar, for that matter). Use the at command, like this:

```
at 11:15 /interactive c:\scripts\myscript.vbs
```

Naturally, you'll want to replace *11:15* with the time you actually want the task to run, and replace *c:\scripts\myscript.vbs* with the full path and filename of the application or script you wish to schedule. You can also use the /every option to specify a repeating day or date, or the /next option to specify only a single day:

```
at 15:45 /interactive /every:tuesday,thursday c:\scripts\myscript.vbs
at 15:45 /interactive /next:saturday c:\scripts\myscript.vbs
```

Type at /? at the Command Prompt for more options. To specify which user account is responsible for running tasks created with the at command, open Task Scheduler, click **Task Scheduler (Local)** on the left, and then click the **AT Service Account Configuration** link in the Actions pane to your right.

Task Scheduler does have its pitfalls. For one, it's a rather passive service, and while that's an aspect I like, at least ideologically, it means that tasks can very easily be missed. Your scheduled tasks will not be performed if your computer is turned off, if Windows isn't running (or has crashed), or if the Task Scheduler service isn't running for some reason. Also, some tasks will only run if you're logged in, and then only if you're running on AC power (not on a battery). These may be obvious, but they can be easy to forget, and Windows won't necessarily tell you whether it missed any tasks; for this, you'll need to check the event log.

 If you're using a laptop, and are worried that some of your tasks aren't being performed when you're running off a battery, you can change this on a task-by-task basis. First, edit a task by double-clicking it, and then choose the **Conditions** tab. Turn off the **Start the task only if the computer is on AC power** option to run it regardless of the power source. If you put your PC to sleep frequently, you may also want to turn on the **Wake the computer to run this task** option. (Naturally, use these options only for vital tasks to prevent needlessly draining your battery.) Click **OK** when you're done.

The use of a scheduler opens up some interesting possibilities. Scheduling helps with repetitive chores, such as running Disk Defragmenter or synchronizing network files; it also helps by taking care of things you may not remember to do yourself, such as backing up or checking the amount of disk space and sending you a text message on your cell phone when it drops below a certain point. And on the flip side of the coin, Task Scheduler is likely doing some things you don't want or need it to do; it's wise to periodically check this tool and eliminate tasks that might be degrading performance or compromising your PC's security.

BIOS Settings

The BIOS, or Basic Input-Output System, is the software—stored in a chip on your motherboard—responsible for booting your computer and starting your operating system. It also handles the flow of data between the operating system and your peripherals (USB devices, PCI/PCIE slots, hard disk controller, video adapter, etc.), manages your PC's power management features, and cooperates with Windows' plug-and-play subsystem. Incorrect settings in your PC's BIOS can prevent Windows from booting, limit performance, and cause all sorts of hardware and driver problems.

 You change BIOS settings in the BIOS setup screen, which you can usually access by pressing a key—such as **Del**, **F2**, or **Esc**—immediately after powering on your system and before the initial beep. The normal boot screen that appears before the Windows logo often identifies the key you need to press; consult your computer's manual if you need further help.

The settings available in a computer's BIOS setup screen vary from one system to another, but there are many settings that are common among them all. Unfortunately, motherboard and computer manufacturers are notorious for poorly documenting BIOS settings, so it can be difficult to determine what the settings mean, let alone how they should be set. For instance, look up *Microcode Updation* in an ASUS motherboard manual, and here's the entire explanation of the entry for that setting:

Microcode Updation [Enabled]
Allows you to enable or disable the microcode updation.
Configuration options: [Disabled] [Enabled]

Thus, the need for this appendix becomes obvious.

When changing BIOS settings, keep the following in mind:

Change one at a time. If you're trying to fix a problem, don't change more than one BIOS setting at a time. Although it may take longer, it means you can determine which setting is responsible for fixing the problem (or causing a new one).

Check for updates. The BIOS is typically stored on a "flash" chip, which means it can be updated with newer versions. Check with your motherboard manufacturer to see whether a newer BIOS is available for your system. In most cases, BIOS updates only fix bugs, but they occasionally can improve performance or add support for new hardware. If you're unable to install Windows (or its successor) on your system, an outdated BIOS may be to blame.

 Flashing (updating) a BIOS can be a risky procedure. If something goes wrong (i.e., the power goes out, or the BIOS turns out to be corrupted or the wrong version), your computer will probably not boot. Now, such occurrences aren't common, but if you encounter a problem after upgrading your BIOS, check with the manufacturer for a "BIOS recovery" method. For obvious reasons, it's wise to familiarize yourself with the procedure *before* you attempt to update your BIOS.

Names may vary. The names of BIOS settings listed here may vary, and one appendix can't possibly accommodate them all. For example, a setting named **Event Log** on one system might be called **System Event Log** on another. If you can't find a particular setting, try looking through the list for variations.

Take snapshots. One of the problems with the BIOS setup screen is that you can't access it from within Windows, which means you can't look up settings on the Web, you can't take screenshots, and you can't take notes without using a pen and paper. However, a digital camera can be very handy in this situation; just take one or more photos of your screen (with the flash turned off, of course) to quickly record all your BIOS settings.

Table A-1 lists many common BIOS settings, along with brief explanations and some tips. For more extensive BIOS setting information and advice, check out the "The Definitive BIOS Optimization Guide" at *http://www.techarp.com/freebog.aspx*.

Table A-1. Common BIOS settings and what they do

Setting	Description
AC Power Recovery	Determines whether or not the computer turns on automatically when power is applied (such as from a power loss or external power switch). Note that many PCs don't reliably start when AC power is restored, even if you set this option to **Always On**. See "Start Windows Instantly (Almost)," in Chapter 5, for the Windows settings necessary to prevent data loss when you use an external switch to cut power to your PC.
ACPI 2.0 Support	This enables or disables your motherboard's support for ACPI (Advanced Configuration and Power Interface), a power management feature. In most cases, this should be set to **Enabled**, but if you change this setting after Windows has been installed, you'll get a Blue Screen of Death the next time you boot. If you enable ACPI, you'll need to reinstall Windows (see Chapter 1).
ACPI APIC Support	This enables or disables the APIC (Advanced Programmable Interrupt Controller), which should be enabled, particularly if you have a multicore processor. Like "ACPI 2.0 Support," you may need to reinstall Windows after changing this setting.
ACPI Aware O/S	Set this to **Yes**; see "Power Management" for details.
AddOn ROM Display Mode	Choose whether the startup screen is handled by the primary BIOS or a secondary "add-on" BIOS. Disable this option unless you have a specific need for it.
Address Range Shadowing	Various hardware address ranges can be "shadowed," which means that pieces of faster system RAM are substituted for them. It's best to disable shadowing for all address ranges; this feature is typically not available on newer PCs.
AGP 2X/4X Mode	The AGP 2X and 4X modes double and quadruple the bandwidth to your AGP video card, respectively, but can only be used if your video card supports 2X or 4X. Not applicable on motherboards with PCI-Express slots.
AGP Aperture/Device Address Space Size	This sets the amount of system memory used to store textures for 3D graphics. The more video memory you have, the lower this setting should be. Many video problems are caused by this value being set too high, but Vista's Glass feature won't work if it's not set at least as high as indicated in "Get Glass" in Chapter 5.
AHCI settings	See "SATA Configuration."
AI Overclocking	See "Overclocking."
AI Quiet	See "Digital Home Mode."
ALPE and ASP	Enables or disables the Aggressive Link Power Management (ALPE) and Aggressive Slumber/Partial (ASP) power management features for SATA drives. **Disabled/Off** is usually the default; enable this setting if you need advanced features like AHCI Port 3 Interlock Switch or Staggered Spinup Support.
AMD Cool 'n' Quiet/ PowerNow!	See "Intel SpeedStep."
Anti-Virus Protection	Actively scans your hard disk for boot sector viruses. Despite the apparent usefulness of a feature like this, you should always disable it, as it typically interferes with Windows and causes all sorts of problems.
APM settings	See "Power Management."
Assign IRQ For USB	See "Legacy USB Support."

Table A-1. Common BIOS settings and what they do (continued)

Setting	Description
Assign IRQ For VGA/ Allocate IRQ to PCI VGA	This should be enabled unless your video card does not need its own IRQ *and* you need an extra IRQ for another device.
Auto Power On	See "AC Power Recovery."
Boot Device Priority/ Boot Sequence	Specifies the order among the various drives in your system that your computer looks for a drive with a bootable operating system. For example, if your CD/DVD drive has a higher boot priority than your hard drive, then your PC will look for a bootable CD or DVD before it attempts to boot off the hard disk. If the CD/DVD drive has a *lower* boot priority, and Windows has already been installed, your PC will ignore bootable CDs. Put your hard disk at the top of the list for faster booting, or promote your CD/DVD drive if you're installing Windows (see Chapter 1).
Boot Graphic Adapter Priority	If you have more than one video card, use this setting to choose which one is the "primary" video adapter. Change this setting if you get no video when you boot, but use the settings in Windows Control Panel if you want to configure multiple monitors.
Boot Other Device	If an operating system isn't found on the first boot drive (see "Boot Device Priority/ Boot Sequence") and this setting is enabled, your computer will attempt to boot off of other drives.
Boot Sector Virus Protection	See "Anti-Virus Protection."
Boot to OS/2	Changes how memory above 64 MB is handled for compatibility with IBM's defunct OS/2 operating system. For obvious reasons, this option should be disabled.
Bootup Numlock Status	See "Numlock State."
C000/C400/C800/CC00 16k Shadow	See "Address Range Shadowing."
Chassis Fan	This shows the RPM of the fan connected to the "Chassis Fan" connector on your motherboard. This is typically a read-only display, not a setting you can change.
CPU Current Temperature	This shows the measured temperature of your processor. For dual-processor systems, you'll see two such settings. This is typically a read-only display, not a setting you can change.
CPU Fan	This shows the RPM of the fan connected to the "CPU Fan" connector on your motherboard. For dual-processor systems, you'll see two such settings. This is typically a read-only setting.
CPU Level 1 Cache/ Level 2 Cache	These settings allow you to disable your processor's primary (level 1) and secondary (level 2) cache, respectively. These settings should always be enabled.
CPU to PCI Write Buffer	Enables or disables the buffer used for data sent to the PCI bus by the processor. This should be enabled.
D000/D400/D800/DC00 16k Shadow	See "Address Range Shadowing."
Delayed Transaction	See "PCI 2.1 Compliance."
Diskette	See all "Floppy" entries.
DRAM CAS Latency	In theory, set this to **CAS2** if your system memory (RAM) is rated at CAS Latency 2; otherwise, use **CAS3**. Interestingly, you should be able to use the faster **CAS2** setting regardless of the type of installed memory; use **CAS3** only if instability results.

Table A-1. Common BIOS settings and what they do (continued)

Setting	Description
DRAM Data Integrity/ECC Mode	If your system memory (RAM) has the ECC (Error Checking and Correction) feature, set this to **ECC**. Otherwise, choose **Non-ECC**.
DRAM Timing by SPD	Enable this option to have the BIOS set memory timing options automatically according to (Serial Presence Detect).
EHCI Hand-Off	This is a USB 2.0 feature newly supported by Vista, and should be enabled unless you're having USB problems.
Event Log	Your motherboard can log errors (such as BIOS problems and hard disk boot problems) it encounters during startup. Settings in this section allow you to enable or disable logging, view the log, erase the log, etc.
Fast Boot	See "Quick Boot."
First Boot Device	See "Boot Device Priority/Boot Sequence."
Flash BIOS Protection	This prevents the BIOS from being overwritten or updated. You'll need to disable this to update your BIOS, as explained at the beginning of this appendix. Otherwise, leave this enabled to protect against viruses that attack BIOSes.
Floppy Drive A/B	Use these settings to define the floppy diskette drives you have connected to your computer; set to **Disabled** if you have no floppy drive.
Floppy Drive Seek	When enabled, this option will send a signal to your floppy drive(s) to help detect certain drive characteristics. Leave this off for a quicker boot.
Floppy Write Protect	This prevents anyone from writing data to a diskette in your floppy drive, which is useful if the computer is in a public place and you don't want people copying data to floppies.
Front Panel Support Type	Set this to match the audio connectors on the front of your PC, if applicable; choose between the older AC97 and newer high-definition standards.
Full Screen Logo	Show your PC or motherboard's corporate logo on screen instead of the POST (Power On Self Test) messages.
GART W2K Miniport Driver	The GART (Graphics Address Remapping Table) is part of the AGP subsystem. In most cases, you want to disable this option.
Green PC Monitor Power State	If you're using an APM (advanced power management)-compliant "Green PC" monitor, this setting allows you to automatically shut it off after a certain period of inactivity, in lieu of a screensaver. With these types of settings, it's best to let Windows Vista control how and when devices are shut off.
Hard Disk Power Down Mode	Windows can shut down your hard disk to save power after a certain period of inactivity. With these types of settings, it's best to let Windows Vista control how and when devices are shut off.
Hard Disk Write Protect	This option write-protects your hard disk so data can't be written to it. You won't want to use this on a Windows PC.
Hard-Disk Drive Sequence	If you have more than one hard disk drive, this option allows you to choose the order in which your computer looks for bootable drives. Used in conjunction with "Boot Device Priority/Boot Sequence."
Hardware Reset Protect	Prevent the computer from being restarted with the **Reset** button on the front of your PC's case (helpful if you have a dog who likes to wag his/her tail while standing next to your computer).

Table A-1. Common BIOS settings and what they do (continued)

Setting	Description
HD Audio	Enable the high-definition audio subsystem on your motherboard. Disable this only if it interferes with a separate audio card.
HDD S.M.A.R.T. Capability	Enables the S.M.A.R.T. (Self Monitoring Analysis and Reporting Technology) feature supported by IDE (parallel ATA) hard disks, that helps predict potential problems before they happen. Most users don't need it, and are probably better off disabling this feature.
Hit DEL Message Display	Turns on or off the message on the POST (Power On Self Test) screen that says "Press DEL to enter Setup."
Hyper Path 3	Set to **Enabled** or **Auto** to shorten latency time during data transfers.
IDE BusMaster	Enables or disables bus mastering for the IDE controller, which helps reduce load on the processor when data is transferred to and from IDE devices. Disable if you're using older drives that don't support bus mastering.
IDE Controller	Despite the name, this feature can apply to both IDE (Parallel ATA) and SATA (Serial ATA) controllers; use this feature to enable or disable said controllers on the motherboard. You can shorten boot times and free IRQs by disabling controllers you don't need. However, on older IDE/PATA systems, you can marginally improve performance by enabling all your IDE controllers and then distributing your hard disks and CD drives so you don't ever have two devices sharing the same controller.
IDE Detect Time Out	Choose how long your PC waits for IDE devices to respond before giving up.
IDE HDD Block Mode	This option should not be used with Windows Vista.
Intel SpeedStep/AMD Cool 'n' Quiet/Power-Now!	These are power-management features that allow processors to run at lower speeds and use less power. Enable the feature to allow Windows to control your processor speed.
Internal Cache	See "CPU Level 1 Cache/Level 2 Cache."
Interrupt 19 Capture	Enable this feature if you need to boot off a hard disk connected to a separate (add-on) hard disk controller, like a RAID or SCSI controller. Otherwise, disable it.
IRQ3, IRQ4, IRQ5, etc.	There are two different settings named for IRQs. One, used with power management, determines whether or not your computer monitors a given IRQ for activity (used to "wake up" the system). The other, typically found in the PCI section, allows you to "reserve" an IRQ and prevent the Plug-and-Play system from automatically assigning it to a device.
JMicron SATA/PATA Controller	This controls the additional (optional) RAID controller on some motherboards. Turn it on only if you have a RAID system connected to this controller.
Legacy USB Support	Enable this option if you're using a USB keyboard or USB mouse and you want to use them in the BIOS setup screen, DOS, or some other environment outside of Windows.
Master/Slave Drive UltraDMA	This should be enabled for IDE (Parallel ATA) drives that support UltraDMA, and disabled otherwise. In most cases, it should be set to **Auto**.
Memory Hole at 15M–16M	Enable this option to reserve this segment of your computer's memory for use by some older ISA cards. Unless you specifically need it, this option should be disabled.
Memory Write Posting	This option may improve performance on older systems, but will likely degrade performance—and even cause video corruption—on newer systems. Disable this option unless you're willing to experiment with it.

Table A-1. Common BIOS settings and what they do (continued)

Setting	Description
Microcode Updation	This permits BIOS updates from the manufacturer to also update certain code in your processor. Set this to **Enabled** if you want all the latest fixes and bugs.
MPS Version Control	This allows you to choose the multiprocessor specification version supported by your operating system. Windows Vista supports version 1.4, although some other operating systems do not.
Numlock State	Turn this on if you want the **Num Lock** keyboard light turned on when the system starts. Turn this off if you typically use the numeric keypad to move your cursor, instead of the "inverted T" cursor keys.
Onboard FDD Controller	This enables or disables the floppy diskette drive controller on your motherboard.
Onboard IR Function	This enables or disables the infrared port on your motherboard.
Onboard SCSI	This enables or disables the SCSI controller on your motherboard. Note that SCSI settings will typically be set with a separate SCSI BIOS utility (e.g., **Ctrl-A** for Adaptec controllers).
Overclocking	See "Overclock Your Processor" in Chapter 5.
Overheat Warning Temperature	This sets the temperature above which the overheat warning is triggered. See "System Overheat Warning," later in this appendix, for more information.
Palette Snooping/ VGA Palette Snoop	Enable this only if you're using an MPEG-2 decoder add-on card that connects to the "Feature Connector" found on older video cards, and then only if the device specifically requires this setting.
Parallel Port	This enables or disables the parallel (printer) port on your motherboard. Disable the parallel port — if your PC even has one — if you have a USB printer.
Parallel Port Mode	Use this to choose among the various parallel (printer) port modes: **ECP, EPP, ECP+EPP, Normal (SPP)**. In most cases, you'll want ECP; only choose one of the lesser options if you run into a compatibility problem. Note that such problems are more commonly caused by incorrect or faulty printer cables.
PEG Buffer Length	This sets the size of the packets sent to your PCI-Express graphics (PEG) card; in most cases, this should be set to **Auto**.
PEG Force X1	Disable this in most cases. Enable this only if you've inserted a PCI-Express X1 card into your PCI-Express X16 slot, the slot normally used for a X16 video card.
PEG Link Latency	Set this to **Normal** or **Auto**; see "PEG Link Mode" for more information.
PEG Link Mode	Used to overclock your PCI-Express video card. Set to **Auto** to be on the safe side, or set to **Faster** for better performance at the risk of frying your video card.
PCI 2.1 Compliance	This should be enabled unless you have one or more PCI cards that are not compatible with the PCI 2.1 specification. Not applicable for PCI-Express slots.
PCI IDE BusMaster	See "IDE BusMaster."
PCI IRQ Assignment	This setting (usually a group of settings) allows you to assign IRQs to specific PCI slots.
PCI Latency Timer	This sets the number of cycles during which a single PCI device can monopolize the PCI bus. Increase this value for better performance, or decrease it if you run into problems. The default is typically 32 cycles, but you may have success with 64 or 128 cycles.

BIOS Settings

Table A-1. Common BIOS settings and what they do (continued)

Setting	Description
PCI Pipelining	Enable this to improve performance with your video adapter. Not applicable for PCI-Express slots.
Plug and Play OS/ PnP OS Installed	Enable this feature to have Vista manage your Plug-and-Play (PnP) devices, or disable it to have the BIOS manage PnP. This should be enabled if Vista is installed.
PME Resume	See "Remote Wake Up."
Power Button Mode	This allows you to choose whether your computer's power button shuts off the computer (after holding it for four seconds) or forces your computer to enter a hibernate state. See "Start Windows Instantly (Almost)," in Chapter 5, for related settings.
Power Lost Control	See "AC Power Recovery."
Power Management	This allows your operating system's APM (Advanced Power Management) feature to turn off the various devices in your system to save power. Enable this option for Windows Vista.
Power On By...	See "Start Windows Instantly (Almost)," in Chapter 5, for ways to use these settings to power on your PC.
Primary Display	Allows you to choose whether your PCI or AGP adapter is used as your primary display when using multiple video cards. Not applicable on systems with PCI-Express slots.
Primary IDE Master/ Slave	Specify the type of drive connected to your primary IDE (Parallel ATA) controller, and set either as the "master" or "slave" (typically with a jumper). Sometimes this option also applies to SATA controllers.
Processor Serial Number	Enable this only if you want your operating system to be able to read the serial number of your processor. Since this can cause substantial security and privacy problems, this option should be disabled unless you specifically need it.
Processor Speed	This is typically a read-only setting that shows the speed of your processor (in Mhz or Ghz). Some motherboards allow you to "overclock" your processor, forcing it to run faster than its rated speed.
Processor Type	This read-only setting tells you what type of processor is currently installed.
PS/2 Mouse Support	Use this to enable or disable your PS/2 mouse port. Disable this if you're using a USB mouse, and wish to free up IRQ 12 for another device.
PXE Resume	See "Remote Wake Up."
Quick Boot	Turn this on to skip the thorough, slow memory test performed when the computer is first turned on, allowing a faster boot. It's a good idea to disable this option and sit through the test when first installing new RAM, but once the memory has been tested, it's fine to set this option to **Enabled** to skip it.
Quiet Boot	A "quiet" boot is one where your motherboard manufacturer's logo is displayed on the screen instead of the details, such as the amount of memory, detected disks, and BIOS revision date. Disable this option (or press **Esc** while looking at the logo) to show this information.
Ratio	See "Overclocking."
Read-Around-Write	When this setting is enabled, your processor can read directly from the cache, without waiting for it to be written to memory first. Enable this feature for better performance.
Remote Wake Up	This feature allows your computer to be turned on a signal from another computer on your network. Disable this feature unless you specifically need this functionality. See "Start Windows Instantly (Almost)," in Chapter 5, for details.

Table A-1. Common BIOS settings and what they do (continued)

Setting	Description
Repost Video on S3 Resume	When you wake your PC from the S3 Sleep state (see "Start Windows Instantly (Almost)" in Chapter 5), your video card will be put through its self test if this option is enabled.
Reset Config Data	If enabled, the PnP subsystem will reset and reconfigure all of your PnP devices every time your system starts. Use this only if one or more devices needs to be reset to function.
Restore on AC Power Loss	See "AC Power Recovery."
SATA Configuration	If you're using SATA drives, then all your SATA settings should be enabled. But be careful adjusting these settings after you've installed Windows.
	For instance, the AHCI (Advanced Host Controller Interface) subsystem allows Vista to take advantage of the higher speeds and hot-plug features of SATA hard drives. In theory, you'll want to enable ACPI 2.0 support with Vista, but if you change this setting after installing Windows, you'll get a Blue Screen of Death (INACCESSABLE_ BOOT_DEVICE) the next time you boot. Microsoft offers a solution in KB article 922976, but it doesn't work. Instead, you'll need to reinstall Windows (see Chapter 1) if you change this setting.
SDRAM settings	See "DRAM settings."
Second Boot Device	See "Boot Device Priority/Boot Sequence."
Secondary IDE Master/ Slave	See "Primary IDE Master/Slave."
Serial Port 1/2 Serial Port A/B	The numbers (or letters) have no correlation to the well-known COM1/COM2 designations, but rather to each of the two physical ports on your motherboard. Set the ports as follows: "3F8/IRQ4" to assign the port to COM1, "2F8/IRQ3" for COM2, "3E8/IRQ4" for COM3, or "2E8/IRQ3 to make it COM4. Disable any port you're not using so it won't consume any resources you can use for other devices. Make sure the two ports don't conflict with each other, or any other devices in your system (such as your modem).
Slot Power	This allows your PC to provide your PCI-Express video card with the power it needs; in most cases, just set this to **Auto**.
Supervisor Password	This setting allows you to password-protect your BIOS setup. Note that if you forget the password (or simply wish to bypass such a restriction), just reset the BIOS configuration; this is typically done with a jumper, but can also be accomplished by disconnecting the motherboard battery for about 20 minutes.
Suspend Mode	Choose whether the computer is placed in Suspend or Hibernate power-saving modes; set to **Auto** if available. In most cases, you should use the settings in the Windows Control Panel instead.
Suspend Timeout	Specifies the number of minutes of inactivity before the system is placed in Suspend power-saving mode. In most cases, you should use the settings in the Windows Control Panel instead.
System BIOS Cacheable	This is similar to "Address Range Shadowing," except that it works with your motherboard's BIOS. Disable this option for best performance.
System Date/Time	Sets your computer's internal clock. This can also be changed in the Windows Control Panel.
System Keyboard	Disable this option if there's no keyboard attached.

BIOS Settings

Table A-1. Common BIOS settings and what they do (continued)

Setting	Description
System Memory	In most computers, this will be a read-only setting that displays the amount of installed RAM. However, as a holdover from older computers, you may have to enter the BIOS setup screen and then exit for the computer to recognize newly installed memory, even though you won't be able to directly modify this setting.
System Overheat Warning	Enable this to sound an alarm or flash a light if your computer's internal temperature exceeds the value set with the "Overheat Warning Temperature."
Third Boot Device	See "Boot Device Priority/Boot Sequence."
Typematic Rate/Delay	Faster settings will make your keyboard more responsive outside of Windows, but within Windows, these settings are overridden by those found in the Windows Control Panel.
USB Function	This enables or disables the USB ports on your motherboard. Since it's unlikely they'd conflict with anything else, you'll probably want to leave them all enabled. See "Legacy USB Support" for related settings.
VCORE Voltage	This is a read-only display indicating the output of your motherboard's voltage regulators.
Video BIOS Shadow/ Video BIOS Cacheable	This is similar to "Address Range Shadowing," except that it works with the BIOS of your video adapter. This is a holdover from early video cards, and should be disabled in any modern system.
Video Power Down	If enabled, your computer will be able to shut down your video card and monitor to save power. Typically, it's best to use the settings in the Windows Control Panel instead.
Video RAM Cacheable	This is similar to "Address Range Shadowing," except that it works with the memory installed on your video card. This option should always be disabled.
Virtualization Technology	This is a set of Intel extensions for hardware-assisted virtual machine management, used to improve performance for Virtual PC software.
Virus Warning	See "Anti-Virus Protection."
Wait for F1 if Error	If this option is disabled, your computer will continue to boot even if an error is found; otherwise, you'll have to press **F1** before the system will start. Such errors include a missing keyboard, a missing video adapter, and an unexpected quantity of installed memory. Enable this option if you want to know about every problem, or disable it if you want the PC to start without interruption (essential for servers).
Write combining	Enable this option for better video performance, but disable it if you encounter video corruption or system crashes.

TCP/IP Ports

When your web browser or email program connects to another computer on the Internet, it does so through a TCP/IP port. If you have a web server or FTP server running on your PC, it opens a port through which other computers can connect to those services. Port numbers are used to distinguish one network service from another.

Mostly, this is done behind the scenes. However, knowing which programs use a specific port number becomes important when you starting considering security. A firewall uses ports to form its rules about which types of network traffic to allow, and which to prohibit. And the Active Connections utility (*netstat.exe*), used to determine which ports are currently in use, allows you to uncover vulnerabilities in your system using ports. Ports, firewalls, and the Active Connections utility are all discussed in Chapter 7.

 Some firewalls make a distinction between TCP (Transmission Control Protocol) and UDP (User Datagram Protocol) ports, which is typically unnecessary. In most cases, programs that use the more common TCP protocol will use the same port numbers as their counterparts that use the less-reliable UDP protocol.

Ports are divided into three ranges:

Well-known ports: 0–1023
Registered ports: 1024–49151
Dynamic and/or private ports: 49152–65535

Since a complete listing of known ports would consume about a hundred pages of this book, only the most commonly used ports are listed here. For a more complete listing, see any of these resources:

http://www.iana.org/assignments/port-numbers
http://www.faqs.org/rfcs/rfc1700.html
http://en.wikipedia.org/wiki/List_of_TCP_and_UDP_port_numbers

Table B-1 lists the more commonly used TCP/IP ports.

 Those ports marked with an ✗ in Table B-1 are commonly exploited by worms and other types of remote attacks. Unless you specifically need them, you should block them in your firewall or router.

Table B-1. Commonly used TCP/IP ports and how they're used

Port Number	Description
20–21	FTP (File Transfer Protocol)
22	SSH (Secure Shell)
23	Telnet
25	SMTP (Simple Mail Transfer Protocol), used for sending email
42	WINS (Windows Internet Name Service)
43	WhoIs
50–51	IPSec (PPTP Passthrough for VPN, Virtual Private Networking)
53	DNS (Domain Name Server), used for looking up domain names
67	DHCP (Dynamic Host Configuration Protocol)
69 ✗	TFTP
70	Gopher
79	Finger
80	HTTP (Hyper Text Transfer Protocol), used by web browsers to download standard web pages
110	POP3 (Post Office Protocol, version 3), used for retrieving email
119	NNTP (Network News Transfer Protocol), used for newsgroups
123	NTP (Network Time Protocol), used for Windows' Internet Time feature
135 ✗	RPC (Microsoft Windows Remote Procedure Call)
137–139 ✗	NETBIOS Services
143	IMAP4 (Internet Mail Access Protocol version 4)
161–162	SNMP (Simple Network Management Protocol)
194	IRC (Internet Relay Chat)
220	IMAP3 (Internet Mail Access Protocol version 3)

Table B-1. Commonly used TCP/IP ports and how they're used (continued)

Port Number	Description
443	HTTPS (HTTP over TLS/SSL), used by web browsers to download secure web pages
445 ✗	Active Directory, file sharing for Microsoft Windows networks (445 UDP used for SMB/Samba)
500	IPSec (PPTP Passthrough for VPN, Virtual Private Networking)
514	RSH (Remote Shell)
531	AOL Instant Messenger (AIM)
554	RTSP (Real Time Streaming Protocol), used for streaming audio and video
563	NNTPS (Network News Transfer Protocol over SSL), used for secure newsgroups
593 ✗	RPC (Microsoft Windows Remote Procedure Call) over HTTP
691	Microsoft Exchange Routing
750	Kerberos IV email authenticating agent
989–990	FTP over SSL (secure File Transfer Protocol)
992	Telnet over SSL (secure Telnet)
993	IMAP4 over SSL (secure Internet Mail Access Protocol version 4)
995	POP3 over SSL (secure Post Office Protocol, version 3)
1026 ✗	Windows Messenger - pop ups (spam)
1194	OpenVPN
1214 ✗	Kazaa peer-to-peer file sharing
1270	Microsoft Operations Manager 2005 agent (MOM 2005)
1352	Lotus Notes/Domino mail routing
1433–1434	Microsoft SQL database system, monitor
1503	Windows Messenger - application sharing and whiteboard
1512	WINS (Windows Internet Name Service)
1701	VPN (Virtual Private Networking) over L2TP
1723	VPN (Virtual Private Networking) over PPTP
1755	MMS (Microsoft Media Services) for Windows Media Player
1812–1813	RADIUS authentication protocol
1863	Windows Live Messenger - instant messenging
1900	Microsoft SSDP Enables discovery of UPnP devices
3074	Xbox Live (Microsoft gaming console)
3306	MySQL database
3389	Remote Desktop Sharing (Microsoft Terminal Services), used for remote control
4444 ✗	W32.BLASTER.WORM virus
5004 and up	Windows Messenger - audio and video conferencing (port is chosen dynamically)
5010	Yahoo! Messenger

Table B-1. Commonly used TCP/IP ports and how they're used (continued)

Port Number	Description
5190	AOL Instant Messenger
5631, 5632	pcAnywhere, used for remote control
5800, 5801 5900, 5901	VNC (Virtual Network Computing), used for remote control
6699	Peer-to-peer file sharing, used by Napster-like programs
6891–6901	Windows Live Messenger - file transfer, voice
6881–6999	BitTorrent peer-to-peer file transfer clients

Index

We'd like to hear your suggestions for improving our indexes. Send email to *index@oreilly.com*.

About the Author

David A. Karp is the author of the bestselling Windows Annoyances series of books and the founder of Annoyances.org. His other books include *eBay Hacks* and *Windows XP Pocket Reference,* and he is the co-author of *Windows XP in a Nutshell.* David also writes for *PC Magazine.*

Colophon

The animal on the cover of *Windows Vista Annoyances* is a horned frog (genus *Ceratophrys*). Named for the triangular flap of skin at the edge of their upper eyelids, horned frogs can grow to a length of six to eight inches and are generally as wide as they are long. Their rotund build, coupled with the fact that they have extremely large mouths, has earned them the nickname "PacMan frog."

The coloration of the horned frog can be quite varied, and helps to camouflage it against the ground of the South American jungles in which it makes its home. Species include the Ornate (*Ceratophrys ornate*; specific to eastern Brazil and Argentina), Cranwell's (*Ceratophrys cranwelli*), and Columbian (*Ceratophrys calcarata*) horned frogs.

Females are generally larger and not as brightly colored as males; they're also less vocal. Unlike the more conventional "ribbit" or "croak," the male's vocalization sounds have been compared to bovine bellowing.

Horned frogs are voracious eaters whose diet consists of insects, lizards, mice, and just about anything they can get their mouths around—in fact, frog owners are encouraged to keep their pet horned frogs separated to minimize the risk of cannibalism. This insatiable appetite can have fatal consequences; they have been found dead in the wild with the remains of an impossible-to-digest victim still protruding from their mouths.

A fiercely aggressive creature, the horned frog will attack anything it sees as a threat, even animals many times its own size and bulk. It can inflict painful bites, and a row of sharp teeth in its upper jaw makes it nearly impossible to let go of its prey once it has captured it. Its vicious reputation has given root to an Argentinean superstition suggesting that if a horned frog bites the lip of a grazing horse, the horse will die (in actuality, horned frog bites are not poisonous). Amazon villagers have been known to wear high leather boots called *botas escuerzas* to repel attacks by the highly territorial Amazon horned frog.

The cover image is from Wood's *Reptiles, Fishes, Insects, &c.* The cover font is Adobe ITC Garamond. The text font is Linotype Birka; the heading font is Adobe Myriad Condensed; and the code font is LucasFont's TheSans Mono Condensed.

Related Titles from O'Reilly

Windows Users

Access Cookbook, *2nd Edition*

Access 2003 Personal Trainer

Access 2003 for Starters:
The Missing Manual

Access 2007: The Missing Manual

Access 2007 for Starters:
The Missing Manual

Access Database Design &
Programming, *3rd Edition*

Analyzing Business Data
with Excel

Excel Annoyances

Excel Hacks, *2nd Edition*

Excel Pocket Guide, *2nd Edition*

Excel 2003 Personal Trainer

Excel 2007: The Missing Manual

Excel 2007 for Starters:
The Missing Manual

Excel Scientific and Engineering
Cookbook

FileMaker Pro 9: The Missing
Manual

Fixing Access Annoyances

Fixing PowerPoint Annoyances

Fixing Windows XP Annoyances

Fonts & Encodings

FrontPage 2003: The Missing
Manual

Microsoft Projects 2007:
The Missing Manual

Outlook 2000 in a Nutshell

Outlook Pocket Guide

PC Annoyances, *2nd Edition*

PCs: The Missing Manual

Photoshop Elements 4:
The Missing Manual

PowerPoint 2003 Personal Trainer

PowerPoint 2007: The Missing
Manual

QuickBooks 2006: The Missing
Manual

Quicken 2006 for Starters:
The Missing Manual

Windows Vista Annoyances

Windows Vista for Starters: The
Missing Manual

Windows Vista Pocket Reference

Windows Vista: The Missing
Manual

Windows XP Annoyances
For Geeks, *2nd Edition*

Windows XP Cookbook

Windows XP Hacks, *2nd Edition*

Windows XP Home Edition: The
Missing Manual, *2nd Edition*

Windows XP in a Nutshell,
2nd Edition

Windows XP Pocket Reference

Windows XP Pro: The Missing
Manual, *2nd Edition*

Windows XP for Starters:
The Missing Manual

Windows XP Unwired

Word Annoyances

Word Hacks

Word Pocket Guide, *2nd Edition*

Word 2003 Personal Trainer

Word 2007 for Starters: The
Missing Manual

Word 2007: The Missing Manual

O'REILLY®

Our books are available at most retail and online bookstores.

To order direct: 1-800-998-9938 • *order@oreilly.com* • *www.oreilly.com*

Online editions of most O'Reilly titles are available by subscription at *safari.oreilly.com*